Dictionary of African Filmmakers

Dictionary
of African
Filmmakers

ROY ARMES

Indiana University Press • *Bloomington and Indianapolis*

This book is a publication of

Indiana University Press
601 North Morton Street
Bloomington, IN 47404-3797 USA

http://iupress.indiana.edu

Telephone orders   800-842-6796
Fax orders   812-855-7931
Orders by e-mail   iuporder@indiana.edu

Library of Congress Cataloging-in-Publication Data

Armes, Roy.
    Dictionary of African filmmakers / Roy Armes.
        p.   cm.
    Includes bibliographical references and index.
    ISBN 978-0-253-35116-6 (cloth : alk. paper)
1. Motion picture producers and directors—
Africa—Biography—Dictionaries. 2. Motion picture
producers and directors—Africa—Credits. I. Title.

PN1998.2.A758 2008
791.43023'309226—dc22
[B]
                                    2007049772

1 2 3 4 5   13 12 11 10 09 08

FOR MARTINE LEROY
*to whom all students of African
film owe a huge debt*

The ability to picture oneself is a vital need. In fact, if a man were to live without the capacity of forging a picture of himself, he would have no aspirations, no desires, no dreams of his own. The same applies to a community, a society and a people. A society daily subjected to foreign images eventually loses its identity and its capacity to forge its own destiny. The development of Africa implies among other things the production of its own images.

GASTON KABORÉ
"THE ABILITY TO
PICTURE ONESELF"

CONTENTS

ACKNOWLEDGMENTS

This book is essentially a work of synthesis, and in compiling it, I have drawn on the full range of resources in my library, listed in the bibliography or at the end of the chronologies in the national listings.

The principal published sources on which I have drawn, and which all contain more information on specific films than can be contained here, are, in order of publication: Guy Hennebelle, ed., *Les Cinémas africains en 1972* (Paris: Société Africaine d'Édition, 1972); Claude-Michel Cluny, *Dictionnaire des nouveaux cinémas arabes* (Paris: Sindbad, 1978); Victor Bachy, "Dictionnaire de 250 cinéastes," in Jacques Binet, Ferid Boughedir, and Victor Bachy, eds., *Cinémas noirs d'Afrique* (Paris: CinémAction 26, 1983); Keyan Tomaselli, "Les Films sud-africains depuis 1910," and Alex Holt, Christo Doherty, and Keyan Tomaselli, "Dictionnaire de trente cinéastes sud-africains," in Keyan Tomaselli, ed., *Le Cinéma sud-africain est-il tombé sur la tête?* (Paris: L'Afrique Littéraire 78/CinémAction 39, 1986); Ibrahim al-Ariss, Mouny Berrah, Claude Michel Cluny, Jacques Lévy, and Yves Thoraval, "Dictionnaire de 80 cinéastes," in Mouny Berrah, Jacques Lévy, and Claude Michel Cluny, eds., *Les Cinémas arabes* (Paris: CinémAction 43/Cerf/Institut du Monde Arabe, 1987); Nancy Schmidt, *Sub-Saharan Films and Film Makers: An Annotated Bibliography* (London: Zell, 1988); Keyan Tomaselli. *The Cinema of Apartheid: Race and Class in South African Film* (London: Routledge, 1989); Hedi Dohoukar, "25 cinéastes plus ou moins beurs," in Guy Hennebelle and Roland Schneider, eds., *Cinémas métis: De Hollywood aux films beurs* (Paris: CinémAction 56/Hommes et Migrations/Corlet/Télérama, 1990); Afolabi Adesanya, ed., *The Nigerian Film/TV Index* (Ikeja: A-Productions Nigeria, 1992); Johan Blignaut and Martin Botha, *Movies Moguls Mavericks: South African Cinema 1979–1991* (Cape Town: Showdata, 1992); Keith Shiri, ed., *Directory of African Film-Makers and Films* (Trowbridge, England: Flicks Books, 1992); Alberto Elena, *El cine del tercer mundo: diccionario de realizadores* (Madrid: Ediciones Turfan, 1993); Andrea Morini, Erfan Rashid, Anna Di Martino, and Adriano Aprà, *Il cinema dei paesi arabi* (Venice: Marsilio Editori, 1993); Luciana Fina, Cristina Fina, and António Loja Neves, "Os realizadores e os filmes," in *Cinemas de África* (Lisbon: Cinemateca Portugesa & Culturgest, 1995); Touti Moumen, *Films tunisiens, long métrages 1967–1998* (Tunis: Touti Moumen, 1998); L'Association des Trois Mondes/Fespaco, *Les Cinémas d'Afrique* (Paris: Éditions Karthala and Éditions ATM, 2000); Khalid El Khodari, *Guide des réalisateurs marocains* (Rabat, Morocco: Khalid El Khodari, 2000); Hyginus Ekwuazi, *Nigerian Cinema: Pioneers and Practitioners* (Jos, Nigeria: National Film Institute, 2004); Youssef Chérif Rizkallah, "Répertoire des réalisateurs," Kamal Ramzi, "Répertoire des acteurs," and Ali Abou Chadi and Layanne Chawaf, "Répertoire des films," in Magda Wassef, ed., *Egypte, 100 ans de cinéma* (Paris: Institut du Monde Arabe and Éditions Plume, 2005); Rebecca Hillauer, *Encyclopedia of Arab Women Filmmakers* (Cairo: American University in Cairo Press, 2005); Alberto Elena, ed., *Balcón Atlantico: las mil y una imágenes de cine marroquí* (Las Palmas/Madrid: Festival Internacional de Cine de las Palmas de Gran Canaria/T&B Editores, 2007).

Equally indispensable are Olivier Barlet's *Africultures* website (http://www.africultures.com); the *Africiné* website of the Fédération Africaine de la Critique Cinématographique (http://www.africine.com); that of the Guild of African Filmmakers (www.cinemasdafrique .com); the Association des Trois Mondes (www .cine3mondes.fr); *Images Nord-Sud,* edited by Martine Leroy and Dominique Sentilhes; and the meticulous documentation of South African mainstream feature films, compiled by Trevor T. Moses and held at the South African National Film Video and Sound Archive (SANFVSA) in Pretoria.

Individuals to whom I owe a very real and specific debt for information and encouragement (beyond the call of duty) include Seham Abdel Salam, Afolabi Adesanya, Steve Ayorinde, Imruh Bakari, Olivier Barlet, Martin P. Botha, Kevin Dwyer, Alberto Elena, Kedmon Hungwe, Jacqueline Mainguard, Zunaid Man-soor, Martin Mhando, Trevor T. Moses, Ogova Ondego, Jeffrey Ruoff, Keith Shiri, Joanna Sterkowitz, Trevor Taylor, Keyan Tomaselli, and Angela van Schalkwyck.

I am very grateful to the Leverhulme Trust for the award of a second Leverhulme Emeritus Fellowship, which helped finance this dictionary and has provided funding for the research to be undertaken for the companion volume, a discussion of *Issues in African Film.*

Though I have made every effort to check information, errors and omissions are inevitable in a work of this nature and I would welcome contact from any readers who can help correct the mistakes and fill the gaps.

Dictionary
of African
Filmmakers

INTRODUCTION: Mapping the Field— Feature Filmmaking in Africa

There is no single entity called "African cinema," and the films produced in Africa over the past hundred years offer at best a very partial (if totally fascinating) image of the history and current development of the continent. Africa itself can be defined unambiguously in geographical terms: an enormous land mass, stretching over 4,500 miles at its widest point and measuring some 5,000 miles from north to south, with which are associated a range of widely spread and totally diverse islands, from Madagascar and the Seychelles in the Indian Ocean to St. Helena in the South Atlantic and the Cape Verde Islands and the Canaries in the North Atlantic. But as soon as we depart from the geography of the continent, problems of definition—both cultural and national—become acute. The heritage of colonialism is everywhere apparent. Arbitrary boundaries inherited from the colonial era divide some communities into two, while elsewhere artificially yoking together totally divergent groups into newly defined nation-states. To the north there are recurring tensions between Arabs and non-Arabs (as in the issue of the Berber communities) and between Muslims and Christians (particularly in Nigeria and Sudan). To the south there is the anomaly of the white population of South Africa and the question of its place in a wider Africa. Across Africa the all-too-prevalent dictatorships drive artists and intellectuals into exile, and at the same time the whole continent is shaken both by mass migrations of whole populations fleeing recurrent wars and famines and by tens of thousands of mostly young men annually seeking to emigrate to Europe for economic survival. African cinemas—and the writings about them—inevitably reflect these tensions and ambiguities.

At the time when the cinematograph and its successors were first introduced into Africa—as early as 1896 in Algeria and South Africa, 1897 in Morocco and Tunisia,

1903 in Nigeria—the continent was suffering the aftermath of the 1894–1895 Berlin conference on the partition of Africa, where European states carved out African empires for themselves. Before the outbreak of World War I, France had annexed Algeria, set up protectorates in Tunisia and Morocco, and established its two "super colonies," French West Africa and French Equatorial Africa, while Great Britain had conquered Sudan and unified Nigeria. Local filmmaking in Africa is one of the developments which has occurred as this process of colonization has been gradually reversed and independent African states have emerged. The first feature film (now unfortunately lost) was made in South Africa in 1910, the year in which "Louis Botha became prime minister of a British Dominion with a population of 4 million Africans, 300,000 Coloureds, 150,000 Indians, and 1,275,000 Whites."[1] Egypt became a (notionally) independent monarchy in 1922, and the first experiments with filmmaking occurred there in the mid-1920s. When, beginning in the late 1950s, former French colonies began to achieve independence, one of the first actions of the many new governments was to set up a local film production monopoly, modeled on the lines of the Parisian Centre National de la Cinématographie and equipped with the requisite French-language acronym. The exception was Morocco, where the new government discovered a Moroccan film center—the Centre Cinématographique Marocain (CCM)—already in existence and fully functional. The center is still the focus of Moroccan film activity today.

The first locally produced feature films tended to be made by foreigners. Feature production in South Africa between 1916 and 1925 was the product of an Anglo-American enterprise headed by U.S. businessman Isadore W. Schlesinger. Early film production in Egypt was largely the work of cosmopolitan expatriate elites in Cairo and Alexandria. In Algeria, Morocco, and Nigeria, the first locally produced features after independence were directed by Europeans or Americans. But gradually the directing role was taken over by African nationals. Egypt led the way with the founding of the locally financed Misr studios in the mid-1930s. This, as Kristina Bergmann aptly notes, was a moment of transformation for Egyptian films: "at first financed by Lebanese and Greeks, shot by Italians, designed and acted by the French, films then became Egyptian."[2] Elsewhere we find the beginnings of indigenous film production occurring in the wake of independence: Algeria, Ghana, Guinea, the Ivory Coast, Morocco, Senegal, Somalia, Sudan, and Tunisia in the 1960s; Angola, Benin, Burkina Faso, Cameroon, Congo, the Democratic Republic of Congo (ex-Zaire), Ethiopia, Gabon, Libya, Madagascar, Mali, Mauritania, Mauritius, Mozambique, Niger, Nigeria, and Zimbabwe in the 1970s. Other African countries gradually followed suit: Guinea-Bissau and Kenya in the 1980s; Burundi, Cape Verde, Chad, Tanzania, and Togo in the 1990s; and, most recently, the Central African Republic in 2003. Whatever the complexities of its funding and whatever foreign cultural influences may be present, these productions are usually clearly separable from those big budget foreign productions (from *Raiders of the Lost Ark* to *The English Patient*) which use Africa as a mere backdrop for non-African narratives. Only in South Africa before 1994—when the majority was denied a voice, and the attitudes, assumptions, and divisions of colonial rule persisted under the apartheid system—did national film output remain inextricably linked, creatively as well as financially, with European and American interests, so that genuinely South African films and foreign films using South African locations are virtually indistinguishable.

Under the colonial system, the prejudices of the colonizers made it impossible for them to imagine that an African could actually make *any* sort of film, let alone a feature film. The assumption, chillingly spelled out by Notcutt and Latham in their account of the 1930s Bantu Educational Cinema Experiment, was that, at best, "intelligent young Africans" could be trained "to do much of the routine work of the darkroom and the sound studios, and even some of the semi-skilled work."[3] Twenty years later, Paulin Soumanou Vieyra, born in Dahomey (now Benin) but later living and working in Senegal, was able to graduate from the major French film school, Institut des Hautes Études Cinématographiques (IDHEC), in Paris, but that did not mean that, under existing French law, he could shoot film in Africa. As a result, Vieyra's first, collaboratively made, work had to be the 20-minute short *Africa on Seine* (1957), shot in Paris. But the racist assumptions of Notcutt and Latham had already been refuted in the 1920s by one of African cinema's most remarkable pioneers, Albert Samama Chikly (1872–1934), a Tunisian Jew who was fascinated by Western technology and had arranged screenings of the Lumière cinematograph in Tunis in 1897. After shooting footage, from the Turkish side, of the Italian invasion of Libya in 1911, Chikly became one of the dozen cameramen employed by the French Army film service (along with

Abel Gance—future creator of *Napoléon*—and Louis Feuillade—author-to-be of both the *Fantômas* and *Judex* series), filming at the front at Verdun in 1916. Subsequently, with the aid of his daughter Haydée, as actress, scriptwriter, and editor, he made a first fictional short, *Zohra* (1922), and then a second, feature-length, film, *The Girl from Carthage / Aïn el-Ghezal* (1924).[4]

* * *

This dictionary is concerned with fictional feature films (16mm or 35mm or shot on video and subsequently transferred to—and distributed on—film) made by Africans in Africa or in exile. Though television companies throughout the world help to co-finance films which have an initial commercial distribution in cinemas (and therefore deserve an entry here), I have not listed films shot purely for television screening—what the French call "téléfilms" (though, where possible, I have mentioned significant television work in the filmmaker entries). Also omitted are purely video works of feature-length fiction. This is due in part to the logistical difficulties caused by the Nigerian situation (Pierre Barrot gives an estimate of seven thousand video features made between 1992 and the beginning of 2005).[5] But, in any case, these Nigerian home videos are destined not for public projection but for domestic consumption within a family context. Though technological developments and new promotional strategies are likely to lead to a totally different situation in the coming decade, at the present time the economic base for video work—as well as its shooting and distribution strategies—is totally different from that shaping any sort of true film activity. As the veteran filmmaker Eddie Ugbomah, who later turned to video, put it: "a (video) film made with three million on Monday can bring you back ten million on Friday. What other activity can equal that in Nigeria?"[6] The transition is fully reflected in the catalogues of the twenty-first edition of the Journées Cinématographiques de Carthage (JCC, 2006) and the twentieth edition of the Festival Panafricain du Cinéma et de la Télévision de Ouagadougou (FESPACO, 2007), not only by the continued strength and importance of 35mm filmmaking across the continent but also by the growing number of works, even by established filmmakers, which are digitally produced and reflect television formats: 52-minute documentaries and fictional works in a mini-series pattern of three 26-minute episodes.[7]

In general I have omitted feature-length documentaries, but I have included in the filmmaker listings (though without indexing their films) half-a-dozen or so documentarists who have made truly significant contributions to African filmmaking, without mention of whom any overview of African film production would be deficient—among them Simon Bright (Zimbabwe), Issa Genina (Morocco), Nana Mahomo (South Africa), Samba Félix Ndiaye (Senegal), and António Ole (Angola). A place has also been found in these chronologies for a handful of important feature-length documentaries—to leave out Ahmed Rachedi's masterly *Dawn of the Damned,* the first feature produced in a newly independent Algeria, just because it is a compilation film would have been absurd. I have also included works in the growing category of docudramas or pseudo-documentaries (such as Mahamat Saleh Haroun's *Bye-Bye Africa,* chronicling a return to his native Chad), along with films which are treated

as features by the organizers of African and Arab film festivals but which do not, strictly speaking, fulfill the conventional length requirements of a feature film (such as Abderrahmane Sissako's 61-minute meditation on the new millennium, *Life on Earth*).

As far as individual filmmakers are concerned, the guiding principle of this dictionary is that every filmmaker is equal: black or white, Muslim or Christian, speaking English, Afrikaans, or Zulu. The dictionary is therefore concerned with everyone from Niazi Mostafa, who made more than a hundred features over a period of 50 years within the genre constraints of the Egyptian film industry, to Didier Ouenangare, whose co-directed debut feature, *The Silence of the Forest* (2003), is the first to be made by someone born in the Central African Republic. Of necessity, it ranges from Med Hondo, who struggled for many years and endured huge financial problems to create a masterpiece of African filmmaking, *Sarraounia,*[8] to Kamal Abou al-Ela, a respected Egyptian film editor, who was amazed to receive his sole co-directing credit for his work on *Zohra* (1947), when he had just shot the last few scenes after a dispute between the film's producer and star, Bahiga Hafez, and its director, Hussein Fawzi.[9] The listing here includes some filmmakers who have forged successful careers and others (perhaps the majority outside Egypt) whose work has been constantly frustrated by financial and production constraints. There are both those endowed with a genius for audio-visual organization and storytelling, and also a few whose hesitant efforts have never, it would seem, merited any sort of commercial release. In general, in compiling this dictionary, I have tried to be as flexible and inclusive as possible and I have adopted the very liberal definition used by festivals like the JCC in Tunis and FESPACO in Ouagadougou as to what constitutes an "African" film. The result, at the moment of going to press, is a list of over 5,400 feature films made by about 1,250 filmmakers from 37 countries.

* * *

A real problem has been how to classify the 1,250 or so filmmakers who have some claim to have produced an African film. I have in general used the nationality of the filmmaker as a shorthand for identifying and grouping films, since this is the way in which they are circulated in the film marketplace and listed at international film festivals. This has allowed me to include the work in France and in the French language of such exiled Algerian filmmakers as Merzak Allouache (though he is becoming more and more of a French filmmaker, viewing the Maghreb from outside). Also included is the entire feature production of both Khaled al-Hagar, whose second, semi-autobiographical, feature, *Room to Rent,* is omitted from official Egyptian listings, since it is a film shot and produced in London and uses the English language, and Youri Nasrallah, whose 2005 double feature *The Gate of the Sun* is technically a French film. I have similarly included both feature-length diploma films shot at European film schools, such as Elaine Proctor's *On the Wire,* her graduation film at the National Film and Television School at Beaconsfield in the United Kingdom, and the work in exile of such young Nigerian filmmakers as Newton I. Aduaka (*Rage,* 2000, and *Ezra,* 2006), Branwen Okpako (*Valley of the Innocent,* 2002), and Adaora Nwandu (*Rag Tag,* 2006).

But there is a problem in that certain films regarded as nationally significant in Africa have not been made by Africans. Even after the founding of the Misr studios in Egypt (where the first feature to be produced, *Weddad,* was directed by the German Fritz Kramp), foreigners have continued to play a part in Egyptian filmmaking. Surveying the postwar era (1945–1953), Samir Farid notes that the list of mainstream "Egyptian" directors of the period "included Palestinians, Hungarians, and Italians."[10] Subsequently Japanese, American, and Lebanese names figure among the directors of officially listed Egyptian films. In many of the newly independent African states of the 1950s and 1960s, local production often began with feature films directed by outsiders. This was the case in Algeria, Tunisia, and Nigeria, for example. Throughout the history of South African filmmaking, South African producers have imported English and American directors for their own productions or been involved, as co-producers, in films directed by foreigners. Thus the listings by South African critics and historians include routine films by British directors such as Ken Annakin, Harry Watt, Cy Enfield, Val Guest, Dan Chaffrey, Peter Collinson, Peter Hunt, and J. Lee Thompson, many of which, from a UK perspective, would seem to be essentially British films shot on location.

The problem is aggravated in the case of South Africa by the fact that three of the films which are key to any definition of filmmaking in South Africa were in fact directed by foreigners. The silent Afrikaner epic *De Voortrekkers* (1916) was produced by the South African–based American businessman Schlesinger and directed by Harold Shaw, an American imported from London. The first South African feature to show (if only hesitantly) the realities of black urban life, *Cry the Beloved Country* (1951), was directed by the Hungarian-born Zoltan Korda and produced by his brother Alexander's London Film Company. *Come Back Africa* (shot in 1958 but not screened in South Africa until 30 years later) was the first feature to document black township life, with its mix of rural migrants and urbanized intellectuals, but it was independently produced and directed by a wealthy New York Jew, Lionel Rogosin. While the "Africanness" of these films can be endlessly debated, to omit them here would be to distort totally the development of filmmaking in South Africa. So are Harold Shaw, Zoltan Korda, and Lionel Rogosin to be regarded as African filmmakers? A recent attempt to rework the history of South African filmmaking, Isabel Balseiro and Ntongela Masilela's *To Change Reels: Film and Film Culture in South Africa*,[11] complicates matters still further, in that while devoting chapters to each of the three films listed above, it ignores totally all Afrikaans-language filmmaking, so that major figures such as Manie van Rensberg, Jans Rautenbach, and Katinka Heyns fail to get even a mention in the index. Are we therefore (presumably for political purposes) to exclude the work of Afrikaners, though Afrikaans is a language spoken only in Africa and many Afrikaners have roots in Africa going back generations (the first Dutch settlers reached the Cape 342 years before Nelson Mandela took his oath of office[12])?

A further problem is posed by the films made by second generation immigrants in France. A third of the films listed here as "Algerian" were made by members of the so-called "beur" community in France. While to include such films might, at first sight, seem to constitute an avoidable blurring of the already complex notion of African identity, these films are in fact an inevitable reflection of the current twin forces of world population migration and media globalization, which have resulted in the development of transnational forms of cinema and ever-increasing cultural hybridity. These are, after all, films which are recognized as "African" by African and other international film festivals. *Days of Glory / Indigènes*, for example, the film chosen to open the 40th Journées Cinématographiques de Carthage in 2006, was directed by Rachid Bouchareb, who was born in France, has French nationality, and has always lived in Europe. As Amin Maalouf eloquently points out in his book *On Identity*, within a young man born in France of Algerian parents, "French, European and other western influences mingle with Arab, Berber, African, Muslim and other sources, whether with regard to language, beliefs, family relationships or to tastes in cooking and the arts. This represents an enriching and fertile experience if the young man in question feels free to live it fully."[13] The role for all those, men or women, who share this "peculiar rather than privileged situation" is "to act as bridges, go-betweens, mediators between the various communities and cultures"[14]—a truly creative situation for a potential filmmaker.

As a result, the list of Algerian films given here includes *Mirka* (Mohamed Rachid Benhadj's international co-production with French-Spanish-Italian backing, shot by the Italian cinematographer Vittorio Storaro and starring Vanessa Redgrave and

Gérard Depardieu) and *Living in Paradise / Vivre au paradis* (a French-Belgian-Norwegian co-production, adapted by two French writers from a French-language novel, shot in Tunisia but set in France, in the slums of Nanterre). Bourlem Guerdjou, the director of *Living in Paradise,* is not one's idea of a typical African—his family is of Algerian origin, but he himself was born in France, has French nationality, and works as a writer-director in French television. But this did not prevent his first feature from winning one of the top prizes for any African film, the *Tanit d'or,* at the JCC in Tunis in 1998.

Guerjou's situation is not unique, and for a number of filmmakers born in francophone Africa,[15] the stated nationality of a film may in fact amount to little more than that of its foreign-trained director, now living in semi-permanent exile (or even, in extreme cases, the nationality of one or more of his or her parents). The paradoxical notion that the filmmaking of a first African generation born after independence would, in many parts of Africa, be essentially a cinema in exile could never have been foreseen in the 1960s. Yet the younger francophone filmmakers in both the Maghreb and south of the Sahara are virtually all European film school trained and many are now residing in Paris or Brussels. At first sight they seem to constitute a typical exile group of the kind so ably chronicled by Hamid Naficy,[16] and certainly many of their films carry the marks of exile and diaspora. But these Paris-based African filmmakers have an advantage not shared by other exiles, in that their decision to reflect cinematically on life in the countries where they were born has intermeshed precisely with the French government's desire to maintain its cultural links with all its former African colonies. Their problem is less exile than potential integration and loss of African identity.

* * *

The end credits (and press book) of any film made by a European-based filmmaker show the enormous financial contribution made by European organizations to much African filmmaking. Abderrahmane Sissako has built up an international reputation with films shot in Mali and Mauritania. But his second feature, *Waiting for Happiness,* for example, was produced by his own (Paris-based) production company Duo Films in association with ARTE France and gave thanks to the participation of the European Development Fund, a number of French funding bodies (including the French Foreign Ministry, the Agence Intergouvernementale de la Francophonie, and the Centre National de la Cinématographie), and the Locarno-based Montecinema Verità Foundation. Similarly, Flora Gomes's internationally shown *The Blue Eyes of Yonta* is the third of six features made in Guinea-Bissau. But it was produced by the Portuguese Vermedia company in cooperation with the Cooperativa Cultural Arco-Íris (Bissau), Eurocreation Production (Paris), the Instituto Português de Cinema, and RTP (Rádiotelevisão Portuguesa), in association with Channel Four (London), and with support from the Guinea-Bissau Finance Ministry, the French Ministry of Cooperation, and D.D.A., a Swiss organization for cooperation in development and humanitarian aid. The fact that these films have absolutely no possibility of recovering their costs in Guinea-Bissau or Mauritania (or indeed through any likely distribution in Africa) means that they must of necessity be shaped to meet the demands of European audiences.

Even for those still living in Africa, the diversity of contemporary funding sources may make the national identity of their films in many ways problematic. To take just one example: unlike so many other Algerian cultural workers, Yamina Bachir-Chouikh remained in Algeria, working as a film editor, throughout the murderous upheavals of the 1990s. In 2002 she was finally able to realize a long-cherished project, her first feature film, *Rachida*. But the fact that 100 percent of the film's funding was French has led some Algerians to question the extent to which it can be regarded as an Algerian film, with Tewfik Fares (whose 1969 feature, *The Outlaws,* was made for the Algerian state organization Office National du Commerce et de l'Industre Cinématographiques [ONCIC]) arguing that describing *Rachida* as an Algerian film is like "calling Roman Polanski's *Rosemary's Baby* a Polish film."[17]

Much current African filmmaking is in fact determined by French cultural policies. The response of successive governments in France to the increasing dominance of Hollywood cinema in France itself has been to establish Paris as the hub of a worldwide network of "cultural" filmmaking. Whatever language is actually used for the films' dialogue, the sponsored films can—given French funding—be dubbed "francophone" and thereby contribute to the status of France as a key player in the international film cultural scene. This process began in the 1960s, when the French Ministry of Cooperation funded a scheme for low-budget 16mm filmmaking by would-be directors from francophone Sub-

Saharan Africa. While undoubtedly well intentioned, this resulted in the production of ghettoized works which were totally unsuited to the normal 35mm commercial film distribution networks in Africa and which found their limited screenings mainly in the French cultural centers maintained by France in most of its ex-colonies in Africa or, at best, in Parisian art cinemas.[18]

A new impetus was given in 1984 when three French ministries (Culture, Cooperation, and Foreign Affairs) came together to establish a fund specifically to help 35mm filmmaking "in the South" (the Fonds Sud Cinéma). In the first 20 years of its existence, the fund has helped finance some 322 films worldwide, 137 of these in Africa, with assistance going to filmmakers from 27 African countries.[19] Most of this aid has naturally gone to filmmakers from the Maghreb (Algeria, Morocco, and Tunisia) and to those from the twelve states formed from the two giant former French colonies in West and Equatorial Africa. There the fund has aided the careers of many who have emerged as major figures during the past 20 years: Nouri Bouzid and Naceur Khemir (Tunisia), Mohamed Chouikh (Algeria), Nabil Ayouch (Morocco), Ousmane Sembene (Senegal), Idrissa Ouedraogo and Gaston Kabore (Burkina Faso), and many others. But significant help has also been given to filmmakers from countries lacking this direct connection with French culture: Ramadan Suleiman (South Africa), Youssef Chahine and Yousri Nasrallah (Egypt), Flora Gomes (Guinea-Bissau), Ingrid Sinclair (Zimbabwe), and Wanjiru Kinyanjui (Kenya) among them. This range is impressive, but there is a strong argument that, to quote Raphaël Millet, "it is less the case of a

French aid policy serving the cinemas of the South, than of the latter being used to assist French cultural policy."[20]

In most countries of the world filmmaking is controlled by governments through various forms of censorship and by visa schemes authorizing public exhibition. In some African countries this control has extended at times to total state control of funding, production, and distribution. The extreme form of this was to be found in Algeria in the 1970s, when only salaried employees of the state film monopoly, ONCIC, could make films, and when ONCIC defined the subject matter, if not the style, of all the films produced. More recently, in Morocco in the 1980s and 1990s, it has proved virtually impossible to produce or distribute commercially a film which has not received initial approval and funding through the government aid scheme (the "fonds d'aide"). But wherever such funding schemes have been introduced without some sort of quality control—as, initially, in Morocco in 1980 and in South Africa from 1975 and again in the late 1980s—the result has been a surge in the production of low-quality films whose reason for existence is not to reach as wide an audience as possible but simply to fulfill the requirements necessary to receive the state subsidy. Moreover, state funding does not necessarily assure that films are a true expression of real (as opposed to officially asserted) national identity. In Algeria, for example, any use of the Berber language, Tamazight, was forbidden (in the name of the national ideology of "one nation, one language, one religion") until the national control of filmmaking fell apart in the mid-1990s. Only then were Azzeddine Meddour, Belkacem

Hadjadj, and Ghaouti Bendeddouche able to make linguistically authentic films set in the Atlas Mountains. Similarly, many Afrikaans, English, and African-language films funded or aided by the apartheid government in Pretoria are very dubious expressions of any true sense of a real "national" identity.

Official lists of films rarely tell the whole story. The list regularly updated by the CCM in Morocco lists all films given state support, whether or not the films in question have ever received any sort of commercial screening in Morocco or elsewhere. Interestingly, the listing now even includes Fatima Jebli Ouazzani's Dutch-produced *In My Father's House* (1997), which unexpectedly won the top prize in 1998 at the Fifth Moroccan National Film Festival. Jebli Ouazzani, though born in Meknès in 1959, has lived in the Netherlands since the age of 11 and the subject matter of her film (female sexuality) precludes it from ever getting a commercial release in Morocco. In South Africa under apartheid, the National Film Archive in Pretoria produced lists which excluded the (government-funded) films made for black audiences, while simultaneously claiming as "South African" a range of productions—from the Gaumont-British *Rhodes of Africa* (shot by the Austrian emigré Berthold Viertel for Michael Balcon in 1936) to David Lean's *Ryan's Daughter* (1970)—which, though shot—at least in part—in South Africa, were unquestionably UK or U.S. films. As far as possible (and this is not always the case with South Africa), the myriad international films that simply use Africa as a location are ignored here, even if there is some minimal local production involvement (usually for tax—not creative—purposes). It should be noted, however, that the investment in such foreign production activity often far exceeds that in local or national film production (in a ratio of fourteen to one in Morocco in the 1990s, for example).

The impact of one aspect of what is perhaps best understood as an internal colonial rule—that of the white government in South Africa over the indigenous black majority after the triumph of the Nationalist Party in the 1948 elections—cannot be ignored. There was a real question of whether to include here the large number of films produced from the mid-1970s—mostly by white filmmakers who spoke no African languages—specifically to entertain (and possibly indoctrinate) segregated black audiences and, of course, to recoup government subsidies. I concluded that, despite their widely perceived gross inadequacies, such films should, as far as possible, be included.[21] Though many South African critics despise this whole area of production, even a cursory glance shows that, like the "quota quickies" produced in Britain in the 1920s, it does deserve consideration. *U-Deliwe* (1975), for example, was the first feature to be shot by a black South African, Simon Sabela, and, as the second Zulu-language film ever produced, it reached a black audience estimated at some two million spectators.[22] However, it was produced by Heyns Films, subsequently exposed as a company covertly funded by the South African Department of Information (and therefore, ironically, able to offer the directors of its films for black audiences higher than usual budgets). A decade later, after the refusal of a "normal" commercial distribution (that is to say, in whites-only cinemas) for his widely praised first feature on the workings

of the pass laws, *My Country My Hat* (1983), David Bensusan turned almost exclusively to low-budget African-language production. More recently, Darrell Roodt, one of the dominant figures in South African production over the past 15 years, began his career (though this is not usually acknowledged) with Zulu- and Xhosa-language features.

* * *

If the nationality of a specific film is problematic, the notion of a national cinema is even more so. In most African states production levels are too low for the notion of a national cinema to be meaningful: we have at best a collection of disparate films made by dedicated but diverse individuals. Ironically, the particular flavor of a "national" production may be given by the nature of the foreign training received: of thirteen Malian filmmakers, five were sent to the Vsesoyuznyi gosudarstvennyi institut kinematografii (VGIK) in Moscow and one to (what was then) the German Democratic Republic, whereas most Cameroonian filmmakers were Paris-trained, a third at Conservatoire Libre du Cinéma Français (CLCF). Even the production of many hundreds of films within the national boundaries may arguably not truly constitute a national cinema. Jacqueline Maingard unequivocally asserts that, despite the production of more than 1,400 feature films, "there is no national cinema in South Africa, even though some cinema might seem—or seek —to represent or evoke a sense of the 'national.'"[23] As Masilela and Balseiro note, Thelma Gutsche, author of the first scholarly study of film in South Africa, *The History and Social Significance of Motion Pictures in South Africa, 1895–1940* (1972), "refused to engage with features made by white South Africans," who, they claim, "saw themselves, in any case, as Europeans in Africa."[24]

Certainly the particular situation of South Africa within the world economy and the huge rifts within its social and political structures have produced a bewildering succession of largely unrelated blocks of film production: more than forty silent features aimed at the world market between 1916 and 1925 followed, after an 8-year gap, by a seemingly unambitious Afrikaans-language cinema aimed at the local market from 1933 to the early 1960s. Thereafter there has been a largely English-language and partially state-funded cinema, often aimed at an international audience, of around ten to twenty films a year. But this latter has been distorted by two ill-conceived government interventions. The first was a funding initiative which led to the production of more than 450 cheap and exploitative so-called "B" films made ostensibly for an exclusively segregated black audience (but increasingly produced largely to pick up the government subsidy). This began with the production of a single Zulu-language film in 1974, peaked at some 90 films in 1985, and came to an end only with the cancellation of the scheme in 1990. The second government intervention was an ill-drafted 1985 tax incentive scheme for exporters, a loophole which led in the late 1980s to the making of an additional 200 English-language films, again aimed at exploiting available government rebates rather than seeking to develop a South African film audience (most were destined for video or cable release). This scheme also ended in 1990. But at least in the 1990s and early 2000s, exciting new possibilities for South African filmmaking have emerged with the appearance of a growing number of black filmmakers.

There is, however, one country about which it is meaningful to speak of a national cinema; this is Egypt, which has produced around 56 percent of all African feature films. Though notionally an independent monarchy from 1922, Egypt remained under British economic dominance from 1882 until the Officers' Coup in 1952 that eventually brought Gamal Nasser to power. Though the very early days of Egyptian cinema reflect the interests and enthusiasms of members of its thriving cosmopolitan urban communities, the creation of a film industry was intimately associated with the sociopolitical developments linking industrialization to the growing sense of national identity in the early part of the twentieth century. The Bank Misr, which set up the Misr studios in the mid-1930s, was the institution at the heart of Egyptian efforts to foster industrial development, and indeed by the end of the 1970s it had come to dominate the whole Egyptian economy. The nationalization of the bank's assets in 1980 was rapidly followed by the state takeover of the film sector—under the General Organisation for Egyptian Cinema— just as the subsequent return of the national economy to private enterprise was fully reflected in the changed structures of the film industry. Contemporary Egyptian cinema has an organized infrastructure and a direct link to its national audience, as well as a thriving export trade. It is not an elite cinema shaped by foreign funding, critics, and festivals, but rather a popular medium of expression which became central to mid-twentieth-century notions of Egyptian identity, so as to constitute, for millions of Arabs outside Egypt, "the object of Arab desire and pride."[25] As Bergmann notes, "There is not an Arab from the Gulf to the Maghreb who is unaware of Egyptian cinema, who doesn't have a favorite Egyptian film or is not a fan of one Egyptian actress or other."[26] In addition, Egyptian filmmaking has offered a working context (with all the tensions to be found in any industrial complex) in which its creators and technicians can hope to develop their skills over a lifetime, though some filmmakers of real talent—such as Shadi Abdel Salem—have found their efforts frustrated. It has its own training for access to the industry—through the Cairo Higher Film Institute—and a recognized path to the role of director through years of work as assistant director. Hardly any Egyptian filmmakers have trained abroad and the country is stable enough for its artists and intellectuals not to need to go into exile. By any common definition, Egyptian cinema is a national cinema.

LAYOUT

The layout of the dictionary itself is, I hope, self-explanatory. Part 1 comprises an alphabetical listing of all 1,250 or so filmmakers who have completed at least one fictional feature film which can be considered African. Where available, date and place of birth, training and/or film industrial experience, and an indication of other creative activities (such as short or documentary filmmaking, television work, video productions, publications) are given, together with a list of feature films. Part 2 sets out to list in alphabetical order the thirty-seven countries to which these filmmakers are conventionally aligned. In each case, a summary list of filmmakers is followed by a chronology of feature film output. The dating given here can be no more than approximate, however, since I have used a wide variety of sources, some employing production dates and others using release dates. In any case, there may be a wide gap between a film's foreign festival screenings and its eventual release at home (particularly if there are censorship problems), and a number of films, for whatever reason, have obtained no local commercial release at all. In the South African entries from 1974 to 1990 I have attempted to separate mainstream productions from the (incomplete) listing of low-budget "B" pictures which are set off by a blank line at the end of the year's list. The chronologies of part 2 are supplemented by a list of books and articles relevant to each national output. Part 3 is an index of film titles, using both original titles and distribution variants, together with English translations where appropriate. In each case, the director's name, the film's date, and the country of origin are given. For films from the Maghreb and francophone Africa, both English and French versions of the title are given and indexed. Similarly, South African films are indexed under both main and alternative release titles. In the case of Nigeria and South Africa, the language used in the film is also indicated. The Arabic transcriptions of Egyptian and Libyan film titles are very simplified forms (largely based—because of my principal source—on the French transcription system) and are intended merely to identify and differentiate films which, in most cases, do not have formal English titles. These transcriptions are not indexed. The names of filmmakers from the Democratic Republic of Congo are set out differently from all the others because when President Mobutu came to power in 1971, he not only changed the name of the country to Zaire, he also banned Christian names (along with neckties and miniskirts). The main bibliography lists books on relevant aspects of world cinema and general studies of African film (monographs on specific countries, filmmakers, and films are given in reference lists in part 2).

NOTES

1. Leonard Thompson, *A History of South Africa* (New Haven, Conn.: Yale University Press, 2001), pp. 152–153.

2. Kristina Bergmann, *Filmkultur und Filmindustrie in Ägypten* (Darmstadt, Germany: Wissenschaftliche Buchgesellschaft, 1993), p. 6.

3. L. A. Notcutt and G. C. Latham, *The African and the Cinema* (London: Edinburgh House Press, 1937), p. 183.

4. See my brief discussion of Chikly in Roy Armes, *African Filmmaking: North and South of the Sahara* (Edinburgh: Edinburgh University Press; Bloomington: Indiana University Press, 2006), pp. 24–25, and, for a much fuller account, in French, Guillemette Mansour, *Samama Chikly: un tunisien à la rencontre du XXième siècle* (Tunis: Simpact Editions, 2000).

5. Pierre Barrot, ed., *Nollywood: Le Phénomène vidéo au Nigeria* (Paris: Éditions L'Harmattan, 2005), p. 5.

6. Ibid., p. 20. There were signs in 2005–2006, with videos like Fred Amata's *Before the Sunrise,* Jimi Odumosu's *The Mourning After,* and, above all, Tunde Kelani's *Abeni,* that budgets and production standards are rising.

7. The current problems of distribution for 35mm films, faced throughout Africa, are set out clearly by Olivier Barlet in "Cinéma: un public sans marché," *Africultures* 69 (2007): 76–86.

8. See Ibrahima Signaté, *Med Hondo—un cinéaste rebelle* (Paris: Présence Africaine, 1994), pp. 44–47.

9. Kamal Abou al-Ela, quoted in Magda Wassef, ed., *Egypte: cent ans de cinéma* (Paris: Institut du Monde Arabe, 1995), p. 83.

10. Samir Farid, "Periodisation of Egyptian Cinema," in Alia Arasoughly, ed., *Screens of Life: Critical Film Writing from the Arab World* (Quebec: World Heritage Press, 1998), p. 8.

11. Isabel Balseiro and Ntongela Masilela, *To Change Reels: Film and Film Culture in South Africa* (Detroit: Wayne State University Press, 2003).

12. Thompson, *History,* p. 264.

13. Amin Maalouf, *On Identity* (London: Harvill Press, 2000), p. 4.

14. Ibid., p. 6.

15. "Francophone" is used here and throughout in the sense of those countries, usually former colonies or protectorates, which have close economic and cultural ties with France, the latter characterized by a national literature (novels, plays, poems) in French.

16. Hamid Naficy, *An Accented Cinema: Exilic and Diasporic Filmmaking* (Princeton, N.J.: Princeton University Press, 2001).

17. Tewfik Fares, cited in *Où va le cinéma algérien?* (Paris: *Cahiers du cinéma,* hors-série, February–March 2003), p. 71.

18. Claire Andrade-Watkins, "France's Bureau of Cinema: Financial and Technical Assistance between 1961 and 1977," *Framework* 38–39 (1992), pp. 27–46.

19. See Jean-Pierre Frodon, ed., *Au Sud du Cinéma* (Paris: Cahiers du Cinéma/Arte Editions, 2004).

20. Raphaël Millet, "(In)dépendance des cinémas du Sud &/vs France," *Théorème* 5 (1998), p. 163.

21. My listing is, however, incomplete. Johan Blignaut and Martin Botha in *Movies, Moguls, Mavericks: South African Cinema 1979–1991* (Cape Town: Showdata, 1992), p. 81, calculate that 944 films were produced in the years 1979–1991. I have only been able to locate 861, and for many of these I have found no more than a title and possible indication of the language used.

22. Keyan Tomaselli, *The South African Film Industry* (Johannesburg: University of Witwatersrand, 1981), p. 105. Tomaselli's chapter "Films for Blacks," in *The Cinema of Apartheid: Race and Class in South African Film* (London: Routledge, 1989), pp. 53–82, points out the ideological complexities of the South African situation.

23. Jacqueline Mainguard, "Framing South African National Cinema and Television," in Balseiro and Masilela, *To Change Reels,* p. 115.

24. Balseiro and Masilela, *To Change Reels,* p. 3.

25. Magda Wassef, ed., *Égypte: 100 ans de cinéma* (Paris: Éditions Plume/Institut du Monde Arabe, 1995), p. 14.

26. Bergmann, *Filmkultur und Filmindustrie in Ägypten,* p. 1.

Part One

African Feature Filmmakers

Abalo, Kilizou Blaise. Togo filmmaker. Trained teacher and filmmaker who taught at Ouagadougou University and the Institut Africain d'Education Cinématographique (INAFEC). Made a feature-length documentary, *President Eyadema's 10 Years in Power / 10 ans de pouvoir du Président Eyadema* (1976). Feature film: *Kawilasi* (1992)

Abaza, Mohamed. Egyptian filmmaker. Feature films: *Beware of the Women's Gang / Ihtaris ʿisâbat al-nisâʾ* (1986), *Wife on Approval / Imraʾah taht al-ikhtibâr* (1986), *The Musician / al-Mazzîkâtî* (1988), *A Serious Police Record / Arbâb sawâbiq* (1988), *Stop / Stop* (1989), *The Wounded Bird / al-Tâʾir al-garîh* (1990)

Abbazi, Mohamed (b. 1938 in Khémisset). Moroccan filmmaker. Studied film direction at the University of California at Los Angeles (UCLA) and cinema studies at Harvard. Worked extensively as assistant on foreign films shot in Morocco. Also worked in Moroccan television and made a number of shorts in the 1960s and 1970s. Feature films: *From the Other Side of the River / De l'autre côté du fleuve* (1982), *The Treasures of the Atlas / Les Trésors de l'Atlas* (1997)

Abboud, Taysir. Egyptian filmmaker. Feature films: *The Folly of Adolescent Girls / Gounoun al-mourâhiqât* (1972), *Resolute Nights / Layâlî lan taʾoud* (1974), *Shore of Violence / Châti al-ʾounf* (1975), *Our Days Are Numbered / Ayyâm al-ʾoumr maʾdoudah* (1978), *Let Me Avenge Myself / Daʾounî antaqim* (1979), *The Girls' Father / Abou al-banât* (1980), *The Thieves / al-Lousous* (1981), *A Dangerous Liaison / ʿAlâqah khatirah* (1981), *I Shall Return without Tears / Sa aʾoud*

bilâ doumouʾ (1981), *Deviation / Inhirâf* (1985), *Farewell My Child / Wadâʾan yâ waladî* (1986)

Abdel Aziz, Mohamed (b. 1940 in Cairo). Egyptian filmmaker. Elder brother of Omar Abdel Aziz. Graduated from the Cairo Higher Film Institute in 1964 and worked as assistant director to, among others, Salah Abou Seif. Active as a director for 30 years, he made his reputation with a long series of comedies. Feature films: *Forbidden Images / Souwar mamnouʿah* (one episode) (1972), *A Woman from Cairo / Imraʾah min al-Qâhirah* (1973), *In Summer You Have to Love / Fî-l-sayf lâzim nihibb* (1974), *A World of Kids / ʿÂlum ʿiyâl ʿiyâl* (1976), *Heartbeat / Daqqat qulb* (1976), *Good Children / al-ʾIyâl al-tayyibîn* (1976), *The Weaker Sex / Guins nâʾim* (1977), *A Million and One Kisses / Alf bousah wa bousah* (1977), *Some People Get Married Twice / al-Baʿd yadhhab ilâ al-maʾdhoun marratayn* (1978), *Hello, Captain / Ahlan yâ kabtin* (1978), *The Purse Is with Me / al-Mihfazah maʾâya* (1978), *A Murderer Who Has Killed No-One / Qâtil mâ qatalch hadd* (1979), *Beware of Your Neighbors / Khallî bâlak min Guîrânak* (1979), *Take Care, Gentlemen / Intabihou ayyouhâ al-sâdah* (1980), *A Man Who Has Lost His Mind / Ragoul faqada ʿaqlahou* (1980), *The Clumsy Man / Ghâwî machâkil* (1980), *Lips Which Do Not Know How to Lie / Chifâh lâ taʾrif al-kadhib* (1980), *Vote for Dr. Soleymane Abdel Basset / Intakhibou al-doktor Soulaymân ʿAbd al-Bâsit* (1981), *Journey of Terror / Rihlat al-rouʾb* (1981), *Hamada and Toutou's Gang / ʿIsâbat Hamâdah wa Toutou* (1982), *The Sparkle in Your Eyes / Barîq ʿaynayki* (1982), *Morsi from Above, Morsi from Below / Moursî fawq Moursî taht* (1982), *Journey of Suffering and Love / Rih-*

lat al-chaqâ³ wa-l-houbb (1982), *The Realm of Hallucinations / Mamlakat al-halwasah* (1983), *Our Daughters Abroad / Banâtounâ fî-l-khârig* (1984), *The Fox and the Grape / al-Tha³lab wa-l-³inab* (1984), *Your Day Will Come, Bey / Lak youm yâ bîh* (1984), *But There Is Still Something Left / Wa lâkin chay³an mâ yabqâ* (1984), *Who, of the Two of Us, Is the Thief? / Mîn fînâ al-Harâmî* (1984), *Beware of Your Intelligence / Khallî bâlak min ᶜaqlak* (1985), *Ten Out of Ten / ᶜAchrah ᶜalâ ᶜachrah* (1985), *The Judgment at the End of the Audience / al-Houkm âkhir al-galsah* (1985), *The Alarm Bells / Agrâs al-khatar* (1986), *Extremely Confidential / Sirrî li-l-ghâyah* (1986), *The Password / Kalimat al-sirr* (1986), *The Secret Session / al-Galsah al-sirriyyah* (1986), *Do Not Destroy Me Along with Yourself / Lâ toudammirnî ma³ak* (1986), *The House of the Poisoned Family / Manzil al-³â³ilah al-masmoumah* (1986), *Cry of Remorse / Sarkat nadam* (1988), *The Night of Bakiza and Zaghloul's Arrest / Laylat al-qabd ᶜalâ Bakîzah wa Zaghloul* (1988), *We Share Your Joys / Nouchâtiroukoum al-afrâh* (1988), *Matron Samah / al-Mou³allimah Samah* (1989), *The Bad Boy / al-Fatâ al-chirrîr* (1989), *Hanafi the Magnificent / Hanafi al-oubbahah* (1990), *Night of Honey / Laylat ᶜasal* (1990), *The Devil Finds a Solution / al-Chaytân youqaddim hallan* (1991), *Beware of Charbate / Âh . . . we âh min Charbât* (1992), *The Game of Revenge / Lou³bat al-intiqâm* (1992), *Round Up! / Hallaq hoosh!* (1997), *Afrotto / Afrotto* (2001)

Abdel Aziz, Omar (b. 1952). Egyptian filmmaker. Graduated from the Cairo Higher Film Institute in 1976 and worked as assistant director to, among others, his brother, Mohamed Abdel Aziz, and Salah Abou Seif. Like his brother he has specialized in comedy. Feature films: *A Very Special Invitation / Da³wah khâssah guiddan* (1982), *Sympathy for the Dead Man / Li-l-faqîd al-rahmah* (1982), *Nothing to Do, It's the Way Things Are / Tiguîbhâ kidah, tiguîlhâ kidah, hiyya kidah* (1983), *The Lout / al-Qifl* (1983), *Provided It Is a Son / Yâ rabb walad* (1984), *The Lucky Guy / al-Mahzouz* (1984), *Here Is Cairo / Hounâ al-Qâhirah* (1985), *The Flat Goes to the Wife / al-Chiqqah min haqq al-zawgah* (1985), *The Man Who Had Sneezed / al-Ragoul alladhî*

ᶜatas (1985), *The Mad Woman / al-Mag³nounah* (1985), *The Banner / al-Bandîrah* (1986), *The Trainee Lawyer / Mouhâmî taht al-tamrîn* (1986), *The Players / al-La³îbah* (1987), *One July Night / Laylah fî chahr sab³ah* (1988), *Bric-à-brac / Karâkîb* (1989), *Mr. Dessouqi on Holiday / Dessouqi afandî fî-l-masyaf* (1992), *Why Pyramids? / Lîh yâ haram* (1993), *Summer Love Is Crazy / Fil seif al-hubb gonoon* (1995), *Talking about Taboos / al-Kalaam fil mamnoo³* (2000), *Fruit Ice / Graneeta* (2001), *Heaven Save Us! / Ashtatan Ashtoot* (2004), *Farhan Mulazem Adam / Farhan Mulazem Adam* (2005)

Abdel Aziz, Sameh. Egyptian filmmaker. Feature films: *Private Lesson / Dars khusussi* (2005), *Dreams of a Reckless Young Man / Ahlam al-Fata al ta³ish* (2007), *A Lion and Four Cats / Asad wa 4 qitat* (2007)

Abdel Gawad, Mohamed. Egyptian filmmaker. Feature films: *Love Story / Qissat gharâm* (with Kamal Selim, 1945), *The Gipsies's Town / madînat al-ghagar* (1945), *Old People's Love / Gharâm al-chouyoukh* (1946), *The Return of the Magic Cap / ᶜAwdat tâqiyyat al-ikhfâ* (1946), *Return to the Departure Point / ᶜÂdat ilâ qawâ³idihâ* (1946), *Flowers and Thorns / Azhar wa achwâk* (1947), *The Vagabond / al-Moutacharridah* (1947), *The Great Sacrifice / al-Tad³hiyah al-koubrâ* (1947), *The Escaped Prisoner / Hârb min al-sig³n* (1948), *The Countryside in Mourning / al-Rîf al-hazîn* (1948), *Gawaher / Gawâhir* (1949), *When Life Smiles at You / al-Douniâ limma tidhak* (1953), *Between Two Hearts / Bayn qalbayn* (1953), *Victim of Injustice / al-Mazloumah* (1950), *The Outlaw / al-Khârig ᶜalâ al-qânoun* (1951), *The Wretched Man / Qalîl al-bakht* (1952), *April Fool / Kidbad abril* (1954), *Women Don't Know How to Lie / al-Sittât mâ ya³rafouch yikdibou* (1954), *No-One's Worth Anything in the Grave / Mâhaddichwâkhid minhâ hâgah* (1955), *Happiness Is a Promise / al-Sa³d wa³d* (1955), *Kiss Me in the Shadows / Qabbilnî fî-l-zalîm* (1959), *Husband on Holiday / Zawg fî agâzar* (1964), *The Unknown Man / al-Ragoul al-mag³houl* (1965)

Abdel Ghani, Rachad. Egyptian filmmaker. Feature film: *The Three Tough Guys / al-Guid³ân al-thâlathah* (1988)

Abdel Khalek, Ali (b. 1944). Egyptian film-maker. Graduated from the Cairo Higher Film Institute in 1966 and made a number of noted documentaries. A member of the New Cinema group. Feature films: *Song on the Way / Ough-niyah ͨâla al-mamarr* (1972), *Home without Tenderness / Bayt bilâ hanân* (1976), *The Dev-ils / al-Abâlisah* (1980), *The Suffering of Love / ͨAdhâb al-houbb* (1980), *Traveller without a Road / mousâfir bilâ tarîq* (1981), *Love Alone Is Not Enough / al-Houbb wahdahou lâ yakfî* (1981), *And My Heart Ended Down There / Wa dâ'a houbbî hounak* (1982), *Disgrace / al-'Âr* (1982), *Gentlemen You Are Corrupt / al-Sâdah al-mourtachoun* (1983), *Daughters of Satan / Banât Iblîs* (1984), *The Execution of a Dead Man / I'dâm mayyit* (1985), *The Drug / al-Kîf* (1985), *The Fish Kettle / Châdir al-samak* (1986), *The Debauched / al-Hanâkîch* (1986), *Furnished Cemeteries to Let / Madâfin mafrouchah li-l-îgâr* (1986), *Mud / al-Wahl* (1987), *Four on a Diffi-cult Mission / Arba'ah fî mouhimmah rasmiyyah* (1987), *The Well of Treason / Bi'r al-khiyânah* (1987), *The Deer Run / Garî al-wouhouch* (1987), *Help! / Ilhaqounâ* (1989), *Rape / Ightisâb* (1989), *The Egg and the Stone / al-Baydah wa-l-hugar* (1990), *The Route of Terror / Darb al-rahbah* (1990), *Humour / al-Mizâg* (1991), *Maid Ser-vant, but . . . / Khâdimah wa lâkin* (1993), *Wom-en's Threshold / ͨAtabet el settaat* (1995), *The Gentleman / el-Gentel* (1996), *The Empress / Al-imbratoura* (1999), *Al Kafeer / al-Kafeer* (1999), *Al Nims / al-Nims* (2000), *Fine, Fine / Bono, bono* (2000), *Rendezvous / Rendezvous* (2001), *An Oath of Divorce / Yameen talaq* (2001), *Whale Hunting / Said al-heitaan* (2002), *May God Make It Up to Us / ͨAlih al-ͨawad* (2003), *The Day of Dignity / Youm El Karama* (2004), *Zaza / Zaza* (2006)

Abdel Muti, Tarek. Egyptian filmmaker. Fea-ture film: *Agamista / 'Agamista* (2007)

Abdel Salam, Ahmed. Egyptian filmmaker. Feature film: *Mister Dollar / Mister Dollar* (1993)

Abdel Salam, Chadi (b. 1930 in Alexandria; d. 1986). Egyptian filmmaker. Studied architec-ture at the Cairo Fine Art School and drama in Oxford. Worked as designer on a number of Egyptian productions of the 1950s and, in the 1960s, collaborated on films with Youssef Cha-hine (on *Saladin*) and three foreign directors (J. L. Mankiewicz, Jerzy Kawalerowicz, and Roberto Rossellini). His debut feature, *The Mummy*, was followed by three short films made in the early 1970s and a series of historical docu-mentaries for children in the 1980s *The Mummy* is universally regarded as one of the master works of Egyptian cinema. He was subsequently unable to made his long-planned second fea-ture, *Akhanaton*. Feature film: *The Mummy* aka *The Night of Counting the Years / al-Moumyâ'* (1969)

Abdel Sayed, Daoud (b. 1946 in Cairo). Egyp-tian filmmaker. Graduated from the Cairo Higher Film Institute in 1967, worked as assis-tant director with Youssef Chahine and Kamal Al-Cheikh, and made a number of shorts in the 1970s. A key director of the 1980s when he turned to feature filmmaking. Feature films: *The Hooligans / al-Sa'âlîk* (1985), *Kit Kat / al-Kît Kât* (1991), *Looking for Sayyed Marzouq / Al Bahth 'an Sayyed Marzouk* (1991), *Land of Dreams / Ard al-ahlâm* (1993), *The Man Who Stole Joy / Sarek al-farah* (1995), *Land of Fear / Ard el khouf* (2000), *A Citizen, a Detective and a Thief / Mowa-ten wa mukhber wa haraamy* (2001)

Abdel Wahab, Fatine (b. 1913 at Damiette; d. 1972). Egyptian filmmaker. Married to the singer Leïla Mourad. Studied at military school but was drawn to the cinema and worked as as-sistant director in the Misr studios from the be-ginning of the 1940s. A prolific director in the 1960s and 1970s, he is regarded as Egyptian cinema's finest specialist in comedy. Feature films: *Nadia / Nâdiâ* (1949), *The Husband of the Four / Gouz al-arbba'ah* (1950), *Tears of Hap-piness / Doumou' al-farah* (with Ahmed Salem, 1950), *The House of Ghosts / Bayt al-achbâh* (1951), *Fatma the Lawyer / al-Oustâdhah Fat-mah* (1952), *The Slaves of Money / ͨAbîd al-mâl* (1953), *The Law of a Tyrant / Houkm qa-râqouch* (1953), *The Truth / Kalimat al-haqq* (1953), *Miss Hanafi / al-Ânissah* (1954), *Hello / Nahârak sa'îd* (1955), *Ishmael Yassine in the*

Army / Ismâ³îl fî-l-gaych (1955), *I Have Given You My Life / Wahabtouka hayâtî* (with Zouheir Bekir, 1956), *Ishmael Yassine in the Police / Ismâ³îl Yâsîn fî-l-bolîs* (1956), *Women in My Life / Nisâ³fî hayâtî* (1957), *Tachera / Tâhirah* (1957), *Hamido's Son / Ibn Hamido* (1957), *Ishmael Yassine in the Navy / Ismâ³îl Yâsîn fî-l-oustoul* (1957), *Stop Thief / Imsik harâmî* (1958), *The Seducer of Women / Sâhir al-nisâ³* (1958), *Ishmael Yassine in the Military Police / Ismâ³îl Yâsîn bolis harbî* (1958), *The Elder Brother / al-Akhkh al-kabîr* (1958), *Al-Atba al-Khadraa / al-³Atbah al-khadrâ³* (1959), *Ishmael Yassine in Flying / Ismâ³îl / Yâsîn fî-l-tayarân* (1959), *Ishmael Yassine in the Secret Police / Ismâ³îl Yâsîn bolis sirrî* (1959), *They Will Drive Me Mad / Hayganninounî* (1960), *Ladies' Hairdresser / Hallâq al-sayyidât* (1960), *Girls and Summer / Banât wa-l-sayf* (one episode) (1960), *And Love Returns / Wa ³âda al-houbb* (1960), *The Magic Lamp / al-Fânous al-sihrî* (1960), *Rumour of Love / Ichâ³at houbb* (1960), *The Filtered Light / al-Daw³ al-khâfit* (1961), *Wife No. 13 / al-Zawgah raqam talata³ch* (1962), *The Three Cavaliers / al-Foursân al-thalâthah* (1962), *Beware of Hawa / Âh min Hawwâ* (1962), *Zizi's Family / ³Â³ilat Zizi* (1963), *The Fiancée from the Nile / ³Arous al-Nîl* (1963), *His Majesty / Sâhib al-galâlah* (1963), *The Honorable Family / al-³Â³ilah al-kârimah* (1964), *Me, Him and Her / Anâ wa houwa wa hiya* (1964), *Confessions of a Husband / I³tirâfât zawg* (1964), *The Artistic Director / al-Moudîr al-fannî* (1965), *Driven from Paradise / Tarîd al-Fardous* (1965), *Three Thieves / Thalâthat lousous* (one episode) (1966), *My Wife Is Managing Director / Mirâtî moudîr ³âmm* (1966), *Adam's Apple / Touffâhat Adam* (1966), *When We Love / ³Indamâ nouhibb* (1967), *My Wife's Honor / Karâmat zawgatî* (1967), *Land of Hypocrites / Ard al-nifâq* (1968), *My Wife's Ghost / ³Ifrît mirâtî* (1968), *Eve's Lies / Akâdhîb Hawwâ* (1969), *Seven Days in Paradise / Sab³ayyâm fî-l-gannah* (1969), *Half-an-Hour of Marriage / Nouss sa³at zawâg* (1969), *My Life / Hayâti* (1970), *The Joyous Troupe / Firqat almarah* (1970), *Mummy's Suitor / Khatîb mâmâ* (1971), *A Pleasant Trip / Rihla ladhîdhah* (1971), *The Lights of the City / Adwâ al-madînah* (1972)

Abdel Wahab, Hamada. Egyptian filmmaker. Feature films: *The Honest Burglar / al-Liss al-charîf* (1953), *Ishmael Yassine Meets Raya and Sekina / Ismâ³îl Yâsîn youqâbil Rayyâ Sakînah* (1955), *Trip on the Moon / Rihlah ilâ al-qamar* (1959)

Abdel Wahab, Hassan. Egyptian filmmaker. Feature films: *Broken Hearts / Qouloub dâmiyah* (1945), *If Youth . . . / Layta al-chabâb* (1948)

Abdel Wahab, Zaki Fatin. Egyptian filmmaker and actor. Son of Fatine Abdel Wahab. Actor and assistant on Youssef Chahine's *Alexandria Now and Forever*. Feature film: *Romantic / Romantica* (1996)

Abdelilah, Badr (b. 1963 in Casablanca). Moroccan filmmaker. Martial arts specialist working as actor and stunt coordinator in Europe and Morocco. Based in Brussels, he made his feature film debut with a comedy which is the first Moroccan film in the Berber language, Amazigh. Feature film: *Bouksasse Boutfounaste* (2006)

Abdelwahab, Ali (b. 1938 in Tozeur). Tunisian theatre director and filmmaker. Worked as assistant to Jacques Baratier and Omar Khlifi. Feature film: *Om abbes* (1970)

Abidi, Ali (b. 1950 in Redeyef). Tunisian filmmaker. Studied film and theatre in Romania. Three shorts before beginning his feature film career. Feature films: *Barg Ellil / Éclair nocturne* (1990), *Redeyef 54* (1997)

Abikanlou, Pascal (b. 1935 in Pobé). Benin filmmaker. Photographer and designer. Trainee in France. Ten documentaries before and after his sole feature film. Feature film: *Under the Sign of the Vaudon / Sous le signe du vaudon* (1974)

Abou al-Ela, Kamal. Egyptian filmmaker. Worked as film editor. His sole directing credit arose when he completed the shooting after a quarrel between the director and the producer/star, Bahiga Hafez. Feature film: *Zohra / Zohrah* (with Hussein Fawzi, 1947)

Abou al-Nasr, Hicham (b. 1944 in Cairo). Egyptian filmmaker. Graduated from the Cairo Higher Film Institute in 1964 and subsequently studied film at the University of California at Los Angeles (UCLA). Feature films: *Al-Akmar / al-Aqmar* (1978), *Mawardi's Café / Qahwat al-Mâwardî* (1982), *Girls and the Unknown / al-Banât wa-l-mag³houl* (1986), *The Gang / al-³Isâbah* (1987)

Abou Laban, Osman. Egyptian filmmaker. Feature films: *Our Life's Dreams / Ahlaam ᶜumrena* (2005), *Open Your Eyes / Fattah ᶜinak* (2006)

Abou Seif, Mohamed (b. 1950 in Cairo). Egyptian filmmaker. Son of Salah Abou Seif. Studied psychology first at university and then filmmaking at the Cairo Higher Film Institute, graduating in 1976. Worked as assistant director. Feature films: *The Apple and the Skull / al-Touffâhah wa-l-goumgoumah* (1986), *The River of Fear / Nahr al-khawf* (1988), *Hell 2 / Gahîm itnîn* (1990), *First Grade, Secondary School / ᶜUla thanawy* (2001), *A Hero from the South / Batal min al-ganoob* (2001), *Be Alert / Khalli el demaagh sahi* (2002), *The Ostrich and the Peacock / al-Na³aama wa al-tawooss* (2002), *Cholesterol Free / Khaly min al-cholesterol* (2005)

Abou Seif, Salah (b. 1915 in Cairo; d. 1996). Egyptian filmmaker. Without film training, he began as an assistant (most notably on Kamal Selim's *The Will* in 1939). Active as a director for almost 50 years, he is a key figure in Egyptian realist cinema. Collaborated with the Nobel Prize–winning novelist Naguib Mahfouz, whom he introduced to cinema, on eight feature films in eight years, including *Dead among the Living* and *Cairo 30*. Director of the General Organisation of Egyptian Cinema from 1963 to 1965, when he founded the Script Institute. Feature films: *Always in My Heart / Dâyman fî qalbî* (1946), *The Avenger / al-Mountaqim* (1947), *The Adventures of Antar and Abla / Moughâmarât b³Antar wa ᶜAbla* (1948), *Pulchinello Street / Châri³ al-bahlawân* (1949), *The Falcon / al-Saqr* (1950), *Your Day Will Come / Lak Youm yâ zâlim* (1951), *Love Is a Scandal / al-Houbb bah-*

dalah (1952), *Hassan the Foreman / al-Oustâ Hasan* (1952), *Raya and Sakina / Rayyâ wa Sakînah* (1953), *The Monster / al-Wahch* (1954), *The Leech / Chabâb imra³ah* (1956), *The Tough Guy / al-Foutouwwah* (1957), *The Empty Pillow / al-Wisâdah al-khâliyah* (1957), *Nights without Sleep / Lâ anâm* (1957), *A Criminal on Holiday / Mougrim fî agâzah* (1958), *The Dead End / al-Tarîq al-masdoud* (1958), *That's Love / Hâdhâ houwa al-houbb* (1958), *I Am Free / Anâ hourrah* (1959), *Between Heaven and Earth / Bayn al-samâ³ wa-l-ard* (1959), *Anguish of Love / Law³at al-houbb* (1960), *Girls and Summer / Banât wa-l-sayf* (one episode) (1960), *Dead among the Living / Bidâyah wa nihâyah* (1960), *Don't Extinguish the Sun / Lâ toufi³ al-chams* (1961), *Letter from an Unknown Woman / Risâlah min imra³ah mag³houlah* (1962), *No Time for Love / Lâ waqt li-l-houbb* (1963), *Cairo 30 / al-Qâhirah talâtîn* (1966), *The Second Wife / al-Zawgah al-thâniyah* (1967), *Trial 68 / al-Qadiyyah 68* (1968), *Three Women / Thalâth nisâ³* (one episode) (1969), *A Little Suffering / Chay³ min al-³adhâb* (1969), *The Dawn of Islam / Fagr al-Islâm* (1971), *The Malatilli Baths / Hammâm al-Malâtîli* (1973), *The Liar / al-Kaddâb* (1975), *First Year of Love / Sanah oulâ houbb* (one episode) (1976), *She Fell into a Sea of Honey / Wa saqatat fî bahr al³asal* (1977), *The Watercarrier Is Dead / al-Saqqâ mât* (1977), *The Criminal / al-Mougrim* (1978), *Satan's Empire / al-Bidâyah* (1986), *Citizen Masri / al-Mouwâtin Masrî* (1991), *Mr. D / al-Sayyed kâf* (1994)

Abou Seif, Youssef. Egyptian filmmaker. Feature films: *Days of Evil / Ayyaam al-charr* (1995), *Rebel Woman / Imra³ah moutamarridah* (1986), *Abou Khatwa / Abou Khatwa* (1998), *The Female and the Wasp / Al-untha wa al-dabbour* (1998), *Bab Charq / Bâb Charq* (1989), *The Fugitive's Return / ᶜAwdat al-hârib* (1990)

Abou Zeid, Ahmed. Egyptian filmmaker. Feature film: *The Devils / Al-chayateen* (2007)

Abou Zikri, Kamla. Egyptian filmmaker. Studied at the Cairo Higher Film Institute, graduating in 1994. She worked as an assistant director and in documentary before turning to fiction, with three short films. Feature films: *Swindlers, First Grade / Sana ula nasb* (2004), *Heads or Tails / Makel wa ketaba* (2005), *Love and Passion / ʿAnn al-ʿishk wal hawa* (2006)

Aboulouakar, Mohamed (b. 1946 in Marrakesh). Moroccan painter and filmmaker. Studied filmmaking at the Vsesoyuznyi gosudarstvennyi institut kinematografii (VGIK; All-Union State Cinema Institute) in Moscow and made a number of fictional and documentary shorts. Feature film: *Hadda* (1984)

Achouba, Abdou (b. 1950 in Rabat). Moroccan filmmaker, resident in France, working as teacher and critic. Studied filmmaking at the Institut des Hautes Études Cinématographiques (IDHEC) in Paris. Made a number of short films and documentaries from the 1970s, including *La Confession des possédés* (1983). Feature film: *Taghounja / Tarounja* (1980)

Adams, Catlin. South African filmmaker. Feature film: *Sticky Fingers* (English, 1977)

Adeeb, Adel. Egyptian filmmaker. Studied at the Cairo Higher Film Institute. Several documentaries and commercials. Feature films: *Hysteria / Hysteria* (1998), *The Most Elegant Guy in Roxy / Ashyak waad fi roxy* (1999)

Adenuga, Adewale. Nigerian filmmaker. Feature film: *Papa Ajasco* (Pidgin English, 1984)

Aderohunmu, Bayo. Nigerian filmmaker. Feature film: *Kanna Kanna* (Yoruba, 1986)

Adesanya, Afolabi (b. 1956 in Kano). Nigerian filmmaker and critic. Managing director of the Nigerian Film Corporation in Jos from 2005. Studied filmmaking at the San Francisco Art Institute. Made a number of Yoruba documentaries and videos and worked as assistant on Ladi Ladebo's films *Pariah* (1994), *Power* (1998), and *Baba Zak* (1999). Feature films: *Vigilante* (English, 1988), *Ose Sango* (Yoruba, 1991)

Adewusi, Gbenga. Nigerian filmmaker. After making his only feature film in 16mm, turned to video and worked as director and producer (Bayowa Films). Feature film: *Itunu* (Yoruba, 1992)

Adjesu, Egbert (b. 1931 at Odumase Krobo). Ghanaian filmmaker. Lived in London and worked at Pinewood studios. Worked from 1952 at the Gold Coast Film Unit and became one of its first directors when it became the Ghana Film Industry Corporation. Feature film: *I Told You So* (1970)

Adu, Jab (b. in Lagos). Nigerian filmmaker. An actor in radio and television, he appeared in Ossie Davies's Nigerian-produced *Count Down at Kusini* (1976). Feature film: *Bisi Daughter of the River* (English, 1977)

Aduaka, Newton I. (b. 1966 in Ogidi, Eastern Nigeria). Moved to Lagos in 1970 and to London in 1985. Currently based in Paris. Studied at the London International Film School, graduating in 1990. His three short films and his feature film debut all received acclaim at international festivals and his second feature, *Ezra,* won the top prize, the Étalon de Yennenga. at the Festival Panafricain du Cinéma de Ouagadougou (FESPACO) in 2007. Feature films: *Rage* (English, 2000), *Ezra* (2007)

Afifi, Ibrahim. Egyptian filmmaker. Feature films: *The Dose of Hashish / al-Qirch* (1981), *The Baker's Shop / al-Fourn* (1984), *The Hippopotamus / al-Sayyed qichtah* (1985), *Izbat al-Safih / ʿIzbat al-safîh* (1987), *The Old Man and the Crook / al-ʾAgouz wa-l-baltaguî* (1989), *Chawadder / Chawâdir* (1990), *Hilali's Grip / Qabdat al-Hilâlî* (1991), *The Gypsies / al-Ghagar* (1996), *Sons of the Devil / Abnaʾ al-Chaytaan* (2000)

Afolayan, Adeyemi [Ade Love] (b. Agbamu, 1940; d. 1996). Nigerian filmmaker. Founder of the Ade Love Theatre. Played the leading role in Balogun's *Ajani Ogun* (1975) and was producer/writer/lead performer of the same director's *Ija Ominira* (1978). Feature films: *Kadara* (Yoruba, 1980), *Ija Orogun* (Yoruba, 1982). *Taxi Driver* (Yoruba, 1983), *Iya ni Wura* (Yoruba, 1984), *Taxi Driver II* (Yoruba, 1986),

Mosebolatan (Yoruba, 1986), *Ori Olori* (Yoruba, 1989), *Ehin Oku* (Yoruba, 1992)

Aglane, Nabawi. Egyptian filmmaker. Feature film: *A Lost Woman / Imra'ah dallat al-tarîq* (1990)

Agrama, Farouk. Egyptian filmmaker. Feature film: *Bitter Grape / al'Inab al-mourr* (1965)

Ahmed, Mohsen. Egyptian filmmaker. Feature film: *Al-Sayyed Abou El-Araby Is Here / al-Sayyed Abu El-Araby wasal* (2005)

Ahmed Ali, Magdi (b. 1952 at Mansourah). Egyptian filmmaker. Graduated from the Cairo Higher Film Institute in 1981. Made several documentaries and scripted Tarek al-Telmessani's *Laughs, Games, Seriousness and Love* (1993). Feature films: *Oh, Life, My Love / Ya donya ya gharamy* (1996), *The Champion / al-Batal* (1998), *Girls' Secrets / Asraar al-banat* (2001)

Ajaga, Mukaila. Nigerian filmmaker. Feature films: *Egunleri* (Yoruba, 1985), *Akoni* (Yoruba, 1989)

Akdi, Ahmed Kacem (b. 1942 in Chefchaouen). Moroccan filmmaker. Worked as a trainee in Gibraltan television and made a number of shorts. Returned to television after two feature films. Feature films: *The Drama of the 40,000 / Le Drame des 40,000* (1982), *What the Winds Have Carried Away / Ce que les vents ont emporté* (1984)

Akika, Ali (b. 1945 in Gigel in Algeria). French-based filmmaker of Algerian descent who has lived in France since 1965. Studied political economy at university and became a school-teacher and film critic. Participated in the 85-minute collective film *The Olive Tree / L'Olivier* (1976) and made several shorts and a number of video documentaries. Feature films: *Journey to the Capital / Voyage en capital* (with Anne-Marie Autissier, 1977), *Tears of Blood / Larmes de sang* (with Anne-Marie Autissier, 1980)

Akin, Mohamed Lamine (b. 1927 in Treichville, Ivory Coast). Guinean filmmaker. Studied at the Institut des Hautes Études Cinématographiques (IDHEC) in Paris and worked as a trainee in Germany. The pioneer of Guinean cinema. Feature film: *Sergeant Bakary Woolen / Le Sergent Bakary Woolen* (1966)

Aknash, Mourad. Turkish director of one Egyptian feature film: *Runaway Mummy / Horoob mumia* (2003)

Akomfrah, John (b. 1957 in Ghana). Ghanaian filmmaker based in the United Kingdom. Teacher, journalist, founding member of the Black Audio Film Collective in London. Maker of about twenty documentaries, beginning with *Handsworth Songs* in 1986, some of them of feature length: *Speak Like a Child* (1998), *Urban Soul* (2003). Fictional features: *Testament* (1988), *Who Needs a Heart* (1991)

Al-Aassar, Adel. Egyptian filmmaker. Feature films: *A Deal Made with a Woman / Safqah ma' imra'ah* (1985), *The Fatal Dream / al-Houlm al-qâtil* (1986), *Operation 42 / al-'Amaliyyah tinîn wa arba'în* (1987), *A Woman's Claws / Makhâlib imra'ah* (1988), *A Life's Scandal / Fadîhat al-'oumr* (1989), *The Fall / al-Souqout* (1990), *Al-Gablawi / al-Gablâwî* (1991), *Satan's Gates / Bawwâbat Iblîs* (1993), *Rubbish / Qadhârah* (1994), *Escape to the Summit / al-Horoob ila al-qimma* (1996), *Suspicious Liaisons / 'Ilaqaat mashbouha* (1996), *Daytime Devil / 'Afreet al-nahaar* (1997), *Anbar and the Colours / 'Anbar wa al-alwaan* (2001), *Gaafar al-Masri's Disappearance / Ikhtifaa' Gaafar al-Masr* (2002), *The Sea-Drill / Haffaar el bahr* (2003)

Alabi Huneyin, Tunde. Nigerian filmmaker. Feature film: *Ireke Onibudo* (Yoruba, 1983)

Al-Alami, Yehya. Egyptian filmmaker. Feature films: *The Woman Who Conquered the Devil / al-Mar'ah allatî ghalabat al-chaytân* (1973), *Meeting with the Past / Liqâ' ma' al-mâdî* (1975), *The Taxi King / Malik al-taxi* (1976), *With Hot Tears / al-Doumou' al-sâkhinah* (1976), *The Gang of Bonviveurs / Chillat al-ouns* (1976), *The*

Sad Bird of Night / Tâ³ir al-layl al-hâzin (1977), *The Sins of Love / Khatâyâ al-houbb* (1977), *Night and Desire / Layl wa raghbah* (1977), *Love You Are Beautiful / Hilwah yâ douniâ al-houbb* (1977), *Youth Dancing on Fire / Chabâb yarqous fawq al-nâr* (1978), *Hearts in an Ocean of Tears / Qouloub fî bahr al-doumou³* (1978), *An Angel's Sin / Khatî³at malâk* (1979), *Men Knowing Nothing of Love / Rigâl lâ ya³rifoun al-houbb* (1979), *The Hidden Trap / al-Khoud³ah al-khafiyyah* (1979), *Something Frightens Him / Khâ³ifah min chay³in mâ* (1979), *The Tough Guys from Boulak / Foutouwwât Boulâq* (1981), *Dandach / Dandach* (1981), *The Lovers' Struggle / Sirâ³ al-³ouchchâq* (1981), *One Fiancée and Two Suitors / ʿArousah wa gouz ʿoursân* (1982), *The Promised Night / al-Laylah al-maw³oudah* (1984), *Falsification of Official Papers / Tazwîr fî awrâq rasmiyyah* (1984), *The Masters of the Port / Gabâbirat al-minâ³* (1985), *Nagwa Madam Chatlata / Nagwâ madame Chalâtah* (1986), *Roots in the Air / Goudhour fî-l-hawâ³* (1986), *Khalil after the Changes / Khalîl ba³d al-ta³dîl* (1987)

Alan, Jordon. South African filmmaker. Feature film: *Terminal Bliss* (English, 1988)

Al-Ansari, Mouhannad. Egyptian filmmaker. Feature film: *Trial No. 1 / al-Qadiyyah raqam wâhid* (1983)

Al-Aqqad, Mohamed. Egyptian filmmaker. Feature film: *Reasonable People / Ashâb al-³ouqoul* (1940)

Al-Aryane, Tarek (b. 1963). Egyptian filmmaker of Palestinian origin. The son of a film producer established in Egypt, he studied in the United States. Feature films: *The Emperor / al-Ambarâtour* (1990), *The Pasha / al-Bâchâ* (1993)

Al-Asfoury, Samir. Egyptian filmmaker. Feature films: *Bluffing / Alabanda* (with Mohamed Fadel, 1999), *That's OK / Keda OK* (with Osama Al-Asi, 2003)

Al-Asi, Osama. Egyptian filmmaker. Feature film: *That's OK / Keda OK* (with Samir Al-Asfoury, 2003)

Alassane, Mustapha (b. 1942 in N'Dougou). Niger filmmaker. A pioneer of African cinema since the early 1960s, he has made about twenty films in a wide variety of genres: documentaries and short fictions, as well as feature films and a number of animated films. His first animation, *The Boatman / Le Piroguier,* dates from 1962, and he returned to the genre with *Gandji's Death / La Mort de Gandji* (1965), *Bon voyage Sim* (1966), *Samba the Great / Samba le grand* (1977), and *Kokoa* (1985). Feature films: *FVVA* (1972), *Toula / Toula ou le Génie des eaux* (1973), *Kankamba / Kankamba ou Le Semeur de discorde* (1982)

Al-Badri, Ahmed. Egyptian filmmaker. Feature films: *Love Fan / Ghawy hubb* (2005), *I Swear Thrice by Songs / ³Alayya al-tarab bil talaata* (2006), *Touched in the Head / Lakhmet raas* (2006), *I Am Not With Them / Ana mush ma³ahum* (2007)

Al-Badri, Khaled. Egyptian filmmaker. Feature film: *Ouija / Ouija* (2006)

Al-Bagouri, Sameh. Egyptian filmmaker. Feature film: *Ruining the Party / Kursi fil koloob* (2000)

Al-Bahhat, Imad. Egyptian filmmaker. Feature films: *Hide and Seek / Ustughummaaya* (2007), *The Clown / Al-beliatshu* (2007)

Al-Bakri, Asma (b. 1947 in Alexandria). Egyptian filmmaker. She studied French literature at Alexandria University and history at Cairo before becoming assistant to Youssef Chahine and Salah Abou Seif, among others. Also worked on foreign productions (including *Death on the Nile*) and made documentaries. Worked as a freelance writer and book illustrator. Has made a number of video works in the 2000s. Her third feature, shot on video and transferred to film, seems not to have had a commercial release. Feature films: *Beggars and Proud People / Chahhâtîn wa noubalâ* (1991), *Concerto in the Street of Happiness / Concerto fî darb sa'aada* (2000), *Violence and Hate / al'Unf wa-l-sukhriya* (2005)

Al-Bechir, Mohamed. Egyptian filmmaker. Feature film: *Samira's Death / Mawt Samîrah* (1985)

Albou, Karin (b. 1968 in Paris). French-based filmmaker of (Jewish) Algerian descent. Initial studies of theatre, dance, French, and Arabic literature, followed by Paris-based studies of film. Worked for television and made a widely shown 35-minute short, *Aid el Kabir*, in 1999. Teaches at the École Internationale de Création Audiovisuelle et Réalisation (EICAR) in Paris. Feature film: *Little Jerusalem / La Petite Jérusalem* (2005)

Albrecht, Joseph. South African veteran filmmaker and the only person to make both silent and sound features in South Africa. Feature films: *A Border Scourge* (Silent, 1917), *The Voice of the Waters* (Silent, 1918), *The Stolen Favourite* (Silent, 1919), *Copper Mask* (Silent, 1919), *With Edged Tools* (Silent, 1919), *Isban Israel* (Silent, 1920), *The Man Who Was Afraid* (Silent, 1920), *Reef of Stars* (Silent, 1924), *Sarie Marais* (Afrikaans, 1931), *Moedertjie* (Afrikaans, 1931), *Die Bou van 'n Nasie / They Built a Nation* (Afrikaans/English, 1939)

Al-Chakankiri, Ibrahim. Egyptian filmmaker. Feature film: *Ayn Al-hayat / 'Ayn al-hayât* (1970)

Al-Chami, Mohamed. Egyptian filmmaker. Feature films: *The Snake / al-Thou'bân* (1985), *A Seventy-Year-Old Joker / Chaqâwah fî-l-sab'în* (1988)

Al-Chamma, Essam. Egyptian filmmaker. Feature film: *Maganino / Magânîno* (1993), *A Very Important Man / Ragoul mohemm geddann* (1996)

Al-Charkawi, Fahmi. Egyptian filmmaker. Feature film: *A Peasant in Congress / Fallah fî el-kongress* (2002)

Al-Charkawi, Galal. Egyptian filmmaker. Feature films: *A Widow and Three Daughters / Armalah wa thatlâth banât* (1965), *Shame / al-'Ayb* (1967), *People from the Interior / al-Nâs illî gouwwah* (1969)

Al-Chazli, Abdel Hamid. Egyptian filmmaker. Feature film: *The Terrible Hours / al-Sâ'ât al-rahîbah* (1970)

Al-Cheikh, Kamal (b. 1919 in Cairo). Egyptian filmmaker. Began as a film editor in the Misr studios and went on to direct literary adaptations, thrillers, and films with a political background. Also worked from 1980 at the Egyptian Ministry of Culture. Feature films: *House No. 13 / al-Manzil raqam talatta'char* (1952), *The Plot / Mou'âmarah* (1953), *Life or Death / Hayât aw mawt* (1954), *Love and Tears / Houbb wa doumou'* (1955), *Love and Execution / Houbb wa i'dâm* (1956), *The Outsider / al-Gharîb* (1956), *Land of Peace / Ard al-salâm* (1957), *The Land of Dreams / Ard al-ahlâm* (1957), *Merchants of Death / Touggâr al-mawt* (1957), *The Little Angel / al-Malâk al-saghîr* (1958), *The Lady from the Castle / Sayyidat al-qasr* (1958), *For a Woman / Min agli imra'ah* (1959), *For My Love / Min agl houbbî* (1959), *A Burning Heart / Qalb yahtariq* (1959), *Angel and Demon / Malâk wa chaytân* (1960), *I Shall Not Confess / Lan a'tarif* (1961), *Escaped from Hell / al-Liss wa-l-kilâb* (1962), *The Last Night / al-Laylah al-akhîrah* (1963), *The Little Demon / al-Chaytân al saghîr* (1963), *The Infidel / al-Khâ'inah* (1965), *Three Thieves / Thalâthat lousous* (one episode) (1966), *The Saboteurs / al-Moukharriboun* (1967), *The Man Who Had Lost His Shadow / al-Ragoul alladhî faqada zillahou* (1968), *Miramar / Miramar* (1969), *The Well of Privation / Bi'r al-hirmân* (1969), *Dusk and Dawn / Ghouroub wa chourouq* (1970), *Something in My Heart / Chay' fî sadrî* (1971), *The Fugitive / al-Hârib* (1974), *Who Are We Shooting At? / 'Alâ man noutliq al-rasâs* (1975), *First Year of Love / Sanah oulâ houbb* (one episode) (1976), *Between Them the Devil / Wa thâlithhoum al-chaytân* (1978), *Mounting toward the Abyss / al-Sou'oud ilâ al-hâwiyah* (1978),

The Peacock / al-Tâwous (1982), *The Conqueror of Time / Qâhir al-zaman* (1987)

Al-Chennawi, Kamal. Egyptian filmmaker. Feature films: *Undecided Hearts / Qouloub hâ᾽irah* (1956), *My Only Love / Houbbî al-wahîd* (1960), *The Idle / Tanabilat al-soultân* (1965), *The Mirage / al-Sarâb* (1970), *Anger / al-Ghadab* (1972), *The Devil and Autumn / al-Chaytân wa-l-kharîf* (1972), *If Only I᾽d Not Known Love / Laytanî mâ ᶜaraftou al-houbb* (1976), *Thirteen and One Lies / Talatata᾽ch kidbah wa kidbah* (1977), *The Bill, Miss / al-Hisâb yâ mademoiselle* (1978), *The Last Confession / al-I᾽tirâf al-akhîr* (1978)

Al-Cherif, Medhat. Egyptian filmmaker. Feature film: *The Most Courageous / Agda᾽ al-nâs* (1993)

Al-Cherif, Nour (b. 1946 in Cairo). Egyptian actor and filmmaker. Appeared in over two hundred Egyptian films, working especially with Atef Al-Tayeb and Youssef Chahine. Just one feature film as director: *The Lovers / al-ᶜAshiqaan* (2001)

Al-Deghidi, Inas (b. 1954). Egyptian filmmaker. One of the rare female directors active in Egyptian cinema (with Nadia Hamza and Asma al-Bakri), she has gone on to make over a dozen films. She graduated from the Cairo Higher Film Institute in 1975 and worked as assistant to directors such as Henri Barakat and Salah Abou Seif. Feature films: *Sorry, It᾽s the Law / ᶜAfwan ayyouhâ al-qIanoun* (1985), *The Era of Prohibitions / Zaman al-mamnou᾽* (1988), *The Challenge / al-Tahaddî* (1988), *One Wife Is Not Enough / Imra᾽ah wâhidan lâ takfî* (1990), *The Samiha Badran Affair / Qadiyyat Samîhah Badrân* (1990), *The Murderess / al-Qâtilah* (1992), *Disco . . . Disco / Disco . . . disco* (1994), *Cheap Flesh / Lahm rakhis* (1995), *Lobster / Istakoza* (1996), *Lace / Dantiella* (1998), *Night Talk / Kalaam el lil* (1999), *The Red Rose / al-Warda al-hamra* (2000), *Diaries of a Teenage Girl / Muzakkeraat muraheqa* (2002), *Women in Search of Freedom / al-Bahethaat ᶜan al-hurreyya* (2005), *Let᾽s Dance / Ma tigi norqus* (2006)

Al-Demerdache, Nour. Egyptian filmmaker. Feature films: *The Cost of Liberty / Thaman al-hourriyya* (1964), *The Intruder / al-Dakhîl* (1967), *The Elegant, the Noble and the Greedy / al-Zarîf wa-l-charhm wa-l-tammâ᾽* (1971), *Music . . . Love and Espionage / Mousîqâ . . . houbb . . . wa Gâsousiyyah* (1971)

Al-Dik, Bechir (b. 1945 at Damietta). Egyptian filmmaker. A writer who published stories in the press before becoming involved in cinema, he became one of the preferred scriptwriters for the new generation of 1980s filmmakers, such as Mohamed Khan and Atef al-Tayeb. He also worked as a director on two films in the late 1980s. Feature films: *The Flood / al-Tawafân* (1985), *The Journey᾽s Route / Sikkat safar* (1987)

Alessandrini, Goffredo. Italian director of one Egyptian feature film: *Amina / Amînah* (1949)

Al-Gabali, Mazen. Egyptian filmmaker. Feature films: *Pizza Pizza / Pizza pizza* (1998), *Abracadabra / Gala gala* (2001), *Volcanic Rage / Borkaan al-ghadab* (2002)

Al-Gazaerli, Fouad. Egyptian filmmaker. Feature films: *Congratulations / Mabrouk* (1937), *Bahbah Pasha / Bahbah bâchâ* (1938), *The Lineage of the Beloved / Khalaf al-habâyib* (1939), *Dreams of Love / Ahlâm al-houbb* (1945), *Good Luck / al-Hazz al-sa᾽îd* (1945), *Scheherazade / Chahrazade* (1946), *The Orphan / al-Yatîmah* (1946), *A Bedouin Girl᾽s Love / Gharâm badawiyyah* (1946), *Marouf the Shoemaker / Ma᾽rouf al-iskâfî* (1947), *Goha and the Seven Girls / Gohâ wa-l-sab᾽banât* (1947), *The Conquest of Egypt / Fat᾽h Misr* (1948), *Hassan the Brave / al-Châtir Husan* (1948), *Hassan, Morcos and Cohen / Hasan wa Morqos wa Kohîn* (1954)

Al-Guendi, Ahmed. Egyptian filmmaker. Feature film: *Watch Out! You᾽ve Dropped Something / Housh illi wei᾽e᾽ mennak* (2007)

Al-Guindi, Farid. Egyptian filmmaker. Feature films: *Do Not Deny Your Ancestors / Man fâta qadîmouh* (1943), *Bride for Hire / ᶜArousah li-l-îgâr* (1946), *Lost Hopes / Amal dâ᾽i᾽* (1947)

Al-Hagar, Khaled (b. 1963 in Suez). Egyptian filmmaker, resident for a time in London. Studied law at the University of Cairo and then worked in the Egyptian film industry (as assistant to Youssef Chahine) and for the BBC before studying at the National Film and Television School in the United Kingdom, graduating in 1989. He also made his second, semi-autobiographical, feature in the United Kingdom. Made three shorts before his feature debut. Feature films: *Little Dreams / Ahlâm saghîragh* (1993), *Room to Rent* (English-language, 2000), *Women's Love / Houbb al-banat* (2004), *None but That / Mafesh gher kada* (2006)

Al-Hakim, Amine. Egyptian filmmaker. Feature film: *The Way of Vengeance / Tarîq al-intiqâm* (1972)

Al-Halbawi. Hassan. Egyptian silent filmmaker. Feature film: *Drugs / al-Moukhaddarât* (1929)

Al-Hawwaari, Magdi. Egyptian filmmaker. Feature films: *Ambulance 55 / 55 is'aaf* (2001), *Lover Boys / ʿEyaal habbiba* (2005), *The Kids Ran Away / al-ʿEyaal herbet* (2006)

Alheit, Willie. South African filmmaker. Feature films: *Vrou uit die Nag* (Afrikaans, 1974), *Die Ridder van die Grootpad* (Afrikaans, 1976), *Thaba / Terug na Thaba* (Afrikaans, 1977)

Ali, Mohamed. Egyptian filmmaker. Feature films: *The Game of Love / Leibet al-hubb* (2006), *First Thing in Love / Al-awwela fil gharaa* (2007)

Alim, Abdel. Egyptian filmmaker. Feature films: *The Mixed School Is Banned / al-Ihktilât mamnou'* (1986), *The Women's Police / al-Bolîs al-nisâ'i* (1988), *Everything . . . Except My Mother / Illâ . . . oummî* (1989)

Al-Imam, Hassan (b. 1919 at Mansourah; d. 1988). Egyptian filmmaker. Worked as an actor before serving as assistant director from 1944. With Niazi Mostafa, one of the most prolific Egyptian directors, making films in all genres. Feature films: *Angels in Hell / Malâ'ikah fî gannam* (1947), *Women Are Devils / al-Sittât ʿafrârît* (1947), *A Good Reputation Is Worth More than*

Riches / al-Sît wa-lâ al-guinâ (1948), *The Two Orphans / al-Yatîmatayn* (1948), *An Hour for Your Heart / Sâ'ah li-qalbak* (1950), *People's Victims / Zalamounî al-nâs* (1950), *The Strongest Reason / houkm al-qawî* (1951), *I'm from a Good Family / Anâ bint nâs* (1951), *People's Secrets / Asrâr al-nâs* (1951), *The Cup of Suffering / Kâs al-'adhâb* (1952), *Who Is My Father? / Anâ bint mîn* (1952), *Parents' Anger / Ghadab al-wâlidayn* (1952), *The Strange Era / Zaman al-'agâyib* (1952), *By What Right? / Fî char' mîn* (1953), *The Scandal Merchant / Tâguir al-fadâ'ih* (1953), *Love in the Shadows / Houbb fî-l-zalâm* (1953), *The Baker's Wife / Bâ'i'at al-khoubz* (1953), *Human Hearts / Qouloub al-nâs* (1954), *The Unjust Angel / al-Malâk al-zâlim* (1954), *A Wife's Confessions / I'tirâfât zawgah* (1955), *Women of the Night / Banât al-layl* (1955), *The Body / al-Gasad* (1955), *Dawn Farewells / Wadâ' fî-l-fagr* (1956), *Lawahez / Lawâhiz* (1957), *I Shall Never Cry / Lan abkî abadan* (1957), *The Great Love / al-Houbb al-'adhîm* (1957), *Ighraa / Ighrâ'* (1957), *The Haunt of Pleasure / Wakr al-maladhdhât* (1957), *The Little She-Devil / al-Chuytânah al-saghîrah* (1958), *Burning Love / Houbb min nâr* (1958), *Maidens' Hearts / Qouloub al-'adhârâ* (1958), *Awatef / ʿAwâtif* (1958), *The Seducer of Men / Sâ'idat al-rigâl* (1960), *I Accuse / Innî attahim* (1960), *Love and Adoration / Houbb hattâ al-'ibâdah* (1960), *Street Wife / Zawgah min al-châri'* (1960), *Money and Women / Mâl wa nisâ'* (1960), *The Mute Girl / al-Kharsâ'* (1961), *My Life Is the Cost of It / Hayâtii hiya al-thaman* (1961), *The Pupil / al-Timîdhah* (1961), *The Miracle / al-Mou'guizah* (1962), *Sins / al-Khatâyâ* (1962), *Chafiqa the Copt / Charfîqah al-qibtiyya* (1963), *The Alley of Miracles / Zouqâq al-Midaqq* (1963), *A Woman on the Margins / Imra'ah ʿalâ al-hâmich* (1963), *The Newspaper Vendor / Bayyâ'at al-garâyid* (1963), *The Dead End of the Two-Palaces / bayn al-qasrayn* (1964), *The Arabian Nights / Alf laylah wa laylah* (1964), *The Woman and Men / hiya wa-l-rigâl* (1965), *The Nun / al-Râhibah* (1965), *Three Thieves / Thalâthat lousous* (one episode) (1966), *The Man and Women / Houwa wa-l-nisâ'* (1966), *The Palace of Desires / Qasr al-Chawq* (1967), *The Beggars' Strike / Idrâb al-chahhâtiin* (1967), *One of Those Girls / Bint min al-banât* (1968), *Beau-*

tiful Aziza / al-Hilwah ᶜAzîzah (1969), *Dalal the Egyptian Woman / Dalâl al-misriyyah* (1970), *Furnished Flat / Chiqqah mafrouchah* (1970), *Love and Money / al-Houb wa-l-foulous* (1971), *Forbidden Love / al-Houbb al-Mouharram* (1971), *Imtithal / Imtithâl* (1972), *Love and Pride / Houbb wa kibriyâ* (1972), *Beware of Zouzou / Khallî bâlak min Zouzou* (1972), *Badia's Daughter / Bint Badîah* (1972), *My Story with Life / Hikâyatî maᵓ al-zamân* (1973), *Al-Soukkariyyah / al-Soukkariyyah* (1973), *Bamba Kachar / Bamba Kachchar* (1974), *Strange O Time / ᶜAgâyib yâ zaman* (1974), *Suffering on Smiling Lips / al-ᵓAdhâb fawqa chifâh tabtasim* (1974), *The Princess of My Love / Amîrat houbbî anâ* (1974), *I Love This One but I Want That One / Hâdhâ ouhibbouh wa hâdhâ ourîdouh* (1975), *And Love Came to an End / Wa intahâ al-houbb* (1975), *Badia Massabni / Badîᵓah Masâbni* (1975), *Don't Leave Me Alone / La tatrouknî wahdî* (1975), *The All-Time Beauty / Qamar al-zamân* (1976), *You Must Venerate Your Parents / Wa bi-l-wâlidayn ihsânan* (1976), *The Curlew Has Lips / al-Karawân louh chafâyif* (1976), *The Oppressed's Prayer / Douᵓâᵓ al-madhloumîn* (1977), *The Famous Affair / al-Qadiyyah al-machhourah* (1978), *Love on a Volcano / Houbb fawq al-bourkân* (1978), *The Queen of Tarab / Soultânat al-tarab* (1979), *Paradise Is at His Feet / al-Gannah tahta qadamayhâ* (1979), *Do Not Oppress Women / Lâ tadhlimou al-nisâᵓ* (1980), *Whose Son Is He? / Ibn mîn fî-l-mougtamâᵓ* (1982), *Blood on the Pink Dress / Dimâᵓ ᶜalâ al-thawb al-wardî* (1982), *Layal / Layâl* (1982), *Their Wiles Are Great / Kaydahounna ᶜadhîm* (1983), *God's World / Douniâ Allâh* (1985), *Tomorrow Will Be More Beautiful / Boukra ahlâ min al-nahâr dah* (1986), *The Time of Love / ᶜAsr al-houbb* (1986)

Al-Iryaan, Tarek. Egyptian filmmaker. Feature films: *Snakes and Ladders / al-Sellem wa el teᵓbaan* (2001), *Tito / Tito* (2004)

Aliu, Jimoh. Nigerian filmmaker. Veteran actor. Feature films: *Fopomoyo* (Yoruba, 1991)

Al-Kachef, Radwane (b. 1952 in Cairo; d. 2002). Egyptian filmmaker. Studied scriptwriting at the Cairo Higher Film Institute and philosophy at Cairo University. Twelve years of work as as-

sistant and as film critic. Feature films: *Violets Are Blue / Lîh yâ banafsig* (1993), *Date Wine / ᶜaraᵓ el balah* (1999), *The Magician: The Notion of Joy / al-Saher: nazareyet al-bahga* (2002)

Al-Kalioubi, Mohamed Kamal (b. 1948 in Cairo). Egyptian filmmaker. Graduated from the Cairo Higher Film Institute (where he now teaches) in 1972, then took his PhD in film at the Vsesoyuznyi gosudarstvennyi institut kinematografii (VGIK; All-Union State Cinema Institute) in Moscow in 1986. Began with documentary films (*Tales of What Happened in the City* [1975], *Three Special Moments* [1980], *Diary of a Window* [1982], *Sketches for a City* [1984], and *Chronicle of Lost Time* [1991], on the pioneer filmmaker Mohamed Bayoumi). Feature films: *Three on the Road / Thalâthah ᶜalâ al-tarîq* (1993), *Why Does the Sea Laugh? / al-Bahr beyedhak lih* (1995), *Roll Up, Roll Up / Itfarrag ya salaam* (2001), *Adam's Autumn / Kharif Adam* (2002)

Al-Kawadri, Anwar. Egyptian filmmaker. Feature film: *Gamal Abdel Nasser / Gamal Abdel Nasser* (1998)

Al-Kayyali, Mohamed Saleh. Egyptian filmmaker: Feature film: *The Girl from the Beach / Bint al-châtîᵓ* (1952)

Al-Kerdawi, Oussama. Egyptian filmmaker. Feature film: *Red Card / Kârt ahmar* (1994)

Al-Khamissi, Abdel Rahman. Egyptian filmmaker. Feature films: *The Reward / al-Gazâ* (1965), *Respectable Families / ᶜÂᵓilât moutaramah* (1969), *Love and Its Cost / al-Houbb wal-thhaman* (1970), *The Violet / Zahrat al-banafsag* (1977)

Al-Khatib, Ahmed. Egyptian filmmaker. Feature films: *The Son of Taheya Azouz / Ibn Tahiyyah ᶜAzzouz* (1986), *The Cursed House / al-Bayt al-malᵓoun* (1987)

Allam, Talaat. Egyptian filmmaker. Feature film: *A Madman's Testimony / Chahâdat magᵓnoun* (1978)

Allan, James. South African filmmaker. Feature film: *Burndown* (English, 1988)

Alli, Segun. Nigerian filmmaker. Feature films: *Ofa Oro* (Yoruba, 1992), *Ogun Idile* (Yoruba, 1986)

Allouache, Merzak (b. 1944 in Algiers). Algerian filmmaker, resident in France since 1995. Studied at the Institut National de Cinéma (INC) in Algiers and the Institut des Hautes Études Cinématographiques (IDHEC) in Paris. Worked at the Office des Actualités Algériennes (OAA) and the Centre National de la Cinématographie (CNC) before becoming a director with the Office National du Commerce et de l'Industre Cinématographique (ONCIC) in Algeria. Numerous short films throughout his career. Published a novel, *Bab el-Oued*, in 1996. His two films on Algiers (*Omar Gatlato* and *Bab el-Oued City*) are among the sharpest studies of Algerian everyday life. In 1978 he won the top prize, the *Tanit d'or*, at the Journées Cinématographiques de Carthage (JCC) with *The Adventures of a Hero*, and he repeated this success with *Salut Cousin!* in 1996. But since he settled in France, he has virtually become a French filmmaker, looking at the Maghreb from outside. Feature films: *Omar Gatlato* (1976), *The Adventures of a Hero / Les Aventures d'un héros* (1978), *The Man Who Looked at Windows / L'Homme qui regardait les fenêtres* (1982), *A Parisian Love Story / Un amour à Paris* (1986), *Bab el-Oued City* (1994), *Hello Cousin! / Salut Cousin!* (1996), *Algiers-Beirut: In Remembrance / Alger-Beyrouth, pour mémoire* (1998), *The Other World / L'Autre monde* (2001), *Chouchou* (2003), *Bab el Web* (2004)

Al-Mihi, Raafat (b. 1940 in Cairo). Egyptian filmmaker. First studied English literature, then scriptwriting at the Cairo Higher Film Institute Began work as a scriptwriter in 1966, before turning to direction 15 years later. Feature films: *Ever-Open Eyes / ʿOuyoun lâ tanâm* (1981), *The Lawyer / al-Avocato* (1984), *The Last Love Story / Li-l-houbb qissah akhîrah* (1986), *These Men Are Gentlemen / al-Sâdah al-rigâl* (1987), *Fish, Milk and Tamarind / Samak laban tamr hindî* (1988), *Ladies, Young Ladies / Sayyidâtî ânisâtî* (1990), *A Little Love, a Lot of Violence / Qaleel mina al-hubb katheer min al-ʿunf* (1995), *All Hail / Mit foll* (1996), *Apple / Toffaha* (1997), *Lady among Ladies / Set el settaat* (1998), *How to Please God / ʿAlashaan rabbena yehebbak* (2001)

Al-Mogui, Ibrahim. Egyptian filmmaker. Feature films: *The Informer / al-Mourchid* (1989), *The Falcon's Eyes / ʿOuyoun al-saqr* (1992)

Al-Mouhandès, Hussein Helmi. Egyptian filmmaker. Feature films: *Sun without Twilight / Chams lâ taghîb* (1959), *Storm of Love / ʿÂsifah min al-houbb* (1961), *The Cat's Claw / Mikhlab al-qitt* (1961), *My Daughters and I / Anâ wa banâtî* (1961), *Under the City Sky / Tahta samâʾ al-madînah* (1961), *I Love This Man / Hâdhâ al-ragoul ouhibbou* (1962), *Girls and Boys / Sibyân wa banât* (1965), *The Pledge / al-Wadîʾah* (1965), *Eve on the Road / Hawwâʾ ʿalâ al-tarîq* (1968), *Count Down / Saʾat al-sifr* (1972), *The Lights / al-Adwâʾ* (1972), *Night's Murmurs / Hamsat al-laykl* (1977), *For Whom the Sun Rises / Liman touchriq alchams* (1979)

Al-Naggar, Mohamed. Egyptian filmmaker. Feature films: *An Upper Egyptian Back and Forth / Seʾeedy rayeh gayy* (2001), *Journey of Love / Rehlet hubb* (2001), *Brave Heart / Qalb gareeʾ* (2002), *I Love You; Me Too / Bahebbak; wʾana kamaan* (2003), *Mido the Troublemaker / Mido mashakel* (2003), *Okal / ʿOkal* (2004), *The Era of Hatem Zahran / Zaman Hâtim Zahrân* (1988), *Humiliation / al-Dhoull* (1990), *The Cry / al-Sarkhah* (1991), *Al-Haggama / al-Haggâmah* (1992), *Spicy Ali / Aly Spicy* (2005), *A Day of Telling Lies / Sabahu Kedb* (2007)

Al-Nahhas, Abdel Halim. Egyptian filmmaker. Feature film: *The Wolves / al-Dhiʾâb* (1993)

Al-Nahhas, Ahmed. Egyptian filmmaker. Feature films: *The Lost Plane / al-Tâʾirah al-mafqoudah* (1984), *The Louts / al-Awghâd* (1985), *Illusions / al-Awhâm* (1988), *The Two Female Prisoners / al-Saguinatân* (1988), *The She-Devil / al-Chaytânah* (1990), *They've Robbed Oum Ali / Saraqou Oumm ʿAlî* (1994), *The Boss-Woman and the Gentleman / al-Meʾallemma wal ustaaz* (1995), *As the Heart Loves / al-Qalb wi ma yeʾshaq* (1996)

Al-Nahri, Tarek. Egyptian filmmaker. Feature films: *A Father's Revolt / al-Abb al-thâʾir* (1988), *The Courageous / al-Chougʾân* (1992), *A Woman's Hell / Gahîm imraʾah* (1992), *Playing with the Evil / al-Liʾb maʾ al-achrâr* (1993), *The Enraged / al Ghadeboon* (1996), *Cash OK / el-Cash mashi* (2000), *If This Is a Dream / Law kaan da helm* (2001)

Al-Qadi, Ismaïl. Egyptian filmmaker. Feature films: *Reserved for Husbands / Li-l-moutazawwiguîn faqat* (1969), *The Divorced / al-Moutaalaqât* (1975)

Al-Rachidi, Farouk. Egyptian filmmaker. Feature film: *The Scandal / al-Fadîhah* (1992)

Al-Rihani, Naguib (b. 1887; d. 1949). Egyptian veteran filmmaker and actor. Brought up by his Egyptian mother in Cairo, he learned French as well as Arabic and was much influenced by French drama. His theatre company was established in 1918 and he made his film debut in a silent film which he co-directed with Stephane Rosti and which was subsequently sonorized. Made many later film appearances as one of the most popular of Egyptian actors. Silent feature: *The Clerk Kish Kish Bey / Sâhib al-saʾâdah Kichkich bek* (with Stephane Rosti, 1931). Sound feature film: *The Clerk Kish Kish Bey / Sahib al-saʾadah Kichkich bek* (with Stephane Rosti, 1934).

Al-Sabaawi, Ahmed. Egyptian filmmaker. Feature films: *A Single Life Is Best / Bidoun zawâg afdal* (1978), *The Composition of Time / Hisâb al-sinîn* (1978), *All in Hell / Koullouhoum fî-l-nâr* (1978), *The Malediction of Time / Laʾnat al-zaman* (1979), *The Challenge of the Powerful / Tahaddî al-aqwiyâʾ* (1980), *And the Days Pass / Wa tamdî al-ayyâm* (1980), *The Mute / al-Akhras* (1980), *Breakdown / Inhiyâr* (1982), *Al-Salakhana / al-Salakhânah* (1982), *Antar Wears His Sword / ʿAntar châyil sîfouh* (1983), *Prison without Bars / Sigʾn bilâ qoudbân* (1983), *The Tower of the Tanneries / Bourg al-madâbigh* (1983), *The Beggar / al-Moutasawwil* (1983), *Naïma Is a Forbidden Fruit / Naʾîmah fâkihah mouharramah* (1984), *Mr Tayyeb / al-Tayyib afandî* (1984), *The Hooligans / al-Achqiyâʾ*

(1984), *The Judge's House / Bayt al-qâdî* (1984), *The Good and the Bad / al-Âyqah wa-l-dirrîsa* (1985). *I'm the One Who Killed al-Hanach / Anâ illî qatalt al-Hanach* (1985), *Legitimacy Sweeps It Away / al-Halâl yiksab* (1985), *Me / Anâ* (1985), *The Professor Always Knows More / al-Oustâdh yaʾrif akthar* (1985), *Ramadan on a Volcano / Ramadân fawqa al-Bourkân* (1985), *Denunciation of a Woman / Balâgh didd imraʾah* (1986), *The Inheritors / al-Warathah* (1986), *The Rhinoceros / al-Khirtît* (1987), *The Confrontation / al-Mouwâgahah* (1987), *The Giant / al-ʾImlâq* (1987), *The Genie and Love / al-ʾAbqarî wa-l-houbb* (1987), *Youth in Hell / Chabâb fî-l-gahîm* (1988), *How's the World Doing? / al-Douniâ garâ fîhâ îh?* (1988), *Money and Monsters / al-Foulous wa-l-wouhouch* (1988), *Unruly Girls in Danger / al-Mouchâghibât fî khatar* (1989), *Notice to Public Opinion / Balâgh li-l-raʾî al-ʾâm* (1990), *The Fool / al-Ahtal* (1990), *Forbidden Wife / Zawgah mouharramah* (1991), *A Very Unruly Girl / Bint mouchâghibah guiddan* (1991), *The Bloody Trace / al-Khoutwah al-dâmiyah* (1992), *The Deserter / Hârib min al-tagʾnîd* (1992), *My Wife and the Wolf / Zawgatî wa-l-dhiʾb* (1992), *Girls in a Jam / Banât fi wartah* (1992), *The Strongest of Men / Aqwâ al-rigâl* (1993), *The Foxes / al-Thaʾâlib* (1993), *Abou Zeid of His Time / Abou Zeid zamanu* (1995), *The Jewelry Market / al-Sagha* (1996), *Time for Revenge / Saʾat el-intekam* (1998)

Al-Sabahi, Magda. Egyptian filmmaker. Feature film: *Who Do I Love? / Man ouhibb?* (1966)

Al-Sahn, Ibrahim. Egyptian filmmaker. Feature film: *Three Stories / Thalâth qisas* (one episode) (1968)

Al-Saïfi, Hassan (b. 1927). Prolific Egyptian filmmaker. Worked as assistant to Anwar Wagdi. Feature films: *The Young Thief / Nachchâlah hânim* (1953), *You Are Witnesses / Ichhadou yâ nâs* (1953), *Son of Aristocrats / Ibn dhawât* (1953), *He Kidnapped My Wife / Khataf mirâtî* (1954), *Ishmael Yassine and the Ghost / ʿIfrîtat Ismâʾîl Yâsîn* (1954), *Don't Be Unjust / al-Dhoulm harâm* (1954), *The Girl from the Country / Bint al-balad* (1954), *Young Girls at Auction / ʿArâyis fî-l-mazâd* (1955), *The Un-*

known Lover / al-Habîb al-mag'houl (1955), Who Is the Killer? / Man al-qâtil (1956), Samara / Samârah (1956), Zannouba / Zannoubah (1956), Madam Hold the Power / Sâhibat al-'ismah (1956), The Charming Postmistresses / al-Koumsariyyât al-fâtinât (1957), The End of a Love / Nihâyat al-houbb (1957), My Dark-Haired Love / Habîbî al-asmar (1958), The Girl with the Bold Look / Abou 'ouyoun garî'ah (1958), Touha / Touhah (1958), The Highway Robber / Qâtî tarîq (1959), Beware of Love / Ihtaris min al-houbb (1959), Hassan and Marika / Hasan wa Mârîkâ (1959), The Poor Millionnaire / al-Millionnaire al-faqîr (1959), Sad Melody / al-Nagham al-hazîn (1960), The Girls from Alexandria / Banât Bahrî (1960), Ishmael Yassine in Prison / Ismâ'îl Yâsîn f-l-sig'n (1960), Love and Suffering / Houbb wa 'adhâb (1961), Fattouma / Fattoumah (1961), The Guide / al-Tourgmân (1961), The King of Petrol / Malik al-Bitroul (1962), The Association of Wife Killers / Gam'iyyat qatl al-zawgât (1962), The Love Judge / Qâdî al-gharâm (1962), The Madmen Are Happy / al-Magânîn fî na'îm (1963), The Black Suitcase / al-Haqîbah al-sawdâ' (1964), The Fugitive from Marriage / Hârib min al-zawâg (1964), The Girl from the District / Bint al-hittah (1964), For Hanafi / Min agl Hanifî (1964), The Story of a Marriage / Hikâyat zawâg (1964), The Two Brothers / al-Chaqîqân (1965), Kill Me Please / Iqtinî mn fadlak (1965), Lovers' Tears / Mabkâ al-'ouchâq (1966), The Bachelor Husband / al-Zawg al-'âzib (1966), Love in August / Gharâm fî Aghoustous (1966), The Second Suitor / al-'Arîs al-thânî (1967), The Second Meeting / al-Liqâ' al-thânî (1967), Hamza's Suitcase / Chantat Hamzah (1967), The False Millionnaire / al-Millionnaire al-mouzayyaf (1968), The Bravest Man in the World / Achga' ragoul fî-l-âlam (1968), Son of the District / Ibn al-hittah (1968), Battle of Professionals / Sirâ' al-mouhtarifîn (1969), Pickpocket in Spite of Himself / Nachchâl raghmâ anfih (1969), Mummy's Secretary / Secrétaire mâmâ (1969), Young Girls' Frivolity / Dala' al-banât (1969), The Three Madmen / al-Magânîn al-thalâthah (1970), The Deer in the Night / Sab' al-layl (1971), The Haunt of the Wretched / Wakr al-achrâ (1972), The Obstinate One / al-'Anîd (1973), The Voyage of Marvels / Rihlat al-'agâyib (1974), Forbidden during the Wedding Night / Mamnou fî laylat al-doukhlah (1976), The Respectable Husband / al-Zawg al-mouhtaram (1977), The Best Days of Life / Ahlâ ayyâm al-'oumr (1978), The Good Guys / Awlâd al-halâl (1978), The Lovers' Route / Sikkat al-'âchiqîn (1978), One Type of Women / Naw' min al-nisâ' (1979), The Alien Brothers / al-Ilhwah al-ghourabâ (1980), What Do Girls Want? / al-Banât 'âyzah îh (1980), A Man in the Women's Prison / Ragoul fî sign al-nisâ' (1982), A Dog Bite / 'Addat kalb (1983), The Shore of Chance / Châti' al-hazz (1983), I Am Not a Thief / Anâ mouch harâmiyyah (1983), Hadi Badi / Hâdî bâdî (1984), It's All My Fault / Anâ illî astâhil (1984), Meghawri at the University / Mighâwrî fî-l-koulliyyah (1985), Angels of the Streets / Malâ'ikat al-chawârî' (1985), Honey Devil / Chaytân min 'asal (1985), Lord, Deliver Us! / Satrak yâ rab (1986), A Woman in Prison / Imra'ah fî-l-sig'n (1986), My Daughter and the Wolves / Ibnatî wa-l-dhi'âb (1986), Some Enjoy and Others Confect / Nâs hâysah wa nâs lâysah (1986), The Girls of Our Alley / Banât haritnâ (1987), The Clerk Caught in a Story of Fraud / al-Arda hâluî fî qadiyyat nash (1987), Lovers' Lane / Hârat al-habâyib (1989), It's Fate / Qismah wa nasîb (1990), The Three Idiots / al-Aghbiyâ' al-thalâthah (1990), A Strange Story / Hikâyah laha la-'agab (1990), Husbands Beware / Intabihou ayyouhâ al-azwâg (1990), The Trap / al-Matabb (1990), The Minister's Daughter / Bint al-Bâchâ al-wazîr (1991), Criminal Despite Himself / Mougrim raghm anfih (1991), Half-a-Dozen Madmen / Nouss dastat magânîn (1991), Husbands in a Jam / Azwâg fî wartah (1992), Without You / Lawlâki (1993)

Al-Sayed, Ibrahim. Egyptian filmmaker. Feature film: God Is Great / Allah akbar (1959)

Al-Seifi, Manal. Egyptian filmmaker. Feature film: Life Is Delightful / al-Hayat muntaha al-lazza (2005)

Al-Sibaï, Medhat. Egyptian filmmaker. Feature films: Unidentified Culprit / Wa qouyyidat didd mag'houl (1981), The Poor Who Don't Go to Paradise / Fouqarâ' la yadkhouloun al-gannah (1984), The Wounded Man / al-Garîh (1985), A Man with Seven Lives / Ragoul bi-sab' arwâh

(1988), *Nawaem / Nawâ²im* (1988), *We're the Ones Who Robbed the Robbers / Ihna illî saraqnâ al-harâmiyyah* (1989), *Agent No. 13 / al-²Amîl raqam talata²ch* (1989), *Fallen Woman / Imra²ah âyilah li-l-souqout* (1992), *Women / al-Sittât* (1992), *Gawhari Alleyway / Hârat al-gawharî* (1992), *The Knights of Old / Foursân âkhir zaman* (1993), *Disorder / Khaltabîtah* (1994), *The Good, the Ugly and the Beauty / al-Tayyib wa-l-charis wa-l-Gamîlah* (1994), *Three Around a Table of Blood / Thalâthah ᶜalâ mâ²idat al-dam* (1994), *Criminal with Honors / Mogrem ma²a martabet el sharaf* (1998), *All Well and Good / Foll el foll* (2000)

Al-Tabei, Gamal. Egyptian filmmaker. Feature films: *No to Violence / Lâ yâ ᶜounf* (1993), *City Dogs / Kelaab al-madina* (1995)

Al-Tayeb, Atef (b. 1947; d. 1995). Egyptian filmmaker. Graduated from the Cairo Higher Film Institute in 1970, worked as assistant and made a few documentaries. Achieved huge reputation with his second feature, *The Bus Driver*, and became a leading Egyptian director of the 1980s and 1990s, specializing in the realist treatment of social and political subjects. Died after a heart operation. Feature films: *Fatal Jealousy / al-Ghîrah al-qâtilah* (1982), *The Bus Driver / Sawwâq al-otobus* (1983), *On Close Watch / al-Takhchîbah* (1984), *The Flute Player / al-Zammâr* (1984), *Love at the Foot of the Pyramids / al-Houbb fawqa hadabat al-Haram* (1986), *On the Vice Squad Files / Malaff fî-l-âdâb* (1986), *The Innocent / al-Barî²* (1986), *Sons and Murderers / Abnâ² wa qatalah* (1987), *The Basement / al-Badroun* (1987), *Master Stroke / Darbat mou²allim* (1987), *The World on a Dove's Wing / al-Douniâ ᶜalâ ganâh yamâmah* (1989), *The Execution Squad / kaîbat al-I²dâm* (1989), *In the Middle of the Night / Qalb al-layl* (1989), *The Escape / al-Houroub* (1991), *Nagui al-Ali / Nâguî al-²Alî* (1992), *Against the Government / Didd al-houkoumah* (1992), *Blood on the Asphalt / Dimâ² ᶜalâ al-isfalt* (1992), *Summons to Reintegrate the Family Home / Indhâr bi-l-Tâ²ah* (1993), *Lifting the Veil / Kachf al-mastour* (1994), *Hot Night / Laila sakhena* (1996), *Consolation / Gabr el khawater* (1998)

Al-Telmessani, Kamel (b. 1915; d. 1972). Egyptian filmmaker. One of three brothers who all worked in the film industry: one of his brothers, Abdel Kader, was a documentary director, and the other, Hassan, a cinematographer. He was first active as a photographer and involved in the Egyptian surrealist movement. He worked at the Misr studios from 1943, but after a striking debut achieved little commercial success. After writing two books on the cinema, he abandoned his career as film director and emigrated to Lebanon in 1961. Feature films: *The Black Market / al-Souq al-sawdâ²* (1945), *The Jackpot / al-Brimo* (1947), *Samson the Magnificent / Chamchoun al-gabbâr* (1948), *Women's Wiles / Kayd al-nisâ* (1950), *My Love and Me / Anâ wa habîbî* (1953), *Professor Charaf / al-Oustâdh Charf* (1954), *Girls' School / Madrasat al-banât* (1955), *Rendezvous with Satan / Maw²îd ma ᶜIblîs* (1955), *The People from Down There / al-Nas illî taht* (1960)

Al-Telmessani, Tarek. Egyptian filmmaker. Feature film: *Laughs, Games, Seriousness and Love / Dihk wa lou²b wa gadd wa houbb* (1993)

Al-Toukhi, Ahmed. Egyptian filmmaker. Feature films: *The Triumph of Islam / Intisâr al-islâm* (1952), *Bilal, The Prophet's Muezzin / Bilâl mou²adhdhin al-rasoul* (1953), *Mecca / Bayt Allah al-harâm* (1957)

Al-Touni, Mounir. Egyptian filmmaker. Feature films: *The Three Liars / al-Kaddâbîn al-thalâthah* (1970), *Innocent at the Gallows / Barî fî-l-machnaqah* (1971)

Al-Wakil, Hussein. Egyptian filmmaker. Feature films: *The Curse / al-La²nah* (1984), *Mr. Hassan's Flat / Chiqqat al-oustâdh Hasan* (1984), *Beans Are My Favorite Dish / al-Foul sadîqî* (1985), *The Vamp / al-Ounthâ* (1986), *Before the Farewells / Qabl al-wadâ²* (1986)

Amacha, Saïd. Egyptian filmmaker. Feature film: *Moment of Danger / Lahzat khatar* (1991)

Amadangoleda, Louis Balthazar. Cameroonian filmmaker. Studied filmmaking at the École

Supérieure des Études Cinématographiques (ESEC) in Paris. Feature film: *The Three Little Shoeblacks / Les Trois Petits Cireurs* (1985)

Amari, Raja (b. 1971 in Paris). Tunisian filmmaker. She studied filmmaking at the Fondation Européenne des Métiers de l'Image et du Son (FEMIS) in Paris. Made three shorts from 1995 and a video documentary, *Tracking Oblivion / Sur les traces de l'oubli*, about the traveller Isabelle Eberhardt, in 2004. One of the brightest talents of the post-independence generation. Feature film: *Red Satin / Satin Rouge* (2002)

Amata, Jeta (b. 1974). Nigerian filmmaker. Made over thirty video features before completing his debut 35mm feature, shot with a full British crew. Feature film: *The Amazing Grace* (English, 2005)

Amer, Hassan. Egyptian filmmaker. Feature films: *The Marriage Photo / Sourat al-zifzâf* (1952), *Out of Work / Khâlî choughl* (1955)

Ameur-Zaïmèche, Rabah (b. 1966 in Beni Zid). French-based filmmaker of Algerian descent and Algerian nationality, living in France since the age of 2. Studied social sciences in Paris and is self-taught as a filmmaker. His films explore the lives of characters caught between two cultures. His first feature was shot on video and transferred to 35mm for cinema release. Feature films: *Wesh Wesh—What's Happening? / Wesh Wesh, Qu'est-ce qui se passe?* (2002), *Bled Number One* (2005)

Amin, Mohamed. Egyptian filmmaker. Graduated from the Cairo Higher Film Institute in 1985. Made numerous commercials and one short film. Feature films: *Cultural Film / Film thaqaafi* (2000), *The Night Baghdad Fell / Laylat suqoot Baghdaad* (2005)

Amir, Aziza (b. 1901; d. 1952). Egyptian actress and veteran filmmaker. Real name: Moufida Mohamed Ghoneim. She was an actress with Youssef Wahbi's Ramses company when she produced and starred in the first Egyptian silent feature, *Leila*, shown in Cairo on 16 November

1926. She went on to star in *The Girl from the Nile* (1929) and some two dozen further films, the first of which she directed herself. She produced most of these films through her production company, Isis Films. Many were made with her husband, the actor-director Mahmoud Zoulficar. Feature films: *The Girl from the Nile / Bint al-Nîl* (1929), *Atone for Your Sins / Kaffirî ʿan khatiʾatik* (1933)

Amir, Gideon [Gidi]. South African filmmaker. Feature film: *Accident* (English, 1988)

Ammar, Gamal. Egyptian filmmaker. Feature films: *A Man in the Eyes of a Woman / Ragoul fi ʿouyoun imraʾah* (1987), *This Marriage Must Not Take Place / al-Gawâzah di mouch lâzim titim* (1988), *Everyone Deceives Everyone Else / Loullouh biyilʾab ʿalâ koullouh* (1992), *Nannousa / Nannoussah* (1992)

Amoussou, Sylvestre (b. 1964 in Benin). Benin filmmaker and actor. Living in France since the mid-1980s. Several short films. Feature film: *Africa Paradis* (2006)

Ampaw, King (b. 1940 in Ghana). Ghanaian filmmaker. Studied film in Potsdam-Babelsberg and Vienna and at the Film and Television School in Munich, where his graduation film was *They Call It Love* (1972). Various production activities in Germany. Returned to Ghana in 1976. Appeared as actor in Werner Herzog's *Cobra Verde* (1987). Feature films: *Kukurantumi: The Road to Accra* (1983), *Nana Akoto / Juju* (with Ingrid Metner, 1986), *The Last Respect* (2006)

Anderson, Gordon. South African filmmaker. Feature film: *Insident op Paradysstrand / Incident on Paradise Beach* (Afrikaans, with Grenville Middleton, 1973)

Anglo, Nagui. Egyptian filmmaker. Feature films: *The Last Chase / al-Moutâradah al-akhîrah* (1986), *The Innocent Man and the Gallows / al-Barîʾ wa-l-machnaqah* (1986), *The Fugitives / al-Hâribât* (1987), *Meeting during the Honeymoon / Liqâʾ fî chahr ʿasal* (1987), *The Vir-*

gin and the Scorpion / al-ʾAdhrâ ʾ wa-l-ʾaqrab (1990), *Can't Make Up Their Minds* (literally: *Those Who Dance in the Stairways) / Illâ raqa-sou ʿalâ al-sillim* (1994)

Annakin, Ken. British director of two films included in some listings of South African feature films: *Nor the Moon by Night* (English, 1958), *The Hellions* (English, 1961)

Ansah, Kwah Paintsil (b. 1941 at Agona Swedra). Ghanaian filmmaker. Studied music and drama in the United Kingdom and film production at the RKO studios in Hollywood. Wrote two plays while in the United States. Founder of Film Africa Ltd. and of Target Advertising. Produced commercials. One of the few Ghanaian filmmakers to make an international impact with his feature films, in 1989 he became the first filmmaker from an "anglophone" country to win the top prize, the Étalon de Yennenga, at the Festival Panafricain du Cinéma de Ouagadougou (FESPACO). Feature films: *Love Brewed in the African Pot* (1980), *Heritage Africa* (1989)

Antonio, Jorge. Angolan filmmaker (Portuguese by birth). Feature film: *The Watchtower of the Moon / Miradouro da Lua* (1992)

Aoulad Syad, Daoud (b. 1953 in Marrakesh). Moroccan photographer and filmmaker. Completed a doctorate in physical sciences in Nancy and teaches in the Faculty of Science in Rabat. Attended courses in filmmaking at the Fondation Européenne des Métiers de l'Image et du Son (FEMIS) and worked as a photographer, publishing three books of photographs: *Marocains* (1989), *Boujaâd, espace et mémoire* (1996), and *Territoires de l'instant* (with poems by his fellow director Ahmed Bouanani, 2000). Made a number of internationally shown fictional shorts in the early 1990s, often in collaboration with Bouanani, who also scripted his first two features. A leading figure among the new generation which renewed Moroccan filmmaking at the end of the 1990s. Feature films: *Bye-bye Souirty / Adieu forain* (1998), *The Wind Horse / Le Cheval de vent* (2001), *Tarfaya* (2004), *Waiting for Pasolini / En attendant Pasolini* (2007)

Aptekman, Maurice. Egyptian filmmaker. Feature films: *A Son of the People / Ibn al-Chaʾb* (1934), *The Black Hand / al-Yad al-sawdâ ʾ* (1936), *Doctor Ibraham's Secret / Sirr al-doktor Ibrâhîm* (1937)

Arafa, Amr. Egyptian filmmaker. Feature film: *Africano / Afrikano* (2001), *The Embassy in the Building /al-Sefara fil ʿemara* (2005), *She Made Me a Criminal / Gaʾalatny mugreman* (2006), *The Ghost / Al-Chabah* (2007)

Arafa, Cherif (b. 1960 in Cairo). Egyptian filmmaker. Son of Saad Arafa, he graduated from the Cairo Higher Film Institute in 1983. Subsequently he worked as assistant director and made documentaries. Feature films: *The Dwarves Arrive / al-Aqzâm qâdimoun* (1987), *Third Class / al-Daragah al-thâlithah* (1988), *Hush, They're Listening / Sammiʾ his* (1991), *Playing at the Court of the Great / al-Louʾb maʾ al-kibâr* (1991), *Ya Mehalabiyyah ya / Yâ mihal-labiyyah yâ* (1991), *Terrorism and Kebabs / al-Irhâb wa-l-kabâb* (1992), *The Forgotten Man / al-Mansî* (1993), *Birds of the Darkness / Tuyour al-zalaam* (1995), *Sitting on Their Hands / al-Noum fî al-ʿasal* (1996), *Say Cheese for the Photo to Be Beautiful / Idhak el sourah tetlaʾ helwa* (1998), *Abboud on the Borders / Abboud ʿala al-hodood* (1999), *The Leader / al-Zaʾim* (with Mohamed Fadel, 1999), *The Headmaster / al-Nazer* (2000), *Son of Ezz the Rich Man / Ibn Ezz* (2001), *Mafia / Mafia* (2002), *Great Beans of China / Fuul el sein al-ʿazeem* (2004), *Halim / Halim* (2006)

Arafa, Saad (b. 1923 in Cairo). Egyptian filmmaker. Began work as assistant director. Feature films: *Meeting at Dusk / Liqâ ʾ fî-l-ghouroub* (1960), *With the Memories / Maʾ al-dhrikrayât* (1961), *The Universe of Girls / Douiniâ al-banât* (1962), *Unforgettable Love / Houbb lâ an-sâh* (1963), *The Confession / al-Pʾtirâf* (1965), *Summer Holiday / Agâzat sayf* (1967), *Just One Night / Laylah wâhidah* (1969), *A Woman's Confessions / Pʾtirâfât imraʾah* (1971), *House of Sand / Bayt min al-rimâl* (1972), *Foreigners / Ghourabâ ʾ* (1973), *The Voyage of Life / Rihlat al-ʾoumr* (1974), *Love before Bread Sometimes /*

al-Houbb qabla al-khoubz ahyânan (1977), *Tears on a Wedding Night / Doumou² fî laylat al-zifâf* (1981), *I See Myself in His Eyes / Anâ fî ᶜaynayh* (1981), *Aggression / I²tidâ²* (1982), *Marzouka / Marzouqah* (1983), *The Game of the Great / lou²bat al-kibâr* (1987), *Angels Do Not Live on Earth / al-Malâ²ikah lâ taskoun al-²ard* (1987), *Story of Half-a-Million Dollars / Hikâyat nisf million dollar* (1988), *The Thief / al-Liss* (1990), *Angels Do Not Live on Earth / al-Mala²ika lâ taskun al-ᶜard* (1995)

Arayes, Ibrahim. Egyptian filmmaker. Feature film: *The Wrongdoer / al-Chaqî* (1992)

Aryeety, Sam (b. 1929 in Accra). Ghanaian filmmaker. Studied at the Colonial Film Unit and trained as an editor in London. Feature film: *No Tears for Ananse* (1968)

Ascafare, Abdoulaye (b. 1949 in Gao). Malian filmmaker. Studied filmmaking at the Vsesoyuznyi gosudarstvennyl Institut kinematografii (VGIK; All-Union State Cinema Institute) in Moscow. He worked in radio until 1978, then taught at the Institut National des Arts in Bamako and made several shorts. His first feature is a highly stylized study of grinding poverty, told with great physical intensity. Feature film: *Faraw! / Faraw! Une mère des sables* (1996)

Asli, Mohamed (b. 1957 in Casablanca). Moroccan filmmaker. Studied filmmaking in Milan and worked as assistant on numerous documentaries and téléfilms in Italy. On return to Morocco, founded the Kanzaman studios in Ouazzarte and a film training centre in collaboration with Cinecittà and the Luce Institute. His first feature won the top prize, the *Tanit d'or*, at the Journées Cinématographiques de Carthage (JCC) in 2004. Feature film: *In Casablanca Angels No Longer Fly / À Casablanca, les anges ne volent pas* (2004)

Atallah, Amine. Egyptian silent filmmaker. Silent feature: *Boot Making / Sâni² al-qabâqîb* (1928)

Atef, Ahmed. Egyptian filmmaker. Graduated from the Cairo Film Institute in 1993. Subse-quently made half-a-dozen shorts, worked as a film critic and in festival organization. Feature films: *Omar 2000/ Omar 2000* (2000), *Talk to Mom / Kallem Mama* (2003), *How to Make Girls Love You / I zaay el banat tehebbak* (2003)

Ateyya, Kamal. Egyptian filmmaker. Feature films: *My Lovers Are Numerous / Habâybî kitîr* (1950), *The Criminal / al-Mougrim* (1954), *I Killed My Wife / Qatalt zawgati* (1956), *The Accused / al-Mouttaham* (1957), *The Lovers of the Night / ᶜOuchchâq al-layl* (1957), *The Seventeen-Year-Old Girl / Bint sabata²ch* (1958), *The Last to Be Told / Âkhir man ya²lam* (1959), *The Arms Trade / Souq al-silâh* (1960), *The End of the Path / Nihâyat* (1960), *Letter to God / Risâlah ilâ Allah* (1961), *Slaves of the Flesh / ᶜAbîd al-gasad* (1962), *The Absent Man's Secret / Sirr al-ghâ²îb* (1962), *The Path of the Demon / Tarîq al-chaytân* (1963), *With the People / Ma² al-nâs* (1964), *The Whole Town Is Talking about It / Hadîth al-madînah* (1964), *The Girls' Revolt / Yhawrat al-banât* (1964), *Oum Hatchem's Lantern / Qindîl Oumm Hâchim* (1968), *Some People Have Two Lives / al-Ba²d ya²îch marratayn* (1971), *The City of Silence / Madînat al-samt* (1973), *Secondary Roads / al-Chawâri² al-khalfiyyah* (1974), *After Love / Mâ ba²da al-houbb* (1976), *The Degenerate / al-Ma²touh* (1982), *The Mild Man's Anger / Ghadab al-halîm* (1985), *Our Gang Has No Branch / Laysa li-²isâbatinâ far² âktar* (1990)

Aufort, Didier (b. 1951 in Djibouti, of French-Ivorian descent). Ivorian filmmaker. Feature film: *Love's Gamble / Le Pari de l'amour* (2002)

Augé, Simon (b. 1944 in Port-Gentil). Gabonese filmmaker and journalist. Studied filmmaking at the Institut National de l'Audiovisuel (INA) and the Office de Radiodiffusion et de Télévision Française (ORTF) in Paris. Assistant head of Gabonese television and director general of the film centre, Centre National du Cinéma (CENACI), from 1985. One short film and one documentary. His sole feature film was originally shot as a thirteen-part television series. Feature film: *Where Are You Going Koumba? / Où vas-tu Koumba?* (with Alain Ferrari, 1971)

August, Billie. Danish maker of one feature film included in some South African filmographies. Feature film: *Goodbye Bafana* (English, 2006)

Austin, Chris (b. 1948 in Cape Town). South African documentary filmmaker, journalist, and photographer. Began studies at Stellenbosch University but was expelled for political activities. Numerous documentaries, some of feature length: *House of Hunger* (English, 1983), *Keita—Destiny of a Noble Outcast* (English, 1989), *Brenda Fassie—Not a Bad Girl* (English, 1993)

Austin, Ray. British director of a film included in some South African film listings. Feature film: *House of the Living Dead / Skadus oor Brugplaas* (English/Afrikaans, 1973)

Autissier, Anne-Marie. French co-director, with Ali Akika, of two Algerian films. Feature films: *Journey to the Capital / Voyage en capital* (with Ali Akika, 1977), *Tears of Blood / Larmes de sang* (with Ali Akika, 1980)

Aw, Cheikh Tidiane (b. 1935 in Kébémer). Senegalese filmmaker. Studied filmmaking in Germany and at the Office de Copération Radiophonique (OCORA) in Paris. One of the pioneers of Senegalese cinema. Feature films: *The Bronze Bracelet / Le Bracelet de bronze* (1974), *The Certificate / Le Certificat* (1982)

Awad, Adel. Egyptian filmmaker. Feature films: *Below Zero / Taht al-sifr* (1990), *The Scorpion / al-ʾAqrab* (1990), *Christal / Kristâl* (1993), *Youth On-Air / Shabaab ʿala el hawa* (2002)

Awad, Ahmed. Egyptian filmmaker. Feature films: *Likewise in Zamalek / Kazalik fi el Zamalk* (2002), *I Want a Divorce / Ureedo kholʾan* (2005), *Chick / Katkoot* (2006)

Ayad Driza, Mohamed. Libyan filmmaker. Feature film: *The Battle of Taghrift / Maʾrakat Taqraft* (with Khaled Khachim, 1979)

Ayite, Madjé (b. 1981 in Lomé). Togo filmmaker. Studied scriptwriting at EICAR in Paris, then returned home to work in television and make several shorts and documentaries. Fea-

ture film: *Vanessa and Sosie / Vanessa et Sosie* (2006)

Ayouch, Hichem (b. 1976 in Paris). Moroccan filmmaker. Younger brother of Nabil Ayouch. Began his career in journalism and subsequently made commercials and documentaries. His first feature was originally shot for television but shown at the Journées Cinématographiques de Carthage (JCC) in 2006. Feature film: *Edges of the Heart / Les Arêtes du cœur* (2006)

Ayouch, Nabil (b. 1969 in Paris). Moroccan filmmaker based in Paris. Older brother of Hichem Ayouch. Studied drama and directing in Paris. Made shorts and commercials, then a series of fictional shorts in Morocco. All his early work has been co-funded by the Centre Cinématographique Marocain (CCM) in Rabat. His second feature won the top prize at the Festival Panafricain du Cinéma de Ouagadougou (FESPACO) in 1991 and his co-scriptwriter, Nathalie Saugeon, published a version of it as a children's story in 2001. Feature films: *Mektoub* (1997), *Ali Zaoua / Ali Zaoua, prince de la rue* (1999), *A Minute of Sunshine Less / Une minute de soleil en moins* (2002), *Whatever Lola Wants* (2007)

Azevedo, Licínio (b. 1951 in Brazil). Mozambican filmmaker and journalist, living in Mozambique since 1975. Studied at the Instituto Nacional de Cinema (INC). Journalist and maker of educational videos for the Instituto de Comunicaçao Social. Over a dozen documentaries since 1986 and a medium-length video fiction, *The Big Bazaar / O grande bazar* (2005). Feature-length documentary: *The Fight for Water / A guerra de agua* (1995)

Azizi, Mohamed Nadir (b. 1941 at Miliana). Algerian filmmaker. Co-directed the documentary feature *So That Algeria May Live / Pour que vive l'Algérie* (with Ahmed Kerzabi, 1972). Feature film: *The Olive Tree of Boul'Hilet / L'Olivier de Boul'Hilet* (1978)

Ba, Cheikh Ngaïdo (b. 1949 in Pire). Senegalese filmmaker. Worked in television and made a number of short documentaries. Feature film: *Xew Xew / La Fête commence* (1983)

Babai, Brahim (b. 1936 in Béja). Tunisian filmmaker. Studied at the Institut des Hautes Études Cinématographiques (IDHEC) in Paris, worked as a trainee in the Office de Radiodiffusion et de Télévision Française (ORTF), and served as assistant on a number of French and Italian features. Back in Tunisia worked for television and made some short films. Also made a feature-length documentary, *A People's Victory / Victoire d'un peuple* (1975). His first feature is one of the pioneering works of Tunisian cinema. Fictional features: *And Tomorrow? / Et demain?* (1972), *The Night of the Decade / La Nuit de la décennie* (1991), *An Odyssey / Une Odysée* (2004)

Baccar, Elyes (b. 1971 in Tunis). Tunisian filmmaker. Studied at the Conservatoire Libre du Cinéma Français (CLCF) and the Fondation Européenne des Métiers de l'Image et du Son (FEMIS) in Paris. Worked as assistant director with Ferid Boughedir and Ridha Behi. Made two shorts and a documentary for Al-Jazeera TV and directed two stage plays. Feature film: *Him and Her / Elle et lui* (2004)

Baccar, Selma (b. 1945 in Tunis). Tunisian filmmaker. A product of the Fédération Tunisienne des Cinéastes Amateurs (FTCA), she studied filmmaking at the Institut Français de Cinéma (IFC) in Paris. Worked as assistant director in Radio-Télévision Tunisienne (RTT) and on several feature films. Made two short films. The first Tunisian woman to complete a feature film. Features: *Fatma 75* (1978), *The Fire Dance / La Danse du feu* (1995), *Flower of Forgetfulness / Fleur de l'oubli* (2005)

Bachir-Chouikh, Yamina (b. 1954 in Algiers). Algerian editor and filmmaker. Wife of Mohamed Chouikh. Joined the Office National du Commerce et de l'Industre Cinématographique (ONCIC) in 1974 and worked, first as script girl and then as editor, on numerous documentaries and features, including Chouikh's *The Citadel* and *The Desert Ark*. Stayed in Algeria throughout the troubles of the 1990s,

waiting years to make her first film, which is the first 35mm feature to be shot by a woman in Algeria. Feature film: *Rachida* (2002)

Badie, Mustapha (b. 1928 in Algiers). Algerian television director and filmmaker. His epic debut feature, the first to be shot by an Algerian in independent Algeria, was co-produced by Radiodiffusion Télévision Algérienne (RTA), and he has since worked largely in television. Features: *The Night Is Afraid of the Sun / La Nuit a peur du soleil* (1965), *Hassan Terro's Escape / L'Évasion de Hassan Terro* (1974)

Badish, Ken. South African filmmaker. Feature film: *Pirates of the Plains* (with John Cherry, English, 1998)

Badrakhan, Ahmed (b. 1909 in Cairo; d. 1969). Egyptian filmmaker. Sent to study in France in 1931 by Talaat Harb (founder of Misr studios). On his return, published a book on cinema and scripted *Wedad*, the first film made at Misr. During his career he worked extensively with Oum Kalthoum and Farid Al-Attrache. Later artistic director of the General Organization of Egyptian Cinema. Feature films: *The Song of Hope / Nachîd al-amal* (1937), *Something fom Nothing / Chay' min lâ chay* (1938), *A Humble Life / Hayât al-zalâm* (1940), *Dananir / Danânîr* (1940), *The Victory of Youth / Intisâr al-chabâb* (1941), *Storm over the Province / 'Âsfah 'alâ al-rîf* (1941), *On the Stage of Life / 'Alâ masrah al-hayâh* (1942), *Aida / 'Aïda* (1942), *Who Is Guilty? / Man al-gânî* (1944), *The Innocent / al-Abriyâ'* (1944), *A Kiss in Lebanon / Qoublah fî Loubnan* (1945), *The New Generation / al-Guîl al-gadîd* (1945), *Open Taxi / Taxi hantour* (1945), *The Honeymoon / Chahr al-'asal* (1945), *I Cannot / Ma 'darch* (1946), *Glory and Tears / Magd wa doumou'* (1946), *Deceptive Appearances / al-Nafkhah al-kaddâbah* (1946), *The Caravan's Return / 'Awdat al-qâfilah* (1946), *Cairo Baghdad / al-Qâhiran Baghdad* (1947), *Kiss Me Daddy / Qabbilnî yâ 'abî* (1947), *Fatma / Fatmah* (1947), *It's You I Love / Ahibbak inta* (1949), *You and Me / Anâ wa anta* (1950), *Last Lie / Âkhir Kidbah* (1950), *Night of Love / Laylat gharâm* (1951), *Honor Is Precious / al-Charaf ghâli*

(1951), *Faith / al-Imân* (1952), *I Want to Get Married / ʿAyza atgawwiz* (1952), *Mostafa Kamel / Mostafa Kâmil* (1952), *My Love's Song / Lahn houbbî* (1953), *For Your Beautiful Eyes / ʿAlachân ʿouyounak* (1954), *Promise / Waʾd* (1954), *Oath of Love / ʿAhd al-hawâ* (1955), *God Is with Us / Allah maʾnâ* (1955), *How Can I Forget You? / Izzây ansâk* (1956), *The Little Doll / al-ʾArousah al-saghîrah* (1956), *Ghariba / Gharîbah* (1958), *Sayyed Darwish / Sayyed Darwich* (1966), *The Other Half / al-Nisf al-âkhar* (1967), *Afrah / Afrâh* (1968), *Nadia / Nadia* (1969)

Badrakhan, Ali (b. 1946 in Cairo). Egyptian filmmaker. Son of Ahmed Badrakhan, he graduated from the Cairo Higher Film Institute in 1967. Worked as assistant to a number of directors, including his father, Youssef Chahine, and Chadi Abdel Salem. Teaches at the Cairo Higher Film Institute. Feature films: *Past Love / al-Houbb alladhî kân* (1973), *Al-Karnak / al-Karnak* (1975), *Exchange of Courtesies / Chayilnî wa achayyilak* (1977), *Chafika and Metwalli / Chafîqah wa Mitwallî* (1978), *People at the Top / Ahlou al-qimmah* (1981), *Hunger / al-Gouʾ* (1986), *The Shepherd and Women / al-Râʾî wa-l-nisâʾ* (1991), *The Third Man / al-Ragoul al-thaleth* (1995), *Caprice / Nazwa* (1996), *Desire / al-Raghba* (2002)

Badrakhan, Salah. Egyptian filmmaker. Feature film: *A Night's Dream / Hilm laylah* (1949)

Baghdadi, Ibrahim. Egyptian filmmaker. Feature film: *Al-Labbana Street / Darb al-Labbânah* (1984)

Bahloul, Abdelkrim (b. 1950 in Rebahia in Algeria). French-based filmmaker of Algerian descent. Came to France in 1970 at the age of 20 but still has Algerian nationality. Studied first modern languages and then film at the Institut des Hautes Études Cinématographiques (IDHEC) in Paris from 1972 to 1975. Worked in television and made two shorts. Has also made occasional film appearances, as in Merzak Allouache's *The Other World*. One of the trio of filmmakers (with Mehdi Charef and Rachid Bouchareb) to give an authentic and distinctive voice to the Algerian immigrant community in the mid-1980s. Feature films: *Mint Tea / Le Thé à la menthe* (1984), *A Vampire in Paradise / Un vampire au paradis* (1991), *The Hamlet Sisters / Les Soeurs Hamlet* (1996), *The Night of Destiny / La Nuit du destin* (1997), *The Assassinated Sun / Le Soleil assassiné* (2004)

Bahnasi, Amali. Egyptian filmmaker. Feature film: *Railway Switch / al-Tahwila* (1996)

Bakaba, Sidiki (b. 1949 in Ben Abengourou). Ivorian actor and filmmaker. Also theatre actor and director. Appeared in a number of films, including Désiré Écaré's *Visages de femmes* (1972), Jacques Champreux's *Bako, l'autre rive* (1979), Ousmane Sembene's *Camp de Thiaroye* (1987), Mustapha Diop's *Le Médecin de Gafiré* (1987) and *Mamy Wata* (1990), as well as his own features. In 1994 he also produced a Beta SP fictional feature, *Tanowe des lagunes,* about social conditions in the Ivory Coast. Feature films: *Aduefue / Les Guérisseurs* (1988), *Freewheeling / Roues libres* (2002)

Bakabe, Mahamane (b. 1947 in Gazoua). Niger filmmaker. Worked in television and made five shorts before his feature debut, a film about failed resistance to French occupation in 1905. Feature film: *If the Horsemen . . . / Si les cavaliers . . .* (1981)

Bakhti, Benamar (b. 1941 in Tlemcen). Algerian filmmaker and television director. Studied filmmaking at the Institut des Hautes Études Cinématographiques (IDHEC) and worked for Radiodiffusion Télévision Algérienne (RTA), directing a number of téléfilms. His second feature, a comedy, found a wide audience. Feature films: *The Epic of Cheikh Bouamama / L'Épopée de Cheikh Bouamama* (1983), *Moonlighting / Le Clandestin* (1991)

Bakupa-Kanyinda, Balufu (b. 1957 in Kinshasa). Democratic Republic of Congo filmmaker. Writer and journalist. Studied sociology, history, and philosophy in Brussels and filmmaking in France, England, and the United States. Currently lectures on film in New York.

Nine short films, mostly documentaries. Feature film: *Juju Factory* (2005)

Baldi, Fernandino. Maker of Egyptian feature film: *Cleopatra's Son / Ibn Cléobâtra* (1965)

Balewa, Sadick (b. 1955 in Bauchi). Nigerian filmmaker. Studied at Ahmado Bello University, Zaria (where he now teaches) and at the National Film & Television School in London. Made four shorts and a feature-length documentary. Feature film: *Kasarmu Ce* (Hausa, 1991)

Balima, Armand. Burkinabè filmmaker. Two short films. Feature film: *The Dizziness of Passion / Le Vertige de la passion* (1985)

Balogun, Baba. Nigerian filmmaker. Feature film: *Orogun Orun* (Yoruba, 1992)

Balogun, Ola (b. 1945 in Aba). Nigerian filmmaker. Studied at the universities of Dakar, Caen, and Paris. Then film studies at the Institut des Hautes Études Cinématographiques (IDHEC) in Paris. Based for a time in France, he worked for the Nigerian Embassy and published two French-language plays, *Shango* and *Le Roi-Éléphant* (Paris: Pierre Jean Oswald, 1968). Made a dozen or more documentary films throughout his career from 1969. Fictional features: *Alpha* (English, 1972), *Amadi* (Ibo, 1975), *Ajani Ogun* (Yoruba, 1975), *Musik Man* (English, 1976), *Ija Ominira* (Yoruba, 1978), *Black Goddess / A Deusa Negra* (Portuguese, 1978), *Aiye* (Yoruba, 1979), *Cry Freedom* (English, 1981), *Orun Mooru* (Yoruba, 1982), *Money Power* (Yoruba, 1982)

Barakat, Abdallah. Egyptian filmmaker. Feature films: *My Child / Waladî* (1949), *Hated Love / al-Houbb makrouh* (1953), *The Frivolous Woman / al-Moustahtirah* (1953)

Barakat, Henri (b. 1914 in Cairo). Egyptian filmmaker. Initially studied law, then went to France to learn about cinema. Worked as editor and assistant director before making his first feature. A prolific director active for over 50 years, he was successful in a wide range of film styles within the Egyptian industry. Feature

films: *The Tramp / al-Chârid* (1942), *If I Were Rich / Law Kount ghanî* (1942), *The Accused / al-Mouttahamah* (1942), *What Madness! / Imma guinân* (1944), *The Heart Has Only One Love / al-Qalb louh wâhid* (1945), *The Paternal Lack / Hâdhâ ganâhou abî* (1945), *The Lady / al-Hânim* (1947), *The Love of My Life / Habîb al-ʾoumr* (1947), *The Punishment / al-ʾIqâb* (1948), *Duty / al-Wâguib* (1948), *Peaceful Night / Sagâ al-layl* (1948), *Madam Devil / ʿIfrîtah hânim* (1949), *The Shore of Love / Châtiʾ al-gharâm* (1950), *It's Just My Luck / Maʾlich yâ zahr* (1950), *The Prince of Vengeance / Amîr al-Intiqâm* (1950), *Love's Roses / Ward al-gharâm* (1951), *Heart to Heart / Min al-qalb li-l-qalb* (1952), *Don't Tell Anyone / Mâ tʾoulch li-hadd* (1952), *A Father's Mistake / Ghaltat ʿabb* (1952), *I Am Alone / Anâ wahdî* (1952), *The Immortal Song / Lahn al-khouloud* (1952), *I Fear for My Son / Qalbî ʿalâ waladî* (1953), *The Law of Life / Houkm al-zamân* (1953), *I Am Love / Anâ al-houbb* (1954), *Love Letter / Risâlat gharâm* (1954), *It Happened One Night . . . / Hadatha dhâta laylah* (1954), *With You Always / Dâyman maʾâk* (1954), *Have Pity on Me / Irham doumouʾî* (1954), *Story of My Love / Qissat houbbî* (1955), *Days and Nights / Ayyâm wa layâlî* (1955), *Lovers' Rendezvous / Mawʾid gharâm* (1956), *Modern Young Girls / banât al-yawm* (1957), *Till Our Meeting / Hattâ naltaqî* (1958), *I Have only You / Mâlîch gheirak* (1958), *Take Pity on My Heart / Irham houbbî* (1959), *Hassan and Naima / Hasan wa Naʾîmah* (1959), *The Curlew's Call / Douʾâʾ al-karawân* (1959), *The Shore of Love / Châtiʾ al-houbb* (1961), *A Man in Our Home / Fî baytinâ ragoul* (1961), *Day without Tomorrow / Yawm bilâ ghad* (1962), *Chains of Silk / Salsîl min harîr* (1962), *The Open Door / al-Bâb al-maftouh* (1963), *The Prince of Tricks / Amîr al-dahâʾ* (1964), *The Sin / al-Harâm* (1965), *The Wedding Night / Laylat al-zifâf* (1966), *Something in My Life / Chayʾ fî hayâti* (1966), *Three Women / Thalâth nisâʾ* (one episode) (1969), *Lost Love / al-Houbb al-dâʾiʾ* (1970), *My Sister / Oukhtî* (1971), *The Fine Thread / al-Khayt al-rafî* (1971), *The Story of a Girl Called Marmar / Hikâyat bint ismouhâ Marmar* (1972), *The Woman Visitor / al-Zâʾirah* (1972), *Woman with a Bad Reputation / Imrʾah sayyiʾat al-soumʾah* (1973), *The Clock Strikes Ten / al-Sâʾah tadouqq al-âchirah* (1974), *My Love / Habîbatî* (1974), *A Question with Love / Souʾâl fî-l-houbb* (1975), *Song of My Life / Nagham fî hayâtî* (1975), *The Voyage in Life / Rihlat al-ayyâm* (1976), *His Sisters / Ikhwâtouh al-banât* (1976), *Mouths and Rabbits / Afwâh wa arânib* (1977), *Rendezvous with Soussou / Miʾâd maʾ Sousou* (1977), *With My Love and Tenderness / Maʾ houbbî wa achwâqi* (1977), *Remember Me / Idhkourînî* (1978), *Yasmine's Nights / Layâlî Yasmîn* (1978), *A Woman Is a Woman / al-Marʾah hiya al-marʾah* (1978), *Doubt, My Love / al-Chak yâ habîbî* (1979), *Lovers Younger than Twenty / ʿOuchchâq tahta al-ʾichrîn* (1979), *No Condolences for the Ladies / Wa lâ ʿazâʾ li-l-sayyidât* (1979), *I Am Neither Angel Nor Devil / Lastou chaytânan walâ malâkan* (1980), *Women without Chains / Imraʾah bilâ qayd* (1980), *Chaabane Below Zero / Chaabân tahta al-sifr* (1980), *The Valley of Memories / Wâdî al-dhikrayât* (1981), *At the Minister's Door / ʿAlâ bâb al-wazîr* (1982), *Poor Mr. Hassan / Hasan bîh al-ghalbân* (1982), *Chabrawi the Soldier / al-ʾAskarî chabrâwî* (1982), *The Widow and the Devil / al-Armalah wa-l-chaytân* (1984), *The Night of Fatima's Arrest / Laylat al-qabd ʿalâ Fatmah* (1984), *Melodies / Anghâm* (1986), *Nawwara and the Monster / Nawwârah wa-l-wahch* (1987), *Caught in the Act / Hâlat talabbous* (1988), *The Rebel / al-Moutamarrid* (1988), *Widow of a Living Man / Armalat ragfoul hayy* (1989), *The Game of the Wicked / Louʾbat al-achrâr* (1991), *The Accused Woman / al-Mouttahamah* (1992), *Enquiry with a Citizen / Tahqîq maʾ mouwâtinah* (1993)

Barakat, Kamal. Egyptian filmmaker. Feature films: *The Little Millionnairess / al-Millionnairah al-saghîrah* (1948), *Vagabond Souls / Arwâh hâʾimah* (1949)

Barkan, Yuda. South African filmmaker. Feature film: *The Big Gag / Candid Camera* (English, with Igal Shilon, 1986)

Barker, John. South African filmmaker. A graphic designer before turning to film. Produced several films, including South Africa's first musical documentary, *Blu Cheez*. Feature film: *Bunny Chow: Know Thyself* (English, 2006)

Barnard, Laurens. South African filmmaker. Feature films: *The Stay Awake* (English, 1987), *Run to Freedom* (English, 1989), *Déjà Vu, Vanessa* (English, 1990)

Barretto, Viriato. South African filmmaker. Feature film: *Knockout* (English, 1970)

Barsaoui, Khaled W. (b. 1955 in Souk El Arba). Tunisian filmmaker. Studied sociology at the University of Algiers, where he attended the Cinémathèque. Made his first amateur films in Super 8 and 16mm in the context of the Fédération Tunisienne des Cinéastes Amateurs (FTCA). Since 1990, several shorts and a télé-film, *La Fille du kiosque*, for Tunisian television. Feature film: *Beyond the Rivers / Par delà des rivières* (2006)

Barton, Sean. South African filmmaker. Feature film: *The Curse III: Blood Sacrifice / Panga Chance* (English, 1989)

Bassek Ba Kobhio (b. 1957 in Ninje). Cameroonian writer and filmmaker. His novel, *Sango Malo*, was published in Paris to coincide with the release of his first feature. One of the most forceful voices among the younger generation, specializing in studies of flawed idealists. Feature films: *The Village Teacher / Sango Malo* (1991), *The Great White Man of Lambaréné / Le Grand blanc de Lambaréné* (1995), *The Silence of the Forest / Le Silence de la forêt* (with Didier Ouenangare, 2003)

Bassiouni, Mohamed. Egyptian filmmaker. Feature films: *The Other Man / al-Ragoul al-âkhar* (1973), *One Smile Is Enough / Ibtismâmah wâhidah takfî* (1978)

Bathily, Moussa Yoro (b. 1946 in Bakel). Senegalese filmmaker. Worked as a history teacher and began with a solidly realist approach to Senegalese society. Several shorts, best known of which is *Poverty Certificate / Certifical d'indigence* (1981). Feature films: *Tiyabu Biru* (1978), *White Beans with Cassava or Gombo Sauce / Petits blancs au manioc ou à la sauce gombo* (1989), *Biliyaane* (1993)

Baxmeister, Florian. South African filmmaker. Feature film: *The Three Investigators* (English, 2007)

Bayoumi, Mohamed (b. 1894 at Tanta; d. 1963). Egyptian film pioneer. Studied filmmaking in Berlin and returned to found the first Egyptian studio, Films Amon, in 1923. Shot pioneering silent films and was involved in the building of the Misr studios and the establishment of the first Egyptian film training institute. Abandoned the cinema shortly after making his sole feature. Feature film: *Fiancé No. 13 / alᵓKhatîb nimrah tala-taᵓch* (1933)

Bechara, Khaïri (b. 1947 at Tanta). Egyptian filmmaker. Studied at the Cairo Higher Film Institute and worked as assistant director before completing further study of film in Poland. Made numerous documentaries in the 1970s as the release of his first feature, shot in 1971, was delayed for 10 years. Became a key figure in the new 1980s generation of Egyptian filmmakers. Feature films: *Barge 70 / al-ᵓAw wâmuh sabᵓîn* (1982), *Bloody Fates / al-Aqdâr al-dâmiyah* (1982), *The Necklace and the Bracelet / al-Tawk wa-l-iswirah* (1986), *Sweet Day . . . Bitter Day / Yawm mourr . . . yawm hilou* (1988), *Crab / Kabouria* (1990), *Savage Desire / Raghbah moutawahhichah* (1991), *Ice Cream in Glim / Ice cream fî glîm* (1992), *America Cadabra / Amérika chîkâ bîkâ* (1993), *The Strawberry War / Harb al-farâwlah* (1994), *Nutshells / Qeshr el bunduk* (1995), *Traffic Light / Isharet muroor* (1996). Bechara also shot a digitally produced feature which was not transferred to celluloid in the 2000s: *What's Wrong with You, Sweety / Maal al amar*

Bedeir, al-Sayed (b. 1915; d. 1986). Egyptian filmmaker. Began as an extra in the 1930s and entered filmmaking as screenwriter and dialoguist, especially for Salah Abou Seif. In the 1960s he combined filmmaking with extensive work for television and later became a senior administrator. Feature films: *Night of Horror / Laylah rahîbah* (1957), *Glory / al-Magd* (1957), *Kahramanah / Kahramânah* (1958), *My Beloved's Fault / Ghaltat habiibî* (1958), *The Virgin Wife / al-Zawgah al-ᵓadhrâᵓ* (1958), *She Lived for Love / ᶜÂchat li-l-houbb* (1959), *Oum Ratiba / Oumm Ratîbah* (1959), *Giants of the Sea / ᶜAmâliqat al-bihâr* (1960), *Madam Sokkar / Soukkar hânim* (1960), *Three Heiresses / Thalâth warîthât* (1960), *Half Virgin / Nisf ᶜadhrâ* (1961), *Salwa in the Storm / Salwa fî mahabb al-rîh* (1962), *The Olive Branch / Ghousn al-zaytoun* (1962), *The Idiot / al-ᵓAbît* (1966), *Love and Betrayal / Houbb wa khiyânah* (1968), *The Beauty from the Airport / Hasnâ al-matâr* (1971), *Adam and Women / Adam wa-l-nisâᵓ* (1971), *5 Love Street / Khamsah chârîᵓal-habâyib* (1971), *Widowed on Her Wedding Night / Armalay laylat al-zifâf* (1974)

Beheiri, Ali. Egyptian filmmaker. Feature films: *The Memories of Our Schoolboy Life / Dhikrayât al-talmadhah* (1965), *Reserved for Women / Li-l-nisâ faqat* (1966)

Behi, Ridha (b. 1947 in Kairouan). Tunisian filmmaker. A product of the Fédération Tunisienne des Cinéastes Amateurs (FTCA). Made his reputation with his second short, *Forbidden Thresholds / Seuils interdits*. After a widely successful debut, his career shows a struggle to maintain links with an international audience, with one film shot in Egyptian Arabic and others made using French star players. Feature films: *Hyena's Sun / Soleil des hyènes* (1977), *The Angels / Les Anges* (1984), *Bitter Champagne / Champagne amer* (1988), *Swallows Don't Die in Jerusalem / Les Hirondelles ne meurent pas à Jérusalem* (1994), *The Magic Box / La Boîte magique* (2002)

Bekir, Medhat. Egyptian filmmaker. Feature films: *The Three Faces of Love / Thalâth wougouh li-l-houbb* (one episode) (1969), *Invitation to Life / daᵓwah li-l-hayât* (1973), *Chase into the Forbidden / Moutâradah f-l-mamnouᵓ* (1993)

Bekir, Zouheir. Egyptian filmmaker. Feature films: *I Gave You My Life / Wahabtouka hayâtî* (with Fatine Abdel Wahab, 1956), *Struggle against Life / Sirâᵓ maᵓ al-hayât* (1957), *A Woman's Life / Hayât imraᵓah* (1958), *Return to Life / ᶜAwdat al-hayât* (1959), *Life and Hope / Hayât wa amal* (1961), *The Battle of Tyrants / Sirâᵓ* *al-gabâbirah* (with Raymond Nassour, 1962), *Lost Youth / Hîrah wachabâb* (1962), *Eternal Love / al-Houbb al-khâlid* (1965), *The Last-born / Âkhir al-ʾounqoud* (1966), *A Madman's Loves / Gharâmiyyât magʾnoun* (1967), *The Pickpocket / Sâriq al-mihfazat* (1970), *Honeymoon Trip / Rihlat chahr ʿasal* (1970), *The Language of Love / Loughat al-houbb* (1974)

Bekolo, Jean-Pierre (b. 1966 in Yaoundé). Cameroonian filmmaker who has lived recently in France, Canada, and Durham, North Carolina. Studied filmmaking at the Institut National de l'Audiovisuel (INA) in Paris. His films, which are unclassifiable experiments playing inventively with narrative in a highly personal fashion, set the tone for one important strand of filmmaking by the post-independence generation. Several short films, including one on the Senegalese filmmaker Djibril Diop Mambety. Feature films: *The Mozart District / Quartier Mozart* (1992). *Aristotle's Plot / Le Complot d'Aristote* (1996), *Bloody Women / Les Saignantes* (2005)

Belabbes, Hakim (b. 1961 in Boujaad). Moroccan filmmaker. Studied at the universities of Rabat, Lyon, and Chicago. Made four shorts in early 1990s. Teaches film at Columbia University in Chicago. Feature films: *Fibres of the Soul / Les Fibres de l'âme* (2003), *Why the Sea? / Pourquoi la mer?* (2006)

Belhachmi, Ahmed (b. 1927 in Casablanca). Moroccan filmmaker. Studies in Paris and Cambridge followed by training at the Institut des Hautes Études Cinématographiques (IDHEC) in Paris. Worked as assistant to Paolo Pasolini. First director of the Centre Cinématographique Marocain (CCM) in Rabat. Made a first feature, *The Violin / Le Violon* (1959), which was lost at the studio. Subsequently worked as an actor and settled in Switzerland

Belhiba, Fitouri (b. 1950 in Zarzis). Tunisian filmmaker. Trained as a teacher and worked in the theatre. A self-taught filmmaker, he continued to make short films after his feature debut, including *Sacrées bouteilles* (2006). Feature film: *Wandering Heart / Cœur nomade* (1990)

Belkadhi, Néjib (b. 1972 in Tunis). Tunisian filmmaker. Studied economics. Actor in film, television, and theatre. For 10 years (1992–2002) producer, director, and presenter for a fiction series on Canal Horizon and Canal 21. Also made commercials and documentaries. Feature film: *VHS—Kahloucha* (2006)

Bello, Bankole (b. 1945 in Igaara). Nigerian filmmaker. Academic studies in Nigeria and New York. Worked as assistant to Ola Balogun and as a feature film cinematographer. Made several documentaries. Feature films: *Efunsetan Aniwura* (Yoruba, 1982), *Oselu* (Yoruba, 1996)

Belmejdoub, Jamal (b. 1956 in Sidi Kacem). Moroccan scriptwriter and filmmaker. Studied filmmaking at the Institut National des Arts du Spectacle et Techniques de Diffusion (INSAS) in Brussels. Co-scripted Saâd Chraïbi's *Women . . . and Women / Femmes . . . et femmes* (1998) and Abdelhaï Laraki's *Mona Saber* (2001). Made three shorts. Feature films: *Yacout* (2000), *Moroccan Dream* (2007)

Belouad, Naguel. French-based filmmaker of Algerian descent. Studied communications at the American University in Washington, D.C., and shot a first short documentary in Maryland in 1991. Worked as assistant director on a number of Centre Algérien pour l'Art et Industrie Cinématographiques (CAAIC) productions. Feature film: *Women's Expectations / L'Attente des femmes* (2000)

Beloufa, Farouk (b. 1947 in Oued Fodda). Algerian filmmaker. Studied at the Institut National de Cinéma (INC) in Algiers and the Institut des Hautes Études Cinématographiques (IDHEC) in Paris, where he also followed courses taught by Roland Barthes. His feature-length compilation film, *Insurrectionary / Insurrectionelle* (1973), was banned and the material was re-edited and released unsigned. His sole feature is one of the rare Algerian films to deal with life elsewhere in the Arab world and established him as a filmmaker of real talent. Unfortunately he did not make a second film. Feature film: *Nahla* (1979)

Ben Aicha, Sadok (b. 1936 in Sidi Alouane). Tunisian filmmaker. Studied at the Institut des Hautes Études Cinématographiques (IDHEC) in Paris and the Centro sperimentale di cinematografia in Rome. A trainee at the Office de Radiodiffusion et de Télévision Française (ORTF) and professional film editor. Made several short films. One of the pioneers of Tunisian cinema. Feature films: *Mokhtar* (1968), *The Mannequin / Le Mannequin* (1978)

Ben Ammar, Abdellatif (b. 1943 in Tunis). Tunisian producer and filmmaker. He studied at the Institut des Hautes Études Cinématographiques (IDHEC) in Paris and the Centro sperimentale di cinematografia in Rome. Worked for the Tunisian newsreel company and as assistant on a number of foreign productions shot in Tunisia. Later worked as producer through his company Latif Productions, producing, among other films, Nacer Khemir's *Searchers of the Desert*. His masterly study of the situation of women in Tunisia, *Aziza*, which won the top prize, the *Tanit d'or*, at the Journées Cinématographiques de Carthage (JCC) in 1980, is one of the major works of Tunisian cinema. Feature films: *Such a Simple Story / Une si simple histoire* (1970), *Sejnane* (1974), *Aziza* (1980), *The Noria's Song / Le Chant de la noria* (2002)

Ben Brahim, Rachid (b. 1951 in La Lambèse). Algerian television director and filmmaker. Made shorts and documentaries before working in television. Contributed an episode to the collectively made *The Other Algeria: Views from Within / L'Autre Algérie: regards intérieurs* (1998). Feature film: *The Third Act / Le Troisième acte* (1991)

Ben Halima, Hamouda (b. 1935 in Mknine). Tunisian filmmaker. Studied at the Institut des Hautes Études Cinématographiques (IDHEC) in Paris. Worked as editor for the Tunisian newsreel company and as producer for Radio-Télévision Tunisienne (RTT). Contributed an episode to *In the Land of the Tararani / Au pays de Tararani* (1972). A pioneer of Tunisian cinema. Feature film: *Khlifa Ringworm / Khlifa le teigneux* (1969)

Ben Mabrouk, Nejia (b. 1949 in El-Oudiane). Tunisian filmmaker. She studied filmmaking at the Institut National des Arts du Spectacle et Techniques de Diffusion (INSAS) in Brussels and worked as a trainee in Belgian television. Contributed an episode to *After the Gulf? / La Guerre du Golfe . . . et après?* (1992). Her feature is the second to be made by a woman in Tunisia. Feature film: *The Trace / La Trace* (1988)

Ben Mahmoud, Mahmoud (b. 1947 in Tunis). Tunisian filmmaker. Studied filmmaking at the Institut National des Arts du Spectacle et Techniques de Diffusion (INSAS) and art and communication at the Free University of Brussels in Belgium. Made a big impact with his debut feature and has continued making an impressive series of documentaries, including the feature-length *A Thousand and One Voices / Les Mille et une voix* (2001) on music in the Islamic world. His debut feature, made in English, is a highly sophisticated parable about emigration. Feature films: *Crossing Over / Traversées* (1982), *Chichkhan / Poussière de diamants* (with Fadhel Jaïbi, 1992), *The Pomegranate Siesta / Les Siestes grenadine* (1999)

Ben Mokhtar, Rabie (b. 1944 in Amalou). Algerian filmmaker. Studied filmmaking at ENTA in France. In Algeria, he made documentaries and worked as cinematographer. Feature film: *Marathon Tam* (1992)

Ben Salah, Mohamed (b. 1945 in Algeria). Belgian-based filmmaker of Algerian descent. Writer and academic. Author of a book on cinema in the Mediterranian area. Made his sole 16mm feature-length film as his diploma film at the Institut National des Arts du Spectacle et Techniques de Diffusion (INSAS), where he studied. Feature film: *Some People and Others / Les Uns, les autres* (1972)

Ben Smaïl, Mohamed (b. 1953 in La Goulette). Tunisian actor and filmmaker. Studied first biology and then dramatic arts at the University of Paris VIII and in Los Angeles. Worked as an actor in the 1980s, including playing one of the leads in Mehdi Charef's *Miss Mona.* He stars in his own debut feature. Feature film: *Tomorrow I Burn / Demain je brûle* (1998)

Benallel, Rachid (b. 1946 in Algiers). Algerian editor and filmmaker. Studied filmmaking at the Institut des Hautes Études Cinématographiques (IDHEC) in Paris. From the 1970s edited some of the most significant Algerian feature films. Two films as director. Feature films: *Ya ouled* (1993), *Si Mohand U M'hand / L'Insoumis / The Rebel* (with Liazid Khodja, 2004)

Benayat, Mohamed (b. 1944 in Algeria). French-based filmmaker of Algerian descent. Arrived in France at the age of 4 and retains Algerian nationality. One short film. Stands apart from his more socially committed contemporaries. Feature films: *The Mask of an Enlightened Woman / Le Masque d'une éclaircie* (1974), *Savage Barricades / Barricades sauvages* (1975), *The New Romantics / Les Nouveaux romantiques* (1979), *Child of the Stars / L'Enfant des étoiles* (1985), *Arizona Stallion* (1988)

Benbarka, Souheil (b. 1942 in Timbuktu in Mali). Moroccan filmmaker and administrator. Studied sociology and then filmmaking at the Centro sperimentale di cinematografia in Rome. Worked as assistant director in Italy, including on two films by Pier Paolo Pasolini. Head of the Centre Cinématographique Marocain (CCM) from 1986. Has his own production and distribution complex, Dawliz. He has been a key figure in Moroccan cinema since the 1970s, when his first feature, *A Thousand and One Hands,* won the top prize, the Étalon de Yennenga, at the 1973 Festival Panafricain du Cinéma de Ouagadougou (FESPACO). His later features are big-budget international co-productions, unlike any other Moroccan features. Feature films: *A Thousand and One Hands / Mille et une mains* (1972), *The Oil War Will Not Happen / La Guerre du pétrole n'aura pas lieu* (1974), *Blood Wedding / Noces de sang* (1977), *Amok* (1982), *Horsemen of Glory / Les Cavaliers de la gloire* (1993), *Shadow of the Pharaoh / L'Ombre du pharaon* (1996), *The Lovers of Mogador / Les Amants de Mogador* (2002)

Benchrif, Hamid (b. 1949 in Fez; d. 1986). Moroccan editor and filmmaker. Also worked in radio and television in Senegal and Morocco. Feature film: *Steps in the Mist / Des pas dans le brouillard* (1982)

Bendeddouche, Ghaouti (b. 1936 in Tlemcen). Algerian filmmaker. Studied at the Institut des Hautes Études Cinématographiques (IDHEC) in Paris. Back in Algeria, worked for 10 years as assistant and documentarist. Contributed one episode to the collective film *Hell for a Ten-Year-Old / L'Enfer à dix ans* (1968). Feature films: *The Fishermen / Les Pêcheurs* (1976), *Dead the Long Night / Morte la longue nuit* (compilation film, with Mohamed Slim Riad, 1979), *Harvests of Steel / Moissons d'acier* (1983), *Hassan niya* (1989), *The Neighbour / La Voisine* (2002)

Benegal, Shyam. Indian director of one film included in some lists of South African feature films: *The Making of the Mahatma* (English, 1994)

Benguigui, Yamina (b. 1957 in Lille). French-based filmmaker of Algerian descent. Work in television includes two series on women's issues each comprising three 52-minute videos: *Women of Islam / Femmes d'Islam* (1994) and *Immigrants' Memories: The Maghreb Inheritance / Mémoires d'immigrés, l'héritage maghrébin* (1997). Also made *Kate's House, A Place of Hope / La Maison de Kate, un lieu d'espoir* (1995), the 52-minute video *The Perfumed Garden / Le Jardin parfumé* (2000), and the feature-length documentary *The Glass Ceiling / Le Plafond de verre* (2005). Published a novel, *Inch'allah dimanche,* in Paris in 2001. Her whole output focuses on women's issues, especially those of concern to Muslim women. Feature film: *Inch'Allah Sunday / Inch'Allah dimanche* (2001)

Benhadj, Mohamed Rachid (b. 1949 in Algiers). Algerian filmmaker and painter, resident in Italy. Studied architecture in Paris and filmmaking at the Université de Paris. His first film was a strikingly original debut within a largely conformist Algerian cinema, but his later work is increasingly international in outlook. Feature films: *Desert Rose / Rose des sables / Louss* (1989), *Touchia* (1992), *The Tree of Suspended Fates / L'albero dei destini sospesi* (in Italy, 1997), *Mirka* (in Italy, 1999)

Béni, Alphonse. Cameroonian actor and filmmaker. Studied filmmaking at the Conservatoire Libre du Cinéma Français (CLCF) in Paris. His work has been accurately defined as comprising "erotico-disco thrillers." Feature films: *The Guys, the Cops and the Whores / Les Mecs, les flics et les p . . .* aka *Les Tringleuses* (1974), *Girls in the Sun / Les Filles au soleil* (1975), *Dance My Love / Danse mon amour* (1979), *Anna Makossa* (1980), *Crooked Saint / Saint-Voyou* (1982), *A Hard Blow / Coup Dur* (1982), *Cameroon Connection / Cameroun Connection* (1985), *African Fever* (1985), *The Tear / La Déchirure* (2005)

Benjelloun, Hassan (b. 1950 in Settat). Moroccan filmmaker. Studied pharmacy, then filmmaking at the Conservatoire Libre du Cinéma Français (CLCF) in Paris, graduating in 1983. Made short films in the 1980s. His 1990s features are a continuation of the realist tradition in Moroccan cinema. Features: *Other People's Celebrations / La Fête des autres* (1990), *Yarit* (1993), *Yesterday's Friends / Les Amis d'hier* (1997), *A Woman's Judgment / Jugement d'une femme* (2000), *The Lips of Silence / Les Lèvres du silence* (2001), *The Pal / Le Pote* (2002), *The Black Room / La Chambre noire* (2004), *The Red Moon / La Lune rouge* (2006), *Where Are You Going, Moshe? / Où vas-tu Moshe?* (2007)

Benlyazid, Farida (b. 1948 in Tangier). Moroccan scriptwriter and filmmaker. She studied filmmaking at the École Supérieure des Études Cinématographiques (ESEC) in Paris. One of the few professional scriptwriters in the Maghreb, she worked as screenwriter with Jillali Ferhati (*A Breach in the Wall*, 1977, and *Reed Dolls*, 1981), Mohamed Abderrahman Tazi (*Badis*, 1990, and *In Search of My Wife's Husband*, 1993), and Abdelmajid Rchich (*The Story of a Rose*, 2000). Made a number of shorts and contributed one episode to the collective feature *Five Films for a Hundred Years / Cinq films*

pour cent ans (1995). Feature films: *Gateway to Heaven / Une porte sur le ciel* (1987), *Women's Wiles / Ruses de femmes / Keid Ensa* (1999), *Casablanca Casablanca* (2003), *Juanita from Tangier / Juanita de Tanger* (2005)

Bennani, Hamid (b. 1942 in Meknes). Moroccan filmmaker. Studied at the Institut des Hautes Études Cinématographiques (IDHEC) in Paris. Made short films, worked as a critic on the journal *Cinéma 3,* and was a member of the film collective Sigma 3. Features: *Traces / Wechma* (1970), *A Prayer for the Absent / La Prière de l'absent* (1995)

Bennani, Larbi (b. 1930 in Fez). Moroccan filmmaker. Studied filmmaking at the Institut des Hautes Études Cinématographiques (IDHEC) in Paris. Joined the Centre Cinématographique Marocain (CCM) in 1959 and made a dozen shorts there before co-directing the second Moroccan feature film to be released. Waited 27 years to complete his second film. Feature films: *When the Dates Ripen / Quand mûrissent les dattes* (with Abdelaziz Ramdani, 1968), *The Unknown Resistance Fighter / Le Résistant inconnu* (1995)

Bennet, Arthur. South African filmmaker. Feature films: *Die Wildsboudjie* (Afrikaans, with Louis Knobel, 1946), *Die Skerpioen* (Afrikaans, 1946), *Pantoffelregering* (Afrikaans, 1947)

Bensaïd, Hamid (b. 1948 in Meknès). Moroccan filmmaker. Studied filmmaking at Lodz in Poland. Worked at the Cinémathèque Française in Paris. In Morocco made several shorts and documentaries and worked in television. Feature film: *The Bird of Paradise / L'Oiseau du paradis* (1981)

Bensaidi, Faouzi (b. 1967 in Meknès). Moroccan actor and filmmaker. Studied drama at the Insitut Supérieur d'Art Dramatique et d'Animation Culturelle de Rabat (ISADAC) and at the Conservatoire National Supérieur d'Art Dramatique (CNSAD) Paris, and filmmaking at the Fondation Européenne des Métiers de l'Image et du Son (FEMIS). Appeared as an actor in features made by Nabil Ayouch (*Mektoub*), Jillali Ferhati (*Braids*), and Daoud Aoulad Syad (*The Wind Horse*). Made three acclaimed short films, which gave him an international reputation even before his feature debut. Feature films: *A Thousand Months / Mille mois* (2003), *WWW: What a Wonderful World* (2006)

Bensusan, David. South African filmmaker. Studied filmmaking at the Polytechnic of Central London. One short, while teaching at the University of Witwatersrand. His independently produced and critically successful first film, a study of the workings of the pass law, was refused distribution as a "white" film, but classified as a "black" film and as such shown largely to black audiences. Most of his later work is in native African languages. Feature films: *My Country My Hat* (English, 1983), *The Banana Gang* (Zulu, 1984), *Bank Busters* (Zulu, 1984), *Innocent Revenge* (English, 1985), *The Taste of Blood* (Zulu, 1985), *The Taste of Blood II* (Zulu, 1986), *Mountain of Hell* (Zulu, 1986), *Hotter than Snow* (Zulu, 1986), *Revenge of Q* (English, 1987), *Ho Llelo Thuso* (Zulu, 1987), *The Unforgiving* (Zulu, 1987), *The Dark Warrior* (Zulu, 1987), *Disco Marathon* (Sotho, 1988), *Sam* (Sotho, 1988), *Mahlokolobe / Pigs' Eyes* (Sotho, 1989), *Molori / Dreamer* (Tswana, 1989), *Midnite Rush* (Zulu, 1990), *The Chicken Man* (Sotho, 1990), *The Deserter* (English, 1990)

Bergman, Robert. South African filmmaker. Feature films: *From a Whisper to a Scream* (English, 1988), *Whispers* (English, 1988)

Bernard, John [Johan Barnard]. South African filmmaker. Feature film: *The Stay Awake* (English, 1987), *'n Pot vol Winter* (Afrikaans, 1991)

Berry, John. South African filmmaker. Feature film: *Boesman and Lena* (English, 1999)

Beye, Ben Diogaye (b. 1947 in Dakar). Senegalese filmmaker. Also journalist. Began with a satire on young Africans in Paris: *Les Princes noirs de Saint-Germain-des-Prés* (1975). His two features are 22 years apart. Feature films: *Sey*

Seyeti / Un homme, des femmes (1980), *A Child's Love / Un amour d'enfant* (2002)

Biggs, Charles. South African filmmaker. Feature film: *Backtrack* (English/Xhosa, 1989)

Birkinshaw, Allan. South African filmmaker. Feature films: *Sweeter than Wine* (English, 1988), *Ten Little Indians / Death on Safari* (English, 1988), *The Fall of the House of Usher* (English, 1988), *Love Me Leave Me* (English, with Charles Mariott, 1988), *The Masque of the Red Death* (English, 1989)

Blair, Les. British director of one film included in some South African film listings. Feature film: *Jump the Gun* (English, 1996)

Blignaut, Johan (b. 1953 in Benoni, Transvaal). South African filmmaker. Began his career as an actor, later working in community theatre in the colored townships. Work as producer on a number of South African features. Developed the media data-base Showdata. Co-author of a study of South African cinema 1979–1991, *Movies Moguls and Mavericks*. Neither of his innovative features was fully distributed. Feature films: *Mamza* (Afrikaans, 1985), *Tojan* (Afrikaans, 1986)

Block, Thomas. South African filmmaker. Feature film: *Donker Spore* (Afrikaans, 1944)

Bobba, Carlo. Italian maker of Egyptian feature films: *The Shop for Lovers / Makhzan al-ᵓouchchâq* (1932), *Everything but That / Koullouh alla kidah* (1936), *Omar and Gamilla / ᶜOmar wa Gamîlah* (1937)

Bode, Peter. South African filmmaker. Feature film: *Prisoners of the Lost Universe* (English, 1984)

Bokala Nkolobise. Democratic Republic of Congo filmmaker. Feature film: *Bakanja* (1988)

Boll, Uwe. South African filmmaker. Feature film: *Tunnel Rats* (English, 2007)

Bond, Anthony. South African filmmaker. Feature films: *An African Affair* (English, 1990), *Fatal Mission / Kwavinga Run / The Rat* (English, with Tonie van der Merwe, 1990)

Boonzaaier, Johannes J. South African filmmaker. Feature film: *Newels Oor Mont-Aux-Sources* (Afrikaans, 1942)

Boorman, John. British maker of one feature film included in some South African feature film listings: *Country of My Skull* (English, 2004)

Bornaz, Kaltoum (b. 1945 in Tunis). Tunisian editor and filmmaker. She studied at the Institut des Hautes Études Cinématographiques (IDHEC) in Paris and subsequently worked as assistant on foreign productions and as editor on Tunisian films, including some features. Feature films: *Keswa—The Lost Thread / Keswa, le fil perdu* (1997), *The Other Half / L'Autre moitié* (2006)

Botha, Immel. South African filmmaker. Feature film: *The Desert Inn* (English, 1959)

Botha, Kappie. South African filmmaker. Has worked exclusively in Afrikaans-language films. Feature film: *Ek sal Opstaan* (Afrikaans, 1958), *Kyk na die Sterre* (Afrikaans, 1960), *Die Hele Dorp Weet* (Afrikaans, 1961), *Vortreflike Familie Smit* (Afrikaans, 1965), *Bennie-Boet* (Afrikaans, 1967), *Twee Broeders Ry Saam* (Afrikaans, 1968), *Hulda Versteegh MD* (Afrikaans, 1970), *K9 Basspatrolliehond* (Afrikaans, 1972)

Botha, Pierre D. South African filmmaker. Feature films: *Die Goddelose Stad* (Afrikaans, 1958), *Die Bubbles Schroëder Storie / The Bubbles Schroëder Story* (Afrikaans, 1961), *Moord in Kompartement 1001E* (Afrikaans, 1961), *Die Reen kom Weer* (Afrikaans, 1963)

Bouamari, Mohamed (b. 1941 in Setif). Algerian filmmaker. Self-taught, he was a leading figure in 1970s Algerian cinema, mixing documentary precision with constant stylistic innovation. His first feature was widely shown and very well received. Feature films: *The Charcoal Burner / Le Charbonnier* (1972), *The Inheritance / L'Héritage* (1974), *First Step / Premier pas* (1979), *The Refusal / Le Refus* (1982)

Bouanani, Ahmed (b. 1938 in Casablanca). Moroccan scriptwriter, editor, and filmmaker. Studied at the Institut des Hautes Études Cinématographiques (IDHEC) in Paris and was part of the Sigma 3 collective. A pioneer of Moroccan filmmaking, he worked as a film editor after completing his sole feature (working with Hamid Bennani, Mohamed Osfour, Nabyl Lahlou, and Mohamed Abbazi). Made a number of short films, published a collection of poems, *Les Persiennes* (1980), and co-authored *Territoires de l'instant* (2000) with Daoud Aoulad Syad, whose first two features he scripted. Feature film: *Mirage* (1979)

Bouassida, Abdellatif (b. 1947 in Sfax). Tunisian filmmaker. A product of the Fédération Tunisienne des Cinéastes Amateurs (FTCA), he studied at the Filmov Akademie Múzickych Umení (FAMU; the Film & Television Faculty of the Academy of Performing Arts) in Prague. His sole feature was an ambitious historical epic, made as a Tunisian-Czechoslovakian co-production. Feature film: *The Ballad of Mamelouk / La Ballade de Mamelouk* (1981)

Bouberras, Rabah (b. 1950 in Algeria). Algerian filmmaker. Studied at the Vsesoyuznyi gosudarstvennyi institut kinematografii (VGIK; All-Union State Cinema Institute) in Moscow. Worked largely in television, making a number of téléfilms for Radiodiffusion Télévision Algérienne (RTA). Feature film: *Sahara Blues* (1991)

Bouchaâla, Ahmed (b. 1956 in Algeria). French-based filmmaker of Algerian descent. Has lived in France since the age of 6 and has Algerian nationality. Worked as assistant director and made a first short in 1984. Co-scripted his first film with his wife, Zakia, who co-directed his second. Together they also collaborated on the script of Abdelhaï Laraki's first Moroccan feature, *Mona Saber* (2001). Feature films: *Krim* (1995), *Control of Origin / Origine contrôlée* (with Zakia Bouchaâla, 2001)

Bouchaâla, Zakia (b. 1963 in Lille and née Tahiri). French-based filmmaker and actress. She co-wrote her husband Ahmed's first feature, *Krim,* and co-directed the second. Together they also collaborated on the script of Abdelhaï Laraki's first Moroccan feature, *Mona Saber* (2001). Feature film: *Control of Origin / Origine contrôlée* (with Ahmed Bouchaâla, 2001)

Bouchareb, Rachid (b. 1956 in Paris). French-based filmmaker of Algerian descent but French nationality. Began his career in French television, working as an assistant, and making a number of shorts. One of the trio of filmmakers (with Mehdi Charef and Abdelkrim Bahloul) to give an authentic and distinctive voice to the Algerian immigrant community in the mid-1980s. His ambitious later work has a wider focus. Feature films: *Bâton Rouge* (1985), *Cheb* (1990), *Segou* (1992), *Shattered Years / Des années déchirées* (1992), *Life Dust / Poussière de vie* (1994), *My Family's Honor / L'Honneur de ma famille* (1997), *Little Senegal* (2000), *Days of Glory / Indigènes* (2005)

Boucif, Mourad (b. 1967 in Algeria). Belgian-based filmmaker of Moroccan descent. Arrived in Belgium at the age of 5. Self-taught filmmaker engaged in community work. All his initial films—two shorts and a feature—were made in collaboration with his childhood friend, a fellow Belgian immigrant, Taylan Barman from Istanbul. His first solo film is the documentary *The Color of Sacrifice / La Couleur du sacrifice* (2006). Feature film: *Beyond Gibraltar / Au delà de Gibraltar* (with Taylan Barman, 2001),

Boughedir, Ferid (b. 1944 in Mammam-Lif). Tunisian film critic, historian, and filmmaker, he contributed one episode to the collective feature *In the Land of the Tararani / Au pays de Tararani* (1972). Made two key documentaries, *African Camera / Caméra d'Afrique* (1983) and *Arab Camera / Caméra arabe* (1987). A key figure in the appeciation of African filmmaking, he has worked tirelessly as a critic and published a number of books including *Le Cinéma en Afrique et dans le monde* and *Le Cinéma africain de A à Z.* His first solo feature, the uninhibited comedy *Halfaouine,* which won the

top prize, the *Tanit d'or,* at the Journées Cinématographiques de Carthage (JCC) in 1990, remains one of the most popular and successful of all Tunisian films. Feature films: *Murky Death / La Mort trouble* (with Claude d'Anna, 1970), *Halfaouine / Halfaouine, l'enfant des terrasses* (1990), *One Summer at La Goulette / Un été à la Goulette* (1995)

Bouguermouh, Abderrahmane (b. 1938 in Akbou). Algerian filmmaker. Studied filmmaking at the Institut des Hautes Études Cinématographiques (IDHEC) in Paris. Contributed one episode to the collective feature *Hell for a Ten-Year-Old / L'Enfer à dix ans* (1968) and made two 16mm television features, *Summer Birds / Les Oiseaux de l'été* (1978) and *Black and White / Noir et blanc* (1980). His second feature is one of the first to be made in the Berber language. Feature films: *Cry of Stone / Cri de pierre* (1986) and *The Forgotten Hillside / La Colline oubliée* (1996)

Boukhitine, Lyèce (b. 1965 in Digoin, France). French-based filmmaker of Algerian descent. Studied drama in Lyon and Paris and appeared in a number of films. Made three short fictional films. Feature film: *The Mistress in a Swimming Costume / La Maîtresse en maillot de bain* (2001)

Boulane, Ahmed (b. 1956 in Salé). Moroccan actor and filmmaker. Studied drama in Rabat and then (briefly) filmmaking in Italy. After his return to Morocco in 1981, he worked as an actor and as assistant on Moroccan and foreign productions. Made shorts and documentaries from the 1990s. Feature films: *Ali, Rabia and the Others / Ali, Rabia et les autres* (2000), *Satan's Angels / Les Anges de Satan* (2007)

Bourquia, Farida (b. 1948 in Casablanca). Moroccan television director and filmmaker. She studied drama in Moscow. Worked in Moroccan television on a wide variety of dramatic productions throughout the 1980s and 1990s. The first woman to complete a feature film in Morocco but had to wait 25 years to complete a second. Feature films: *The Embers / La Braise* (1982), *Two Women on the Road / Deux femmes sur la route* (2007)

Bouzid, Nouri (b. 1945 in Sfax). Tunisian scriptwriter and filmmaker. Studied filmmaking at the Institut National des Arts du Spectacle et Techniques de Diffusion (INSAS) in Brussels. Arrested for political activities on his return and imprisoned for 5 years. On his release he resumed his career, making three feature films in 1986–1992, beginning with *Man of Ashes,* which won the top prize, the *Tanit d'or,* at the Journées Cinématographiques de Carthage (JCC) in 1986. These put him in the forefront of Maghrebian filmmaking, with work of great power and sensitivity. He repeated this JCC success with *Making Of* in 2006. Bouzid increased his impact on Arab cinema by working as scriptwriter for Ferid Boughedir (*Halfaouine*), Moufida Tlatli (*Silences of the Palace),* Moncef Dhouib (*The Sultan of the Medina*), and others. He contributed an episode to the collective feature *After the Gulf? / La Guerre du Golfe . . . et après?* (1992). Feature films: *Man of Ashes / L'Homme de cendres* (1986), *Golden Horseshoes / Les Sabots en or* (1989), *Bezness* (1992), *Girls from a Good Family / Tunisiennes / Bent familia* (1997), *Clay Dolls / Poupées d'argile* (2002). *Making Of,* (2006)

Bowden, Weston. South African silent filmmaker. Feature film: *The Blue Lagoon* (Silent, 1923)

Bowey, John R. South African filmmaker. Feature film: *Time of the Beast / Mutator* (English, 1989)

Breccia, Alfonso. Italian maker of one Egyptian feature film: *The Victor of Atlantis / Qâhir al-Atlants* (1966)

Breytenbach, Jan. South African filmmaker. Feature films: *Die Afspraak* (Afrikaans, 1974), *Wat Maak Oom Kallie Daar?* (Afrikaans, 1975)

Bright, Simon (b. 1952 in Harare). Zimbabwean filmmaker. Studied English literature at Cambridge and sociology at Reading University in England. Co-founder of the production company Zinmedia with Ingrid Sinclair. Made a number of well-received documentaries: *Corridors of Freedom* (1987), *Limpopo Line* (1990),

The Sanctions Debate (1990), *M'Bira Music— Spirit of the People* (1990). Produced the collective film *Mama Africa* (2002)

Brijmohun Brothers. Mauritian filmmakers. Feature films: *Lost Dream / Bikre Sapne* (1975), *The Egotist / Khudgarz* (1988)

Bristow, Douglas. South African filmmaker. Feature film: *Crystal Eye* (English, with Joe Tornatore, 1988)

Burke, Louis. South African filmmaker. Feature film: *Follow That Rainbow* (English, 1980)

Buys, Bernard. South African filmmaker. Feature film: *Savage Encounter* (English, 1980)

Calasto, Gianpietro. South African filmmaker. Feature film: *Vulture Is a Patient Bird* (1988)

Camara, Cheik Fantamady (b. 1960 in Conakry). Guinean filmmaker. Self-taught as a filmmaker, he worked as assistant director on Cheikh Oumar Sissoko's Malian film *Genesis* (1999). Several shorts in the early 2000s. Feature film: *It'll Rain in Conakry / Il va pleuvoir sur Conakry* (2006)

Camara, Dansogho Mohamed (b. 1945). Guinean filmmaker. Worked as a teacher before studying filmmaking in Germany. Feature films: *Give and Take / Du donner et du recevoir* (1977), *Ouloukoro* (1983), *The Witness / Sere / Le Témoin* (1990)

Camara, Mohamed (b. 1959 in Conakry). Guinean actor and filmmaker. Studied drama in Paris. Noted for his outspoken fictional shorts, *Denko* (1992) and *Minka* (1994), he made a formalized study of the taboo subject of homosexuality as his feature debut. Feature film: *Destiny / Dakan* (1997)

Campbell, Martin. South African filmmaker. Feature film: *Beyond Borders* (English, 2003)

Canes, George. South African filmmaker. Feature films: *Pressure Burst* (English, 1971), *Next Stop Makouvlei* (English, 1972)

Cardiff, Jack. English cinematographer and director of one feature film included in some South African film lists: *Dark of the Sun / The Mercenaries* (English, 1968)

Cardos, John. American director of three films included in some South African film listings. Feature films: *Outlaw of Gor* (English, 1987), *Skeleton Coast* (English, 1987), *Act of Piracy* (English, 1988), *Barracuda* (English, 1988)

Cardoso, José (b. 1930 at Figueira de Castelo Rodrigo in Portugal). Mozambican filmmaker. Emigrated to Mozambique with his parents in 1937. Chemist and self-taught fimmaker. Began with Super 8 films in the late 1960s. A number of documentaries and fictional shorts in 16mm and video. Feature films: *Sing My Brother, Help Me to Sing / Canta meu irmao, ajuda-me a cantar* (1982), *The Wind from the North / O vento sopra do norte* (1987)

Carlsen, Henning. Danish director of one film included in some South African feature film lists: *Dilemma* (1962)

Carvalho, Sol de (b. 1953 in Beira). Mozambican filmmaker. Studied at the National Conservatory of Cinema in Madrid and worked as a journalist and photographer. From 1984 he worked in the film and television industries and directed several shorts and documentaries. Feature film: *O Jardim do Outro Homen* (2006)

Carver, Steve. American director of a film included in some South African film listings. Feature film: *River of Death* (English, 1988)

Cawood, Bromley. South African filmmaker. Feature films: *Wolhaarstories* (Afrikaans, 1983), *Tawwe Tienies* (Afrikaans, 1984), *Skating on Thin Uys* (English, 1985), *The Devil and the Song* (English, 1987)

Chaaban, Cherif. Egyptian filmmaker. Feature films: *Jeans / al-Jînz* (1994), *Tata, Reeka and Kazem Bey / Ta'ta wa Reeka wa Kazem Bey* (1995), *A Fish and Four Sharks / Samaka wa arba' quroosh* (1997), *All-Girl Band / Ferqet banaat wi bass* (2000)

Chaaban, Mohamed. Egyptian filmmaker. Feature film: *Honour / al-Charaf* (2000)

Chaabane, Youssef. Libyan filmmaker. Feature film: *The Road / al-Tariq* (1973)

Chaath, Ghaleb. Egyptian filmmaker. Feature film: *Shadows on the Other Bank / al-Zilâl fî-l-gânib al-âkhar* (1975)

Chaffey, Don. British director of two films included in some South African film lists: *A Twist of Sand* (English, 1969), *Creatures the World Forgot* (English, 1972)

Chafik, Sobhi. Egyptian filmmaker. Feature film: *The Meeting / al-Talâqî* (1977)

Chahine, Youssef (b. 1926 in Alexandria). Egyptian filmmaker. Born into a Catholic family, he studied at the English-language Victoria College and then, for a year, at university in Alexandria. Further study of direction and acting at Pasadena Playhouse near Los Angeles. He was one of Egypt's youngest directors at his debut in the 1950s, but rapidly established himself as one of the major figures in Egyptian cinema. Subsequently became a key influence on the younger generation, winning the top prize, the *Tanit d'or,* at the second Journées Cinématographiques de Carthage (JCC) in Tunis in 1970. From the late 1970s, he has been one of the few Arab filmmakers to make openly autobiographical films. Features: *Papa Amine / Bâbâ Amîn* (1950), *Son of the Nile / Ibn al-Nîl* (1951), *The Great Clown / al-Mouharrig al-kabîr* (1952), *The Lady from the Train / Sayyidat al-qitâr* (1952), *Women without Men / Nisâ' bilâ rigâl* (1953), *Sky of Hell / Sirâ fii-l-wâdî* (1954), *The Demon of the Desert / Chaytân al-sahrâ* (1954), *Black Waters / Sirâ fî-l-mînâ* (1956), *Farewell My Love / Wadda'tou houbbak* (1956), *You Are My Love / Anta habîbî* (1957), *Central Station / Bâb al-hadîd* (1958), *Gamila the Algerian Woman / Gamîlah* (1958), *For Ever Yours / Houbb îla al-abad* (1959), *In Your Hands / Bein îdek* (1960), *The Lovers' Call / Nidâ al-'ouchchâq* (1960), *A Man in My Life / Ragoul fî hayâtî* (1961), *Saladin / al-Nâsir Salah Eddine* (1963), *The Dawn* of a New Day / Fagr yawm gadîd (1965), The Earth / al-Ard (1970), The Choice / al-Ikhtiyâr (1971), The People and the Nile / al-Nâs wa-l-Nîl (1972), The Sparrow / al-ɔOusfour (1974), The Return of the Prodigal Son / ᶜAwdat al-ibn al-dâll (1976), Alexandria . . . Why? / Iskandariyyah lîh (1979), An Egyptian Story / Haddoutah masriyyah (1982), Farewell Bonaparte / al-Wadâɔ yâ Bonaparte (1985), The Sixth Day / al-Yawm al-sâdis (1986), Alexandria Now and Forever / Iskandariyyah kamân we kamân (1990), The Emigrant / al-Moughâguir (1994), Destiny / al-Masseer (1997), The Other / al-Akhar (1999), Silence! We're Filming / Sukoot ha nsawwar! (2001), Alexandria-New York / Iskendereya New York (2004), Chaos / Heya fawda (with Khaled Youssef, 2007)

Chamiyya, Chafik. Egyptian filmmaker. Feature film: Crime of Honour / Hâdithat charaf (1971)

Charaf, Bahaa Eddine. Egyptian filmmaker. Feature films: Elham / Elham (1950), Al-Sayyed Ahmad al-Baadawi / al-Sayyed Ahmad al Badawî (1953), Captain Misr / Kabtin Misr (1955), Whoever Is Happy with a Little / Man radiya bi-qalîhih (1955), Lost Days / Ayyâm dâˀiˀah (1965)

Charaf Eddine, Youssef. Egyptian filmmaker. Feature films: The Days' Struggle / Sirâɔ al-ayyâm (1985), The Professionals / al-Moutharifoun (1986), We Still Have Love / Wa yabqâ al-houbb (1987), The Last Game / al-Louɔbah al-akhîrah (1990)

Charef, Mehdi (b. 1952 at Maghnia in Algeria). French-based filmmaker of Algerian descent. Arrived in France at the age of 10, but retains Algerian nationality. Trained as a mechanic and worked in a factory from 1970 until 1983. That year he published the first of four French-language novels, Le Thé au harem d'Archi Ahmed, followed by Le Harki de Meriem (1989), La Maison d'Alexina (1999), and À bras-le-cœur (2006). He also made several téléfilms for La Sept Arte in the 1990s, including Pigeon volé (1995) and a version of La Maison d'Alexina (1998). One of the trio of filmmakers (with Abdelkrim

Bahloul and Rachid Bouchareb) to give an authentic and distinctive voice to the Algerian immigrant community in the mid-1980s. He continued in this vein through to 2000. Features: Tea in the Harem / Le Thé au harem d'Archimède (1985), Miss Mona (1987), Camomile / Camoumille (1988), In the Land of the Juliets / Au pays des Juliets (1992), Marie-Line (2000), Keltoum's Daughter / La Fille de Keltoum (2002), Gallic Cartridges / Cartouches gaulois (2007)

Charkas, Wael. Egyptian filmmaker. Feature films: I'll Let Go If You Will / Seeb wa ana aseeb (2004), Abdou Seasons /ɔAbdu mawasem (2006)

Chatta, Nidhal (b. 1959 in Tunis). Tunisian filmmaker. Studied ecology and oceanography in the United Kingdom. Worked for the BBC and made a number of short underwater films. Feature film: No Man's Love (2000)

Chawkat, Seif Eddine. Egyptian filmmaker. Feature films: The Intelligent Person / al-Nâsih (1949), Felfel / Felfel (1950), The Heart's Elect / Ibn al-halâl (1951), Samson and Leblcb / Chamchoun wu Liblib (1952), Life . . . Love / al-Hayât . . . al-houbb (1954), The Hope of My Life / Amânî al-ɔoumr (1955), Birds of Paradise / ᶜAsâfîr al-gannah (1955), Ishmael Yassine at the Zoo / Ismâɔîl Yâsîn fi guininet al-haywân (1957), Secret Love / al-Houbb al-sâmit (1958), A Heartless Man / Ragoul bilâ qalb (1960), Love, Love / Houbb fi houbb (1960), Woman and Demon / Imraɔah wa chaytân (1961), The Two Adolescent Girls / al-Mourâhigân (1964), One Wife for Five Men / Zawgah li-khamsat riggâlah (1970), The Thieving Millionairess / al-Millionnairah al-nachchâlah (1978)

Chawki, Khalil (b. 1928 at Port-Tawfiq). Egyptian filmmaker. Studied literature in Egypt, then (unusually for an Egyptian filmmaker) followed a course in filmmaking at the Centro sperimentale di cinematografia in Rome. Worked initially in documentary and television. Unable to complete more than a handful of films, he abandoned cinema for television. Feature films: The Mountain / al-Gabal (1965), The Girls' Camp / Mouɔaskar al-banât (1967), The Everyday

Toy / lou³bat koull yawm (1971), *The Madness of Youth / Gounoun al-chabâb* (1980), *The Wife Knows More / al-Zawgah ta³rif akthar* (1987)

Chebl, Fouad. Egyptian filmmaker. Feature films: *According to Your Means / ᶜAlâ ᶜad lihâfak* (1949), *Your Mother-in Law Loves You / Hamâtak tihibbak* (1950)

Chebl, Mohamed (b. 1949 in Cairo). Egyptian filmmaker. Studied English (as well as Chinese) in Moscow and has continued to work in English-language radio and journalism. His handful of features reflect an interest in the supernatural. He has also made a lengthy documentary series on Youssef Chahine. Feature films: *Fangs / Anyâb* (1981), *The Amulet / al-Ta³wîdhah* (1987), *Nightmare / Kâbous* (1989), *Love and Cruel Revenge / Gharâm wa intiqâm bi-l-sâtour* (1992)

Cheferani, Oswaldo. Maker of one Egyptian feature film: *The Desert Horseman / Fâris al-sahrâ³* (1966)

Chenouga, Chad (b. 1962 in Paris). French-based filmmaker of Algerian descent. He studied economics, then drama at the Cours Florent in Paris, where he later became a teacher. Acted in a number of French films and television dramas and made four shorts in the 1990s. One of many filmmakers at the beginning of the 2000s to adopt an autobiographical approach. Feature film: *17 rue Bleue* (2001)

Cherabi-Labidi, Nadia (b. 1954 in Algiers). Algerian filmmaker. Studied drama at the Sorbonne in Paris. Works as assistant director and teaching at the University of Algiers. Documentary films from 1993. Feature film: *The Other Side of the Mirror / L'Envers du miroir* (2007)

Cherif, Abdel Rahman. Egyptian filmmaker. Feature films: *Come Back Mummy / ᶜOudî yâ oummî* (1961), *Day of Judgment / Yawm al-hisâb* (1962), *The First Love / Awwal houbb* (1964), *The Flames / al-Lahab* (1964), *Love for All / Houbb li-l-gamî* (1965), *The Good Guys of Our Street / Gid³ân haritnâ* (1965), *Wife without a Man / Zawgah bilâ ragoul* (1969), *The Trickster / al-Ghachchâch* (1970), *The Pardon / al-*

Ghoufrân (1971), *The Most Honest of Sinners / Achraf khâti³a* (1973), *The Authentic One / al-Asîl* (1973), *Love and Silence / al-Houbb wa-l-samt* (1973), *Life Is a Song / al-Hayât na³ham* (1976)

Cherry, John. South African filmmaker. Feature films: *Ernest in the Army* (English, 1997), *Ernest in Africa* (English, 1997), *Laurel and Hardy—The Movie* (English, with Larry Harmon, 1998), *Pirates of the Plains* (with Ken Badish, English, 1998)

Chiarini, Telio [or Stelio]. Italian maker of two Egyptian feature films: *The Radio Song / Ounchoudat al-radio* (1936), *My Second Wife / Mirâtî nimrah itnîn* (1937)

Chibane, Malek (b. 1964 in Saint-Vallier, in France). French-based filmmaker of Algerian descent. Born of Kabyle parents, he has French nationality and lives in France. His first two films are modestly funded independent features looking at the immigrant community. Feature films: *Hexagon / Hexagone* (1993), *Sweet France / Douce France* (1995), *Neighbours / Voisins, Voisines* (2005)

Chigorimbo, Stephen (b. 1951 in Chegutu). Zimbabwean filmmaker. Co-founder of the Film Worker Association and Union. Feature film: *Pfuma Yedu* (1991)

Chimi, Saîd. Egyptian filmmaker. Feature film: *The Treasure / al-Kanz* (1993)

Chouika, Driss (b. 1953 in Kalaa Sraona). Moroccan filmmaker. A product of the Moroccan cine-club movement, the Fédération Nationale des Ciné-Clubs au Maroc (FNCCM), and one of the organizers of Khouribga film festival. He underwent a technical training in Paris studios and laboratories. Worked as magazine editor and, from 1996, in Moroccan television, making dramas and a series about cinema. Cowrote Mohamed Lotfi's *Rhésus, Another Person's Blood*. Feature films: *Mabrouk* (1999), *The Game of Love / Le Jeu de l'amour* (2006)

Chouikh, Mohamed (b. 1943 in Mostaganem). Algerian actor and filmmaker. Played the lead in one of the first Algerian features, Mohamed Lakhdar Hamina's *Wind from the Aurès,* and in a number of other important films for Tewfik Farès (*The Outlaws*) and Sid Ali Mazif (*The Nomads*), as well as French films such as Michel Drach's *Elise, or Real Life.* Directed two Algerian téléfilms, *The River Mouth / L'Embouchure* (1972–1974) and *The Wrecks / Les Paumés* (1974). One of the few major directors to remain in Algeria during the troubles, he created a remarkable trio of films in 1988–1997 which explored the potential of parable and allegory. Feature films: *Breakdown / La Rupture* (1982), *The Citadel / La Citadelle* (1988), *Youssef—The Legend of the Seventh Sleeper / Youcef, la légende du septième dormant* (1993), *Desert Ark / L'Arche du désert* (1997), *Hamlet of Women / Douar de femmes* (2005)

Choukri, Abdel Meneim. Egyptian filmmaker. Feature films: *Quiet Honeymoon / Chahr ʿasal bidoun izʾâg* (1968), *A Criminal Put to the Test / Mougrim taht al-ikhtibâr* (1968), *Hello My Dear Wife / Sabâh al-khatr yâ zawgatî al-ʾazîzah* (1969), *The Street of Roundabouts / Chârîʾ al-mahâhî* (1969), *How to Get Rid of Your Wife / Kayfa tatakhallas min zawgatik* (1969), *My Wife, My Mistress and I / Anâ wa mirâtî wa-l-gaww* (1969), *I Love You, My Beauty / Bahibbik yâ hiulwah* (1970), *Love on an Agricultural Road / Gharâm fî-l-tarîq al-zieâʾî* (1971), *The Important Thing Is Love / al-Mouhimm al-houbb* (1974), *Dounia / Douniâ* (1974), *The Charmer of Women / Sâʾid al-nisâ* (1975), *The Love Thief / Harâmî al-houbb* (1977), *Terrorized / Ahdân al-khawf* (1986)

Choukri, Atef. Egyptian filmmaker. Feature film: *Cool, Man! / Ishta yaba* (2004)

Choukri, Mamdouh (b. 1939 at Wadiʾn Nana in Upper Egypt; d. 1973). Egyptian filmmaker. Abandoned studies of fine arts to join the Cairo Higher Film Institute. After working as assistant director and making a first documentary, he began his feature career by writing the three sketches of *The Three Faces of Love* and directing one of them. The release of his final feature was delayed because of censorship problems until 2 years after his early death from brain fever.

Feature films: *The Three Faces of Love / Thalâth wougouh li-l-houbb* (one episode) (1969), *The Illusions of Love / Awhâm al-houbb* (1970), *The Yellow Valley / al-Wâdi al-asfar* (1970), *The Evening Visitor / Zâʾir al-fagr* (1975)

Choukri, Osman. Egyptian filmmaker. Feature film: *The Swindle / al-Malʾoub* (1987)

Chraïbi, Omar (b. 1961 in Casablanca). Moroccan filmmaker. Younger brother of Saâd Chraïbi. Studied photography in Liège, communication studies in Grenoble, and film at the Sorbonne and the Fondation Européenne des Métiers de l'Image et du Son (FEMIS) in Paris. Worked as assistant director and contributed an episode to the collective feature *Five Films for a Hundred Years / Cinq films pour cent ans* (1995). Three short films. Feature films: *The Man Who Embroidered Secrets / L'Homme qui brodait des secrets* (2000), *Rahma* (2003), *Woven by Hands from Material / Tissée de mains et d'étoffe* (2007)

Chraïbi, Saâd (b. 1952 in Fez). Moroccan filmmaker. Older brother of Omar Chraïbi. Studied medicine and was a product of the Fédération Nationale des Ciné-Clubs au Maroc (FNCCM), the Moroccan film club movement. A member of the collective which made *Cinders of the Vineyard / Les cendres du clos* (1977). Made a variety of short films. His second feature was a major commercial hit. Feature films: *Chronicle of a Normal Life / Chronique d'une vie normale* (1991), *Women . . . and Women / Femmes . . . et femmes* (1998), *Thirst / Soif* (2000), *Jawhara* (2003), *Islamour* (2007)

Chrigui, Tijani (b. 1949 in Azemmour). Moroccan painter and filmmaker. Co-scripted Mohamed Aboulouakar's *Hadda* (1984). He has described his only feature as "a series of situations in which it is difficult to know what the characters do or say." Feature film: *Ymer or the Flowering Thistles / Ymer ou les chardons florifières* (1991)

Chung, Lee Isaac. Rwandan filmmaker. Feature film: *Munyurangabo* (2007)

Cisse, Mamo (b. 1951 in Kayes). Malian novelist and filmmaker, who began his literary career with *La Roue de la vie* in 1984. His first feature deals with the discovery of school by a young orphan. Feature films: *Falato* (1989), *Yelema* (1992), *Yelema II* (1997)

Cisse, Souleymane (b. 1940 in Bamako). Malian filmmaker. Studied filmmaking at the Vsesoyuznyi gosudarstvennyi institut kinematografii (VGIK; All-Union State Cinema Institute) in Moscow. He began with two socially committed realist studies of Malian life, the second of which, *Baara,* won the top prize, the Étalon de Yennenga, at the Festival Panafricain du Cinéma de Ouagadougou (FESPACO) in 1979. He made a huge reputation in the 1980s with his two powerful and varied features which allowed aspects of fantasy and magic to enter the field. With *Finye,* in 1983, he became the only filmmaker ever to win a second Étalon de Yennenga, as well as the first to combine this win with the *Tanit d'or* at the Journées Cinématographiques de Carthage (JCC) in 1984. *Yeelen,* one of the most powerful and influential of 1980s African films, is a visually complex and resplendent retelling of a Bambara legend. His career seems to have stalled after his ambitious but commercially unsuccessful English-language study of apartheid, *Waati.* Feature films: *Den muso / La Jeune fille* (1975), *Baara* (1978), *Finye* (1982), *Yeelen* (1987), *Waati* (1995)

Clarence, Trevor. South African filmmaker. Feature film: *Crazy Monkey Presents: Straight Outta Benoni* (English, 2005)

Clegg, Tom. South African filmmaker. Feature films: *Any Man's Death* (English, 1988), *Bravo Two Zero* (English, 1998)

Clinton, B. F. South African silent filmmaker. Feature films: *A Kract Affair* (Silent, 1916), *The Water Cure* (Silent, 1916), *£20,000* (Silent, 1916)

Cloete, Franz. South African filmmaker. Produced as well as directed his sole feature. Feature film: *Die Sewende Horison* (Afrikaans, 1958)

Coelo, Issa Serge (b. 1967 in Biltine). Chadian filmmaker, currently resident in France. Studied history at the University of Paris I and filmmaking at the Ecole Supérieure de Réalisation Audiovisuelle (ESRA) in Paris. Worked in television. Made an appearance in his compatriot Mahamat Saleh Haroun's *Bye Bye Africa.* Feature films: *Daresalam* (2000), *Tartina City* (2006)

Coertze, François. South African filmmaker. Feature films: *Desert Diners* (English, 1999), *Lyk Lollery* (Afrikaans, 2000)

Coetzer, Morné. South African filmmaker. Feature film: *Lag met Wena* (Afrikaans, 1977)

Cohen, Norman. Irish director of two films included in some South African film listings. Feature films: *Burning Rubber* (English, 1980), *The Lion's Share* (English, 1985)

Coley, Francis. South African filmmaker. Feature film: *Sarie Marais* (Afrikaans, 1949)

Collinson, Peter. British director of one feature included in some lists of South African features: *Tigers Don't Cry* (English, 1976)

Conradie, Franz. South African filmmaker. Feature film: *Die Jakkels van Tula Metsi* (Afrikaans, 1967)

Coulibaly, Mambaye (b. 1957 at Kayes). Malian filmmaker and composer. Studied first law, and then cinema with Jean Rouch in Paris. Made a first animated short, *Segou Janjo,* in 1989 and then, 15 years later, black Africa's first animated feature film. Feature film: *Segou's Power / Segu fanga* (2006)

Coulibaly, Sega (b. 1950 in Dakar, Senegal). Malian filmmaker. Studied filmmaking at the Conservatoire Libre du Cinéma Français (CLCF) in Paris. Feature films: *Fate / Mogho Dakan* (1976), *Den Kasso* (1978)

Cox, Vincent G. South African filmmaker. Feature films: *Return to Justice / The Last Cowboy / White Dust* (English, 1988), *Voice in the Dark* (English, 1989)

Crampton, Hazel. South African filmmaker. Feature film: *Blood City* (English, 1989)

Crawford, Wayne. South African filmmaker. Feature films: *Jake Speed* (English, 1986), *Devil Fish* (English, 1987), *The Crime Lords* (English, with Franck Schaeffer, 1990), *Snake Island* (English, 2003)

Cruchten, Pol. Cape Verde filmmaker. Feature film: *Black Dju* (1997)

Cruikshanks, Dick. South African veteran filmmaker and actor. The most prolific of all South African silent filmmakers. Feature films: *The Major's Dilemma* (Silent, 1917), *The Piccanin's Christmas* (Silent, 1917), *The Mealie Kids* (Silent, 1917), *Zulu-Town Comedies* (Silent, 1917), *Bond and Word* (Silent, 1918), *The Bridge* (Silent, 1918), *Fallen Leaves* (Silent, 1919), *Prester John* (Silent, 1920), *The Vulture's Prey*, (Silent, 1921)

Cunningham, Tony. South African filmmaker. Feature film: *Black Crusader* (English, 1990)

Curling, Chris. South African filmmaker. Feature film: *Dark City* (English, 1989)

Dagher, Assia (b. 1908 in Lebanon; d. 1986). Egyptian actress and veteran film producer. Real name: Almazer Dagher, the aunt of Mary Queeny. She was an extra in *Leila* and went on to produce and star in *The Beauty from the Desert / Ghâdat al-sahrâ²* (directed by Wedad Orfi). After playing the lead in sixteen films up to 1947, she continued to work as a producer until 1970. In this role she was responsible for some of the major works of Egyptian cinema, including Youssef Chahine's *Saladin* and Tewfik Saleh's *Diary of a Deputy Country Prosecutor*

Dahms, Heinrich (b. 1954). South African filmmaker. Studied philosophy and lingistics at Cape Town and Witwatersrand universities. Worked as a cameraman on documentaries and in television. Feature films: *City Wolf* (English, 1987), *Dune Surfer / Kalahari Surfer* (English, 1989), *Au Pair* (English, 1990)

D'Almeida e Silva, Fernando (b. 1945). Mozambican filmmaker. Studied audio-visual production in London. Fictional shorts from 1973. Feature film: *The Earth's Storm / A tempestade da terra* (1996)

Damak, Mohamed (b. 1952 in Sfax). Tunisian filmmaker. A product of the Fédération Tunisienne des Cinéastes Amateurs (FTCA), he studied filmmaking at the Conservatoire Libre du Cinéma Français (CLCF) and the École Pratique des Hautes Études in Paris. Worked on foreign features shot in Tunisia and made several noted shorts. Feature films: *The Cup / La Coupe* (1986), *The Villa / La Villa* (2004)

Damardjji, Djafar (b. 1934 in Algiers). Algerian filmmaker. Studied theatre at the Berlin Humboldt University in the DDR and taught at the Institut National de Cinéma (INC) in Algiers. Short films in Algeria and the Arab Emirates. Feature films: *The Good Families / Les Bonnes familles* (1972), *Wanderings / Errances* (1993)

Daneel, Richard. South African filmmaker. Feature films: *Oupa for Sale* (Afrikaans, 1968), *Vrolike Vrydag* (Afrikaans, 1969), *Stadig oor die Klippe* (Afrikaans, 1969)

Dangarembga, Tsitsi (b. at Mutoko). Zimbabwean filmmaker and actress. She studied psychology and filmmaking, the latter at the Berlin Film and TV Academy. She has written a play, *She No Longer Weeps*; a novel, *Nervous Conditions*; and the script for Godwin Mawuru's *Neria*. She also made a video documentary, *Growing Stronger*, in 2006. Feature films: *Everyone's Child* (1996), *Kare Kare Zvako / The Survival of the Butchered Woman* (2004)

Darwich, Ahmed Fouad. Egyptian filmmaker. Feature films: *The Execution of a Secondary School Boy / I'dâm tâlib thânawî* (1982), *The Beauty of the Soul / Halâwat al-rouh* (1990)

Darwich, Wasfi. Egyptian filmmaker. Feature films: *The Last Word / al-Kalimah al-akhîrah* (1982), *The Traitors / al-Khawanah* (1984), *I Am Not a Criminal / Lastou mougriman* (1985), *The Village of the Greedy / Kafr al-tammâ²în* (1992)

Davidson, Boaz. Israeli-born director of several films included in some South African film listings. Feature films: *Ben Bonzo and Big Bad Joe / My African Adventure* (English, 1987), *Crazy Camera / Crazy People* (English, with Zvi Shisel, 1988), *Lunar Cop* (English, 1994)

Davies, Robert (b. in Cape Town). South African filmmaker. Worked at RAI and lived in Italy in the 1970s, then active in the South African industry. Feature films: *Saturday Night at the Palace* (English, 1986), *Dark Mountain* (English, 1988), *In the Name of Blood* (English, 1989)

Davis, Beau. South African filmmaker. Feature films: *American Ninja II: The Confrontation* (English, with Sam Firstenberg, 1987), *White Ghost* (English, 1987), *Laser Mission* (English, 1988)

Day, Robert. British director of a film included in some South African film listings. Feature film: *The Big Game* (English, 1973)

De Cordova, Leander. South African silent filmmaker. Feature film: *The Swallow* (Silent, 1922)

De Medeiros, Richard (b. 1940 in Ouidah). Benin filmmaker. Studied literature in Cotonou and Paris. Two documentaries and a short fictional film before his feature debut. Feature film: *The Newcomer / Le Nouveau venu* (1976)

De Villiers, Dirk. South African filmmaker. With Elmo de Witt, one of the few South African directors to be active over a 30-year period. Feature films: *Jy is my Liefling* (Afrikaans, 1968), *Geheim van Nantes* (Afrikaans, 1969), *Die Drie van der Merwes* (Afrikaans, 1970), *A New Life* (English, 1971), *Die Lewe Sonder Jou* (Afrikaans, 1971), *My Broer se Bril* (Afrikaans, 1972), *Die Wit Sluier* (Afrikaans, 1973), *Pens en Pootjies* (Afrikaans, 1974), *Tant Ralie se Losieshuis* (Afrikaans, 1974), *Met Liefde van Adele / Wikus en Adele* (Afrikaans, 1974), *The Virgin Goddess* (English, 1974), *The Diamond Hunters* (English, 1975), *My Naam is Dingertjie* (Afrikaans, 1975), *Daan en Doors oppie Diggins* (Af-

rikaans, 1975), *Glenda / The Snake Dancer* (English, 1976), *Crazy People* (English/Afrikaans, 1977), *Dingertjie en Idi* (Afrikaans, 1977), *Die Spaanse Vlieg* (Afrikaans, 1978), *Decision to Die / The Dr. Walters Trial* (English, 1978), *Witblits and Peach Brandy* (English/Afrikaans, 1978), *Abashokobezi* (Zulu, 1978), *Charlie Word 'n Ster* (Afrikaans, 1979), *That Englishwoman* (English, 1989), *Kalahari Harry* (English, 1994), *Kaalgat Tussen Die Daisies* (Afrikaans, 1997)

De Wet, Pierre. South African filmmaker, actor, and producer. Feature films: *Pinkie se Erfenis* (Afrikaans, 1946), *Geboortegrond* (Afrikaans, 1946), *Simon Beyers* (Afrikaans, 1947), *Kaskenades van Dr Kwak* (Afrikaans, 1947), *Kom Saam Vanaand* (Afrikaans, 1949), *Hier's Ons Weer* Afrikaans, (1950), *Alles sal regkom* (Afrikaans, 1951), *Altyd in my Drome* (Afrikaans, 1952), *'n Plan is 'n Boerdery* (Afrikaans, 1954), *Vadertjie Langbeen / Daddy Long-Legs* (Afrikaans, 1954), *Matieland* (Afrikaans, 1955), *Dis Lekker om te Lewe* (Afrikaans, 1957), *Fratse van die Vloot* (Afrikaans, 1958), *Piet se Tante* (Afrikaans, 1959), *Nooi van my Hart* (1959), *Oupa en die Plaasnooientjie* (Afrikaans, 1960), *En die Vonka Spat* (Afrikaans, 1961)

De Witt, Elmo. South African filmmaker and producer. Like Dirk de Villiers, active for over 30 years in the South African film industry. Feature films: *Satanskoraal* (Afrikaans, 1959), *Debbie* (Afrikaans, 1965), *Die Kavaliers / The Cavaliers* (Afrikaans, 1966), *Hoor My Lied / Hear My Song* (Afrikaans, 1967), *Danie Bosman* (Afrikaans, 1969), *Sien Jou Môre* (Afrikaans, 1970), *Zebra* (Afrikaans, 1971), *Die Wiltemmer* (Afrikaans, 1972), *The Last Lion* (English, 1972), *Spergebied: Diamond Area No. 1* (Afrikaans, 1972), *Snip en Rissiepit* (Afrikaans, 1973), *Môre Môre* (Afrikaans, 1973), *Kwikstertjie* (Afrikaans, 1974), *Liefste Veertjie* (Afrikaans, 1975), *Ter wille van Christine* (Afrikaans, 1975), *Vergeet my Nie* (Afrikaans, 1976), *'n Beeld vir Jeannie* (Afrikaans, 1976), *Kom tot Rus* (Afrikaans, 1977), *Mooimeisiefonten* (Afrikaans, 1977), *Someone Like You / Iemand Soos Jy* (Afrikaans/English, 1978), *Grensbasis 13* (Afrikaans, 1979), *You Must Be Joking* (English, 1986), *Croc* (English,

1989), *Enemy Unseen / Lost Valley* (English, with Robert Smawley, 1989), *The Toothman and the Killer* (English, 1990), *Van der Merwe Strikes Back* (English, 1990), *Tolla is Tops* (Afrikaans, 1991), *Tolla is Tops II* (Afrikaans, 1992)

De Witt, Louis. South African filmmaker. Feature film: *Joe Bullet* (English, 1974)

Debbo, Al. South African filmmaker. Actor from the 1950s. Feature films: *Boerboel de Wet* (Afrikaans, 1961), *Tom, Dirk en Herrie* (Afrikaans, 1962), *Gevaalike Spel / Dangerous Deals* (Afrikaans/ English, 1962), *Die Geheim van Onderplaas* (Afrikaans, 1962), *Die Wonderwêreld van Kammie Kamfer* (Afrikaans, 1964), *Haak Vrystaat* (Afrikaans, 1976)

Debboub, Yahia (b. 1940 in Algeria). Algerian filmmaker. Studied at the Institut National de Cinéma (INC) in Algiers and worked in television, initially as an administrator. Features: *The Old Lady and the Child / La Vielle dame et l'enfant* (1991–1997), *The Resistance Fighters / Les Résistants* (1997)

Dehane, Kamal (b. 1954 in Algeria). Algerian filmmaker based in Belgium. Studied at the Institut National des Arts du Spectacle et Techniques de Diffusion (INSAS) in Brussels. From 1984 made an international reputation with a number documentaries investigating social issues or dealing with key literary figures, such as Kateb Yacine and Assia Djebar. Feature film: *The Suspects / Les Suspects* (2004)

Delbeke, Jean. South African filmmaker. Feature film: *The Schoolmaster* (English, 1988)

Delgardo, Clarence T. (b. 1953 in Dakar). Senegalese filmmaker. Studied filmmaking in Algeria and Portugal. His sole feature is an adaptation of one of Ousmane Sembene's short stories. Feature film: *Niiwam* (1991)

Demissie, Yemane I. Ethiopian filmmaker. Studied at the University of California at Los Angeles (UCLA). Half-a-dozen fictional shorts before his feature debut. Feature film: *Tumult / Gir Gir* (1996)

Derkaoui, Mohamed Abdelkrim (b. 1945 in Oujda). Moroccan cinematographer and filmmaker. Studied film at Lodz in Poland. A member of the collective responsible for *Cinders of the Vineyard / Les Cendres du clos*. Became one of Morocco's leading cinematographers, working on some twenty features from the mid-1980s, for his brother Mostafa and such leading directors as Jillali Ferhati, Moumen Smihi, and Hakim Noury. Feature films: *The Travelling Showman's Day / Le Jour du forain* (with Driss Kettani, 1984), *Cairo Street / Rue le Caire* (1998)

Derkaoui, Mostafa (b. 1944 in Oujda). Moroccan filmmaker. Studied drama at the Conservatoire d'Art Dramatique in Casablanca and filmmaking at Lodz in Poland. A member of the collective responsible for *Cinders of the Vineyard / Les Cendres du clos* in 1977 and contributed one episode to the Tunisian-produced collective film *After the Gulf? / La Guerre du Golfe . . . et après?* (1992). Made short films and documentaries. His experimental, innovatory early features found smaller and smaller audiences in Morocco, but he achieved a huge popular success with *The Loves of Hadj Mokhtar Soldi*. Feature films: *About Some Meaningless Events / De quelques événements sans signification* (1974), *The Beautiful Days of Sheherazade / Les Beaux jours de Charazade* (1982), *Provisional Title / Titre provisoire* (1984), *First Fiction / Fiction première* (1992), *(Ga)me in the Past / Je(u) au passé* (1994), *The Seven Gates of the Night / Les Sept portes de la nuit* (1994), *The Great Allegory / La Grande allégorie* (1995), *The Loves of Hadj Mokhtar Soldi / Les Amours de Hadj Mokhtar Soldi* (2001), *Casablanca by Night* (2003), *Casablanca Daylight* (2004)

Devenish, Ross (b. 1939 in Polokwane [Pietersburg]). South African filmmaker. Studied at the London School of Film Technique. Made a number of documentaries about ongoing wars for UK television companies. His first three 1970s features, made with the playwright Athol Fugard, put him in the front rank of South African filmmakers. But finding it impossible to work in South Africa after 1974, he moved to

England, where he directed numerous television dramas, including an eight-part version of *Bleak House.* Returned to South Africa in 2002. Feature films: *Boesman en Lena* (Afrikaans/English, 1973), *The Guest / Die Besoeker* (Afrikaans/English, 1977), *Marigolds in August* (English/Afrikaans, 1980)

Dhouib, Moncef (b. 1952 in Sfax). Tunisian filmmaker. A product of the Fédération Tunisienne des Cinéastes Amateurs (FTCA), he studied in Paris and worked in puppetry and street theatre. Made a series of four very remarkable short films in the 1980s. Feature films: *The Sultan of the City / Soltane el medina!* (1993), *The TV Arrives / La Télé arrive* (2006)

Di Leo, Mario. South African filmmaker. Feature films: *The Final Alliance* (English, with David Goldstein, 1988), *Rough Justice* (English, 1988)

Dia Mokouri, Urbain (b. 1935 in Douala). Cameroonian filmmaker. Studied filmmaking at the Conservatoire Libre du Cinéma Français (CLCF) in Paris. Feature films: *The Burning / La Brûlure* (1982), *The Lucky Guy / Le Veinard* (1983)

Diaa Eddine, Ahmed (b. 1912; d. 1976). Egyptian filmmaker. Studied art at the Leonardo da Vinci Institute in Cairo in 1929 and worked as a caricaturist before becoming an assistant director. A prolific director over his almost 30-year career. Feature films: *The Hypocrite / Dhou al-wag²hayn* (with Wali Eddine Sameh, 1949), *Without Farewells / Min Ghayr wadâ²* (1951), *After the Farewells / Ba²da al-wadâ²* (1953), *Window on Paradise / Nâfidhah ʿalâ al-gannah* (1953), *And the Days Pass By / Marrat al-ayyâm* (1954), *The Lovers' Village / Qaryat al²ouchchâq* (1954), *Let Me Live / Da²ounî a²îch* (1955), *Where Is My Life? / Ayna ʿoumrî* (1956), *Our Green Earth / Ardounâ al-khadrâ²* (1956), *My Happy Days / Ayyâmî al-saʿîdah* (1958), *With Time / Ma²al-ayyâm* (1958), *Every Beat of My Heart / Koull daqqah fî qalbî* (1959), *Qaïs and Leila / Qays wa Layla* (1960), *The Adolescent Girls / al-Mourâhiqât* (1960), *These Are All My Children /*

Koullouhoum awlâdî (1962), *A Schoolgirl's Memoirs / Moudhakkarat tilmîdhad* (1962), *Forever Faithful / Wafâ² ilâ al-abad* (1962), *Without a Rendezvous / Min gheir mî²âd* (1962), *A Husband for My Sister / ʿArîs li-ouktî* (1963), *The Beauty and the Students / al-Hasnâ wa-l-talabah* (1963), *Am I Mad? / Hal âna mag²nounah?* (1964), *An Abnormal Girl / Fatât châdhdhah* (1964), *Leave Me with My Tears / Da²nî wal-l-doumou²* (1964), *If I Were a Man / Law kountou ragoulan* (1964), *Personal Professor / Moudarris khousousî* (1965), *The Storm Has Eased / Soukoun al-²âsifah* (1965), *Looking for Love / al-Bâhithah ʿan al-houbb* (1965), *The Three Friends / al-Asdiqâ al-thalâthah* (1966), *Girls Boarding School / Bayt al-Tâlibât* (1967), *The Long Nights / al-Layâlî al-tawîlah* (1967), *Madam Headmaster / al-Sitt al-nâzirah* (1968), *The Schoolgirl and the Professor / al-Tilmîdhah wa-l-oustâdh* (1968), *No . . . No . . . My Love / Lâ . . . lâ . . . yâ habîbî* (1970), *The Mirror / al-Mirâyah* (1970), *Things That Are Not for Sale / Achiyâ² la touchtarâ* (1970), *And Then the Sun Rises / Thoumma touchriqou al-chams* (1971), *From Home to School / Min al-bayt li-l-madrasa* (1972), *The Lover of the Soul / ʿÂchiq al-rouh* (1973), *Desire and Perdition / al-Raghbah wa-l-dayâ²* (1973), *A Woman for Love / Imra²ah li-l-houbb* (1974), *We Live for Love / ʿAychîn li-l-houbb* (1974), *A Meeting Down There / Liqâ² hounâk* (1976), *Tears in Eyes That Smile / al-Doumou²fî²ouyoun dIahikah* (1977)

Diaa Eddine, Karim (b. in Cairo). Egyptian filmmaker. Studied business at the American University in Cairo and in California. Worked as assistant director during 3 years in France. Feature films: *Love and Terror / al-Houbb wa-l-rou²b* (1992), *Desires / Raghbât* (1994), *Abou El Dahab / Abou el Dahab* (1996), *Ismailia Round Trip / Ismailia rayeh . . . gayy* (1997), *I Never Intended to Be a . . . / Wa la fî el neyya ab²aa . . .* (1999), *Hassan and Aziza: State Security Case / Hassan wi ʿAzeeza, qadeyet amn dawla* (1999), *In Arabic, Cinderella / Bil araby Cinderella* (2006)

Diabi, Lanciné (b. 1956 in Ivory Coast). Ivorian filmmaker. Studied filmmaking at the Conservatoire Libre du Cinéma Français (CLCF) in

Paris. Made a number of fictional shorts before his feature debut. Feature film: *The Twin Girl / La Jumelle* (1996)

Diakite, Moussa Kemoko (b. 1940 in Mamou). Guinean filmmaker. Studied drama in Germany. His debut feature, after a dozen short documentaries, is a ballet film based on a traditional story and featuring the Ballets de la République de Guinée, produced for the state organization, Syli-Cinéma. Feature film: *Naitou* (1982)

Diallo, Boubakar (b. 1963). Burkinabè filmmaker, journalist, and novelist. Director of two newspapers, *Journal de jeudi* and *24 heures,* and author of two thrillers. Self-taught as a filmmaker, he began as a screenwriter and documentarist. A pioneer of very low-budget commercial video filmmaking. *Phoenix Code* was transferred to 35mm film and shown in competition at the Festival Panafricain de Cinéma de Ouagadougou (FESPACO) in 2007. Feature-length video films: *Sofia* (2004), *A Hot File / Dossier brûlant* (2005), *Phoenix Code / Code Phénix* (2005), *The Youngas' Gold / L'Or des Younga* (2006)

Diegu, Omah. Nigerian filmmaker based abroad. His feature was shot in Germany and Nigeria. Feature film: *The Snake in My Bed* (1994)

Dieng, Massaër. Senegalese filmmaker. Studies in France. Feature film: *Bul déconné!* (with Marc Picavez, 2005)

Dienta, Kalifa (b. 1940 in Macina). Malian filmmaker. Studied filmmaking at the Vsesoyuznyi gosudarstvennyi institut kinematografii (VGIK; All-Union State Cinema Institute) in Moscow. Feature film: *A Banna / C'est fini* (1980)

Diffenthal, Henry. South African filmmaker. Feature film: *Runaway Hero* (English, 1990)

Dikongue-Pipa, Jean-Pierre (b. 1940 in Douala). Cameroonian filmmaker. Studied filmmaking at the Conservatoire Libre du Cinéma Français (CLCF) in Paris. His first pioneering

film, *Muna Moto,* was a highly regarded analysis of traditional culture, which won the top prize, the Étalon de Yennenga, at the Festival Panafricain du Cinéma de Ouagadougou (FESPACO) in 1976. Like several other Cameroonian filmmakers he has since turned to comedy. Feature films: *Muna Moto* (1975), *The Cost of Freedom / Le Prix de la Liberté* (1978), *Histoires drôles, Histoires de gens* (1983), *Short Illness / Badyaga / Courte Maladie* (1987)

Diop, Moustapha (b. 1945 in Cotonou). Niger filmmaker. The only Niger filmmaker to attend a film school—the Conservatoire Libre du Cinéma Français (CLCF) in Paris—and the only one to work in 35mm (on his second feature). His two features are studies of the clash of tradition and modernity. Feature films: *Le Médecin de Gafire* (1982), *Mamy Wata* (1989)

Diop-Mambety, Djibril (1945–1988). Senegalese actor and filmmaker. Made several short films and just two features, 19 years apart, which have given him his reputation as one of the greatest African filmmakers. His work is always original and innovative and marked by a very real sense of humor. Feature films: *Touki Bouki* (1973), *Hyenas / Hyènes* (1992)

Dippenaar, Coenie. South African filmmaker and producer. Feature films: *The Musicmaker* (Zulu/English, 1984), *The Hitch-Hikers* (Zulu, 1984), *Iso Ngeso* (Zulu/English, 1984)

Dirie, Idriss Hassan. Somalian filmmaker. Feature film: *Reality and Myth / Dan Iyo Xarrago* (1973)

Djadjam, Mostéfa (b. 1952 in Oran). French-based filmmaker of Algerian descent who has retained his Algerian nationality. Orginally an actor, he played the lead in Merzak Allouache's *The Adventures of a Hero* (1978). In addition to his appearances as an actor on screen and stage, he has worked as assistant director (for Werner Schroeter and Mahmoud Zemmouri) and as scriptwriter. He began making short films and documentaries in 1982. Feature film: *Frontiers / Frontières* (2000)

Djebar, Assia (b. 1936 in Cherchell). Algerian French-language novelist and filmmaker. Studied at the Ecole Normale Supérieure at Sèvres in France. A major French-language novelist, she is the author of a dozen novels (four of them translated into English)—*La Soif* (1957), *Les Impatients* (1958), *Les Enfants du monde nouveau* (1962), *Les Alouettes naïves* (1967), *L'Amour, la fantasia / Fantasia: An Algerian Cavalcade* (1985), *Ombre sultane / A Sister to Scheherazade* (1987), *Loin de Médine / Far from Madina* (1991), *Vaste est la prison / So Vast the Prison* (1995), *Le Blanc de l'Algérie / Algerian White* (1996), *Les Nuits de Strasbourg* (1997), *La Femme sans sépulcre* (2002), *La Disparition de la langue française* (2003), *Nulle part dans la maison de mon père* (2007)—and three books of stories—*Femmes d'Alger dans leur appartement / Women of Algiers in Their Apartment* (1980), *Chronique d'un été algérien* (1983), *Oran, langue morte* (1997). She published her memoirs, *Ces voix qui m'assiègent*, in 1999. Elected to the Académie Française in 2004 (the first writer from the Maghreb and only the fifth woman). She currently teaches at New York University. Her two feature-length films, both given international festival screenings, are poetic meditations, commissioned by Radiodiffusion Télévision Algérienne (RTA) and shot on 16mm. Feature films: *La Nouba / La Nouba des femmes du mont Chenoua* (1978), *The Zerda / La Zerda ou les chants de l'oubli* (1980)

Djemai, Ahmed. Tunisian filmmaker, resident in France. Learned filmmaking in the French film industry and showed his debut feature at the Journées Cinématographiques de Carthage (JCC) in 1994. Feature film: *Wind of Destinies / Vent du destin* (1994)

Djim Kola, Mamadou (b. 1940 in Ouagadougou). Burkinabè filmmaker. Studied filmmaking at the Conservatoire Libre du Cinéma Français (CLCF) in Paris. His first feature was the first to be made in Burkina Faso. His second is one of the largely Burkinabè-financed educative features which have not received European distribution. Feature films: *Blood of the Outcasts / Le Sang des parias* (1971), *The Foreigners / Tougan / Les Étrangers* (1992)

Dong, Pierre-Marie (b. 1945 in Libreville). Gabonese filmmaker and actor. Several short films. After a personal first feature, he co-directed two films made from scripts written by the wife of President Omar Bongo and then, solo, a version of the president's memoirs. Feature films: *Identity / Identité* (1972), *Obali* (1976, with Charles Mensah), *Ayouma* (1977, with Charles Mensah), *Tomorrow Is Another Day / Demain un nouveau jour* (1978)

Dornford-May, Mark. UK-born South African filmmaker. Twenty-five years as theatre director in the United States, Europe, Australia, and South Africa. Feature films: *U-Carmen ekhayelitsha* (2005), *Son of Man / Jezile* (English, 2005)

Dosso, Moussa (b. 1946 in Lakota). Ivorian filmmaker. Studied fine art in Paris. His feature details the familiar subject of the consequences of a forced marriage. Feature film: *Dalokan / La Parole donnée* (1982)

Dosunmu, Sanya. Nigerian filmmaker. Early work in television and subsequent activity as film distributor. Feature film: *Dinner with the Devil* (English, 1975)

Doukoure, Cheik (b. 1943 in Kankan). Guinean filmmaker and actor. Studied literature in Paris, where he has lived for 40 years. While the first two of his three French-language films are set in Guinea, the third reflects life in the Parisian immigrant community. Feature films: *Ebony White / Blanc d'Ebène* (1991), *The Golden Ball / Le Ballon d'or* (1993), *Paris According to Moussa / Paris Selon Moussa* (2002)

Douwes, Jay. South African filmmaker. Feature film: *Lost Valley* (English, 1989)

Drabo, Adama (b. 1948 in Bamako). Malian filmmaker. Studied filmmaking at the Centre National de Production Cinématographique (CNPC) in Mali. His first feature is a wide-ranging study of a young idealist's confrontation with traditional society, while the second is a frequently hilarious retelling of a traditional tale of role reversal in an African village. He made a three-part television series, *Kokadje,* in 2006. Feature films: *Fire! / Ta Dona* (1991), *Skirt Power / Taafe Fanga* (1997)

Dridi, Karim (b. 1961 in Tunis). French-based filmmaker of Tunisian descent. Produced various industrial films and directed a number of short films before beginning his feature film career. His second feature is a fascinating study of the immigrant community in France. Features: *Pigalle* (1994), *Bye-Bye* (1995), *Out of Play / Hors jeu* (1998)

Du Toit, Chris. South African filmmaker. Feature films: *Elsa se Geheim* (Afrikaans, 1979), *Gemini* (Afrikaans, 1980), *Edge of Innocence / Eendag vir Altyd* (Afrikaans, 1987), *Hippo Pool / Big Game* (English, 1988), *Ransom* (Zulu, 1989)

Du Toit, Marie. South African filmmaker. Feature film: *Nicolene* (Afrikaans, 1978)

Duarte de Carvalho, Ruy (b. 1941 at Satarem, in Portugal). Angolan filmmaker. Spent his childhood in Angola and became an Angolan citizen in 1975. Poet, writer, and agricultural engineer. Twenty documentaries, including ten in the *Presente Angolano* series and some of feature length: *Courage, Comrade / Faz lá coragem, camarada* (docu-drama) (1977), *Moia—The Message of the Islands / Moia—O Recado das Ilhas* (1989). His sole fictional feature film, the first to made in Angola, drew succesfully on traditional oral story-telling techniques. Feature film: *Nelisita* (1982)

DuChau, Frederick. South African filmmaker. Feature film: *Racing Stripes* (2004)

Duparc, Henri (b. 1940 in Forecariah, Guinea; d. 2006). Ivorian filmmaker. Studied filmmaking in Belgrade and at the Institut des Hautes Études Cinématographiques (IDHEC) in Paris. Appeared as an actor in Désiré Écaré's *Concerto for an Exile* (1967). The best known of all Ivorian filmmakers with seven features during a 30-year career. One of the few African filmmakers to specialize in comedy, he achieved great popular

successes with his later exuberant features. Feature films: *Abusuan* (1972), *Wild Grass / L'Herbe sauvage* (1977), *Bal Poussière* (1988), *The Sixth Finger / Le Sixième doigt* (1990), *Rue Princesse* (1994), *Coffee-Coloured / Une couleur café* (1997), *Caramel* (2005)

Dyter, M. South African filmmaker. Feature films: *Point of Return* (English/Zulu, 1984), *Usiko Lwbafana* (Zulu, 1984), *Run for Freedom* (English, 1984), *Isithixo Segolide* (Zulu, 1984)

Eastman, Allan. South African filmmaker. Feature film: *Danger Zone* (English, 1995)

Écaré, Désiré (b. 1939 in Abidjan). Ivorian filmmaker. Studied filmmaking at the Institut des Hautes Études Cinématographiques (IDHEC) in Paris. A pioneer of African filmmaking, he made his name with his first short film, *Concerto for an Exile / Concerto pour un exil* (1967). Provoked a scandal with his uninhibited second feature. Feature films: *It's Up to Us, France / À nous deux France* (1969), *Women's Faces / Visages de femmes* (1985)

Eddine, Hassan Seif. Egyptian filmmaker. Feature film: *We Regret This Mistake / Na'saf li-hâhhâ al-khata'* (1986)

Eddine, Mohsen Mohi. Egyptian filmmaker. Feature film: *Insecure Youth / Chabâb ᶜalâ kaff ᶜifrît* (1990)

Egan, William. South African filmmaker. Feature film: *Liewe Hemel, Genis!* (Afrikaans, with Hannes Roets, 1988)

El Fani, Nadia (b. 1960 in Paris). Tunisian filmmaker, resident in France. Brought up in Tunisia, she worked as assistant director on foreign productions (including films directed by Roman Polanski and Franco Zefferelli), as well as Nouri Bouzid's *Man of Ashes*. Four very personal short films. Feature film: *Bedwin Hacker* (2002)

El Maânouni, Ahmed (b. 1944 in Casablanca). Moroccan filmmaker. Studied drama in Paris at the Université du Théâtre des Nations and filmmaking in Brussels at the Institut National des Arts du Spectacle et Techniques de Diffusion (INSAS). Worked as cinematographer and made videos and documentaries. His first feature was a key contribution to the Moroccan realist strand of filmmaking. Feature films: *The Days, The Days / O les jours* (1978), *Trances / Transes* (1981), *Broken Hearts / Cœurs brûlés* (2006)

El Mejoub, Mohamed Ali. Moroccan filmmaker. Studied filmmaking at the École Supérieure des Études Cinématographiques (ESEC) in Paris. Travelled widely, making half-a-dozen short films. Also worked as scriptwriter for Moroccan television series. Feature film: *The White Wave / La Vague blanche* (2006)

El Okbi, Mohamed Ali (b. 1948 in Tunis). Tunisian filmmaker. Studied film in Paris—at the Institut des Hautes Études Cinématographiques (IDHEC) and the Sorbonne—and in Los Angeles. Worked as assistant on a number of foreign films. His first feature is a semi-documentary featuring the 1978 Tunisian football team, his second is one of the rare Tunisian comedies. Feature films: *A Ball and Some Dreams / Un ballon et des rêves* (1978), *The Teddy Boys / Les Zazous de la vague* (1992)

Ellenbogen, Nicholas. South African filmmaker. Feature film: *The Angel, the Bicycle and the Chinaman's Finger* (English, with Roos Koets, 1992)

Emara, Hussein. Egyptian filmmaker. Feature films: *The Beauty and the Crook / al-Fâtinah wa-l-souʾlouk* (1976), *Where Is the Way Out? Ayna al-Mafarr* (1977), *Step . . . False Step / Wâhdah baʾd wâhdah wa nouss* (1978), *God Is Great / Yâ mâ inta karîm yâ rabb* (1983), *The Terrace / al-Soutouh* (1984), *And Fate Laughs at It / Wa tadʾhek al-aqdâr* (1985), *The Virgin Widow / al-Armalah al-ʾadhrâ* (1986), *The Killer of Karmouz / Sahhâh Karmouz* (1987), *Very Difficult Mission / Mouhimmah saʾbah guiddan* (1987), *The Midnight Policeman / Châwîch nouss al-leil* (1991), *The Orphan and the Wolves / al-Yatîm wa-l-dhiʾâb* (1993)

Emara, Ibrahim. Egyptian filmmaker. Feature films: *The Women Are in Danger / al-Sittât fî khatar* (1942), *The White Penny / al-Qirch al-abyad* (1945), *The Big Mistake / al-Zallah al-koubrâ* (1945), *The Sin / al-Khatîʾah* (1946), *L'Écervelée / al-Tâʾichah* (1946), *The White Angel / al-Malâk al-abyad* (1946), *The Wisdom of the Arabs / Ahkâm al-lâthah* (1947), *The Enemy of Society / ʿAdouww al-mougtamaʾ* (1947), *The Bigamist / Gouz al-itnîn* (1947), *Halawa / Halâwah* (1949), *I Wish You Numerous Offspring / ʿOʾbâl al-bakârî* (1949), *The Seventh Wife / al-Zawgah al-sâbiʾah* (1950), *You're Thinking of Another Woman / Machghoul bighayrî* (1951), *I Have Sacrificed My Love / Dahhayt gharâmî* (1951), *To Whom Might I Complain? / Achkî li-mîn* (1951), *Goha's Star Turn / Mismâr Gohâ* (1952), *Heaven Is Watching / al-Samâʾ lâ tanâm* (1952), *I Have Done Myself an Injustice / Zalamt rouhi* (1952), *Written on His Forehead / Maktoub ʿalâ al-guibîn* (1953), *Is It My Fault? / Anâ dhanbî îh* (1953), *I Have No-One / Mâlîch had* (1953), *Money and Children / al-Mâl wa-l-banoun* (1954), *You Have Done Me an Injustice / Yâ zâlimnî* (1954), *We Are Human Beings / Nahnou bachar* (1955), *The Song of Fidelity / Lan al-wafâʾ* (1955), *Tears in the Night / Doumou ʿ fî-l-layl* (1955), *Police File / sahiifat al-sawâbiq* (1956), *The Spring of Love / Rabîʾal-houbb* (1956), *Crime and Punishment / al-Garîmah wa—ʾiqâb* (1957), *The Girl from the Desert / Bint al-bâdiyah* (1958), *The Prison of Virgins / Sigʾn al-ʾadhârâ* (1959), *Love and Privations / Houbb wa hirmân* (1960), *Why Am I Living? / Limâdhâ aʾîch* (1961), *The Prophet's Migration to Medina / Higrat al-rasoul* (1964), *For a Handful of Children / Min aglhifnât awlâd* (1969), *Struggle against Death / Sirâʾ maʾ al-mawt* (1970), *My Pretty Schoolteacher / Moudrarrisatî al-hasnâ* (1971)

Enfield, Cy. British director of one feature film included in some lists of South African features: *Sands of the Kalari* (1965)

Engels, Mark. South African filmmaker. Feature film: *The Endangered* (English, 1989)

Epstein, H. South African filmmaker. Feature films: *U-Lindiwe* (Sotho, with Jimmy Murray, 1984), *Inyoka* (Sotho, with Jimmy Murray, 1984)

Essawy, Sayyed. Egyptian filmmaker. Feature film: *I Love You So /Bahebbak wi bamoot fik* (2005)

Essid, Lofti (b. 1952 in Tunisia). Tunisian filmmaker. Studied literature and cinema and worked as an actor. Two short films. Feature film: *What Are We Doing This Sunday? / Que fait-on ce dimanche?* (1983)

Esterhuizen, Willie. South African filmmaker. Feature films: *Orkney Snork Nie—Die Movie* (Afrikaans, 1992), *Orkney Snork Nie 2—Nog 'n Movie* (Afrikaans, 1993), *Lipstiek, Dipstiek* (Afrikaans, 1994), *Oh Schuks I'm Gatvol* (English, with Leon Schuster, 2004), *Poena is Koning!* (2007)

Eyres, John. South African filmmaker. Feature films: *Project Shadowchaser 2* (English, 1994), *Project Shadowchaser 3* (English, 1995)

Ezz Eddine, Ibrahim. Egyptian filmmaker. Feature film: *The Birth of Islam / Zouhour al-islâm* (1951)

Fabian, Anthony. South African filmmaker. Feature film: *Skin* (2007)

Fadel, Mohamed (b. 1938). Egyptian filmmaker. Studied agriculture before becoming a successful television director. Made just a couple of feature films in the 1970s and 1980s, but achieved intenational success with his television-produced documentary on Nasser. Feature films: *A Flat in Town / Chaqqah wast al-balad* (1977), *Love in Prison / Houbb fi-l-zinzânah* (1983), *Nasser '56 / Nasser 56* (1996), *Bluffing / Alabanda* (with Samir Al-Asfoury, 1999), *The Leader / al-Za'im* (with Cherif Arafa, 1999), *The Star of the Orient / Kawkab al-sharq* (1999)

Fadika, Kramo-Lanciné (b. 1948 in Danané). Ivorian filmmaker. Studied filmmaking at the École Louis Lumière in Paris. His first and most striking feature is a sensitive study of the impact of university education on a young woman from a traditionally minded family, which won the top prize, the Étalon de Yennenga, at the Festival Panafricain du Cinéma de Ouagadougou (FESPACO) in 1981. Feature films: *Djeli* (1981), *Wariko* (1994)

Fahmi, Achraf (b. 1936 in Cairo). Egyptian filmmaker. After graduating from history studies at Cairo University, he turned to cinema. Studied first at the Cairo Higher Film Institute, then at the University of California at Los Angeles (UCLA), where he obtained a master's degree. A prolific director over his 30-year career. Feature films: *The Killers / al-Qatalah* (1971), *One in a Million / Wâhiid fi-l-million* (1971), *Forbidden Images / Souwar mamnou'ah* (one episode) (1972), *Night and Barred Windows / Layl wa qoudbân* (1973), *Woman in Love / Imra'ah 'âchiqah* (1974), *Until the End of My Life / Hattâ âkhir al-'oumr* (1975), *Waves without Border / Amwâg bilâ châti'* (1976), *Chawq / Chawq* (1976), *Come and See What Sokkar Is Doing / Bouss chouf Soukkar bi-ta'mil ih* (1977), *Voyage to a Woman's Depths / Hihlah dâkhil imra'ah* (1978), *The Other Woman / al-Mar'ah al-oukhrah* (1978), *A Woman Killed by Love / Imra'ah qatalahâ al-houbb* (1978), *With Premeditation / Ma' sabq al-isrâr* (1979), *My Dignity / Karâmatî* (1979), *And the Investigation Continues / Wa Lâ yazâl al-tahqîq moustamirran* (1979), *The Vagabond / al-Charîdah* (1980), *The Devil Preaches / al-Chaytân ya'îz* (1981), *A Monster Makes Man / al-Wahch dâkhil al-insân* (1981), *Bitter Bread / al-Khoubz al-mourr* (1982), *The Powerful / al-Aqwiyâ'* (1982), *The Half-Meter Accident / Hâdith al-nisf mitr* (1983), *The Dancer and the Percussionist / al-Râqisah wa-l-tabbâl* (1984), *The Unknown / al-Mag'houl* (1984), *The Maidservant / al-Khâdimah* (1984), *Do Not Ask Me Who I Am / Lâ tas'alnî man anâ* (1984), *Saad the Orphan / Sa'd al-yatîm* (1985), *A Divorced Woman / Imra'ah moutallaqah* (1986), *Dishonour / Wasmat 'âr* (1986), *For Lack of Proof / Li-'adam kifâyat al-'adillah* (1987), *The Killing of a Schoolmistress / Ightiyâl moudarissah* (1988), *Garden of Blood / Boustân al-dam* (1989), *The Corridor of Death / 'Anbar al-mawt* (1989), *Traitors in the Night / Layl wa khawanah* (1990), *Execution of a Judge / I'dâm qâdî* (1990), *Ika's Law / al-Qânoun îkâ* (1991), *The Spy Trap /*

Fakhkh al-Gawâsîs (1992), *Five-Star Thieves /
Lousous khamsat nougoum* (1994), *The Night of
the Murder / Laylat al-qatl* (1994), *The Red Flag /
al-Râyah al-hamrâ* (1994), *Penalty / Darbet
gazza*ʾ (1995), *Woman at the Top / Imraʾa fawq
al-qemma* (1997), *A Police Officer Resigns / Istiqalet dabet shurta* (1997), *Delicious Killing / al
Katl el lazeez* (1998), *A Woman under Observation / Imraʾa taht el muraqba* (2000), *Love and
Blood / al-ʿIshk wa al-damm* (2002)

Fahmi, Ahmed. Egyptian filmmaker. Feature
film: *Crazy People ½ dot com / Maganeen ½ com*
(2007)

Faleti, Adebayo. Nigerian filmmaker. Feature
film: *Agba Arin* (1989)

Fani-Kayode, Lola. Nigerian filmmaker. Feature film: *Iwa* (1989)

Farag, Ahmed Samir. Egyptian filmmaker. Feature film: *Code 36 / Code 36* (2007)

Fares, Tewfik (b. 1937 in Bordj-Bou-Arreridj).
Algerian scriptwriter and filmmaker. Studied at
the Sorbonne in Paris. On his return, worked
for the Office des Actualités Algériennes (OAA)
and in Algerian television, as well as collaborat-
ing on a number of short films. Scripted two features directed by Mohamed Lakhdar Hamina,
The Wind from the Aurès and *Chronicle of the
Years of Embers*. Feature film: *The Outlaws / Les
Hors-la-loi* (1969)

Farghal, Ehsane. Egyptian filmmaker. Feature
films: *You Only Live Once / al-ʾOumr wâhid*
(1954), *The Women's Realm / Mamlakat al-nisâʾ*
(1955)

Fargo, James. American director of a film included in some South African film listings. Feature film: *Game for Vultures* (English, 1979)

Farid, Akram. Egyptian filmmaker. Feature
films: *Farah / Farah* (2004), *Does He Think
That . . . / Ayazun* (2006), *Haha and Tuffaha /
Haha wa Tuffaha* (2006), *Like Wishes / Zayy El-
Hawa* (2006), *Such is Love / Al-hubb kida* (2007),
Omar and Selma / ʾAmr wa Selma (2007)

Farid, Mahmoud. Egyptian filmmaker. Fea-
ture films: *The Pickpocket / al-Nachchâl* (1963),
Prisoner of the Night / saguîn al-layl (1963), *We
Want a Wife Straightaway / Matloup zawgah
fawran* (1964), *The Three Bachelors / al-ʾOuzzâb
al-thalâthan* (1964), *The Great Adventure / al-
Moughâmarah al-koubrâ* (1964), *The Troublemakers / al-Mouchâghiboun* (1965), *The Three
Wise Men / al-ʾOuqalâʾ al-thalâthah* (1965), *The
Terror / al-Rouʾb* (1969), *We Are Not Angels /
Lasnâ malâʾikah* (1970), *Men Trapped / Rigâl fî-
l-misyadah* (1971), *The Return of the Most Dangerous Man in the World / ʿAwdat akhtar ragoul fî-l-ʾâlam* (1972), *A Youth Which Is Eaten
Up / Chabâb yahtariq* (1972), *The Cheats / al-
Moukhâdiʾoun* (1973), *The Devils and the Balloon / al-Chayâtîn wa-l-kourah* (1973), *The Expected Husband / ʿArîs al-hanâ* (1974), *Devils
for Ever / Chayâtîn ilâ al-abad* (1974), *Beware
of Men, Mummy / Ihtarisî min al-rigâl yâ mâmâ*
(1975), *The Kings of the Gag / Moulouk al-dahik*
(1975), *Looking for Problems / al-Bahth ʿan al-
mataâʾib* (1975), *The Music Is in Danger / al-
Mazzîkah fî khatar* (1976), *Women in Love /
al-Âchiqât* (1976), *The Cabaret of Life / Kabârîh
al-hayât* (1977), *Let's Get Married Quickly My
Love / Ilâ al-maʾdhoun yâ habîbî* (1977), *Adventurers Around the World / Moughâmiroun
hawl al-ʾâlam* (1979), *The Beautiful Thieves / al-
Nachchalât al-fâtinât* (1985), *The Poor People /
al-Nâs al-ghalâbah* (1986), *The Orphan and
Love / al-Yâtim wa-l-houbb* (1993)

Faridi, Hamid (b. 1968 in Casablanca). Moroccan filmmaker. Studied journalism in Rabat and
worked in advertising. Made short films and published a first novel, *La Poussière des sentiments*,
in 2006. Feature film: *The Bike / Le Vélo* (2006)

Farkache, Alexandre. Egyptian filmmaker. Feature films: *The Concierge / Bawwâr al-ʾimârah*
(1935), *The Gentleman Wants to Get Married /
Bisalamtouh ʿIawiz yitgawwiz* (1936)

Farouk, Ahmed. Egyptian filmmaker. Feature
film: *Men Never Marry Beautiful Women / al-
Rigâl lâ yatazawwagoun al-gamîliat* (1965)

Farouq, Ismaïl. Egyptian filmmaker. Feature
film: *90 Minutes / 90 Daqeeqa* (2006)

Fathallah, Farid. Egyptian filmmaker. Feature film: *The Man from Upper Egypt / al-Ragoul al-saʾîdî* (1987)

FauntleRoy, Don E. South African filmmaker. Feature film: *Mercenary for Justice* (English, 2005)

Faure, William C. South African filmmaker. Feature film: *'n Plekkie in die Son* (Afrikaans, 1979)

Faurie, Wanna. South African filmmaker. Feature film: *The Black Ninja* (English, 1990)

Fawzi, Hussein (b. 1909; d. 1962). Egyptian filmmaker. Brother of Ahmed Galal and Abbas Kamel. Studied fine arts in Italy and worked as an illustrator and designer. Worked as an actor, beginning with *Leila* in 1927, before becoming a director. His many films include a commercially successful series of musicals with his wife, Naïma Akef. Directed the first Egyptian color film, *Daddy's Getting Married,* in 1950. Feature films: *The Apple Seller / Bayyâʾat al-touffâh* (1939), *I Love Mistakes / Ahibb al-ghalat* (1942), *Wedding Night / Laylat al-farah* (1942), *Bahbah in Baghdad / Bahbah fi Baghdâd* (1942), *Nadouga / Nadougâ* (1944), *I Love What's Popular / Ahibb al-baladî* (1945), *Patience Is Golden / al-Sabr tayyib* (1945), *I Have Destroyed My Household / Hadamt baytî* (1946), *A Day of Greatness / Yawm fî-l-âlî* (1946), *The Love Express / Express al-houbb* (1946), *A Lebanese at the University / Loubnânî fî-l-gâmiʾah* (1947), *It's Me Sattaouta / Anâ Sattaouta* (1947), *Zohra / Zohrah* (with Kamal Abou al-Ela, 1947), *Hello / Sabâh al-khayr* (1947), *Mr Boulboul / Boulboul afandî* (1948), *Shared Bread / al-ʾIch wa-l-milh* (1949), *Midnight / Nouss al-layl* (1949), *Lahalibo / Lahâlibo* (1949), *My Sister Steita / Oukhtî Steitah* (1950), *Popular and Sympathetic / Baladî wa-khiffah* (1950), *Let Me Sing / Sîbounî aghannî* (1950), *Daddy's Getting Married / Bâbâ ʿâris* (1950), *Everything Is OK / Fourigat* (1951), *The Girl from the Circus / Fatât al-sîrk* (1951), *The Tiger / al-Nimr* (1952), *Love Is Beautiful / Yâ halâwat al-houbb* (1952), *Heaven and Hell / Gannah wa nâr* (1952), *Uncle Abdou's Ghost / ʿIfrît ʿamm ʿAbdou* (1953), *A Million Pounds / Million guinîh* (1953), *The Barber of Baghdad / Hallâq Baghdâd* (1954), *Light of My Eyes / Nour ʿouyounî* (1954), *Aziza / Azîzah* (1954), *An Ocean of Love / Bahr al-gharâm* (1955), *Love and Humanity / Houbb wa insâniyyah* (1956), *Henna Flower / Tamr henna* (1957), *I Love You Hassan / Ahibbak yâ Hasan* (1958), *Leila, the Girl from the Beach / Layla bint al-châtiʾ* (1959), *The Police Inspector / Moufattich al-mabâhith* (1959), *My Love / Yâ habîbî* (1960), *Love at the Circus / Gharâm fî-l-sîrk* (1960), *Achour the Lionheart / ʿAchur qalb alasad* (1961), *Pretty and Lying / Hilwah wa kaddâbah* (1962)

Fawzi, Osama (b. 1961 in Cairo). Egyptian filmmaker. Studied at the Cairo Higher Film Institute. Feature films: *Road Devils / ʿAfarit al-asphalt* (1996), *Devils' Paradise / Gannat al-chayatin* (2000), *I Love the Movies / Baheb el seema* (2004)

Faye, Safi (b. 1943 in Dakar). Senegalese ethnographer and filmmaker. Began as a teacher. Her first contact with cinema was when she appeared in Jean Rouch's *Petit à petit* (1969). She studied ethnography at the École Pratique des Hautes Études and then filmmaking at the École Louis Lumière in Paris. All her work is marked by a fusion of fictional and documentary approaches, focused on her native village and her Serer background. Numerous documentaries. The first woman in francophone West Africa to make a feature film. Feature films: *Letter from My Village / Kaddu beykat / Lettre paysanne* (1975), *FadʾJal* (1979), *Mossane* (1996)

Fayek, Ashraf. Egyptian filmmaker. Feature films: *The Costumer / al-Labbeess* (2001), *Slum Side Story / Qessat al-hayy al-shaʾby* (2006)

Fazaî Mellitti, Ezzedine (b. 1957 in Tunis). Tunisian filmmaker. Worked as an actor in Europe and the United States. His debut film was shown at the Journées Cinématographiques de Carthage (JCC) in 1994 but not distributed in Tunisia. Feature film: *The Magic Box / Le magique* (1994)

Fedler, Dov. South African filmmaker. Feature film: *Botsotso II* (Zulu, 1983)

Ferchiou, Rachid (b. 1941 in Bardo). Tunisian filmmaker. Studied filmmaking in Berlin and worked as a trainee in television in France and Italy. Subsequently worked for Tunisian television. Feature films: *Yusra* (1972), *The Children of Boredom / Les enfants de l'ennui* (1975), *Autumn '86 / Automne '86* (1991), *Check and Mate / Échec et mat* (1995)

Ferhati, Jillali (b. 1948 in Khemisset). Moroccan filmmaker. Studied literature, sociology, and drama in Paris, where he lived for 10 years. Made two short films and contributed an episode to the collective feature *Five Films for a Hundred Years / Cinq films pour cent ans* (1995). Ferhati is a key figure in the social realist trend of Moroccan cinema in the 1980s and 1990s. Feature films: *A Hole in the Wall / Une brèche dans le mur* (1978), *Reed Dolls / Poupées de roseau* (1981), *The Beach of Lost Children / La Plage des enfants perdus* (1991), *Make-Believe Horses / Chevaux de fortune* (1995), *Braids / Tresses* (2000), *Memory in Detention / Mémoire en détention* (2004)

Ferjani, Mohamed Ali. Libyan filmmaker. Feature film: *The Splinter / al-Shadhiya* (1986), *The Four Seasons / al-Fusul al-Arba'a* (documentary, 1990)

Fernandes, Joao. South African filmmaker. Feature film: *Red Scorpion* (English, with Joe Zito, 1987)

Fero, Norbert. Zimbabwean filmmaker. Feature film: *Matters of the Spirit* (1998)

Ferroukhi, Ismaïl (b. 1962 in Kenitra). Moroccan filmmaker. Studied film in France, where he now lives, following courses at the Établissement Cinématographique et Photographique des Armes at Ivry. In 1990s: two shorts, two feature scripts with French director Cédric Kahn, and two téléfilms. Feature film: *The Long Journey / Le Grand voyage* (2004)

Fettar, Sid Ali (b. 1943 in Algiers). Algerian filmmaker. Studied at the Institut National de Cinéma (INC) in Algiers and then at Lodz in Poland, where he also worked as a trainee in television. On his return, worked for Radiodiffusion Télévision Algérienne (RTA). Feature films: *Rai* (1988), *Forbidden Love / Amour interdit* (1993)

Fila, David-Pierre (b. 1954 in Brazzaville). Congolese filmmaker, resident in France. Studied at the technological university in Bordeaux and then filmmaking at the École Louis Lumière in Paris. A dozen shorts, mostly documentaries, before his first feature and half-a-dozen further shorts since its completion. Feature film: *Matanga* (1995)

Firstenberg, Sam. U.S.-born filmmaker who has worked extensively on South African commercial films. Feature films: *American Ninja I: The Confrontation* (English, with Beau Davis, 1987), *American Ninja II: The Domination* (English, 1988), *Cyborg Cop* (English, 1992), *Cyborg Cop 2* (English, 1993), *Operation Delta Force* (English, 1996)

Florentine, Isaac. South African filmmaker. Feature film: *Cold Harvest* (English, 1998)

Fofana, Gahité (b. 1965 in France). Guinean filmmaker. Studied literature and filmmaking in Paris. After five documentaries about various aspects of West African life from the mid-1990s, his first feature is a fictionalized account of a possible return from Paris. Feature films: *Temporary Registration / Immatriculation temporaire* (2001), *Early One Morning / Un matin de bonne heure* (2005)

Ford, Amalia. South African filmmaker. Feature film: *The Body* (English, 1988)

Ford, Joe [Joey]. South African filmmaker. Feature films: *The Juggernaut* (English, 1985), *Death Walker* (English, 1988), *Raw Vengeance* (English, 1988), *Baby Brown* (English, 1989), *My Brother My Enemy* (English, 1990)

Fortunato, Orlando (b. 1946 in Benguela in Angola). Angolan filmmaker. Supported the liberation struggle from exile. Feature-length documentary: *Memory of a Day / Memoria de um dia* (1982)

Fotso, Ghislain. Cameroonian filmmaker. Feature film: *The Broken Dream / Le Rêve brisé* (2006)

Fouad, Ahmed. Egyptian filmmaker. Feature films: *Just One Day's Honeymoon / Yawm wâhid ᶜasal* (1969), *Dangerous Life / Hayât khatirah* (1971), *The School for Adolescents / Madrasat al-mourâhiqîn* (1973), *A Little Love / Chayᵓ min al-houbb* (1973), *Twenty-Four Hours of Love / Arbaᵓah wa-ichrîn sâᵓah houbb* (1974), *Everyone Would Like to Fall in Love / al-Koull ᶜâwiz yihibb* (1975), *Who Can Tame Aziza? / Mîn yiqdar ᶜalâ ᶜAzîzah* (1975), *Face to Face / Wagᵓhan li wagᵓh* (1976), *Husbands Are Devils / al-Azwâg al-chayâtîn* (1977), *The Beauty and the Idiot / al-Houlwah wa-l-ghabî* (1977), *A Woman Who Runs through My Veins / Imraᵓah fî damî* (1978), *Ragab on a Burning Roof / Ragab fawqa safihin sâkhin* (1979), *Who Will Drive Us Mad? / Mîn yigannin mîn* (1981), *4-2-4 / 4-2-4* (1981), *A Hot Summer Night / laylat chitâᵓ dâfiᵓah* (1981), *The Girl Who Said No / al-Bint illîᵓâlit laᵓ* (1982), *The Madmen's Strike / Idrâb ul-magânîn* (1983), *Raya and Sekina / Rayyâ wa Sakînah* (1983), *Take Care / al-Ihtiyât wâguib* (1983), *The Coachman / al-ᵓArbaguî* (1983), *The House of Correction / Bayt al-qâsirât* (1984), *The Villain Gets It / al-Hidiq yifham* (1986), *The Thugs / al-Awbâch* (1986), *The Train / al-Qitâr* (1986), *Playing with Demons / al-Louᵓb maᵓ al-chayâtîn* (1991), *Love at Taba / al-Houbb fî Tâbâ* (1992)

Fox, Revel. South African filmmaker. Feature film: *The Flier* (2005)

Francis, Freddie. British director and cinematographer who completed one South African feature film after the director walked out. Feature film: *The Golden Rendezvous* (with Ashley Lazarus, 1977)

Francis, Youssef (b. 1934 in Cairo). Egyptian filmmaker. Studied fine art and worked as a painter before studying at the Cairo Higher Film Institute. On graduating, worked as a film critic and scriptwriter. Made a first feature in 1973 but had to wait 10 years to complete a second. Feature films: *Wild Flowers / Zouour barriyyah* (1973), *The Drug Addict / al-Moudmin* (1983), *Bird of the Orient / ᶜOusfour al-charq* (1986), *How Much Are You Worth, My Friend? / Yâ sadîqî kam tousâwi* (1987), *The Women's Market / Souq al-nisaᵓ* (1994)

Freimond, Craig. South African filmmaker. Feature film: *Gums and Noses* (English, 2005)

Friedberg, Lionel. South African filmmaker. Feature film: *Hot Snow* (English, 1989)

Frites, Mahmoud. Moroccan filmmaker. Feature film: *Nancy and the Monster / Nancy et le monstre* (2007)

Fugard, Athol (b. 1932 in Middleburg of an Irish father and Afrikaaner mother). South African dramatist and filmmaker. Studied philosophy and anthropology at Cape Town University. Spent some time in London. A major playwright with an international reputation. His plays, which show intense sympathy and admiration for South Africa's black population, include *Nogogo* (1960), *The Blood Knot* (1961), *People Are Living There* (1968), *Boesman and Lena* (1970), and the trilogy *The Island* (1973), *Sizwe Banzi Is Dead* (1973), and *Statements after an Arrest under the Immorality Law* (1974). Three films adapted from his plays—*Boesman and Lena*, *The Guest / Die Besoeker*, and *Marigolds in August*—were made in collaboration with Ross Devenish in the 1970s. His only novel was adapted to make the Oscar-winning *Tsotsi*, directed by Gavin Hood in 2005. He made his directing debut in 1991. Feature film: *The Road to Mecca* (English, with Peter Goldsmid, 1991)

Gabriel, Ian. South African filmmaker. Work across the audio-visual spectrum. Prolific maker of commercials (more than four hundred ads). Co-directed *The Motor Gang*. Feature film: *Forgiveness* (English, 2004)

Galal, Ahmed. Egyptian filmmaker. Feature films: *I Want My Rights / ʿAwez haqqy* (2003), *Abou Ali / Abu Ali* (2005), *An Ordinary Man / Wahid min al naas* (2006), *At Cairo Central Station / Fi mahatet masr* (2006), *That is Satisfactory / Keda reda* (2007)

Galal, Ahmed (b. 1897 in Port-Said; d. 1947). Egyptian veteran filmmaker. Elder brother of Hussein Fawzi and Abbas Kamel and husband of the actress Mary Queeny. Work as journalist and then as scriptwriter for Aziza Amir on her pioneering features. Appeared as an actor in a number of the films he directed. Silent feature: *The Beauty from the Desert / Ghâdat al-sahrâʾ* (with Wedad Orfi, 1929). Sound feature films: *When a Woman Loves / ʿIndamâ tou-hibb al-maraʾah* (1933), *Bewitching Eyes / ʿOuyoun sâhirah* (1934), *Chagarat al-Darr / Chagarat al-Dourr* (1935), *The Bank Note / al-Banknot* (1936), *Interim Wife / Zawgah bi-l-niyâbah* (1936), *The Director's Daughter / Bint al-bâchâ al-moudîr* (1938), *Cherchez la femme / Fattich ʿan al-marʾah* (1939), *Zalikha Loves Achour / Zilîkhah touhibb ʿAchour* (1940), *Young Girls in Revolt / Fatât mouta marridah* (1940), *A Dangerous Woman / Imraʾah khatirah* (1941), *The Fifth Suitor / al-ʾArîs al-khâmis* (1942), *Rabab / Rabâb* (1942), *Magda / Magda* (1943), *The Dream Princess / Amîrat al-ahlâm* (1945), *Oum al-Saad / Oumm al-Saʾd* (1946), *The Return of the Absent One / ʿAwdat al-ghâʾib* (1947)

Galal, Nader (b. 1941 in Cairo). Egyptian filmmaker. Son of Ahmed Galal and the actress Mary Queeny. His graduation from the Cairo Higher Film Institute in 1964 was followed by 6 years work as assistant director. A prolific director over his 30-year career. Feature films: *Tomorrow Love Will Return / Ghadan yaʾoud al-houbb* (1972), *My Son / Waladî* (1972), *Men Who Do Not Fear Death / Rigâl lâ yakhâfoun al-mawt* (1973), *Abou Rabie / Abou Rabîʾ* (1973), *Boudour / Boudour* (1974), *No Time for Tears / Lâ waqta li-l-doumouʾ* (1976), *And Life Returns / Wa ʿâdat al-hayât* (1976), *When the Body Slides / ʿIndamâ yascout al-gasad* (1977), *A Girl Who Is Looking for Love / Fatât tabhath ʿan al-houbb* (1977), *Woman of Glass / Imraʾah min*

Zougâg (1977), *The Follies of Love / Gounoun al-houbb* (1977), *Remorse / al-Nadam* (1978), *The Judge and the Executioner / al-Qâdî wa-l-gallâd* (1978), *Stronger than Time / Aqwâ mîn al ayyâm* (1979), *The Illusion / al-Wahm* (1979), *A Man in the True Sense of the Word / Ragoul bi-maʾnâ al-kalimah* (1981), *The Tough Guys from the Mountains / Foutouwwat al-gabal* (1982), *The Trial / al-Moukâkamah* (1982), *They Steal Rabbits / Innahoum yasriqoun al-arânib* (1983), *Neither Seen, Nor Recognized / Lâ min châf wa-lâ min dirî* (1983), *Gate Five / Khamsah bâb* (1983), *An Eye for an Eye, a Tooth for a Tooth / Wâhdah bi-Wâhdah* (1984), *The Power of a Woman / Gabarout imraʾah* (1984), *A Man for These Times / Ragoul li-hâdhâ al-zaman* (1986), *Hello Friend / Salâm yâ sâhibî* (1986), *The Snakes / al-Thaʾâbîn* (1986), *Paper Hero / Batal min waraq* (1988), *Samia Chaarawi's Dossier / Malaff Samia Chaʾrâwî* (1988), *The Cost of Emigration / Thaman al-ghourbah* (1989), *Hell Under Water / Gahîm taht al-mâʾ* (1989), *Terrorism / al-Irhâb* (1989), *The Devil's Island / Gazirat al-chaytân* (1990), *The Network of Death / Chabakat al-mawt* (1990), *The Era of the Powerful / ʿAsr al-qouwwah* (1991), *The Wicked Person / al-Charis* (1992), *Mission in Tel-Aviv / Mouhimmah fî Tall Abîb* (1992), *The Wicked / al-Chouttâr* (1993), *131, Forced Labour / 131 Achghâl* (1993), *The Terrorist / al-Irhâbî* (1994), *A Woman Who Shook Egypt's Throne / Imaraʾa hazzat ʿarsh masr* (1995), *Bekhit and Adila / Bekheet wa ʿAdeela* (1995), *Assassination / Ighteyaal* (1996), *Bekhit and Adila: The Bucket and the Coffee Pot / Bekheet wi ʿAdeela / al-Gardal wi al-kanaka* (1997), *Hassan El Loll / Hassan el loll* (1997), *48 Hours in Israel / 48 saʾa fî Israel* (1998), *A Message to the Ruler / Resala ela al-wali* (1998), *Mahrous, the Shadow of the Minister / al-Waad Mahrous betaaʾ el wazeer* (1999), *State Security / Amn dawla* (1999), *Hello America / Hallo Amrika* (2000), *Smart Bilya / Bilya we demagho el ʾalya* (2000), *Underground Hell / Gaheem that al ʿard* (2001)

Gamal, Ismaïl. Egyptian filmmaker. Feature films: *Bloody Encounter / al-Liqâʾ al-dâmî* (1992), *The Politician / al-Siyâsî* (1993), *A Woman's Revenge / Intiqâm im raʾah* (1994), *The Wolf Trap /*

Misyadat al-dhiʾâb (1994), *Goodbye to Bachelorhood / Wadaʾan lel ʿuzubeyya* (1995), *Jailbird / al-Lumangi* (1996), *Empire of Evil / Imbratoureyet el sharr* (1998), *Waves of Anger / Amwaag al-ghadab* (1999), *Going Cheap in Taht El Rab / Taht el rabʾ Be gnih wi rubʾ* (2000)

Gamba, Sao (b. 1940 in Uganda; d. 2004). Kenyan filmmaker. After training at the Polish film school in Lodz, he spent some time in Uganda. Back in Kenya in 1973 he first joined the Voice of Kenya Television, where he made twenty-five documentaries, and then the Kenyan Film Corporation. After completing his first feature, he abandoned filmmaking for painting and sculpture. Feature film: *Kolormask* (1986)

Gamboa, Zézé (b. 1955 in Luanda). Angolan filmmaker. Worked in Angolan television from 1974 to 1980, then studied film directing and sound editing in Paris. Has lived in Belgium from 1980. Made two documentaries in the 1990s and then a first feature film which received wide international festival screening. Feature film: *A Hero / O Heroi* (2004)

Ganda, Oumarou (b. 1931 in Niamey; d. 1981). Niger filmmaker. Also actor. One of the true pioneers of African filmmaking, he fought as a volunteer in the French army in the Far East, and appeared as an actor in Jean Rouch's *Me, a Black Man / Moi, un noir* (1957) while he was working as an unskilled laborer. Subsequently worked at the French cultural centre in Niger and turned to directing in 1968. Some of his most striking works—*Cabascabou* (1968) and *Le Wazzou polygame* (1970)—are medium-length works which were very well received. The 50-minute *Le Wazzou polygame,* for example, won the top prize, the Étalon de Yennenga, at the first Festival Panafricain du Cinéma de Ouagadougou (FESPACO) in 1972. His second feature is a skilled adaptation of oral story-telling techniques to film. Feature films: *Le Wazzou polygame* (1970), *Saitane* (1972), *The Exile / L'Exilé* (1980)

Ganga, Maria João (b. 1964 at Huambo in Angola). Angolan filmmaker. She studied at the École Supérieure des Études Cinématographiques (ESEC) in Paris. Playwright. Assistant director (including on Abderrahmane Sissako's *Rostov-Luanda*). Feature film: *Hollow City / Na Cidade vazia* (2004)

Garcia, George. South African filmmaker. Feature film: *The Adventures of a Heidelberg Press* (English, with Michael Garcia, 1990)

Garcia, Michael. South African filmmaker. Feature films: *The Adventures of a Heidelberg Press* (English, with George Garcia, 1990), *Armageddon—The Final Challenge* (English, 1994)

Gaye Ramaka, Joseph (b. 1952 in Saint Louis). Senegalese filmmaker. Studied anthropology in Paris and filmmaking at the University of Paris VIII. After a number of documentaries, including the feature-length *Nitt . . . Ndoxx!* (1988), his sole fictional feature, adapted from Prosper Mérimé's story, is a striking tale of passion, desire, and death. In 2006 he made a feature-length documentary on video: *And If Latif Was Right? / Et si Latif avait raison.* Feature film: *Karmen Geï* (2000)

Genini, Izza (b. 1942 in Casablanca). Moroccan filmmaker of Jewish descent. She studied languages in Paris, where she has lived since 1960. Formed her own production and distribution company, Sogeav, to produce and distribute her own and others' films. Co-producer of feature films by Ahmed El-Maânouni, Mohamed Aboulouakar, and Tayeb Saddiki. A major figure in Maghrebian documentary, she is best known for her twelve-part series *Morocco: Bodies and Souls / Maroc: corps et âmes* (1987–1992). Has continued with further single documentaries on aspects of traditional life in Morocco. Also published two books, *Maroc* (with photographs by Jean du Boisberranger, 1995) and *Maroc: Royaume des mille et une fêtes* (with photographs by Jacques Bravo and Xavier Richer, 1998)

George, Terry. South African filmmaker. Feature film: *Hotel Rwanda* (English, 2004)

Gerard, Francis. South African filmmaker. Feature films: *A Private Life / Jack and Stella* (English, 1988), *The Fever / Township Fever* (English, with David Thompson, 1990)

Gerima, Haile (b. 1946 in Gondar). Ethiopian filmmaker, based in the United States. Actor. Studied at Goodman School of Drama in Chicago and at the University of California at Los Angeles (UCLA). Teaches at Howard University, Washington, D.C. A major figure in African, and also in Black American, cinema, his debut feature remains a striking pioneering work of African cinema. Feature films: *Harvest 3000 Years / Birt sost shi amit* (1976), *Bush Mama* (1976), *Wilmington 10—USA 10,000* (documentary, 1976), *Ashes and Embers* (1982), *Sankofa* (1993), *Adwa* (documentary, 1999)

Ghalem, Ali (b. 1943 in Constantine). Algerian filmmaker. Also a novelist who adapted his own French-language novel (*Une femme pour mon fils*, 1979) as his third feature, the only one he has made in Algeria. Self-taught, he began his filmmaking in France, taking the immigrant community as his subject. Feature films: *Mektoub* (1970), *The Other France / L'Autre France* (1975), *A Wife for My Son / Une femme pour mon fils* (1982)

Ghorab-Volta, Zaïda (b. 1966). French-based filmmaker of Algerian descent. She began with work in the social sector before turning to cinema. Made three short fiction films and co-scripted Romain Goupil's French feature, *Her Life / Sa vie à elle* (1995). Feature films: *Leave a Little Love / Laisse un peu d'amour* (1998), *Gilded Youth / Jeunesse dorée* (2001)

Ghorbal, Khaled (b. 1950 in Tunisia). Tunisian theatre director and filmmaker. Studied drama in Tunis (at the Centre d'Art Dramatique) as well as extensively in Paris (at the Université Internationale du Théâtre de Paris, Université Paris VIII, and the École Jacques Lecoq). Has worked as actor, writer, and director in theatre and been involved in bringing films into schools and running art cinemas. Feature film: *Fatma* (2001)

Gibson, Angus. South African filmmaker. Feature film: *Heartlines* (English, 2006)

Ginsberg, Diana. South African filmmaker. Feature film: *Die Spook van Donkergat* (Afrikaans, 1973)

Ginty, Robert. South African filmmaker. Feature film: *A Woman of Desire* (English, 1992)

Giumale, Hadj Mohamed. Somalian filmmaker. Feature film: *Town and Village / Miyi Iyo Magaalo* (1968)

Gold, Jeff. South African filmmaker. Feature film: *Tattoo Chase / Bottom Line* (English, 1988)

Goldsmid, Peter. South African filmmaker. Feature film: *The Road to Mecca* (English, with Athol Fugard, 1991)

Goldstein, David. South African filmmaker. Feature film: *Crossing the Line* (English, with Dean Goodhill, 1988)

Gom³a, Khaled. Egyptian filmmaker. Feature film: *Ouija* (2006)

Gom³a, Mohamed. Egyptian filmmaker. Feature film: *Real Dreams / Ahlam haqiqeyya* (2007)

Gomes, Flora (b. 1949 in Cadique). Guinea-Bissau filmmaker. Studied film at the Instituto Cubano de Arte e Industria Cinematográficos (ICAIC) in Cuba, graduating in 1972. Worked as a cinematographer and made short films from 1976, some in collaboraton with Sana Na N³Hada. His features have been widely seen and well received on the international festival circuit. Feature films: *Mortu nega* (1988), *The Blue Eyes of Yonta / Udju azul di Yonta* (1990), *Po di sangui* (1996), *Nha Fala* (2002)

Gomis, Alain (b. 1972 in Paris, of French-Senegalese descent). Senegalese filmmaker, resident in France. Studied filmmaking at the University of Paris I. Four short films before his first feature, which reflects on his growing up in Paris. Feature film: *L'Afrance* (2001)

Goosen, Anton. South African filmmaker. Feature film: *'n Brief vir Simone* (Afrikaans, with F. C. Hamman, 1980)

Gounajjar, Nour Eddine (b. 1946 in Berguent). Moroccan filmmaker. Studied filmmaking at the Institut des Hautes Études Cinématographiques (IDHEC) in Paris. Part of the collective responsible for *Cinders of the Vineyard / Les cendres du clos* in 1977. Made a number of video documentaries and fictional pieces. Feature film: *The Waiting Room / La Salle d'attente* (1991)

Grädler, Theodore. South African filmmaker. Feature film: *Find Livingstone / Finden Sie Livingstone* (Afrikaans, 1968)

Graver, Gary. U.S. director of two features listed in some South African filmographies. Feature films: *Dust* (English, 1988), *Crossing the Line* (English, with David Goldstein, 1990)

Gravevolik, Zika. South African filmmaker and producer. Feature films: *Crime Doesn't Pay* (English, 1984), *Maphata* (Sotho, 1984)

Greene, Tim. South African filmmaker. Feature film: *A Boy Called Twist* (English, 2004)

Greyson, John. South African filmmaker. Feature film: *Proteus* (2004)

Griffith, Chuck. South African filmmaker. Feature film: *A Little Adventure* (English, 1988)

Grünbauer, Werner. South African filmmaker. Feature films: *Paul Kruger* (Afrikaans, 1956), *Die Vervlakste Tweeling* (Afrikaans, 1969)

Gubara, Gadalla (b. 1921 at Omdurman). Pioneer Sudanese filmmaker. Studied at the University of California. Director and producer, who founded his own studio in 1970. Made numerous documentaries. Feature films: *Congratulations / Mabruk alik* (1974), *Tajour* (1982), *Viva Sara* (1988), *The Cheikh's Baraka* (1998)

Guemei, Omar. Egyptian filmmaker. Feature films: *Call of the Heart / Nidâ' al-qaib* (1943), *Ragaa / Ragâ'* (1945), *The Mother / al-Oumm* (1945), *The Father / al-Abb* (1947), *Playing with Fire / al-Li'b bi-l-nâr* (1948), *Prisoner No. 17 / al-Saguînah raqm sab'at 'achar* (1949), *Farewell My Love / Wadâ'an yâ gharâmî* (1951), *My Children / Awlâdî* (1951)

Guerdjou, Bourlem (b. 1965 in Asnières, Paris). French-based filmmaker of Algerian descent, but French nationality. Works in French television. Directed a number of short films and appeared as an actor in Mehdi Charef's *Tea in Archimedes' Harem* (1985). His films are international co-productions, the first of which remarkably won the top prize, the *Tanit d'or*, at the Journées Cinématographiques de Carthage (JCC) in Tunis in 1998. Feature films: *Living in Paradise / Vivre au paradis* (1998), *Zaida, Horsewoman from the Atlas / Zaïda, cavalière de l'Atlas* (2005)

Guerra, Ruy (b. 1931 in Lourenço Marquez [Maputo]). Mozambican filmmaker. Educated in Portugal and Mozambique and studied film at the Institut des Hautes Études Cinématographiques (IDHEC) in Paris, where he also worked as assistant director. He has also appeared as an actor in several films, including Werner Herzog's *Aguirre, Wrath of God* (1972). Spent a decade in Brazil and became one of the key figures of the Brazilian Cinema Novo [*Os Cafajestes / The Hustlers*, 1962; *Os Fuzis / The Guns*, 1964; *Sweet Hunters*, 1969; *Os Deuses e os Mortos / The Gods and the Dead*, 1971; *A Queda / The Fall*, 1978]. Returned to Mozambique after independence to reorganize its film centre, the Instituto Nacional de Cinema (INC). His first Mozambican feature is the restaging of a notorious massacre, shot as a real event. Mozambican feature films: *Mueda, Memory and Massacre / Mueda, memoria e massacre* (1979), *Mixed Up / Estorvo* (2003)

Guest, Val. English director of one feature film included in some South African film listings: *Killer Force* (English, 1976)

Guirguiss, Raffi. Egyptian filmmaker. Feature film: *Lost in America / Tayeh fî Amrika* (2002)

Habib, Salah. Egyptian filmmaker. Feature film: *The Unfortunate / al-Manhous* (1987)

Hachem, Anouar (b. 1946 in Khartoum). Sudanese filmmaker. Studied agronomy at Cairo University, then turned to filmmaking and studied at the Cairo Higher Film Institute, graduating in 1973. Made a number of medium-length documentaries. Feature film: *Eye Trip* (1984)

Haddad, Moussa (b. 1937 in Algiers). Algerian filmmaker. Worked extensively on foreign productions, serving as assistant to Gillo Pontecorvo and Luchino Visconti, and in television. Made a number of téléfilms and a video feature, *Mad In* (1999). Feature films: *Three Guns against Caesar / Trois pistolets contre César* (with Enzo Peri, 1967), *Beside the Poplar Tree / Auprès du peuplier* (1972), *Inspector Tahar's Holiday / Les Vacances de l'inspecteur Tahar* (1973)

Hadjadj, Belkacem (b. 1950 in Algiers). Algerian filmmaker. Studied filmmaking at the Institut National des Arts du Spectacle et Techniques de Diffusion (INSAS) in Brussels. Television work in Belgium and Algeria, where he made three téléfilms. His debut feature was one of the first shot in the Berber language. Feature films: *Once upon a Time / Il était une fois / Machaho* (1995), *El Manara* (2004)

Hafez, Bahiga (b. 1908; d. 1983). Egyptian actress and filmmaker. Born into an aristocratic family linked to the monarchy, she was a talented musician and linguist. Chosen by Mohamed Karim to play the lead in his adaptation of Mohamed Hussein Heykal's novel *Zeinab* (1930), she wrote a score recorded onto disk to accompany screenings of the film. She set up her own production company in 1932, producing Ibrahim Lama's *The Victims* and Mario Volpi's *The Accusation*, before embarking on the direction of an expensive version of *Leila, the Girl from the Desert*, which ruined her when it was initially banned by the government after protests from Iran (whose ruler was about to marry the king's sister). Feature films: *The Victims / al-Dahâyâ* (with Ibrahim Lama, 1935), *Leila, the Girl from the Desert / Layla bint al-sahrâ* (1937), *Leila the Bedouin / Layla al-badawiyyah* (1944)

Hafez, Hassen. Egyptian filmmaker. Feature films: *Viva Zalata / Viva Zalata* (1976), *God Is Patient, but Do Not Forget / Youmhil wa lâ youhmil* (1979)

Hafez, Nagdi. Egyptian filmmaker. Feature films: *The Cunning Man / al-Ragoul al-tha'lab* (1962), *A Bachelor's Life / Hayât ᶜâzib* (1963), *The Hilarious Crime / al-Garîmah al-dâhikah* (1963), *Love, Joy and Youth / Houbb wa-marah wa-chabîb* (1964), *Compulsory Holiday / Agâzah bi-l-'âfiyah* (1966), *A Man and Two Women / Ragoul waimra'atân* (1966), *How to Rob a Millionnaire? / Kayfa tasriq millionnaire* (1968), *Amorous Pursuit / Moutâradah gharmâmiyyah* (1968), *The Thief / al-Harâmî* (1969), *Reda Bond / Ridâ Bond* (1970), *A Quarter of a Dozen Bad People / Rib' dasta achrâr* (1970), *The Beauty and the Thief / al-Hasnâ wa-l-liss* (1971), *Gentle Embrace / al-Ahdân al-dâfi'ah* (1974), *I Want Love and Tenderness / Ourîd houbban wa hanânan* (1978), *Behind the University Walls / Khalf aswâr al-Gâmi'ah* (1981), *Marriage—It's for the Worthy / al-Gawâz li-l-guid'ân* (1983), *The Years of Danger / Sanawât al-khatar* (1985), *The Dancer and the Undertaker (al-Râqisah wa-l-hânoutî* (1992), *The Men Are in Danger / al-Rigâl fî khatar* (1993)

Hafez, Samir. Egyptian filmmaker. Feature films: *Sammoura and the Pretty Girl / Sammourah wa-l-bint al-'ammourah* (1984), *The Police Devils / Chayâtîn al-chourtah* (1992), *Rare Coins / al'Imlah al-nâdirah* (1992), *Our Beautiful Dreams / Ahlâmounâ al-hilwah* (1994)

Hakkar, Amor (b. 1958 at Khenchela in Algeria). French-based filmmaker of Algerian descent. Grew up as the child of immigrants in Besançon. Feature film: *Bad Weather for a Crook / Sale temps pour un voyou* (1992)

Halgryn, Chris. South African filmmaker. Feature films: *Utotsi* (Zulu, 1978), *Phindesela* (Zulu, 1979)

Halilu, Adamu (b. 1936 at Gardika). Nigerian filmmaker. Studied at the Overseas Film & Television Centre in London and worked for RAI in Italy. After his return to Nigeria in 1963, he collaborated on some seventy documentaries, including the feature-length *Mama Learns a Lesson* (1963) and *Child Bride* (1971). Founding chief executive of the Nigerian Film Corporation (1979–1985). Feature films: *Shehu Umar* (Hausa, 1976), *Kanta of Kebbi* (Hausa, 1978), *Moment of Truth* (English, 1981)

Halim, Helmi (b. 1916; d. 1971). Egyptian filmmaker. Originally a film critic, he worked as assistant on Kamal Selim's *The Will* (1939) and later became head of scripting and production at the Misr studios. He wrote and directed his own features. Taught scriptwriting at the Cairo Higher Film Institute from 1959 till his death. Feature films: *Our Best Days / Ayyâmounâ al-houlwah* (1955), *The Heart Has Its Reasons / al-Qalb louh ahkâm* (1956), *Greet Those Whom I Love / Salltm ʿalà al-habâyib* (1958), *Story of a Love / Hikâyat houbb* (1959), *Three Men and a Woman / Thalâthat rigâl wa Imraʾah* (1960), *The Way of Tears / tariiq al-doumouʾ* (1961), *Story of a Life / Hikâyat alʾoumr koullouh* (1965), *Life Is Beautiful / al-Hayât houlwah* (1966), *Days of Love / Ayyâm al-houbb* (1968), *My Wife Is Completely Mad / Mirâtî magʾnounah magʾnounah* (1968), *A Story from Home / Hikâyah min baladinâ* (1969), *It Was the Good Time / Kânat ayyâm* (1970), *Lovers of Life / ʿOuchchâq al-hayât* (1971), *A Student's Love / Gharâm tilmîdhah* (1973)

Hall, Ivan. South African filmmaker. Feature films: *Die Kruger-miljoene / The Kruger Millions* (Afrikaans, 1967), *Dr. Kalie* (Afrikaans, 1968), *Lied in My Hart* (Afrikaans, 1970), *Vicki* (Afrikaans, 1970), *Flying Squad* (English, 1971), *Gold Squad* (English, 1971), *Boemerang 11.15* (Afrikaans, 1972), *Lokval in Venesie* (Afrikaans, 1972), *Aanslag op Kariba* (Afrikaans, 1973), *Dans van die Vlamink* (Afrikaans, 1974), *Funeral for an Assassin* (English, 1974), *Dingertjie is Dynamite!* (Afrikaans, 1975), *Die Troudag van Tant Ralie* (Afrikaans, 1975), *Kill and Kill Again* (English, 1981), *The Riverman / Return to*

Eden (English, 1983), *Skollie* (Afrikaans, 1985), *Back to Freedom* (English, 1986), *Trackers / Bush Shrink* (English, 1988)

Hamed, Marwan (b. 1977 in Cairo). Egyptian filmmaker. Studied at the Cairo Higher Film Institute, graduating in 1999, and then worked as asssistant director. Over 60 commercials, plus three documentaries and two fictional shorts since 1997. Achieved international success with his big-budget first feature. Feature film: *The Yacoubian Building / Omaret Yacoubian* (2006)

Hamed, Saïd (b. in Sudan). Egyptian filmmaker. Studied at the Cairo Higher Film Institute and worked as assistant before making his feature debut. Feature films: *Love in a Fridge / al-Houbb fî-l-thallâgah* (1993), *An Upper Egyptian Goes to the American University / Saʾidi fi el gamʾa al merekeya* (1998), *Hammam in Amsterdam / Hammaam fî Amesterdam* (1999), *Shorts, a T-Shirt and a Cap / Short wa ʃunellu wa cap* (2000), *Throwing It About / Rashsha gareeʾa* (2001), *We Interrupt this Programme to Bring You the Following Announcement / Gaʾana al-bayaan al tali* (2001), *A True Friend / Saheb Sahbo* (2002), *Mind Your Face! / Iwʾa weshak!* (2003), *Kimo and His Best Friend / Kimo wi antimo* (2004), *Hamada Plays / Hamada yelʾab* (2005), *Me or My Aunt / Yana ya khalty* (2005), *Return of the Wicked Woman / ʿAwdat al-nadla* (2005)

Hamilton, Ian. South African filmmaker. Feature film: *Sell a Million* (English, with Clive Harding, 1975)

Hammami, Abderrazak (b. 1935 in Kairouan). Tunisian actor and filmmaker. Studied theatre in Strasbourg, worked as an actor in theatre, television and film. After working as a trainee at the Office de Radiodiffusion et de Télévision Française (ORTF) in Paris, he became a director for Radio-Télévision Tunisienne (RTT), working on a whole range of dramas. Feature film: *Omi traki* (1973)

Hammami, Mohamed (b. 1951 in Tunis). Tunisian filmmaker. Studied filmmaking at the Vsesoyuznyi gosudarstvennyi institut kinematografii (VGIK; All-Union State Cinema Institute) and journalism at the Patrice Lumumba University in Moscow. Worked in television for Radio-Télévision Tunisienne (RTT), directing shorts, documentaries, and two téléfilms. *Land of Sacrifice / Terre des sacrificiés* (1974) and *The Spark / L'Étincelle* (1976). Feature film: *My Village / Mon village* (1979)

Hamman, F. C. South African filmmaker. Feature films: *'n Brief vir Simone* (Afrikaans, with Anton Goosen, 1980), *Sing vir die Harlekyn* (Afrikaans, 1980)

Hammon, Michael (b. 1955). South African filmmaker. Studied painting and photography in Cape Town and television in Berlin. Reporter and cameraman. Several short films. Documentaries: *Trekking to Utopia, Hillbrow Kids* (1999) and the feature-length *Wheels and Deals* (English, 1991)

Hammouda, Cherif. Egyptian filmmaker. Feature films: *The Last Visit / al-Ziyârah al-akhîrah* (1986), *The Wretched / al-Safalah* (1986), *A Man Who Is a Victim of Love / Ragoul qate lahou al-houbb* (1986), *The Last Look / al-Nazrah al-akhîrah* (1987), *What Neighbours / Guîrân âkhir zaman* (1989), *Betrayal / Khiyânah* (1989), *Three Critical Hours / Talât sâ'ât harigah* (1990), *Taht al-Rabaa / Tahta al-rab'* (1991), *Madmen on the Road / Magânîn 'alâ al-tarîq* (1991), *The Kidnapped Woman / al-Makhtoufah* (1991), *The Heroes of Upper Egypt / Batal min al-Sa'îd* (1991)

Hamza, Nadia (b. 1939 in Port Saïd). Egyptian filmmaker. She trained as a scriptwriter and worked as assistant and producer before directing her first feature. She founded her own production company, Seven Stars Studio, in 1994. All her films have a female lead and focus on the problems and aspirations of women. Feature films: *Sea of Fantasy / Bahr al-awhâm* (1984), *Women / al-Nisâ'* (1985), *Women Behind Bars / Nisâ' khalfa al-qoudbân* (1986), *A Woman's Greed / Hiqd imra'ah* (1987), *The Woman and the Law / al-Mar'ah wa-l-qânoun* (1988), *A Woman, Alas! / Imra'ah li-l-asaf* (1988), *Lieutenant Nadia's Battle / Ma'rakat al-naqîb Nadiâ* (1990), *Women Outlaws / Nisâ' didd al-qânoun*

(1991), *Female Crooks / Nisâ' sa'âlîk* (1991), *The Female Slaves' Murmurs / Hams al-Gawârî* (1992)

Hanafi, Mohamed. Egyptian filmmaker. Feature film: *The Dancer and the Devil / al-Râqisah wa-l-chaytân* (1992)

Harding, Clive. South African filmmaker. Feature films: *Sell a Million* (English, with Ian Hamilton, 1975), *Shamwari* (English, 1982)

Harmon, Larry. South African filmmaker. Feature film: *Laurel and Hardy: The Movie* (English, with John Cherry, 1998)

Haroun, Mahamat Saleh (b. 1963, in Abéché). Chadian filmmaker, currently resident in France. Studied filmmaking at the CLFC in Paris and journalism at the IUT in Bordeaux. Worked for 5 years in provincial French journalism and radio. From 1991 made short films—both fiction and documentary in a range of formats (35mm and 16mm film, Beta SP). He is a key figure in the new generation of African filmmakers. Made a personal short film, *Kalala*, about his best friend, Hissein Djibrine, who died of AIDS, in 2005. Feature films: *Bye-Bye Africa* (1999), *Our Father / Abouna* (2001), *Dry Season / Daratt* (2006)

Hassan, Abdel Fattah. Egyptian filmmaker. Feature films: *The Last Solution / al-Hall al-akhîr* (1937), *The Gaiety Station / Mahattat al-ouns* (1942), *A Heavenly Love / Houbb min al-samâ* (1944), *Night of Chance / Laylat al-hazz* (1945), *The First Day of the Month / Awwal al-Chahr* (1945), *Me and My Cousin / Anâ wa ibn 'ammî* (1946), *Storms / 'Awâsif* (1946), *Land of the Nile / Ard al-Nîl* (1946), *An Enemy of Women / 'Adouww al-mar'ah* (1946), *Jealousy / al-Ghîrah* (1946), *The Midnight Ghost / Chabah nisf al-layl* (1947), *The Last Dernier Round / al-Gawlah al-akhîrah* (1947), *The Tombola Seller / Bayyâ'at al-yânasîb* (1947), *Ward Chah / Ward Chah* (1948), *The Owner of the Flat / Sâhibat al-'imârah* (1948), *A Peasant's Son / Ibn al-fallâh* (1948), *Narguis / Narguis* (1948), *The Lucky Girl / Bint hazz* (1948), *Woman Is a Devil / al-Mar'ah chaytân* (1949), *Congratulations / Mabrouk 'alîkî*

(1949), *The Woman / al-Mar°ah* (1949), *His Family's Favorite / Mahsoub al-°â°ilah* (1950)

Hassan, Elhami. Egyptian filmmaker. Feature films: *Don't Think About It / Ou°â tifakkar* (1954), *My Companion / Charîk hayâtî* (1953), *Fate's Laughter / Dihkât al-qadar* (1955), *The Call of Love / Nidâ° al-houbb* (1956), *Forget the World / Insâ al-douniâ* (1962)

Hassan, Fardous. Egyptian silent filmmaker. Feature film: *Souad the Gipsy / Sou°âd al-ghagariyya* (with Abdel Aziz Khalil, 1928)

Hassan, Ismaïl. Egyptian filmmaker. Feature films: *Smart but Lost / Fâlih wa mouhtâs* (1954), *I Call You / Banâdî °alîk* (1955),

Hassan, Ismaïl. Egyptian filmmaker. Feature films: *The Commander / al-Komandân* (1986), *Sergeant Hassan / al-Châwîch Hasan* (1988), *A Very Unruly Family / °Â°ilah mouchâghibah guiddan* (1989), *Lottery Claimant / °Arîs fî-l-yânusîb* (1989). *A Mother's Mistake / Ghaltat oumm* (1989), *Mahrous the Foreman / al-Oustâ Mahrous* (1990), *The Faithless Friend / Sahbak min bakhtak* (1990), *The Stroke of My Life / Khabtat al°oumr* (1991), *The Corruptors / al-Moufsidoun* (1991), *The Tea Seller / Bâ°i°at al-chây* (1991), *The Woman and the Giant / Hiya wa-l-°imlâq* (1993), *The Two Fugitives / al-Hâribân* (1993), *Stranger at the Harbour / Gharib fil mina* (1995), *Excuse Me, Debes / La mu°akhza ya de°bes* (2000)

Hassan, Mohamed Kamel. Egyptian filmmaker. Feature films: *Charting Troubled Waters / al-Sâbihah fî-l-nâr* (1959), *The Last Love / al-Houbb al-akhîr* (1959), *Stronger than Life / Aqwâ min al-hayât* (1960), *Wahida / Wahîdah* (1961), *The Lost Son / al-Ibn al-mafqoud* (1964), *The Last Message / al-Risâlah al-akhîraah* (1964)

Hassan, Mostafa. Egyptian filmmaker. Feature films: *The Unknown Singer / al-Moughanni al-mag°houl* (1946), *Wedding Night / Laylat al-doukhlah* (1950)

Hassib, Mohamed. Egyptian filmmaker. Feature films: *God Watches / Inna rabbaka la-bi-*

l-mirsâd (1983, *The Hand / al-Kaff* (1985), *Appeal for Help from the Other World / Istighâthah min al-°âlam al-âkhar* (1985), *Sad Street / Châri° al-sadd* (1986), *Abou Kartona / Abou kartounah* (1991), *Hard Times / al-Zaman al-sa°b* (1993)

Hattingh, A. South African filmmaker. Feature film: *Double Deal* (English, 1984)

Hawkins, Roger (b. Zimbabwe). Zimbabwean filmmaker. Studied at the University of Natal in South Africa and subsequently in the United States and England. Wide-ranging career (school teacher, soil surveyor, advertising copywriter, lounge pianist, research assistant). Cartoons and animated television serials. Feature-length fiction on video: *Dr Juju* (2001). Feature film (animated): *The Legend of the Sky Kingdom* (2003)

Hawl, Qassem. Libyan filmmaker. Feature film: *Searching for Layla al-°Amiriya / al-Bahth °An Layla al-°Amiriya* (1990)

Hay, Rod. South African filmmaker. Feature films: *Ungavimbi Umcolo* (Zulu, 1981), *A Way of Life* (English, 1981), *Will to Win* (English, 1982), *Stoney, the One and Only* (English, 1984)

Hébié, Missa (b. 1951 in Orodara). Burkinabè filmmaker. Studied audiovisual production, then film at the Institut Africain d'Education Cinématographique (INAFEC), in Quebec and in Bordeaux. Half-a dozen short films and videos in the 1990s. Three-part television series, *Commissariat de Tampy* in 2006. Feature film: *Diarabi* (2003)

Hefnawi, Ahmed Kamel. Egyptian filmmaker. Feature films: *Nagaf / Nagaf* (1946), *The Island Princess / Amirat al-gazîrah* (with Hassan Ramzi, 1948), *Path of Happiness / Rarîq al-sa°âdah* (1953), *Long Live Men! / Tahyâ al-riggâlah* (1954), *The Innocent's Prayer / Da°wat al-mazloum* (1956)

Hellal, Abderrazak (b. 1951 in Algeria). Algerian novelist and filmmaker. Novels include *Place de la Régence,* published in Paris in 1989.

Worked largely in television. Feature film: *Question of Honour / Question d'honneur* (1997)

Helmi, Hassan. Egyptian filmmaker. Features: *The Pasha's Wife / Haram al-bâchâ* (1946), *Good and Evil / al-Khayr wa-l-charr* (1946), *Five Pounds / al-Khamsah Guinîh* (1946), *The Hunchback / al-Ahdab* (1946), *Heaven's Light / Nour min al-samâ* (1947), *The Three Suitors / al-ʾOursân al thalâthah* (1947), *Al-Zanati Khalifa / al-Zanâtî Khalîfah* (1948), *Long Live Art / Yahyâ al-fann* (1948), *I Love to Dance / Ahibb al-raqs* (1948), *Gossip / Kalâm al-nâs* (1949), *Women Are Made Like That / al-Sittât kidah* (1949), *The Love Agency / Maktab al-gharâm* (1950), *The Crook's House / Bayt al-nattâch* (1952), *A Well-kept Secret / al-Sirr fî bîr* (1953)

Helmi, Ibrahim. Egyptian filmmaker. Feature films: *The Son of the East / Ibnal-charq* (1947), *Abou Halmous / Abou Halmous* (1947), *Slave of Her Eyes / Asîr al-ʾouyoun* (1949), *A Dance Tour / ʿAchrah baladî* (1952), *Kilo 99 / Kilo tisʾah wa-tisʾîn* (1956)

Hendawi, Saad. Egyptian filmmaker. Feature film: *In Love / Halet hubb* (2004)

Henkel, Peter. South African filmmaker. Feature films: *Scotty Smith* (English, 1970), *Three Bullets for a Long Gun* (English, 1971)

Herbst, Ed. South African filmmaker. Feature films: *Bird Boy* (English, 1984), *The Cross* (English, 1984), *Umdobi* (Zulu, 1984)

Hessler, Brian. British filmmaker who codirected one film listed in some South African filmographies. Feature film: *Out on Bail* (English, with Gordon Hessler, 1988)

Hessler, Gordon. British filmmaker who codirected one film listed in some South African filmographies. Feature film: *Out on Bail* (English, with Brian Hessler, 1988)

Hetata, Atef (b. 1965). Egyptian filmmaker. Studied at Cairo Polytechnic and directed three

shorts. Also wrote short stories. Feature film: *Closed Doors / al-Abwaab al-mughlaqa* (2001)

Hetherington, Neil. South African filmmaker. Feature films: *Those Naughty Angels* (English, 1974), *Olie Kolonie* (Afrikaans, 1975), *Terrorist* (English, 1978), *The Tangent Affair* (English, 1987)

Heunis, Dupreez. South African filmmaker. Feature film: *Dark Horse* (English, 1996)

Heyns, Katinka (b. 1947). South African filmmaker and actress. She studied drama at the University of Pretoria and made her name from 1969 onwards as an actress in a succession of films directed by Jans Rautenbach. Also acted in television, especially in Manie van Rensberg's comedy series *Willem*. Turned to television directing after 1976, making both documentaries and drama series and continuing after her feature film debut. Made her film reputation with three major Afrikaans features. Much of her work is scripted by her husband, Chris Barnard. Feature films: *Fiela se Kind* (Afrikaans, 1988), *Fiela's Child* (Dubbed English version, 1989), *Die Storie van Klara Viljee* (Afrikaans, 1991), *Paljas* (Afrikaans, 1996)

Hickox Anthony. South African filmmaker. Feature film: *Blast* (2004)

Hickox, Douglas. British director of one feature film included in some listings of South African feature films: *Zulu Dawn* (English, 1979)

Hickson, David. South African filmmaker. Grew up in Cape Town. Worked as architect in South Africa and London. Studied film in South Africa. Several shorts. Feature film: *Beat the Drum* (English, 2003)

Hilmi, Mohamed (b. 1931 in Azzefoun). Algerian filmmaker. Worked as an actor and television director, making numerous téléfilms. Feature film: *El Ouelf essaib* (1990)

Hodi, Jeno. South African filmmaker. Feature film: *Deadly Obsession* (English, 1985)

Hofmeyr, Gray. South African filmmaker. Trained and worked in British television before moving to SABC, where he made some notable dramas in the 1980s. Feature films: *Jock of the Bushveld* (English, 1986), *In Harm's Way* (English, 1988), *Lambarene* (English, 1989), *Sweet 'n Short* (English, 1991), *There's a Zulu on My Stoep* (English, 1993), *Mr Bones* (2001), *Mama Jack* (English, 2005)

Hondo, Med (b. 1936 in Aïn Ouled Beni Mathar). Mauritanian filmmaker, resident in France. His powerful series of socially and politically committed works put him in the forefront of African filmmakers and he deservedly won the top prize, the Étalon de Yennenga, at the Festival Panafricain du Cinéma de Ouagadougou (FESPACO) in 1987 with his historical epic *Sarraounia*. Feature films: *Soleil O* (1971), *The Black Wogs, Your Neighbours / Les Bicots-nègres, vos voisins* (1973), *West Indies / West Indies ou les nègres marrons de la liberté* (1979), *Sarraounia* (1986), *Black Light / Lumière noire* (1994), *Watani / Watani, un monde sans mal* (1997), *Fatima / Fatima, l'Algérienne de Dakar* (2004), *First Among Blacks: Toussaint Louverture / Premier des noirs: Toussaint Louverture* (2007)

Hood, Gavin. South African filmmaker. Studied law in South Africa and filmmaking at the University of California. Actor and scriptwriter as well as director. Won an Oscar in the States with his third feature, which is based on Athol Fugard's only novel. Feature films: *A Reasonable Man* (English, 1999), *W pustyni i w puszczy* (2001), *Tsotsi* (Zulu, Xhosa, and Afrikaans, 2005), *Rendition* (2007)

Hookham, John. South African filmmaker. Feature film: *Sky Blue* (English, 1980)

Hool, Lance. American director of a film included in some South African film listings. Feature film: *Steel Dawn / Nomands* (English, 1987)

Hooper, Tobe. South African filmmaker. Feature film: *The Mangler* (English, 1993)

Hooper, Tom. South African filmmaker. Feature film: *Red Dust* (English, 2004)

Hope, Harry. South African filmmaker. Feature film: *Pop's Oasis* (English, 1987)

Hopkins, Stephen. South African filmmaker. Feature film: *The Ghost and the Darkness* (English, 1996)

Howard, Sandy. South African filmmaker. Feature film: *King of Africa / One Step to Hell* (English, with Nino Scolari, 1969)

Hudson, Hugh. English director of one film listed in some South African feature film listing: *I Dreamed of Africa* (1998)

Hughes, Bronwen. South African filmmaker. Feature film: *Stander* (English, 2003)

Hugo, Henk. South African filmmaker. Feature film: *Nommer Asseblief* (Afrikaans, 1981)

Hulette, Don. American director of a film included in some South African film listings. Feature film: *Ipi Tombi* (English, with Tommie Meyer, 1993)

Humphrey, J. South African silent filmmaker. Feature film: *And Then?* (1917)

Hunsicker, Jason. South African filmmaker. Feature film: *Odd Ball Hall* (English, 1989)

Hunt, Peter. British director of two feature films included in some lists of South African feature films: *Gold* (English, 1974), *Shout at the Devil* (English, 1976)

Huntington, Lawrence. British filmmaker who co-directed one film listed in some South African filmographies. Feature film: *Sanders of the River / Death Drums Along the River* (English, 1964)

Hurwitz, Harry. South African filmmaker. Feature films: *Rally / Safari 3000* (English and Afrikaans, 1980), *Fleshtone* (English, 1993)

Hussein, Adel Aziz. Egyptian filmmaker. Feature film: *Love / Houbb* (1948)

Hussein, Farid Chawki. Egyptian filmmaker. Feature film: *Oh My Country . . . / Ah yâ balad ah . . .* (1986)

Hussein, Nasser. Egyptian filmmaker. Feature films: *No, Mummy / Lâ yâ oummî* (1979), *Poor, My Children / al-Fouqarâ awlâdii* (1980), *What Love Did to Daddy / ᶜAmalîh al-houbb fî bâbâ* (1980), *He Who Has Duped the Devils / Illî dihik ᶜalâ al-chayâtîn* (1981), *Soutouhi Is Perched in the Tree / Soutouhî fawq al-chagarah* (1983), *They Kill Honest People / Innahoum yaqtouloun al-chourafâ* (1984), *The Market / al-Souq* (1987), *The Past Surges Up Again / ᶜAwdat al-mâdî* (1987), *A Smile in Sad Eyes / Ibtisâmah fî ᶜouyoun hazînah* (1987), *Drums in the Night / Touboul fî-l-layl* (1987), *Fatality / al-Nasîb maktoub* (1987), *Youth for All Ages / Chabâb li-koull al-Agyâl* (1988), *Conqueror of the Horsemen / Qâhir al-foursân* (1988), *The Secondaryschool Teacher's Suicide / Intihâr moudarris thâniawî* (1989), *The Provincials Arrive / al-Saᵓâydah goum* (1989), *The Tough Guys from the Slaughterhouse / Foutouwwat al-Salakhânah* (1989), *Hello Soussou / Sallim lî ᶜalâ Sousou* (1990), *When the Cat's Away, the Mice Play / Mouled w-sâhbouh ghâyib* (1990), *Sayyed the Crook / al-Wâd Sayyed al-nassâb* (1990), *The Crook and the Lady / al-Souᵓlouk wa-l-hânim* (1991), *The Fool / al-Ghachîm* (1991), *The She-Devils in Prison / al-Mouchâghibât fî-l-sigᵓn* (1991), *The Hunter of Tyrants / Sâᵓid al-Gabâbirah* (1991), *The Wolf's Lair / Wakr al-dhiᵓb* (1992), *The Troublemakers in the Navy / al-Mouchâghiboun fî-l-bahriyyah* (1992), *The Massacre of the Honest / Madhbahat al-chourafâᵓ* (1992), *The Road to the Asylum / al-Tarîq li-moustachfâ al-magânîn* (1992), *The Troublemakers at Nouibi / Mouchâghiboun fî nouibiᵓ* (1992), *The Peasants Arrive / al-Fallâhîn ahom* (1992), *Beware of Azouz / Khallî bâlak min ᶜAzzouz* (1992), *A Provincial in the Army / Saᵓîdî fî-l-gaych* (1993), *The Dancers' Alley / Darb al-ᵓawâlim* (1994)

Ibrahim, Hassan. Egyptian filmmaker. Feature film: *Save this Family / Anqidhou hâdhini al-ᵓâᵓilah* (1979), *A Story in Two Words / Hikâyah fî kalimatayn* (1985), *The Resort for Bonviveurs /* *Mahattat al-ouns* (1985), *The Cat was a Lion / al-Qitt aslouh asad* (1985), *The Doorman / al-Bîh al-bawâb* (1987), *Kill My Wife and You'll Have My Gratitude / Iqtil mirâtî we lak tahiyyâti* (1990), *A Woman Pays the Price / Imraᵓah tadfaᵓ al-thaman* (1993), *Madam's Chauffeur / Sawwâq al-hânim* (1994)

Ibrahim, Youssef. Egyptian filmmaker. Feature film: *Oleich in the Army / ᶜOleich dakhal al-gueich* (1989)

Ide, Kamal. Egyptian filmmaker. Feature films: *Hot Line / al-Khatt al-sâkhin* (1986), *Marriage with Premeditation / Gawâz maᵓ sabq al-isrâr* (1987)

Idris, Ali. Egyptian filmmaker. Graduated the Cairo Higher Film Institute in 1987. Feature films: *Friends or Buisness / Ashaab walla buisiness* (2001), *The Danish Experiment / al-tagruba al-Danemarkeya* (2003), *Security Police Bridegroom / ᶜArees min geha amneya* (2004), *Karim's Harem / Hareem Kareem* (2005), *Love Talk / Kalaam fil hubb* (2006), *Dr. Omar's Gang / ᶜIsabet al-Doktoor Omar* (2007), *Morgan Ahmed Morgan / Morgaan Ahmed Morgaan* (2007)

Ihsaan, Wael. Egyptian filmmaker. Feature films: *Al-Lemby / al-Lemby* (2002), *You-Know-Who / Illy baly balak* (2003), *The Pasha Is a Student / al-Basha telmiz* (2004), *Zaki Chan / Zaki Chan* (2005), *Criminal Countenance / Wesh igraam* (2006), *Emergency / Zarf Tarek* (2006), *Speed Bump / Matabb senaaᵓy* (2006), *Dukki's Nightingale / ᵓAndaleeb al-dukki* (2007)

Imam, Rami. Egyptian filmmaker. Son of the star actor Adel Imam. Feature films: *Prince of Darkness / Ameer al-zalaam* (2002), *Inherently Stupid / Ghaby menno fih* (2004), *Booha* (2005), *Eighth of a Dozen Thugs / 1/8 Dastet Ashrar* (2006)

Imunga Ivanga, Léon (b. 1967 in Libreville). Gabonese screenwriter and filmmaker. Studied literature at university in Libreville and filmmaking at the Fondation Européenne des Métiers de l'Image et du Son (FEMIS) in Paris.

Made half-a-dozen varied shorts in the 1990s and achieved an international reputation and the top prize, the *Tanit d'or*, at the Journées Cinématographiques de Carthage (JCC) with his debut feature, the first made in Gabon for 20 years. Feature films: *Money / Dôlè* (1999), *The Shadow of Liberty / L'Ombre de Liberty* (2006)

Inglesby, Mike. South African filmmaker. Feature film: *The Rat* (English, 1988)

Irving, David. South African filmmaker. Feature film: *Perfume of the Cyclone* (English, 1990)

Isaacs, Ronnie. South African filmmaker. Specialist producer and director of African-language films. Feature films: *Umzingeli* (Zulu, 1979), *Botsotso* (Zulu, 1979), *Umghlali* (Zulu, 1980), *Botsotso II* (Zulu, 1980), *Umdhale* (Zulu, 1980), *Biza Tzimtombi* (Zulu, 1981), *Vimba Isipoko* (Sotho, 1981), *So-Manga* (Zulu, 1981), *Pina Ya Qetelo* (Sotho, 1982), *Umjuluko Me Gazi* (Zulu / English, 1982), *Johnny Tough* (English / Zulu, 1983), *The Spin of Death* (English, 1984), *Snap* (Zulu, 1984), *One More Shot* (English, 1984), *Fanakalo* (Sotho, 1984), *Starbound* (English / Zulu, 1985), *Rhino* (English, 1988), *Warriors from Hell* (English, 1989)

Ismaïl, Fayek. Egyptian filmmaker. Feature films: *From a Good Family / Awlâd al-Ousoul* (1985), *Vengeance / al-Intiqâm* (1986)

Ismaïl, Hassan. Egyptian filmmaker. Feature film: *Daddy Is the Last to be Told / Bâbâ âkhir man ya'lam* (1975),

Ismaïl, Mahmoud. Egyptian filmmaker. Feature films: *Fitna / Fitnah* (1948), *Watch Out for Your Wallet / Ou'a al-mahfazah* (1949), *Love and Coaxing / Houbb wa dala'* (1959), *The Flower-seller / Bayyâ'at al-ward* (1959), *The Bridge of the Immortals / Guisr al-khâlidîn* (1960), *The Hero's Path / Tarîq al-abtâl* (1961)

Ismaïl, Mohamed (b. 1951 in Teuan). Moroccan filmmaker. Studied law in Rabat and then worked in Moroccan television, directing dramas, films and variety shows. Active as a feature

film producer through his company Mia Production. Feature films: *Aouchtam* (1998), *And Afterwards... / Et après...* (2002), *Here and There / Ici et là* (2004), *Farewell Mothers / Adieu les mères* (2007)

Issa, Sayed (b. 1935 in Bishra; d. 1985). Egyptian filmmaker. Studied at the Vsesoyuznyi gosudarstvennyi institut kinematografii (VGIK; All-Union State Cinema Institute) in Moscow before his first film, and again after his third. Shot his last film in a studio he built in his native village. Feature films: *Zézette / Zézette* (1961), *The Giant / al-Mârid* (1964), *The Rains have Dried Up / Gaffat al-amtâr* (1967), *The Singer / al-Moughannawâti* (1983)

Issa, Youssef. Egyptian filmmaker. Feature film: *Life Is Short / al-'Oumr ayyâm* (1964)

Jaïbi, Fadhel (b. 1945 in Ariana). Tunisian filmmaker. Studied drama in Paris and, from the early 1970s founded a succession of theatrical groups. Co-founder, with Fadhel Jaziri of the Nouveau Théâtre de Tunis. Actively engaged in the company's activities, he co-directed the video productions of some of the performances. Feature films: *The Wedding / La Noce* (Collectif du Nouveau Théâtre de Tunis, 1978), *Arab / 'Arab* (with Fadhel Jaziri, 1988), *Chichkhan / Poussière de diamants* (with Mahmoud Ben Mahmoud, 1992)

Jaziri, Fadhel (b. 1948 in Tunis). Tunisian actor filmmaker and actor. Co-founder with Fadhel Jaïbi of the Nouveau Théâtre de Tunis. Actively engaged in the theatre's stage productions, he was also involved, as co-director, in the video versions of these. Appeared as actor, most notably in Mahmoud Ben Mahmoud's *Crossing Over*. Also made a feature-length documentary on Soufi ceremonies, *Hadra* (2001). Feature films: *The Wedding / La Noce* (Collectif du Nouveau Théâtre de Tunis, 1978), *Arab / 'Arab* (with Fadhel Jaïbi, 1988)

Jebli Ouazzani, Fatima (b. 1959 in Meknes). Dutch-based filmmaker of Moroccan descent.

Emigrated in 1970 with her parents to the Netherlands, where she has lived since. Studied psychology, then filmmaking at NFTVA in Amsterdam. From 1983 worked as a reporter in Dutch radio and television and made a number of short documentaries on social issues. Though an outsider to Moroccan production structures, her first feature won the top prize at the Fifth Moroccan National Film Festival in Casablanca in 1998. Feature film: *In My Father's House / In het Huis van mijn Vader* (1997)

Jerdaan, Johan. South African filmmaker. Feature film: *Winner Take All* (English, 1984)

Jindi, Mohamed. Libyan filmmaker. Feature film: *Love in Narrow Alleys / Hub Fi al-Aziqa al-Dayiqa* (1986)

Joannou, Phil. South African filmmaker. Feature film: *Entropy* (1998)

Joffa, Bernard. South African filmmaker. Studied film and fine art at the American Film Institute in Los Angeles. Feature films: *A Woman of Colour* (English, 1996) *Letting Go* (English, 1997)

Johnson, Kwame Robert (b. 1961). Ghanaian filmmaker. Feature: *Black Home Again* (with Koffi Zokko Nartey, 1994)

Johnston, Lorrimer. South African veteran filmmaker. A major figure in South African silent film production. Feature films: *A Zulu's Devotion* (Silent, 1916), *The Silver Wolf* (Silent, 1916), *The Illicit Liquor Seller* (Silent, 1916), *The Gun-Runner* (Silent, 1916), *Sonny's Little Bit* (Silent, 1916), *Gloria* (Silent, 1916), *A Story of the Rand* (Silent, 1916)

Jones, Dominique. South African filmmaker. Feature film: *Dragonard* (English, with Gerard Kikoine, 1987)

Joubert, Danie. South African filmmaker. Feature film: *Jock / Jock of the Bushveld* (English, 1995)

Kaba, Alkaly (b. 1936 in Bamako). Malian filmmaker. Studied filmmaking at the National Film Board of Canada in Montreal. A number of documentaries. Feature films: *Walanda* (1974), *Wamba* (1976)

Kaboré, Gaston (b. 1951 in Bobodioulasso). Burkinabè filmmaker. Studied history in Ouagadougou and Paris and then filmmaking at the École Supérieure des Études Cinématographiques (ESEC) in Paris. Director of cinema in Burkina Faso (1977–1988); secretary general of the Fédération Panafricaine des Cinéastes (FEPACI; 1985–1997). Has made short films throughout his career. A major figure in African filmmaking, he initiated the 1980s trend for setting films in an imagined (and often idyllic) past. He won the top prize, the Étalon de Yennenga, at the Festival Panafricain du Cinéma de Ouagadougou (FESPACO) in 1997 with *Budd Yam*. All four of his feature films explore questions of memory, identity, and the need to be true to oneself. Feature films: *God's Gift / Wend Kuuni* (1982), *Zan Boko* (1988), *Rabi* (1992), *Buud Yam* (1996)

Kabouche, Azize (b. 1960 in Lyon). French-based filmmaker of Algerian descent. Studied drama in Paris and made numerous appearances on stage and in films. Two short films. Feature film: *Letters from Algeria / Lettres d'Algérie* (2002)

Kalarytis, Konstandino. South African filmmaker. Feature film: *Sanctuary* (English, 2005)

Kamal, Hussein (b. 1932 in Cairo). Egyptian filmmaker. Graduated from the Institut des Hautes Études Cinématographiques (IDHEC) in Paris in 1956. Worked as assistant to Youssef Chahine on *Central Station*. Has also worked in television and as stage director. His career combines critically acclaimed realist dramas and huge box-office hits. Feature films: *The Impossible / al-Moustahîl* (1965), *The Postman / al-Bostaguî* (1968), *My Father Is Perched in the Tree / Abî fawq al-chagarah* (1969 Hussein Kamal), *A Trace of Fear / Chayʾ min al-khawf* (1969), *We Don't Plant Thorns / nahnou lâ nazraʾ al-chawk* (1970), *Discussions on the Nile / Thartharah fawq al-Nîl* (1971), *The Empire of M / Am-*

bratouriyyat mîm (1972), *One Nose and Three Eyes* / *Anf wa thalâth ᶜouyoun* (1972), *My Blood, My Tears and My Smile* / *Damî wa doumouʾî wa ibtisâmatî* (1973), *Nothing Is Important* / *Lâ chayʾ yahoumm* (1975), *On a Sheet of Cellophane* / *ᶜAlâ waraq silloufân* (1975), *The Siren* / *al-Naddahah* (1975), *Love Beneath the Rain* / *al-Houbb tahta al-matar* (1975), *What a Mess* / *Moulid yâ douniâ* (1975), *Far from the Land* / *Baʾîdan ᶜan al-ard* (1976), *Those of Us from the Bus* / *Ihna, btouʾ al-otobus* (1979), *A Story Behind Every Door* / *Hikâyah warâʾ koull bâb* (1979), *My Love for Ever? Habîbî dâʾiman* (1980), *The Virgin and the White-Haired* / *al-ʾAdhrâʾ wa-l-chaʾr al-abyad* (1983), *I Beg You, Give me this Medecine* / *Argouk aʾtinî hâdhâ al-dawâʾ* (1984), *Living Legitimately* / *Ayyâm fî-l-halâl* (1985), *The Bars of the Harem* / *Qafas al-harîm* (1986), *All This Great Love* / *Koull hâdhâ al-houbb* (1988), *Berwan Alley* / *Hârat Bergwan* (1989), *The Drug Addicts* / *al-Masâtîl* (1991), *Light in the Eyes* / *Nour al-ʾouyoun* (1991), *The Cock and His Harem* / *Dîk al-barâbir* (1992), *Sayyed the Servant* / *al-Wâd Sayyed al-chaghghâl* (1993), *Tie the Scarf Around My Hips . . .* / *Hazzemny ya* (1997)

Kamal, Kamal (b. 1961 in Berkane). Moroccan filmmaker. After initial university studies in Oujda, he studied film at the Conservatoire Libre du Cinéma Français (CLCF) in Paris. Television work and video commercials. Feature films: *Tayf Nizar* (2002), *Moroccan Symphony* / *Symphonie marocaine* (2005)

Kamba, Sébastien (b. 1941 in Congo). Congolese filmmaker. Studied at the Office de Copération Radiophonique (OCORA) in Paris and worked as a trainee in French television. Also work as a teacher. A dozen documentaries before and after his sole pioneering feature. Feature film: *The Price of a Marriage* / *La Rançon d'une alliance* (1973)

Kamel, Abbas. Egyptian filmmaker. Younger brother of Ahmed Galal and Fawzi Hussein. Feature films: *He Who Kisses Too Much* / *Sâhib bâlayn* (1946), *The Siren* / *ᶜArousat al-bahr* (1947), *The Boss's Daughter* / *Bint al-mouʾallim* (1947), *It Was an Angel* / *Kânat malâkan* (1947),

The Beautiful Woman's Handkerchief / *Mandîl al-hilou* (1949), *The Mayor's Daughter* / *Bint al-ʾoumdah* (1949), *The Horseshoe* / *Hadwat al-hisân* (1949), *The Handsome Dark-haired Man* / *Asmar wa gamîl* (1950), *My Eye Is Blinking* / *ᶜAynî bi-triff* (1950), *Good News* / *Khabar abyad* (1951), *Madam Feyrouz* / *Fayrouz hânim* (1951), *The Window of My Love* / *Choubbâk habîbî* (1951), *The Beauty's Cheek* / *Khadd al-gamîl* (1951), *Respected Sir* / *Hadrat al-mouhtaram* (1952), *The Administrative Council* / *Maglis al-idârah* (1953), *Fate* / *al-Mouqaddar wa-l-maktoub* (1953), *Hold Your Tongue* / *Lisânak hisânak* (1953), *A Dozen Handkerchiefs* / *Dastit manâdîl* (1954), *The Sugar Doll* / *ᶜArousat al-moulid* (1955), *Your Health* / *Fî sihhitak* (1955), *Unappeased Vengeance* / *Târ bâyit* (1955), *Heaven's Mercy* / *Rahmah min al-samâʾ* (1958), *My Wife's Husband* / *ᶜArîs mirâtî* (1959), *My Mother and I* / *Anâ wa oummî* (1960), *Elixir H 3* / *H 3* (1961), *Martyr of the Divine Love* / *Chahîdat al-houbb al-ilâhî* (1962), *The Reason and Money* / *al-ʾAql wa-l-mâl* (1965), *Take Me Away with You* / *Khoudnî maʾâk* (1966), *I'm the Doctor* / *Anâ al-doktor* (1968), *Miss Manal's Diary* / *Moudhakkarât al-ânisar Manâl* (1971), *It Was Another Time . . .* / *Kân wa kân wa kân* (1977)

Kamel, Mostafa. Egyptian filmmaker. Feature film: *Victims of the Feudal System* / *Dahâyâ al-iqtâ* (1955)

Kamoun, Moez (b. 1962 in Tunis). Tunisian filmmaker. Studied at the École Supérieure des Études Cinématographiques (ESEC) in Paris. Worked as assistant to numerous Tunisian and foreign directors. Several short films. Feature film: *Men's Words* / *Parole d'hommes* (2004)

Kamwa, Daniel (b. 1943 in Nkongsamba). Cameroonian filmmaker. Studied filmmaking at the University of Paris VIII and dance at the Académie Internationale de Danse. Also studied at the Actors Studio and worked as an actor. His first two features were highly sucessful comedies. Feature films: *Pousse-Pousse* (1975), *Our Daughter* / *Notre fille* (1980), *Totor* (1993), *The Circle of Powers* / *Le Cercle des pouvoirs* (1997, with Jules Takam)

Kaplan, Ken. South African filmmaker. Feature film: *Pure Blood* (English, 1999)

Karama, Issa. Egyptian filmmaker. Feature films: *You Deserve It / Halâl ʿalayk* (1952), *Take Pity on Me / Harâm ʿalayk* (1953), *For Love / Fî sabîl al-houbb* (1955), *Take Your Chance / Garrab hazzak* (1956), *Ishmaell Yassine in the Waxworks / Ismâʾîl Yâsîn fî moutʾhaf al-chamʾ* (1956), *Ishmael Yassine in the Asylum / Ismâʾîl Yâsîn fî moustachfa al-magânîn* (1958), *The Guesthouse of Surprises / Loukândat al-moufâgaʾât* (1959), *My Mother-in-Law Is an Angel / Hamâtî malâk* (1959), *Moon of Honey and Gall / Chahr ʿasal basal* (1960), *Husband for Hire / Zawg li-l-lîgâr* (1961), *Husbands and Summer / al-Azwâg wa-l-sayf* (1961), *Marriage in Danger / Gawâz fî khatar* (1963), *Reckless Youth / Âkhir chaqâwah* (1964), *The Midnight Story / Hikâyat nouss al-leil* (1964), *The Pupils' Notes / Nimar al-talâmidhah* (1964), *The Ultimate Madness / Âkhir guinân* (1965), *A Widow Is Requested / Matloub armalah* (1966), *That Man Will Drive Me Mad / al-Râguil dah hayganninni* (1968), *A Pretty, Boisterous Girl / Hilwah wa chaqiyyah* (1968), *Youthful Adventure / Moughâmarat Chabâb* (1970)

Karim, Alaa. Egyptian filmmaker. Feature films: *Suspicion / Ichtibâh* (1991), *85 at the Crime / 85 Guinâyat* (1993), *The Garage / al-Garage* (1995), *A Woman and Five Men / Imraʾa wa khamas regaal* (1997), *Zanqet El Settaat / Zanqet el settaat* (2000), *The First Time You Fall in Love / Awwel marra teheb* (2003)

Karim, Mohamed (b. 1896 in Cairo; d. 1972). Egyptian veteran filmmaker. Appeared in two short films in 1918, then studied filmmaking in Rome and Berlin. Made a silent feature, *Zeinab / Zeinab* (1930), and the first real Egyptian sound film, *Sons of Aristocrats / Awlâd al-Dhawât* (1932), as well as a series with the singer Abdel Wahab. Head of the Cairo Higher Film Institute from 1959 till 1967. Features: *Zeinab / Zeinab* (1930), *Sons of Aristocrats / Awlâd al-Dhawât* (1932), *The White Rose / al-Wardah al-baydâʾ* (1933), *Tears of Love / Doumouʾ al-houbb* (1935), *Long Live Love / Yahyâ al-houbb* (1938),

Happy Day / Yawm saʾîd (1940), *Forbidden Love / Mamnouʾ al-houbb* (1942), *Love at First Sight / Rasâsah fî-l-qalb* (1944), *Dounia / Douniâ* (1946), *Their Excellencies / Ashâb al-saʾâdah* (1946), *I'm No Angel / Lastou Malâkan* (1946), *Eternal Love / Houbb lâ Yamout* (1948), *Nahed / Nâhid* (1952), *Zeinab / Zeinab* (1952), *Love's Madness / Gounoun al-houbb* (1954), *Dalila / Dalîlah* (1956), *Heart of Gold / Qalb min dhadhab* (1959)

Kassari, Yasmine (b. 1968 in Jerada). Morrocan filmmaker. Studied at the Institut National des Arts du Spectacle et Techniques de Diffusion (INSAS) in Brussels, graduating in 1997. She still lives in Belgium. Made two short films and a documentary which were widely shown at international festivals. Her first feature won the top prize at the 2005 National Morocain Film Festival. Feature film: *The Sleeping Child / L'Enfant endormi* (2004)

Kassem, Chirine. Egyptian filmmaker. Feature film: *The Player / al-Mouqâmir* (1994)

Kassem, Gamal. Egyptian filmmaker. Feature film: *Coming Soon / Gayy fil sareeʾ* (2005)

Kateb, Mustapha. Algerian actor and filmmaker. Appeared in several of the early films of Mustapha Badie (*The Night Is Afraid of the Sun*), Mohamed Lakhdar Hamina (*The Wind from the Aurès, Hassan Terro*), and Ahmed Rachedi (*Opium and the Stick*). Feature film: *El Ghoula* (1972)

Katelman, Michael. South African filmmaker. Feature film: *Primeval* (English, 2006)

Keating, Lulu. South African filmmaker. Feature film: *The Midday Sun* (English, 1988)

Kechiche, Abdellatif (b. 1960 in Tunis). French-based filmmaker of Tunisian descent. Worked as an actor, in the theatre and on screen, taking leading roles in Abdelkrim Bahloul's *Mint Tea* (1984) and André Téchiné's *The Innocents*. Won four of the French film industry's top annual awards (the césars) with his second feature.

Feature films: *Voltaire's Fault / La Faute à Voltaire* (2000), *The Scam / L'Esquive* (2004), *The Secret of the Grain / La Graine et le mulet* (2007)

Keïta, Mama (b. 1956, in Dakar, Senegal). Guinean filmmaker. Studied law at the Université Paris I and worked as a writer for both theatre aand screen. Began with short fictional films in the early 1980s. His second feature is the completion of a film begun, shortly before his death, by David Achkar (1960–98). Feature films: *The Eleventh Commandment / Le 11e commandement* aka *Choose a Friend / Choisis-toi un ami* (1997), *The River / Le Fleuve* (2003), *The Snake's Smile / Le Sourire du serpent* (2004)

Kente, Gibson. South African filmmaker. Co-directed one anti-apartheid feature film which was not released in South Africa: *How Long?* (English, with Ben Nanoyi, 1976)

Kettani, Driss (b. 1947 in Salé; d. 1994). Moroccan filmmaker. Trained in the theatre in Paris, he worked as an actor and television director. Further training at the Office de Radiodiffusion et de Télévision Française (ORTF) in Paris and at the BBC in London. Work as theatre director after his return to Morocco in 1978. In the 1980s taught at the Insitut Supérieur d'Art Dramatique et d'Animation Culturelle de Rabat (ISADAC). Feature film: *The Travelling Showman's Day / Le Jour du forain* (with Mohamed Abdelkrim Derkaoui, 1984)

Kettle, Ross. South African filmmaker. Feature film: *After the Rain* (English, 1998)

Keyser, Anthony. South African filmmaker. Feature film: *Skadu van Gister* (Afrikaans, with Hendrick Kotze, 1961)

Khachim, Khaled. Libyan filmmaker. Feature film: *The Battle of Taghrift / Ma'rakat Taqraft* (with Mohamed Ayad Driza, 1979)

Khalifa, Hani (b. 1970 at Sohaj in Upper Egypt). Egyptian filmmaker. Studied law at the University of Asiout and then filmmaking at the Cairo

Higher Film Institute. Three short films. Feature film: *Sleepless Nights / Sahar al-layali* (2003)

Khalil, Abdel Aziz. Egyptian silent filmmaker. Silent feature: *Souad the Gipsy / Sou'âd al-ghagariyya* (with Fardous Hassan, 1928)

Khalil, Adli. Egyptian filmmaker. Feature films: *Heart in the Night / qalb fi-l-zalâm* (1960), *Women Who Flee Love / Hâribât min al-houbb* (1970), *Chahira / Chahîrah* (1975), *Love . . . in a Dead End / al-Houbb . . . fi tarîq masdoud* (1977), *Wanted Dead or Alive / Matloub hayyan aw mayyitan* (1984), *The Car Thief / Sâriq al-sayyârât* (1986), *A Smile between the Tears / Ibtisâmah fi nahr al-doumou'* (1988), *This Kind of Men / Naw'min al-rigâl* (1988), *The Prosecution Pleads Not Guilty / al-Niyâbah tatloub al-barâ'ah* (1990), *The Game of Crime / Lou'bat al-qatl* (1994)

Khalil, Hala (b. 1967 in Cairo) Egyptian filmmaker. She abandoned engineering studies to enrol in the Cairo Higher Film Institute, graduating in 1992. Work as film critic and television director. Feature films: *The Best Times / Ahla aliawqaat* (2004), *Cut and Paste / Qass wa lazq* (2007)

Khalil, Mahmoud. Egyptian filmmaker. Feature film: *Mustapha or The Little Magician / Mostafa aw al-sâhir al-saghîr* (1932)

Khan, Feroz. South African filmmaker. Feature film: *Gandhi My Father* (2007)

Khan, Mohamed (b. 1942 in Cairo). Egyptian filmmaker. Studied at the London School of Film Technique and worked as assistant in Beirut in the mid-1960s. Wrote a book, *An Introduction to the Egyptian Cinema*. A leading figure among the new generation of the 1980s. Feature films: *A Glimpse of Sunshine / Darbat chams* (1980), *Desire / al-Raghbah* 1980), *Rendezvous for Dinner / Maw'id 'alâ al-'achâ'* (1981), *A Bird on the Path / Tâ'ir 'alâ al-tartîq* (1981), *Vengeance / al-Tha'r* (1982), *Half-a-Million / Nisf arnab* (1983), *The Professional / al-Hirrîf* (1984), *Reported Missing / Kharaga wa lam ya'oud*

(1985), *The Ballad of Omar / Michwâr ʿOumar* (1986), *A Citizen's Return / ʿAwdat mouwâtin* (1986), *The Wife of an Important Man / Zawgat ragoul mouhim* (1988), *Dreams of Hind and Camellia / Ahlâm Hind wa Kâmîliya* (1988), *Supermurket / Super Market* (1990), *The Knight of the City / Fâris al-madînah* (1992), *Mister Karate / Mister Karaté* (1993), *Al-Ghaqana / al-Gharqânah* (1993), *A Very Hot Day / Youm harr gedan* (1995), *Days of Sadat / Ayyaam El Sadat* (2001), *Downtown Girls / Banaat wist al-balad* (2005), *In the Heliopolis Flat / Fi chaqqet masr el gedeeda* (2007). Khan also shot a digitally produced feature film in 2004 which was not transferred to celluloid: *The Crook / Klefty*

Khattab, Abdel Alim. Egyptian filmmaker. Feature films: *Salwa / Salwa* (1946), *Island of Dreams / Gazîrat al-ahlâm* (1951), *El-Alamain / al-ʾAlamayn* (1965)

Khayat, Mustapha (b. 1944 in Casablanca). Moroccan filmmaker. Studied filmmaking at the Office de Radiodiffusion et de Télévision Française (ORTF) in Paris. On his return worked in Moroccan television, first as cameraman, then as producer-director. Feature film: *Dead End / L'Impasse* (1984)

Khechine, Ahmed (b. 1940 in Kairouan). Tunisian filmmaker. Initially worked as a teacher and is a product of the Tunisian amateur film movement, the Fédération Tunisienne des Cinéastes Amateurs (FTCA). Made a number of shorts in the 1960s. Feature film: *Under the Autumn Rain / Sous la pluie d'automne* (1970)

Khemir, Nacer (b. 1948 in Korba). Tunisian filmmaker. Worked in a variety of media, active as sculptor, writer and performing storyteller. Author of a series of children's stories: *Le Conte des conteurs* (1984), *Gran-père est né* (1985), *Chahrazade* (1988), *L'Ogresse* (1991), *L'Alphabet des sables* (1998), *Le Juge, la mouche et la grand-mère* (2000), *J'avale le bébé du voisin* (2000), *Le Chant des génies* (2001), *Le Livre des djinns* (2002), *La Quête d'Hassan de Samarkand* (2003). Also made a two-hour video: *In Search of the Thousand and One Nights / À la recher-* che des mille et une nuits (1991). Khemir's exquisite visions of the lost glory of Andalousia make him a unique poet of African cinema. Feature films: *The Searchers of the Desert / Les Baliseurs du désert* (1984), *The Dove's Lost Necklace / Le Collier perdu de la colombe* (1990), *BabʾAziz / BabʾAziz, le prince qui contempaît son âme* (2005)

Khidr, Ahmed. Egyptian filmmaker. Feature film: *Who Does That Lady Represent? / al-Hânim bi-l-niyâbah* (1988)

Khlifi, Omar (b. 1934 in Soliman). Tunisian filmmaker. He studied in Tunisia and France, but learned his filmmaking in the Fédération Tunisienne des Cinéastes Amateurs (FTCA), the Tunisian amateur film movement, in the context of which he made a dozen short films. Subsequently, the pioneer of Tunisian feature film who gave it a forceful voice in the 1960s. He published a history of cinema in Tunisia in 1970. Feature films: *The Dawn / L'Aube* (1966), *The Rebel / Le Rebelle* (1968), *The Fellagas / Les Fellagas* (1970), *Screams / Hurlements* (1972), *The Challenge / Le Défi* (1986)

Khodja, Liazid. Algerian filmmaker. Studied first sociology and then filmmaking at the Institut National de Cinéma (INC) in Algiers and at the Institut des Hautes Études Cinématographiques (IDHEC) in Paris. Worked widely in audio-visual media and film production in Algeria. Feature film: *Si Mohand U M'hand / L'Insoumis / The Rebel* (with Rachid Benallel, 2004)

Khorchid, Ahmed. Egyptian filmmaker. Feature film: *A Hard Man / al-Sabʾ afandî* (1951)

Kiersch, Fritz. South African filmmaker. Feature film: *Gor* (English, with Harry Towers, 1986)

Kikhya, Abdel Rahman. Egyptian filmmaker. Feature films: *Three Adolescent Girls / Thalâth fatayât mourâhiqât* (1973), *Farewell for Ever / Wadâʾan ilâ al-abad* (1976)

Kikoine, Gerard. South African filmmaker. Feature films: *Dragonard* (English, with Dominique

Jones, 1987), *Master of Dragonard Hill* (English, 1987), *Buried Alive / Ravenscroft* (English, 1988)

Kinyanjui, Wanjiru (b. 1958 in Kiambu). Kenyan filmmaker. Initially studied English and German literature, then filmmaking at the German Film and Television School in Berlin. She has worked as editor, theatre director, and radio and television journalist in Berlin. At the same time she has made a dozen short films in Kenya. Feature film: *The Battle of the Sacred Tree* (1994)

Kirstein, Hyman. South African filmmaker and producer. His sole feature is a backstage musical featuring black performers. Feature film: *Zonk* (English, 1950)

Klimovski, Léon. Maker of Egyptian feature film: *Love in the Desert / Gharâm fî-l-sahrâ* (with Gianni Vernuccio, 1959)

Knobel, Louis. South African filmmaker. Feature film: *Die Wildsboudjie* (Afrikaans, with Arthur Bennet, 1946)

Kondo, K. South African filmmaker. Feature film: *A New World Travels* (English, 1988)

Korayyem, Salah. Egyptian filmmaker. Feature films: *Modern Marriage / al-Zawâg ʿalâ al-tarîqah al-hadîthah* (1968), *We Are the Ambulance Men / Ihna boutouʾ al-isʾâf* (1984)

Korda, Zoltan. Hungarian-born director of a (British-produced) film included in all listings of South African feature films: *Cry the Beloved Country* (1951)

Kostanov. Maker of one Egyptian feature film: *The Hell of Jealousy / Gahîm al-gîrah* (1953)

Kotze Hendrick. South African filmmaker. Feature film: *Skadu van Gister* (Afrikaans, with Anthony Keyser, 1961)

Koula, Jean-Louis (b. 1950 in Mona). Ivorian filmmaker. Studied filmmaking at the Conser-vatoire Libre du Cinéma Français (CLCF) in Paris. Worked as assistant director and made a number of documentaries. His first feature explores the tradition / modernity divide by examining a drama caused by the difference between traditional and modern rules of inheritance. Feature film: *Adja Tio* (1980)

Koumba-Bididi, Henri-Joseph (b. 1957 in Omboué). Gabonese filmmaker. Studied film-making at the École Supérieure des Études Cinématographiques (ESEC) in Paris. Assistant director general of Gabonese television (RTG). A number of short films. With Léon Imunga Ivanga, part of the renewal of Gabonese cinema after a 20-year gap. Feature film: *The Elephant's Balls / Les Couilles de l'éléphant* (2001)

Kouyaté, Assane (b. 1954 in Bamako). Malian filmmaker. Studied filmmaking at the Vsesoyuznyi gosudarstvennyi institut kinematografii (VGIK; All-Union State Cinema Institute) in Moscow. His debut feature revives the tradition / modernity theme with the tale of a rejected youth who returns to transform the life of his village, told in a classic visual style. Feature film: *Kabala* (2002)

Kouyaté, Dani (b. 1961 in Bobodioulasso). Burkinabè filmmaker. Son of the actor and griot Sotigui Kouyaté. Studied filmmaking at the University of Paris VIII and at the Sorbonne. Some work in television. His first two features are major works: imaginative evocations of the African past, drawing on oral story-telling techniques. He made a 50-minute documentary on the African historian *Joseph Ki-Zerbo* in 2005. Feature films: *Keita, The Heritage of the Griot / Keïta, l'héritage du griot* (1994), *Sia, le rêve du python* (2000), *Ouaga Saga* (2004)

Kouyate, Djibril (b. 1942 in Bamako). Malian filmmaker. Studied filmmaking at the Vsesoyuznyi gosudarstvennyi institut kinematografii (VGIK; All-Union State Cinema Institute) in Moscow. A number of documentaries for the Ministry of Information. Feature film: *Tiefing* (1963)

Kramp, Fritz. German filmmaker hired to make the first features at the new Misr studios in Cairo. Egyptian feature films: *Weddad / Wedad* (1936), *Lachine / Lachine* (1938)

Krim, Rachida (1955 at Alès). French-based filmmaker of Algerian descent. She studied painting at the schools of fine art in Montpellier and Nîmes. Made a number of short films from 1992 and a five-part television series on sexuality and AIDS in 2002. Feature film: *Under Women's Feet / Sous les pieds des femmes* (1996)

Kruger, Kobus. South African filmmaker. Son-in-law of Jamie Uys who produced his first feature. Feature film: *Funny People* (Afrikaans/English, 1976)

Ktari, Naceur (b. 1943 in Sayada). Tunisian filmmaker. Studied filmmaking in Paris (at the Institut des Hautes Études Cinématographiques [IDHEC], the CCF, and the Sorbonne) and in Rome (at the Centro sperimentale di cinematografia). Worked as assistant on Tunisian films and also foreign films shot in Tunisia, including Steven Spielberg's *Raiders of the Lost Ark* in 1981. There is a 20-year gap between his first (Libyan co-produced) film, *The Ambassadors*, which won the top prize, the *Tanit d'or*, at the Journées Cinématographiques de Carthage (JCC) in 1976, and his second. Feature films: *The Ambassadors / Les Ambassadeurs* (1975), *Be My Friend / Sois mon amie* (2000)

Ktiri Idrissi, Naguib (b. in Casablanca). US-based filmmaker of Moroccan descent. Studied at the University of California at Los Angeles (UCLA) and taught film at Loyola Marymount College in San Francisco. He was producer, director, scriptwriter, editor, sound recordist, and co-cameraman for his first (16mm) feature, which was shown at the Journées Cinématographiques de Carthage (JCC) in 1992 as a Moroccan film, but is not included in the official Centre Cinématographique Marocain (CCM) listings. Feature film: *Aziz and Ito: A Moroccan Wedding / Aziz et Ito, un mariage marocain* (1991)

Kuhle, Hans. South African filmmaker. Feature films: *Danger Coast* (English, 1986), *Quiet Thunder* (English, 1987)

Kuhn, Gustav. South African filmmaker. Feature film: *Ouma Se Slim Kind* (Afrikaans, 2005)

Labib, Raid. Egyptian filmmaker. Feature film: *Zakeya Zakareya Goes to Parliament / Zakeya Zakareya fi al barlamaan* (2001)

Lachine, Hani (b. 1951 in Cairo). Egyptian filmmaker. Graduated from the Cairo Higher Film Institute in 1976. His debut feature was the first film made by Egyptian television for cinema release (and marked the return to Egyptian cinema of Omar Sharif, after a 20-year absence). Feature films: *Ayoub / Ayyoub* (1984), *The Puppeteer / al-Aragoz* (1989), *Why, Dunia? / Lîh yâ douniâ* (1994)

Ladebo, Ladi (Olasubomi Oladipupo Loladere) (b. 1943 at Ijebu Odi). Nigerian filmmaker. Studied businesss at Yaba College of Technology, then business administration at Bowling State University, Ohio. Also received an MBA at New York University Graduate School and worked in advertising. Producer and/or scriptwriter on Ossie Davies's *Countdown at Kusini* and Jab Adu's *Bisi, Daughter of the River*. Feature films: *I Too Sing Nigeria* (English, 1985), *Children of God* (English, 1985), *Vendor* (1988), *Eewo / Taboo* (English, 1989), *Pariah* (English, 1994), *Power*, aka *The Throne* (English, 1998), *Baba Zak* (English, 1999), *Heritage* (English, 2002)

Ladjimi, Moktar (b. 1975 in Monastir). Tunisian filmmaker. Studied at the Institut des Hautes Études Cinématographiques (IDHEC) in Paris, where he now lives. Numerous shorts and videos, best known of which is his compilation, *Colonial Cinema / Le Ciné colonial* (1997). Feature film: *Summer Wedding / Noce d'été* (2004)

Lagtaâ, Abdelkader (b. 1948 in Casablanca). Moroccan filmmaker. Studied filmmaking at the Lodz film school in Poland. Some television work. Formed part of the collective which made

Cinders of the Vineyard / Les cendres du clos in 1977. His forceful work from the 1990s adds a new political edge to Moroccan realist filmmaking. Feature films: *A Love Affair in Casablanca / Un amour à Casablanca* (1991), *The Closed Door / La Porte close* (1995, released 2000), *The Casablancans / Les Casablancais* (1998), *Face to Face / Face à face* (2003), *Yasmine and Men / Yasmine et les hommes* (2007)

Laham, Doureid. Syrian director of one Egyptian feature film: *Little Fathers / al-Abaaʾ al-sighaar* (2005)

Lahlou, Latif (b. 1939 in El Jadida). Moroccan filmmaker. Studied filmmaking at the Institut des Hautes Études Cinématographiques (IDHEC) and sociology at the Sorbonne in Paris. Worked for a time in French television. One of the pioneers of the Moroccan realist tradition of filmmaking. Feature films: *Spring Sunshine / Soleil de printemps* (1969), *The Compromise / La Compromission* (1986), *Samira's Garden / Le jardin de Samira* (2007)

Lahlou, Nabyl (b. 1945 in Fez). Moroccan playwright and filmmaker. Studied drama in Paris at the Théatre National Populaire. Numerous plays produced but not published, in French: *Ophélie n'est pas morte* (1972), *Schrischamatury* (1974), and in Arabic: *Les Milliardaires* (1968), *Les Tortues* (1970), *La Grande Kermesse* (1971), *Stop* (1971), *Le Bal n'aura pas lieu sur la plage* (1971), *Asseyez-vous sur les cadavres* (1974). His films, which show clearly his theatrical inclinations are often sardonic fables, bristling with ideas and invention. Feature films: *Al Kanfoudi* (1978), *The Governor-General of Chakerbakerben Island / Le gouverneur-général de l'île de Chakerbakerben* (1980), *Brahim Who? / Brahim qui?* (1982), *The Soul That Brays / L'Âme qu braît* (1984), *Komany* (1989), *The Night of the Crime / La Nuit du crime* (1992), *The Years of Exile / Les Années de l'exil* (2002), *Tabite or Not Tabite* (2006)

Lakhdar Hamina, Malek (b. 1962 in Algeria). Algerian filmmaker, son of Mohamed Lakh-dar Hamina. Child actor in his father's films. Studied drama in the United States. His first feature was well received but he has not made a second. Feature film: *Autumn—October in Algiers / Automne—octobre à Alger* (1992)

Lakhdar Hamina, Mohamed (b. 1934 in M'sila). Algerian filmmaker. Worked for the GPRA in Tunis. Studied briefly at the Filmov Akademie Múzickych Umení (FAMU; the Film & Television Faculty of the Academy of Performing Arts) in Prague and worked in the Czech studios. Head of the Office des Actualités Algériennes (OAA) and later of the Office National du Commerce et de l'Industre Cinématographique (ONCIC) and one of the most prominent and dominating personalities in early Algerian filmmaking. Won the Palme d'or at Cannes, with his super-production *Chronicle of the Years of Embers,* becoming the first Arab director to achieve such a distinction. Feature films: *The Wind from the Aurès / Le Vent des Aurès* (1966), *Hassan Terro* (1968), *December / Décembre* (1972), *Chronicle of the Years of Embers / Chronique des années de braise* (1975), *Sand Storm / Vent de sable* (1982), *The Last Image / La Dernière image* (1986)

Lakhmari, Nour-Eddine (b. 1964 at Safi). Moroccan filmmaker resident in Norway since 1986. Studied chemistry in France and Norway, before turning to film which he studied at CNED in Paris and at the Oslo Film & TV Akademie. Also studied Method Acting at the Lee Strasberg School in New York. From the mid-1990s he made a number of short films and videos which were shown at various festivals. Feature film: *The Look / Le Regard* (2004)

Lallem, Ahmed (b. 1940 in Sétif). Algerian filmmaker. An FLN militant, he studied briefly at the Institut des Hautes Études Cinématographiques (IDHEC) in Paris and then at the Lodz film school in Poland. Author of a number of striking documentary films after his feature debut, including *Women / Elles* (1966) and its sequel *Algerian Women Thirty Years On / Algériennes,* *trente ans après* (1996). Feature films: *Forbidden Zone / Zone interdite* (1974), *Barriers / Barrières* (1977)

Lama, Ibrahim (b. 1904 in Chili, of Palestinian origin; d. 1953). Veteran Egyptian filmmaker. His first film, *A Kiss in the Desert,* was inspired by the Hollywood film *Son of the Sheikh* and starred his brother Badr Lama, who appeared in twenty of his features. A specialist in historical films and bedouin dramas. Silent features: *A Kiss in the Desert / Qoublah fî-l-sahrâ* (1928), *Drama at the Pyramides / Fâguiʾah fawq al-haram* (1928), *The Miracle of Love / Mouʾguizat al-haubb* (1930). Sound feature films: *The Victims / al-Dahyâyâ* (1932), *The Shadow of the Past / Chabah al-mâdi* (1934), *The Victims / al-Dahâyâ* (with Bahiga Hafez, 1935), *Marouf the Bedouin / Maʾrouf al-badawî* (1935), *The Escaped Prisoner / al-Hârib* (1936), *As Requested / Izz al-talab* (1937), *Souls in Distress / Noufous hâʾirah* (1938), *The Lost Treasure / al-Kanz al-mahfqoud* (1939), *Cairo Nights / Layâli al-Qâhirah* (1939), *Qays and Leila / Qays wa Layla* (1939), *A Man between Two Women / Ragoul bayna imraʾatayn* (1940), *A Cry in the Night / Sarkhah fî-layl* (1940), *Saladin / Salah Eddine al-Ayyoubî* (1941), *The Son of the Desert / Ibn al-sahrâ* (1942), *The Mysteries of Life / Khafâyâ al-douniâ* (1942), *Cleopatra / Cléôbatra* (1943), *The Call of Blood / Nidâ al-dam* (1943), *Down with Love / Yasqout al-houbb* (1944), *The Ideal Suitor / ʿArîs al-hanâ* (1944), *Wahida / Wahîdah* (1944), *Money / al-Foulous* (1945), *The False Bey / al-Beh al-mouzayyat* (1945), *The Girl from the East / Bint al-charq* (1946), *The Beautiful Bedouin Girl / al-Badawiyya al-hasnâʾ* (1947), *The Treasure of Happiness / Kanz al-saʾâdah* (1947), *The Safest Route / Sikkat al-salâmah* (1948), *The Missing Link / al-Halqah al-mafqoudah* (1948), *Spring Storm / ʿÂsifah fî-l-rabî* (1951), *The Caravan Passes By / alʾQâfilah tasîr* (1951)

Lamei, Ihaab. Egyptian filmmaker. Feature films: *At First Sight / Min nzret ain* (2003), *The Day I Fell in Love / Kaan youm houbbak* (2004), *Private Affairs / ʿIlaqaat khassa* (2007)

Lamy, Benoît. Belgian co-director of Mweze Ngangura's debut feature: *Life is Good / La Vie est belle* (1987)

Lane, Andrew. South African filmmaker. Feature film: *Jake Speed* (English, with Martin Walters, 1986)

Laplaine, José Zeka (b. 1960 at Iiebo in Congo, of mixed Congolese and Portuguese descent). Democratic Republic of Congo filmmaker. Studied in various European cities (the American University in Rome, Lisbon, Brussels and Paris). Resident in Paris. Film work as actor and assistant director (to Roger Vadim). His very varied feature films have earned him an international reputation. Co-directed a feature-length documentary, *The Black Child / L'Enfant noir,* with Laurent Chevallier in 2004. Feature films: *Macadam Tribu* (1996), *The Illegal Worker / Le Clandestin* (1996), *Paris xy* (2001), *Daddy's Garden / Le Jardin de papa* (2003), *Kinshasa Palace* (2006), *The Sacred Lake / Le Lac Sacré* (2007)

Laradji, Rabah (b. 1943 in Bordj-Benaim). Algerian filmmaker. Studied filmmaking at the Institut National de Cinéma (INC) in Algiers. Contributed an episode to the collective fictional feature, *Stories of the Revolution / Histoires de la révolution* (1970) and was part of the collective team that made the feature-length documentary *So That Algeria May Live / Pour que vive l'Algérie* (1972). Feature film: *A Roof, a Family / Un toit, une famille* (1982)

Laraki, Abdelhaï (b. 1949 in Fez). Moroccan filmmaker. Studied filmmaking at the École Louis Lumière and film history at the Sorbonne in Paris. Made a number of fictional and documentary short films., as well as commercials. Also worked in Moroccan television. Feature film: *Mona Saber* (2001), *The Scent of the Sea / Parfum de mer* (2007)

Larson, Larry. South African filmmaker. Feature films: *Deadly Passion* (English, 1985), *Double X / Deadly Licence* (English, 1989), *Para-*

noid (English, 1990), *The King's Messenger* (English, 1990)

Laskri, Amar (b. 1942 in Aïn Berda). Algerian filmmaker. Studied film in Belgrade. Contributed an episode to the collective fictional feature, *Hell for a Ten-Year-Old / L'Enfer à dix ans* (1968). He was head of the Centre Algérian pour l'Art et l'Industrie Cinématographiques (CAAIC), just before it was closed down, in 1996–1997. Feature films: *Patrol in the East / Patrouille à l'est* (1972), *The Benevolent / Al Moufid* (1978), *Gates of Silence / Les Portes du silence* (1987), *Lotus Flower / Fleur de lotus* (1998)

Lazarus, Ashley (b. 1941 in Durban). South African filmmaker. Studied economics at Cape Town University. Began his film career with documentaries and commercials. His 1977 feature was completed by the cinematographer Freddie Francis after a dispute with the producer. Feature films: *Soul Africa* (English, 1971), *'e Lollipop / Lollipop* (English, 1975), *The Golden Rendezvous* (English, with Freddie Francis, 1977)

Le Péron, Serge. French filmmaker and member of the editorial committee of *Cahiers du Cinéma* who co-directed one Moroccan feature film: *I Saw Ben Barka Get Killed / J'ai vu tuer Ben Barka* (with Saïd Smihi, 2005)

Lebcir, Mohamed (b. in Algeria). Algerian filmmaker. Studied at the École Berlioz in Paris. Worked in Algerian television. Numerous short films. Feature film: *My Friend, My Sister / Mon amie ma soeur* (2003)

Lee, Norman V. South African silent filmmaker. He made four animated films in 1917: *The Adventures of Ranger Focus, The Second Adventures of Ranger Focus, Don't You Believe It,* and *Crooks and Christmas*. Feature films: *A Tragedy of the Veldt* (Silent, 1916), *Virtue in the City* (Silent, 1920)

Legzouli, Hassan (b. 1963 in Adrej). Moroccan filmmaker. Studied in France, where he has lived since 1980, and at the Institut National des Arts du Spectacle et Techniques de Diffusion (INSAS) in Belgium, where he graduated in 1994. Seven shorts from 1990, many of which were shown at international festivals. Feature film: *Tenja* (2004)

Leonard, Don. South African filmmaker. Feature film: *Confetti Breakfast* (English, 1980)

Levey, William A. South African filmmaker. Feature film: *Committed / The Intruder* (English, 1988), *Hellgate / Ghost Town* (English, 1989)

Levring, Kristin. South African filmmaker. Feature film: *The King Is Alive* (English, 1999)

Lister, David. South African filmmaker. Prominent television director. Feature films: *Killer Instinct* (English, 1989), *Oh Shucks Here Comes UNTAG* (English, 1990), *Sport Crazy* (English, 1991), *The Rutanga Tapes* (English, 1991), *Tough Luck* (English, 1992), *Soweto Green* (English, 1995), *Panic Mechanic* (English, 1996), *The Last Leprechaun* (English, 1998), *The Story of un African Farm* (English, 2004)

Lledo, Jean-Pierre (b. 1947 in Tlemcem). Algerian filmmaker. Studied at the Vsesoyuznyi gosudarstvennyi institut kinematografii (VGIK; All-Union State Cinema Institute) in Moscow. On his return, made a number of documentaries. Has recently made well-received video documentaries, some of feature-length (such as *An Algerian Dream / Un rêve algérien*. 2004). Feature films: *The Empire of Dreams / L'Empire des rêves* (1982), *Lights / Lumières* (1992)

Locoque, H Lisle. South African silent filmmaker. Feature films: *King Solomon's Mines* (Silent, 1918), *Allan Quartermaine* (Silent, 1919)

Lomberg, Lothar. South African filmmaker. Feature film: *Gevaarlike Reis / Heisses Land* (Afrikaans, with Alfredo Medori, 1961)

Lopez, Leão (b. 1948 in Ilha de Santo Antão, Cape Verde). Cape Verde filmmaker. Studied design in Lisbon. Worked as painter and ceramist before turning to writing and filmmaking. Feature: *Island of Strife / Ilhéu do contenda* (1994)

Lopez, Temi. South African filmmaker. Feature film: *Chain of Desire* (English, 1991)

Lotfi, Ibrahim. Egyptian filmmaker. Feature films: *Gentlemen Burglars / Lousous lâkin zourafî* (1969), *We Men Are Good / Nahnou al-rigâl tayyiboun* (1971)

Lotfi, Mohamed (b. 1939 in Oujda). Moroccan producer and filmmaker. Studied at the Institut des Hautes Études Cinématographiques (IDHEC) in Paris. Occupied a wide range of production and assistant roles in Moroccan filmmaking, made shorts and worked in television. For many years president of the Moroccan Chamber of Film Producers, he directed his first feature at the age of 57. Feature film: *Rhesus or Another Person's Blood / Rhésus, ou le sang de l'autre* (1996)

Louhichi, Taïeb (b. 1948 in Mareth). Tunisian filmmaker. A product of the Fédération Tunisienne des Cinéastes Amateurs (FTCA), he studied the Institut Français de Cinéma (IFC) and the École Louis Lumière in Paris. Made over a dozen short or medium-length films in addition to his features. His debut film is an exemplary tale of the decline of traditional rural life. Feature films: *Shadow of the Earth / L'Ombre de la terre* (1982), *Leïla My Reason / Layla ma raison* (1989), *Moon Wedding / Noces de lune* (1998), *The Wind Dance / La Danse du vent* (2004)

Louw, Derrick. South African filmmaker. Feature films: *Queen of the Castle* (English, 1991), *Death Dance* (English, 1993)

Lupo, Michele. South African filmmaker. Feature film: *Bomber / The Knock-Out Cop* (English, 1984)

Luzolo Mpwati N'Tima Nsi (b. 1951 at Kimuela). Democratic Republic of Congo filmmaker. Drama training. Feature: *There's No Such Thing as Chance / Le Hasard n'existe pas* (1976)

Lynn, Robert. British director of two films included in some South African film listings. Feature films: *Code 7, Victim 5 / Table Mountain* (1964), *Coast of Skeletons* (1965), *Mocambique* (1966)

Maake, Norman. South African fimmaker. Studied at South African School of Motion Picture Medium and Live Performance (AFDA). One short and one documentary. Feature films: *Soldiers of the Rock* (English, 2003), *Homecoming* (English, 2005)

Maalouf, Youssef. Egyptian filmmaker. Feature films: *Equal in Misfortune / Fî-l-hawâ sawâ* (1951), *Life Is Beautiful / a-Douniâ hilwah* (1951), *Amal / Amâl* (1952), *Love Has No Cure / al-Hawâ mâlouch dawâ* (1952), *You Are My Life / Hayâtî inta* (1953), *Ishmael Yassine / Moughâmarât Ismâ'îl Yâsîn* (1954), *Mr Bahbouh / Bahbouh afandî* (1958), *Madam Nawaem / al-Sitt Nawâ'im* (1958), *Young Girls' Dreams / Ahlâm al-banât* (1959), *Dearest to My Heart / A'azz al-habâyib* (1961)

Mabhikwa, Isaac Meli (b. 1962 at Kwekwe). Zimbabwean filmmaker. Work as film actor and assistant. Feature: *More Time* (1992)

MacDonald, David. British director of a film included in some South African film listings. Feature film: *The Adventurers* (English, 1950)

MacFarlane, Bruce. South African filmmaker. Feature films: *Freedom Fighters* (English, with Ricki Shelach, 1986), *Kill Slade* (English, 1987), *African Express* (English,, 1988), *Burns / Under Suspicion* (English, 1988). *Voices in the Wind* (English, 1990)

Mack, Joanna. South African filmmaker. Feature film: *Lost Children of the Empire* (English, 1988)

MacKendrick, Alexander. British filmmaker of one film listed in some South African filmographies. Feature film: *Sammy Going South* (English, 1962)

Mackenzie, Peter. South African filmmaker. Feature film: *Merchants of War* (English, 1988)

MacLachlan [McLachlan], Duncan. South African filmmaker. Feature films: *Scavengers* (English, 1986), *Running Wild* (English, 1993)

MacNellie, Duncan. South African filmmaker. Feature film: *Black Gold* (English, 1988)

Madbouli, Abdel Fattah. Egyptian filmmaker. Feature films: *Al-Darb al-Ahmar / al-Darb al-Ahmar* (1985), *Rawd al-Farag / Rawd al-Farag* (1987)

Madenda Kiesse Masekela (b. 1948 at Masi-Manimba). Democratic Republic of Congo filmmaker. Half-a-dozen short films. Feature film (funded by Catholic Church): *Sister Anuarite: A Life for God / Sœur Anuarite, une vie pour dieu* (1982)

Madi, Choukri. Egyptian veteran filmmaker. Silent feature: *In the Moonlight / Tahta daw' al-qamar* (1930). Sound feature film: *Master Bahbah / al-Mou'allim Bahbah* (1935)

Madkour, Gamal. Egyptian filmmaker. Feature films: *At Last I've Got Married / Akhîran tazawwagl* (1942), *Between Two Fires / Bayn nârayn* (1945), *First Love / al-Houbb al-awwal* (1945), *I Killed My Son / Qatalt waladî* (1945), *Casino 'al-Latafa' / Casino al-latâfah* (1945), *Life Is a Struggle / al-Haydâh kifâh* (1945), *My Heart and My Sword / Qalbî wa sayfî* 1947), *When I Was Young / Ayyâm chabâbî* (1950), *The Lissener-in / Sammâ'at al-telefon* (1951), *The Beautiful Flowers / al-Zouhour al-Fâtinah* (1952), *Orphans' Possessions / Amwâl al-yatâmâ* (1952), *Aicha / 'Âichah* (1953), *Traces in the Sand / Âthar fî-l-rimâl* (1954)

Mahdi, Tozri. Egyptian filmmaker. Feature film: *Hello, It's Me, the Cat / Allo, anâ al-qittah* (1975)

Mahgoub, Alaa. Egyptian filmmaker. Feature films: *Witness for the Prosecution / Châdid ithbât* (1987), *Achmawi / 'Achmâwî* (1987), *Dance with Satan / al-Raqs ma' al-chaytân* (1993)

Mahomo, Nana (b. 1930 in Johannesburg). South African documentary filmmaker. Initially studied law and is a self-taught filmmaker.

A member of the Pan African Congress, he was one of the few black South Africans active in the 1970s, but had to spend much of his time in exile. Documentaries include *The End of Dialogue* (1970), *The Dumping Grounds* (1973) and *Last Grave at Dimbaza* (1974)

Maiga, Djingary (b. 1939 in Ouatagouna). Niger filmmaker. Actor and self-taught director. Against all the odds he persisted with 16mm feature filmmaking, with four films in 25 years. Feature films: *The Black Star / L'Etoile noire* (1975), *Black Clouds / Nuages noirs* (1979), *Black Dawn / Aube noire* (1983), *Black Friday / Vendredi noir* (1999)

Mailer, Basil. South African filmmaker. Feature film: *Africa Shakes* (English, 1966)

Makram, Ayman. Egyptian filmmaker. Feature film: *Mind Your Own Business / Khalleek fi halak* (2007)

Maldoror, Sarah (b. 1939 in Candou in the South of France). Angolan filmmaker of French-Guadeloupan descent. Married to the poet Mário de Andrade, one of the leaders of the Angolan liberation movement. Studied filmmaking at the Vsesoyuznyi gosudarstvennyi institut kinematografii (VGIK; All-Union State Cinema Institute) in Moscow. Short films on a variety of African states and subjects made from a base in Paris, beginning with *Monangambee* in 1968. Her sole fictional feature, based on a story by the novelist Luandino Vieira, who became head of the Angolan Film Institute, is a film totally committed to the independence struggle, vigorously told in a traditional narrative style. Feature film: *Sambizanga* (1972)

Mandour, Cherif. Egyptian filmmaker. Feature films: *Mediterranean Man / al-Ragoul al-abyad al-mutawasset* (2002), *What's Going on? / Howwa feeh eih?* (2002), *Excuse Us, We're Being Humiliated / La Mu'akhza i'na benetbahdel* (2005)

Mankinwa, Dr Ola. Nigerian filmmaker. Feature film: *Agbo meji* (Yoruba, 1993)

Manoughehri, Farid Fathallah. Egyptian film-maker. Feature film: *The Lions of Sinaï / Ousoud Sinâ* (1984)

Manso, Francisco. Cape Verde filmmaker (Portuguese by birth). Feature film: *Señor Napumoceno's Will / O testamento do Senhor Napumoceno* (1996)

Mansour, Ali (b. 1944 in Mahdia). Tunisian filmmaker. Studied for about 10 years in Paris, first graphic design, then drama and eventually filmmaking at the CICF. Worked in Tunisian television. Feature film: *Two Crooks in Madness / Deux larrons en folie* (1980)

Mansour, Youssef. Egyptian filmmaker. Feature film: *Desert Cat / Qett al-saharaa* (with Saïd Marzouk, 1995), *Badr: Enter in Peace / Badr: idkholouha ameneen* (2002)

Marcel, Terence. South African filmmaker. Feature film: *Jane and the Lost City* (English, 1985)

Marie, Khaled. Egyptian filmmaker. Feature film: *Taymour and Safika / Taymour wa Shafika* (2007)

Mariott, Charles. South African filmmaker. Feature film: *Love Me Leave Me* (English, with Allan Birkinshaw, 1988)

Marnham, Christian. British director of a film included in some South African film listings. Feature films: *Lethal Woman* aka *The Most Dangerous Woman Alive* (English, 1988)

Marrakchi, Laïla (b. 1975 in Casablanca). Moroccan filmmaker. She studied filmmaking at the University of Paris III from 1993. Worked as assistant director and made three shorts in 2000–3, one of which, *200 Dirhams,* was shown at Cannes. Feature film: *Marock* (2005)

Marsh, Donovan. South African filmmaker. Feature film: *Dollars and White Pipes* (English, 2005)

Marshall, Neil. South African filmmaker. Feature film: *Doomsday* (2007)

Martin, Paul. Director of one film included in some South African film lists: *Diamond Walkers / Jagd auf die blauen* Diamenten (English / German, 1965)

Martinez, Phillipe. South African filmmaker. Feature film: *Wake of Death* (English, 2004)

Martino, Sergio. South African filmmaker. Feature film: *African Fever* (English, 1989)

Marton, Andrew. American director hired to make one Egyptian film: *O Islam / Wâ islâmâh* (1961)

Maruma, Olley (b. 1953 in Bulawayo). Zimbabwean filmmaker. Studied law and audio-visual production in London. made a number of documentaries, including the feature-length *Quest for Freedom* (1981). Also *The Assegaï* (1982, filmed play for television). Co-directed *Consequences* (1988) on teenage pregnancy with John Riber. Feature film: *The Big Time* (2004)

Marx, Franz (b. in Pretoria). South African actor and filmmaker. Studied drama at Stellenbosch University and scriptwriting in Hollywood. Feature films: *Jakalsdraai se Mense* (Afrikaans, 1975), *Seuns van die Wolke* (Afrikaans, 1975), *Ma Skryf Matriek* (Afrikaans, 1975), *Liefste Madelein* (Afrikaans, 1976), *Die Vlindervanger / Murder on Holiday* (Afrikaans, 1976), *Netnou Hoor die Kinders* (Afrikaans, 1977), *Dit was Aand en dit was Môre* (Afrikaans, 1978), *'n Seder Val in Waterkloof* (Afrikaans, 1978), *Weerskant die Nag* (1978), *Forty Days* (English, 1979), *Weerskant die Nag* (Afrikaans, 1979), *Verkeerde Nommer* (Afrikaans, 1982), *Agter Elke Man* (Afrikaans, 1990), *Die Prince van Pretoria / Die Prins van Lichtenstein* (Afrikaans, 1991), *Geel Trui vir 'n Wenner* (Afrikaans, 1983)

Marzouk, Mohamed. Egyptian filmmaker. Feature films: *Playing with Fire / al-Lou'b bi-l-nâr* (1989), *The Good, the Ugly and the Monster / al-Tayyib, al-charis, al-wahch* (1990), *The Innocent Culprits / al-Moudhniboun al-abriyâ* (1990),

The Innocent Man and the Executioner / al-Barî² wa-l-gallâd (1991), *Flight Towards Hell / al-Hâribah ilâ al-gahîm* (1991), *The Man from the Mountains / Ibn al-Gabal* (1992), *Man of Fire / Ragoul min nâr* (1992), *The Battle of the Beauties / Sirâ² al-hasnâwât* (1993), *Evil Road / Tarik al-charr* (1995)

Marzouk, Saïd (b. 1940 in Cairo). Egyptian filmmaker. Began his career in television. Experienced censorship problems with two features dealing with corruption. Feature films: *My Wife and the Dog / Zawgâtî wa-l-kalb* (1971), *Fear / al-Khawf* (1972), *I Ask for a Solution / Ouridou hallan* (1975), *Those Who Are at Fault / al-Moudhniboun* (1976), *Saving What can still be Saved / Inqâdh mâ youmkin inqâdhouh* (1985), *Time of Terror / Ayyâm al-rou²b* (1988), *The Rapists / al-Moughtasiboun* (1989), *Dr Manal Dances / al-Doktorah Nanâl tarqous* (1991), *Ouch . . . Ouch / Aïe . . . Aïe* (1992), *Houda and His Excellency the Minister / Huda wa Ma²aal² al-wazir* (1995), *The Woman And the Cleaver / al-Mar²a wa al-satoor* (1997), *Crazy Life / Gunoon al-hayah* (2000), *Lovers' Snippets / Qusaqis al-ᶜushaq* (2003)

Marzouk, Saïd Mohamed. Egyptian filmmaker. Feature films: *Explosion / Infigâr* (1990), *The City Demons / Chayâtîn al-madînah* (1991), *Fathiyyah and the Mercedes / Fathiyyah wa-l-marsîdès* (1992), *Desert Cat / Qett al-saharaa²* (with Youssef Mansour, 1995)

Marzouk, Youssef. Egyptian filmmaker. Feature film: *The Market in Women / Souq al-hârim* (1970),

Maseko, Zola (b. 1967 to South African parents in exile). South African filmmaker. Studies in Swaziland, Tanzania and at the National Film and Television School in the UK. ANC activist. Shorts and documentaries from 1992, beginning with *Dear Sunshine* (1992) and *Scenes from Exile* (1993). His first feature, *Drum*, was internationally successful and with it he became the first South African filmmaker to win the top prize, the Étalon de Yennenga, at the Festival Panafricain du Cinéma de Ouagadougou

(FESPACO) in 2005. Feature film: *Drum* (English / Afrikaans / German, 2004)

Masso, Cyrille. Cameroonian filmmaker. Took distance-learning projects at several film schools and worked as a trainee in Cameroonian television, then studied at FEMIS in Paris. He made numerous shorts, commericals, and documentaries. Feature film: *Confidences* (2006)

Mastandrea, Nicholas. South African filmmaker. Feature film: *The Breed* (English, 2005)

Matabane, Khaolo. South African filmmaker. Feature film: *Conversations on a Sunday Afternoon* (English, 2006)

Mattera, Teddy (b. Johannesburg). Studied filmmaking both in the United States and in Europe (in Amsterdam and at the London International Film School). Debut film: *Hoop Dreams* (1993). Since then, documentaries and shorts plus two personal short films, *Waiting for Valdez* and *Norman comes to Jozi*. Has worked largely in South African television since his sole feature. Feature film: *Max and Mona* (English, 2004)

Matthews, Paul. South African filmmaker. Feature film: *The Little Unicorn* (English, 1998)

Mayer, Harry. South African filmmaker. Feature film: *Divided Loyalties* (English, 1989)

Mayersberg, Paul. American director (born in the UK) of a film included in some South African film listings. Feature film: *The Last Samurai* (English, 1988)

Mawuru, Godwin (b. 1961 in Zimbabwe). Zimbabwean filmmaker. Actor in theatre, television and film. Feature films: *Neria* (1992), *I Am the Future* (1994)

Mazhar, Ahmed (b. 1918). Egyptian actor and filmmaker. An army officer and contemporary of Nasser, he turned to film acting in 1951 and appeared in over a hundred roles. Wrote and directed just two films, in which he played the lead. Feature films: *Lost Souls / Noufous hâ²irah* (1968), *Another's Love / Habîbat ghayrî* (1976)

Mazif, Sid Ali (b. 1943 in Algiers). Algerian filmmaker. Studied at the Institut National de Cinéma (INC) in Algiers. Made numerous short films and contributed episodes to two collective features, *Hell for a Ten-Year-Old / L'Enfer à dix ans* (1969) and *Stories of the Revolution / Histoires de la révolution* (1970). Feature films: *Black Sweat / Sueur noire* (1972), *The Nomads / Les Nomades* (1975), *Leila and the Others / Leila et les autres* (1978), *I Exist / J'existe* (documentary for the Arab League, 1982), *Houria* (1986)

Mbala, Gnoan Roger (b. 1943 in Grand Bassam). Ivorian filmmaker. Studied filmmaking at the Conservatoire Libre du Cinéma Français (CLCF) in Paris. Made a number of forceful and ambitious village dramas, winning the top prize, the Étalon de Yennenga, at FESPACO with *In the Name of Christ* in 1993. Feature films: *The Hat / Le Chapeau* (1975), *Ablakon* (1984), *Bouka* (1988), *Adanggaman* (2000), *In the Name of Christ / Au nom du Christ* (1992)

McCarthey, Michael. British director of a film included in some South African film listings. Feature film: *Chameleon* (English, 1989)

McKenzie, Peter M. South African filmmaker. Feature film: *Merchants of War* (English, 1988)

McLaglan, Andrew. American director of one feature film included in some listings of South African features: *The Wild Geese* (English, 1978)

Meddour, Azzedine (b. 1947 in Sidi Aich; d. 2000). Algerian filmmaker. Studied at the Vsesoyuznyi gosudarstvennyi institut kinematografii (VGIK; All-Union State Cinema Institute) in Moscow. Made numerous documentaries and the compilation series *Colonialism without Empire / Le Colonialisme sans empire* (1978). Also contributed to the collectively made *The Other Algeria: Views from Within / L'Autre Algérie: regards intérieurs*. A Fench-language novel based on his only feature film, *La Montagne de Baya, ou la 'diya'*, was published in Algeria in 1999. The film itself was one of the first to be made in the Berber language. Feature film: *Baya's Mountain / La Montagne de Baya* (1997)

Medhat, Ahmed. Egyptian filmmaker. Feature film: *El-Turbini / El-turbini* (2007)

Medi, Rachid. Sudanese filmmaker. Feature film: *Hopes and Dreams* (1969)

Medori, Alfredo. South African filmmaker. Feature film: *Gevaarlike Reis / Heisses Land* (Afrikaans, with Lothar Lomberg, 1961)

Meehan, Tom. South African filmmaker. Feature film: *The Men from the Ministry* (English, 1971)

Mefti, Tayeb (b. 1942 in Algiers). Algerian filmmaker. No formal film training, but made three shorts. Feature film: *Moussa's Wedding / Le Mariage de Moussa* (1982)

Mehrem, Magdi. Egyptian filmmaker. Feature film: *He Has Finished His Statement / Wa tammat aqwâlouh* (1992)

Mekhiemar, Wahid. Egyptian filmmaker. Feature film: *The Maggot in the Fruit / al-Fâs fî-l-râs* (1992)

Mekky, Ahmed. Egyptian filmmaker. Feature film: *Seventh Sense / Al-Hassa Al-Sab'a* (2005)

Mensah, Charles (b. 1948 in Libreville). Gabonese filmmaker. Studied filmmaking at the École Supérieure des Études Cinématographiques (ESEC) in Paris. Worked as director in Gabonese television and as assistant head of the Centre National du Cinéma (CENACI). With Pierre-Marie Dong he began his career co-directing two films scripted by the wife of President Omar Bongo. Feature films: *Obali* (with Pierre-Marie Dong, 1976), *Ayouma* (with Pierre-Marie Dong, 1977), *Ilombe* (1978)

Merbah, Mohamed Lamine (b. 1946 in Thigenif). Algerian filmmaker. Studied first sociology, and then filmmaking at the Institut National de Cinéma (INC). A spell as a trainee in Polish television. Combined work for the Algerian publishing house Société Nationale d'Edition et de Diffusion (SNED) with work for Radiodiffusion Télévision Algérienne (RTA), for which he made numerous téléfilms. Head of Entreprise Nationale de Productions Audiovisuelles (ENPA) in the 1990s. Feature films: *The Plunderers / Les Spoliateurs* (1972), *The Uprooted / Les Déracinés* (1976), *Radhia* (1992)

Mernich, Mohamed. Moroccan filmmaker. Feature film: *Tilila* (2006)

Mesbahi, Abdellah (b. 1936 in El Jadida). Moroccan filmmaker. Studied filmmaking at the École Supérieure des Études Cinématographiques (ESEC) in Paris. Journalist and administrator. His third and fourth features were co-productions with the General Organisation for Cinema in Libya. Feature films: *Silence: No Entry / Silence, sens interdit* (1973), *Tomorrow the Land Will Not Change / Demain la terre ne changera pas* (1975), *The Green Light / Feu vert* (1976), *Where Are You Hiding the Sun / Où cachez-vous le soleil* (1979), *Land of Challenge / La Terre du défi* aka *I Shall Write Your Name in the Sand / J'écrirai ton nom sur le sable* (1989)

Mesbahi, Imane (b. 1964 in Tetouan). Moroccan filmmaker. Child actor in the first two features directed by her father, Abdellah Mesbahi, who scripted her first feature which she began in 1994. Studied in Cairo: filmmaking at the Higher Institute of Cinema and psychology at the Univerity of Aïn Chams. Work as assistant director. Feature film: *The Paradise of the Poor / Paradis des pauvres* (1994–2002)

Mesnaoui, Ahmed (b. Rabat in 1926; d. 1996). Moroccan filmmaker. Self-taught filmmaker and co-director of the first Moroccan feature film. Made numerous documentaries for the Centre Cinématographique Marocain (CCM), which he joined in 1962 and worked for until his retirement in 1986. Feature film: *Conquer to Live / Vaincre pour vivre* (with Mohamed BA Tazi, 1968)

Metner, Ingrid. German co-director of one Ghanaian film. Feature film: *Juju / Nana Akoto* (with King Ampaw, 1986)

Metsing, Simon. South African filmmaker. Began as a rural film distributor. Had a lengthy collaboration with Jimmy Murray at a time when links between blacks and whites were rare. Feature films: *Tommy* (Zulu, 1981), *Blood Money* (Zulu/English, with Jimmy Murray, 1982)

Meyer, Rudi. South African filmmaker. Specialist in African-language films. Feature films: *Isoka* (Zulu, 1979), *Ighawe* (Zulu, 1980), *Uzenzile Akakhalelwa* (Zulu, 1981), *Isigangi* (Sotho, 1981), *Ukuklupela* (Sotho, 1982), *Ubude Abuphangwa* (Sotho, 1982), *Inyembezi Zami* (Sotho, 1983), *Impumelelo* (Sotho, 1983), *Ighawe II* (Zulu, 1984)

Meyer, Tommie. South African filmmaker. Studied mechanical engineering at the University of Witwatersrand and worked as a mining engineer. General Secretary of FAK, he was an outspoken advocate of the Afrikaans language. He became involved in the production of the nationalistic *Doodkry is Min* (1961) and subsequently joined Jamie Uys Films Ltd as president. Feature films: *Springbok* (Afrikaans, 1976), *Birds of Paradise* (English, 1981), *Ipi Tombi* (English, with Don Hulette, 1993)

Mhando, Martin (b. 1952 in Mbulu). Tanzanian filmmaker. Studied at the University of Dar es Salaam and worked as a journalist. Film studies at the Institute of Theatre and Film Art in Bucharest. Directed documentaries in the 1980s for the Tanzanian Film Company. His sole feature film was co-directed with the American Ron Mulvihill and scripted by the latter's wife, the dramatist Quennae Taylor-Mulvihill. Feature film: *Maangamizi: The Ancient One* (with Ron Mulvihill, 1996)

Middleton, Grenville. South African filmmaker. Feature film: *Insident of Paradysstrand / Incident on Paradise Beach* (Afrikaans, with Gordon Anderson, 1973)

Millin, David (b. Cape Town). South African filmmaker. Joined African Film Productions in 1940 and worked as cinematographer from early 1950s. Two documentaries. Feature films:

Donker Afrika (Afrikaans, 1957), *The Last of the Few* (English, 1960), *Stropers van die Laeveld* (Afrikaans, 1962), *Seven against the Sun* (English, 1964), *Ride the High Wind / African Gold* (English, 1965), *The Second Sin* (English, 1966), *Majuba* (Afrikaans, 1968), *Petticoat Safari* (English, 1969), *Banana Beach* (English, 1970), *Shangani Patrol* (English, 1970), *Die Banneling* (Afrikaans, 1971), *The Brave the Rough and the Raw* (English, 1973), *Die Voortrekkers* (Afrikaans, 1973), *Suster Theresa* (Afrikaans, 1974)

Mire, Soraya (b. 1961 at Belet Huen). Somalian filmmaker. Feature film: *Fire Eyes* (1994)

Misiorowski, Bob. South African filmmaker. Feature film: *Point of Contact* (English, 1992), *Shark Attack* (English, 1998)

Mizrahi, Togo (b. 1905 in Alexandria; d. 1986). Egyptian veteran filmmaker. Developed a passion for cinema while in Europe, visiting studios in Italy, France and Germany. Made the silent feature: *Cocaine / al-Kokaïn* aka *The Abyss / al-Hâwiyah* (1930), and built his own studios, first in Alexandria and then in the Guizeh district of Cairo. The most prolific of all 1930s directors, he moved to Italy when his career ended. Sound feature films: *5001 / Khamsat âlaf wa wâhid* (1932), *Sons of Egypt / Awlâd Misr* (1933), *The Two Delegates / al-Mandoubân* (1934), *Doctor Farhat / al-Doktor Farhât* (1935), *Shalom the Interpreter / Chalom al-tourgmân* (1935), *The Sailor / al-Bahhâr* (1935), *A Hundred Thousand Pounds / Mît alf guinîh* (1936), *The Policeman / Khafiral-darak* (1936), *Wealth Is a Scandal / al-ʾIzz bahdalah* (1937), *Shalom the Sportsman / Chalom al-riyâdî* (1937), *At Seven O'Clock / al-Sâ-ah sabʾah* (1937), *The Telegram / al-Telegraf* (1938), *The Way I'm Made / Anâ tabʾî kidah* (1938), *Osman and Ali / ʿOthman wa ʿAlî* (1939), *Lend Me Threee Pounds / Sallifnî talâtah guinîh* (1939), *Stormy Night / Laylah moumtirah* (1939), *The Contractor / al-Bâchmouqâwil* (1940), *A Woman's Heart / Qalb imraʾah* (1940), *The Three Musketeers / al-Foursân al-thalâthah* (1941), *Leila, The Country Girl / Layla bint al-rîf* (1941), *The Arabian Nights / Alf laylah wa laylah* (1941, *Leila, The School Girl / Layla bint al-madâris* (1941), *Leila / Layla* (1942), *Ali Baba* *and the Forty Thieves / ʿAli Bâbâ wa-l-arbaʾîn harâmî* (1942), *The Right Path / al-Tariq al-moustaqîm* (1943), *Long Live Women / Tahyâ al-sittât* (1943), *Leila in the Shadows / Layla fî zalâm* (1944), *What Lies! / Kidb fî kidb* (1944), *Nour Eddine and the Three Sailors / Nour Eddine wa-l-bahhârah al-thalâthah* (1944), *Sallama / Sallâmah* (1945), *Long Live Men / Tahyâ al-riggâlah* (1945), *The Beauty Queen / Malikat al-gamâl* (1946)

Mogotlane, Thomas. South African filmmaker and actor. Feature film: *Mapantsula* (English / Afrikaans / Zulu / Sotho, with Olivier Schmitz, 1987)

Mohamed, Amina (1908–1985). Egyptian filmmaker. Her only feature film was the product of a group that included the director Salah Abou Seif and two painters, Salah Taher and Abdel Salam Al Cherif. Feature film: *Tita and Wong / Tita wa Wong* (1937)

Mohamed, Saïd. Egyptian filmmaker. Feature films: *Silence of the Sheep / Samt al-kherfaan* (1995), *The Turtles / al-Salahef* (1996)

Mohamed, Youssef Chabaane. Egyptian filmmaker. Feature film: *Desire and Its Cost / al-Raghbah wa-l-thaman* (1978)

Mohamed, Yussuf. Nigerian filmmaker. Feature film: *Ruwan bagaja* (Hausa, 1989)

Möhr, Hanro. South African filmmaker. Feature films: *Baeng* (Tswana, 1980), *U-Mona* (Zulu, 1980), *Hostage* (English, 1986)

Moknèche, Nadir (b. 1965 in Paris). French-based filmmaker of Algerian descent. Though born in Paris, he grew up in Algiers from the age of one month. Left Algeria at the age of 18 and studied law in Paris, where he now lives. Studied in London, Paris and at the New School of Social Research in New York, where he specialised in film. Two short films in the United States. His subsequent work has been made from a production base in France, using French language for his features. Feature films: *Madam Osmane's Harem / Le Harem de Mme Osmane* (2000),

Viva Laldjérie (2004), *A Paloma Sweet / Délice Paloma* (2007)

Monat, Donald. South African filmmaker. Feature film: *Fraud* (English, 1974)

Montaldo, Giuliano. South African filmmaker. Feature film: *The Short Cut / Time to Kill* (1988)

Montgomery, George. American director of a film included in some South African film listings. Feature film: *Satan's Harvest* (English, 1970)

Moore, Michael. South African filmmaker. Feature film: *Mr Deathman* (English, 1978)

Mora-Kpaï, Idrissou (b. 1967, in Benin). Benin filmmaker. Left Benin at the age of 19 for Germany. Currently resident in France. Studied American civilisation at the Free University of Berlin and then filmmaking at the Babelsberg Film and Television Institute in Germany, where he made a fictional short. A typical member of the post-independence generation, his work mixes documentary and fiction. Feature films: *Si-Guériki / Si-Guériki, la reine-mère* (2001), *Arlit, A Second Paris / Arlit, deuxième Paris (2004)*

Morris, Clive. South African filmmaker. Feature film: *A Case of Murder* (English, 2003)

Morsi, Ahmed Kamel (b. 1909 in Cairo; d. 1987). Egyptian filmmaker. Began as film critic and assistant director. Turned first to radio and then to television. Later head of direction at the Cairo Higher Film Institute and co-author of the first Arab-language Technical Dictionary of Cinema (with 3,000 entries). Feature films: *Return to the Land / al'Awdah ilâ al-rîf* (1939), *The Workman / al-'Âmil* (1943), *The Cheikh's Daughter / Bint al-cheikh* (1943), *The Weaker Sex / al-Guinsa al-latîf* (1945), *The Procurator General / al-Nâ'ib al-'âmm* (1946), *Sunset / Ghouroub* (1947), *Divine Justice / ʿAdl al-samâ* (1948), *The Big House / al-Bayt al-Kabîr* (1949), *The Mistress of the House / Sitt al-bayt* (1949), *Every Houshold Has Its Man / Koull bayt louh Râguil* (1949), *The Thoughtlessness of Youth / Taych al-chabâb* (1951), *the Murderous Mother / al-Oumm al-qâtlah* (1952), *Give Me Your Reason / Iddînî ʿaqlak* (1952), *I Al-*

most *Destroyed My Home / Kidtou ahdoumou baytî* (1954), *An American from Tantah / Amrikânî min Tantah* (1954), *The Rendezvous / al-Mîʾâd* (1955)

Mory, Philippe (b. 1932 in Batanga). Gabonese filmmaker. Studied in France where he worked as an actor in the theatre and as assistant to Michel Drach. Scripted Robert Darène's *La Cage* (1962), the first French-Gabonese co-production. Director general of the film centre Centre National du Cinéma (CENACI), 1975–1985. Made various short films after his sole feature. Feature film: *The Tam-tams Are Silent / Les Tam-tams se sont tus* (1972)

Mostafa Kamal, Mohamed (b. 1956 in Cairo). Egyptian filmmaker. Graduated from the Cairo Higher Film Institute in 1979. Worked as assistant to Khaïri Bechara, Atef Al-Tayeb, and Osma Fawzi. Director of production on numerous short, long, and documentary films for foreign television organizations. Feature film: *Leisure Time / Awqat farugh* (2006)

Mostafa, al-Saïd. Egyptian filmmaker. Feature films: *The Two Tramps / al-Moutacharridân* (1983), *Forbidden to Students / Mamnouʾ li-l-talabah* (1984), *Poor but Happy / Fouqarâʾ wa lâkin souʾadâʾ* (1986), *The Thirsty Woman / ʿAtchânah* (1987), *Rich Man, Poor Man / al-Ghanâ wa-l-faqîr* (1989), *The Lucky Ones / Awlâd hazz* (1989)

Mostafa, Galal. Egyptian filmmaker. Feature film: *Bouthayna's Love / Gharâm Bouthayna* (1953)

Mostafa, Houssam Eddine (b. 1926 in Port Said). Egyptain filmmaker. He studied filmmaking in the United States and worked in the Hollywood studios. His huge output, spread over almost 40 years, includes numerous adaptations. Feature films: *Cry No More, My Eyes / Kifâyah yâʾayn* (1956), *A Courtisan's Life / Hayât ghâniyah* (1957), *Must I Kill My Husband / Hal aqtoul zawguî* (1958), *Ishmael Yassine for Sale / Ismâʾîl Yâsîn li-l-bayʾ* (1958), *I Think of the Man Who Has Forgotten Me / Bafakkar fî-llî nâsînî* (1959), *I Am Innocent / Anâ barîʾah* (1959), *Abou al-*

Layl / Abou al-Layl (1960), *Men in the Storm /
Rigâl fî-l-ʾâsifah* (1960), *Farewell to Love /
Wadâʾan yâ houbb* (1960), *Women and Wolves /
Nisâʾ wa dhiʾâb* (1960), *Struggle in the Moun-
tain / Sirâʾ fî-l-gabal* (1961), *The Cream of Girls /
Sitt al banât* (1961), *The Three Rogues / al-
Achqiyâ al-thalâthah* (1962), *The Remains of a
Virgin / Baqâyâ ʿadhrâʾ* (1962), *Days without
Love / Ayyâm bilâ houbb* (1962), *Heroes to the
Very End / Batal li-l-nahâyah* (1963), *The Fugi-
tive Woman's Secret / Siaa al-hâribah* (1963), *Dark
Glasses / al-Nadhdhârah al-sawdâʾ* (1963), *Tur-
bulent Young Girls / Chaqâwat banât* (1963), *No
Way Out / al-Tarîq* (1964), *The Girl from the
Port / Fatât al-mînâ* (1964), *The Three Devils /
al-Chaytâtîn al-thalâthah* (1964), *Adham al-
Charkawi / Adham al-Charqâwi* (1964), *Free
from the Days / Hârib min al-ayyâm* (1965),
*The Three Adventurers / al-Moughâmiroun al-
thalâthah* (1965), *The Terrible Children / Chaqâ-
wat riggâlah* (1966), *A Turbulent Girl / Bint
chaqiyyah* (1967), *Thrushes and Autumn / al-
Simân wa-l-kharîf* (1967 1967), *The Shores of
Gaiety / Châti al-marah* (1967), *Crime in a Quiet
District / Garîmah fî-l-hayy al-hâdiʾ* (1967), *A
Very Ridiculous World / ʿÂlam moudhik guiddan* (1968), *The Three Prisoners / al-Masâguîn
al-thlâthah* (1968), *Chanabo Trapped / Chanabo
fî-l-misyadah* (1968), *The Three Good Guys / al
Chougʾân al-thalâthah* (1969), *Son of Satan /
Ibn al-chaytân* (1969), *The Woman and the Demons / Hiya wa-l-chayâtîn* (1969), *The Devils'
End / Nihâyat al-chayâtîn* (1970), *The Fox and
the Chameleon / al-Thaʾlab wa-l-harbâʾ* (1970),
The Wicked / al-Achrâr (1970), *Thieves' Rendezvous / Lousous ʿalâ Mawʾid* (1970), *A Woman
and a Man / Imraʾah wa ragoul* (1971), *The Devil's Gang / ʿIsâbat al-chattân* (1971), *The Demons
of the Sea / Chayâtîn al-bahr* (1972), *The Kings
of Evil / Moulouk al-charr* (1972), *Word of Honour / Kalimat charaf* (1972), *The Kidnappers /
al-Khattâfin* (1972), *Al-Chaymaa / al-Chaymâʾ*
(1972), *The School for Troublemakers / Madrarsat al-mouchâghibîn* (1973), *The Girls and the
Mercedes / al-Banât wal-l-marsîdès* (1973), *The
Devils on Holiday / al-Chayâtîn fî agâzah* (1973),
The Woman with Two Faces / Dhât al-wagʾhayn
(1973), *The Beggar / al-Chahhât* (1973), *The Hostile Brothers / al-Ikhwah al-aʾdâʾ* (1974), *The
Slums of the City / Qâ al-madînah* (1974), *Young

Girls and Love / al-Banât wa-l-houbb* (1974),
The Giants / al-ʾAmâliqah (1974), *The Ball Is
Still in My Pocket / al-Rasâsah lâ tazâl fî gaybî*
(1974), *The Heroes / al-Abtâl* (1974), *A Forest
of Legs / Ghâbah min al-sîqân* (1974), *Sabrine /
Sabrîn* (1975), *The Victims / al-Dahâyâ* (1975),
Lost Women / Nisâʾ dâʾiʾât (1975), *I Am nei-
ther Reasonable nor Mad / Anâ lâ ʿâqlah wa-lâ
magʾnounah* (1976), *Tawhida / Tawhîdah* (1976),
My Lord, It Is Your Will / Hikmitak yâ rab (1976),
Sonia and the Madman / Sonia wa-l-magʾnoun
(1977), *The Devils / al-Chayâtîn* (1977), *There
Are Loves That Kill / Wa min al-houbb mâ qa-
tal* (1978), *Al-Batiniyya / al-Bâtiniyyah* (1980),
Wekalat al-Balah / Wakâlat al-balah (1982), *The
Alleyway of Love / Darb al-hawâ* (1983), *When
Men Weep / ʿIndamâ yabkî al-rigâl* (1984),
The Queen's Juice / Chahd al-malikhah (1985),
The Slaughterhouse / al-Madbah (1985), *Al-
Harafish / al-Harâfich* (1986), *Al-Sakakini / al-
Sakâkînî* (1986), *The Path of Regrets / Sikkat al-
naddâmah* (1987), *The Three Troublemakers /
al-Mouchâghibât al-thalâthah* (1987), *Bird in
the Sky / Tayr fî-l-samâ* (1988), *Vipers' Love /
Gharâm al-fâʾî* (1988), *The Devils / al-ʾAfârit*
(1990), *The Kingdom of God / al-Moulk li Al-
lah* (1990), *The She-Devils and the Captain / al-
Mouchâghibât wa-l-kâbtin* (1991), *Crime at the
Bottom of the Sea / Garîmah fî-l-aʾmâq* (1992),
The Bulldozer / al-Buldozer (1992), *Bitter Love /
al-Houbb al-mourr* (1992), *Dirty Game / al-
Louʾbah al-qadhirah* (1993), *Hekmat Fahmi the
Spy / al-Gâsousah Hikmat Fahmî* (1994)

Mostafa, Houssam Eddine. Egyptian filmmaker.
Feature film: *The Unjust and the Wronged / Al
Zalim Wa Al Mazloom* (1999)

Mostafa, Niazi (b. 1911 at Assiout; d. 1986).
Egyptian filmmaker. Studied in Germany at the
Munich Film Institute and was apprenticed in
the UFA studios. Editor in the early years at the
Misr studios (including Fritz Kramp's *Wedad* and
Lachine). The most prolific of all Egyptian direc-
tors, making up to five films a year at times, he
explored every genre in over 100 feature films
during 50 years of filmmaking. Feature films:
Salama Is Fine / Salama fî khayr (1937), *The
Doctor / al Doktor* (1939), *Mr. Omar / Sî
ʿOmar* (1941), *The Wife Factory / Masnaʾ al-

zawgât (1941), *The Valley of the Stars / Wâdî al-nougoum* (1943), *Rabha / Râbha* (1943), *The Magic Cap / Tâqiyyat al-ikhfâ᾽* (1944), *My Daughter / Ibnatî* (1944), *Hababa / Habâbah* (1944), *Hassan and Hassan / Hasan wa Hasan* (1944), *Mohamed-Ali Street / Chârĩ᾽ Mouhammad ᶜAlî* (1944), *Miss Boussa / al-Ânisah Boussah* (1945), *The Human Being / al-Banî âdam* (1945), *Antar and Abla / ᶜAntar wa ᶜAblah* (1945), *The Victims of Modernity / Dahâyâ al-madaniyyah* (1946), *Rawiya / Râwiya* (1946), *The First Glance / Awwal nazrah* (1946), *The Parvenu / Ghanî harb* (1947), *Nights of Pleasure / Layâli al-Ouns* (1947). *The Queen of the Desert / Soultânat al-sahrâ* (1947), *Love and Youth / al-Hawâ wa-l-chabâb* (1948), *Leila the American / Layla al-᾽âmiriyyah* (1948), *The Princess's Secret / Sirr al-amîrah* (1949), *More Beautiful than the Moon / Qamar abata᾽ch* (1950), *Afrah / Afrâh* (1950), *The Beauty / Sitt al-housn* (1950), *Soussou My Love / Habîbatî Soussou* (1951), *Wahiba, Queen of the Gipsies / Wahîbu malikat al-ghagar* (1951), *Patience Pays / al-Sabr gamîl* (1951), *Where Does All That Come From / Min ayna laka hâdhâ* (1952), *Land of Heroes / Ard al-abtâl* (1953), *Hamido / Hamido* (1953), *The Love Taxi / taxi al-gharâm* (1954), *Daughters of Eve / Banât Hawwâ* (1954), *The Black Horseman / al-Fâris al-aswad* (1954), *Al-Houseiniyya's Tough Guys / Foutouwwat al-Houseiniyyah* (1954), *A Glass and a Cigarette / Sigârah wa kâs* (1955), *Platform 5 / Rasîf nimra khamsah* (1956), *First Love / Awwal gharâm* (1956), *Demons of Heaven / Chayâtîn al-gaww* (1956) *Abou Zouboul's Prisoner / Saguîn Abou Zou᾽boul* (1957), *Abou Hadid / Abou Hadîd* (1958), *The Midnight Driver / Sawwâq nisf al-layl* (1958), *Ishmael Yassine as Tarzan / Ismâ᾽îl Yâsîn Tarazân* (1958), *The Love of My Life /Habîbî al-asmar* (1958), *Sultan / Soultân* (1958), *Scandal in Zamalek / Fadîhah fî-l-Zamâlik* (1959), *The Mystery of the Magic Cap / Sirr tâqiyyat al-ikhfâ᾽* (1959), *The Dark-haired Girl from the Sinaï / Samrâ᾽ Sinâ᾽* (1959), *Daily Bread / louqmat al-᾽aych* (1960), *The Crook / al-Nassâb* (1961), *Blood on the Nile / Dimâ᾽ ᶜalâ al-Nil* (1961), *My Wife's Husband / gouz mirâti* (1961), *Antar Ibn Chadad / ᶜAntar bin chaddâd* (1961), *The Last Chance / Âkhir foursah* (1962), *I am the Fugitive / anâ al-hârib* (1962), *Rabea al-Adawiyya / Rabi᾽ah al-᾽Adawiyyah* (1963), *The*

Princess of the Arabs / Amîrat al-᾽arab (1963), *The Little Magician / al-Sâhirah al-sagghîrah* (1963), *The Amorous Bedouin / al-Badawiyyah al-᾽âchiqah* (1963), *The Fiancé will arrive tomorrow / al-Arîs yasil ghadam* (1963), *The Game of Love and Marriage / Lou᾽bat al-houbb-wa-l-zawâg* (1964), *The Spy / al-Gâsous* (1964), *The Agitator / al-Mouchâghib* (1965), *Too Young to Love / Saghîrah ᶜAlâ al-houbb* (1966), *Farès Bani Hamdan / Fâris banî Hamdân* (1966), *Demons of the Night / Chayâtîn al-luyl* (1966), *Kounouz / Kounouz* (1966), *His Excellency the Ambassador / Ganâb al-safîr* (1966), *Thirty Days in Prison / Thalathoun yawm fî-l-sig᾽n* (1966), *The Most Dangerous Man in the World / Akhtar ragoul fî-l-âlam* (1967), *Very Mad Youth / Chabâb mag᾽noun guiddan* (1967), *Eve and the Gorilla / Hawwâ᾽ wa-l-qird* (1968), *Daddy Wants It Like This / Bâbâ ᶜâyiz kidah* (1968), *Agent 77 / al-᾽Amîl sab᾽ah wa sab᾽în* (1969), *Al-Ataba Gazaz / al-᾽Atabah gazâz* (1969), *The Suitor of the Minister's Daughter / ᶜArîs bint al-wâzir* (1970), *The Killer of Women / Saffâh al-nisâ᾽* (1970), *It's You Who Killed My Daddy / Inta illî qatalt bâbâyâ* (1970), *Without Pity / Bilâ rahmah* (1971), *The Pleasure and the Suffering / al-Mout᾽ah wa-l-᾽adhâb* (1971), *Satan Is a Woman / al-Chaytân imra᾽ah* (1972), *Son for Sale / Abnâ li-l-bay᾽* (1973), *The Gang of Adolescents / Chillat al-mourâhiqîn* (1973), *When Love Sings / ᶜIndamâ youghanni al-houbb* (1973), *Looking for a Scandal / al-Bahth ᶜan al-fadîhah* (1973), *A Woman's Curse / La᾽nat imra᾽ah* (1974), *My Beloved Is Very Mischievous / Habîbatî chaqiyyah guiddan* (1974), *A Girl Called Mahmoud / Bint ismouhâ Mahmoud* (1975), *Bloody Sunday / Yawm al-ahad al-dâmî* (1975), *Hereditary Madness / Magânîn bi-l-wirâthah* (1975), *The Woman and the Wolves / al-Ounthâ wa-l-dhi᾽âb* (1975), *Women under Pressure / Nisâ tahta al-tab᾽* (1976), *The Delinquents / al-Mounharifoun* (1976), *Thoughtless Husbands / Azwâg tâ᾽ichoun* (1976), *First Year of Love / Sanah oulâ houbb* (one episode) (1976), *Dearest Uncle Ziou / Oncle Zizou habîbî* (1977), *Intelligent but Stupid / Adhkiyâ lâkin aghbiyâ* (1980), *I'm the Madman / Anâ al-magnoun* (1981), *The Man Who Sold the Sun / al-Ragoul alladhî bâ᾽a al-chams* (1983), *The Monsters of the Port / Wouhouch al-minâ᾽* 1983), *The Defender of Poor People / Foutouwwat al-nâs al-ghalâbah*

(1984), *The Troublemakers in the Army / al-Mouchâghiboun fî-l-gaych* (1984), *The Mountain of Scorpions / Tall al-ʾAqârib* (1985), *The Mulberries and the Cudgel / al-Tout wa-l-babbout* (1986), *The Monkey Trainer / al-Qirdâtî* (1987), *The Killer / al-Dabbâh* (1987)

Moufti, Hassan (b. 1935 in Tetouan). Moroccan filmmaker. Studied script-writing at the Cairo Higher Film Institute and worked as assistant to several leading Egyptian directors, including Youssef Chahine, Salah Abou Seif and Henri Barakat. He also worked in television. Feature film: *Tears of Regret / Les Larmes du regret* (1982)

Mourad, Ismaïl (b. 1962 in Cairo). Egyptian filmmaker. Studied at the Cairo Higher Film Institute and made several shorts. Feature films: *The Assassination of Faten Tawfik / Ighteyaal Faten Tawfiq* (1995), *Surface to Surface / Ard ard* (1998)

Mouyeke, Camille (b. 1962 in Congo). Congolese filmmaker, currently resident in France. Studied filmmaking at the University of Paris VIII. Two fictional shorts. Feature film: *Trip to Ouaga / Voyage à Ouga* (2001)

Mrini, Driss (b. 950 in Salé). Moroccan filmmaker. Studied mass communications in Hamburg and worked in German television (NDR). Further television work and short films after his return to Morocco. Feature film: *Bamou* (1983)

Mrozowski, Janusz (b. 1948 in Poland of French-Burkinabè descent). Burkinabè filmmaker, resident in France. Feature film: *Lucy's Revenge / La Revanche de Lucy* (1998)

Mselmani, Habib (b. in Tunisia). Tunisian filmmaker. Worked in television. His first feature is one of the few Maghrebian films to be addressed directly to a child audience. Feature film: *Sabra and the Monster from the Forest / Sabra et le monstre de la forêt* (1986)

Mulvihill, Ron. American co-director of one Tanzanian film, scripted by his wife, the dramatist Quennae Taylor-Mulvihill. Feature film: *Maangamizi: The Ancient One* (with Martin Mhando, 1996)

Munga, Djo [Djo Tunda wa Munga] (b. 1972 in Kinshasa). Democratic Republic of Congo filmmaker. Studied first art, and then filmmaking at the Institut National des Arts du Spectacle et Techniques de Diffusion (INSAS) in Brussels. Two documentaries. Feature film: *Viva Riva!* (2006)

Mungai, Anne (b. 1957 in Bunyala). Kenyan filmmaker. She is a graduate of the Kenyan Institute for Mass Communications, where she now works. She is also founder-director of the Shagilia Street Children's Theatre and, at the same time, director of a dozen short and medium-length films. Feature: *Saikati the Enkabaani* (1992)

Murlowski, John. South African filmmaker. Feature film: *Return of the Family Man* (English, 1988)

Murray, Jimmy. South African filmmaker and producer. Also active in television. Began making wildlife, documentary and training films before turning to African-language features in 1975. Unlike many directors of such films, he is fluent in Zulu, South Sotho and Tswana and has a working knowledge of Xhosa, Swazi and Pedi. Feature films: *Ingilosi Yofuka* (Zulu, 1979), *Sonto* (Sotho, 1981), *Dumela Sam* (English/Sotho, with Clive Scott 1981), *Doctor Luke* (English, 1982), *Blood Money* (Zulu / English, with Simon Metsing, 1982), *Boiphetetso* (Sotho, 1984), *Yonna Lefatseng* (Sotho, 1984), *U-Lindiwe* (Sotho, with H Epstein, 1984), *Inyoka* (Sotho, with H Epstein, 1984), *Imali* (Sotho, with Regardt van den Berg, 1984), *Nag van Vrees / Night of Terror* (Afrikaans, with Stanley Roup, 1986), *Grader Murphy* (English, 1988)

Musa, Hatem. Egyptian filmmaker. Feature film: *What's the Plan? / Ieeh al-nizaam* (2006).

Mustafa, Mohamed. Egyptian filmmaker. Feature film: *Magic / al-Magic* (2007)

Na N'Hada, Sana (b. 1950 at Enxalé). Guinea-Bissau filmmaker. Studied filmmaking at the Instituto Cubano de Arte e Industria Cinematográficos (ICAIC) in Cuba and at the Institut des Hautes Études Cinématographiques (IDHEC) in Paris. Head of the National Film Corporation in Guinea-Bissau. Several short films, the first two co-directed with Flora Gomes. Feature: *Xime* (1994)

Nabih, Mohamed. Egyptian filmmaker. Feature films: *Three Stories / Thalâth qisas* (one episode) (1968), *The Most Difficult Marriage / As'ab gawâz* (1970), *The Troublemakers No. 6 / al-Mouchâghib sittah* (1991)

Naciri, Saïd (b. 1960 in Casablanca). Moroccan filmmaker and actor. Studied at the Los Angeles Film School. Made several shorts in the 1990s and also directed sit-coms and a téléfilm, *Kasbah City* (2002), for Moroccan television. Scripted Hassan Benjelloun's *The Pal* (2002). Feature films: *The Bandits / Les Bandits* (2004), *Abdou with the Almohades / Abdou chez les Almohades* (2006)

Nacro, Régina Fanta (b. 1962 in Tenkodogo). Burkinabè filmmaker. The first female film director active in Burkina Faso, she studied at the Institut Africain d'Education Cinématographique (INAFEC) in Ouagadougou and subsequently in Paris. Numerous well-received, prize-winning short films from 1992, including *A Certain Morning / Un certain matin* (1991), *Puk Nini* (1995), and *Konate's Trick / Le Truc de Konate* (1999). Her first feature is a very ambitious study of violence and dictatorship in Africa. Feature film: *The Night of Truth / La Nuit de la vérité* (2004)

Naguib, Albert. Egyptian filmmaker. Feature film: *Tomorrow Will Be Another Day / Ghadan yawmoun âktar* (1961)

Naguib, Ramses. Egyptian filmmaker. Worked largely as a film producer. Feature films: *Hada / Houda* (1959), *Bahiyya / Bahiyyah* (1960), *The Masters' Love / Gharâm al-asyâd* (1961)

Nakahira, Ko. Director of one Egyptian film: *On the Banks of the Nile / ʿAlâ difâf al-Nîl* (1963)

Nanoyi, Ben. South African filmmaker. Co-directed one anti-apartheid feature film which was not released in South Africa: *How Long?* (with Gibson Kente, 1976)

Nartey, Koffi Zokko. Ghanaian filmmaker. Feature: *Black Home Again* (with Kwame Robert Johnson, 1994)

Nashaat, Sandra (b. 1970 in Cairo). Egyptian filmmaker. Her mother was Lebanese, her father Syrian. Studied French at Cairo University and filmmaking at the Cairo Higher Film Institute. Worked as assistant on several Egyptian features and one US film. Feature films: *Mabrouk and Bolbol / Mabrouk wa Bolbol* (1998), *Why Did You Make Me Love You? / Lih khalletny ahebbak?* (2000), *Thieves in KG II / Harameya fî kg II* (2002), *Thieves in Thailand / Harameyya fî Thailand* (2003), *Alexandria Private / Alexandria prive* (2005), *The Hostage / al-Rahina* (2006), *Number Plate: Alexandria / Malaki Eskandriya* (2007)

Nasr, Abdel Halim (b. 1913). Egyptian filmmaker. A leading Egyptian cinematographer who began his career with Togo Mizrahi in the mid-1930s and subsequently shot dozens of films, working with many leading directors. Directed just one film himself. Feature film: *A Castle in Spain / Qasr fî-l-hawâ'* (1980)

Nasrallah, Yousri (b. 1952 in Cairo). Egyptian filmmaker. Studied economics and polical science in Cairo, then filmmaking at the Cairo Higher Film Institute. Four years of work as film critic in Beirut. Assistant to Volker Schlöndorf, Omar Amiralay, and Youssef Chahine. Co-scripted *Alexandria Now and Forever* for Chahine, who produced his first feature. His documentary, *About Boys, Girls and the Veil* (1995), received international screening. His 2005 double feature is not included in official Egyptian listings as it is regarded as a French film. Feature films: *Summer Thefts / Sariqât sayfiyyah* (1988), *Mercedes / Marsîdès* (1993), *The*

City / al-Madina (2000), *The Gate of the Sun* / *Bab al-Chams* [*Departure* (142') + *Return* (137')] (2005)

Nassour, Raymond. Egyptian filmmaker. Feature films: *Night's Light* / *Nour al-layl* (1959), *Without Return* / *Bilâ ʿawdah* (1961), *The Battle of Tyrants* / *Sirâ ʾ al-gabâbirah* (with Zouheir Bekir, 1962), *The Vindictive Man* / *al-Haqîd* (1962)

Nathanson, Alan. South African filmmaker. Feature films: *Claws* / *The Beast* (English, 1982), *Sanna* / *Torn Allegiance* (English, 1984)

Nawwar, Samir. Egyptian filmmaker. Feature film: *X Is a Sign of Error* / *X ʾalâmah maʾnâhâ al-khataʾ* (1980)

Ndiaye, Cheik (b. 1962 in Dakar). Senegalese filmmaker. Trained as cameraman and editor at the Conservatoire Libre du Cinéma Français (CLCF) in Paris. Several short films and documentaries from 1994. Feature film: *The Wrestling Grounds* / *L'Appel des arènes* (2005)

Ndiaye, Samba Félix (b. 1945 in Dakar). Senegalese filmmaker. Studied filmmaking at the Université de Paris VIII. Also studied law and economics in Dakar. One of Africa's leading documentary filmmakers, he has made about twenty documentaries films, beginning with *Perantal* in 1975 and including the feature-length *Ngor, The Spirit of the Places* / *Ngor, l'esprit des lieux* (1994) and a video on Africans' views on their continent's development, *Question à la terre natale* (2006)

Ndomaluele Mafuta Nlanza. Democratic Republic of Congo filmmaker. Feature film: *For an Infidelity* / *Pour une infidélité* (1994)

Nee Owoo, Kwaté (b. 1945 in Ghana). Ghanaian filmmaker. Studied at the London International Film School and made his first short in London. Also worked at the University of Ghana. Four short documentaries. Feature film: *Ama* (with Kwesi Owusu, 1991)

Neethling-Pohl, Anna. South African filmmaker. Feature film: *Afspraak in die Kalahari* (Afrikaans, 1973)

Negeda, Fakhr Eddine. Egyptian filmmaker. Feature films: *Harmonica* / *Harmonica* (1998), *Magic of the Eyes* / *Sehar al-ʿuyoun* (2002), *The Actor* / *al-Meshakhasati* (2003), *The Diver* / *al-Ghawwaas* (2006)

Nejjar, Narjiss (b. 1971 in Tangier). Moroccan filmmaker. Studied filmmaking at ESRA in Paris. Three short films, one of which (like her first feature) was screened at Cannes. She published her first novel, *Cahiers d'empreintes*, in 1999. Feature films: *Cry No more* / *Les Yeux secs* (2002), *Wake Up, Morocco* (2006)

Nel, Frans. South African filmmaker. Studied at the Pretoria Film School. Feature films: *'n Wêreld sonder Grense* (Afrikaans, 1987), *Final Cut* (English, 1988), *Death Force* (English, 1988), *Impact* (English, 1989), *Let the Music Be* (English, 1989), *American Kickboxer* (English, 1991)

Nel, Fred. South African filmmaker. Feature film: *Bosveldhotel—Die Moewie* (Afrikaans, 1982)

Ngabo, Léonce (b. 1951 in Burundi). Burundi filmmaker, Studied chemistry at the University of Algiers. Director of the National School of Telecommunications in Burundi. Feature film: *Gito the Ungrateful* / *Gito l'ingrat* (1992)

Ngangura, Mweze D. (b. 1950 in Bukavu). Democratic Republic of Congo filmmaker. Studied film at the Institut National des Arts du Spectacle et Techniques de Diffusion (INSAS) in Brussels and subsequently taught at the Institut National des Arts in Kinshasa. A number of short films, including the widely seen documentary about life in Kinshasa, *Kin Kiesse* (1982). His features have been equally successful, with *Identity Papers* winning the top prize, the Étalon de Yennenga, at the Festival Panafricain du Cinéma de Ouagadougou (FESPACO) in 1999. Feature films: *Life Is Good* / *La Vie est belle* (with Benoît Lamy, 1987), *Identity Papers* / *Pièces d'identité* (1998), *The Governor's New Clothes* / *Les Habits neufs du gouverneur* (2005)

Niccol, Andrew. South African filmmaker. Feature film: *The Lord of War* (English, 2004)

Nkieri Ngunia Wawa (b. 1946 in Kinshasa). Democratic Republic of Congo filmmaker. Work in television. Feature film: *Fame in the Street / La Gloire dans la rue* (1980)

Nofal, Emil (b. in Johannesburg; d. 1985?). South African filmmaker and producer. Trained in the industry and began work in documentary. His first film features a Zulu jazz band. Went on to become a leading director and producer for over 30 years, specialising in Afrikaans films, most notably directing *The Wild Season* and producing Jans Rautenbach's *Die Kandidat* (1968) and *Katrina* (1969). Features: *Song of Africa* (English, 1951), *Rip van Wyk* (Afrikaans, 1960), *Hou die Blinkkant Bo* (Afrikaans, 1960), *Voor Sononder* (Afrikaans, 1962), *Kimberley Jim* (Afrikaans, 1963), *King Hendrik* (English, 1965, *Die Wilde Seisoen / The Wild Season* (Afrikaans, 1967), *The Winners* (English, with Roy Sargeant, 1972), *You're in the Movies* (English, 1984), *You Gotta Be Crazy* (English, 1986)

Nogueira, Helena. South African filmmaker. One of South Africa's few women filmmakers, she studied first at the University of Natal and then at the Institut des Hautes Études Cinématographiques (IDHEC) in Paris. Began with a documentary about Athol Fugard, *Fugard's People* (1985). Feature films: *Quest for Love* (English, 1987), *The Good Fascist* (English, 1991)

Norris, Aaron. South African filmmaker. Feature film: *Platoon Leader* (English, 1987)

Norton, Charles. South African filmmaker. Feature film: *No Hard Feelings / Kick or Die* (English, 1987)

Norval, James. South African filmmaker. Feature film: *Spore in die Modder* (Afrikaans, 1961)

Noury, Hakim (b. 1952 in Casablanca). Moroccan filmmaker. Studied drama at the Conservatoire National Supérieur d'Art Dramatique (CNSAD) in Paris and worked as assistant director (in particular with Souheil Benbarka) and in television. Contributed one episode to *Five Films for a Hundred Years / Cinq films pour cent ans* (1995). A key figure in the realist strand of 1990s Moroccan filmmaking who achieved great commercial success when he turned to comedy in 2000. Feature films: *The Postman / Le Facteur* (1980), *The Hammer And the Anvil / Le Marteau et l'enclume* (1990), *Stolen Childhood / L'Enfance volée* (1993), *The Dream Thief / Le Voleur de rêves* (1995), *A Simple News Item / Un simple fait divers* (1997), *A Woman's Fate / Destin de femme* (1998), *She Is Diabetic and Hypertensive and She Refuses to Die / Elle est diabétique et hypertendue et elle refuse de crever* (2000), *Love Story / Histoire d'amour* (2001), *She Is Diabetic and Hypertensive and Still She Refuses to Die / Elle est diabétique et hypertendue et elle refuse toujours de crever* (2005)

Noury, Imad (b. 1983 in Casablanca). Moroccan filmmaker, son of Hakim Noury. Work in various assistant production roles. Also a rock guitarist. Short films with his brother Sohael from 1999. Based in Madrid since 2001. Feature film: *Heaven's Doors / Les Portes du ciel* (with Swel Noury, 2005)

Noury, Sohael (b. 1978 in Casablanca). Moroccan filmmaker, son of Hakim Noury. Studied economics, languages and oriental civilisation in Paris.. Worked as assistant on his father's films. Short films with his brother Imad from 1999. Based in Madrid since 2001. Feature film: *Heaven's Doors / Les Portes du paradis* (with Imad Noury, 2005)

Novolcci, André. Director of one Egyptian feature film: *How to Steal an Atomic Bomb / Kayfa tasrouq qounboulah dharriyyah* (1968)

Noyce, Phillip. Australian-born filmmaker of one feature film included in some South African fim listings: *Catch a Fire* (English, 2006)

Ntsimenkou, Jude. Cameroonian filmmaker. Feature film: *Urban Jungle* (2006)

Nwandu, Adaora. Nigerian filmmaker. After graduating from Oxford University in 1999, she worked on documentaries for Communicating for Change. Studied filmmaking for a year in France and at USC in the United States. Made her first feature in London. Feature film: *Rag Tag* (2006)

Odendaal, Sias. South African filmmaker. Feature films: *Pikkie* (Afrikaans, 1972), *Sonneblom uit Parys* (Afrikaans, 1974), *Somer* (Afrikaans, 1975), *Nukie* (English, with Michael Pakleppa, 1987), *Vyfster: Die Slot* (Afrikaans, 1988)

Odidja, Bernard (b. 1960). Ghanaian filmmaker. Studied at the Overseas Film & Television Centre in London. Worked as editor for the Ghana Film Unit, Ghanaian television and the BBC. Editor and documentary filmmaker for the Ghana Film Corporation. Feature film: *Do Your Own Thing* (1971)

Odoutan, Jean (b. 1965 in Cotonou). Benin actor, filmmaker and musician, currently resident in France. Seven short fictional films. After a first feature set in his native Benin, he has made three features set within the immigrant community in Paris. Feature films: *Barbecue Pejo* (1999), *Djib* (2000), *Mama Aloko* (2001), *The Waltz of the Fat Bottoms / La Valse des gros derrières* (2003)

Odunsi, Tubosun [*aka* Paadi Mukaila]. Nigerian filmmaker. Feature film: *Ejo Ngboro* (Yoruba, 1989)

Ogunde, Chief Hubert (b. 1916; d. 1990). Nigerian filmmaker and actor. Initially worked in the police force before becoming a leading figure in the Yoruba Travelling Theatre. Produced and starred in Balogun's *Aiye* (1979) and in his own films. Also appeared in Bruce Bereford's *Mister Johnson* (1990). His three features were all co-directed with the English cameraman Freddie Goode. Feature films: *Jaiyesimi* (Yoruba, 1980), *Aropin 'N'tenia.* (Yoruba, 1982), *Ayanmo* (Yoruba, 1988)

Ogundipe, Moyo. Nigerian filmmaker. Feature film: *The Songbird* (English, 1986)

Ogunmola, Yomi. Nigerian filmmaker. Feature films: *Panpe Aiye* (Yoruba, 1988), *Ha! Enia* (Yoruba, 1989), *Kirakita* (Yoruba, 1991)

Ogunsola, Isola [*aka* I-Show Pepper]. Nigerian filmmaker. Feature film: *Ogun Laye* (Yoruba, 1993)

Oguri, Kenichi. South African filmmaker. Feature film: *Love Towards Children of Southern Africa* (English, 1988)

Okioh, François Sourou (b. 1950 in Léma). Benin filmmaker and writer. Studied filmmaking at the Filmov Akademie Múzickych Umení (FAMU; the Film & Television Faculty of the Academy of Performing Arts) in Prague. Five short films and a 50-minute video, *Crânes épais... lèvres fausses* (2006). Feature film: *Ironu* (1985)

Okpako, Branwen (b. 1969 in Lagos). Nigerian filmmaker based abroad. Studied politics and economics in Bristol, then filmmaking from 1992 at the DFFB in Berlin, where her graduation film was the feature-length documentary *Dreckfresser / Dirt for Dinner* (German, 2000). She has a Nigerian father and a German mother and both her films deal with mixed marriages. Feature film: *Valley of the Innocent* (English, 2003)

Olaiya Adejumo, Moses (also known as **Baba Sala**). Nigerian filmmaker. Nigeria's best known Yoruba comic actor of the 1980s. Producer and star of Balogun's *Orun Mooru* (1982) and Ade Afolayan's *Mosebolatan* (1986). Made video features in the 1990s: *Agba Man* (Yoruba, 1992) and *Return Match* (Yoruba, 1993). Feature film: *Aare Agbaye* (Yoruba, with Oyewole Olowomojuore, 1983)

Ole, António (b. 1951 in Luanda). Angolan filmmaker. Painter. From 1975 worked in television and made documentaries, including *Conceição Tchimbula, A Day, A Life / Conceição Tchimbula, Um Dia, Uma Vida* (1982), In 1983–86 studied at the American Film Institute and at the University of California at Los Angeles (UCLA), but on his return experienced difficulties in resuming his career and returned to painting and sculpture. Feature documentary: *The Rhythm of the N'Gola Ritmos / O Ritmo do N'Gola Ritmos* (1978)

Olowomojuore, Oyewole. Nigerian filmmaker. Feature films: *Anikura* (Yoruba, 1983), *Aare Agbaye* (Yoruba, with Moses Olaiya Adejumo, 1983), *Lisabi* (Yoruba, 1986)

Oloyede, Tunde. Nigerian filmmaker. Feature film: *Eri Okan* (Yoruba, 1990)

Olwagen, J. O. O. South African filmmaker. Feature film: *Die Wilde Boere* (Afrikaans, 1959)

Omonitan, Ola (also known as Ajimajasan). Nigerian filmmaker. Feature film: *Ogun Ajaye* (Yoruba, 1986)

Omotehinse, Rufus. Nigerian filmmaker. Feature film: *The Wrath of Agbako* (English, 1983)

Omotso, Akin. South African filmmaker. Studied drama at the University of Cape Town and worked as an actor in television. His first feature was shot on video and transferred to film. Feature film: *God Is African* (English, 2001)

Onwurah, Ngozi. Nigerian filmmaker based abroad. She studied in England, at Manchester Polytechnic and at the National Film School. Short films, including *Shoot the Messenger* (2006). Feature film in the United Kingdom: *Welcome II the Terrordome* (English, 1994)

Orfanelli, Alvisi. Versatile Italian-born pioneer Egyptian filmmaker. Worked first with Aziz Bandarli and Umberto Dorès who founded one of the first cinemas in Alexandria in 1906. Subsequently became an important producer who invented the production formula of 'Egyptians in front of the camera and foreigners behind it'. Directed seven features between 1936 and 1940. Also worked as cinematographer until 1961. Cofounder, with two foreign residents, the Frenchman Jacques Schutz and the Italian Giaccomo Puccini, of the Egyptian Artistic Film Company in 1928. Feature films: *Abou Zarifa / Abou Zarîfah* (1936), *White and Black / al-Abyad wa-l-aswad* (1936), *A NIght in Life / Laylah fi-l-ʾoumir* (1937), *My Servant / Khaddâmtî* (1938), *The Long-Awaited Day / Yawm sl-mounâ* (1938), *The Price of Happiness / Thaman al-saʾâdah* (1939), *Under the Sheets / Tahtâ al-silâh* (1940)

Orfi, Wedad (b. 1900; d. 1969). Egyptian silent filmmaker of Turkish origin. Sent to Egypt by a German company to shoot a film on the Prophet Mohamed (abandoned because of religious objections), he made a first version of a film he wrote, directed and starred in with the stage actress Aziza Amir (who produced it), *The Hand of God*. But Aziza Amir was dissatisfied with the result and had it remade by Stephane Rosti as *Leila*. He was also involved with producer/actress Assia Dagher on *The Beauty from the Desert*, He returned to Turkey at the beginning of the 1930s. Silent features: *Leila / Layla* (with Stephane Rosti, 1927), *The Victim / al-Dahiyyah* (1928), *The Beauty from the Desert / Ghâdat al-sahrâ* (with Ahmed Galal, 1929), *The Drama of Life / MaʾSât al-hayât* (1929)

Orpen, Roger. South African filmmaker. Feature film: *Mark of the Jackal* (English, 1989)

Osfour, Mohamed (b. 1927 in Casablanca; d. 2005). Moroccan filmmaker. Received no formal film training and began by making amateur films. Worked on a large number of foreign films as actor or assistant. His fifty-minute silent black-and-white 16mm film, *The Cursed Son / Le Fils maudit* (1958), is listed by the Centre Cinématographique Marocain (CCM) as the first Moroccan feature. Feature film: *The Devil's Treasure / Le Trésor infernal* (1970)

Ouedraogo, Idrissa (b. 1954 in Banfora). Burkinabè filmmaker. Studied filmmaking at the Institut Africain d'Education Cinématographique (INAFEC) in Burkina Faso and at the Institut des Hautes Études Cinématographiques (IDHEC) and the Sorbonne in Paris. His first three 'village' films earned him an international reputation, with *Tilai* taking the top prize, the Étalon de Yennenga at the Festival Panafricain du Cinéma de Ouagadougou (FESPACO) in 1991. He has struggled to maintain this reputation, working in a variety of forms and styles. His seventh feature, *Kini and Adams,* was made in English and shot in Zimbabwe. He remains a major figure in African cinema. Feature films: *Yam Daabo* (1987), *Yaaba* (1989), *Tilai* (1989), *Karim and Sala / Karim et Sala* (1991), *Samba Traore* (1992), *A Cry from the Heart / Le Cri de cœur* (1994), *Kini and Adams* (1997), *The Gods' Anger / La Colère des dieux* (2003), *Kato Kato / Un malheur n'arrive jamais seul* (2006)

Ouedraogo, Tahiru Tasséré (b. 1966). Burkinabè filmmaker. After a technical training at Aformav, he studied directing at CPAF and scriptwriting at the Institut National de l'Audiovisuel (INA) all in Paris. Three shorts from 2000. Feature film: *Djanta* (2007)

Ouenangare, Didier (b. 1953 in Bambari; d. 2006). Central African Republican filmmaker. Studied in Rennes and Paris and worked as a cinematographer. Co-directed the first feature film made in his country. Feature film: *The Silence of the Forest / Le Silence de la forêt* (with Bassek Ba Kobhio, 2003)

Ould Khelifa, Saïd (b. in Tunisia). Algerian filmmaker. Worked as a critic. Feature films: *White Shadows / Ombres blanches* (1991), *Ania's Tea / Le Thé d'Ania* (2004)

Oussama, Mohamed. Egyptian filmmaker. Feature film: *Golden Girl / Bint min dahab* (1988)

Owusu, Kwesi (b. in Ghana). Ghanaian filmmaker. Studied at LSE in London and is now professor at the University of London. Writer. Feature film: *Ama* (with Kwate Nee Owoo, 1991)

Oyewole, Olowomujore. Nigerian filmmaker. Feature film: *Oju Oro* (1986)

Pakleppa, Michael (b. in Namibia). South African filmmaker. Worked in the South African film industry from 1990. Numerous documentaries. Feature film: *Nukie* (English, with Sias Odendaal, 1987)

Panou, Sanvi. Benin filmmaker and actor, resident in France. Founder of the 'Images d'ailleurs' cinema and festival in Paris. Shorts in 1980s and 1990s. Feature film: *The Amazonian Candidate / L'Amazone candidate* (2007)

Parr, John. South African filmmaker. Studied at the Technikon Film School in Pretoria and began in 1985 as assistant to Ronnie Isaacs. Feature films: *Nightslave* (English, 1988), *Cry Vengeance* (English, 1988), *Hunted* (English, 1988), *The Pin-Up Girl* (Zulu, 1988), *The Pin-Up Girl II*

(Zulu, 1989), *Prey for the Hunter* (English, 1989), *The Assassin* (English, 1989), *King of the Road* (Zulu, 1989), *Deadly Hunter / Pursuit* (English, 1990)

Peake, Bladon. South African filmmaker. Feature films: *Hans-Die-Skipper* (Afrikaans, 1953), *Inspan* (Afrikaans, 1953)

Perold, Jan. South African filmmaker. Feature films: *As ons Twee eers Getroud is* (Afrikaans, 1962), *Die Ruiter in die Nag* (Afrikaans, 1963), *Piet my Niggie* (Afrikaans, 1964)

Persson, Sven. Danish-born South African filmmaker. Studied photography in Denmark. Worked in Swedish documentary and was sent to South Africa by the Svensk Documentary Film Unit in 1946. Worked as cinematographer and in early 1950s went to Hollywood to polish his skills. Began as a director with tourist and wildlife films, but is best known for his anti-apartheid documentaries of the mid-1970s. Feature films: *Raka* (English, 1968), *Makulu / Rogue Lion* (English, 1972), *Land Apart* (English, 1974), *The South Africans* (English, 1976)

Pescatino, Luigi. Italian-born director of one Egyptian film: *The Glass Sphinx / Abou al-Hol al-Zougâguî* (1968)

Peterson, Kristine. South African filmmaker. Feature film: *The Redemption* (English, 1995)

Phillip, Harald. South African filmmaker. Feature films: *Vreemde Wêreld* (Afrikaans, 1974), *Voortvlugtige Spioen* (Afrikaans, 1974)

Picavez, Marc. French founder of the audiovisual company MAKIZ'ART and co-director of one Senegalese feature: *Bul déconné!* (with Massaër Dieng, 2005)

Pienaar, Andries A. South African filmmaker. Feature film: *Lig van 'n Eeu* (Afrikaans, 1942)

Pillay, Maganthrie. South African filmmaker. Feature film: *34 South* (2005)

Pohl, Truida. South African filmmaker. Feature films: *Man in die Donker* (Afrikaans, 1962), *Huis op Horings* (Afrikaans, 1963)

Pretorius, Hein. South African filmmaker. Feature film: *Cold Blood* (Zulu, 1984)

Pretorius, Henk. South African filmmaker. Feature film: *Bakgat* (2007)

Pringle, Stuart. South African filmmaker. Began his film career in 1960 as an actor in Howard Hawks's *Hatari* in Tanganyika and worked on a number of wild life and hunting-inspired projects, some for television. Feature film: *Leatherlip* (English, 1972)

Prior, David. South African filmmaker. Feature film: *Dangerous Curves* (English, 1987)

Proctor, Elaine (b. 1962 in Johannesburg). South African filmmaker. One of only a handful of women South African filmmakers, she studied at the National Film and Television School at Beaconsfield in the UK, in the context of which she made her first fictional feature. She had earlier made three documentaries, *Forward to a People's Republic* (1981), *Re Tia Bona* (1985) and *Sharpeville Spirit* (1987). Feature films: *On the Wire* (English, 1990), *Friends* (English, 1992)

Prowse, Peter. South African filmmaker. Feature film: *Tokolosche* (English, 1965)

Purcell, Evelyn Maud. South African filmmaker. Feature film: *Borderline* (English, 2003)

Puren, Etienne. South African filmmaker. Feature films: *Kampus* (English, 1987), *Little Man Big Trouble / Nonpopi Nodambusa* (English, 1990)

Pyamooto, Barlen. Mauritian filmmaker. Feature film: *Bénarès* (2006)

Pyun, Albert. South African filmmaker. Feature films: *Journey* (English, 1987), *Alien from LA* (English, 1987), *Journey II* (English, 1987), *Journey to the Centre of the Earth* (English, 1987), *American Kickboxer II / The Road Back* (English, with Darrell Roodt, 1991)

Qamar, Abdel Ghani. Egyptian filmmaker. Feature film: *The Fisherman's Daughter / Bint al-sayyad* (1957)

Qawadri, Anwar. Egyptian filmmaker. Feature film: *Race against Time / Sibâq maʾ al-zaman* (1993)

Qissi, Michael. South African filmmaker. Feature films: *Backlash* (English, 1991), *Terminator Woman* (English, 1993)

Rached, el-Hadj. Libyan filmmaker. Feature film: *No!* (documentary, 1985)

Rachedi, Ahmed (b. 1938 in Tebessa). Algerian filmmaker. Worked in the film section of the FLN in Tunis. First director general of the Office National du Commerce et de l'Industre Cinématographiques (ONCIC). Contributed to the collective documentary, *So That Algeria May Live / Pour que vive l'Algérie* (1972). Later directed two television series on the Algerian war, one for Radiodiffusion Télévision Algérienne (RTA) (1981) and one for the French Antenne 2 (1992). His first feature is a major work and his later films mix satire and social engagement. Feature films: *Dawn of the Damned / L'Aube des damnés* (documentary, 1965), *Opium and the Stick / L'Opium et le bâton* (1969), *A Finger in the Works / Le Doigt dans l'engrenage* (1974), *Ali in Wonderland / Ali au pays des mirages* (1979), *Monsieur Fabre's Mill / Le Moulin de Monsieur Fabre* (1984)

Radi, Hatem. Egyptian filmmaker. Feature film: *A Man against the Law / Ragoul didd al-qânoun* (1988)

Radi, Ihab. Egyptian filmmaker. Feature films: *A Girl from Israel / Fatat min Israel* (1999), *Burning Love / Hobbak naar* (2004), *Difficult Task / Mohemma saʾba* (2007)

Radi, Mohamed (b. 1939). Egyptian filmmaker. Brother of Mounir Radi. Feature films: *The Bar-*

rier / al-Hâguiz (1972), *My Daughter, Love and Me / Anâ wa ibnâtî wa-l-houbb* (1974), *Children of Silence / Abnâ² al-samt* (1974), *The Innocents / al-Abriyâ²* (1974), *The Star Maker / Sâni² al-nougoum* (1977), *Life Is Short / al-²Oumr lahzar* (1978), *Behind the Sun / Warâ² al-chams* (1978), *Hell / al-Gahîm* (1980), *Mothers in Exile / Oummahât fî-l-manfâ* (1981), *Human Beings and Genies / al-Ins wa-l-guinn* (1985), *Rendezvous with Fate / Maw²id ma² al-qadar* (1986), *To Escape from the Asylum / al-Houroub min al-khânkah* (1987), *Rendezvous with the President / Maw²id ma² al-ra²îs* (1990), *The Wheel Turns / al-Hagar dâyir* (1992)

Radi, Mounir (1947 in Cairo). Egyptian filmmaker. Brother of Mohamed Radi. Feature films: *Time of Anger / Ayyâm al-ghadab* (1989), *The President's Visit / Ziyârat al-Sayyed al-ra²îs* (1994), *Indian Movie / Film Hindi* (2003)

Radwane, Tolba. Egyptian filmmaker. Feature films: *A Woman's Love / Gharâmiyyât imra²ah* (1960), *Aziza the Ambassadress / al-Safîrah ʿAzîzah* (1961), *The Trap / al-Misyadah* (1962), *Forbidden Story / Qissah mamnou²ah* (1963), *The Students' Flat / Chiqqat al-talabah* (1967)

Raeburn, Michael (b. 1948 in Cairo). Zimbabwean filmmaker, who lived in what was then Rhodesia from the age of three. After University of Rhodesia, studied in London (BA in French Literature), Aix-en-Provence (PhD) and at the Institut des Hautes Études Cinématographiques (IDHEC) in Paris. Banned from Rhodesia after his medium-length satiric fiction *Rhodesia Countdown* (1969), he now divides his time between Harare and Paris. Numerous documentary and short fictional films. Several British produced feature-length films: *Beyond the Plains Where Man Was Born* (1976) and *Requiem for a Village* (1976), then *The Grass Is Singing* (1981) shot in Zambia. *Jit* (1990) is his first true Zimbabwean feature, followed by *Soweto* (1991), *Winds of Rage* (1998), *Home Sweet Home* (with Heidi Draper, 1999), *Zimbabwe, From Liberation to Chaos* (2003) *Let's Hit the Streets* (2005)

Rafla, Helmi. Egyptian filmmaker. Feature films: *The World Is Alright / al-Douniâ bi-kheir*

(1946), *My Head Is on Holiday / al-Aql² fî agâzah* (1947), *The Dove of Peace / hamâmat al-salâm* (1947), *Love and Madness / Houb wa gounoun* (1948), *Body and Soul / al-Rouh wa-l-gasad* (1948), *Hoda / Houda* (1949), *Fatma, Marika and Rachel / Fatmah wa-Mârîkâ wa-Rachel* (1949), *Party Evening / Laylat al-²îd* (1949), *The Mad Woman / al-Mag²nounah* (1949), *Beware of Men / Âh min al-riggâlah* (1950), *The Hero / al-Batal* (1950), *The Girl from Paris / Bint Paris* (1950), *Mademoiselle Maman / al²Ânisah Mâmâ* (1950), *The Millionnaire / al-Millionnaire* (1950), *A Dancer's Love / Gharâm râqisah* (1950), *The Beloved's Country / Balad al-mahboub* (1951), *Love in Danger / al-Houbb fî khatar* (1951), *Girls Are Sweet / al-Banât charbât* (1951), *The End of a Story / Nihâyat qissah* (1951), *Come and Say Hello / Ta²âla sallim* (1951), *My Mother-in-Law Is an Atomic Bomb / Hamâtî qounboulah dharriyyah* (1951), *In Good Humor / Fâyeq wa râyeq* (1951), *The Victor / al-Mountasir* (1952), *In Your Way / ʿAlâ keifak* (1952), *Auspicious / Qadam al-khayr* (1952), *The Love of My Soul / Habîb qalbi* (1952), *A Benefactor / Fâ²il Khatr* (1953), *Your Horoscope This Week / Hazzak hâdhâ al-ousbou²* (1953), *Those Who Love Me Have Done Me an Injustice / Zalamounî al-habâyib* (1953), *Woman Is Everything / al-Mar²ah koull chay²* (1953), *Son for Hire / Ibn li-l-igâr* (1953), *The Pretty Mothers-in-Law / al-Hamawât al-Fâtinât* (1953), *The Young Girl's Honour / Charaf al-bint* (1954), *Who Are You in Love With? / Li-miin hawâk* (1954), *Have Condidence in God / Khallîk ma² Allah* (1954), *The Impostor / al-Mouhtâl* (1954, *Let Me Get Married, Quickly / Ilhaqounî bi-l-ma²dhoun* (1954), *Abou al-Dahab / Abou al-Dahab* (1954), *A Poor Man / Insân ghalbân* (1954), *Adored Soul / ʿÂchiq al-rouh* (1955), *The City's Revolt / Thawrat al-madînah* (1955), *Nights of Love / Layâlî al-houbb* (1955), *The Merry Widow / al-Armalah al-taroub* (1956), *The Inspector General / al-Moufattich al-²âmm* (1956), *The Prince of My Dreams / Fatâ ahlâmi* (1957), *The Festival of Love / mahragân al-houbb* (1958), *Ishmael Yassine in Damascus / Ismâ²îl Yâsîn fî Dimachq* (1958), *The Love Nest / ʿIchch al-gharâm* (1959), *Melody of Happiness / Lahn al-sa²âdah* (1960), *Almaz and Abdou al-Hamouli / Almaz wa ʿAbdou al-Hâmoulî* (1962), *The Public Idol / Ma²boudat al-gamâhîr* (1967), *A*

Very Jealous Wife / Zawgah ghayourah guiddan (1969), *Tender Gesture / Lamsat hanân* (1971), *Rendezvous with the Beloved / Maw²id ma² al-habîb* (1971), *My Dearest Daughter / Ibnatî al-²azîzah* (1971), *Housing Crisis / Azmat sakan* (1972), *One Last Night of Love / Laylat houbb akhîrah* (1972), *The Gang of Swindlers / Chillat al-mouhtâlîn* (1973),*The Voice of Love / Sawt al-houbb* (1973), *Women of the Night / Nisâ al-layl* (1973), *It Was Love / Wa kâna al-houbb* (1974), *Great Fidelity / al-Wafâ² al-azîm* (1974), *The Happy Marriage / al-ZawIag al-sa²îd* (1974), *My First and Last Love / Houbbî al-awwal wa-l-akhîr* (1975), *The Tears Dry Up / Gaffat al-doumou²* (1975), *Love . . . Even More Beautiful than Love / Houbb ahlâ min al-houbb* (1975), *No, to You whom I Loved / Lâ yâ man kounta habîbî* (1976), *First Year of Love / Sanah oulâ houbb* (one episode) (1976), *Love on the Miami Beach / Houbb ʿalâ² châtiʾ Miami* (1976), *Women in the City / Nisâ fî-l-madînah* (1977), *A Call after Midnight / Moukâlamah ba²du mountasuf al-layl* (1978), *The Thief / al-Nachchâlah* (1985)

Ragab, Ali. Egyptian filmmaker. Feature films: *Action Movie Hero / Shagi² el sima* (2000), *The Red Notebook / al-Agenda al hamraa²* (2000), *Beach Bum / Saye² bahr* (2004), *Aunty Faranssa / Khalty Faranssa* (2004), *Sentimental Sayyed / Sayyed al-ʿAtify* (2005), *Karkar / Karkar* (2007)

Rahim, Hadj. Algerian filmmaker. Received no formal film training, but worked in Algerian television, making numerous téléfilms. Feature film: *The Portrait / Le Portrait* (1994)

Rajaonarivelo, Raymond (b. 1949 in Antanarivo). Madagascan filmmaker. Studied filmmaking at the University of Montpellier and at the Université de Paris. Two Madagascan short films in the 1970s. Features: *Tabataba* (1988), *When the Stars Meet the Sea / Quand les étoiles rencontrent la mer* (1996), *Mahaleo* (2004)

Ramampy, Benoît (b. 1947 in Ambalavao). Madagascan filmmaker. Trained at the Office de Copération Radiophonique (OCORA) and Radio France in Paris. On his return home he studied at the Malagasy Production Centre and made educational shorts. Feature films: *Dahalo,*

Dahalo . . . (1984), *The Price of Peace / Le Prix de la paix* (1987)

Ramdani, Abdelaziz (b. 1937 in Saïdia). Moroccan filmmaker. Studied at the Institut des Hautes Études Cinématographiques (IDHEC) in Paris and, on his return to Morocco, joined the Centre Cinématographique Marocain (CCM) in 1959. Worked on a number of foreign films shot in Morroco. Made numerous short documentaries before co-directing the second Moroccan feature film. Feature film: *When the Dates Ripen / Quand murissent les dattes* (with Larbi Bennani, 1968)

Ramsis, Amir. Egyptian filmmaker. Feature films: *An Account / Kashf hesaab* (2007), *The Furthest End of the World / Akher el dunia* (2007)

Ramzi, Hassan. Egyptian filmmaker. Feature films: *Souleymane's Ring / Khâtim Soulaymân* (1947), *The Island Princess / Amirat al-gazîrah* (with Abdel Kamel Hefnawi, 1948), *It Wasn't Foreseen / Mâ kânch ʿalâ al²bâl* (1950), *Boulboul the Lawyer / al-Mou²allim Boulboul* (1951), *Good News / Bouchret khayr* (1952), *Love's Victory / Intisâr al-houbb* (1954), *Spring Dreams / Ahlâm al-rabî²* (1955), *The Fugitive / alHâribah* (1958), *Together for Always / Ma²an ilâ al-abad* (1960), *Hot Nights / al-Layâlî al-dâfi²ah* (1962), *The Queen of the Night / Mlikat al-layl* (1971), *Feelings and Body / al-Âtifah wa-l-gasad* (1972), *The White Dress / al-Ridâ² al-abyad* (1975), *I Shall Never Return / Abadan lan a²oud* (1975), *Two Women / Imra²atân* (1975)

Randrasana, Ignace-Solo. Madagascan filmmaker. Studied film at the Malagasy Production Centre and worked as assistant director. Feature films: *Very Remby / Le Retour* (1973), *Mad 47 / Ilo Tsy Very* (1987)

Rautenbach, Jans (b. 1936 in Boksburg). South African filmmaker. Studied first theology and then criminology. Self-taught filmmaker who began his career working for Jamie Uys Films. A pioneering figure in Afrikaans filmmaking, his first two 1960s features were produced by Emil Nofal. He abandoned filmmaking in 1984. It was later revealed that he secretly made propaganda films funded by the South African Defence Force. Feature-length documentary: *Sestig Jaar van John Vorster* (1976) Feature films: *Die Kandidaat* (Afrikaans, 1968), *Katrina* (Afrikaans, 1969), *Jannie Totsiens* (Afrikaans, 1970), *Pappalap* (1971), *Ongewensde Vreemdeling* (Afrikaans, 1974), *Eendag op in Reëndag / Die Rousseaus van La Rochelle* (Afrikaans, 1975), *Erfgoed is Sterfgoed* (Afrikaans, 1976), *The Winners II / Again My Way* (English, 1977), *Blink Stefaans* (Afrikaans, 1981), *No-one Cries Forever / Tears in the Dry Wind* (1983), *Broer Matie* (Afrikaans, 1984), *Die Groen Faktor* (Afrikaans, 1984)

Rchich, Abdelmajid (b. 1942 in Kinetra). Moroccan filmmaker. Studied filmmaking at the Institut des Hautes Études Cinématographiques (IDHEC) in Paris, and later anthropology and the history of art in Brussels. Joined the Centre Cinématographique Marocain (CCM) in 1964 and became a noted documentary filmmaker for many years. Made his feature debut at the age of 58. Feature films: *The Story of a Rose / L'Histoire d'une rose* (2000), *Broken Wings / Les Ailes brisées* (2006)

Reda, Ali. Egyptian filmmaker. Feature films: *The Winter Holidays / Agâzat nisf al-sanah* (1962), *Love at Karnak / Gharâm fî-l-Karnak* (1967), *The Thief Who Stole the Lottery Ticket / Harâmîal-waraqah* (1970), *Girls Ought to Get Married / al-Banât lâzim titgawwiz* (1973), *Never Again, good heavens / Yâ rabb toubah* (1975), *O Night . . . O Time / Al yâ layl yâ zaman* (1977), *Masters and Slaves / Asyâd wa ʿabîd* (1978), *My Life Is Suffering / Hayâyî ʿadhâb* (1979), *The Trial of "The Uncle Ahmed" / Qadiyyat ʿamm Ahmad* (1985)

Reda, Hassan. Egyptian filmmaker. Feature films: *The Adventurer / al-Moughâmir* (1948), *A / Khayâl imraʾah* (1948), *The Murdress / al-Qâtilah* (1949), *Intelligence Is a Good Thing / al-Aql zînah* (1950), *Between Ourselves / Baynî wa Baynak* (1953), *The Happiest Days / Asʾad al-ayyâm* (1954), *Forgive Mei / Samihnî* (1958), *The Matron / al-Mouʾallimah* (1958), *I Shall Not Return / Lan aʾoud* (1959), *Samara's Ghost / ʿIfrît Samârah* (1959), *Al-Mabrouk / Al-Mabrouk* (1959), *Abou Ahmed / Abou Ahmad* (1960), *My*

Beloved's Khoulkhal / Khoulkhâl habîbî (1960), *The Accursed Castle / al-Qasr al-malʾoun* (1962), *A Man in the Shadows / Ragoul fî-l-zalâm* (1963), *Without Hope / Min gheir amal* (1963), *Fire in My Heart / Nâr fii sadrî* (1963), *The River of Life / Nahr al-hayât* (1964), *Farewell to the Night / Wadâʾan ayyouhâ al-layl* (1966), *Three Stories / Thalâth qisas* (one episode) (1968), *Lovers Island / Gazîrat al-ʾouchchâq* (1968), *The Gates of the Night / Abwâb al-layl* (1969), *Evasion / Houroub* (1970), *Moments of Fear / Lahzât khawf* (1972)

Reggab, Mohamed (b. 1942 in Safi; d. 1990). Moroccan filmmaker. Studied film at the École Louis Lumière in Paris and then at VGIK in Moscow. Also studied psychology in Brussels and audio-visual studies in Germany. Joined Moroccan television in 1967 and made a number of short films. Part of the collective that made *Cinders of the Vineyard / Les Cendres du clos* (1977). Imprisoned for the debts incurred by the making of his sole feature. Feature film: *The Barber of the Poor Quarter / Le Coiffeur du quartier des pauvres* (1982)

Reinhl, Harold. South African filmmaker. Feature films: *Jungle Paradise* (English, 1982), *Just Desserts* (English, 1986), *Just for the Money* (English, 1987)

Reinhl, Heinz. South African filmmaker. Feature film: *Dooie Duikers Deel Nie* (Afrikaans, 1974)

Rennie, Howard. South African filmmaker. Worked as assistant to Cy Enfield, Nicholas Roeg and Cornell Wilde. Feature films: *Forgotten Summer* (English, 1970), *Stop Exchange* (English, 1970), *De Wet's Spoor* (Afrikaans, 1975)

Retief, Bertrand. South African filmmaker. Feature films: *Groetnis vir die Eerste Minister* (Afrikaans, 1973), *Die Seun van die Wiltemmer* (Afrikaans, 1973), *Boland!* (Afrikaans, 1974), *Mirage Eskader* (Afrikaans, 1975), *Ses Soldate / Six Soldiers* (Afrikaans, 1975), *My Liedjie van Verlange* (Afrikaans, 1975), *Hank, Hennery and Friend* (English, 1976), *Pretoria O Pretoria* (Afrikaans, 1979)

Retief, Daan. South African filmmaker. Feature films: *Staal Burger* (Afrikaans, 1969), *Breekpunt* (Afrikaans, 1971), *Salomien* (Afrikaans, 1972), *Jamie 21* (Afrikaans, 1973), *Soekie* (Afrikaans, 1975), *Die Rebel / Sending vir 'n Voortvlugtige* (Afrikaans, 1976), *Sonja* (Afrikaans, 1978), *Night of the Puppets* (English, 1979), *Beloftes van Môre* (Afrikaans, 1981)

Rezzoug, Abdellah. Libyan filmmaker. Feature films: *When Fate Hardens / ʿIndama Yaqsu al-Zaman* (1973), *Song of the Rain / Maʾazufatu al-matar* (1991)

Rhanja, Hassan. Moroccan filmmaker. Feature film: *Argana* (2007)

Riad, Mohamed Slim (b. 1932 in Cherchell). Algerian filmmaker. Received no formal film training. Worked for French television and was imprisoned in France as an FLN supporter. Made short films for CNC and one téléfilm, *Inspector Tahar / Inspecteur Tahar* (1969). Feature films: *The Way / La Voie* (1968), *Sanaʾoud* (1972), *Wind from the South / Vent du sud* (1975), *Autopsy of a Plot / Autopsie d'un complot* (1978), *Dead the Long Night / Morte la longue nuit* (documentary, with Ghaouti Bendeddouche, 1979), *Hassan Taxi* (1982)

Riad, Nagui. Egyptian filmmaker. Feature film: *The Three Faces of Love / Thalâth wougouh li-l-houbb* (one episode) (1969)

Ribeiro, Tom (b. 1935 in Ghana). Ghanaian filmmaker. Studied at the City University of New York and worked first as assistant, then as director, on various commercials, documentaries and features, including Denis Sanders's *Soul to Soul* (1971). Feature films: *Genesis Chapter X* (1977), *The Visitor* (1983), *Dede* (1983), *Out of Sight* (1983)

Riber, John. US-born filmmaker resident in Zimbabwe. Began as producer with the Media for Development Trust, responsible, for example, for *Consequences* (a documentary on teenage pregnancy, co-directed with Olley Maruma), as well as Godwin Mawuru's *Neria*, Isaac Meli Mabhikwa's *More Time* and Tsitsi Dangarembga's *Everyone's Child*. Feature film: *Yellow Card* (2000)

Richard, Christian. French maker of one Burkinabè feature film, the second to be produced by the short-lived private company Sociétété Africaine de Cinéma (CINAFRIC). At the time he was teaching at the Institut Africain d'Education Cinématographique (INAFEC). Feature film: *Other People's Courage / Le Courage des autres* (1982)

Robinson, Roland. South African filmmaker. Feature film: *Wastelands / The Wasteland* (English, 1989)

Roets, Hannes. South African filmmaker. Feature film: *Liewe Hemel, Genis!* (Afrikaans, with William Egan, 1988)

Roets, Koos (b. Prieska). South African filmmaker. Began his film career in 1962 as assistant cameraman on Jamie Uys's *Lord Oom Piet* and became a leading cinematographer. Feature films: *Die Erfgenaam* (Afrikaans, 1971), *Vlug van die Seemeeu* (Afrikaans, 1972), *Die Sersant en die Tiger Moth* (Afrikaans, 1973), *Babblekous en Bruidegom* (Afrikaans, 1974), *Daar Kom Tant Alie* (Afrikaans, 1976), *Kootjie Emmer* (Afrikaans, 1977), *Wie Laaste Lag / Danger Games* (Afrikaans, 1985), *Brutal Glory / Kid McCoy* (English, 1988), *Liewe Hemel Genis* (Afrikaans, 1988), *For Better for Worse / The Gentile Wedding* (English, 1990), *The Sandgrass People* (English, 1990), *Die Nag van die 19de* (Afrikaans, 1991), *The Angel, the Bicycle and the Chinaman's Finger* (English, with Nicholas Ellenbogen, 1992), *Running Riot* (English, 2006)

Rogeogian, Gabriel. Egyptian silent filmmaker. Silent feature: *The Strange Adventure / al-Moukhâtarach al-ʾaguîbah* (1929)

Rogers, John. South African filmmaker. Feature film: *The Gift* (English, 1990)

Rogosin, Lionel (1928–2000). US-born filmmaker who achieved initial fame with his US documentary, *On the Bowery* (1956). Equally known for his clandestinely filmed study of black township life (included in all listings of South African feature films): *Come Back Africa* (English, 1958)

Roodt, Darrell (b. 1963 in Johannesburg). South African filmmaker. Abandoned his studies at the Drama Department of the University of Witwatersrand to move directly into filmmaking. Began as assistant to Gray Hofmeyr and Elmo de Witt, before beginning his directing career with two African-language features. He is the most prolific of the South African filmmakers who came to the fore in the 1980s. Feature films: *Mr TNT* (Zulu, 1984), *Wind Rider* (Zulu/ Xhosa, 1985), *Tenth of a Second* (1986). *City of Blood* (1986), *Place of Weeping* (1987), *The Stick* (1988), *Jobman / Devil's Land* (1988), *American Kickboxer II / The Road Back* (English, with Albert Pyun, 1990), *To the Death* (English, 1991), *Sarafina* (English, 1991), *Fatherhood* (1993), *Cry the Beloved Country* (English, 1994), *Dangerous Ground* (English, 1997), *The Second Skin* (English, 2000), *Pavement* (English, 2003), *Sumuru* (English, 2003), *Yesterday* (English, 2004), *Number Ten* (English, 2005), *Faith's Corner* (English, 2005), *Prey* (English, 2006), *Lullaby* (English, 2007)

Roper, Mark. South African filmmaker. Feature films: *Dancing in the Forest* (English, 1988), *Human Timebomb* (English, 1994), *War Head* (English, 1995), *Delta Force 3—Clear Target* (English, 1997)

Rosito, Victor. Italian maker of a pioneering Egyptian silent feature: *In the Land of Tutankhamen / Fî bilâd Tout Ankh Amon* (1923)

Rosti, Stephane (1891–1964). Veteran Egyptian filmmaker and actor. Born in Cairo of an Italian mother and aristicratic Austrian father. Worked as a actor in Cairo from 1917. Completed the first Egyptian fictional feature film, *Leila,* after a dispute between the star and producer Aziza Amir and the original director, Wedad Orfi. In his acting career, which continued until his death, he specialised in playing villains. Silent feature films: *Leila / Layla* (with Wedad Orfi, 1927), *Why Is the Sky Laugh-*

ing? / al-Bahr biyidhak lîh (1928), *The Clerk Kish Kish Bey / Sâhib al-saʾâdah Kichkich bek* (with Naguib al-Rihani, 1931). Sound feature films: *The Clerk Kish Kish Bey / Sahib al-saʾadah Kichkich bek* (with Naguib al-Rihani, 1934), *Mr Antar / ʿAntar afandi* (1935), *The Factory / al-Warchah* (1940), *Son of the Country / Ibn al-balad* (1942), *The Most Beautiful Woman / Ahlâhoum* (1945), *Gamal and Dalal / Gamâl wa Dalâl* (1945)

Rothig, Thomas. South African filmmaker. Feature film: *Sky Full of Diamonds* (English, 1989)

Rouchdi, Fatma (b. 1908). Egyptian filmmaker and actress. Brought up in Cairo, she met and married the stage director Aziz Ide, who guided her career. After achieving fame on the stage and starring in Ibrahim Lama's *Drama at the Pyramids* (1928), she went on to direct a feature. Also starred in twenty films, including Kamal Selim's *The Will* (1939). Feature film: *The Marriage / al-Zawâg* (1933)

Rouchdi, Neimat. Egyptian filmmaker. Feature film: *The Battle between the Wives / Sirâʾ al-zawgât* (1992)

Roup, Stanley. South African filmmaker. Feature film: *Nag van Vrees / Night of Terror* (Afrikaans, with Jimmy Murray, 1986)

Roux, Jean-Pierre. South African filmmaker. Feature film: *The Piano Player* (English, 2002)

Rowley, Christopher. South African filmmaker. Feature film: *Death of a Snowman* (English, 1982)

Rubens, Percival. South African filmmaker and producer. Feature films: *The Forster Gang* (English, 1964), *The Long Red Shadow / Three Days of Fire* (English, 1968), *Strangers at Sunrise* (English, 1969), *Mr Kingstreet's War* (English, 1971), *Die Saboteurs* (Afrikaans, 1974), *Mightyman 1 and 2* (Zulu, 1979), *The Demon / Midnight Caller* (English, 1980), *Survival Zone* (English, 1984),

Hostage (English, with Hanro Möhr, 1986), *Okavango / Wild Country* (English, 1989), *Sweet Murder* (English, 1989)

Ryan, Terence. South African filmmaker. Feature film: *Hold My Hand, I'm Dying* (English, with Duncan McLachlan, 1988)

Saab, Jocelyne. Lebanese director of one Egyptian feature film included in official listings: *Dunia / Dunia* (2006)

Saadi, Jilani (b. 1962 in Bizerte). Tunisian filmmaker. Studied filmmaking in Paris. One short film and a medium-length work in the mid-1990s. Feature films: *Khorma: Stupidity / Khorma, la bêtise* (2002), *Wolf's Kindness / Tendresse du loup* (2006)

Sabela, Simon (b. 1931 in Durban). South African filmmaker. Self-taught filmmaker, actor, musician. For many years he was the only black South African able to work as a film director. It is estimated that his first film (the second feature in the Zulu langage) was seen by two million spectators. Feature films: *U-Deliwe* (Zulu,1975), *Inkedama* (Xhosa, 1975), *The Boxer* (Zulu, 1976), *Ngwanaka / My Child* (Sotho,1976), *I-Kati Elimnyana / The Black Cat* (Zulu, 1976), *The Eagle* (Zulu, 1976), *Ngata* (Tswana, 1976), *Inyakanyaka* (Zulu, 1977), *The Advocate* (Zulu, 1978), *Isuvemelwano* (Zulu, 1978), *Setipana* (Sotho, 1978), *Setipana* (Zulu, 1979), *Umunt Akalahlwa* (Zulu, 1979)

Sabet, Madkour. Egyptian filmmaker. Feature films: *Forbidden Images / Souwar mamnou'ah* (one episode) (1972), *The Idiot Boy / al-Walad al-ghâbi* (1977)

Sabri, Cherif. Egyptian filmmaker. Feature film: *7 Playing Cards / 7 waraqaat kutsheena* (2004)

Sabri, Mohamed. Egyptian silent filmmaker. Silent feature: *The Midnight Crime / Guinâyat mountasaf al-layl* (1930)

Saddiki, Tayeb (b. 1937 in Essaouira). Moroccan playwright, actor and filmmaker. Has written many dramas for stage and television and also worked extensively as an actor in film, theatre and television. Founded a succession of theatre groups in Morocco. A number of his plays have been published in Morocco, including *Le Dîner de gala*, (1990), *Les Sept grains de beauté*, (1994), *Molière, ou Pour l'amour de l'humanité*, (1994), *Nous sommes faits pour nous entendre* (1997). He also published a book of notes and aphorisms, *Par cœur*, in 2002. Scripted and directed numerous commercials and téléfilms. Feature film: *Zeft* (1984)

Sadek, Adel. Egyptian filmmaker. Feature films: *My Love in Cairo / Houbbî fî-l-Qâhirah* (1966), *Young People in the Storm / Chabâb fi 'âsifah* (1971), *The Story of the West Quarter / Qissat al-hayy al-gharbî* (1979), *The Wolves / al-Dhi'âb* (1983), *The End of a Married Man / Nihâyat ragoul moutazawwig* (1983), *Husbands at Your Service / Zawg taht al-talab* (1985), *The Crook and the Dog / al-Nassâb wa-l-kalb* (1990), *Two Outlaws / Ithnân didd al qânuun* (1992)

Safo, Socrat. Ghanaian filmmaker. Video feature: *Stand by Me* (1996)

Saheb-Ettaba, Nawfel (b. 1937 in Essaouira). Tunisian filmmaker. Studied visual communication and film at the University of Quebec. Directed documentaries, commercials, institutional films and television programs. Also worked as scriptwriter and made a medium-length documentary, *Stambali*, in Tunisia. Feature film: *The Bookstore / El-Kotbia* (2002)

Sahraoui, Djamila (b. 1950 in Algiers). Algerian filmmaker. She studied literature in Algiers and filmmaking at the Institut des Hautes Études Cinématographiques (IDHEC) in Paris, where she has lived since 1975. From 1990 made seven documentaries, including the feature-length works *The Other Half of Allah's Heaven / L'Autre moitié du ciel d'Allah* (1995), *Algeria, Life in Spite of It All / Algérie la vie quand même* (1999), *Algeria Life Still / Algérie la vie toujours* (2001) and *Trees Grow in Kabylia / Les Arbes poussent en Kabylie* (2003), which have been widely shown at international festivals. Fictional feature: *Barakat!* (2005)

Saïd, Hamed. Egyptian filmmaker. Feature films: *First Love / al-Hubb al-awwal* (2000), *Criminal Troop 16 / al-Firqa 16 igraam* (2006)

Saïd, Sayed. Egyptian filmmaker. Feature film: *The Captain / Al-qubtaan* (1997)

Salah Eddine, Kamal. Egyptian filmmaker. Feature films: *Adaweyya / ʿAdawiyyah* (1968), *Flowers and Thorns / Ward wa chawk* (1970), *Wolves on the Road / Dhiʾâb ʿalâ al-tarîq* (1972), *Young Girls and Ladies / Ânisât wa sayyidât* (1974), *A Different Girl / Bint ghayr koull al-banât* (1978), *The Window / al-Choubbâk* (1980), *Pity / al-Rahman yâ nâs* (1981), *Gharib Is a Strange Boy / Gharîb walad ʿaguîb* (1983), *The Tough Guys from Bab al-Cheiriyyah / Guyidʾân Bâb al-Chiʾriyyah* (1983), *Ragab the Monster / Ragab al-wahch* (1985), *The Midnight Patrol / Dawriyyat nouss al-layl* (1986), *The Liars / Kaddâbîn al-zaffah* (1986)

Salah, Said. Somalian filmmaker and dramatist. Feature film: *The Somali Darwish* (with Amar Sneh, 1984)

Salami, Adebayo. Nigerian filmmaker. Feature film: *Omo Orukan* (Yoruba, 1987)

Saleh, Ahmed. Egyptian filmmaker. Feature film: *Italian War /Harb Italia* (2005)

Saleh, Fadel. Egyptian filmmaker. Feature film: *The Prince / al-Prince* (1984)

Saleh, Saïd. Egyptian filmmaker. Feature film: *The Lion's Share / Nasîb al-asad* (1992)

Saleh, Simon. Egyptian filmmaker. Feature films: *Virgin, but . . . / ʿAdhrâʾ wa lâkin* (1977), *Suzy, Love Merchant / Suzy bâʾiʾat al-houbb* (1978), *A Man Only Lives Once / al-Insân yaʾîch marrah wâhidah* (1981), *Love in Difficult Circumstances / al-Hubb fî zoroof saʾba* (1996)

Saleh, Tewfik (b. 1926 in Alexandria). Egyptian filmmaker, widely recognized as a maor figure

in Arab cinema. He studied at the English-language Victoria College and then took a degree in English Literature at Alexandria University. In 1950 traveled to France where he stayed 2 years, exploring the world of the arts and frequenting the Cinémathèque Française. Back in Cairo, he worked with Naguib Marfouz on the script for his first feature, which he had great difficulty in setting up. Never truly part of the Egyptian film scene of the 1950s, it was 7 years before he could direct a second feature. With the founding of the General Organisation of Egyptian Cinema he was able to make three features in 4 years, but his direct expression of his political views led to real censorship problems. Exasperated, Saleh went abroad, first to Syria where he made *The Dupes* (1973), which won the top prize, the *Tanit d'or*, at the Journées Cinématographiques de Carthage (JCC) in 1972, and then to Iraq where he directed *The Long Days* (1980). After his eventual return to Egypt, he has made no further films, but taught at the Cairo Higher Film Institute. Egyptian feature films: *Street of Fools / Darb al-Mahâbîl* (1955), *The Heroes' Struggle / Sirâʾ al-abtâl* (1962), *The Rebels / al-Moutamarridoun* (1968), *Diary of a Deputy Country Prosecutor / Yawmiyyât nâʾib fî-l-aryâf* (1969), *Al-Sayyed Al-Bolti / al-Sayyed al-Boltî* (1969)

Saleh, Zaki. Egyptian filmmaker. Feature films: *The Boss's Empire / Ambaratouriyyat al mouʾallim* (1974), *A Bachelor's Loves / Gharâmiyyât ʿâzib* (1976), *The Pretty Liar / al-Bint al-hilwah al-kaddâbah* (1977), *A Flat and a Woman, dear Lord / Chiqqah wa ʿarousa yia rabb* (1978), *The Circle of Doubt / Dâʾirat al-chakk* (1980), *Take Care, We're the Mad Ones / Ihtaris nahnou al-magânîn* (1981)

Salem, Ahmed (b. 1910; d. 1949). Egyptian filmmaker and actor. Son of a rich family, he studied engineering in Cambridge and became a pioneer of Egyptian aviation. An early participant in Egyptian radio in 1934, he became director general of the Misr studios the following year. In 1939 he resigned to write, direct, and star in his first personal film. He died at the age of 39 while directing his seventh feature. *Tears* *of Happiness,* completed by Fatine Abdel Wahab. Feature films: *Wings of the Desert / Agnihat al-sahrâ* (1939), *The Unknown Past / al-Mâdî al-mag³houl* (1946), *Man of the Future / Ragoul al-moustaqbal* (1946), *Antar's Son / Ibn ᶜAntar* (1947), *A Crippled Life / Hayâh hâ³irah* (1948), *The Unknown Future / al-Moustaqbal al-mag³houl* (1948), *Tears of Happiness / Doumou³ al-farah* (with Fatine Abdel Wahab, 1950)

Salem, Atef (b. 1927 in Kordofan in Sudan). Egyptian filmmaker. Introduced to the cinema by Ahmed Galal, whose assistant he became in 1948. He subsequently worked with Ahmed Badrakhan. He also appeared as an actor in a number of films. His most striking films were made from scripts by Naguib Mahfouz. Feature films: *Wretchedness / al-Hirmân* (1953), *They have Made me a Killer / Ga³alounî mougriman* (1954), *A Night in My Life / Laylah min³oumrî* (1954), *Fagr / Fagr* (1955), *Voices from the Past / Sawt min al-mâdî* (1956), *Divine Miracle / Mou³guizat al-samâ³* (1956), *The Rebel / al-Namroud* (1956), *A Millionnaire's Love / Gharâm al-millionaire* (1957), *Teach Me Love / ᶜAllimounî al houbb* (1957), *The Shore of Secrets / Châti³ al-asrâr* (1958), *Struggle on the Nile / Sirâ³ fî-l-Nîl* (1959), *Crime of Love / garîmat houbb* (1959), *We the Students / Ihnâ al-talâmdhah* (1959), *Rendezvous with the Unknown / Maw³id ma³ al-mag³houl* (1959), *A Woman's Secret / Sirr imra³ah* (1960), *No Understanding / Mâ fîch tafâhoum* (1961, *Seven Girls / al-Sab³banât* (1961), *One Day in My Life / Yawm min ᶜoumrî* (1961), *The Naked Truth / al-Haqîqah al-³âriyah* (1963), *The Bride's Mother / Oumm al-arousah* (1963), *Escaped from Life / Hârib min al-hayât* (1964), *The Mamelouks / al-Mamâlîk* (1965 Atef Salem), *Khan al-Khalili / Khân al-Khalîlî* (1966), *The Revolution in Yemen / Thawrat al-Yaman* (1966), *A Woman from Paris / Zawgah min Paris* (1966), *The Circus / al-Sîrk* (1968), *Girls at University / Banât fîl-gâmi³ah* (1971), *The Service Stairs / al-Soullam al-khalfî* (1973), *Lost Love / Zamân al-houbb* (1973), *Where Is My Reason? / Ayna ᶜaqlî?* (1974), *The Grandson / al-Hafîd* (1974), *The Queen and I / al-Malikah wa anâ* (1975), *Young People Today / Choubbân hâdhihi al-ayyâm* (1975), *And the*

Train of My Life Passes / Wa madâ qitâr al-³oumr (1975), *The Peaceful Nest / al-³Ichch al-hâdi* (1976), *Legs in the Mud / Siqân fî-l-wahl* (1976), *First Year of Love / Sanah oulâ houbb* (one episode) (1976), *Barefoot on a Golden Bridge / Hâfiyah ᶜalâ Guisr min-al-dhahab* (1977), *Bye bye My Pretty One / Bay bay yâ helwah* (1977), *That's How Life Goes / Hâkadhâ al-ayyâm* (1977), *Life Is Over, My Son / Dâ³ al-oumr yâ waladî* (1978), *The Wretched / al-Bou³asâ³* (1978), *Conqueror of the Darkness / Qâhir al-zalâm* (1979), *Storm of Tears / ᶜAsifah min al-doumou³* (1979), *The Woman in Love / al-³Âchiqah* (1980), *The Clairvoyant / al-³Arrâfah* (1981), *The Black Panther / al-Nimr al-aswad* (1984), *The House of the Irreproachable / Bayt al-kawâmil* (1986), *The Edge of the Sword Blade / Hadd al-sayf* (1986), *Completely Lost / al-Dâ³i³ah* (Atef Salem), *Oh People / Yâ nâs yâ hou* (1991), *His Majesty's Tears / Doumou³ sahibat al-galâlah* (1992), *Toot Toot / Tout tout* (1993), *I Forgot That I Was a Woman / Wa nasîtou annî imra³ah* (1994)

Salem, Mohamed. Egyptian filmmaker. Feature films: *Cairo by Night / al-Qâhirah Desore / Nâr al-chawq* (1970), *Amacha in the Jungle / ᶜAmâchah fî-l-adghâl* (1972)

Salem, Nadia. Egyptian filmmaker. Feature film: *The Doorman Is at Your Service / Sâhib al-idârah bawwâb al-³imârah* (1985)

Salmane, Mohamed. Egyptian filmmaker. Feature films: *The Demon / al-Chaytân* (1969), *Where Does the Story Begin? / Nibtidî minîn al-hikâyah* (1976), *Who Will Extinguish the Fire? / Man youtfî³ al-nâr* (1982), *Beauty of the Night / Qamar al-layl* (1984), *The Celebrity World / ᶜÂlam al-chouhrah* (1985), *I Suffer from Love for You / Anâ wa-l-³adhâb wa hawâk* (1988)

Salomon, Mikael. South African filmmaker. Feature film: *A Far Off Place* (English, 1993)

Samama Chikly, Albert (b. 1872; d. 1934). Pioneer Tunisian filmmaker. An enthusiast for all aspects of western scientific development, he organised the first film screenings in Tunisia in 1897, explored radio and x-ray technology, shot film from a balloon and underwater. During the 1914–1918 war he was a photographer with the French army, shooting film at the front at Verdun in 1916. A life-long photographer, documenting all aspects of Tunisian life, his film work comprises a pioneering short, *Zohra* (1922) as well as a first feature. Both films were made in close collaboration with his daughter, who wrote the scripts and starred in both, as well as being in charge of the editing. Feature film: *The Girl from Carthage / La Fille de Carthage / Aïn el-Ghezal* (1924)

Samb-Makharam, Ababacar (b. 1934 in Dakar; d. 1987). Senegalese filmmaker. Studied drama at the Centre d'Art Dramatique de la rue Blanche in Paris and trained at the Centro sperimentale di cinematografia in Rome. On his return to Senegal in 1964 he worked for the Ministry of Information. One of the pioneers of Senegalese cinema, his first feature explores the conventional opposition between tradition and modernity, while the second, through its pioneering treatment of the role of the griot and its narrative cut loose from restraints of time and place, anticipates later developments in francophone African filmmaking. Feature films: *Kodou* (1971), *Jom / Jom ou l'histoire d'un peuple* (1981)

Sameh, Wali Eddine. Egyptian filmmaker. Feature films: *The Woman and the Puppet / Liʾbat al-sitt* (1946), *My Father's Secret / Sirr abî* (1946), *Lipstick / Ahmar chafâyif* (1946), *The Hypocrite / Dhou al-wagʾhayn* (with Ahmed Diaa Eddine, 1949)

Sanon, Emmanuel Kalifa (b. 1954 in Burkina Faso). Burkinabè filmmaker. Studied at the Institut Africain d'Education Cinématographique (INAFEC) in Ouagadougou and at the Sorbonne in Paris. Worked in television and made short documentaries. His only feature film is one of the largely Burkinabè-financed educative features which have not received European distribution. Made a feature-length video, *L'Amour est encore possible* in 2006. Feature film: *Desebagato / Le Dernier salaire* (1987)

Sanou, Kollo Daniel (b. 1949, in Borodougou). Burkinabè filmmaker. Studied filmmaking at the Conservatoire Libre du Cinéma Français (CLCF) in Paris. His first two films, the first melodramatic, the second educative, are largely Burkinabè-financed films which have not received European distribution. His third feature, the study of a former soldier in the French army, did, however, get a wider, successful distribution. Feature films: *The Emigrant / Paweogo / L'Émigrant* (1982), *Jiji* (1992), *Tasuma* (2002)

Santry, Denis. South African silent filmmaker. Feature film: *An Artist's Inspiration / The Artist's Dream* (Silent, with Harold Shaw, 1916)

Saqr, Ahmed. Egyptian filmmaker. Feature films: *Man Caught in a Women's Trap / Ragoul fî fakh al-nisâʾ* (1987), *The Dancers' Machinations / Kayd alʾawâlim* (1991), *Gaber's Resignation / Istiqâlat Gaber* (1992), *The Shrew / al-Charisah* (1993), *The Truth Is Called Salem / al-Haqîqah ismouha Sâlim* (1994)

Sargeant, Roy. South African filmmaker. Feature films: *The Winners* (English, with Emil Nofal, 1972), *Oh Brother* (English, 1974), *Kniediep* (Afrikaans, 1975)

Sarwat, Ahmed. Egyptian filmmaker. Feature films: *Live marriage / Gawiz ʿalâ al-hawâ* (1976), *For Life / Min agl al-hayât* (1977), *Bayada / Bayyâdah* (1981), *Moukhaymer Is Always Ready / Moukhaymir gâhiz dâʾiman* (1982), *Five in Hell / Khamsah fî-l-gahîm* (1982), *Why Is Massoud Happy / Masʾoud saʾîd lîh* (1983), *Forbidden Games / Alʾâb mamnouʾah* (1984), *All Is Well / Koullouh tamân* (1984), *To Avenge Ragab / al-Intiqâm la-Ragab* (1984), *The Tough Guy from Darb al-Assal / Foutouwwat Darb al-ʾAssâl* (1985), *The Accusation / al-Ittihâm* (1987), *Fire Woman / Imraʾah min nâr* (1987), *A Genie on Stamped Paper / ʿAbqarî ʿalâ warqah damghah* (1987), *A Madman's Testament / Wasiyyat ragoul magʾnoun* (1987), *The Troublemakers' Excursion / Rihlat al-mouchâghibîn* (1988), *The Liar and His Friend / al-Kaddâb wa sahibouh* (1989), *The Captain Has Arrived / al-Kâbtin wasal* (1991), *Memories and*

Regrets / Dhikrayât wa nadam (1992), *Nights of Waiting / Laylâlî al-sabr* (1992)

Schadeberg, Jurgen. South African filmmaker. Feature film: *Have You Seen Drum Recently* (English, 1988)

Schaeffer, Frank. South African filmmaker. Feature films: *Bloodshot* (English, 1988), *Headhunter* (English, 1988), *Ship of the Desert / Renegades* (English, 1988), *The Crime Lords* (English, with Wayne Crawford, 1990)

Schiess, Mario. South African filmmaker. Feature films: *Onwettige Huwelik* (Afrikaans, 1970), *Bait* (English, 1974)

Schlesinger, Isidore W. South African silent filmmaker. An American businessman with extensive British-based interests, he set up African Film Productions (AFP) in 1916 and produced over 40 silent features. He later controlled film distribution throughout South Africa. One film as director. Feature film: *Symbol of Sacrifice* (1918)

Schmitz, Oliver (b. 1960 in Cape Town). South African filmmaker, currently resident in Berlin. Studied fine art at the University of Cape Town. Work in underground left-wing documentary in the 1980s. Numerous internationally shown documentaries since his feature debut. Feature films: *Mapantsula* (English/Afrikaans/Sotho/Zulu, with Thomas Mogotlane, 1987), *Hijack Stories* (English, 2000)

Scholz, Jan (b. Boksburg). South African filmmaker. Worked as a teacher before joining the SABC as a journalist, while also writing scripts and novels. Head of Afrikaans drama when television was launched in the 1970s. Feature films: *'n Sondag in September* (Afrikaans, 1976), *Die Winter van 14 Julie* (Afrikaans, 1977), *Diamant en die Dief* (Afrikaans, 1978), *Die Eensame Vlug* (Afrikaans, 1979), *Herfsland* (Afrikaans, 1979), *Skelms* (Afrikaans, 1980), *April 1980* (Afrikaans/English, 1980), *Kiepie en Kandas* (Afrikaans, 1980), *Magic Is Alive My Friends*

(English, 1985), *Dada en Die Flower* (Afrikaans, 1988), *Paradise Road / Traitors* (English, 1988), *The Emissary* (English, 1988)

Schroeder, Michael. South African filmmaker. Feature film: *Damned River* (English, 1988)

Schuster, Leon. South African filmmaker. Popular South African comedian. Feature films: *You Must Be Joking Too* (English, 1987), *Oh Shucks, It's Schuster* (English, 1989), *The Millennium Menace* (English, 1999), *Oh Schucks I'm Gatvol* (English, with Willie Esterhuizen, 2004)

Schutz, Jacques. Frenchman resident in Egypt and co-founder, with Alvisi Orfanelli and Giaccomo Puccini, of the Egyptian Artistic Film Company in 1928. Maker of one Egyptian silent feature: *Goha / Goha* (1929)

Scolari, Italo. South African filmmaker. Feature film: *King of Africa / One Step to Hell* (English, with Sandy Howard, 1969)

Scott, Clive. South African filmmaker. Feature films: *Dumela Sam* (English/Sotho,1981 with Jimmy Murray, 1981), *Mathata* (English/Sotho, with Jimmy Murray, 1984)

Scully, Dennis. South African filmmaker. Feature films: *Tremor / As die Aarde Skeur* (English/Afrikaans, 1961), *Hands of Space* (English, 1961), *Journey to Nowhere* (English, 1963), *The Zambezi Kid* (English, 1988), *Diamonds High* (English, 1988), *Chasing Namibia* (English, 1989)

Se Phuma, Peter. South African filmmaker. Feature film: *Tommy 2* (Zulu, 1983)

Seck, Amadou Saalum (b. 1952 in Dakar). Senegalese filmmaker. Studied filmmaking in Munich, Germany. Feature films: *Utopia / Saaraba* (1988), *Ndobine* (2003)

Sedki, Hussein (b. 1917; d. 1961). Egyptian filmmaker and actor. One of the first Egyptian film stars not previously to have been a stage performer or singer. Up to his death in 1961 he appeared in about sixty films, some directed by himself. Feature films: *Betrayal and Suffering / Ghadr wa ᶜadhâb* (1947), *The Killer / al-Qâtil* (1948), *Towards Fame / Nahw al-magd* (1948), *Mr Egypt / al-Masrî afandî* (1949), *A Path Strewn with Thorns / Tarîq al-chawk* (1950), *Life Is a Struggle / Maᵓrakat al-hayâh* (1950), *Adam and Eve / Adam wa Hawwâᵓ* (1951), *The Night of Destiny / Laylat al-qadr* (1952), *The Unfortunate / al-Masâkîn* (1952), *The Happy Family / al-Bayt al-saᵓîd* (1952), *Down with Colonialism / Yasqout al-istiᵓmâr* (1952), *Cheikh Hassan / al-Chaykh Hasan* (1954), *My Heart Loves You / Qalbî yahwâk* (1955), *Khaled Ibn al-Walid / Khâlid bin al-Walid* (1958), *My Fatherland and My Love / Watanî wa houbbî* (1960), *I am Justice / Anâ al-ᵓadâlah* (1961)

Sefrioui, Najib (b. 1948 in Fez). Moroccan filmmaker. Studied Arab literature at the Sorbone and filmmaking at the École Louis Lumière in Paris. Worked as a critic and completed a feature-length 16mm documentary, *The Children of Ben Barka / Les Enfants de Ben Barka* (1981). Feature films: *Chams* (1985), *Love without a Visa / Amour sans visa* (2001)

Seif, Samir (b. 1947 in Cairo). Egyptian filmmaker. Graduated from the Cairo Higher Film Institute in 1969 and worked as assistant director (including on Chadi Abdel-Salam's *The Mummy*). He worked as a film critic and taught direction at the Cairo Higher Film Institute. Feature films: *The Circle of Vengeance / Dâᵓirat al-intiqâm* (1976), *Cat on a Hot Tin Roof / Qittah ᶜalâ nâr* (1977), *Satan in the City / Iblîs fî-l-madîna* (1978), *The Savage / al-Moutawahhichah* (1979), *The Suspect / al-Machbouh* (1981), *A Foreigner at Home / Gharîb fî baytî* 1982), *The Ogre / al-Ghoul* (1983), *Beware of Khott / Ihtaris min al-Khott* (1984), *Streets of Fire / Chawâriᵓ min nâr* (1984), *The Last Respectable Man / Âkhir al-rîgal al-mouhtaramîn* (1984), *The Fugitive / al-Moutârad* (1985), *The Mediocrity / al-Halfout* (1985), *The Time of Wolves / ᶜAsr al-dhiᵓâb* (1986), *The Tiger and the Woman / al-Nimr wa-l-ounthâ* (1987), *The Fair / al-Mouled* (1989), *The She-Devil Who Loved Me / al-Chaytânah al-latî ahabbatnî* (1990), *The Dancer and the Poli-*

tician / al-Râqisah wa-l-siyâsi (1990), *Branded Dangerous / Mousaggal khartar* (1991), *Zanati's Sun / Chams al-Zanâti* (1991), *Flame of Vengeance / Lahîb al-intiqâm* (1993), *Time and the Dogs / al-Zaman wal kelaab* (1996), *Mushroom / ᶜEish el ghuraab* (1997), *Pleasure Market / Souq al-Mutᵓa* (2000), *His Excellency the Minister / Maᵓaly el wazeer* (2002), *Fishtail / Deil al-samaka* (2003)

Seif, Sayed. Egyptian filmmaker. Feature films: *Guard Dogs / Kilâb al-hirâsah* (1984), *The Licit and the Illicit / al-Halâl wa-l-harâm* (1985), *A Virgin and Three Men / ᶜAdhrâ wa thalâth rigâl* (1986), *Desire, Malice and Violence / Raghbahj wa hiqd wa intiqâm* 1987), *Bab al-Nasr / Bâb al-Nasr* (1988), *Khamis Conquers Cairo / Kharmîs yaghzou al-Qâhirah* (1990), *Foxes . . . Rabbits / Taᵓâlib . . . arânib* (1994)

Selim, Kamal (b. 1913; d. 1945). Egyptian filmmaker. After a short visit to Paris, he returned to Egypt to work as assistant director, scriptwriter, and eventually director at the Misr studios. His major film as a director, *The Will* (1939), is regarded as a key work in Egyptian film history. He also pioneered the adaptation of Western classics to the screen, making versions of works by Victor Hugo, Shakespeare, and Emily Bronte. Feature films: *In the Shadows / Warâ al-sitâr* (1937), *The Will / al-Azîmah* (1939), *For Ever / Ilâ al-abad* (1941), *Dreams of Youth / Ahlâm al-chabâb* (1942), *The Wretched / al-Bouᵓasâ* (1943), *The Day's Business / Qadiyyat al-yawm* (1943), *Hanane / Hanane* (1944), *Martyrs of Love / Chouhadâᵓ al-gharâm* (1944), *Appearances / al-Mazâhir* (1945), *Friday Night / Laylat al-goumᵓah* (1945), *Love Story / Qissat gharâm* (with Mohamed Abdel Gawad, 1945)

Selim, Osman Choukri. Egyptian filmmaker. Feature film: *The Prey / al-Fârisah* (1986)

Sembene, Ousmane (b. 1923 in Ziguinchor; d. 2007). Senegalese novelist and filmmaker. Sembene is a major French-language novelist with eight novels (five translated into English)—*Le Docker noir / Black Docker* (1956), *O pays, mon beau peuple* (1957), *Les Bouts de bois de dieu / God's Bits of Wood* (1960), *Le Mandat, précédé* de Véhi Ciosane / The Money Order with White Genesis (1966), Xala / Xala (1973), L'Harmattan (1980), Le Dernier de l'empire / The Last of Empire (1981), Guelwaar (1996)—and two books of stories—Voltaïque / Tribal Scars (1962) and Niiwam, suivi de Taaw / Niiwam and Taw (1987). Regarded by many as 'the father of African cinema', his first feature, Black Girl, was fittingly the first winner of the top prize, the Tanit d'or, at the first pan-African film festival, the Journées Cinématographiques de Carthage (JCC) in Tunis in 1966. Sembene has nine feature films and a number of shorts to his credit. He studied filmmaking with Mark Donskoi and Sergei Gerassimov in Moscow at the age of thirty-eight in 1961. Four short films, including Borom Sarret (1963) which marks the birth of cinema in Francophone West Africa. All his work is marked by his strong social commitment and Marxist view of society. Feature films: Black Girl / La Noire de... (1964), The Money Order / Mandabi / Le Mandat (1968), Emitai (1971), Xala (1974), Ceddo (1977), Camp de Thiaroye (with Thierno Faty Sow, 1988), Guelwaar (1992), Faat-Kine (1999), Moolade (2002)

Sene Absa, Moussa (b. 1958 in Dakar). Senegalese filmmaker, painter, writer, stage actor and musician. Studied filmmaking at the Université de Paris VIII. He has made films in an array of formats, mixing documentary and fiction. Best known to critics for the fluent camerawork and exuberant storytelling of his second feature, he achieved real popular success with his third. Feature films: Ken Bugul (1991), Tableau ferraille (1996), Madame Brouette (2002), Teranga Blues (2006)

Serri, Salah. Egyptian filmmaker. Feature films: The Lorry / al-Trîllâ (1985), Al-Fahamine / al-Fahhâmîn (1987), Al-Charabiyyah / al-Charâbiyyah (1987), Boulteyya, a Girl from Bahary / Boulteyya bent Bahary (1995)

Serri, Taïmour. Egyptian filmmaker. Feature films: Permission to Kill / Tasrîh bi-l-qatl (1991), A Hero of His Time / ʿAntar zamanouh (1994)

Shackleton, Michael. South African filmmaker. Feature film: The Survivor (English, 1988)

Shaw, Harold. South African silent filmmaker. Born in England, he worked for Vitagraph and London Films and was invited to South Africa to work for Isidore W Schlesinger's African Film Production. His second feature is a key film in South African film history. South African silent feature films: An Artist's Inspiration / The Artist's Dream (Silent, with Denis Santry, 1916), De Voortrekkers / Winning a Continent (Silent, 1916), The Splendid Waster (Silent, 1916), The Rose of Rhodesia (Silent, 1917)

Shehu, Brendan (b. 1942). Nigerian filmmaker. Studied at the Overseas Film and Television Training School in London. From 1962 producer, director and editor for Northern Nigeria Broadcasting Corporation. Head of the Kaduna State Film Unit from 1976 (30 documentaries). Subsequently Chief Executive of the Nigerian Film Corporation (from 1985 to 1999), setting up studio facilities and founding the National Film Institute (NFI). Kulba Na Barna is the first (and so far only) feature film produced by the NFC. Feature film: Kulba Na Barna (Hausa, 1992)

Shelach, Ricki. South African filmmaker. Feature film: Freedom Fighters (English, with Bruce MacFarlane, 1986)

Sherman, George. American director of one film included in some South African film lists: The Fiercest Heart (English, 1961)

Shilon, Igal. South African filmmaker. Feature film: The Big Gag / Candid Camera (English, with Yuda Barkan, 1986)

Shisel, Zvi. South African filmmaker. Feature film: Crazy Camera / Crazy People (English, with Boaz Davidson, 1988)

Si Bita, Arthur (b. 1948 in San Melina). Cameroonian film critic and filmmaker. Studied modern theatre and literature and trained as a teacher. Self-taught filmmaker. Four early films in super-8 and one 16mm short before his socially concerned feature. Feature film: The Cooperative Effort / Les Coopérants (1983)

Simon, Barney. South African filmmaker. Feature film: *City Lovers* (English, 1981)

Sinclair, Andrew. South African filmmaker. Feature films: *Secret of the Planet Earth* (English, 1983), *Tuxedo Warrior* (English, 1985)

Sinclair, Ingrid (b. 1948 in Zimbabwe). Zimbabwean filmmaker. Studied medecine in the UK. Began filmmaking in context of Bristol Filmmakers Cooperative. Collaborated with Simon Bright to set up The Black and White Film Company and Zinmedia. Numerous documentaries. Feature films: *Flame* (1996) *Riches* (2003)

Sinclair, J. South African filmmaker. Feature film: *'n Dogter van die Veld* (Afrikaans, 1933)

Sissako, Abderrahmane (1961 in Kiffa). Mauritanian filmmaker, resident in France. Studied filmmaking at the VGIK in Moscow. His work since 1991 (five shorts and three features) makes him one of the leaders of the post-independence generation and he won the top prize, the Étalon de Yennenga, with *Heremakono* at the Festival Panafricain du Cinéma de Ouagadougou (FESPACO) in 2003. Feature films: *Life on Earth / La Vie sur terre* (1998), *Waiting for Happiness / Heremakono / En attendant le bonheur* (2002), *Bamako / The Court* (2006)

Sissoko, Cheikh Oumar (b. 1945 in San). Malian filmmaker. Studied African history and sociology in Paris and film at the École Louis Lumière. Director of the CNPC and later Malian Minister of Culture. Put himself—alongside his compatriot Souleymane Cisse—in the forefront of African filmmaking with his two colourful and visually complex 1990s films drawing on local traditions. He won the top prize, the Étalon de Yennenga, at the Festival Panafricain du Cinéma de Ouagadougou (FESPACO) in 1995 with *Guimba*. Earlier, again like Cisse, he had explored the life of the poor with sensitive realist studies. Feature films: *Nyamanton* (1986), *A Dance for Heroes / Finzan* (1989), *Guimba the Tyrant / Guimba, un tyran, une époque* (1995), *Genesis / La Genèse* (1999), *Bàttu* (2000)

Skiredj, Bachir (b. 1939 in Tangier). Moroccan actor and filmmaker. A major star in both Moroccan theatre and cinema, best known for his leading role in Mohamed Abderrahman Tazi's *Looking for My Wife's Husband*, the biggest commercial success in the history of Moroccan cinema. Feature film: *Once Upon a Time, Twice Upon a Time / Il était une fois, il était deux fois* (2007)

Smallcombe, John. South African filmmaker. Feature film: *An African Dream* (English, 1988)

Smawley, Robert J. South African filmmaker. Feature films: *Murphy's Fault* (English, 1987), *American Eagle / Rescue* (English, 1989), *Enemy Unseen / Lost Valley* (English, with Elmo de Witt, 1989), *River of Diamonds* (English, 1989)

Smihi, Moumen (b. 1945 in Tangier). Moroccan filmmaker. Studied philosophy at the University of Rabat and filmmaking at the Institut des Hautes Études Cinématographiques (IDHEC) in Paris, where he attended Roland Barthes's seminars. Also made two short films and a video. His first feature was one of the key experimental features with which Morocco made its first international impact. His later work follows the dominant realist tradition. Feature films: *El Chergui* (1975), *Forty-Four, or Tales of the Night / Quarante-quatre ou les récits de la nuit* (1981), *Caftan of Love / Caftan d'amour* (1987), *The Lady from Cairo / La Dame du Caire* (1991), *Moroccan Chronicles / Chroniques marocaines* (1999), *The Boy from Tangier / Le Gosse de Tanger* (2005)

Smihi, Saïd. Moroccan filmmaker and journalist. Worked in various production roles in cinema and television and made a few documentaries. Feature film: *I Saw Ben Barka Get Killed / J'ai vu tuer Ben Barka* (with Serge Le Péron, 2005)

Smit, Louise. South African filmmaker. Feature film: *Davey* (English, 1987)

Sneh, Amar. Somalian filmmaker. Feature film: *The Somali Darwish* (with Salah Said), 1984)

Snyman, Gerrie. South African filmmaker. Feature films: *Die Leeu van Punda Maria / The Lion of Punda Maria* (Afrikaans, 1954), *Die Skelm van die Limpopo* (Afrikaans, 1962), *As ons Twee eers Getroud is* (Afrikaans, 1962)

Sokhona, Sidney (b. 1952 in Tachott). French-based filmmaker of Mauritanian origin. Studied filmmaking at Vincennes. All his work focuses in the immigrant community in France. Feature films: *Nationality Immigrant / Nationalité Immigré* (1975), *Safran or The Right to Speak / Safran ou le Droit à la Parole* (1978)

Sonnekus, Neil. South African filmmaker. Feature film: *A.W.O.L* (English, 1989)

Sou, Jabob (b. 1948 in Burkina Faso). Burkinabè filmmaker. Self-taught filmmaker who has worked as actor, reporter and cultural worker. His solo feature film is one of the largely Burkinabè-financed educative features which have not received European distribution. Feature films: *The Story of Orokia / Histoire d'Orokia* (with Jacques Oppenheim, 1987), *The Grotto / Le Grotto* (1989)

Souda, Saïd (b. 1945 in Tangier). Moroccan filmmaker. Received no formal film training, but worked in cinema in Hong Kong (at the Shaw Brothers studio) and in Japan. A martial arts specialist, he appeared in numerous films, including both of those he has directed. Feature films: *Shadow of the Guardian / L'Ombre du gardien* (1985), *From Heaven to Hell / Du paradis à l'enfer* (2000)

Soudani, Mohamed (b. 1949 at El Asman in Algeria). Swiss-based filmmaker of Algerian origin. Studied at the Institut des Hautes Études Cinématographiques (IDHEC) in Paris. Worked in Algerian television before moving to Switzerland in 1972, where he has worked as photographer and made numerous documentaries, some of feature length, such as *The Story-tellers / Les Diseurs d'histoires* (1998) and *Wars without Images / Guerres sans images* (2002). His sole feature film was set within the immigrant Senegalese community in Milan. Feature film: *Waalo Fendo* (1997)

Sousa, Camilo de (b. 1953 in Lourenço Marquez [Maputo]). Mozambican filmmaker. An active figure with the Front for the Liberation of Mozambique (FRELIMO) in the independence struggle, he began work as editor and documentary filmmaker at the Instituto Nacional de Cinema (INC) in 1980. Feature film: *Time of Leopards / O tempo dos leopardos* (with Zravko Velimorovic, 1965)

Sow, Abdoulaye D. (b. 1945; d. 1996). Burkinabè filmmaker. Born in Ouagadougou in 1945, he began his career with a short film, Lotto promo, in Bucharest in 1975. He subsequently appeared as an actor in films in Romania and Burkina Faso, and also scripted and directed a number of short documentary and fictional films. Feature film: *Yelbeedo* (1991)

Sow, Thierno Futy (b. 1941 in Thiès). Senegalese filmmaker. Studied filmmaking at the Conservatoire Libre du Cinéma Français (CLCF) in Paris and later worked in French and Senegalese television. Best known for his collaboration with Ousmane Sembene. Feature films: *The Option / L'Option* (1974), *The Eye / L'Oeil* (1981), *Camp de Thiaroye* (with Ousmane Sembene, 1988)

Soyinka, Wole (b. 1934 in Abeokuta). Nigerian writer and filmmaker. Followed his degree at Ibadan University with further study in Leeds and work at the Royal Court Theatre in London. After his return to Nigeria in 1960, his involvement in politics led to a term of imprisonment and 5 years of voluntary exile in Europe. For many years he was professor at the University of Ife, and visiting professor at several U.S. universities. Poet, novelist, and playwright, he was winner of the Nobel Prize for Literature in 1986, but again forced into exile. His best known recent writings are autobiographical: *The Man Died* and *Aké*. In film, he worked on the adaptation of his play *Kongi's Harvest* (directed by the black American, Ossie Davis, 1970). Feature film: *Blues for a Prodigal* (English, 1984)

Spencer, Josh. South African filmmaker. Feature films: *Easy Kill* (English, 1988), *Forced Alliance* (English, 1988)

Spicer, Edwina (b. 1948). Zimbabwean documentary filmmaker. Films include *Biko, Breaking the Silence* (1987), *No Need to Blame* (1993), *A Place for Everybody* (1993), *Keeping a Live Voice* (1995), *Dancing Out of Tune* (1999)

Spiegel, Scot. Director of one film included in some South African feature film listings: *Texas Blood Money* (1998)

Spring, Tim. South African actor and filmmaker. Debut as an actor in Swanson's *The Magic Garden*. Worked in a wide variety of technical roles in South Africa and Rhodesia. Feature films: *Gee My Jou Hand* (Afrikaans, 1963), *Dog Squad* (English, 1973), *Vang vir my 'n Droom* (Afrikaans, 1974), *Billy Boy* (English, 1978), *Dr Marius Hugo* (Afrikaans, 1978), *Wat Jy Saal* (Afrikaans, 1979), *Reason to Die* (English, 1989), *No Hero / Cupid* (English, 1992)

Stadt, Herman. South African filmmaker. Feature film: *Diamonds Are Dangerous* (English, 1961)

Stanley, Richard. South African filmmaker. Feature film: *Dust Devil* (English, 1991)

Stapleton, Oliver. South African filmmaker. Feature film: *Shadowplay* (English, 1980)

Stein, Nico. South African filmmaker. Feature film: *Lenny* (English, 1997)

Stephenson, Lynton. South African filmmaker. His first feature is a version of *Macbeth* with Xhosa actors. Feature films: *Maxhosa* (English, 1975), *The Stronger* (English, 1983)

Stevens, Wallie. South African filmmaker. Feature film: *Lindie* (Afrikaans, 1971)

Stewardson, Joe. South African filmmaker. Feature films: *Taxi* (English, 1970), *The Baby Game* (English, 1973), *Lelik is my Offer* (Afrikaans, 1975), *Lucky Strikes Back* (English, 1988)

Stewart, Jean. South African filmmaker. Feature film: *The Long Run* (English, 2000)

Stewart, Rod. South African filmmaker. Feature film: *Heel against the Head* (English, 1999)

Steyn, D. B. South African filmmaker. Feature film: *Sieraad Uit As* (Afrikaans, 1970), *Die Skat van Issie* (Afrikaans, 1972), *Gebroke Kontrak* (Afrikaans, 1975), *En die Dag Ontwaak* (Afrikaans, 1977), *Liefde wat Louter* (Afrikaans, 1978)

Strauss, Herman. South African filmmaker. Feature film: *Man van Buite* (Afrikaans, 1972)

Stromin, Stuart. South African filmmaker. Feature film: *Spice* (English, 1989)

Strydom, Juanita. South African filmmaker. Feature film: *Mr Moonlight* (English, 1984)

Suleman, Ramadan (b. 1955 in Durban). South African filmmaker, living in France since the 1980s. Work in South African alternative theatre including the Dhlomo Theatre in Johannesburg. Studied film at the London International Film School (1987–90). Shorts include *The Devil's Child* (1990). Feature films: *Fools* (English, 1997), *Zulu Love Letter* (2005)

Sundström, Cedric (b. 1952). South African filmmaker. Began with two short avant-garde works, *The Hunter* (1972) and *Suffer Little Children* (1977), and went on to work as assistant director on foreign features shot in South Africa. His features are largely designed for video and cable release. Feature films: *American Ninja III—The Cobra Strikes* (English, 1988), *Fair Trade / Flight to Hell* (English, 1988), *The Shadowed Mind* (English, 1988), *American Nija IV—The Annihation* (English, 1989), *The Revenger / Saxman* (English, 1989), *Treasure Hunters* (English, 1989), *Force of the Ninja* (English, 1990)

Sundström, Neal. South African filmmaker. Feature films: *Tyger, Tyger, Burning Bright / Autumn Concerto* (English, 1988), *Space Mutiny / Southern Sun* (English, with David Winters,

1989), *Sonja and* Johnny (English, 1991), *Inside Out* (English, 1999), *Dead Easy* (English, 2004)

Swanepoel, Lourens. South African actor and filmmaker. Feature films: *The Sandpiper* (English, 1984), *Die Strandloper* (Afrikaans, 1985), *Love in the Wood* (English, 1985), *Love in the Wood II* (English, 1986), *Naughty Camera* (English, 1988),

Swanson, Donald. British-born South African filmmaker. While working for Rank on the script of a film shot in South Africa, he made a pioneering independent English-language film with actor Eric Rutherford as producer—the first to show life in a black township and draw on the talents of black performers. Features: *Jim Comes to Jo'burg* (English, 1949), *The Magic Garden / Pennywhistle Blues* (English, 1961)

Swart, François. South African filmmaker. Feature films: *Siener in die Suburbs* (Afrikaans, 1973), *Skadu's van Gister* (Afrikaans, 1974)

Sycholt, Stefanie. South African filmmaker. Feature film: *Malunde* (Afrikaans, 2001)

Szabo, Mohsen. Egyptian filmmaker. Feature film: *Bamba / Bamba* (1952)

Taha, Abdel Hadi. Egyptian filmmaker. Feature films: *To Whom by Law / Ilâ man yahoummouhou al-ʾamr* (1985), *The Cunning / al-Dâhiyah* (1986), *The Stabbing / al-Taʾnah* (1987), *A Chance of Thunder / Hazz min al-samâ'* (1987), *I am Not a Killer / Lastou qâtilan* (1989), *Priceless Men / Rigâl bilâ thaman* (1993)

Takam, Jules (b. 1947 in Yaoundé). Cameroonian filmmaker. Studied filmmaking at the CLFC in Paris. Worked as film editor and made one short film in the 1970s. Feature films: *The Taste for Profit / L'Appât du gain* (1981), *The Circle of Powers / Le Cercle de pouvoirs* (with Daniel Kamwa, 1997)

Tantawi, Sayed. Egyptian filmmaker. Feature films: *My Daughter and the Wolf / Ibnatî wa-l-dhiʾb* (1977), *It's Shameful, Lulu . . . Lulu, It's Shameful / ʿEib yâ Loulou . . . Yâ Loulou ʿEib* (1978), *A Woman Has Deceived Me / Khadaʾatnî imarʾah* (1979), *Moment of Weakness / Lahzat daʾf* (1980), *I Shall Never Forgive You / Lan aghfir abadan* (1981), *The Charlatans / al-Awantaguiyyah* (1987), *The Case of an Adolescent Girl / Hâlat mourâhiqah* (1990), *Beware of That Woman / Indharou hâdhihi al-marʾah* (1991), *We Are Children of Today / Ihna welaad el naharda* (1995)

Taylor, Jane. South African filmmaker. Feature film: *Testament to the Bushmen* (English, 1983)

Tazi, Mohamed Abderrahman (b. 1942 in Fez). Moroccan filmmaker. Studied film at the Institut des Hautes Études Cinématographiques (IDHEC) in Paris and mass media communication at Syracuse University in New York. Part of the Sigma 3 collective, founded in 1970 with Ahmed Bouanani and Hamid Benanni. Work at the Centre Cinématographique Marocain (CCM) and on foreign productions shot in Morocco. Numerous short films, some experimental, some commercial. Also work as cinematographer on on various shorts and features (including films by Hamid Benanni and Abdou Achouba). A key figure in Moroccan realist filmmaking and also the director of one of its biggest box office successes with his comedy, *In Search of My Wife's Husband*. Feature films: *The Big Trip / Le Grand voyage* (1981), *Badis* (1988), *Looking for My Wife's Husband / A la recherche du mari de ma femme* (1993), *Lalla Hobby* (1997), *Abou Moussa's Neighbours / Les Voisines d'Abou Moussa* (2003)

Tazi, Mohamed B. A. (b. 1936 in Fez). Moroccan filmmaker. Studied filmmaking at the Institut des Hautes Études Cinématographiques (IDHEC) in Paris and obtained a doctorate in information and communication sciences at Grenoble. Senior production and administrative roles in the Centre Cinématographique Marocain (CCM) and in Moroccan television. Variously credited as scriptwriter or co-director (with the Italian Nino Zanchini) on a 1966 feature known as both *The Kif Road / La Route du Kif* and *Drug Alert / Alerte à la drogue,* made 2 years before Moroccan national production began. Feature films: *Conquer to Live / Vaincre pour vivre* (with Ahmed Mesnaoui, 1968), *Amina* (1980), *Medecine Woman / Madame la guérisseuse / Lalla chafia* (1982), *Abbas or Jouha Is Not Dead / Abbas ou Jouha n'est pas mort* (1986)

Tchissoukou, Jean-Michel (b. 1942 in Pointe-Noire; d. 1988). Congolese filmmaker. Studied filmmaking at the Institut National de l'Audio-visuel (INA) and the Office de Copération Radiophonique (OCORA) in Paris. Assistant to Sarah Maldoror for *Sambizanga* (1972). Two 16mm fictional shorts. Feature films: *The Chapel / La Chapelle* (1979), *The Wrestlers / Les Lutteurs / M'Pongo* (1982)

Tchuilen, Jean-Claude (b. 1955 in Bajou). Cameroonian filmmaker. Studied filmmaking at CLFC in Paris. Work as an actor. Two short films in the early 1980s. Feature film: *Suicides* (1983)

Tekoit, Ramesh. Mauritian filmmaker. Feature films: *And the Smile Returns / Et le Sourire revient* (1980), *Goodbye My Love* (1988)

Teno, Jean-Marie (b. 1954 in Famleng). Cameroonian filmmaker, currently resident in France. Studied filmmaking at the University of Valenciennes in France and worked as an editor in French television. A major figure in African documentary filmmaking. Numerous documentaries from 1983, including *Head in the Clouds / La Tête dans les* nuages (1994), *Chief! / Chef!* (1999), *Holiday Back Home / Vacances au pays* (2000), *The Colonial Misunderstanding / Le Malentendu colonial* (2004). Feature films: *Bikutsi Water Blues* (documentary, 1988), *Africa I Will Fleece You / Afrique je te plumerai* (documentary, 1992), *Clando* (1996)

Tewfik, Hassan. Egyptian filmmaker. Feature film: *Struggle against the Angels / Sirâ' ma'al-malâ'ikah* (1962)

Theodros, Teshome Kebede (b. 1970 at Jimma). Ethiopian filmmaker. Worked originally as a

photographer and made his first short in 1996. Made two feature-length documentaries before completing his first fictional feature. Feature films: *Kezkaka Wolofen* (documentary) (2003), *Fikir Siferd* (documentary) (2004), *Red Mistake* (2006)

Thiam, Momar (b. 1929 in Dakar). Senegalese filmmaker. Studied photography in Paris and worked in the Boulogne film studios. On his return worked at the Ministry of Information. His three features are the best known of his dozen or so films made over a period of 20 years. Feature films: *Karim* (1971), *Baks* (1974), *Sa Dagga / Le M'Bandakatt* (1982)

Thior, Amadou (b. 1951 in Kaffrine). Senegalese filmmaker. Studied filmmaking at the École Louis Lumière in Paris. His 1983 short *Xareek Maral* received international distribution. Feature film: *Almodou* (2000)

Thompson, David. South African filmmaker. Feature film: *The Fever / Township Fever* (English, with Francis Gerard, 1990)

Thompson, J. Lee. English director of one film included in some South African film listings: *King Solomon's Mines* (English, 1985)

Thompson, Russell. South African filmmaker. Studied photography and filmmaking at Pretoria Film School. Writer. Feature film: *The Sexy Girls* (English, 1997)

Timité, Bassori (b. 1933 in Aboisso). Ivorian filmmaker. Studied filmmaking at the Institut des Hautes Études Cinématographiques (IDHEC) in Paris. One of the pioneers of Ivorian cinema, his first feature is the tale of a young intellectual's traumatised return from exile. Feature film: *The Woman with the Knife / La Femme au couteau* (1969)

Timothy, Ebulus. South African filmmaker. Feature film: *Othello* (English, 2001)

Tissari, Doccio. Italian director of one Egyptian feature film: *The Sphinx's Smile / Ibtisâmat Abou al-Hol* (1966)

Tlatli, Moufida (b. 1947 in Sidi Bou Said). Tunisian editor and filmmaker. She studied at the Institut des Hautes Études Cinématographiques (IDHEC) in Paris and worked as trainee and assistant at the Office de Radiodiffusion et de Télévision Française (ORTF). Between 1974 and 1992 she established herself as one of the leading film editors in the Arab world, editing many of the major films of the period: Abdellatif Ben Ammar's *Sejnane* and *Aziza*, Taïeb Louhichi's *The Shadow of the Earth* and *Leila My Reason*, Mahmoud Ben Mahmoud's *Crossing Over*, Ferid Boughedir's *Halfaouine* and Nacer Khemir's *The Searchers of the Desert*. She also assisted three women directors with their first features by undertaking the editing: Selma Baccar with *Fatma 75*, Nejia Ben Mabrouk with *The Trace* and the Moroccan Farida Benlyazid with *Gateway to Heaven*. Outside Tunisia, she also edited films by the Algerians, Merzak Allouache (*Omar Gatlato*) and Farouk Beloufa (*Nahla*), and the Palestinian director Michel Khleifi (*Fertile Memory*). Her own first feature, *Silences of the Palace*, which won the top prize, the *Tanit d'or*, at the Journées Cinématographiques de Carthage (JCC) in 1994, put her in the very first rank of African and Arab filmmakers. She made the feature-length *Nadia et Sarra* on video in 2004. Feature films: *Silences of the Palace / Les Silences du palais* (1994), *The Men's Season / La Saison des hommes* (2000)

Tolbi, Abdelaziz (b. 1938 in Tamlouka). Algerian filmmaker. Fought in the ranks of the ALN and, when wounded, was sent to Tunis. Studied film in Cologne and worked in German television. Television work for Radiodiffusion Télévision Algérienne (RTA) in the 1960s and 1970s. His sole 16mm feature film is a major work. Feature film: *Noua* (1972)

Tornatore, Joe. South African filmmaker. Feature film: *Crystal Eye* (English, with Douglas Bristow, 1988)

Tors, Ivan. British director (born in Hungary) of a film included in some South African film listings. Feature film: *Rhino* (English, 1964)

Touita, Okacha (b. 1943 in Mostaganem). Algerian filmmaker. Studied filmmaking at the Institut Français de Cinéma (IFC) in Paris. Work as assistant on French and Algerian features. Feature films: *The Sacrificed / Les Sacrifiés* (1982), *The Survivor / Le Rescapé* (1986), *The Cry of Men / Le Cri des hommes* (1990), *Morituri* (2007)

Toukhi, Ahmed. Libyan filmmaker. *A People's Revolt / Intifadat sh'ab* (1970)

Touré, Drissa (b. 1952 in Banfora). Burkinabè filmmaker. A self-taught filmmaker whose two films offer an idyllic view of village life and a harsher insight into shanty-town society respectively. Feature films: *Laada* (1990), *Haramuya* (1993)

Touré, Kitia (b. 1956 in Ayama). Ivorian filmmaker. Studied filmmaking in Paris. Also novelist (*Destins parallèles*, 1995). Director of the Compagnie Ivoirienne de Cinéma et d'Audiovisuel (CIVCA). His first feature looks at the impact of a young ethnographer on the traditional community he wishes to explore. Feature film: *Exotic Comedy / Comédie exotique* (1984)

Touré, Moussa (b. 1958 in Dakar). Senegalese filmmaker. Self-taught, worked in various capacities, including as an electrician, on various French and Senegalese films (François Truffaut's *Adèle H*, Bertrand Tavernier's *Coup de Torchon* and Ousmane Semene's *Camp de Thiaroye*). He made his first short in 1987, followed by two features, the first tracing the adventures of an African in Paris, the second looking at travel and borders within Africa itself. He also made a number of medium and feature-length video documentaries in the 2000s, including *Nosaitres* (2006). Feature films: *Toubab Bi* (1991), *TGV* (1997)

Towers, Harry. South African filmmaker. Feature film: *Gor* (English, with Fritz Kiersch, 1986)

Traïdia, Karim (b. 1949 in Annaba). Dutch-based filmmaker of Algerian descent who has lived in Holland since 1980. Studied sociology in Paris and film at the NFTVA in Amsterdam, graduating in 1991. Made a number of short films and worked as an actor. In 1996 he published a collection of short stories written in Dutch. Feature films: *The Polish Bride / De Poosle Bruid* (1998), *The Truth Tellers / Les Diseurs de vérité* (2000)

Traore, Apolline (b. 1976 in Ouagadougou). Burkina Faso filmmaker. She moved to Boston at 17 and studied film at Emerson College. Four short films from 2001. Feature film: *Under the Moonlight / Sous la clarté de la lune* (2004)

Traore, Issa de Brahima (b. 1962 in Abidjan). Burkinabè filmmaker. Though born in the Ivory Coast, he is a Burkinabè citizen. Studied film at the Institut Africain d'Education Cinématographique (INAFEC) and at the University of Paris. First short film in 1994. Feature films: *Siraba / La Grande voie* (2000), *The World Is a Ballet / Le Monde est un ballet* (2006)

Traore, Issa Falaba (b. 1930 in Bougouni). Malian filmmaker. Studied filmmaking at the Institut Africain d'Education Cinématographique (INAFEC) and in Germany. He has worked in a variety of media—theatre, radio, literature, music—and became the first director of the national theatre. Feature films: *We Are All Guilty / Am Be Nodo / Nous sommes tous coupables* (1980), *The Sacred Loincloth / Bamunan / Le Pagne sacré* (1990)

Traore, Mahama [Johnson] (b. 1942 in Dakar). Senegalese filmmaker. Studied filmmaking at the Conservatoire Libre du Cinéma Français (CLCF) in Paris. Made his first two short films in 1969. One of the pioneers of Senegalese cinema, his career stalled after four socially committed features made in quick succession in the early 1970s. Feature films: *Diegue-Bi* (1970), *Lambaaye* (1972), *Garga M'Bosse* (1974), *Njangaan / N'Diangane* (1975)

Traore, Mory (b. in Ivory Coast). Ivorian filmmaker. Studied first law in Ivory Coast and then drama at the Conservatoire National Supérieur d'Art Dramatique (CNSAD) in Paris. Work as stage director in Ivory Coast. His sole feature traces the decline of a young black man sub-jected to racist pressures in Japan. Feature film: *The Man from Elsewhere / L'Homme d'ailleurs* (1979)

Traore, Nissi Joanny (b. 1952 at Takalédougou). Burkinabè filmmaker. Studied filmmaking in Germany and at the Institut National de l'Audiovisuel (INA) in Paris. Trained as a sound engineer. Director of Direction de la Production Cinématographique (DIPROCI). Two short films in the 1980s and a feature-length video documentary, *Mamio, Exile of the Gods / Mamio, l'exil des dieux* (2005). His feature film is one of the largely Burkinabè-financed educative features which have not received European distribution. Feature film: *Sababu* (1992)

Traore, Salif (b. 1954 at San). Malian filmmaker. Studied at the Institut National des Arts de Bamako and at the Institut Africain d'Education Cinématographique (INAFEC) in Burkina Faso. Two fictional short films in the 1990s. Feature Film: *Faro, Queen of the Waters / Faro, la reine des eaux* (2006)

Travers, Alfred. South African filmmaker. Feature film: *One for the Pot* (English, 1968)

Trichardt, Carl. South African filmmaker. Feature film: *Sononder* (Afrikaans, 1971)

Tsaki, Brahim (b. 1946 in Sidi Bel Abbes). Algerian filmmaker. Studied filmmaking at the Institut National des Arts du Spectacle et Techniques de Diffusion (INSAS) in Brussels. Work for the Office National du Commerce et de l'Industrie Cinématographiques (ONCIC). His second feature which won the top prize, the Étalon de Yennenga, at the Festival Panafricain du Cinéma de Ouagadougou (FESPACO) in 1985 marks the move away from a concentration on the independence struggle and the agrarian revolution in Algerian cinema. Feature films: *Children of the Wind / Les Enfants du vent* (1981), *Story of a Meeting / Histoire d'une rencontre* (1983), *The Neon Children / Les Enfants des néons* (1990)

Turner, Clive. South African filmmaker. Feature film: *Howling IV / Ghoul* (English, 1988)

Ugbomah, Eddie (b. 1943 in Lagos). Nigerian filmmaker. Studied journalism and drama in London, where he also worked for the BBC and ITV. Appeared as an actor in several noted films (*Doctor No, No Guns at Batasi, Sharpeville Massacre*). Studied at the London School of Television Production. Second Chairman of the Nigerian Film Corporation (1988–91). Feature films: *The Rise and Fall of Doctor Oyenusi* (English, 1977), *The Mask* (English, 1979), *Oil Doom* (English, 1981), *The Boy Is Good* (English, 1982), *Bolus 80* (English, 1982), *Vengeance of the Cult* (English, 1984), *Death of the Black President* (English, 1984), *Esan Ake* (Yoruba, 1985), *Apalara* (Yoruba, 1986), *Omiran* (Yoruba, 1988), *Tori Ade* (Yoruba, 1991). Videos include: *The Great Attempt* (English, 1990), *America or Die* (English, 1996)

Ukset, Umban (b. in Guinea-Bissau). Guinea-Bissau filmmaker. Brought up since childhood in Senegal, he studied at the École de Arts in Dakar and then at the Sorbonne in Paris. Active as an actor in Paris, where he is now based. Also singer and musician with his group West African Cosmos. His sole feature was the first to be made in Guinea-Bissau. Feature film: *N'Tturudu* (1987)

Umar, Sule. Nigerian filmmaker. Studied chemical engineering in the United States before turning to film, studying in Ohio and at the University of Southern California. Worked for the Kano State Agency for Mass Education, where he made a documentary on adult education. Used a full American crew for his sole 35mm feature. Subsequently worked for NACB, NDA and Shiroro Dam. Feature film: *Maitatsine* (Hausa, 1988)

Uys, D. W. South African filmmaker. Feature film: *Ons Staan 'n Dag Oor* (Afrikaans, 1942)

Uys, Gerhard. South African filmmaker. Feature film: *A Fire in Africa* (English, 1987)

Uys, Jamie (= Jacobus Johannes Uys). (b. 1921 in Boksburg; d. 1996). South African filmmaker. The most commercially successful—and most controversial—of all South African filmmakers, he studied at the University of Pretoria. He has always proclaimed himself apolitical, but his films, like the internationally shown *The Gods Must Be Crazy*, are deeply impregnated with apartheid ideology. Feature films: *Daar Doer in die Bosveld* (Afrikaans, 1951), *Fifty / Vyftig* (Afrikaans/English, 1953), *Daar Doer in die Stad* (Afrikaans, 1954), *Geld Soos Bossies / Money to Burn* (Afrikaans, 1955), *Die Bosvelder* (Afrikaans, 1958), *Doodkry is Min* (Afrikaans, 1961), *Hans en die Rooinek / Sidney and the Boer* (English/Afrikaans, 1961), *Lord Oom Piet* (Afrikaans, 1962), *Dingaka* (English, 1964), *All the Way to Paris / After You, Comrade* (English, 1966), *Die Professor en die Prikkelpop* (Afrikaans, 1967), *Dirkie* (Afrikaans, 1969), *Beautiful People* (English, 1974), *Funny People* (Afrikaans/English, 1976—produced only), *The Gods Must Be Crazy* (English, 1980), *Funny People II* (English, 1983), *The Gods Must Be Crazy II* (English, 1989)

Van de Coolwyk, Robert. South African filmmaker. Feature films: *Getting Lucky* (English, 1985), *Jewel of the Gods / Grinder's War* (English, 1987), *Bloodriver* (English, 1989), *The Gold Cup* (English, 1990)

Van den Berg, Regardt. South African actor and filmmaker. Feature films: *Imali* (Sotho, with Jimmy Murray, 1984), *Boetie Gaan Border Toe* (Afrikaans/English, 1984), *Boetie of Manoevres* (Afrikaans, 1985), *Van der Merwe, P I* (Afrikaans, 1985), *Circles in a Forest* (English, 1988), *The Sheltering Desert* (English, 1990), *Faith Like Potatoes* (English, 2006), *Hansie* (2007)

Van den Heever, Hennie. South African filmmaker. Feature film: *Wanneer die Masker Val* (Afrikaans, 1955)

Van der Byl, Philip. South African filmmaker. Feature film: *Birds of Paradise* (English, with Tommie Meyer, 1981)

Van der Merwe, Fanie. South African filmmaker. Feature film: *Rienie* (Afrikaans, 1980)

Van der Merwe, Gary. South African film-maker. Feature films: *Inkada* (Zulu, 1981), *Mmampodi* (Sotho, 1983), *Washo Usbaha* (Sotho, 1983), *Joe Slaughter* (Zulu, 1983), *Isalamusi* (Zulu, 1984), *Slow vs Boner* (Zulu, 1984), *Umfaan II* (Zulu, 1984)

Van der Merwe, Japie. South African film-maker. Feature films: *Ukulwa* (Zulu, 1982), *Amazing Grace* (English, 1983), *Ace of Spades* (Zulu, 1984)

Van der Merwe, Robert. South African film-maker. Feature film: *Never Rob a Magician* (Zulu, 1984)

Van der Merwe, Tonie. South African film-maker. Entrepreneur who employed a wide range of his family. Maker of the first Zulu-language feature and specialist in the production of African-language films. Feature films: *Nogomopho* (Zulu, 1974), *Trompie* (Afrikaans, 1975), *Mahlomola* (Zulu, 1976), *Isimanga* (Zulu, 1976), *Iziduphunga* (Zulu, 1977), *Mapule* (N Sotho, 1977), *Wangenza* (Zulu, 1977), *Nofuka* (Zulu, 1978), *Abafana* (Zulu, 1978), *Vuma* (Zulu, 1978), *Moloyi* (Zulu, 1978), *Luki* (Zulu, 1978), *Botsotso* (Zulu, 1979), *Iwisa* (Zulu, 1981), *Bullet on the Run* (English, 1982), *Impango* (Zulu, 1982), *Isiqwaga* (Zulu, 1982), *Ngavele Ngasho* (Zulu, 1983), *Moloyi* (Sotho, 1983), *For Money and Glory* (English/Sotho, 1984), *Zero for Zeb* (Zulu, 1984), *Bona Manzi* (Zulu, 1984), *Operation Hit Squad* (English,1987), *Barret* (English, 1990), *Fatal Mission / Kwavinga Run / The Rat* (English, with Anthony Bond, 1990), *Fishy Stones* (English, 1990), *Rich Girl* (English, 1990)

Van der Merwe, Wally. South African film-maker. Feature films: *Umnyakazo* (Zulu, 1981), *Umdladlo Umkhulo* (Zulu, 1982), *Umdlado Umbango* (Tswana, 1983), *Why Forsake Me?* (English, 1983), *Bobe mo Motseng* (Tswana, 1984), *Ulaka* (Zulu, 1984), *Bozo and Bimbo* (English, 1984), *Mission Spellbound* (English, 1984), *I Will Repay* (English, 1984), *The Reckoning* (English, 1984), *Mr Moonlight* (English, 1984), *Moon Mountain* (English, 1984), *Playing Dirty* (English, 1984)

Van der Wat, Keith G. South African filmmaker. Feature films: *Liefde vir Lelik* (Afrikaans, 1972), *Weekend* (English, 1972), *Just Call Me Lucky / They Call Me Lucky* (English, 1974), *The Savage Sport* (English, 1974), *Cry Me a Teardrop* (English, 1974), *The Weekend* (English, 1988)

Van Eissen, David. South African filmmaker. Feature film: *Slipstream* (English, 2004)

Van Rensberg, Manie (b. 1945 in Krugersdorp; d. 1993). South African filmmaker. A major figure in South African filmmaking, he studied English and Pyschology at the University of Potchefstroom. A self-taught filmmaker, he worked as cameraman on the popular Afrikaans musical *Hear My Song* (1967). He began in the mainstream of Afrikaner filmmaking and throughout his career probed the realities of the Afrikaner way of life and the social problems of a divided South Africa. Worked for SABC up to 1987, beginning with the comedy series *Willem* (1975) and going on to make a number of impressive television dramas. But after a visit to an anti-apartheid congress in Dakar in 1987, he was barred from working for 2 years. Returned to cinema in 1989 to begin a series of English-language studies of Afrikaner lives and attitudes. He also made a 60-minute video adapted from a Nadine Gordimer story, *Country Lovers* (1983). He took his own life in 1993. Feature films: *Freddie's in Love* (English, 1971), *Die Bankrower* (Afrikaans, 1973), *Geluksdal* (Afrikaans, 1974), *Die Square / Hannes Kruger is U Man* (Afrikaans, 1975), *The Fourth Reich* (English, 1989), *The Native Who Caused All the Trouble* (English, 1989), *The Fourth Reich / Operation Weissdorn* (English, 1989), *Taxi to Soweto* (English, 1991)

Van Rooyen, Johan. South African filmmaker. A specialist in African-language films. Feature films: *Ukusindiswa* Zulu, 1981), *Motusmi* (Sotho, 1983), *Vakasha* (Zulu/English, 1983), *Running Young* (English, 1983), *Charlie Steel* (English, 1984), *Upondo No Nkinsela* (Sotho, 1984), *Umfaan* (Zulu, 1984), *Odirang* (Sotho, 1984), *Modise* (Tswana, 1984)

Vendrell, Fernando. Portuguese-born filmmaker who made a first feature in Cape Verde and a second in Mozambique. Feature films: *Fintar o Destino* (1997), *Light Drops / O Goejar da Luz* (2003)

Venter, Albie. South African filmmaker. Feature film: *Kaptein Caprivi* (Afrikaans, 1972)

Vernuccio, Gianni. Egyptian filmmaker of Italian origin, born in Egypt. Made documentaries as well as features. Feature films: *Fire Woman / Imra'ah min nâr* (1950), *Blood in the Desert / Dimâ fî-l-sahrâ* (1950), *The Loved-One's Vengeance / Intiqâm al-habîb* (1951), *An Egyptian in Lebanon / Masrî fî Loubnân* (1952), *By the Sweat of My Forehead / Min ʿaraq guibînî* (1952), *Spring Festival / Chamm al-nasîm* (1952), *Love in the Desert / Gharâm fî-l-sahrâ* (with Léon Klimovski,1959)

Viertel, Berthold. Austrian-born director of one feature film (produced by Michael Balcon) included in some South African film listings: *Rhodes of Africa* (English, 1936)

Vieyra, Paulin Soumanou (b. 1925 in Porto-Novo in Benin; d. 1987). Senegalese film historian and filmmaker. Studied filmmaking at the Institut des Hautes Études Cinématographiques (IDHEC) in Paris. On his return he worked for the Ministry of Information and made numerous documentaries. A major historian of African cinema, he is author of *Le Cinéma et l'Afrique* (1969), *Sembène Ousmane cinéaste* (1972), *Le Cinéma africain des origines à 1973* (1975), *Le Cinéma au Sénégal* (1983). His collaboratively made short, *Africa on the Seine / Afrique sur Seine,* is one of the pioneering films of francophone West Africa. Feature film: *Under House Arrest / En résidence surveillée* (1981)

Viljoen, Judex C. South African filmmaker. Feature film: *Die Marmerpoel* (Afrikaans, 1972)

Vila, Camillo. US maker of one film included in some South African film listings. Feature film: *Options* (English, 1988)

Vimance, Manuel. Egyptian filmmaker. Feature films: *Goha and Abou Nawwas / Gohâ wa Abou Nawwâs* (1932), *Goha and Abou Nawwas Photographers / Gohâ wa Abou Nawwâs mousawirân* (1933)

Vincent, Chuck. South African filmmaker. Feature film: *Thrilled to Death* (English, 1988)

Volpi, Mario. Egyptian filmmaker. Feature films: *The Song of the Heart / Ounchoudat al-Fou'âd* (1932), *The Accusation / al-Ittihâm* (1934), *The Star / al-Ghandourah* (1935), *Queen of the Footlights / Malikat al-masârih* (1936), *Mad with Love / al-Houbb al-mouristâni* (1937)

Vorster, Gordon. South African filmmaker. Actor, writer, artist. Feature films: *Die Vlugteling* (Afrikaans, 1960), *Die Jagters* (Afrikaans, 1960), *Basie* (Afrikaans, 1961), *Die Tweede Slaapkamer* (Afrikaans, 1962), *Jy's Lieflik Vanaand* (Afrikaans, 1962), *Sarah* (Afrikaans, 1975), *The Fifth Season / Die Vyfde Seisoen* (Afrikaans/English, 1978)

Wa Luruli, Ntshaveni. South African filmmaker. Studied drama at the University of Witwatersrand and film at Columbia University. Extensive work in the film industry in the United States. Playwright and scriptwriter. Teaches film in Witwatersrand and Johannesburg. Feature film: *Chikin Biz'nis—The Whole Story* (English/Zulu/Sotho, 1999), *The Wooden Camera* (2004)

Wade, Mansour Sora (b. 1952 in Dakar). Senegalese filmmaker. Studied filmmaking at the University of Paris VIII. Short films from the mid-1970s. His first feature, a visually resplendent traditional tale, told with telling ambiguity, won the first prize, the *Tanit d'or,* at the Journées Cinématographiques de Carthage (JCC) in 2002. Feature film: *The Price of Forgiveness / Ndeysaan / Le Prix du pardon* (2001)

Wagdi, Anwar (b. 1904; d. 1955). Egyptian filmmaker and actor. Began in Youssef Wahbi's theatre company and eventually made over seventy films as an actor, achieving particular success partnering Leila Mourad. From 1945 wrote and directed his own films. Feature films: *Leila, Daughter of the Poor / Layla bint al-fouqâra*

(1945), *Leila, Daughter of the Rich / Layla bint al-aghniyâ* (1946), *My Heart Is My Guide / Qalbî dalîlî* (1947), *Mrs Souad's Divorce / Talâq Sou²âd hânim* (1948), *Amber / ᶜAnbar* (1948), *Young Girls' Flirtations / Ghazal al-banât* (1949), *Yasmine / Yasmine* (1950), *The Eve of the Wedding / Laylat al-hinnah* (1951), *My Love, My Soul / Habîb al-rouh* (1951), *Katr al-Nada / Qatr al-nadâ* (1951), *The Daughter of Aristocrats / Bint al-akâbir* (1953), *Dahab / Dahab* (1953), *Four Girls and an Officer / Arba² banât wa dâbit* (1954)

Wahbi, Youssef (b. 1898 in Fayoun; d. 1982). Egyptian filmmaker. Drawn to acting (to the surprise of his wealthy family), he spent 2 years in Italy from 1920 studying drama and the arts. On his return after the death of his father in 1922, he found himself a very wealthy man. He founded his own company, Ramses, which performed more than three hundred plays in 40 years from 1923. Director of the National Theatre in the 1950s. Produced Mohamed Karim's silent feature *Zeinab* (1930) and his early partial sound film, *Sons of Aristocrats* in 1932. He also later worked in radio and television. The star of many of his own films, he also acted for other directors. Feature films: *The Defence / al-Difâ* (1935), *Eternal Glory / al-Magd al-khâlid* (1937), *The Time of Execution / Sâ-at al-Tanfidh* (1938), *A Suitor from Istambul / ᶜArîs min Istamboul* (1941), *Son of Poor People / Awlâd al-fouqarâ* (1942), *Gawhara / Gawharah* (1943), *Berlanti / Berlanti* (1944), *The Executioner's Blade / Sayf al-gallârd* (1944), *The Blacksmith's Son / Ibn al-haddâd* (1944), *Love and Vengeance / Gharâm wa inti-qâm* (1944), *The Messenger from Hell / Safîr gahannam* (1945), *Girls from the Countryside / Banât al-rîf* (1945, *The Great Artist / al-Fannân al-²azim* (1945), *God's Hand / Yadu Allah* (1946), *A Candle Burns / Cham²ah tahtariq* (1946), *The Angel of Mercy / Malâk al-rahmah* (1946), *Fate's Blow / Darbat al-qadar* (1947), *The Lark from the Valley / Châdiyat al-wâdî* (1947), *The Red Mask / al-Qinâal-ahmar* (1947), *Man without Sleep / Ragoul lâ yanâm* (1948), *Mr. Bayoumi (Bayoumî afandî* (1949), *The Confessional / Koursî al-tirâf* (1949), *Madiha the Lawyer / al-Avocato Madîhah* (1950), *Children of the*

Streets / Awlâd al-chawâri (1951), *The Prostitute / Bint al-hawâ* (1953), *Home / Bayt al-Tâ²ah* (1953), *The Great Betrayal / al-Khiyânah al-²oudhmâ* (1962), *Advocating Slavery / al-Isti²bâd* (1962), *Former Days / Ayyâm zamân* (1963)

Wali, Chérif. Egyptian filmmaker. Feature film: *The Genetic Tree / Chagarat al-²â²ilah* (1960)

Walker, Roy. South African filmmaker. Feature film: *The House* (Zulu, 1987)

Wallace, Charles. South African filmmaker. Feature film: *The Mind Boggles* (English, 1988)

Walters, Martin. South African filmmaker. Feature film: *Jake Speed* (English, with Andrew Lane, 1986)

Watt, Harry. English director of two films included in some South African film listings: *Where No Vultures Fly* (English, 1951), *West of Zanzibar* (English, 1954)

Waxman, Keoni [Darby Black]. South African filmmaker. Feature film: *Sweepers* (English, 1997)

Webb, Hans. South African filmmaker. Feature film: *The Great Pretender* (English, 1989)

Webb, Robert R. American director of two films included in some South African film lists. Feature films: *Escape Route Cape Town* (1967), *The Jackals / The Scavengers* (1967)

Wein, Yossi [Joseph]. South African filmmaker. Feature film: *American Ninja 5—The Nostadamus Syndrome* (English, 1991), *Never Say Die* (English, 1994), *Cyborg Cop 3* (English, 1995), *Merchant of Death* (English, 1996), *Delta Force 2—Mayday* (English, 1997), *Operation Delta Force 4—Random Fire* (English, 1999)

Wetherell, M. A. [Marmaduke Arundel]. South African silent filmmaker and actor. Played the lead in his sole South African film. Feature film: *David Livingstone* (1925)

Whiteman, Cecil. South African filmmaker. Feature film: *Die Bloedrooi Papawer* (Afrikaans, 1960)

Wicht, David. South African filmmaker. Work for South African television (SABC). Currently lives in London. Feature films: *Satan Shoots* (English, 1986), *Windprints* (English, 1988)

Wiesner, Louis. South African filmmaker. Feature film: *In die Lente van Ons Liefde* (Afrikaans, 1967)

Wilannon, Noukpo. Benin filmmaker. Feature film: *Midjeresso* (2006)

Wilde, Cornell. American actor/director and maker of one film included in some South African film listings. Feature film: *The Naked Prey* (English, 1966)

Williams, Sam. South African filmmaker. Feature film: *Inkunzi* (Xhosa, 1976)

Wilson, Anthony. South African filmmaker. Feature film: *Die Posman* (Afrikaans, 1987)

Wilson, Fred [Marino Girolamo]. South African filmmaker. Feature film: *The Manipulator* (English, 1972)

Wilson-Yelverton, T. A. South African filmmaker. Feature film: *Oom Piet se Plaas* (Afrikaans, 1949)

Winters, David. South African filmmaker. Feature films: *Killmasters* (English, 1987), *Rage to Kill* (English, 1987), *Space Mutiny / Southern Son* (English, with Neal Sundström, 1989)

Witt, Thomas. South African filmmaker. Feature film: *Dance of Death* (English, 1990)

Woolf, Alain D. South African filmmaker. Feature films: *You're Famous* (English, 1988), *Funny Face* (English, 1989)

Worsdale, Andrew. South African filmmaker. Studied drama at the University of Witwatersrand and film at the University of California at Los Angeles (UCLA). His sole feature was initially banned in South Africa. Feature film: *Shot Down* (English, 1988)

Worth, David. South African filmmaker. Feature film: *Shark Attack 2* (English, 1999)

Woukoache, François (b. 1966 in Yaoundé). Cameroonian filmmaker. Studied mathematics and physical sciences, then filmmaking at the University of Paris VII and at the Institut National des Arts du Spectacle et Techniques de Diffusion (INSAS) in Brussels. First made his reputation with the 50-minute docudrama, *Asientos* (1995). Feature films: *Fragments of Life / Fragments de vie* (1998), *Smoke in Your Eyes / La Fumée dans les yeux* (1998)

Wragge, Martin. South African filmmaker. Feature film: *The Last Warrior / Coastwatcher* (English, 1988)

Wright, Alex. South African filmmaker. Feature film: *Styx* (English, 2000)

Wulfson, Jason. South African filmmaker. Feature film: *The Bone Snatcher* (English, 2003)

Wyn, Michel. South African filmmaker. Feature film: *The Visitors* (English, 1979)

Xenopoulos, Jason. South African filmmaker. Studied at New York University. Work in the industry. Work across audio-visual media. Feature films: *Promised Land* (English, 2002), *Critical Assignment* (English, 2003)

Yachfine, Ahmed (b. 1948 in Casablanca). Moroccan filmmaker. Studied design in Rome, Islamic studies in Strasbourg (where he received his doctorate) and film at the University of Indiana at Bloomington. Feature films: *Nightmare / Cauchemar* (1984), *Khafaya* (1995)

Yala, Mohamed Meziane (b. 1946 in Akfadou,). Algerian filmmaker. Studied filmmaking at Lodz in Poland and worked as a trainee for Italian television (RAI). Numerous shorts in the 1970s and 1980s. Feature film: *Autumn Song / Chant d'automne* (1983)

Yaméogo, Pierre S. (b. 1955 in Koudougou). Burkinabè filmmaker. Studied filmmaking at the CLFC and at the University of Paris VIII. Produced the television series *Sita* and a video on refugees in Chad, *Réfugiés mais humains*. His six features show a lively and committed interest in social questions and raise fundamental issues about contemporary Africa. Feature films: *Dunia* (1987), *Laafi* (1990), *Wendemi* (1992), *Silmande / Tourbillon* (1998), *Me and My White Guy / Moi et mon blanc* (2002), *Delwende / Delwende, lève-toi et marche* (2005)

Yane, Hani. Egyptian filmmaker. Feature film: *It Was Written / Waʾd wa maktoub* (1986)

Yarney, Ato (b. 1932 in Beraku). Ghanaian filmmaker. Studied at the London International Film School and attended courses at the BFI and University of London. Later studied film in Poland (1965–66). Worked in various roles for the Ghana Film Industry Corporation and made a number of documentaries. Feature film: *His Majesty's Sergeant* (1983)

Yassin, Mohamed. Egyptian filmmaker. Feature films: *Woman's Divorce Lawyer / Muhami kholʾ* (2002), *Askar in the Camp / ʿAskar fi el-muʾaskar* (2003), *Deer's Blood / Damm El-Ghazaal* (2006)

Yassine, Ahmed. Egyptian filmmaker. Feature films: *The Cursed / al-Malaʾîn* (1979), *And Sadness Passes / Wa tamdî al-ahzân* (1979), *My Greetings to My Dear Professor / Maʾ tahiyyâtî li oustâdhî al-ʾazîz* (1981), *Things against the Law / Achyâ didd al-qânoun* (1982), *The Professor and the Dancer / Âlim wa ʿâlimah* (1983), *Hamza's Baker's Shop / Tâbounat Hamzah* (1984), *Khamsa the Genie / al-ʾAbqarî Khamsah* (1985), *Ali Bey Mazhar and the Forty Thieves / ʿAlî Bîh Mazhar wa-l-arbaʾîn harâmî* (1985), *Daqqet Zar / Daqqat zâr* (1986), *Satan's Friends / Asdiqâʾ al-chattân* (1988)

Yassine, Yassine Ismaïl. Egyptian filmmaker. Feature films: *The Toy / al-Louʾbah* (1978), *A Heartless Woman / Imraʾah bilâ qalb* (1978), *The Devil Sings / al-Chaytân youghannî* (1984), *The Vengeful Masters / al-Mountaquimoun* (1985), *Impressions on Water / Basmât fawq al-mâʾ* (1985), *The Hunter / al-Qannâs* (1986),

My Friend, My Brother, I Shall Kill You / Akhî wa sadîqî sa-aqtoulak (1986), *Under Threat / Taht al-tahdîd* (1986), *The Informer / al-Moukhbir* (1986), *He Returns to Take Revenge / ʿÂda li-yantaqim* (1988), *The Diabolical Plan / Khouttat al-chaytân* (1988), *An Almost Perfect Crime / Garîmah illâ roubʾ* (1990), *Fraud / Iltiyâl* (1990), *The Circle of Terror / Halqat al-rouʾb* (1990), *Three against One / Thalâthah ʿalâ wâdid* (1990), *Blood after Midnight / Demaaʾ baʾd muntasaf al-lail* (1995), *Escapee to Prison / Hareb ila al-sign* (1995), *The Fatal Phone Call / al-Mukalama al-qatela* (1996), *The Fierce Man / al-Ragoul al-chares* (1996)

Yehia, Adel. Egyptian filmmaker. Feature film: *Spicy Kids / Shebr wi nuss* (2004)

Yehya, Ahmed (b. 1947 in Cairo). Egyptian filmmaker. A child actor, he subsequently studied at the Cairo Higher Film Institute, graduating in 1968. Worked as assistant, especially with Helmi Halim (in some of whose films he had appeared as a child). Feature films: *Suffering Is a Woman / al-ʾAdhâb imraʾah* (1977), *The Voyage of Forgetfulness / Rihlat al-nisyân* (1978), *Weep Not, Love of My Life / Lâ tabkî yâ habîb al-ʾoumr* (1979), *Dirty Hands / al-Aydî al-qadhirah* (1979), *A Love without Sunshine / Houbb lâ yarâ al-chams* (1980), *The Night when the Moon will Weep / Laylah bakâ fîhâ al-qamar* (1980), *Farewell to Suffering / Wadâʾan li-l-ʾadhâb* (1981), *Judgment Is Given / Hakamat al-Mahkamah* (1981), *Wedad the Dancer / Widâd al-ghâziyyah* (1983), *Tomorrow I Will Take My Revenge / Ghadan saantaqim* (1983), *The Crooks / al-Nassaâbîn* 1984), *So That the Smoke Doesn't Blow Away / Hattâ lâ yatîr al-doukhân* (1984), *The Land Officials / al-Mouwazzafoun fî-l-ard* (1985), *The Suicide of the Flat's Owner / Infihâr sâhib al-chiqqah* (1986), *Prison in the Street / Karakoun fî-l-Châriʾ* (1986), *Patience in the Salt Mines / al-Sabr fî-l-mallâhât* (1986), *Dearest, We Are All Thieves / Yâ ʿazîzî koullounâ lousous* (1989), *The Servant / al-Khâdim* (1990), *Adolescent Boys and Girls / Mourâhiqoun wa mourâhiqât* (1991), *Samara al-Amir / Samârah al-Amîr* (1992), *Woman Prisoner No. 67 / al-Saguînah sabʾa wa sittîn* (1992), *A Man with a Past / Ragoul laho maadi*

(2000), *Suspicious Journey / Rehala mashbouha* (2002)

Yehya, Cherif. Egyptian filmmaker. Feature films: *The Fences of the Tanneries / Aswâr al-madâbigh* (1983), *The Tyrant / al-Tâghiyah* (1985), *Those Bastards . . . / Wlad al-îh* (1989), *Fleshy Lips / Chifâh ghalîzah* (1992), *We Own the Airport / Ihna ashaab el mataar* (2001)

Yeo, Kozoloa (b. 1950 in Tioro). Ivorian filmmaker. Studied filmmaking at the École Louis Lumière in Paris. Short films from 1976. His first feature looks at the clash of generations under the impact of modern education. Feature films: *Petanqui* (1983), *The Three Bracelets / Les trois bracelets* (2000)

Yonly, René Bernard (b. 1945 in Tansarga). Burkinabè filmmaker. Self-taught filmmaker and one of the pioneers of Burkinabè cinema. Feature film: *On the Path to Reconciliation / Sur le chemin de la réconciliation* (1973)

Yousri, Ahmed. Egyptian filmmaker. Feature film: *45 Days / 45 youm* (2007)

Youssef, Adli. Egyptian filmmaker. Feature films: *The Era of Challenge / Ayyâm al-tahaddî* (1985), *'Uncle' Qandil's Scissors / Miqass ʿamm Qandil* (1985), *Police Record / Fîch wa tachbîh* (1986)

Youssef, Hassan (b. 1934). Egyptian filmmaker and actor. Graduated from the Drama Institute in 1952 and got his first screen role from Salah Abou Seif in 1959. In all he appeared in over eighty films, some of which he directed. Feature films: *A Boy, A Girl and the Devil / Walad wa bint wachaytân* (1971), *The Coward and Love / al-Gabân wa-l-houbb* (1975), *That's Enough My Heart / Kafânî yâ qalb* (1977), *An Unforgettable Night / Laylah lâ tounsâ* (1978), *Migrating Birds / al-Touyour al-mouhîguirah* (1979), *Tears without Sin / Doumopuʾ bilâ khatâyâ* (1980), *The Fat Cats / al-Qitat al-simân* (1981), *Seeds of Evil / Boudhour al-chaytân* (1981), *Two on the Road / Itnîn ʿalâʾ al-tarîq* (1984), *A Bird with Teeth / ʿOusfour louh anyâb* (1987)

Youssef, Khaled. Egyptian filmmaker. Worked as assistant to Youssef Chahine. Feature films: *The Tempest / al-Asefa* (2001), *Marriage by Presidential Decree / Gawaaz bi qaraar goumhoury* (2001), *My Soul Mate / Enta omri* (2005), *Legitimate Betrayal / Kheyana mashruʾa* (2006), *Ouija* (2006), *Chaos / Heya Fawda* (with Youssef Chahine, 2007)

Zaki, Abdel Hamid. Egyptian filmmaker. Feature films: *I am the East / Anâ al-charq* (1958), *The Spider's Web / Khouyout al-ʾankabout* (1985), *Two Women and a Man / Imraʾatân wa ragoul* (1987), *Iron Woman / al-Marʾah al-hadîdiyyah* (1987), *The Claw / al-Kammâchah* (1988), *Fratricidal Struggle / Sirâʾ al-ahfâd* (1989), *The Little Monsters / al-Wouhouch al-saghîrah* (1989), *The Volcano / al-Bourkân* (1990), *Brigade No. 12 / al-Firqah tnaʾchar* (1991), *Dounia Abdel Gabbar / Douniâ Abd al-Gabbâr* (1992), *Karawana / Karawânah* (1993), *Spicy Taamiyya / Taʾmiyyah bi-l-chattah* (1993), *Danger / al-Khatar* (1994), *Either You Love . . . or You Leave / Yâ thibb . . . yâ tʾibb* (1994)

Zaki, Abdel Latif. Egyptian filmmaker. Feature films: *The Seventh Sin / al-Khatiʾa al-sabeʾa* (1996), *We'll Love and Get Rich / Ha nheb wi nʾeb* (1997)

Zayed, Yasser. Egyptian filmmaker. Feature film: *Teach Me How to Love / ʿAllemny al-hubb* (2005)

Zemmouri, Mahmoud (b. 1946 in Boufarik). Algerian filmmaker. Studied film at the Institut des Hautes Études Cinématographiques (IDHEC) and began his career in France, where he now lives. One of the few filmmakers to use comedy as a way of dealing with the contradictions of Algerian and immigrant life. Feature films: *Take a Thousand Quid and Get Lost / Prends dix mille balles et casses-toi* (1981, in France), *The Crazy Years of the Twist / Les Folles années du twist* (1983), *From Hollywood to Tamanrasset / De Hollywood à Tamanrasset* (1990), *The Honour of the Tribe / L'Honneur du tribu* (1993), *100% Arabica* (1997), *Arab, White, Red / Beur, blanc, rouge* (2004)

Zerouali, Abdallah (b. 1939 in Taza). Moroccan filmmaker. Studied filmmaking at the Institut des Hautes Études Cinématographiques (IDHEC) in Paris. His first feature, initially called *The Whirlpool / Le toubillon,* was begun in 1980, but completed—with a new title—only in 1995. Feature films: *Pals for the Day / Les Copains du jour* (1984), *I'm the Artist / Moi l'artiste* (1995)

Ziad, Ahmed. Moroccan filmmaker. Feature film: *Real Premonition* (2007)

Ziman, Ralph. South African filmmaker. Feature film: *Jerusalem Entsja* (English, 2006)

Zinaï-Koudil, Hafsa (b. 1951 in Ain Beïda). Algerian novelist and filmmaker, resident in France. She published three French-language novels—*La Fin d'un rêve* (1984), *Le Pari perdu* (1986), *Le Passé décomposé* (1992)—in Algeria and one—*Sans voix* (1997)—in Paris. Worked for Radiodiffusion Télévision Algérienne (RTA), with which she came into dispute over her first 16mm feature, which deals with the exploitation of a woman. Feature film: *The Female Devil / Le Démon au féminin* (1993)

Zineddaine, Mohamed. Moroccan filmmaker, based in Italy. Studied in Nice and at the Department of Art, Music and Spectacle (DAMS) in the University of Bologna. Worked as a journalist and photographer. Made a number of short fictions and documentaries on 16mm or video in Italy from 1996. Feature film: *Awakening / Le Réveil* (2003)

Zinet, Mohamed (b. 1932 in Algiers; d. 1995). Algerian actor and filmmaker. Fought with the Armée de Libération Nationale (ALN) and, when wounded, was sent to Tunis. Studied drama in East Berlin and Munich and worked as an actor in films made in France, Tunisia, and Algeria, including René Vautier's *Three Cousins / Trois Cousins,* Yves Boisset's *Dupont Lajoie,* and Abdellatif Ben Ammar's masterly Tunisian film *Aziza.* In Algeria he worked as assistant on the films produced by Casbah Films, including Gillo Pontecorvo's *The Battle of Al-*

giers. His own sole feature is a totally idiosyncratic and engaging work. Feature film: *Tahia ya Didou / Alger insolite* (1971)

Zingarelli, Italo. South African filmmaker. Feature film: *I'm for the Hippopotamus* (English, 1980)

Zinoun, Lahcen (b. 1944 in Casablanca). Moroccan filmmaker. An internationally celebrated ballet dancer, working as choreographer first in Belgium and then from 1978 in Morocco. Collaborated on films by Martin Scorsese (*The Last Temptation of Christ*) and Bernardo Bertolucci (*The Sheltering Sky*). A first short film in 2001. Feature film: *Oud al-Ouard* (retitled *Scattered Beauty / La beauté éparpillée* for release in 2007)

Zipman, Ralph. South African filmmaker. Feature film: *Hearts and Minds* (English, 1996)

Zito, Joseph. American director of a film included in some South African film listings. Feature film: *Red Scorpion* (English, with Joao Fernandes, 1987)

Ziyada, al-Sayed. Egyptian filmmaker. Feature films: *The Musician / al-Mousîqar* (1946), *The Fruits of Crime / Thamarat al-gârimah* (1947), *She Lived in the Shadows / ʿÂchat fî-l-zalâm* (1948), *Forbidden Happiness / al-Saʾâdah al-mouharramah* (1948), *Aventures de Khadra's Adventures / Moughâmarât Khadrah* (1950), *Khadra and Sindbad al-Qibli / Khadrah wa-l-sindibâd al-qiblî* (1951), *Call of the Blood / al-Dam yahinn* (1952), *The Last Meeting / al-Liqâ' al-akhîr* (1953), *The Private Lover / al-Âcgiq al-mahroum* (1954), *Everyone According to His Rank / al-Nâs maqâmât* (1954), *Explain to Me, I Beg You / Doullounî yâ nâs* (1954), *The Lovers / ahl al-hawâ* (1955), *The Gipsy / al-Ghagariyyah* (1960), *The Woman in Love / al-Âchiqah* (1960), *Take Me with My Shame / Khoudhnî bi-ârî* (1962), *Forgive Me My Sin / Ighfir lî khatî'atî* (1963), *Thoughtless Youth / Chabâb tâ'ich* (1963), *Wife for a Day / Zawgah li tawm yâhid* (1963), *In the Name of Love / Bism al-houbb* (1965), *Al-Sakkin Street / Hârat al-saqâyîn* (1966), *The*

Dancer from Soumbat / Ghâziyyah min soum-bât (1967), *Six Girls and One Suitor / Sitt banât wa ʿarîs* (1968), *Homes Have Their Secrets / al-Bouyout asrâr* (1971), *Let's Love Each Other / Daʾounâ nouhibb* (1975), *An Adolescent Girl from the Country / Mourâ hiqah min al-aryâf* (1976)

Zoulficar, Ezz Eddine (b. 1919; d. 1963). Egyptian filmmaker. Younger brother of Mahmoud Zoulficar. Abandoned a military career to direct his first feature in 1947. Also appeared as actor in some of his own films. Married for 5 years to the star Faten Hamnama, with whom he continued to work after their divorce. Feature films: *The Prisoner of Darkness / Asîr al-zalâm* (1947), *Abou Zeid al-Hilali / Abou Zayd al-Hilâlî* (1947), *Everyone Is Singing / al-Koull you-ghannî* (1947), *Khouloud / Khouloud* (1948), *Holiday in Hell / Agâzah fî gahannam* (1949), *She Has a Few Pennies / Sâhibat al-malâlîm* (1949), *I Am the Past / Anâ al-mâdi* (1951), *Ask It of My Heart / Salou qalbî* (1952), *The Night Train / Qitar al-layl* (1953), *The Doubt Which Kills / al-Chakk al-qâtil* (1953), *Rendezvous with Life / Mawʾid maʾ al-hayâh* (1953), *A Child from the District / Ibn al-hârah* (1953), *Wafaa / Wafâ* (1953), *Rendezvous with Happiness / Mawʾid maʾ al-saʾâdah* (1954), *Stronger than Love / Aqwâ min al-houbb* (1954), *The Farewell Dance / Taqsat al-wadâʾ* (1954), *Je pars / Innî râhilah* (1955), *Dearer than the Pupils of My Eyes / Aghlâ min ʿaynayya* (1955), *The Shore of Memories / Châtiʾ al-dhikrayât* (1955), *The Absent Woman / al-Gâʾibah* (1955), *Sleepless Night / ʿOuyoun sahrânah* (1956), *A Man Flees Love / Hârib min al-houbb* (1957), *The Path of Hope / Tarîq al-amal* (1957), *Give Me Back My Soul / Roudda qalbî* (1957), *Port Saïd / Port Saʾîd* (1957), *Street of Love / Châriʾ al-houbb* (1958), *A Woman on the Road / Imraʾas fî-l-tarîq* (1958), *The Second Man / al-Ragoul al-thânî* (1959), *Among the Ruins / Bayn al-Atlâl* (1959), *River of Love / Nahr al-houbb* (1960), *Girls and Summer / Banât wa-l-sayf* (one episode) (1960), *Rendezvous in the Tower / Mawʾid fî-l-bourg* (1962), *Black Candles / al-Choumouʾ al-sawdâ* (1962)

Zoulficar, Mahmoud (b. 1914; d. 1970). Egyptian filmmaker. Older brother of Ezz Eddine Zoulficar. Began his career as an actor in 1939 and combined acting with directing from 1947, beginning with *Hadiyyah,* starring his wife, Aziza Amir. Feature films: *Hadiyyah / Hadiyyah* (1947), *On a Cloud / Fawq al-sahâb* (1948), *A Girl from Palestine / Fatât min Filastîn* (1948), *The Night Is Ours / al-Layl lanâm* (1949), *It's Fate / Qismah wa-nasîb* (1950), *Little Virtues / Akhlâq li-l-bayʾ* (1950), *My Father Deceived Me / Khadaʾanî abî* (1951), *I Believed in God / Âmint billah* (1952), *The Mistake of My Life / Ghaltat al-ʾoumr* (1953), *The Neighbors' Daughter / Bint al-guîrân* (1954), *The Good Earth / al-Ard al-tayyibah* (1954), *The Ringing of the Khoulhal / Rannat al-khoulkhâl* (1955), *A Journey of Love / Rihlah gharâmiyyah* (1957), *Me and My Heart / Anâ wa qalbî* (1957), *Young People Today / Chabâb al-yawm* (1958), *Never Again / Toubah* (1958), *Forbidden Women / Nisâ mouharramât* (1959), *The Unknown Woman / al-Marʾah al-magʾhoulah* (1959), *The Giant / al-Iʾmlâq* (1960), *The Sacred Link / al-Ribât al-mouqaddas* (1960), *Without Tears / Bilâ doumouʾ* (1961), *Rendezvous with the Past / Mawʾid maʾ al-mâdî* (1961), *Don't Think of Me Anymore / Lâ tadhkourînî* (1961), *The Big Adolescent / al-Mourâhiq al-kabîr* (1961), *That's What Love Is / al-Houbb kidah* (1961), *Woman in Torment / Imraʾah fî dawwâmah* (1962), *Gentle Hands / al-Aydî al-nâʾimah* (1963), *The Rebel / al-Moutamarridah* (1963), *The Years of Love / Sanawât al-houbb* (1963), *The Price of Love / Thaman al-houbb* (1963), *Reserved for Men / Li-l-rigâl faqat* (1964), *Dearer than My Life / Aghlâ min hayâtî* (1965), *The Three Love Her / al-Thalâthah youhibbounahâ* (1965), *The Woman's Enemy / ʿAdouww al-marʾah* (1966), *The Little Adolescent Girl / al-Mourâhiqah al-saghîrah* (1966), *Noura / Nourâ* (1967), *Driven from Paradise / al-Khouroug min al-gannah* (1967), *The Last Kiss / al-Qoublah al-akhîrah* (1967), *Holiday of Love / Agâzat gharâm* (1967), *The Story of Three Girls / Hikâyat thalâth banât* (1968), *The Beauty of Love / Rawʾat al-houbb* (1968), *Three Women / Thalâth nisâ* (one episode) (1969), *The Girl from the Music Hall / Fatât al-istiʾrâd* (1969), *Girls' Secrets / Asrâr al-banât* (1969), *Love in 1970 / al-Houbb sanat asʾîn* (1969), *My Wife, the Secretary and Me / Anâ wa zawgatî wa-l-secrétaira* (1970), *My Husband's Wife / Imraʾat* *zawguî* (1970), *Adolescent Girls' Love / Houbb al-mourâhiqât* (1970), *Under the Sign of the Virgin / Bourg al-ᵓadhrâ* (1972), *Featureless Men / Rigâl bilâ malâmin* (1972)

Zoumbara, Paul (b. 1949 in Souanky, Congo). Burkinabè filmmaker. Studied literature in Ouagadougou University and filmmaking in Paris. President of the Centre National de la Cinématographie du Burkina (CNCB). Two 16mm shorts in the early 1980s. Feature film: *Days of Torment / Jours de tourmente* (1983)

Zran, Mohamed (b. 1959 in Zarzis). Tunisian filmmaker. Studied filmmaking in Paris. Worked as assistant on two films in France and made three noted short films as well as a feature-length video documentary, *Millennium Song / Le Chant du millénaire* (2002). Feature films: *Essaïda* (1996), *The Prince / Le Prince* (2004)

Part Two

Feature Film Chronologies

ALGERIA

OVERALL STATISTICS: 75 filmmakers—
181 feature films
1960s
Output: 9 films
Filmmakers: 5 + 2 collectively made films
(Mustapha Badie, Tewfik Fares, Mohamed Lakhdar Hamina, Ahmed Rachedi, Mohamed Slim Riad)
1970s
Output: 40 films
Filmmakers: 21 active, 17 new (*) + 2 collectively made films
(*Ali Akika, *Merzak Allouache, *Mohamed Nadir Aziri, Mustapha Badie, *Farouk Beloufa, *Mohamed Ben Salah, *Mohamed Benayat, *Ghaouti Bendeddouche, *Mohamed Bouamari, *Djafar Damardjji, *Assia Djebar, *Moussa Haddad, *Mustapha Kateb, Mohamed Lakhdar Hamina, *Amar Laskri, *Sid Ali Mazif, *Mohamed Lamine Merbah, Ahmed Rachedi, Mohamed Slim Riad, *Abdelaziz Tolbi, *Mohamed Zinet)
1980s
Output: 38 films
Filmmakers: 26 active, 16 new (*) + 1 collectively made film
(Ali Akika, Merzak Allouache, *Abdelkrim Bahloul, *Benamar Bakhti, *Ghaouti Bendeddouche, *Mohamed Rachid Benhadj, Mohamed Benayat, Mohamed Bouamari, *Rachid Bouchareb, *Abderrahmane Bouguermouh, *Mehdi Charef, *Mohamed Chouikh, Assia Djebar, *Sid Ali Fettar, *Ali Ghalem, Mohamed Lakhdar Hamina, *Rabah Laradji, Amar Laskri,

*Jean-Pierre Lledo, Sid Ali Mazif, *Taïeb Mefti, Ahmed Rachedi, Mohamed Slim Riad, *Brahim Tsaki, *Mohamed Meziane Yala, *Mahmoud Zemmouri)
1990s
Output: 54 films
Filmmakers: 37 active, 21 new (*) + 1 collectively made film
(Merzak Allouache, Abdelkrim Bahloul, Benamar Bakhti, *Ahmed Bouchaâla, Rachid Bouchareb, *Rachid Ben Brahim, *Rabie Ben Mokhtar, *Rachid Benallal, Mohamed Rachid Benhadj, *Rabah Bouberras, Abderrahmane Bouguermouh, Mehdi Charef, *Malek Chibane, Mohamed Chouikh, Djafar Damardjji, *Yahia Debboub, Sid Ali Fettar, *Zaïda Ghorab-Volta, *Belkacem Hadjadj, *Amor Hakkor, *Abderrazak Hellal, *Mohamed Hilmi, *Rachida Krim, *Malek Lakhdar Hamina, Amar Laskri, Jean-Pierre Lledo, *Saïd Ould Khelifa, *Azzedine Meddour, Mohamed Lamine Merbah, *Hadj Rahim, *Mohamed Soudani, *Okacha Touita, *Karim Traïdia, Brahim Tsaki, Mahmoud Zemmouri, *Hafsa Zinaï-Koudil)
2000s
Output: 40 films
Filmmakers: 34 active, 16 new (*)
(*Karin Albou, Merzak Allouache, *Rabah Ameur-Zaïmèche, *Yamina Bachir-Chouikh, Abdelkrim Bahloul, *Naguel Belouad, Ghaouti Bendeddouche, *Yamina Benguigui, Ahmed Bouchaâla, *Zakia Bouchaâla, Rachid Bouchareb, *Lyèce Boukhitine, Mehdi Charef, *Chad Chenoua, *Nadia Cherabi-Labidi, Malik Chibane, Mohamed Chouikh, *Kamal Dehane, *Mostéfa Djadjam, Zaïda Ghorab-Volta, Bourlem Guerdjou, Belkacem Hadjadj, *Azize Ka-

bouche, Saïd Ould Khelifa, *Liazid Khodja, *Mohamed Lebcir, Jean-Pierre Lledo, *Nadir Moknèche, * Djamila Sahraoui, Mohamed Soudani, Okacha Touita, Karim Traïdia, Mahmoud Zemmouri)

CHRONOLOGY

In addition to the listing of Algerian-directed films, it is worth noting the 1960s features produced by Youcef Saadi's independent Casbah Films and directed by Italians: Gillo Pontecorvo's *The Battle of Algiers* (1966), Enzo Peri's *Three Pistols against Caesar* (co-directed by Moussa Haddad, 1967), and Luchino Visconti's *The Outsider* (1968). There are also two films directed by French Front de Libération Nationale (FLN) activists, René Vautier's documentary *A People on the March / Peuple en marche* (1963) and Jacques Charby's feature, *Such a Young Peace / Une si jeune paix* (1965).

1965
Dawn of the Damned / L'Aube des damnés (Ahmed Rachedi)
The Night Is Afraid of the Sun / La Nuit a peur du soleil (Mustapha Badie)
1966
The Wind from the Aurès / Le Vent des Aurès (Mohamed Lakhdar-Hamina)
1968
Hassan Terro (Mohamed Lakhdar-Hamina)
Hell for a Ten-Year-Old / L'Enfer à dix ans (collective)
The Way / La Voie (Mohamed Slim Riad)
1969
Opium and the Stick / L'Opium et le bâton (Ahmed Rachedi)
The Outlaws / Les Hors-la-loi (Tewfik Fares)
Stories of the Revolution / Histoires de la révolution (collective)
1971
Tahia ya Didou (Mohamed Zinet)
1972
Beside the Poplar Tree / Auprès du peuplier (Moussa Haddad)
Black Sweat / Sueur noire (Sid Ali Mazif)
The Charcoal Burner / Le Charbonnier (Mohamed Bouamari)
December / Décembre (Mohamed Lakhdar Hamina)

El Goula (Mustapha Kateb)
The Good Families / Les Bonnes familles (Djafar Damardjji)
Noua (Abdelaziz Tolbi)
Patrol in the East / Patrouille à l'est (Amar Laskri)
The Plunderers / Les Spoliateurs (Mohamed Lamine Merbah)
Sana'oud (Mohamed Slim Riad)
So That Algeria May Live / Pour que vive l'Algérie (collective)
Some People and Others / Les Uns, les autres (Mohamed Ben Salah)
1973
Inspector Tahar's Holiday / Les Vacances de l'Inspecteur Tahar (Moussa Haddad)
The War of Liberation / La Guerre de libération (collective)
1974
A Finger in the Works / Le Doigt dans l'engrenage (Ahmed Rachedi)
Forbidden Zone / Zone interdite (Ahmed Lallem)
Hassan Terro's Escape / L'Évasion de Hassan Terro (Mustapha Badie)
The Inheritance / L'Héritage (Mohamed Bouamari)
The Mask of an Enlightened Woman / Le Masque d'une éclaircie (Mohamed Benayat)
1975
Chronicle of the Years of Embers / Chronique des années de braise (Mohamed Lakhdar Hamina)
The Nomads / Les Nomades (Sid Ali Mazif)
Savage Barricades / Barricades sauvages (Mohamad Benayat)
Wind from the South / Vent du Sud (Mohamed Slim Riad)
1976
The Fishermen / Les Pêcheurs (Ghaouti Bendeddouche)
Omar Gatlato (Merzak Allouache)
The Uprooted / Les Déracinés (Mohamed Lamine Merbah)
1977
Barriers / Barrières (Ahmed Lallem)
Journey to the Capital / Voyage en capital (Ali Akiki, with Anne-Marie Autissier)
1978
The Adventures of a Hero / Les Aventures d'un héros (Merzak Allouache)

Autopsy of a Plot / Autopsie d'un complot (Mohamed Slim Riad)

The Benevolent / El Moufid (Amar Laskri)

Leila and the Others / Leïla et les autres (Sid Ali Mazif)

The Nouba of the Women of Mount Chenoua / La Nouba des femmes du Mont Chenoua (Assia Djebar)

The Olive Tree of Boul'Hilet / L'Olivier de Boul'Hilet (Mohamed Nadir Aziri)

1979

Ali in Wonderland / Ali au pays des mirages (Ahmed Rachedi)

Dead the Long Night / Morte la longue nuit (collective)

First Step / Premier pas (Mohamed Bouamari)

Nahla (Farouk Beloufa)

The New Romantics / Les Nouveaux romantiques (Mohamed Benayat)

1980

Tears of Blood / Larmes de sang (Ali Akika, with Anne-Marie Autissier)

The Zerda or Songs of Forgetfulness / La Zerda ou les chants de l'oubli (Assia Djebar)

1981

Children of the Wind / Les Enfants du vent (Brahim Tsaki)

Take a Thousand Quid and Get Lost / Prends dix mille balles et casses-toi (Mahmoud Zemmouri)

1982

Autumn Song / Chant d'Automne (Mohamed Meziane Yala)

Breakdown / Rupture (Mohamed Chouikh)

The Crazy Years of the Twist / Les Folles années du twist (Mahmoud Zemmouri)

The Empire of Dreams / L'Empire des rêves (Jean-Pierre Lledo)

The Epic of Cheikh Bouamama / L'Épopée de Cheikh Bouamama (Benamar Bakhti)

Harvests of Steel / Moissons d'acier (Ghaouti Bendeddouche)

Hassan-Taxi (Mohamed Slim Riad)

I Exist / J'existe (Sid Ali Mazif)

The Man Who Looked at Windows / L'Homme qui regardait les fenêtres (Merzak Allouache)

Moussa's Wedding / Le Mariage de Moussa (Tayeb Mefti)

The Refusal / Le Refus (Mohamed Bouamari)

A Roof, a Family / Un toit, une famille (Rabah Laradji)

Sand Storm / Vent de sable (Mohamed Lakhdar Hamina)

Story of a Meeting / Histoire d'une rencontre (Brahim Tsaki)

A Wife for My Son / Une femme pour mon fils (Ali Ghalem)

1984

M. Fabre's Windmill / Le Moulin de M. Fabre (Ahmed Rachedi)

Mint Tea / Le Thé à la menthe (Abdelkrim Bahloul)

1985

Baton Rouge (Rachid Bouchareb)

Child of the Stars / L'Enfant des étoiles (Mohamed Benayat)

Tea in the Harem / Le Thé au harem d'Archimède (Mehdi Charef)

1986

Cry of Stone / Cri de pierre (Abderrahmane Bouguermouh)

Houria (Sid Ali Mazif)

The Last Image / La Dernière image (Mohamed Lakhdar Hamina)

A Paris Love Story / Un amour à Paris (Merzak Allouache)

1987

The Gates of Silence / Les Portes du silence (Amar Laskri)

Miss Mona (Mehdi Charef)

We Shall Go onto the Mountain / Nous irons à la montagne (collective)

1988

Arizona Stallion (Mohamed Benayat)

Camomile / Camoumille (Mehdi Charef)

The Citadel / La Citadelle (Mohamed Chouikh)

Desert Rose / Rose des sables / Louss (Mohamed Rachid Benhadj)

Raï (Sid Ali Fettar)

1989

Hassan nija (Ghaouti Bendeddouche)

1990

Cheb (Rachid Bouchareb)

The Cry of Men / Le Cri des hommes (Okacha Touita)

El ouelf essaib (Mohamed Hilmi)

From Hollywood to Tanarasset / De Hollywood à Tanarasset (Mahmoud Zemmouri)

The Neon Children / Les Enfants des néons (Brahim Tsaki)

1991

Autumn—October in Algiers / Automne—octobre à Alger (Malek Lakhdar Hamina)

Moonlighting / Le Clandestin (Benamar Bakhti)

Sahara Blues (Rabah Bouberras)

The Third Act / Le Troisième acte (Rachid Ben Brahim)

A Vampire in Paradise / Un vampire au paradis (Abdelkrim Bahloul)

White Shadows / Ombres blanches (Saïd Ould Khelifa)

1992

Bad Weather for a Crook / Sale temps pour un voyou (Amor Hakkor)

In the Land of the Juliets / Au pays des Juliets (Mehdi Charef)

Lights / Lumières (Jean-Pierre-Lledo)

Marathon Tam (Rabie Ben Mokhtar)

Radhia (Mohamed Lamine Merbah)

Segou (Rachid Bouchareb)

Shattered Years / Des années déchirées (Rachid Bouchareb)

1993

The Female Devil / Le Démon au féminin (Hafsa Zinaï-Koudil)

Forbidden Love / Amour interdit (Sid Ali Fettar)

Hexagon / Hexagone (Malek Chibane)

The Honour of the Tribe / L'Honneur du tribu (Mahmoud Zemmouri)

Touchia (Mohamed Rachid Benhadj)

Wanderings / Errances aka *Land of Ashes / Terre en cendres* (Djafar Damardjji)

Ya ouled (Rachid Benallal)

Youssef—The Legend of the Seventh Sleeper / Youcef, la légende du septième dormant (Mohamed Chouikh)

1994

Bab el-Oued City (Merzak Allouache)

Life Dust / Poussière de vie (Rachid Bouchareb)

The Portrait / Le Portrait (Hadj Rahim)

1995

Krim (Ahmed Bouchaâla)

Once upon a Time / Machaho / Il était une fois (Belkacem Hadjadj)

Sweet France / Douce France (Malek Chibane)

1996

The Forgotten Hillside / La Colline oubliée (Abderrahmane Bouguermouh)

The Hamlet Sisters / Les Sœurs Hamlet (Abdelkrim Bahloul)

Hello Cousin! / Salut Cousin! (Merzak Allouache)

Under Women's Feet / Sous les pieds des femmes (Rachida Krim)

1997

Baya's Mountain / La Montagne de Baya (Azzedine Meddour)

The Desert Ark / L'Arche du désert (Mohamed Chouikh)

My Family's Honor / L'Honneur de ma famille (Rachid Bouchareb)

The Night of Destiny / La Nuit du destin (Abdelkrim Bahloul)

The Old Lady and the Child / La Vieille dame et l'enfant (Yahia Debboub)

100% Arabica (Mahmoud Zemmouri)

Question of Honor / Question d'honneur (Abderrazak Hellal)

The Resistance Fighters / Les Résistants (Yahia Debboub)

The Tree of Suspended Fates / L'albero dei destini sospesi (Mohamed Rachid Benhadj)

Waalo fendo (Mouhamed Soudani)

1998

Algiers-Beirut: In Remembrance / Alger-Beyrouth, pour mémoire (Merzak Allouache)

Leave a Little Love / Laisse un peu d'amour (Zaïda Ghorab-Volta)

Living in Paradise / Vivre au paradis (Bourlem Guerdjou)

Lotus Flower / Fleur de lotus (Amar Laskri)

The Other Algeria: Views from Within / L'Autre Algérie: regards intérieurs (collective)

The Polish Bride / De Poolse Bruid / La Fiancée polonaise (Karim Traïdia)

The Story Tellers / Les Diseurs d'histoires (documentary) (Mohamed Soudani)

1999

Mirka (Rachid Benhadj)

2000

Frontiers / Frontières (Mostéfa Djadjam)

Little Senegal (Rachid Bouchareb)

Madam Osmane's Harem / Le Harem de Mme Osmane (Nadir Moknèche)

Marie-Line (Mehdi Charef)
The Truth Tellers / Les Diseurs de vérité (Karim Traïdia)
Women's Expectations / L'Attente des femmes (Naguel Belouad)
2001
Control of Origin / Origine contrôlée (Ahmed and Zakia Bouchaâla)
Gilded Youth / Jeunesse dorée (Zaïda Ghorab-Volta)
Inch'Allah Sunday / Inch'Allah dimanche (Yamina Benguigui)
Keltoum's Daughter / La Fille de Keltoum (Mehdi Charef)
The Mistress in a Swimming Costume / La Maîtresse en maillot de bain (Lyèce Boukhitine)
The Other World / L'Autre monde (Merzak Allouache)
17 rue Bleue (Chad Chenouga)
2002
Letters from Algeria / Lettres d'Algérie (Azize Kabouche)
The Neighbor / La Voisine (Ghaouti Bendeddouche)
Rachida (Yamina Bachir-Chouikh)
Wars without Images / Guerres sans images (documentary) (Mohamed Soudani)
Wesh Wesh—What's Happening? / Wesh Wesh, qu'est-ce qui se passe? (Rabah Ameur-Zaïmèche)
2003
Chouchou (Merzak Allouache)
My Friend, My Sister / Mon amie ma soeur (Mohamed Lebcir)
2004
An Algerian Dream / Un rêve algérien (documentary) (Jean-Pierre Lledo)
Ania's Tea / Le Thé d'Ania (Saïd Ould Khelifa)
Arab, White, Red / Beur, Blanc, Rouge (Mahmoud Zemmouri)
The Assassinated Sun / Le Soleil assassiné (Abdelkrim Bahloul)
El Manara (Belkacem Hadjadj)
The Suspects / Les Suspects (Kamal Dehane)
Viva Laldjérie (Nadir Moknèche)
2005
Bab el Web (Merzak Allouache)
Barakat! (Djamila Sahraoui)

Bled Number One (Rabah Ameur-Zaïmeche)
Days of Glory / Indigènes (Rachid Bouchareb)
Little Jerusalem / La Petite Jérusalem (Karin Albou)
Neighbors / Voisins, Voisines (Malik Chibane)
Village of Women / Douar de femmes (Mohamed Chouikh)
Zaina, Horsewoman from the Atlas / Zaïna, cavalière de l'Atlas (Bourlem Guerdjou)
2006
Si Mohand U M'hand / L'Insoumis / The Rebel (Liazid Khadja and Rachid Benallel, 2006)
2007
Gallic Cartridges / Cartouches gaulois (Mehdi Charef)
Morituri (Okacha Touita)
Paloma Sweets / Délice Paloma (Nadir Moknèche)
The Other Side of the Mirror / L'Envers du miroir (Nadia Cherabi-Labidi)

REFERENCES

Allouache, Merzak. *Omar Gatlato* (script). Algiers: Cinémathèque Algérienne/Éditions LAPHOMIC, 1987.

———. *Salut Cousin!* (script). Paris: *L'Avant-Scène du Cinéma* 457, 1996.

Armes, Roy. *Omar Gatlato*. Trowbridge, England: Flicks Books, 1998. Translated as: *Omar Gatlato de Merzak Allouache, un regard nouveau sur l'Algérie*. Paris: Éditions L'Harmattan, 1999.

———. "History or Myth: *Chronique des années de braise*." In Ida Kummer, ed. *Cinéma Maghrébin*, special issue of *Celaan* 1, no. 1–2 (2002): 7–17.

———. "Youcef ou la Légende du Septième dormant / Youssef or The Legend of the Seventh Sleeper." In *The Cinema of North Africa and the Middle East*, ed. Gönül Dönmez-Colin, pp. 134–142. London: Wallflower Press, 2007.

Ben Aissa, Khelfa. *Tu vivras, Zinet!: Tahia ya Zinet!* Paris: Éditions L'Harmattan, 1990.

Berrah, Mouny. "Algerian Cinema and National Identity." In *Screens of Life: Critical Film Writing from the Arab World*, ed. Alia Arasoughly, pp. 63–83. Quebec: World Heritage Press, 1998.

Bosséno, Christian. "Des maquis d'hier aux luttes d'aujourd'hui: Thématique du cinéma algérien." *La Revue du Cinéma—Image et Son* 340 (1979): 27–52.

Bouchareb, Rachid. *Indigènes* (script). Paris: Avant-Scène du Cinéma 564, 2007.

Boudjedra, Rachid. *Naissance du cinéma algérien.* Paris: François Maspéro, 1971.

Brossard, Jean-Pierre, ed. *L'Algérie vue par son cinéma.* Locarno, Switzerland: Festival International du Film de Locarno, 1981.

Calle-Gruber, Mireille. *Assia Djebar, ou la résistance de l'écriture.* Paris: Maisonneuve and Larose, 2001.

———. *Assia Djebar.* Paris: ADPF and Ministère des Affaires Étrangères, 2006.

———, ed. *Assia Djebar, nomade entre les murs.* Paris: Masonneuve & Larose, 2007.

Chikhi, Beïda. *Assia Djebar: Histoires et fantaisies,* Paris: Presses de l'Université Paris-Sorbonne, 2007.

Choukroun, Jacques, and François de La Bretèche, ed. *Algérie d'hier et d'aujourd'hui.* Perpignan, France: Institut Jean Vigo/*Cahiers de la Cinémathèque* 76, 2004.

Cinéma: production cinématographique 1957–1973. Algiers: Ministère de l'Information et de la Culture, 1974.

Clerc, Jeanne-Marie. *Assia Djebar, écrire, transgresser, résister.* Paris: Éditions L'Harmattan, 1997.

Dadci, Younès. *Dialogues Algérie-Cinéma: première histoire du cinéma algérien.* Paris: Éditions Dadci, 1970.

———. *Première histoire du cinéma algérien, 1896–1979.* Paris: Éditions Dadci, 1980.

Dine, Philip. "Thinking the Unthinkable: The Generation of Meaning in French Literary and Cinema Images of the Algerian War." *Maghreb Review* 19, no. 1–2 (1994): 123–132.

Djebar, Assia. *Ces voix qui m'assiègent* (essays). Paris: Albin Michel, 1999.

Film in Algerien ab 1970. Berlin: *Kinemathek* 57 (1978).

Hadj-Moussa, Rahiba. *Le Corps, l'histoire, le territoire: les rapports de genre dans le cinéma algérien.* Paris/Montreal: Publisud and Edition Balzac, 1994.

———. "The Locus of Tension: Gender in Algerian Cinema." In *African Cinema: Post-Colonial and Feminist Readings,* ed. Kenneth W. Harrow, pp. 255–276. Trenton, N.J.: Africa World Press, 1999.

Hennebelle, Guy, Mouny Berrah, and Benjamin Stora, eds. *La Guerre d'Algérie à l'écran.* Paris: Corlet/Télérama/*CinémAction* 85, 1997.

Images et visages du cinéma algérien. Algiers: ONCIC, Ministère de la Culture et du Tourisme, 1984.

Maherzi, Lotfi. *Le Cinéma algérien: institutions, imaginaire, idéologie.* Algiers: SNED, 1980.

Megherbi, Abdelghani. *Les Algériens au miroir du cinéma colonial.* Algiers: SNED, 1982.

———. *Le Miroir aux alouettes.* Algiers: ENAL, UPU, GAM, 1985.

Mimoun, Mouloud, ed. *France-Algérie, images d'une guerre.* Paris: Institut du Monde Arabe, 1992.

Où va le cinéma algérien? Paris: *Cahiers du Cinéma,* hors-série, February–March 2003.

Quarante Ans de Cinéma Algérien. Algiers: Dar Raïs Hamidou, 2002.

Rocca, Anna. *Assia Djebar, le corps invisible—Voir sans être vue.* Paris: Éditions L'Harmattan, 2004.

Salmane, Hala, Simon Hartog, and David Wilson, eds. *Algerian Cinema.* London: British Film Institute, 1976.

Taboulay, Camille. *Le Cinéma métaphorique de Mohamed Chouikh* (long interview plus script of *L'Arche du désert*). Paris: K Films Éditions, 1997.

Tamzali, Wassyla. *En attendant Omar Gatlato.* Algiers: Éditions EnAP, 1979.

Vautier, René. *Caméra citoyenne, mémoires.* Rennes, France: Éditions Apogée, 1998.

———. *Afrique 50* (script). Paris: Éditions Paris Expérimental, 2001.

Venturini, Fabrice. *Mehdi Charef, conscience esthétique de la génération "beur."* Biarritz, France: Séguier, 2005.

ANGOLA

Output: 10 feature films
Filmmakers: 7
(Jorge Antonio, Ruy Duarte de Carvalho, Or-

lando Fortunato, Zézé Gamboa, Maria João Ganga, Sarah Maldoror, António Ole)

CHRONOLOGY
1974
Sambizanga (Sarah Maldoror)
1977
Courage, Comrade / Faz la couragem, camarada (Ruy Duarte de Carvalho)
1978
The Rhythm of N'Gola Ritmos / Ritmo do N'Gola Ritmos (António Ole).
1982
Conceição Tchimbula, a Day, a Life / Conceição Tchimbula, um dia, uma vida (António Ole)
Memory of a Day / Memoria de um dia (Orlando Fortunato)
Nelisita (Ruy Duarte de Carvalho)
1989
Moia—The Message of the Islands / Moia—O recado das ilhas (Ruy Duarte de Carvalho)
1992
The Watchtower of the Moon / O miradouro da lua (Jorge Antonio) (Portuguese by birth)
2004
A Hero / O heroi (Zézé Gamboa)
Hollow City / Na cidade vazia (Maria João Ganga)

REFERENCES
Andrade-Watkins, Claire. "Portuguese African Cinema: Historical and Contemporary Perspectives, 1969–1993." In *Cinemas of the Black Diaspora: Diversity, Dependence and Oppositionality,* ed. Michael T. Martin, pp. 181–203. Detroit: Wayne State University Press, 1995.

Duarte de Carvalho, Ruy. *O Camarada e a câmera.* Luanda, Angola: INAND, 1984.

Fina, Luciana, Cristina Fina, and António Loja Neves. *Cinemas de África.* Lisbon: Cinemateca Portugesa and Culturgest, 1995.

Pfaff, Françoise. "Sarah Maldoror." In *25 Black African Film Makers,* pp. 205–216. New York: Greenwood Press, 1988.

Rodriguès, Antonio. "Les Cinémas d'Afrique 'lusophone.'" In *Cinémas africains, une oasis dans le désert?* ed. Samuel Lelièvre, pp. 237–238. Paris: Corlet/Télérama/*CinémAction* 106, 2003.

BENIN

Output: 12 feature films
Filmmakers: 8
(Pascal Abikanlou, Sylvstre Amoussou, Richardo De Medeiros, Idrissou Mora-Kpaï, Jean Odoutan, François Sourou Okioh, Sanvi Panou, Noukpo Wilannon)

CHRONOLOGY
1974
Under the Sign of the Vaudon / Sous le signe du vaudon (Pascal Abikanlou)
1976
The Newcomer / Le Nouveau venu (Richard De Medeiros)
1985
Ironu (François Sourou Okioh)
1999
Barbecue Pejo (Jean Odoutan)
2000
Djib (Jean Odoutan)
2001
Mama Aloko (Jean Odoutan)
The Queen Mother / Si-Guériki, la reine-mère (Idrissou Mora-Kpaï)
2003
The Waltz of the Fat Bottoms / La Valse des gros derrières (Jean Odoutan)
2004
Arlit, a Second Paris / Arlit, deuxième Paris (Idrissou Mora-Kpaï)
2006
Africa Paradis (Sylvestre Amoussou)
Midjeresso (Noukpo Wilannon)
2007
The Amazonian Candidate / L'Amazone candidate (Sanvi Panou)

BURKINA FASO

Output: 46 feature films
Filmmakers: 21
(Armand Balima, Boubakar Diallo, Missa Hébié,

Gaston Kaboré, Madou Djim Kola, Sanou Kollo, Dani Kouyate, Régina Fanta Nacro, Idrissa Ouedraogo, Tahirou Tasséré Ouédraogo, Christian Richard, Emmanuel Kalifa Sanon, Kollo Daniel Sanou, Jacob Sou, Abdoulaye Sow, Apolline Traoré, Drissa Touré, Issa de Brahima Traore, Nissy Joanny Traoré, Pierre S. Yaméogo, René Bernard Yonly, Paul Zoumbara)

CHRONOLOGY
1971
Blood of the Outcasts / Le Sang des parias (Mamadou Djim Kola)
1973
On the Path to Reconciliation / Sur le chemin de la réconciliation (René Bernard Yonly)
1982
God's Gift / Wend Kuuni / Le Don de dieu (Gaston Kaboré)
The Immigrant / Paweogo / L'Immigrant (Kollo Daniel Sanou)
Other People's Courage / Le Courage des autres (Christian Richard)
1983
Days of Torment / Jours de tourmente (Paul Zoumbara)
1985
The Dizziness of Passion / Le Vertige de la passion (Armand Balima)
1987
Desebagato / Le Dernier salaire (Emmanuel Kalifa Sanon)
Dunia / Le Monde (Pierre S. Yaméogo)
Story of Orokia / Histoire d'Orokia (Jabob Sou)
Yam Daabo / Le Choix (Idrissa Ouedraogo)
1988
Zan Boko (Gaston Kaboré)
1989
Le Grotto (Jabob Sou)
Tilai (Idrissa Ouedraogo)
Yaaba (Idrissa Ouedraogo)
1990
Laada (Drissa Touré)
Laafi / Tout va bien (Pierre S. Yaméogo)
Yelbeedo (Abdoulaye Sow)
1991
Karim and Sala / Karim et Sala (Idrissa Ouedraogo)

1992
The Foreigner / Toungan / L'Étranger (Mamadou Djim Kola)
Jigi / L'Espoir (Kollo Daniel Sanou)
Rabi (Gaston Kaboré)
Sababu (Nissi Joanny Traore)
Samba Traore (Idrissa Ouedraogo)
Wendemi / L'Enfant du bon dieu (Pierre S. Yaméogo)
1993
Haramuya (Drissa Touré)
1994
A Cry from the Heart / Le Cri de cœur (Idrissa Ouedraogo)
Keita, the Heritage of the Griot / Keïta, l'heritage du griot (Dani Kouyate)
1996
Buud Yam (Gaston Kaboré)
1997
Kini and Adams (Idrissa Ouedraogo)
1998
Lucy's Revenge / La Revanche de Lucy (Janusz Mrozowski)
Silmande / Tourbillon (Pierre S. Yaméogo)
2000
Sia, the Dream of the Python / Sia, le rêve du python (Dani Kouyate)
Siraba / Siraba, la grande voie (Issa de Brahima Traore)
2002
Me and My White Guy / Moi et mon blanc (Pierre S. Yaméogo)
Tasuma (Kollo Daniel Sanou)
2003
Diarabi (Missa Hébié)
The Gods' Anger / La Colère des dieux (Idrissa Ouedraogo)
2004
The Night of Truth / La Nuit de la vérité (Régina Fanta Nacro)
Ouaga Saga (Dani Kouyate)
Under the Moonlight / Sous la clarté de la lune (Apolline Traoré)
2005
Delwende / Delwende, lève-toi et marche (Pierre S. Yaméogo)
Phoenix Code / Code Phénix (Boubakar Diallo)
2006
Kato Kato / Un maleur n'arrive jamais seul (Idrissa Ouédraogo)

The World Is a Ballet / Le Monde est un ballet
(Issa Traoré de Brahima)
2007
Djanta (Tahirou Tasséré Ouédraogo)
NB From 2003 Boubakar Diallo began producing video (DVD) films of all kinds, fictional shorts, documentaries and even feature-length works: *Sofia* (2004), *Dossier brûlant* (2005), *Code Phénix* (2005), *L'Or des Youngas* (2006), *La Belle, la brute et le berger* (2006) and *Mogo-Puissant* (2007). Boubakar Zida (also known as Sidnaaba) followed the same path with *Ouaga Zoodo* (2004) and *Wilbdo* (2005). *Code Phénix* was transferred to 35mm and shown at FESPACO in 2007.

REFERENCES

Amarger, Michel. *Cilia Sawadogo Cinéaste.* Paris: Éditions de l'Oeil, 2003.

Armes, Roy, "Dani Kouyaté (Burkina Faso)." In *African Filmmaking: North and South of the Sahara,* pp. 167–175. Edinburgh: Edinburgh University Press; Bloomington: Indiana University Press, 2006.

Bachy, Victor. *La Haute Volta et le cinéma.* Brussels: OCIC, 1982 and 1983.

Barlet, Olivier. *Idrissa Ouedraogo.* Montreuil, France: Éditions de l'Oeil, 2005.

Chirol, Marie-Magdaleine. "The Missing Narrative in *Wend Kuuni* (Time and Space)." In *African Cinema: Post-Colonial and Feminist Readings,* ed. Kenneth W. Harrow, pp. 115–126. Trenton, N.J.: Africa World Press, 1999.

Guellali, Anna, ed. *Idrissa Ouedraogo.* Tunis: *Cinécrits* 15, 1998.

Jøholt, Eva, "Burkina Faso." In *The Cinema of Small Nations,* pp. 198–212. Eds. Mette Hyort and Duncan Petrie. Edinburgh: Edinburgh University Press, 2007.

Kouyaté, Dani. "*Sia, le rêve du python.*" Bulletin de la guilde africaine des réalisateurs et producteurs 4, May 2001. www.cinemasdafrique.com.

Paré, Joseph. "*Keïta! L'héritage du griot:* l'esthétique de la parole au service de l'image." In *Écritures dans les cinémas d'Afrique noire,* ed. Boulou Ebanda De B'béri, pp. 45–59. Montreal: Cinémas, 2000.

Pfaff, Françoise. "Gaston Kaboré." In *25 Black African Film Makers,* pp. 173–183. New York: Greenwood Press, 1988.

Spass, Lieve. "Burkina Faso." In *The Francophone Film: A Struggle for Identity,* pp. 232–246. Manchester: Manchester University Press, 2000.

Thiers-Thiam, Valérie. "Le Griot à la caméra: *Keita! L'héritage du* griot de Dani Kouyaté." In *À chacun son griot,* pp. 133–160. Paris: Éditions L'Harmattan, 2004.

Turégano, Teresa Hocfert de. *African Cinema and Europe: Close-Up on Burkina Faso.* Florence: European Press Academic, 2005.

Ukadike, Nwachukwu Frank. Interviews with Gaston Kabore and Idrissa Ouedraogo in *Questioning African Cinema.* Minneapolis: University of Minnesota Press, 2002, pp. 109–120, 151–159.

BURUNDI

Output: 1 feature film
Filmmaker: 1
(Léonce Ngabo)

CHRONOLOGY
1992
Gito the Ungrateful / Gito l'ingrat (Léonce Ngabo)

REFERENCES

Otten, Rik. *Le Cinéma au Zaire, au Rwanda et au Burundi.* Brussels: OCIC; Paris: Éditions L'Harmattan, 1984.

CAMEROON

Output: 40 feature films
Filmmakers: 16
(Louis Balthazar Amadangoleda, Bassek Ba

Kobhio, Jean-Pierre Bekolo, Alphonse Béni, Urbain Dia Mokouri, Jean-Pierre Dikongue-Pipa, Ghislain Fotso, Daniel Kamwa, Cyrille Masso, Joseph-Henri Nama, Jude Ntsimenkou, Arthur Si Bita, Jules Takam, Jean-Claude Tchuilen, Jean-Marie Teno, François Woukoache)

CHRONOLOGY
1974
The Guys, the Cops and the Whores / Les Mecs les flics et les p . . . aka *Les Tringleuses* (Alphonse Béni)
1975
Girls in the Sun / Les Filles au soleil (Alphonse Béni)
Muna Moto (Jean-Pierre Dikongue-Pipa)
Pousse-Pousse (Daniel Kamwa)
1978
The Cost of Freedom / Le Prix de la liberté (Jean-Pierre Dikongue-Pipa)
Ribo or the Savage Sun / Ribo ou le soleil sauvage (Joseph-Henri Nama)
1979
Dance My Love / Danse mon amour (Alphonse Béni)
1980
Anna Makossa (Alphonse Béni)
Our Daughter / Notre fille (Daniel Kamwa)
1981
The Taste for Profit / L'Appât du gain (Jules Takam)
1982
The Burning / La Brûlure (Urbain Dia Mokouri)
Crooked Saint / Saint-Voyou (Alphonse Béni)
A Hard Blow / Coup dur (Alphonse Béni)
1983
The Cooperative Effort / Les Coopérants (Arthur Si Bita)
Funny Stories, Stories of People / Histoires drôles, Histoires de gens (Jean-Pierre Dikongue-Pipa)
The Lucky Guy / Le Veinard (Urbain Dia Mokouri)
Suicides (Jean-Claude Tchuilen)
1985
African Fever (Alphonse Béni)
Cameroon Connection / Cameroun Connection (Alphonse Béni)

Quartier Mozart (Jean-Pierre Bekolo)
The Three Little Shoeblacks / Les Trois petits cireurs (Louis Balthazar Amadangoleda)
1987
Badyaga / Courte maladie (Jean-Pierre Dikongue-Pipa)
1988
Bikutsi Water Blues (Jean-Marie Teno)
1991
The Village Teacher / Sango Malo (Bassek Ba Kobhio)
1992
Africa I Will Fleece You / Afrique je te plumerai (documentary) (Jean-Marie Teno)
1993
Totor (Daniel Kamwa)
1995
The Great White Man of Lambarene / Le Grand blanc de Lambaréné (Bassek Ba Kobhio)
1996
Aristotle's Plot / Le Complot d'Aristote (Jean-Pierre Bekolo)
Clando (Jean-Marie Teno)
1997
The Circle of Powers / Le Cercle des pouvoirs (Daniel Kamwa and Jules Takam)
1998
Fragments of Life / Fragments de vie (François Woukoache)
Smoke in Your Eyes / La Fumée dans les yeux (François Woukoache)
2000
Chief! / Chef! (documentary) (Jean-Marie Teno)
2003
The Silence of the Forest / Le Silence de la forêt (Bassek Ba Kobhio, Cameroon—with Didier Florent Ouenangare, Central African Republic)
2004
The Colonial Misunderstanding / Le Malentendu colonial (documentary) (Jean-Marie Teno)
2005
Bloody Women / Les Saignantes (Jean-Pierre Bekolo)
The Tear / La Déchirure (Alphonse Béni)
2006
The Broken Dream / Le Rêve brisé (Ghislain Fotso)
Confidences (Cyrille Masso)
Urban Jungle (Jude Ntsimenkou)

REFERENCES

Baratte-Eno Belinga, Thérèse. *Ecrivains, cinéastes et artistes camerounais: bio-biographie.* Yaoundé: Cameroun Ministry of Information and Culture, 1978.

Bonny, Béatrice. "Grandeur et décadence du cinéma camerounais." In *Cinémas africains, une oasis dans le désert?* ed. Samuel Lelièvre, pp. 194–218. Paris: Corlet/Télérama/*CinémAction* 106, 2003.

Haynes, Jonathan. "African Filmmaking and the Postcolonial Predicament: *Quartier Mozart* and *Aristotle's Plot.*" In *African Cinema: Post-Colonial and Feminist Readings,* ed. Kenneth W. Harrow, ed, pp. 21–43. Trenton, N.J.: Africa World Press, 1999.

Mollo Olinga, Jean-Marie. "Le Numératique va-t-il sauver le cinéma africain?" 5 July 2005. http://www.africine.com.

Ngansop, Guy Jérémie. *Le Cinéma camerounais en crise.* Paris: Éditions L'Harmattan, 1987.

Pfaff, Françoise. "Jean-Pierre Dikongue-Pipa" and "Daniel Kamwa." In *25 Black African Film Makers,* pp. 69–85, 185–194. New York: Greenwood Press, 1988.

Spass, Lieve. "Cameroon." In *The Francophone Film: A Struggle for Identity,* pp. 226–231. Manchester: Manchester University Press, 2000.

Tcheuyap, Alexie, ed. *Cinema and Social Discourse in Cameroon.* Bayreuth, Germany: Bayreuth African Studies, 2005.

Ukadike, Nwachukwu Frank. Interviews with Jean-Pierre Bekolo and Jean-Marie Teno in *Questioning African Cinema,* pp. 217–238, 301–316. Minneapolis: University of Minnesota Press, 2002.

CAPE VERDE

Output: 4 feature films
Filmmakers: 4
(Pol Cruchten, Leão Lopez, Francisco Manso, Fernando Vendrell)

CHRONOLOGY
1994
Island of Strife / Ilheu do contenda (Leão Lopez)
1996
Señor Napumoceno's Will / O testamento do Senhor Napumoceno (Francisco Manso)
1997
Black Dju (Pol Cruchten)
Fintar o destino (Fernando Vendrell)

REFERENCES

Andrade-Watkins, Claire. "Portuguese African Cinema: Historical and Contemporary Perspectives, 1969–1993." In *Cinemas of the Black Diaspora: Diversity, Dependence and Oppositionality,* ed. Michael T. Martin, pp. 181–203. Detroit: Wayne State University Press, 1995.

———. "Le Cinéma et la culture au Cap Vert et en Guinée-Bissau." In *Cinémas africains, une oasis dans le désert?* ed. Samuel Lelièvre, pp. 148–155. Paris: Corlet/Télérama/*CinémAction* 106, 2003.

Fina, Luciana, Cristina Fina, and António Loja Neves. *Cinemas de África.* Lisbon: Cinemateca Portugesa and Culturgest, 1995.

Rodriguès, Antonio. "Les Cinémas d'Afrique 'lusophone.'" In *Cinémas africains, une oasis dans le désert?* ed. Samuel Lelièvre, pp. 237–238. Paris: Corlet/Télérama/*CinémAction* 106, 2003.

CENTRAL AFRICAN REPUBLIC

Output: 1 feature film
Filmmaker: 1
(Didier Florent Ouenangare)

CHRONOLOGY
2003
The Silence of the Forest / Le Silence de la forêt (Didier Ouenangare, with Bassek Ba Kobhio (Cameroon))

REFERENCE

Ouengare, Didier. Interview with Olivier Barlet, 28 May 2003. www.africultures.com.

CHAD

Output: 5 feature films
Filmmakers: 2
(Issa Serge Coelo, Mahamet Saleh Haroun)

CHRONOLOGY
1999
Bye-Bye Africa (Mahamat Saleh Haroun)
2000
Daresalam (Issa Serge Coelo)
2001
Our Father / Abouna / Notre Père (Mahamat Saleh Haroun)
2006
Dry Season / Daratt (Mahamat Saleh Haroun)
Tartina City (Issa Serge Coélo)

REFERENCES

Armes, Roy. "Mahamat Saleh Haroun (Chad)." In *African Filmmaking: North and South of the Sahara*, pp. 158–166. Edinburgh: Edinburgh University Press; Bloomington: Indiana University Press, 2006.

Haroun, Mahamat Saleh. "Un certain esprit de résistance." Bulletin de la guilde africaine des réalisateurs et producteurs, March 2000. www.cinemasdafrique.com.

———. Interview, in Paris: *Africultures* 54 (2003): 164–167

CONGO

Output: 5 feature films
Filmmakers: 4
(Jean-Pierre Fila, Sébastien Kamba, Camille Mouyeke, Jean-Michel Tchissoukou)

CHRONOLOGY
1973
The Price of a Marriage / La Rançon d'une alliance (Sébastien Kamba)
1979
The Chapel / La Chapelle (Jean-Michel Tchissoukou)
1982
The Wrestlers / Les Lutteurs / M'Pongo (Jean-Michel Tchissoukou)
1995
Matanga (David-Pierre Fila)
2001
Trip to Ouaga / Voyage à Ouga (Camille Mouyeke)

REFERENCE

Kamba, Sébastien. *Production cinématographique et parti unique: l'exemple du Congo.* Paris: Éditions L'Harmattan, 1992.

DEMOCRATIC REPUBLIC OF CONGO (EX-ZAIRE)

Output: 16 feature films
Filmmakers: 9
(Balufu Bakupa-Kanyinda, José Zeka Laplaine, Luzolo Mpwati N'Tima Nsi, Kiesse Madenda Kiesse Masekela, Djo Munga, Mweze Dieudonné Ngangura, Bokala Nkolobise, Ndomaluele Mafuta Nlanza, Nkieri Ngunia Wawa)

CHRONOLOGY
1976
There's No Such Thing as Chance / Le Hasard n'existe pas (Luzolo Mpwati N'Tima Nsi)
1980
Fame in the Street / La Gloire dans la rue (Nkieri Ngunia Wawa)
1982
Sister Anuarite: A Life for God / Sœur Anuarite, une vie pour dieu (Kiesse Madenda Kiesse Masekela)
1987
Life Is Good / La Vie est belle (Mweze D. Ngangura)
1988
Bakanja (Bokala Nkolobise)

1994

For an Infidelity / Pour une infidélité (Ndomaluele Mafuta Nlanza)

1996

The Illegal Worker / Le Clandestin (José Zeka Laplaine)

Macadam Tribu (José Zeka Laplaine)

1998

Identity Papers / Pièces d'identité (Mweze D. Ngangura)

2001

Paris xy (José Zeka Laplaine).

2003

Daddy's Garden / Le Jardin de papa (José Zeka Laplaine)

2005

The Governor's New Clothes / Les Habits neufs du gouverneur (Mweze D. Ngangura)

Juju Factory (Balufu Bakupa-Kanyinda)

2006

Kinshasa Palace (José Zeka Laplaine)

Viva Riva! (Djo Munga)

2007

The Sacred Palace / Le Lac Sacré (José Zeka Laplaine)

REFERENCES

Convents, Guido. "Le cinéma zaïrois/congolais, une production culturelle de survie." In *Cinémas africains, une oasis dans le désert?* ed. Samuel Lelièvre, pp. 219–225. Paris: Corlet/ Télérama/*CinémAction* 106, 2003.

——. "La République Démocratique du Congo." In *L'Afrique? Quel cinéma!: Un siècle de propagande coloniale et de films africains*, pp. 250–260. Antwerp: Editions EPO, 2003.

——. *Images et Démocratie: Les Congolais face au Cinéma et à l'Audiovisuel.* Leuven: Association Afrika Filmfestival, 2007.

Jacquemin, Jean-Pierre. *Kibushi Ndjate Wooto.* Paris: Éditions de l'Oeil, 2003.

Otten, Rik. *Le Cinéma au Zaire, au Rwanda et au Burundi.* Brussels: OCIC, 1984.

Spass, Lieve. "Democratic Republic of Congo." In *The Francophone Film: A Struggle for Identity*, pp. 247–249. Manchester: Manchester University Press, 2000.

Ukadike, Nwachukwu Frank. Interview with Ngangura Mweze. In *Questioning African Cinema*, pp. 133–149. Minneapolis: University of Minnesota Press, 2002.

EGYPT

OVERALL STATISTICS: 382 filmmakers— 3,082 feature films

1920s:	14 films	12 directors
1930s:	94 films	30 active directors, 20 new
1940s:	326 films	52 active directors, 37 new
1950s:	530 films	74 active directors, 36 new
1960s:	449 films	86 active directors, 44 new
1970s:	460 films	90 active directors, 43 new
1980s:	573 films	120 active directors, 74 new
1990s:	393 films	123 active directors, 48 new
2000s:	243 films	108 active directors, 68 new

1920s

Output:	14 films
1923:	1
1927:	1
1928:	6
1929:	6

Directors: 12

(Hassan Al-Halbawi, Aziza Amir, Amine Atallah, Ahmed Galal, Fardous Hassan, Abdel Aziz Khalil, Ibrahim Lama, Wedad Orfi, Gabriel Rogeogian, Victor Rosito, Stephane Rosti, Jacques Schutz)

1930s

Output:	94 films
1930	5
1931	2
1932	7
1933	7
1934	6
1935	12
1936	13
1937	17
1938	11
1939	14

Directors: 30 active directors, 20 new (*)
(*Fouad Al-Gazaerli, *Naguib Al-Rihani, Aziza Amir, *Maurice Aptekman, *Ahmed Badrakhan, *Mohamed Bayoumi, *Carlo Bobba, *Telio Chiarini,*Alexandre Farkache, *Hussein Fawzi, Ahmed Galal, *Bahiga Hafez, *Abdel Fattah Hassan, *Mohamed Karim, *Mahmoud Khalil, *Fritz Kramp, Ibrahim Lama, *Choukri Madi, *Togo Mizrahi,*Amina Mohamed,*Niazi Mostafa, *Alvisi Orfanelli, Stephane Rosti, *Fatma Rouchdi, *Mohamed Sabri, *Ahmed Salem,*Kamal Selim,*Manuel Vimance,*Mario Volpi, *Youssef Wahbi)

1940s

Output:	326 films
1940	12
1941	12
1942	22
1943	14
1944	24
1945	42
1946	52
1947	55
1948	49
1949	44

Filmmakers: 52 active directors, 37 new (*)
(*Fatine Abdel Wahab, *Hassan Abdel Wahab, *Salah Abou Seif, *Mohamed Al-Aqqad, Fouad Al-Gazaerli, *Farid Al-Guindi, *Hassan Al-Imam, *Goffredo Alessandrini, *Kamel Al-Termessani, Ahmed Badrakhan, *Salah Badrakhan, *Abdallah Barakat, *Henri Barakat,*Kamal Barakat, *Seif Eddine Chawkat, *Fouad Chebl,*Ahmed Diaa Eddine, *Kamal Abou El-Ela, *Ibrahim Emara, Hussein Fawzi, Ahmed Galal, *Mohamed Abdel Gawad, *Omar Guemei, Bahiga Hafez, Abdel Fattah Hassan, *Mostafa Hassan,*Ahmed Kamel Hefnawi,*Hassan Helmi,*Ibrahim Helmi,*Adel Aziz Hussein,*Mahmoud Ismaïl, *Abbas Kamel, Mohamed Karim, *Abdel Alim Khattab, Ibrahim Lama, *Gamal Madkour, Togo Mizrahi, *Ahmed Kamel Morsi, Niazi Mostafa, Alvisi Orfanelli,*Helmi Rafla, *Hassan Ramzi,*Hassan Reda, Stéphane Rosti, Ahmed Salem,*Hussein Sedki, Kamal Selim, *Anwar Wagdi, Youssef Wahbi, *al-Sayed Ziyada, *Ezz Eddine Zoulficar,*Mahmoud Zoulficar)

1950s

Output:	530 films
1950	48
1951	52
1952	59
1953	62
1954	66
1955	51
1956	39
1957	40
1958	55
1959	58

Filmmakers: 74 active directors, 36 new (*)
(Fatine Abdel Wahab, *Hamada Abdel Wahab, Salah Abouh Seif, *Kamal Al-Cheikh,*Kamal Al-Chennawi, Fouad Al-Gazaerli, Hassan Al-Imam, *Mohamed Saleh Al-Kayyali, *Hussein Helmi Al-Mouhandes, *Hassan Al-Saïfi, *Ibrahim Al-Sayed, *Ahmed Al-Toukhi, *Hassan Amer, *Kamal Ateyya, Ahmed Badrakhan, Abdallah Barakat, Henri Barakat, *al-Sayed Bedeir, *Zouheir Bekir, *Youssef Chahine, *Bahaa Eddine Charaf, Seif Eddine Chawkat, Fouad Chebl, Ahmed Diaa Eddine, *Ibrahim Ezz Eddine, Ibrahim Emara, *Ehsane Farghal, Hussein Fawzi, Mohamed Abdel Gawad, Omar Guemei, *Helmi Halim, Abdel Fattah Hassan, *Elhami Hassan, *Ismaïl Hassan, *Mohamed Kamel Hassan, Mostafa Hassan, Ahmed Kamel Hefnawi, Hassan Helmi, Ibrahim Helmi, Mahmoud Ismaïl, Abbas Kamel, *Mostafa Kamel, *Issa Karama, Mohamed Karim, Abdel Alim Khattab, *Ahmed Khorchid, *Léon Klimovski, *Kostanov, Ibrahim Lama, *Youssef Maalouf, Gamal Madkour, Ahmed Kamel Morsi, *Galal Mostafa, *Houssam Eddine Mostafa, Niazi Mostafa, *Ramsès Naguib, *Raymond Nassour, *Abdel Ghani Qamar, Helmi Rafla, Hassan Ramzi, Hassan Reda, *Tewfiq Saleh, Ahmed Salem, *Atef Salem, Hussein Sedki,*Mohsen Szabo, *Gianni Vernuccio, Anwar Wagdi, Youssef Wahbi, *Abdel Hamid Zaki, al-Sayed Ziyada, Ezz Eddine Zoulficar, Mahmoud Zoulficar

1960s

Output:	449 films
1960	59
1961	52

1962	48	1973	43
1963	48	1974	44
1964	44	1975	50
1965	42	1976	47
1966	39	1977	51
1967	33	1978	52
1968	40	1979	39
1969	44		

Filmmakers: 86 active directors, 44 new (*)
(Fatine Abdel Wahab, Salah Abou Seif, *Farouk Agrama, *Galal Al-Charkawi, Kamal Al-Cheikh, Kamal Al-Chennawi, *Nour Al-Demerdache, Hassan Al-Imam, *Abdel Rahman Al-Khamissi, Hussein Helmi Al-Mouhandès, *Ismaïl Al-Qadi, *Magda Al-Sabahi, *Ibrahim Al-Sahn, Hassan Al-Saïfi, Kamel Al-Telmessani, *Saad Arafa, Kamel Ateyya, Ahmed Badrakhan, *Fernandino Baldi, Henri Barakat, al-Sayed Bedeir, *Ali Beheiri, Zouheir Bekir, *Medhat Bekiri, *Alfonso Breccia, Youssef Chahine, Bahaa Eddine Charaf, Seif Eddiine Chawkat, *Khalil Chawki, *Oswaldo Cheferani, *Abdel Rahman Cherif,* Abel Meneim Choukri, *Mamdouh Choukri, Ahmed Diaa Eddine, *Kamal Salah Eddine, Ibrahim Emara, *Mahmoud Farid, *Ahmed Farouk, Hussein Fawzi, *Ahmed Fouad, Mohamed Abdel Gawad, *Nagdi Hafez, Helmi Halim, Elhami Hassan, Mohamed Kamal Hassan, Mahmoud Ismaïl, *Sayed Issa, *Youssef Issa, *Hussein Kamal, Abbas Kamel, Issa Karama, *Adli Khalil, Abdel Alim Khattab, *Salah Korayyem, *Ibrahim Lotfi, Youssef Maalouf, *Andrew Marton, *Ahmed Mazhar, Houssam Eddine Mostafa, Niazi Mostafa, *Mohamed Nabih, *Albert Naguib, Ramsès Naguib, *Ko Nakahira, Raymond Nassour, *André Novolcci, *Luigi Pescatino, *Tolba Radwane, Helmi Rafla, Hassan Ramzi, *Ali Reda, Hassan Reda, *Nagui Riad, *Adel Sadek, Tewfik Saleh, Atef Salem, *Mohamed Salem, *Mohamed Salmane, Hussein Sedki, *Hassan Tewfik, *Doccio Tissari, Youssef Wahbi, *Cherif Wali, al-Sayed Ziyada, Ezz Eddine Zoulficar, Mahmoud Zoulficar)

Directors: 90 active directors, 43 new (*)
(*Taysir Abboud, *Mohamed Abdel Aziz, *Ali Abdel Khalek, *Chadi Abdel Salam, Fatine Abdel Wahab, Salah Abou Seif, *Yehya al-Alami, *Ibrahim al-Chakankiri, *Abdel-Hamid al-Chazli, Kamal al-Cheikh, Kamal al-Chennawi, Nour al-Dermerdache, *Amine al-Hakim, Hassan al-Imam, Abdel Rahman al-Khamissi, *Talaat Allam, Hussein Helmi al-Mouhandès, *Hicham Abou al-Nasr, Ismaïl al-Qadi, *Ahmed al-Sabaawi, Hassan al-Saïfi, *Mounir al-Touni, Saad Arafa, Kamal Atteya, *Ali Badrakhan, Henri Barakat, *Mohamed Bassiouni, al-Sayed Bedeir, *Medhat Bekir, Zouheir Bekir, *Ghaleb Chaath, *Sobhi Chafik, Youssef Chahine, *Chafik Chamiyya, Seif Eddine Chawkat, Khalil Chawki, Abdel Rahman Cherif, Abdel Meneim Choukri, Mamdouh Choukri, Ahmed Diaa Eddine, Kamal Salah Eddine, *Hussein Emara, Ibrahim Emara, *Mohamed Fadel, *Achraf Fahmi, Mahmoud Farid, Ahmed Fouad, *Youssef Francis, *Nader Galal, *Hassen Hafez, Nagdi Hafez, Helmi Halim, *Nasser Hussein, *Hassan Ibrahim, *Hassan Ismaïl, Hussein Kamal, Abbas Kamel, Issa Karama, Adli Khalil, *Abdel Rahman Kikkya, Ibrahim Lotfi, *Tozri Mahdi, *Saïd Marzouk, *Youssef Marzouk, Ahmed Mazhar, *Youssef Chabaane Mohamed, Houssam Eddine Mostafa, Niazi Mostafa, Mohamed Nabih, *Mohamed Radi, Helmi Rafla, Hassan Ramzi, Ali Reda, Hassan Reda, *Madkour Sabet, Adel Sadek, *Simon Saleh, *Zaki Saleh, Atef Salem, Mohamed Salem, Mohamed Salmane, *Ahmed Sarwat, *Samir Seif, *Sayed Tantawi, *Ahmed Yassine, *Yassine Ismaïl Yassine, *Ahmed Yehya, *Hassan Youssef, Al-Sayed Ziyada, Mahmoud Zoulficar)

1970s

	Output:	460 films	
	1970	47	
	1971	46	
	1972	41	

1980s

	Output:	573 films
	1980	34
	1981	43

1982	41
1983	46
1984	64
1985	75
1986	95
1987	71
1988	56
1989	48

Directors: 120 active, 74 new (*)

(*Mohamed Abaza, Taysir Abboud, Mohamed Abdel Aziz, *Omar Abdel Aziz, *Rachad Abdel Ghani, Ali Abdel Khalek, *Daoud Abdel Sayed, *Mohamed Abou Seif, Salah Abou Seif, *Youssef Abou Seif, *Ibrahim Afifi, *Adel al-Aassar, Yehya al-Alami, *Abdel Alim, *Mouhannad al-Ansari, *Mohamed al-Bechir, *Mohamed al-Chami, Kamal al-Cheikh, *Inas al-Deghidi, *Bechir al-Dik, Hassan al-Imam, *Ahmed al-Khatib, *Raafat al-Mihi, *Ibrahim al-Mogui, *Mohamed al-Naggar, *Ahmed al-Nahhas, *Tarek al-Nahri, Hichem Abou al-Nasr, Ahmed al-Sabaawi, Hassan al-Saïfi, *Medhat al-Sibaï, *Atef al-Tayeb, *Hussein al-Wakil, *Gamal Ammar, *Nagui Anglo, *Cherif Arafa, Saad Arafa, Kamal Ateyya, Ali Badrakhan, *Ibrahim Baghdadi, Henri Barakat, *Khaïri Bechara, Youssef Chahine, Khalil Chawki, *Mohamed Chebl, Abdel Meneim Choukri, *Osman Choukri, *Ahmed Fouad Darwich, *Wasfi Darwich, *Hassan Seif Eddine, Kamal Salah Eddine, *Youssef Charaf Eddine, Hussein Emara, Mohamed Fadel, Achraf Fahmi, Mahmoud Farid, *Farid Fathallah, Ahmed Fouad, Youssef Francis, Nader Galal, *Salah Habib, Nagdi Hafez, *Samir Hafez, *Cherif Hammouda, *Nadia Hamza, *Ismaïl Hassan, *Mohamed Hassib, *Farid Chawki Hussein, Nasser Hussein, Hassan Ibrahim, *Youssef Ibrahim, *Kamal Ide, *Fayek Ismaïl, *Sayed Issa, Hussein Kamal, Adli Khalil, *Mohamed Khan, *Ahmed Khidr, *Salah Korayyem, *Hani Lachine, *Abdel Fattah Madbouli, *Alaa Mahgoub, *Farid Fathallah Manoughehri, *Mohamed Marzouk, Saïd Marzouk, *al-Saïd Mostafa, Houssam Eddine Mostafa, Niazi Mostafa, *Abdel Halim Nasr, *Yousri Nasrallah, *Samir Nawwar, *Mohamed Oussama, *Hatem Radi, Mohamed Radi, *Mounir Radi, Helmi Rafla, Ali Reda, Adel Sadek, *Fadel Saleh, Simon Saleh, Zaki Saleh, Atef Salem, *Nadia Salem, Mohamed Salmane, *Ahmed

Saqr, Ahmed Sarwat, Samir Seif, *Sayed Seif, *Osman Choukri Selim, *Salah Serri, *Abdel Hadi Taha, Sayed Tantawi, *Hani Yane, Ahmed Yassine, Yassine Ismaïl Yassine, Ahmed Yehya, *Cherif Yehya, *Adli Youssef, Hassan Youssef, *Abdel Latif Zaki)

1990s

Output:	393 films
1990	64
1991	58
1992	69
1993	53
1994	35
1995	31
1996	28
1997	17
1998	20
1999	18

Directors: 123 active directors, 48 new (*)

(Mohamed Abaza, Mohamed Abdel Aziz, Omar Abdel Aziz, Ali Abdel Khlalek, *Ahmed Abdel Salam, Daoud Abdel Sayed, *Zaki Fatin Abdel Wahab, Mohamed Abou Seif, Salah Abou Seif, Youssef Abou Seif, *Adel Adeeb, Ibrahim Afifi, *Nabawi Aglane, *Magdi Ahmed Ali, Adel al-Aassar, *Tarek al-Aryane, *Samir al-Asfoury, *Asma al-Bakri, *Essam al-Chamma, *Medhat al-Cherif, Inas al-Deghidi, *Yeyha al-Fakhrani, *Mazen al-Gabali, *Khaled al-Hagar, *Radwane al-Kachef, *Mohamed Kamel al-Kalioubi, *Oussama al-Kerdawi, Raafat al-Mihi, Ibrahim al-Mogui, Mohamed al-Naggar, *Abdel Halim al-Nahhas, Ahmed al-Nahhas, Tarek al-Nahri, *Farouk al-Rachidi, Ahmed al-Sabaati, Hassan al-Saïfi. Medhat al-Sibaï, *Gamal al-Tabei, Atef al-Tayeb, *Tarek al-Telmessani, *Saïd Amacha, Gamal Ammar, Nagui Anglo, Cherif Arafa, Saad Arafa, *Ibrahim Arayes, Kamal Ateyya, *Adel Awad, Ali Badrakhan, *Amali Bahnasi, Henri Barakat, Khaïri Bechara, Medhat Bekir, *Cherif Chaaban, Youssef Chahine, Mohamed Chebl, *Saïd Chimi, Ahmed Fouad Darwich, Wasfi Darwich, *Karim Dia Eddine, *Mohsen Mohi Eddine, Youssef Charaf Eddine, *Anwar El-Kawadri, Hussein Emara, Mohamed Fadel, Achraf Fahmi, Mahmoud Farid, *Osama Fawzi, Ahmed Fouad, Youssef Francis, Nader Galal, *Ismaïl Gamal, Nagdi Hafez, Samir Hafez, *Saïd Hamed, Cherif Hammouda, Nadia Hamza,

*Mahmoud Hanafi, Ismaïl Hassan, Mohamed Hassib, Nasser Hussein, Hassan Ibrahim, Hussein Kamal, *Alaa Karim, *Chirine Kassem, Adli Khalil, Mohamed Khan, Hani Lachine, Alaa Mahgoub, *Youssef Mansour, Mohamed Marzouk, Saïd Marzouk, *Saïd Mohamed Marzouk, *Magdi Mehrem, *Wahid Mekhiemar, Houssam Eddine Mostafa, *Ismaïl Mourad, Mohamed Nabih, *Sandra Nashaat, Yousri Nasrallah, *Fakhr Eddine Negeda, *Anwar Qawadri, *Ihab Radi, Mohamed Radi, Mounir Radi, *Neimat Rouchdi, Adel Sadek, *Sayed Saïd. *Saïd Saleh, Simon Saleh, Atef Salem, Ahmed Saqr, Ahmed Sarwat, Samir Seif, Sayed Seif, Salah Serri, *Taïmour Serri, Abdel Hadi Taha, Sayed Tantawi, Yassine Ismaïl Yassine, Ahmed Yeyha, Cherif Yehya, Abdel Latif Zaki)

2000s

Output:	243 films
2000	32
2001	32
2002	27
2003	21
2004	24
2005	31
2006	41
2007	35

Directors: 108 active: 68 new: (*)
(Mohamed Abdel Aziz, Omar Abdel Aziz, *Sameh Abdel Aziz, Ali Abdel Khalek, *Tarek Abdel Muti, Daoud Abdel Sayed, *Osman Abou Laban, Mohamed Abou Seif, *Ahmed Abou Zeid, *Kamla Abou Zikr, Ibrahim Afifi, *Mohsen Ahmed, Magdi Ahmed Ali, *Mourad Aknash, *Osama al-Asi, Adel al-Aassar, Samir al-Asfouri, *Imad al-Bahhat, *Ahmed al-Badri, *Khaled al-Badri, *Sameh al-Bagouri, Asma al-Bakri, *Fahmi al-Charkawi, *Nour al-Cherif, Inas al-Deghidi, Mazen al-Gabali, *Ahmed al-Guendi, Khaled al-Hagar, *Magdi al-Hawwaari, *Mohamed Ali, *Tarek al-Iryaan, Radwane al-Kachef, Mohamed Kamal al-Kalioubi, Raafat al-Mihi, Mohamed al-Naggar, Tarek al-Nahri, *Manal al-Seifi, Medhat al-Sibaï, *Mohamed Amin, *Amr Arafa, Cherif Arafa, *Ahmed Atef, Adel Awad, *Ahmed Awad, Ali Badrakhan, Cherif Chaaban, *Mohamed Chaaban, Youssef Chahine, *Wael Charkas, *Atef Chukri, Karim Diaa Eddine, *Sayyed Essawy,

*Ahmed Fahmi, Ashraf Fahmi, *Ahmed Samir Farag, *Akram Farid, *Ismaïl Farouq, Osama Fawzi, *Ashraf Fayek, *Ahmed Galal, Nader Galal, Ismaïl Gamal, *Khaled Gomʾa, *Mohamed Gomʾa, *Raffi Guirguiss, *Marwan Hamed, Saïd Hamed, Ismaïl Hassan, *Saad Hendawi, *Atef Hetata, *Ali Idris, *Wael Ihsaan, *Rami Imam, *Alaa Karim, *Gamal Kassem, *Hani Khalifa, *Hala Khalil, Mohamed Khan, *Raid Labib, *Doureid Laham, *Ihaab Lamei, *Ayman Makram, *Cherif Mandour, Youssef Mansour, *Khadel Marie, Saïd Marzouk, *Ahmed Medhat, *Ahmed Mekky, *Mohamed Mostafa Kamal, *Ahmed Musa, *Mohamed Mustapha, Sandra Nashaat, Yousri Nasrallah, Fakhr Eddine Negeda, Ihab Radi, Mounir Radi, *Ali Ragab, *Amir Ramsis, *Jocelyne Saab, *Cherif Sabri, *Hamed Saïd, *Ahmed Saleh, Samir Seif, *Mohamed Yassin, *Adel Yehia, Ahmed Yehya, Cherif Yehya, *Ahmed Yousri, *Khaled Youssef, *Yasser Zayed)

CHRONOLOGY
1923
In the Land of Tutankhamen / Fî bilâd Tout Ankh Amon (Victor Rosito)
1927
Leila / Layla (Wedad Orfi and Stephane Rosti)
1928
Boot Making / Sâniʾ al-qabâqîb (Amine Atallah)
Drama at the Pyramids / Fâguiʾah fawq al-haram (Ibrahim Lama)
A Kiss in the Desert / Qoublah fî-l-sahrâ (Ibrahim Lama)
Souad the Gipsy / Souʾâd al-ghagariyya (Fardous Hassan and Abdel Aziz Khalil)
The Victim / al-Dahiyyah (Wedad Orfi)
Why Does the Sea Laugh? / al-Bahr biyidhak lîh (Stéphane Rosti)
1929
The Beauty from the Desert / Ghâdat al-sahrâʾ (Wedad Orfi and Ahmed Galal)
The Drama of Life / MaʾSât al-hayât (Wedad Orfi)
Drugs / al-Moukhaddarât (Hassan al-Halbawi)
The Girl from the Nile / Bin al-Nîl (Aziza Amir)
Goha / Goha (Jacques Schutz)
Strange Adventure / al-Moukhâtarach al-ʾaguîbah (Gabriel Rogeogian)

1930

Cocaine / al-Kokaïn aka *The Abyss / al-Hâwiyah* (Togo Mizrahi)

In the Moonlight / Tahta daw' al-qamar (Choukri Madi)

The Midnight Crime / Guinâyat mountasaf al-layl (Mohamed Sabri)

The Miracle of Love / Mou'guizat al-haubb (Ibrahim Lama)

Zaynab / Zeinab (Mohamed Karim)

1931

The Clerk, Kish Kish Bey / Sâhib al-sa'âdah Kichkich bek (Naguib al-Rihani and Stephane Rosti)

Remorse / Wakhz al-damir (Ibrahim Lama)

1932

5001 / Khamsat âlaf wa wâhid (Togo Mizrahi)

Goha and Abou Nawwas / Gohâ wa Abou Nawwâs (Manuel Vimance)

Mustapha or The Little Magician / Mostafa aw al-sâhir al-saghîr (Mahmoud Khalil)

The Shop for Lovers / Makhzan al-'ouchchâq (Carlo Bobba)

The Song of the Heart / Ounchoudat al-Fou'âd (Mario Volpi)

Sons of Aristocrats / Awlâd al-Dhawât (Mohamed Karim)

The Victims / al-Dahyâyâ (Ibrahim Lama)

1933

Atone for Your Sins / Kaffirî 'an khati'atik (Aziza Amir)

Fiancé No. 13 / al'Khatîb nimrah tala-ta'ch (Mohamed Bayoumi)

Goha and Abou Nawwas Photographers / Gohâ was Abou Nawwâs mousawirân (Manuel Vimance)

The Marriage / al-Zawâg (Fatma Rouchdi)

Sons of Egypt / Awlâd Misr (Togo Mizrahi)

When a Woman Loves / 'Indamâ tou-hibb al-mara'ah (Ahmed Galal)

The White Rose / al-Wardah al-baydâ' (Mohamed Karim)

1934

The Accusation / alIttihâm (Mario Volpi)

Bewitching Eyes / 'Ouyoun sâhirah (Ahmed Galal)

The Clerk Kish Kish Bey / Sahib al-sa'adah Kichkich bek (Naguib al-Rihani and Stephane Rosti)

The Shadow of the Past / Chabah al-mâdi (Ibrahim Lama)

A Son of the People / Ibn al-Cha'b (Maurice Aptekman)

The Two Delegates / al-Mandoubân (Togo Mizrahi)

1935

Chagarat al-Darr / Chagarat al-Dourr (Ahmed Galal)

The Concierge / Bawwâr al-'imârah (Alexandre Farkache)

The Defence / al-Difâ (Youssef Wahbi)

Doctor Farhat / al-Doktor Farhât (Togo Mizrahi)

Marouf the Bedouin / Ma'rouf al-badawî (Ibrahmin Lama)

Master Bahbah / al-Mou'allim Bahbah (Choukri Madi)

Mr. Antar / 'Antar afandi (Stephane Rosti)

The Sailor / al-Bahhâr (Togo Mizrahi)

Shalom the Interpretor / Chalom al-tourgmân (Togo Mizrahi)

The Star / al-Ghandourah (Mario Volpi)

The Tears of Love / Doumou' al-houbb (Mohamed Karim)

The Victims / al-Dahâyâ (Ibrahim Lama and Bahiga Hafez)

1936

Abou Zarifa / Abou Zarîfah (Alvisi Orfanelli)

The Bank Note / al-Banknot (Ahmed Galal)

The Black Hand / al-Yad al-sawdâ' (Maurice Aptekman)

The Escaped Prisoner / al-Hârib (Ibrahim Lama)

Everything but That / Koullouh alla kidah (Carlo Bobba)

The Gentleman Wants to Get Married / Bisalamtouh 'Iawiz yitgawwiz (Alexandre Farkache)

A Hundred Thousand Pounds / Mît alf guinîh (Togo Mizrahi)

Interim Wife / Zawgah bi-l-niyâbah (Ahmed Galal)

The Policeman / Khafiral-darak (Togo Mizrahi)

The Queen of the Footlights / Malikat al-masârih (Mario Volpi)

The Radio Song / Ounchoudat al-radio (Telio Chiarini)

Weddad / Wedad (Fritz Kramp)

White and Black / al-Abyad wa-l-aswad (Alvisi Orfanelli)

1937

As Requested / Izz al-talab (Ibrahim Lama)

At Seven O'Clock / al-Sâ-ah sab³ah (Togo Mizrahi)

Congratulations / Mabrouk (Fouad al-Gazaerli)

Doctor Ibrahim's Secret / Sirr al-doktor Ibrâhîm (Maurice Aptekman)

Eternal Glory / al-Magd al-khâlid (Youssef Wahbi)

The Final Solution / al-Hall al-akhîr (Abdel Fattah Hassan)

In the Shadows / Warâ al-sitâr (Kamal Selim)

Leila, the Girl from the Desert / Layla bint al-sahrâ (Bahiga Hafez)

Mad Love / al-Houbb al-mouristâni (Mario Volpi)

My Second Wife / Mirâtî nimrah itnîn (Telio Chiarini)

A Night in the Life / Laylah fi-l-³oumir (Alvisi Orfanelli)

Omar and Gamilla / ³Omar wa Gamîlah (Carlo Bobba)

Salama Is Fine / Salama fî khayr (Niazi Mostafa)

Shalom the Sportsman / Chalom al-riyâdî (Togo Mizrahi)

The Song of Hope / Nachîd al-amal (Ahmed Badrakhan)

Tita and Wong / Tita wa Wong (Amina Mohamed)

Wealth Is a Scandal / al-³Izz bahdalah (Togo Mizrahi)

1938

Bahbah Pasha / Bahbah bâchâ (Fouad al-Gazaerli)

The Director's Daughter / Bint al-bâchâ al-moudîr (Ahmed Galal)

Lachine / Lachine (Fritz Kramp)

Long Live Love / Yahyâ al-houbb (Mohamed Karim)

The Long-Awaited Day / Yawm sl-mounâ (Alvisi Orfanelli)

My Servant / Khaddâmtî (Alvisi Orfanelli)

Something from Nothing / Chay³ min lâ chay (Ahmed Badrakhan)

Souls in Distress / Noufous hâ³irah (Ibrahim Lama)

The Telegram / al-Telegraf (Togo Mizrahi)

The Time of Execution / Sâ-at al-Tanfidh (Youssef Wahbi)

The Way I'm Made / Anâ tab³î kidah (Togo Mizrahi)

1939

The Apple Seller / Bayyâ³at al-touffâh (Hussein Fawzi)

Cairo Nights / Layâli al-Qâhirah (Ibrahim Lama)

Cherchez la femme / Fattich ³an al-mar³ah (Ahmed Galal)

The Doctor / al-Doktor (Niazi Mostafa)

Lend Me Three Pounds / Sallifnî talâtah guinîh (Togo Mizrahi)

The Lineage of the Beloved / Khalaf al-habâyib (Fouad al-Gazaerli)

The Lost Treasure / al-Kanz al-mahfqoud (Ibrahminm Lama)

Osman and Ali / ³Othman wa ³Alî (Togo Mizrahi)

The Price of Happiness / Thaman al-sa³âdah (Alvisi Orfanelli)

Qays and Leila / Qays wa Layla (Ibrahim Lama)

Return to the Land / al³Awdah ilâ al-rif (Ahmed Kamel Morsi)

Stormy Night / Laylah moumtirah (Togo Mizrahi)

The Will / al-Azîmah (Kamal Selim)

Wings of the Desert / Agnihat al-sahrâ (Ahmed Salem)

1940

The Contractor / al-Bâchmouqâwil (Togo Mizrahi)

A Cry in the Night / Sarkhah fî-layl (Ibrahim Lama)

Dananir / Danânîr (Ahmed Badrakhan)

The Factory / al-Warchah (Stephane Rosti)

A Girl in Revolt / Fatât mouta marridah (Ahmed Galal)

Happy Days / Yawm sa³îd (Mohamed Karim)

A Humble Life / Hayât al-zalâm (Ahmed Badrakhan)

A Man between Two Women / Ragoul bayna imra³atayn (Ibrahim Lama)

Reasonable People / Ashâb al-³ouqoul (Mohamed al-Aqqad)

Under the Sheets / Tahtâ al-silâh (Alvisi Orfanelli)

A Woman's Heart / Qalb imra³ah (Togo Mizrahi)

Zelikha Loves Achour / Zilîkhah touhibb ³Achour (Ahmed Galal)

1941

The Arabian Nights / Alf laylah wa laylah (Togo Mizrahi)

A Dangerous Woman / Imra'ah khatirah (Ahmed Galal)

For Ever / Ilä al-abad (Kamal Selim)

Leila, the Girl from the Country / Layla bint al-rîf (Togo Mizrahi)

Leila, the School Girl / Layla bint al-madâris (Togo Mizrahi)

Mr. Omar / Sî ʿOmar (Niazi Mostafa)

Saladin / Salah Eddine al-Ayyoubî (Ibrahim Lama)

Storm Over the Province / ʿÂsfah ʿalâ al-rîf (Ahmed Badrakhan)

A Suitor from Istambul / ʿArîs min Istamboul (Youssef Wahbi)

The Three Musketeers / al-Foursân al-thalâthah (Togo Mizrahi)

The Victory of Youth / Intisâr al-chabâb (Ahmed Badrakhan)

The Wife Factory / Masna' al-zawgât (Niazi Mostafa)

1942

The Accused / al-Mouttahamah (Henri Barakat)

Aida / ʿAïda (Ahmed Badrakhan)

Ali Baba and the Forty Thieves / ʿAli Bâbâ wa-l-arba'în harâmî (Togo Mizrahi)

At Last I've Got Married / Akhîran tazawwagt (Gamal Madkour)

Bahbah in Bagdad / Bahbah fi Baghdâd (Hussein Fawzi)

Dreams of Youth / Ahlâm al-chabâb (Kamal Selim)

The Fifth Suitor / al-'Arîs al-khâmis (Ahmed Galal)

Forbidden to Love / Mamnou' al-houbb (Mohamed Karim)

The Gaiety Station / Mahattat al-ouns (Abdel Fattah Hassan)

I Love Mistakes / Ahibb al-ghalat (Hussein Fawzi)

If I Were Rich / Law Kount ghanî (Henri Barakat)

Leila / Layla (Togo Mizrahi)

The Mysteries of Life / Khafâyâ al-douniâ (Ibrahim Lama)

On the Stage of Life / ʿAlâ masrah al-hayâh (Ahmed Badrakhan)

Rabab / Rabâb (Ahmed Galal)

The Son of Poor People / Awlâd al-fouqarâ (Youssef Wahbi)

A Son of the Country / Ibn al-balad (Stephane Rosti)

A Son of the Desert / Ibn al-sahrâ (Ibrahim Lama)

The Tramp / al-Chârid (Henri Barakat)

Wedding Night / Laylat al-farah (Hussein Fawzi)

The Women Are in Danger / al-Sittât fî khatar (Ibrahim Emara)

1943

Call of the Blood / Nidâ al-dam (Ibrahim Lama)

Call of the Heart / Nidâ' al-qaib (Omar Guemei)

Cleopatra / Cléôbatra (Ibrahim Lama)

The Day's Business / Qadiyyat al-yawm (Kamal Selim)

Don't Deny Your Ancestors / Man fâta qadîmouh (Farid al-Guindi)

Gawhara / Gawharah (Youssef Wahbi)

Long Live Women / Tahyâ al-sittât (Togo Mizrahi)

Magda / Magda (Ahmed Galal)

Rabha / Râbha (Niazi Mostafa)

The Right Way / al-Tariq al-moustaqîm (Togo Mizrahi)

The Sheikh's Daughter / Bint al-cheikh (Ahmed Kamal Morsi)

The Valley of Stars / Wâdî al-nougoum (Niazi Mostafa)

The Workman / al-'Âmil (Ahmed Kamel Morsi)

The Wretched / al-Bou'asâ (Kamal Selim)

1944

Berlanti / Berlanti (Youssef Wahbi)

The Blacksmith's Son / Ibn al-haddâd (Youssef Wahbi)

Down with Love / Yasqout al-houbb (Ibrahim Lama)

The Executioner's Blade / Sayf al-gallârd (Youssef Wahbi)

Hababa / Habâbah (Niazi Mostafa)

Hanane / Hanane (Kamal Selim)

Hassan and Hassan / Hasan wa Hasan (Niazi Mostafa)

A Heavenly Love / Houbb min al-samâ (Abdel Fattah Hussein)

Leila in the Shadows / Layla fî-zalâm (Togo Mizrahi)

The Ideal Suitor / ʿArîs al-hanâ (Ibrahim Lama)

The Innocents / al-Abriyâ' (Ahmed Badrakhan)

Leila the Bedouin / Layla al-badawiyyah (Bahiga Hafez)

Love and Vengeance / Gharâm wa inti-qâm (Youssef Wahbi)

Love at First Sight / Rasâsah fî-l-qalb (Mohamed Karim)

The Magic Cap / Tâqiyyat al-ikhfâ' (Niazi Mostapha)

Martyrs of Love / Chouhadâ' al-gharâm (Kamal Selim)

Mohamed-Ali Street / Châri' Mouhammad 'Alî (Niazi Mostafa)

My Daughter / Ibnatî (Niazi Mostafa)

Nadouga / Nadougâ (Hussein Fawsi)

Nour Eddine and the Three Sailors / Nour Eddine wa-l-bahhârah al-thalâthah (Togo Mizrahi)

Wahida / Wahîdah (Ibrahim Lama)

What Lies! / Kidb fî kidb (Togo Mizrahi)

What Madness! / Imma guinân (Henri Barakat)

Who Is Guilty? / Man al-gânî (Ahmed Badrakhan)

1945

Antar and Abla / 'Antar wa 'Ablah (Niazi Mostafa)

Appearances / al-Mazâhir (Kamal Selim)

Between Two Fires / Bayn nârayn (Gamal Madkour)

The Big Mistake / al-Zallah al-koubrâ (Ibrahim Emara)

The Black Market / al-Souq al-sawdâ' (Kamel al-Telmessani)

Broken Hearts / Qouloub dâmiyah (Hassan Abdel Wahab)

Casino "al-Latafa" / Casino al-latâfah (Gamal Madkour)

The Dream Princess / Amîrat al-ahlâm (Ahmed Galal)

Dreams of Love / Ahlâm al-houbb (Fouad al-Gazaerli)

The False Bey / al-Beh al-mouzayyat (Ibrahim Lama)

The First Day of the Month / Awwal al-Chahr (Abdel Fattah Hassan)

First Love / al-Houbb al-awwal (Gamal Madkour)

Friday Night / Laylat al-goum'ah (Kamal Selim)

Gamal and Dalal / Gamâl wa Dalâl (Stephane Rosti)

The Gipsies' Town / Madînat al-ghagar (Mohamed Abdel Gawad)

Girls from the Countryside / Banât al-rîf (Youssef Wahbi)

Good Luck / al-Hazz al-sa'îd (Fouad al-Gazaerli)

The Great Artist / al-Fannân al-'azim (Youssef Wahbi)

The Heart Has Only One Love / al-Qalb louh wâhid (Henri Barakat)

The Honeymoon / Chahr al-'asal (Ahmed Badrakhan)

The Human Being / al-Banî âdam (Niazi Mostafa)

I Love What's Popular / Ahibb al-baladî (Hussein Fawzi)

I've Killed My Son / Qatalt waladî (Gamal Madkour)

A Kiss from the Lebanon / Qoublah fî Loubnan (Ahmed Badrakhan)

Leila, Daughter of Poor People / Layla bint al-fouqâra (Anwar Wagdi)

Life Is a Struggle / al-Haydâh kifâh (Gamal Madkour)

Long Live Men / Tahyâ al-riggâlah (Togo Mizrahi)

Love Story / Qissat gharâm (Mohamed Abdel Gawad and Kamal Selim)

The Messenger from Hell / Safîr gahannam (Youssef Wahbi)

Miss Boussa / al-Ânisah Boussah (Niazi Mostafa)

Money / al-Foulous (Ibrahim Lama)

The Most Beautiful Woman / Ahlâhoum (Stephane Rosti)

The Mother / al-Oumm (Omar Guemei)

The New Generation / al-Guîl al-gadîd (Ahmed Badrakhan)

Night of Chance / Laylat al-hazz (Abdel Fattah Hassan)

The Open Taxi / Taxi hantour (Ahmed Badrakhan)

The Paternal Lack / Hâdhâ ganâhou abî (Henri Barakat)

Patience Is Golden / al-Sabr tayyib (Hussein Fawzi)

Ragaa / Ragâ' (Omar Guemei)

Sallama / Sallâmah (Togo Mizrahi)

The Weaker Sex / al-Guinsa al-latîf (Ahmed Kamel Morsi)

The White Penny / al-Qirch al-abyad (Ibrahim Emara)

1946

Always in My Heart / Dâyman fî qalbî (Salah Abou Seif)

The Angel of Mercy / Malâk al-rahmah (Youssef Wahbi)

A Bride for Hire / ʿArousah li-l-îgâr (Farid al-Guindi)

A Candle Burns / Une bougie brûle / Chamʾah tahtariq (Youssef Wahbi)

The Caravan's Return / ʿAwdat al-qâfilah (Ahmed Badrakhan)

A Day of Greatness / Yawm fî-l-âlî (Hussein Fawzi)

Dounia / Douniâ (Mohamed Karim)

An Enemy of Women / ʿAdouww al-marʾah (Abdel Fattah Hassan)

The First Glance / Awwal nazrah (Niazi Mostafa)

The Five Pounds / al-Khamsah Guinîh (Hassan Helmi)

The Girl from the East / Bint al-charq (Ibrahim Lama)

Glory and Tears / Magd wa doumouʾ (Ahmed Badrakhan)

God's Hand / Yadu Allah (Youssef Wahbi)

Good and Evil / al-Khayr wa-l-charr (Hassan Helmi)

He Who Kisses too Much / Sâhib bâlayn (Abbas Kamel)

The Hunchback / al-Ahdab (Hassan Helmi)

I Cannot / Ma ʿdarch (Ahmed Badrakhan)

I Destroyed My Home / Hadamt baytî (Hussein Fawzi)

I'm No Angel / Lastou Malâkan (Mohamed Karim)

Jealousy / al-Ghîrah (Abdel Fattah Hassan)

Land of the Nile / Ard al-Nîl (Abdel Fattah Hassan)

Leila, Daughter of the Rich / Layla bint al-aghniyâ (Anwar Wagdi)

Lipstick / Ahmar chafâyif (Wali Eddine Sameh)

The Love Express / Express al-houbb (Hussein Fawzi)

The Man of the Future / Ragoul al-moustaqbal (Ahmed Salem)

Me and My Cousin / Anâ wa ibn ʿammî (Abdel Fattah Hassan)

Misleading Appearances / al-Nafkhah al-kaddâbah (Ahmed Badrakhan)

The Musician / al-Mousîqar (al-Sayed Ziyada)

My Father's Secret / Sirr abî (Wali Eddine Sameh)

Nagaf / Nagaf (Ahmed Kamel Hefnawi)

Old People's Love / Gharâm al-chouyoukh (Mohamed Abdel Gawad)

The Orphan / al-Yatîmah (Fouad al-Gazaerli)

Oum al-Saad / Oumm al-Saʾd (Ahmed Galal)

The Pasha's Wife / Haram al-bâchâ (Hassan Helmi)

The Procurator General / al-Nâʾib al-ʾâmm (Ahmed Kamel Morsi)

The Queen of Beauty / Malikat al-gamâl (Togo Mizrahi)

Rawiya / Râwiya (Niazi Mostafa)

The Return of the Magic Cap / ʿAwdat tâqiyyat al-ikhfâ (Mohamed Abdel Gawad)

Return to Starting Point / ʾÂdat ilâ qawâʾidihâ (Mohamed Abdel Gawad)

Salwa / Salwa (Abdel Alim Khattab)

The Scatterbrain / al-Tâʾichah (Ibrahim Emara)

Scheherazade / Chahrazade (Fouad al-Gazaerli)

The Sin / al-Khatîʾah (Ibrahim Emara)   *A Bedouin's Love / Gharâm badawiyyah* (Fouad al-Gazaerli)

Storms / ʿAwâsif (Abdel Fattah Hassan)

Their Excellencies / Ashâb al-saʾâdah (Mohamed Karim)

The Unknown Past / al-Mâdî al-magʾhoul (Ahmed Salem)

The Unknown Singer / al-Moughanni al-magʾhoul (Mostafa Hassan)

Victims of Modernity / Dahâyâ a-madaniyyah (Niazi Mostafa)

The White Angel / al-Malâk al-abyad (Ibrahim Emara)

The Woman and the Puppet / Liʾbat al-sitt (Wali Eddine Sameh)

The World's Alright / al-Douniâ bi-kheir (Helmi Rafla)

1947

Abou Halmous / Abou Halmous (Ibrahim Helmi)

Abou Zeid al-Hilali / Abou Zayd al-Hilâlî (Ezz Eddine Zoulficar)

Angels in Hell / Malâʾikah fî gannam (Hassan al-Imam)

Antar's Son / Ibn ʿAntar (Ahmed Salem)

The Avenger / al-Mountaqim (Salah Abou Seif)

The Beautiful Bedouin Girl / al-Badawiyya al-hasnâʾ (Ibrahima Lama)

Betrayal and Suffering / Ghadr wa ʿadhâb (Hussein Sedki)

The Bigamist / Gouz al-itnîn (Ibrahim Emara)

Blow of Fate / Darbat al-qadar (Youssef Wahbi)

The Boss's Daughter / Bint al-mouʾallim (Abbas Kamel)

Cairo Baghdad / al-Qâhiran Baghdad (Ahmed Badrakahn)

The Dove of Peace / Hamâmat al-salâm (Helmi Rafla)

The Enemy of Society / ʿAdouww al-mougtamaʾ (Ibrahim Emara)

Everyone Is Singing / al-Koull you-ghannî (Ezz Eddine Zoulficar)

The Father / al-Abb (Omar Guemei)

Fatma / Fatmah (Ahmed Badrakhan)

Flowers and Thorns (Azhar wa achwâk (Mohamed Abdel Gawad)

The Fruit of Crime / Thamarat al-gârimah (Al-Sayed Ziyada)

Goha and the Seven Girls / Gohâ wa-l-sabʾbanât (Fouad al-Gazaerli)

The Great Sacrifice / al-Tadʾhiyah al-koubrâ (Mohamed Abdel Gawad)

Hadiyyah / Hadiyyah (Mahmoud Zoulficar)

Hello / Subâh al-khayr (Hussein Fawzi)

It Was an Angel / Kânat malâkan (Abbas Kamel)

It's Me Sattaouta / Anâ Sattaouta (Hussein Fawzi)

The Jackpot / al-Brimo (Kamel al-Telmessani)

Kiss Me Daddy / Qabbilnî yâ ʿabî (Ahmed Badrakhan)

The Lady / al-Hânim (Henri Barakat)

The Lark in the Valley / Châdiyat al-wâdî (Youssef Wahbi)

The Last Round / al-Gawlah al-akhîrah (Abdel Fattah Hassan)

A Lebanese at the University / Loubnânî fî-l-gâmiʾah (Hussein Fawzi)

Lost Hopes / Amal dâʾîʾ (Farid al-Guindi)

The Love of My Life / Habîb al-ʾoumr (Henri Barakat)

Marouf the Shoemaker / Maʾrouf al-iskâfî (Fouad al-Gazaerli)

The Midnight Ghost / Chabah nisf al-layl (Abdel Fattah Hassan)

My Head Is on Holiday / al-Aqlʾ fî agâzah (Helmi Rafla)

My Heart and My Sword / Qalbî wa sayfî (Gamal Madkour)

My Heart Is My Guide / Qalbî dalîlî (Anwar Wagdi)

Nights of Pleasure / Layâli al-Ouns (Niazi Mostafa)

The Parvenu / Ghanî harb (Niazi Mostafa)

The Prisoner of Darkness / Asîr al-zalâm (Ezz Eddine Zoulficar)

The Queen of the Desert / Soultânat al-sahrâ (Niazi Mostafa)

The Red Mask / al-Qinâal-ahmar (Youssef Wahbi)

The Return of the Absent One / ʿAwdat al-ghâʾib (Ahmed Galal)

The Siren / ʿArousat al-bahr (Abbas Kamel)

The Sky's Light / Nour min al-samâ (Hassan Helmi)

The Son of the East / Ibn al-charq (Ibrahim Helmi)

Souleyman's Ring / Khâtim Soulaymân (Hassan Ramzi)

Sunset / Ghouroub (Ahmed Kamel Morsi)

The Three Suitors / al-ʾOursân al thalâthah (Hassan Helmi)

The Tombola Seller / Bayyâʾat al yânasîb (Abdel Fattah Hassan)

The Treasure of Happiness / Kanz al-saʾâdah (Ibrahim Lama)

The Vagabond / al-Moutacharridah (Mohamed Abdel Gawad)

The Wisdom of the Arabs / Ahkâm al-lâthah (Ibrahim Emara)

Women Are Devils / al-Sittât ʿafrârît (Hassan al-Imam)

Zohra / Zohrah (Hussein Fawzi and Kamal Abou el-Ela)

1948

The Adventurer / al-Moughâmir (Hassan Reda)

The Adventures of Antar and Abla / Moughâmarât bʾAntar wa ʿAbla (Salah Abou Seif)

Al-Zanati Khalifa / al-Zanâtî Khalîfah (Hassan Helmi)

Amber / ʿAnbar (Anwar Wagdi)

Body and Soul / al-Rouh wa-l-gasad (Helmi Rafla)

The Conquest of Egypt / Fatʾh Misr (Fouad al-Gazaerli)

The Countryside in Mourning / al-Rîf al-hazîn (Mohamed Abdel Gawad)

Divine Justice / ʿAdl al-samâ (Ahmed Kamel Morsi)

Duty / al-Wâguib (Henri Barakat)

The Escaped Prisoner / Hârb min al-sigᵓn (Mohamed Abdel Gawad)

Eternal Love / Houbb lâ Yamout (Mohamed Karim)

Fitna / Fitnah (Mahmoud Ismaïl)

Forbidden Happiness / al-Saᵓâdahal-mouharramah (al-Sayed Ziyada)

A Girl from Palestine / Fatât min Filastîn (Mahmoud Zoulficar)

A Good Reputation Is Worth More than Riches / al-Sît wa-lâ al-guinâ (Hassan al-Imam)

Hassan the Brave / al-Châtir Husan (Fouad al-Gazaerli)

I Love to Dance / Ahibb al-raqs (Hassan Helmi)

If Youth . . . / Layta al-chabâb (Hassan Abdel Wahab)

The Island Princess / Amirat al-gazîrah (Hassan Ramzi and Abdel Kamel Hefnawi)

Khouloud / Khouloud (Ezz Eddine Zoulficar)

The Killer / al-Qâtil (Hussein Sedki)

Leila the American / Layla al-ᵓâmiriyyah (Niazi Mostafa)

A Life in Distress / Hayâh hâᵓirah (Ahmed Salem)

The Little Millionairess / al-Millionnairah al-saghîrah (Kamal Barakat)

Long Live Art / Yahyâ al-fann (Hassan Helmi)

Love / Houbb (Adel Aziz Hussein)

Love and Madness / Houb wa gounoun (Helmi Rafla)

Love and Youth / al-Hawâ wa-l-chabâb (Niazi Mostafa)

The Lucky Girl / Bint hazz (Abdel Fattah Hassan)

Man without Sleep / Ragoul lâ yanâm (Youssef Wahbi)

The Missing Link / al-Halqah al-mafqoudah (Ibrahim Lama)

Mr. Boulboul / Boulboul afandî (Hussein Fawzi)

Mrs. Souad's Divorce / Talâq Souᵓâd hânim (Anwar Wagdi)

Narguis / Narguis (Abdel Fattah Hassan)

On a Cloud / Fawq al-sahâb (Mahmoud Zoulficar)

The Owner of the Flat / Sâhibat al-ᵓimârah (Abdel Fattah Hassan)

Peaceful Night / Sagâ al-layl (Henri Barakat)

A Peasant's Son / Ibn al-fallâh (Abdel Fattah Hassan)

Playing with Fire / al-Liᵓb bi-l-nâr (Omar Guemei)

The Punishment / al-ᵓIqâb (Henri Barakat)

The Safest Path / Sikkat al-salâmah (Ibrahim Lama)

Samson the Magnificent / Chamchoun al-gabbâr (Kamel al-Telmessani)

She Lived in the Shadows / ᶜÂchat fî-l-zalâm (al-Sayed Ziyada)

Towards Fame / Nahw al-magd (Hussein Sedki)

The Two Orphans / al-Yatîmatayn (Hassan al-Imam)

The Unknown Future / al-Moustaqbal al-magᵓhoul (Ahmed Salem)

Ward Chah / Ward Chah (Abdel Fattah Hassan)

A Woman's Imagination / Khayâl imraᵓah (Hassan Reda)

1949

According to Your Means / ᶜAlâ ᶜad lihâfak (Fouad Chebl)

Amina / Amînah (Goffredo Alessandrini)

The Beautiful Woman's Handkerchief / Mandîl al-hilou (Abbas Kamel)

The Big House / al-Bayt al-Kabîr (Ahmed Kamel Morsi)

The Confessional / Koursî al-tirâf (Youssef Wahbi)

Congratulations / Mabrouk ᶜalîkî (Abdel Fattah Hassan)

Each Household Has Its Man / Koull bayt louh Râguil (Ahmed Kamel Morsi)

Fatma, Marika and Rachel / Fatmah wa-Mârîkâ wa-Rachel (Helmi Rafla)

Gawaher / Gawâhir (Mohamed Abdel Gawad)

Hoda / Houda (Helmi Rafla)

Holiday in Hell / Agâzah fî gahannam (Ezz Eddine Zoulficar)

The Hypocrite / Dhou al-wagᵓhayn (Wali Eddine Saleh and Ahmed Diaa Eddine)

I Wish You Many Offspring / ᶜOᵓbâl al-bakârî (Ibrahim Emara)

The Intelligent Person / al-Nâsih (Seif Eddine Chawkat)

It's You I Love It's You I Love / Ahibbak inta (Ahmed Badrakhan)

Lahalibo / Lahâlibo (Hussein Fawzi)

Madam Devil / ᶜIfrîtah hânim (Henri Barakat)

The Mayor's Daughter / Bint al-ᵓoumdah (Abbas Kamel)

Midnight / Nouss al-layl (Hussein Fawzi)

The Mistress of the House / Sitt al-bayt (Ahmed Kamel Morsi)

Mr. Bayoumi / Bayoumî afandî (Youssef Wahbi)

Mr. Egypt / al-Masrî afandî (Hussein Sedki)

The Murderess / al-Qâtilah (Hassan Reda)

A Night's Dream / Hilm laylah (Salah Badrakhan)

The Night Is Ours / al-Layl lanâ (Mahmoud Zoulficar)

Party Evening / Laylat al-ʾîd (Helmi Rafla)

The Prince's Secret / Sirr al-amîrah (Niazi Mostafa)

Prisoner No. 17 / al-Saguînah raqm sabʿat ʿachar (Omar Guemei)

Punchinello Street / Châriʾ al-bahlawân (Salah Abou Seif)

She Has a Few Pennies / Sâhibat al-malâlîm (Ezz Eddine Zoulficar)

Slave of Her Eyes / Asîr al-ʾouyoun (Ibrahim Helmi)

Vagabond Souls / Arwâh hâʾimah (Kamal Barakat)

Watch Out for Your Wallet / Ouʾa al-mahfazah (Mahmoud Ismaïl)

The Woman / al-Marʾah (Abdel Fattah Hassan)

Women Are Made Like That / al-Sittât kidah (Hassan Helmi)

Young Girls' Flirtations / Ghazal al-banât (Anwar Waghi)

1950

Afrah / Afrâh (Niazi Mostafa)

The Beauty / Sitt al-housn (Niazi Mostafa)

Beware of Men / Âh min al-riggâlah (Helmi Rafla)

Blood in the Desert / Dimâ fî-l-sahrâ (Gianni Vernuccio)

Daddy Gets Married / Let Me Sing / Sîbounî aghannî (Hussein Fawzi)

A Dancer's Love / Gharâm râqisah (Helmi Rafla)

Elham / Elham (Bahaa Eddine Charaf)

The Falcon / al-Saqr (Salah Abou Seif)

Felfel / Felfel (Seif Eddine Chawkat)

Fire Woman / Imraʾah min nâr (Gianni Vernuccio)

The Girl from Paris / Bint Paris (Helmi Rafla)

The Handsome Dark-Haired Man / Asmar wa gamîl (Abbas Kamel)

The Hero / al-Batal (Helmi Rafla)

An Hour for Your Heart / Sâʾah li-qalbak (Hassan al-Imam)

His Family's Favorite / Mahsoub al-ʾâʾilah (Abdel Fattah Hassan)

The Husband of the Four / Gouz al-arbbaʾah (Fatine Abdel Wahab)

Intelligence Is a Great Thing / al-Aql zînah (Hassan Redi)

It Wasn't Foreseen / Mâ kânch ʿalâ alʾbâl (Hassan Ramzi)

It's Fate / Qismah wa-nasîb (Mahmoud Zoulficar)

It's Really My Chance / Maʾlich yâ zahr (Henri Barakat)

Khadra's Adventures / Moughâmarât Khadrah (al-Sayed Ziyada)

Last Lie / Âkhir Kidbah (Ahmed Badrakhan)

The Lawyer Madiha / al-Avocato Madîhah (Youssef Wahbi)

Let Me Sing / Sîbounî aghannî (Hassein Fawzi)

Life Is a Struggle / Maʾrakat al-hayâh (Hussein Sedki)

Little Virtues / Akhlâq li-l-bayʾ (Mahmoud Zoulficar)

The Love Agency / Maktab al-gharâm (Hassan Helmi)

The Millionnaire / al-Millionnaire (Helmi Rafla)

Miss Mother / alʾÂnisah Mâmâ (Helmi Rafla)

More Beautiful than the Moon / Qamar abataʾch (Niazi Mostafa)

My Eye Blinks / ʿAynî bi-triff (Abbas Kamel)

My Lovers Are Numerous / Habâybî kitîr (Kamal Ateyya)

My Sister Steita / Oukhtî Steitah (Hussein Fawzi)

Papa Amine / Bâbâ Amîn (Youssef Chahine)

A Path Strewn with Thorns / Tarîq al-chawk (Hussein Sedki)

Popular and Sympathetic / Baladî wa-khiffah (Hussein Fawzi)

The Price of Vengeance / Amîr al-Intiqâm (Henri Barakat)

The Seventh Wife / al-Zawgah al-sâbiʾah (Ibrahim Emara)

The Shore of Love / Châtiʾ al-gharâm (Henri Barakat)

Tears of Happiness / Doumouʾ al-farah (Ahmed Salem/Fatine Abdel Wahab)

Victim of Injustice / al-Mazloumah (Mohamed Abdel Gawad)

Victim of People / Zalamounî al-nâs (Hassan al-Imam)

The Wedding Night / Laylat al-doukhlah (Mostafa Hassan)

When I Was Young / Ayyâm chabâbî (Gamal Madkour)

Women's Wiles / Kayd al-nisâ (Kamel al-Telmessani)

Yasmine / Yasmine (Anwar Wagdi)

You and Me / Anâ wa anta (Ahmed Badrakhan)

Your Mother-in-Law Loves You / Hamâtak tihibbak (Fouad Chebl)

1951

Adam and Eve / Adam wa Hawwâ' (Hussein Sedki)

The Beauty's Cheek / Khadd al-gamîl (Abbas Kamel)

The Beloved's Country / Balad al-mahboub (Helmi Rafla)

The Birth of Islam / Zouhour al-islâm (Ibrahim Ezz Eddine)

Boulboul the Lawyer / al-Mou'allim Boulboul (Hassan Ramzi)

The Caravan Passes By / al'Qâfilah tasîr (Ibrahim Lama)

Children of the Streets / Awlâd al-chawâri (Youssef Wahbi)

Come and Meet / Ta'âla sallim (Helmi Rafla)

The End of a Story / Nihâyat qissah (Helmi Rafla)

Equal in Misfortune / Fî-l-hawâ sawâ (Youssef Maalouf)

The Eve of the Wedding / Laylat al-hinnah (Anwar Wagdi)

Everything Is Agreed / Fourigat (Hussein Fawzi)

Farewell My Love / Wadâ'an yâ gharâmî (Omar Guemei)

The Girl from the Circus / Fatât al-sîrk (Hussein Fawzi)

Girls Are Sweet / al-Banât charbât (Helmi Rafla)

Good News / Khabar abyad (Abbas Kamel)

The Hard Man / al-Sab' afandî (Ahmed Khorchid)

The Heart's Elect / Ibn al-halâl (Seif Eddine Chawkat)

Honor Is Precious / al-Charaf ghâli (Ahmed Badrakhan)

House of Ghosts / Bayt al-achbâh (Fatine Abdel Wahab)

I Am the Past / Anâ al-mâdi (Ezz Eddine Zoulficar)

I Come from a Good Family / Anâ bint nâs (Hassan al-Imam)

I Sacrificed My Love / Dahhayt gharâmî (Ibrahim Emara)

In Good Humor / Fâyeq wa râyeq (Helmi Rafla)

Island of Dreams / Gazîrat al-ahlâm (Abdel Alim Khattab)

Katr al-Nada / Qatr al-nadâ (Anwar Wagdi)

Khadra and Sindbad al-Qibli / Khadrah wa-l-sindibâd al-qiblî (al-Sayed Ziyada)

Life Is Beautiful / a-Douniâ hilwah (Youssef Maalouf)

The Listener-In / Sammâ'at al-telefon (Gamal Madkour)

Love in Danger / al-Houbb fî khatar (Helmi Rafla)

The Loved One's Vengeance / Intiqâm al-habîb (Gianni Vernuccio)

Love's Roses / Ward al-gharâm (Henri Barakat)

Madam Feyrouz / Fayrouz hânim (Abbas Kamel)

My Children / Awlâdî (Oma Guemei)

My Father Deceived Me / Khada'anî abî (Mahmoud Zoulficar)

My Love, My Soul / Habîb al-rouh (Anwar Wagdi)

My Mother-in-Law Is an Atomic Bomb / Hamâtî qounboulah dharriyyah (Helmi Rafla)

Night of Love / Laylat gharâm (Ahmed Badrakhan)

The Outlaw / al-Khârig ʿalâ al-qânoun (Mohamed Abdel Gawad)

Patience Pays / al-Sabr gamîl (Niazi Mostafa)

People's Secrets / Asrâr al-nâs (Hassan al-Imam)

Son of the Nile / Ibn al-Nîl (Youssef Chahine)

Soussou My Love / Habîbatî Soussou (Niazi Mostafa)

Spring Storm / ʿÂsifah fî-l-rabî (Ibrahim Lama)

The Strongest Reason / Houkm al-qawî (Hassan al-Imam)

The Thoughtlessness of Youth / Taych al-chabâb (Ahmed Kamel Morsi)

To Whom Could I Complain? / *Achkî li-mîn* (Ibrahim Emara)

Wahiba, Queen of the Gipsies / *Wahîba malikat al-ghagar* (Niazi Mostafa)

The Window of My Love / *Choubbâk habîbî* (Abbas Kamel)

With No Farewells / *Min Ghayr wadâ'* (Ahmed Diaa Eddine)

You Are Thinking of Another Woman / *Machghoul bighayrî* (Ibrahim Emara)

Your Day Will Come / *Lak Youm yâ zâlim* (Salah Abou Seif)

1952

Amal / *Amâl* (Youssef Maalouf)

Ask My Heart / *Salou qalbî* (Ezz Eddine Zoulficar)

Auspicious / *Qadam al-khayr* (Helmi Rafla)

Bamba / *Bamba* (Mohsen Szabo)

The Beautiful Flowers / *al-Zouhour al-Fâtinah* (Gamal Madkour)

By the Sweat of My Brow / *Min 'araq guibînî* (Gianni Vernuccio)

The Call of the Blood / *al-Dam yahinn* (al-Sayed Ziyada)

The Crook's House / *Bayt al-nattâch* (Hassan Helmi)

The Cup of Suffering / *Kâs al-'adhâb* (Hassan al-Imam)

A Dance Tour / *'Achrah baladî* (Ibrahim Helmi)

Don't Tell Anyone / *Mâ t'oulch li-hadd* (Henri Barakat)

Down with Colonialism / *Yasqout al-isti'mâr* (Hussein Sedki)

An Egyptian in Lebanon / *Masrî fî Loubnân* (Gianni Vernuccio)

Faith / *al-Imân* (Ahmed Bakdrakhan)

A Father's Mistake / *Ghaltat 'abb* (Henri Barakat)

Fatma the Lawyer / *al-Oustâdhah Fatmah* (Fatine Abdel Wahab)

The Girl on the Beach / *Bint al-châti'* (Mohamed Saleh al-Kayyali)

Give Me Your Reason / *Iddînî 'aqlak* (Ahmed Kamel Morsi)

Goha's Star Turn / *Mismâr Gohâ* (Ibrahim Emara)

Good News / *Bouchret khayr* (Hassan Ramzi)

The Great Clown / *al-Mouharrig al-kabîr* (Youssef Chahine)

The Happy Family / *al-Bayt al-sa'îd* (Hussein Sedki)

Hassan the Foreman / *al-Oustâ Hasan* (Salah Abou Seif)

Heart to Heart / *Min al-qalb li-l-qalb* (Henri Barakat)

Heaven and Hell / *Gannah wa nâr* (Hussein Fawzi)

Heaven Watches / *al-Samâ' lâ tanâm* (Ibrahim Emara)

House No. 13 / *al-Manzil raqam talatta'char* (Kamal al-Cheikh)

I Am Alone / *Anâ wahdî* (Henri Barakat)

I Believed in God / *Âmint billah* (Mahmoud Zoulficar)

I Want to Get Married / *'Ayza atgawwiz* (Ahmed Badrakhan)

The Immortal Song / *Lahn al-khouloud* (Henri Barakat)

I've Done Myself an Injustice / *Zalamt rouhi* (Ibrahim Emara)

The Lady on the Train / *Sayyidat al-qitâr* (Youssef Chahine)

Love Has No Cure / *al-Hawâ mâlouch dawâ* (Youssef Maalouf)

Love Is a Scandal / *al-Houbb bahdalah* (Salah Abou Seif)

Love Is Beautiful / *Yâ halâwat al-houbb* (Hussein Fawzi)

The Love of My Soul / *Habîb qalbi* (Helmi Rafla)

The Marriage Photo / *Sourat al-zifzâf* (Hassan Amer)

Mostafa Kamel / *Mostafa Kâmil* (Ahmed Badrakhan)

The Murderous Mother / *al-Oumm al-qâtlah* (Ahmed Kamel Morsi)

Nahed / *Nâhid* (Mohamed Karim)

Night of Destiny / *Laylat al-qadr* (Hussein Sedki)

Orphans' Property / *Amwâl al-yatâmâ* (Gamal Madkour)

The Parents' Anger / *Ghadab al-wâlidayn* (Hassan al-Imam)

Respected Sir / *Hadrat al-mouhtaram* (Abbas Kamel)

Samson and Lebleb / *Chamchoun wa Liblib* (Seif Eddine Chawkat)

Spring Festival / *Chamm al-nasîm* (Gianni Vernuccio)

The Strange Era / Zaman al-ʾagâyib (Hassan al-Imam)

The Tiger / al-Nimr (Hussein Fawzi)

The Triumph of Islam / Intisâr al-islâm (Ahmed al-Toukhi)

The Unfortunate / al-Masâkîn (Hussein Sedki)

The Unfortunate Man / Qalîl al-bakht (Mohamed Abdel Gawad)

The Victor / al-Mountasir (Helmi Rafla)

Where Do You Get All That From? / Min ayna laka hâdhâ (Niazi Mostafa)

Who Is My Father / Anâ bint mîn (Hassan al-Imam)

You Are My Life / Hayâtî inta (Youssef Maalouf)

You Deserve It / Halâl ʿalayk (Issa Karama)

Your Way / ʿAlâ keifak (Helmi Rafla)

Zeinab / Zeinab (Mohamed Karim)

1953

The Administrative Council / Maglis al-idârah (Abbas Kamel)

After the Farewells / Baʿda al-wadâʾ (Ahmed Dia Eddine)

Aicha / ʿÂichah (Gamal Madkour)

Al-Sayyed Ahmad al-Baadawi / al-Sayyed Ahmad al-Badawî (Bahaa Eddine Charaf)

The Baker's Wife / Bâʾiʾat al-khoubz (Hassan al-Imam)

A Benefactor / Fâʾil Khatr (Helmi Rafla)

Between Ourselves / Baynî wa Baynak (Hassan Reda)

Between Two Hearts / Bayn qalbayn (Mohamed Abdel Gawad)

Bilal, the Prophet's Muezzin / Bilâl mouʾadhdhin al-rasoul (Ahmed al-Touhki)

Bouthayna's Love / Gharâm Bouthayna (Galal Mostafa)

By What Right? / Fî charʾ mîn (Hassan al-Imam)

A Child from the District / Ibn al-hârah (Ezz Eddine Zoulficar)

Dahab / Dahab (Anwar Wagdi)

Daughter of Aristocrats / Bint al-akâbir (Anwar Wagda)

The Doubt Which Kills / al-Chakk al-qâtil (Ezz Eddine Zoulficar)

The Error of My Life / Ghaltat al-ʾoumr (Mahmoud Zoulficar)

Fate / al-Mouqaddar wa-l-maktoub (Abbas Kamel)

The Frivolous Woman / al-Moustahtirah (Abdallah Barakat)

Hamido / Hamido (Niazi Mostafa)

Hated Love / al-Houbb makrouh (Abdallah Barakat)

Have Pity on Me / Harâm ʿalayk (Issa Karama)

The Hell of Jealousy / Gahîm al-gîrah (Kostanof)

Hold Your Tongue / Lisânak hisânak (Abbas Kamel)

Home / Bayt al-Tâʾah (Youssef Wahbi)

The Honest Burglar / al-Liss al-charîf (Hamada Abdel Wahab)

I Fear for My Son / Qalbî ʿalâ waladî (Henri Barakat)

I Have No-One / Mâlîch had (Ibrahim Emara)

Is It My Fault? / Anâ dhanbî îh (Ibrahim Ebara)

The Land of Heroes / Ard al-abtâl (Niazi Mostafa)

The Last Meeting / al-Liqâʾ al-akhîr (al-Sayed Ziyada)

The Law of Life / Houkm al-zamân (Henri Barakat)

Love in the Shadows / Houbb fî-l-zalâm (Hassan al-Imam)

A Million Pounds / Million guinîh (Hussein Fawzi)

My Companion / Charîk hayâtî (Elhami Hassan)

My Love and I / Anâ wa habîbî (Kamel al-Telmessani)

My Love's Song / Lahn houbbî (Ahmed Badrakhan)

The Night Train / Qitar al-layl (Ezz Eddine Zoulficar)

The Path of Happiness / Rarîq al-saʾâdah (Ahmed Kamel Hefnawi)

The Plot / Mouʾâmarah (Kamel al-Cheikh)

The Pretty Mothers-in-Law / al-Hamawât al-Fâtinât (Helmi Rafla)

The Prostitute / Bint al-hawâ (Youssef Wahbi)

Raya and Sakina / Rayyâ wa Sakînah (Salah Abou Seif)

Rendezvous with Life / Mawʾid maʾ al-hayâh (Ezz Eddine Zoulficar)

The Scandal Merchant / Tâguir al-fadâʾih (Hassan al-Imam)

Slaves of Money / ʿAbîd al-mâl (Fatine Abdel Wahab)

Son for Hire / Ibn li-l-igâr (Helmi Rafla)

Son of Aristocrats / Ibn dhawât (Hassan al-Saïfi)

Those Who Love Me Have Wronged Me / Zala-mounî al-habâyib (Helmi Rafla)

The Truth / Kalimat al-haqq (Fatine Abdel Wahab)

A Tyrant's Law / Houkm qarâqouch (Fatine Abdel Wahab)

Uncle Abdou's Ghost / ʿIfrît ʿamm ʿAbdou (Hussein Fawzi)

Wafaa / Wafâ (Ezz Eddine Zoulficar)

A Well-Kept Secret / al-Sirr fî bîr (Hassan Helmi)

When Life Smiles at You / al-Douniâ limma tid-hak (Mohamed Abdel Gawad)

Window on Paradise / Nâfidhah ʿalâ al-gannah (Ahmed Diaa Eddine)

Woman Is Everything / al-Marʾah koull chayʾ (Helmi Rafla)

Women without Men / Nisâʾ bilâ rigâl (Youssef Chahine)

Wretchedness / al-Hirmân (Atef Salem)

Written on His Forehead / Maktoub ʿalâ al-guibîn (Ibrahim Emara)

You Are Witnesses / Ichhadou yâ nâs (Hassan al-Saïfi)

The Young Thief / Nachchâluh hânim (Hassan al-Saïfi)

Your Horoscope This Week / Hazzak hâdhâ al-ousbouʾ (Helmi Rafla)

1954

Abou al-Dahab / Abou al-Dahab (Helmi Rafla)

Al-Houseiniyya's Tough Guys / Foutouwwat al-Houseiniyyah (Niazi Mostafa)

An American fromTantah / Amrikânî min Tan-tah (Ahmed Kamel Morsi)

And the Days Pass / Marrat al-ayyâm (Ahmed Diaa Eddine)

April Fool / Kidbad abril (Mohamed Abdel Gawad)

Aziza / Azîzah (Hussein Fawzi)

The Barber of Baghdad / Hallâq Baghdâd (Hussein Fawzi)

The Black Horseman / al-Fâris al-aswad (Niazi Mostafa)

Cheikh Hassan / al-Chaykh Hasan (Hussein Sedki)

The Criminal / al-Mougrim (Kamal Ateyya)

The Daughters of Eve / Banât Hawwâ (Niazi Mostafa)

The Demon of the Desert / Chaytân al-sahrâ (Youssef Chahine)

Don't Be Unjust / al-Dhoulm harâm (Hassan al-Saïfi)

Don't Think about It / Ouʾâ tifakkar (Elhami Hassan)

A Dozen Handkerchiefs / Dastit manâdîl (Abbas Kamel)

Each According to His Rank / al-Nâs maqâmât (al-Sayed Ziyada)

Explain to Me, I Beg You / Doullounî yâ nâs (al-Sayed Ziyada)

The Farewell Dance / Taqsat al-wadâʾ (Ezz Eddine Zoulficar)

For Your Beautiful Eyes / ʿAlachân ʿouyounak (Ahmed Badrakhan)

Four Girls and an Officer / Arbaʾ banât wa dâbit (Anwar Wagdi)

The Girl from the Country / Bint al-balad (Hassan al-Saïfi)

The Girl's Honor / Charaf al-bint (Helmi Rafla)

The Good Earth / al-Ard al-tayyibah (Mahmoud Zoulficar)

The Happiest Days / Asʾad al-ayyâm (Hassan Reda)

Hassan, Morcos and Cohen / Hasan wa Morqos wa Kohîn (Fouad al-Gazaerli)

Have Confidence in God / Khallîk maʾ Allah (Helmi Rafla)

Have Pity on Me / Irham doumouʾî (Henri Barakat)

He's Kidnapped My Wife / Khataf mirâtî (Hassan al-Saïfi)

Human Hearts / Qouloub al-nâs (Hassan al-Imam)

I Almost Destroyed My Home / Kidtou ahdou-mou baytî (Ahmed Kamel Morsi)

I Am Love / Anâ al-houbb (Henri Barakat)

The Imposter / al-Mouhtâl (Helmi Rafla)

Ishmael Yassine and the Ghost / ʿIfrîtat Ismâʾîl Yâsîn (Hassan al-Saïfi)

Ishmael Yassine's Adventures / Moughâmarât Ismâʾîl Yâsîn (Youssef Maalouf)

It Happened One Night . . . / Hadatha dhâta lay-lah (Henri Barakat)

Let Me Get Married, Quickly / Ilhaqounî bi-l-maʾdhoun (Helmi Rafla)

Life or Death / Hayât aw mawt (Kamal al-Cheikh)

Life . . . Love / al-Hayât . . . al-houbb (Seif Eddine Chawkat)

Light of My Eyes / Nour ᶜouyounî (Hussein Fawzi)

Long Live Men! / Tahyâ al-riggâlah (Ahmed Kamel Hefnawi)

Love Letter / Risâlat gharâm (Henri Barakat)

The Love Taxi / Taxi al-gharâm (Niazi Mostafa)

The Lovers' Village / Qaryat alᵓouchchâq (Ahmed Diaa Eddine)

Love's Victory / Intisâr al-houbb (Hassan Ramzi)

Mademoiselle Hanafi / al-Ânissah (Fatine Abdel Wahab)

The Madness of Love / Gounoun al-houbb (Mohamed Karim)

Money and Children / al-Mâl wa-l-banoun (Ibrahim Emara)

The Monster / al-Wahch (Salah Abou Seif)

The Neighbors' Daughter / Bint al-guîrân (Mahmoud Zoulficar)

A Night in My Life / Laylah minᵓoumrî (Atef Salem)

A Poor Man / Insân ghalbân (Helmi Rafla)

The Private Lover / al-Âcgiq al-mahroum (al-Sayed Ziyada)

Professor Charaf / al-Oustâdh Charf (Kamel al-Telmessani)

Promise / Waᵓd (Ahmed Badrakhan)

Rendezvous with Happiness / Mawᵓid maᵓ al-saᵓâdah (Ezz Eddine Zoulficar)

Resourceful but Lost / Fâlih wa mouhtâs (Ismaïl Hassan)

Sky of Hell / Sirâ fii-l-wâdî (Youssef Chahine)

Stronger than Love / Aqwâ min al-houbb (Ezz Eddine Zoulficar)

They Have Made Me a Killer / Gaᵓalounî mougriman (Atef Salem)

Traces in the Sand / Âthar fi-l-rimâl (Gamal Madkour)

The Unjust Angel / al-Malâk al-zâlim (Hassan al-Imam)

Who Are You in Love With? / Li-miin hawâk (Helmi Rafla)

With You Always / Dâyman maᵓâk (Henri Barakat)

Women Don't Know How to Lie / al-Sittât mâ yaᵓrafouch yikdibou (Mohamed Abdel Gawad)

You Only Live Once / al-ᵓOumr wâhid (Ehsane Farghal)

You've Done Me Wrong / Yâ zâlimnî (Ibrahim Emara)

1955

The Absent Woman / al-Gâᵓibah (EzzEddine Zoulficar)

Adored Soul / ᶜÂchiq al-rouh (Helmi Rafla)

Birds of Paradise / ᶜAsâfîr al-gannah (Seif Eddine Chawkat)

The Body / al-Gasad (Hassan al-Imam)

Captain Misr / Kabtin Misr (Bahaa Eddine Charaf)

The City's Revolt / Thawrat al-madînah (Helmi Rafla)

Days and NIghts / Ayyâm wa layâlî (Henri Barakat)

Dearer than the Pupils of My Eyes / Aghlâ min ᶜaynayya (Ezz Eddine Zoulficar)

Fagr / Fagr (Atef Salem)

Fate's Laughter / Dihkât al-qadar (Elhami Hassan)

For Love / Fî sabîl al-houbb (Issa Karama)

Girls of the Night / Banât al-layl (Hassan al-Imam)

Girls' School / Madrasat al-banât (Kamel al-Termessani)

A Glass and a Cigarette / Sigârah wa kâs (Niazi Mostafa)

God Is with Us / Allah maᵓnâ (Ahmed Badrakhan)

Happiness Is a Promise / al-Saᵓd waᵓd (Mohamed Abdel Gawad)

He Who Is Satisfied with Little . . . / Man radiya bi-qalîhih (Bahaa Eddine Charaf)

Hello / Nahârak saᵓîd (Fatine Abdel Wahab)

The Hope of My Life / Amânî al-ᵓoumr (Seif Eddine Chawkat)

I Call You / Banâdî ᶜalîk (Isnmaïl Hassan)

I'm Leaving / Innî râhilah (Ezz Eddine Zoulficar)

Ishmael Yassine in the Army / Ismâᵓîl fî-l-gaych (Fatine Abdel Wahab)

Ishmael Yassine Meets Raya and Sekina / Ismâᵓîl Yâsîn youqâbil Rayyâ wa Sakînah (Hamada Abdel Wahab)

Let Me Live / Daᵓounî aᵓîch (Ahmed Diaa Eddine)

Love and Tears / Houbb wa doumouᵓ (Kamal al-Cheikh)

The Lovers / ahl al-hawâ (al-Sayed Ziyada)

My Heart Loves You / Qalbî yahwâk (Hussein Sedki)

Nights of Love / Layâlî al-houbb (Helmi Rafla)

No-One's Worth Anything in the Grave / Mâhad-dichwâkhid minhâ hâgah (Mohamed Abdel Gawad)

Oath of Love / ʿAhd al-hawâ (Ahmed Badrakahn)

An Ocean of Love / Bahr al-gharâm (Hussein Fawzi)

Our Best Days / Ayyâmounâ al-houlwah (Helmi Halim)

Out of Work / Khâlî choughl (Hassan Amer)

The Rendezvous / al-Mîʾâd (Ahmed Kamel Morsi)

Rendezvous with Satan / Mawʾîd ma ʿIblîs (Kamel-al-Telmessani)

The Ringing of the Khoulhal / Rannat al-khoulkhâl (Mahmoud Zoulficar)

The Shore of Memories / Châtiʾ al-dhikrayât (Ezz Eddine Zoulficar)

The Song of Fidelity / Lan al-wafâʾ (Ibrahim Emara)

Spring Dreams / Ahlâm al-rabîʾ (Hassan Ramzi)

Story of My Love / Qissat houbbi (Henri Barakat)

Street of Fools / Darb al-Mahâbil (Tewfik Saleh)

The Sugar Doll / ʿArousat al-moulid (Abbas Kamel)

Tears in the Night / Doumouʿ fî-l-layl (Ibrahim Emara)

The Unknown Lover / al-Habîb al-magʾhoul (Hassan al-Saïfi)

Vengeance Unfulfilled / Târ bâyit (Abbas Kamel)

Victims of the Feudal System / Dahâyâ al-iqtâ (Mostafa Kamel)

We're Human Beings / Nahnou bachar (Ibrahim Emara)

A Wife's Confessions / Iʾtirâfât zawgah (Hassam al-Imam)

Women's Realm / Mamlakat al-nisâʾ (Ehsane Farghal)

Young Girls at Auction / ʿArâyis fî-l-mazâd (Hassan al-Saïfi)

Your Health! / Fî sihhitak (Abbas Kamel)

1956

Black Waters / Sirâ fî-l-mînâ (Youssef Chahine)

The Call of Love / Nidâʾ al-houbb (Elhami Hassan)

Dalila / Dalîlah (Mohamed Karim)

Dawn Farewells / Wadâʾ fî-l-fagr (Hassan al-Imam)

The Demons of Heaven / Chayâtîn al-gaww (Niazi Mostafa)

Divine Miracle / Mouʾguizat al-samâʾ (Atef Salem)

Farewell My Love / Waddaʾtou houbbak (Youssef Chahine)

First Love / Awwal gharâm (Niazi Mostafa)

The Heart Has Its Reasons / al-Qalb louh ahkâm (Helmi Halim)

How Can I Forget You? / Izzây ansâk (Ahmed Badrakhan)

I Killed My Wife / Qatalt zawgati (Kamal Ateyya)

The Innocent's Prayer / Daʾwat al-mazloum (Ahmed Kamel Hefnawi)

The Inspector General / al-Moufattich al-ʾâmm (Helmi Rafla)

Ishmael Yassine at the Waxworks / Ismâʾîl Yâsîn fî moutʾhaf al-chamʾ (Issa Karama)

Ishmael Yassine in the Police / Ismâʾîl Yâsîn fî-l-bolîs (Fatine Abdel Wahab)

I've Given You My Life / Wahabtouka hayâtî (Zouheir Bekir and Fatine AbdelWahab)

Kilo 99 / Kilo tisʾah wa-tisʾîn (Ibrahim Helmi)

The Leech / Chabâb imraʾah (Salah Abou Seif)

The Little Doll / al-ʾArousah al-saghîrah (Ahmed Badrakhan)

Love and Execution / Houbb wa iʾdâm (Kamel al-Cheikh)

Love and Humanity / Houbb wa insâniyyah (Hussein Fawzi)

Lovers' Rendezvous / Mawʾid gharâm (Henri Barakat)

Madam Holds the Power / Sâhibat al-ʾismah (Hassan al-Saïfi)

The Merry Widow / al-Armalah al-taroub (Helmi Rafla)

Our Green Land / Ardounâ al-khadrâʾ (Ahmed Diaa Eddine)

The Outsider / al-Gharîb (Kamal al-Cheikh)

Platform 5 / Rasîf nimra khamsah (Niazi Mostafa)

Police Record / Sahiifat al-sawâbiq (Ibrahim Emara)

The Rebel / al-Namroud (Atef Salem)

Samara / Samârah (Hassan al-Saïfi)

Sleepless Night / ʿOuyoun sahrânah (Ezz Eddine Zoulficar)

The Spring of Love / Rabî²al-houbb (Ibrahim Emara)

Try Your Luck / Garrab hazzak (Issa Karama)

Undecided Hearts / Qouloub hâ²irah (Kamal al-Chennawi)

Voices of the Past / Sawt min al-mâdî (Ataf Salem)

Weep Not, My Eyes / Kifâyah yâ²ayn (Houssam Eddine Mostafa)

Where Is My Life? / Ayna ᶜoumrî (Ahmed Diaa Eddine)

Who Is the Killer? / Man al-qâtil (Hassan al-Saïfi)

Zannouba / Zannoubah (Hassan al-Saïfi)

1957

Abou Zouboul's Prisoner / Saguîn Abou Zou²boul (Niazi Mostafa)

The Accused / al-Mouttaham (Kamal Ateyya)

The Charming Postmistresses / al-Koumsariyyât al-fâtinât (Hassan al-Saïfi)

A Courtesan's Life / Hayât ghâniyah (houssam Eddine Mostafa)

Crime and Punishment / al-Garîmah wa—²iqâb (Ibrahim Emara)

The Empty Pillow / al-Wisâdah al-khâliyah (Salah Abou Seif)

The End of a Love / Nihâyat al-houbb (Hassan al Saïfi)

The Fisherman's Daughter / Bint al-sayyad (Abdel Ghani Qamar)

Give Me Back My Soul / Roudda qalbî (Ezz Eddine Zoulficar)

Glory / al-Magd (al-Sayed Bedeir)

The Great Love / al-Houbb al-²adhîm (Hassan al-Imam)

Hamido's Son / Ibn Hamido (Fatine Abdel Wahab)

The Haunt of Pleasure / Wakr al-maladhdhât (Hassan al-Imam)

Henna Flower / Tamr henna (Hussein Fawzi)

I Shall Never Weep / Lan abkî abadan (Hassan al-Imam)

Ighraa / Ighrâ² (Hassan al-Imam)

Ishmael Yassine at the Zoo / Ismâ²îl Yâsîn fi guininet al-haywân (Seif Eddine Chawkat)

Ishmael Yassine in the Navy / Ismâ²îl Yâsîn fi-l-oustoul (Fatine Abdel Wahab)

A Journey of Love / Rihlah gharâmiyyah (Mahmoud Zoulficar)

Land of Dreams / Ard al-ahlâm (Kamal al-Cheikh)

Land of Peace / Ard al-salâm (Kamal al-Cheikh)

Lawahez / Lawâhiz (Hassan al-Imam)

Lovers of the Night / ᶜOuchchâq al-layl (Kamal Ateyya)

A Man Flees Love / Hârib min al-houbb (Ezz Eddine Zoulficar)

Me and My Heart / Anâ wa qalbî (Mahmoud Zoulficar)

Mecca / Bayt Allah al-harâm (Ahmed al-Toukhi)

Merchants of Death / Touggâr al-mawt (Kamal al-Cheikh)

A Millionnaire's Love / Gharâm al-millionaire (Atef Salem)

Modern Young Girls / Banât al-yawm (Henri Barakat)

Night of Horror / Laylah rahîbah (al-Sayed Bedeir)

Nights without Sleep / Lâ anâm (Salah Abou Seif)

The Path of Hope / Tarîq al-amal (Ezz Eddine Zoulficar)

Port Saïd / Port Sa²îd (Ezz Eddine Zoulficar)

Prince of My Dreams / Fatâ ahlâmi (Helmi Rafla)

Struggle against Life / Sirâ² ma² al-hayât (Zouheir Bekir)

Tachera / Tâhirah (Fatine Abdel Wahab)

Teach Me Love / ᶜAllimounî al-houbb (Atef Salem)

The Tough Guy / al-Foutouwwah (Salah Abou Seif)

Women in My Life / Nisâ²fî hayâtî (Fatine Abdel Wahab)

You Are My Love / Anta habîbî (Youssef Chahine)

1958

Abou Hadid / Abou Hadîd (Niazi Mostafa)

Awatef / ᶜAwâtif (Hassan al-Imam)

Burning Love / Houbb min nâr (Hassan al-Imam)

Central Station / Bâb al-hadîd (Youssef Chahine)

A Criminal on Holiday / Mougrim fî agâzah (Salah Abou Seif)

Dead End / al-Tarîq al-masdoud (Salah Abou Seif)

The Elder Brother / *al-Akhkh al-kabîr* (Fatine Abdel Wahab)

Festival of Love / *Mahragân al-houbb* (Helmi Rafla)

Forgive Me / *Samihnî* (Hassan Reda)

The Fugitive / *alHâribah* (Hassan Ramzi)

Gamila the Algerian Girl / *Gamîlah* (Youssef Chahine)

Ghariba / *Gharîbah* (Ahmed Bardakhan)

The Girl from the Desert / *Bint al-bâdiyah* (Ibrahim Emara)

The Girl with the Bold Look / *Abou ʿouyoun garîʾah* (Hassan al-Saïfi)

Greet Those Whom I Love / *Sallim ʿalâ al-habâyib* (Helmi Halim)

Heaven's Pity / *Rahmah min al-samâʾ* (Abbas Kamel)

I Am the East / *Anâ al-charq* (Abdel Hamid Zaki)

I Love You Hassan / *Ahibbak yâ Hasan* (Hussein Fawzi)

I Only Have You / *Mâlîch gheirak* (Henri Barakat)

Ishmael Yassine as Tarzan / *Ismâʾîl Yâsîn Tarazân* (Niazi Mostafa)

Ishmael Yassine for Sale / *Ismâʾîl Yâsin li-l-bayʾ* (Houssam Eddine Mostafa)

Ishmael Yassine in Damascus / *Ismâʾîl Yâsîn fî Dimachq* (Helmi Rafla)

Ishmael Yassine in the Asylum / *Ismâʾîl Yâsîn fî moustachfa al-magânîn* (Issa Karama)

Ishmael Yassine in the Military Police / *Ismâʾîl Yâsîn bolis harbî* (Fatine Abdel Wahab)

Kahramanah / *Kahramânah* (al-Sayed Bedeir)

Khaled Ibn al-Walid / *Khâlid bin al-Walid* (Hussein Sedki)

The Lady from the Castle / *Sayyidat al-qasr* (Kamal al-Cheikh)

The Little Angel / *al-Malâk al-saghîr* (Kamal al-Cheikh)

The Little Devil / *al-Chaytânah al-saghîrah* (Hassan al-Imam)

The Love of My Life / *Habîbî al-asmar* (Niazi Mostafa)

Madam Nawaem / *al-Sitt Nawâʾim* (Youssef Maalouf)

Maiden's Hearts / *Qouloub al-ʾadhârâ* (Hassan al-Imam)

The Matron / *al-Mouʾallimah* (Hassan Reda)

The Midnight Driver / *Sawwâq nisf al-layl* (Niazi Mostafa)

Mr. Bahbouh / *Bahbouh afandî* (Youssef Maalouf)

Must I Kill My Husband? / *Hal aqtoul zawguî* (Houssam Eddine Mostafa)

My Beloved's Fault / *Ghaltat habiibî* (al-Sayed Bedeir)

My Brown-Haired Love / *Habîbî al-asmar* (Hassan al-Saïfi)

My Happy Days / *Ayyâmî al-saʾîdah* (Ahmed Diaa Eddine)

Never Again / *Toubah* (Mahmoud Zoulficar)

Secret Love / *al-Houbb al-sâmit* (Seif Eddine Chawkat)

The Seducer of Women / *Sâhir al-nisâʾ* (Fatine Abdel Wahab)

The Seventeen-Year-Old Girl / *Bint sabataʾch* (Kamal Ateyya)

Shore of Secrets / *Châtîʾ al-asrâr* (Atef Salem)

Stop Thief / *Imsik harâmî* (Fatine Abdel Wahab)

Street of Love / *Chârîʾ al-houbb* (Ezz Eddine Zoulficar)

Sultan / *Soultân* (Niazi Mostafa)

That's Love / *Hâdhâ houwa al-houbb* (Salah Abou Seif)

Touha / *Touhah* (Hassan al-Saïfi)

Until We Meet / *Hattâ naltaqî* (Henri Barakat)

The Virgin Wife / *al-Zawgah al-ʾadhrâ* (al-Sayed Bedeir)

With Time / *Maʾ al-ayyâm* (Ahmed Diaa Eddine)

A Woman on the Road / *Imraʾas fî-l-tarîq* (Ezz Eddine Zoulficar)

A Woman's Life / *Hayât imraʾah* (Zouheir Bekir)

Young People Today / *Chabâb al-yawm* (Mahmoud Zoulficar)

1959

Al-Atba al-Khadraa / *al-ʾAtbah al-khadrâʾ* (Fatine Abdel Wahab)

Al-Mabrouk / *Al-Mabrouk* (Hassan Reda)

Among the Ruins / *Bayn al-Atlâl* (Ezz Eddine Zoulficar)

Between Heaven and Earth / *Bayn al-samâʾ wa-l-ard* (Salah Abou Seif)

Beware of Love / *Ihtaris min al-houbb* (Hassan al-Saïfi)

A Burning Heart / *Qalb yahtariq* (Kamal al-Cheikh)

Charting Troubled Waters / al-Sâbihah fî-l-nâr (Mohamed Kamel Hassan)

Crime of Love / Garîmat houbb (Atef Salem)

The Curlew's Call / Dou'â' al-karawân (Henri Barakat)

The Dark-Haired Girl from the Sinaï / Samrâ' Sinâ' (Niazi Mostafa)

Each Beat of My Heart / Koull daqqah fî qalbî (Ahmed Diaa Eddine)

The Flowerseller / Bayyâ'at al-ward (Mahmoud Ismaïl)

For a Woman / Min agli imra'ah (Kamal al-Cheikh)

For Ever Yours / Houbb îla al-abad (Youssef Chahine)

For My Love / Min agl houbbî (Kamal al-Cheikh)

Forbidden Women / Nisâ mouharramât (Mahmoud Zoulficar)

The Ghost of Samara / 'Ifrît Samârah (Hassan Reda)

God Is Great / Allah akbar (Ibrahim al-Sayed)

The Guest House of Surprises / Loukândat al-moufâga'ât (Issa Karama)

Hada / Houda (Ramsès Naguib)

Hassan and Marika / Hasan wa Mârîkâ (Hassan al-Saïfi)

Hassan and Naima / Hasan wa Na'îmah (Henri Barakat)

Heart of Gold / Qalb min dhadhab (Mohamed Karim)

The Highway Robber / Qâtî tarîq (Hassan al-Saïfi)

I Am Free / Anâ hourrah (Salah Abou Seif)

I Am Innocent / Anâ barî'ah (Houssam Eddine Mostafa)

I Shall Not Return / Lan a'oud (Hassan Reda)

I Think of the Man Who Has Forgotten Me / Bafakkar fî-llî nâsînî (Houssam Eddine Mostafa)

Ishmael Yassine in Flying / Ismâ'îl Yâsîn fî-l-tayarân (Fatine Abdel Wahab)

Ishmael Yassine in the Secret Police / Ismâ'îl Yâsîn bolis sirrî (Fatine Abdel Wahab)

Kiss Me in the Shadows / Qabbilnî fî-l-zalîm (Mohamed Abdel Gawad)

The Last Love / al-Houbb al-akhîr (Mohamed Kamel Hassan)

The Last Person Told / Âkhir man ya'lam (Kamal Ateyya)

Leila, the Girl from the Beach / Layla bint al-châtî' (Hussein Fawzi)

The Light of Night / Nour al-layl (Raymond Nassour)

Love and Coaxing / Houbb wa dala' (Mahmoud Ismaïl)

Love in the Desert / Gharâm fî-l-sahrâ (Gianni Vernuccio and Léon Klimovski)

The Love Nest / 'Ichch al-gharâm (Helmi Rafla)

My Mother-in-Law Is an Angel / Hamâtî malâk (Issa Karama)

My Wife's Husband / 'Arîs mirâtî (Abbas Kamel)

The Mystery of the Magic Cap / Sirr tâqiyyat al-ikhfâ' (Niazi Mostafa)

Oum Ratiba / Oumm Ratîbah (al-Sayed Bedeir)

The Police Inspector / Moufattich al-mabâhith (Hussein Fawzi)

The Poor Millionnaire / al-Millionnaire al-faqîr (Hassan al-Saïfi)

The Prison of Virgins / Sig'n al-'adhârâ (Ibrahim Emara)

Rendezvous with the Unknown / Maw'id ma' al-mag'houl (Atef Salem)

Return to Life / 'Awdat al-hayât (Zouheir Bekir)

Scandal at Zamalek / Fadîhah fî-l-Zamâlik (Niazi Mostafa)

The Second Man / al-Ragoul al-thânî (Ezz Eddine Zoulficar)

She Lived for Love / 'Âchat li-l-houbb (al-Sayed Bedeir)

Story of a Love / Hikâyat houbb (Helmi Halim)

Struggle on the Nile / Sirâ' fî-l-Nîl (Atef Salem)

Sun without Twilight / Chams lâ taghîb (Hussein Helmi al-Mouhandès)

Take Pity on My Heart / Irham houbbî (Henri Barakat)

Trip on the Moon / Rihlah ilâ al-qamar (Hamada Abdel Wahab)

The Unknown Woman / al-Mar'ah al-mag'houlah (Mahmoud Zoulficar)

We the Students / Ihnâ al-talâmdhah (Atef Salem)

Young Girls' Dreams / Ahlâm al-banât (Youssef Maalouf)

1960

Abou Ahmed / Abou Ahmad (Hassan Reda)

Abou Al-Layl / Abou al-Layl (Houssam Eddine Mostafa)

The Adolescent Girls / al-Mourâhiqât (Ahmed Diaa Eddine)

And Love Returns / Wa ⁽âda al-houbb (Fatine Abdel Wahab)

Angel and Demon / Malâk wa chaytân (Kamal al-Cheikh)

Anguish of Love / Law²at al-houbb (Salah Abou Seif)

The Arms Trade / Souq al-silâh (Kamal Ateyya)

Bahiyya / Bahiyyah (Ramsès Naguib)

The Bridge of the Immortals / Guisr al-khâlidîn (Mahmoud Ismaïl)

Daily Bread / Louqmat al-²aych (Niazi Mostafa)

Dead among the Living / Bidâyah wa nihâyah (Salah Abou Seif)

The End of the Path / Nihâyat (Kamel Ateyya)

Farewell to Love / Wadâ²an yâ houbb (Houssam Eddine Mostafa)

The Genetic Tree / Chagarat al-²â²ilah (Chérif Wali)

The Giant / al-²imlâq (Mahmoud Zoulficar)

Giants of the Sea / ⁽Amâliqat al-bihâr (al-Sayed Bedeir)

The Gipsy / al-Ghagariyyah (al-Sayed Ziyada)

Girls and Summer / Banât wa-l-sayf (Ezz Eddine Zoulficar, Salah Abou Seif, and Fatine Abdel Wahab)

The Girls from Alexandria / Banât Bahrî (Hassan al-Saïfi)

Heart in the Night / qalb fî-l-zalâm (Adli Khalil)

A Heartless Man / Ragoul bilâ qalb (Seif Eddine Chawkat)

I Accuse / Innî attahim (Hassan al-Imam)

In Your Hands / Bein îdek (Youssef Chahine)

Ishmael Yassine in Prison / Ismâ²îl Yâsîn f-l-sig²n (Hassan-al-Saïfi)

Ladies' Hairdresser / Hallâq al-sayyidât (Fatine Abdel Wahab)

Love and Adoration / Houbb hattâ al-²ibâdah (Hassan al-Imam)

Love and Privations / Houbb wa hirmân (Ibrahim Emara)

Love at the Circus / Gharâm fî-l-sîrk (Hussein Fawzi)

Love, Love / Houbb fî houbb (Seif Eddine Chawkat)

The Lovers' Call / Nidâ al-²ouchchâq (Youssef Chahine)

Madam Sokkar / Soukkar hânim (al-Sayed Bedeir)

The Magic Lamp / al-Fânous al-sihrî (Fatine Abdel Wahab)

Meeting at Dusk / Liqâ² fî-l-ghouroub (Saad Arafa)

Melody of Happiness / Lahn al-sa²âdah (Helmi Rafla)

Men in the Storm / Rigâl fî-l-²âsifah (Houssam Eddine Mostafa)

Money and Women / Mâl wa nisâ² (Hassan al-Imam)

Moon of Honey and Gall / Chahr ⁽asal basal (Issa Karama)

My Beloved's Khoulkhal / Khoulkhâl habîbî (Hassan Reda)

My Fatherland and My Love / Watanî wa houbbî (Hussein Sedki)

My Love / Yâ habîbî (Hussein Fawzi)

My Mother and I / Anâ wa oummî (Abbas Kamel)

My Only Love / Houbbî al-wahîd (Kamal al-Chennawi)

The People from Down There / al-Nas illî taht (Kamel al-Telmessani)

Qaïs and Leila / Qays wa Layla (Ahmed Diaa Eddine)

River of Love / Nahr al-houbb (Ezz Eddine Zoulficar)

Rumour of Love / Ichâ²at houbb (Fatine Abdel Wahab)

The Sacred Link / al-Ribât al-mouqaddas (Mahmoud Zoulficar)

Sad Melody / al-Nagham al-hazîn (Hassan al-Saïfi)

The Seducer of Men / Sâ²idat al-rigâl (Hassan al-Imam)

Street Wife / Zawgah min al-châri² (Hassan al-Imam)

Stronger than Life / Aqwâ min al-hayât (Mohamed Kamal Hassan)

They Will Drive Me Mad / Hayganninounî (Fatine Abdel Wahab)

Three Heiresses / Thalâth warîthât (al-Sayed Bedeir)

Three Men and a Woman / Thalâthat rigâl wa Imraʾah (Helmi Halim)

Together for Always / Maʾan ilâ al-abad (Hassan Ramzi)

The Woman in Love / al-Âchiqah (al-Sayed Ziyada)

A Woman's Love / Gharâmiyyât imraʾah (Tolba Radwane)

A Woman's Secret / Sirr imraʾah (Atef Salem)

Women and Wolves / Nisâʾ wa dhiʾâb (Houssam Eddine Mostafa)

1961

Achour the Lionheart / ʿAchur qalb alasad (Hussein Fawzi)

Antar Ibn Chadad / ʿAntar bin chaddâd (Niazi Mostafa)

Aziza the Ambassadress / al-Safîrah ʿAzîzah (Tolba Radwane)

The Big Adolescent / al-Mourâhiq al-kabîr (Mahmoud Zoulficar)

Blood on the Nile / Dimâʾ ʿalâ al-Nil (Niazi Mostafa)

The Cat's Claw / Mikhlab al-qitt (Hussein Helmi al-Mouhandès)

Come Back Mummy / ʿOudî yâ oummî (Abdel Rahman Chérif)

The Cream of Girls / Sitt al-banât (Houssam Eddine Mostafa)

The Crook / al-Nassâb (Niazi Mostafa)

Dearest to My Heart / Aʾazz al-habâyib (Youssef Maalouf)

Don't Extinguish the Sun / Lâ toufiʾ al-chams (Salah Abou Seif)

Don't Think of Me Anymore / Lâ tadhkourînî (Mahmoud Zoulficar)

Elixir H 3 / H 3 (Abbas Kamel)

Fattouma / Fattoumah (Hassan al-Saïfi)

The Filtered Light / al-Dawʾ al-khâfit (Fatine Abdel Wahab)

The Guide / al-Tourgmân (Hassan al-Saïfi)

Half Virgin / Nisf ʿadhrâʾ (al-Sayed Bedeir)

The Hero's Path / Tarîq al-abtâl (Mahmoud Ismaïl)

Husband for Hire / Zawg li-l-lîgâr (Issa Karama)

Husbands and Summer / al-Azwâg wa-l-sayf (Issa Karama)

I Am Justice / Anâ al-ʾadâlah (Hussein Sedki)

I Shall Not Confess / Lan aʾtarif (Kamal al-Cheikh)

Letter to God / Risâlah ilâ Allah (Kamal Ateyya)

Life and Hope / Hayât wa amal (Zouheir Bekir)

Love and Suffering / Houbb wa ʿadhâb (Hassan al-Saïfi)

A Man in My Life / Ragoul fî hayâtî (Youssef Chahine)

A Man in Our Home / Fî baytinâ ragoul (Henri Barakat)

The Masters' Love / Gharâm al-asyâd (Ramsès Naguib)

The Mute Girl / al-Kharsâʾ (Hassan al-Imam)

My Daughters and I / Anâ wa banâtî (Hussein Helmi al-Mouhandès)

My Life Is the Cost of It / Hayâtii hiya al-thaman (Hassan al-Imam)

My Wife's Husband / Gouz mirâti (Niazi Mostafa)

No Understanding / Mâ fîch tafâhoum (Atef Salem)

O Islam / Wâ islâmâh (Andrew Marton)

One Day in My Life / Yawm min ʿoumrî (Atef Salem)

The Pupil / al-Timîdhah (Hassan al-Imam)

Rendezvous with the Past / Mawʾid maʾ al-mâdî (Mahmoud Zoulficar)

Seven Girls / al-Sabʾbanât (Atef Salem)

The Shore of Love / Châtiʾ al-houbb (Henri Barakat)

Storm of Love / ʿÂsifah min al-houbb (Hussein Helmi al-Mouhandès)

Struggle in the Mountain / Sirâʾ fî-l-gabal (Houssam Eddine Mostafa)

That's What Love Is / al-Houbb kidah (Mahmoud Zoulficar)

Tomorrow Will Be Another Day / Ghadan yawmoun âktar (Albert Naguib)

Under the City Sky / Tahta samâʾ al-madînah (Hussein Helmi al-Mouhandès)

Wahida / Wahîdah (Mohamed Kamel Hassan)

The Way of Tears / Tarîq al-doumouʾ (Helmi Halim)

Why Am I Living? / Limâdhâ aʾîch (Ibrahim Emara)

With the Memories / Maʾ al-dhikrayât (Saad Afara)

Without Return / Bilâ ʿawdah (Raymond Nassour)

Without Tears / Bilâ doumouʾ (Mahmoud Zoulficar)

Woman and Demon / Imra²ah wa chaytân (Seif Eddine Chawkat)

Zézette / Zézette (Sayed Issa)

1962

The Absent Man's Secret / Sirr al-ghâ²îb (Kamal Ateyya)

The Accursed Castle / al-Qasr al-mal²oun (Hassan Reda)

Advocating Slavery / al-Isti²bâd (Youssef Wahbi)

Almaz and Abdou Al-Hamouli / Almaz wa ʿAbdou al-Hâmoulî (Helmi Rafla)

The Association of Wife Killers / Gam²iyyat qatl al-zawgât (Hassan al-Saïfi)

The Battle of Tyrants / Sirâ² al-gabâbirah (Zouheir Bekir and Raymond Nassour)

Beware of Hawa / Âh min Hawwâ (Fatine Abdel Wahab)

Black Candles / al-Choumou² al-sawdâ² (Ezz Eddine Zoulficar)

Chains of Silk / Salsîl min harîr (Henri Barakat)

The Cunning Man / al-Ragoul al-tha²lab (Nagdi Hafez)

Day of Judgment / Yawm al-hisâb (Abdel Rahman Chérif)

Day without Tomorrow / Yawm bilâ ghad (Henri Barakat)

Days without Love / Ayyâm bilâ houbb (Houssam Eddine Mostafa)

Escaped from Hell / al-Liss wa-l-kilâb (Kamal al-Cheikh)

For Ever Faithful / Wafâ² ilâ al-abad (Ahmed Diaa Eddine)

Forget the World / Insâ al-douniâ (Elhami Hassan)

The Great Betrayal / al-Khiyânah al-²oudhmâ (Youssef Wahbi)

The Heroes' Struggle / Sirâ² al-abtâl (Tewfik Saleh)

Hot Nights / al-Layâlî al-dâfi²ah (Hassan Ramzi)

I Am the Fugitive / Anâ al-hârib (Niazi Mostafa)

I Love This Man / Hâdhâ al-ragoul ouhibbou (Houssein Helmi al-Mouhandès)

The King of Petrol / Malik al-Bitroul (Hassan al-Saïfi)

The Last Chance / Âkhir foursah (Niazi Mostafa)

Letter from an Unknown Woman / Risâlah min imra²ah mag²houlah (Salah Abou Seif)

Lost Youth / Hîrah wachabâb (Zouheir Bekir)

The Love Judge / Qâdî al-gharâm (Hassan al-Saïfi)

Martyr of the Divine Love / Chahîdat al-houbb al-ilâhî (Abbas Kamel)

The Miracle / al-Mou²guizah (Hassan al-Imam)

The Olive Branch / Ghousn al-zaytoun (al-Sayed Bedeir)

Pretty and Lying / Hilwah wa kaddâbah (Hussein Fawzi)

The Remains of a Virgin / Baqâyâ ʿadhrâ² (Houssam Eddine Mostafa)

Rendezvous in the Tower / Maw²id fî-l-bourg (Ezz Eddine Zoulficar)

Salwa in the Storm / Salwa fî mahabb al-rîh (al-Sayed Bedeir)

A Schoolgirl's Memoirs / Moudhakkarat tilmîdhad (Ahmed Diaa Eddine)

Sins / al-Khatâyâ (Hassan al-Imam)

Slaves of the Flesh / ʿAbîd al-gasud (Kamal Ateyya)

Struggle against the Angels / Sirâ² ma²al malâ²ikah (Hassan Tewfik)

Take Me with My Shame / Khoudhnî bi-ârî (al-Sayed Ziyada)

These Are All My Children / Koullouhoum awlâdî (Ahmed Diaa Eddine)

The Three Cavaliers / al-Foursân al-thalâthah (Fatine Abdel Wahab)

The Three Rogues / al-Achqiyâ al-thalâthah (Houssam Eddine Mostafa)

The Trap / al-Misyadah (Tolba Radwane)

The Universe of Girls / Douiniâ al-banât (Saad Arafa)

The Vindictive Man / al-Haqîd (Raymond Nassour)

Wife No. 13 / al-Zawgah raqam talata²ch (Fatine Abdel Wahab)

The Winter Holidays / Agâzat nisf al-sanah (Ali Reda)

Without a Rendezvous / Min gheir mî²âd (Ahmed Diaa Eddine)

Woman in Torment / Imra²ah fî dawwâmah (Mahmoud Zoulficar)

1963

The Alley of Miracles / Zouqâq al-Midaqq (Hassan al-Imam)

The Amorous Bedouin / al-Badawiyyah al-²âchiqah (Niazi Mostafa)

A Bachelor's Life / Hayât ᶜâzib (Nagdi Hafez)

The Beauty and the Students / al-Hasnâ wa-l-talabah (Ahmed Diaa Eddine)

The Bride's Mother / Oumm al-arousah (Atef Salem)

Cairo by Night / al-Qâhirah fii-l-layl (Mohamed Salem)

Chafika the Copt / Charfîqah al-qibtiyya (Hassan al-Imam)

*Dark Glasses / al-Nadhdhârah al-sawdâ*ᵓ (Houssam Eddine Mostafa)

The Fiancé Will Arrive Tomorrow / al-Arîs yasil ghadam (Niazi Mostafa)

The Fiancée from the Nile / ᶜArous al-Nîl (Fatine Abdel Wahab)

Fire in My Heart / Nâr fî sadrî (Hassan Reda)

*Forbidden Story / Qissah mamnou*ᵓ*ah* (Tolba Radwane)

*Forgive Me My Sin / Ighfir lî khatî*ᵓ*atî* (Al-Sayed Ziyada)

Former Days / Ayyâm zamân (Youssef Wahbi)

The Fugitive Woman's Secret / Siaa al-hâribah (Houssam Eddine Mostafa)

*Gentle Hands / al-Aydî al-nâ*ᵓ*imah* (Mahmoud Zoulficar)

Heroes to the Very End / Batal li-l-nahâyah (Houssam Eddine Mostafa)

The Hilarious Crime / al-Garîmah al-dâhikah (Nagdi Hafez)

His Majesty / Sâhib al-galâlah (Fatine Abdel Wahab)

A Husband for My Sister / ᶜArîs li-ouktî (Ahmed Diaa Eddine)

The Last Night / al-Laylah al-akhîrah (Kamal al-Cheikh)

The Little Demon / al-Chaytân al saghîr (Kamal al-Cheikh)

The Little Magician / al-Sâhirah al-sagghîrah (Niazi Mostafa)

*The Madmen Are Happy / al-Magânîn fî na*ᵓ*îm* (Hassan al-Saïfi)

A Man in the Shadows / Ragoul fî-l-zalâm (Hassan Reda)

Marriage in Danger / Gawâz fî khatar (Issa Karama)

*The Naked Truth / al-Haqîqah al-*ᵓ*âriyah* (Atef Salem)

*The Newspaper Vendor / Bayyâ*ᵓ*at al-garâyid* (Hassan al-Imam)

No Time for Love / Lâ waqt li-l-houbb (Salah Abou Seif)

On the Banks of the Nile / ᶜAlâ difâf al-Nîl (Ko Nakahira)

The Open Door / al-Bâb al-maftouh (henri Barakat)

The Path of the Demon / Tarîq al-chaytân (Kamal Ateyya)

The Pickpocket / al-Nachchâl (Mahmoud Farid)

The Price of Love / Thaman al-houbb (Mahmoud Zoulficar)

*The Princess of the Arabs / Amîrat al-*ᵓ*arab* (Niazi Mostafa)

Prisoner of the Night / Saguîn al-layl (Mahmoud Farid)

*Rabea Al-Adawiyya / Rabi*ᵓ*ah al-*ᵓ*Adawiyyah* (Niazi Mostafa)

The Rebel / al-Moutamarridah (Mahmoud Zoulficar)

Saladin / al-Nâsir Salah Eddine (Youssef Chahine)

Supreme Happiness / Mountahâ al-farah (Mohamed Salem)

*Thoughtless Youth / Chabâb tâ*ᵓ*ich* (al-Sayed Ziyada)

Turbulent Young Girls / Chaqâwat banât (Houssam Eddine Mostafa)

Unforgettable Love / Houbb lâ ansâh (Saad Arafa)

Wife for a Day / Zawgah li tawm yâhid (al-Sayed Ziyada)

Without Hope / Min gheir amal (Hassan Reda)

*A Woman on the Margins / Imra*ᵓ*ah ᶜalâ al-hâmich* (Hassan al-Imam)

The Years of Love / Sanawât al-houbb (Mahmoud Zoulficar)

*Zizi's Family / ᶜÂ*ᵓ*ilat Zizi* (Fatine Abdel Wahab)
1964
An Abnormal Girl / Fatât châdhdhah (Ahmed Diaa Eddine)

Adham al-Charkawi / Adham al-Charqâwi (Houssam Eddine Mostafa)

*Am I Mad? / Hal âna mag*ᵓ*nounah?* (Ahmed Diaa Eddine)

The Arabian Nights / Alf laylah wa laylah (Hassan al-Imam)

*The Black Suitcase / al-Haqîbah al-sawdâ*ᵓ (Hassan al-Saïfi)

*Confessions of a Husband / I*ᵓ*tirâfât zawg* (Fatine Abdel Wahab)

The Cost of Liberty / Thaman al-hourriyya (Nour al-Demerdache)

The Dead End of the Two Palaces / bayn al-qasrayn (Hassan al-Imam)

Escaped from Life / Hârib min al-hayât (Atef Salem)

The First Love / Awwal houbb (Abdel Rahman Chérif)

The Flames / al-Lahab (Abdel Rahman Chérif)

For Hanafi / Min agl Hanifî (Hassan al-Saïfi)

The Fugitive from Marriage / Hârib min al-zawâg (Hassan al-Saïfi)

The Game of Love and Marriage / Lou⁾bat al-houbb-wa-l-zawâg (Niazi Mostafa)

The Giant / al-Mârid (Sayed Issa)

The Girl from the District / Bint al-hittah (Hassan al-Saïfi)

The Girl from the Port / Fatât al-mînâ (Houssam Eddine Mostafa)

The Girls' Revolt / Yhawrat al-banât (Kamal Ateyya)

The Great Adventure / al-Moughâmarah al-koubrâ (Mahmoud Farid)

The Honorable Family / al-⁾Â⁾ilah al-kârimah (Fatine Abdel Wahab)

Husband on Holiday / Zawg fî agâzar (Mohamed Abdel Gawad)

If I Were a Man / Law kountou ragoulan (Ahmed Diaa Eddine)

The Last Message / al-Risâlah al-akhîraah (Mohamed Kamel Hassan)

Leave Me with My Tears / Da⁾nî wal-l-doumou⁾ (Ahmed Diaa Eddine)

Life Is Short / al-⁾Oumr ayyâm (Youssef Issa)

The Lost Son / al-Ibn al-mafqoud (Mohamed Kamel Hassan)

Love, Joy and Youth / Houbb wa-marah wa-chabîb (Nagdi Hafez)

Me, Him and Her / Anâ wa houwa wa hiya (Fatine Abdel Wahab)

The Midnight Story / Hikâyat nouss al-leil (Issa Karama)

No Way Out / al-Tarîq (Houssam Eddine Mostafa)

The Prince of Tricks / Amîr al-dahâ⁾ (Henri Barakat)

The Prophet's Migration to Medina / Higrat al-rasoul (Ibrahim Emara)

The Pupils' Notes / Nimar al-talâmidhah (Issa Karama)

Reckless Youth / Âkhir chaqâwah (Issa Karama)

Reserved for Men / Li-l-rigâl faqat (Mahmoud Zoulficar)

The River of Life / Nahr al-hayât (Hassan Reda)

The Spy / al-Gâsous (Niazi Mostafa)

The Story of a Marriage / Hikâyat zawâg (Hassan al-Saïfi)

The Three Bachelors / al-⁾Ouzzâb al-thalâthan (Mahmoud Farid)

The Three Devils / al-Chaytâtîn al-thalâthah (Houssam Eddine Mostafa)

The Two Adolescent Girls / al-Mourâhigân (Seif Eddine Chawkat)

We Want a Wife Straightaway / Matloup zawgah fawran (Mahmoud Farid)

The Whole Town Is Talking about It / Hadîth al-madînah (Kamal Ateyya)

With the People / Ma⁾ al-nâs (Kamal Ateyya)

1965

The Agitator / al-Mouchâghîb (Niazi Mostafa)

The Artistic Director / al-Moudîr al-fannî (Fatine Abdel Wahab)

Bitter Grape / al⁾Inab al-mourr (Farouk Agrama)

Cleopatra's Son / Ibn Cléobâtra (Fernandino Baldi)

The Confession / al-I⁾tirâf (Saad Arafa)

The Dawn of a New Day / Fagr yawm gadîd (Youssef Chahine)

Dearer than My Life / Aghlâ min hayâtî (Mahmoud Zoulficar)

Driven from Paradise / Tarîd al-Fardous (Fatine Abdel Wahab)

El-Alamain / al-⁾Alamayn (Abdel Alim Khattab)

Eternal Love / al-Houbb al-khâlid (Zouheir Bekir)

Free from the Days / Hârib min al-ayyâm (Houssam Eddine Mostafa)

Girls and Boys / Sibyân wa banât (Hussein Helmi al-Mouhandès)

The Good Guys of Our Street / Gid⁾ân haritnâ (Abdel Rahman Cherif)

The Idle / Tanabilat al-soultân (Kamal al-Chennawi)

The Impossible / al-Moustahîl (Hussein Kamal)

In the Name of Love / Bism al-houbb (al-Sayed Ziyada)

The Infidel / al-Khâ⁾inah (Kamal al-Cheikh)

Kill Me Please / Iqtinî mn fadlak (Hassan al-Saïfi)

Looking for Love / al-Bâhithah ᶜan al-houbb (Ahmed Diaa Eddine)

Lost Days / Ayyâm dâᵓiᵓah (Bahaa Eddine Charaf)

Love for All / Houbb li-l-gamî (Abdel Rahman Chérif)

The Mamelouks / al-Mamâlîk (Atef Salem)

The Memories of Our Schoolboy Life / Dhikrayât al-talmadhah (Ali Beheiri)

Men Never Marry Beautiful Women / al-Rigâl lâ yatazawwagoun al-gamîliat (Ahmed Farouk)

The Mountain / al-Gabal (Khalil Chawki)

The Nun / al-Râhibah (Hassan al-Imam)

Personal Professor / Moudarris khousousî (Ahmed Diaa Eddine)

The Pledge / al-Wadîᵓah (Hussein Helmi al-Mouhandès)

The Reason and Money / al-ᵓAql wa-l-mâl (Abbas Kamel)

The Reward / al-Gazâ (Abdel Rahman al-Khamissi)

The Sin / al-Harâm (Henri Barakat)

The Storm Has Eased / Soukoun al-ᵓâsifah (Ahmed Diaa Eddine)

Story of a Life / Hikâyat alᵓoumr koullouh (Helmi Halim)

The Three Adventurers / al-Moughâmiroun al-thalâthah (Houssam Eddine Mostafa)

The Three Love Her / al-Thalâthah youhibbou-nahâ (Mahmoud Zoulficar)

The Three Wise Men / al-ᵓOuqalâᵓ al-thalâthah (Mahmoud Farid)

The Troublemakers / al-Mouchâghiboun (Mahmoud Farid)

The Two Brothers / al-Chaqîqân (Hassan al-Saïfi)

The Ultimate Madness / Âkhir guinân (Issa Karama)

The Unknown Man / al-Ragoul al-magᵓhoul (Moamned Abdel Gawad)

A Widow and Three Daughters / Armalah wa thatlâth banât (Galal al-Charkawi)

The Woman and Men / Hiya wa-l-rigâl (Hassan al-Imam)

1966

Adam's Apple / Touffâhat Adam (Fatine Abdel Wahab)

Al-Sakkin Street / Hârat al-saqâyîn (Al-Sayed Ziyada)

The Bachelor Husband / al-Zawg al-ᵓâzib (Hassan al-Saïfi)

Cairo 30 / al-Qâhirah talâtîn (Salah Abou Seif)

Compulsory Holiday / Agâzah bi-lᵓâfiyah (Nagdi Hafez)

Demons of the Night / Chayâtîn al-layl (Niazi Mostafa)

The Desert Horseman / Fâris al-sahrâᵓ (Oswaldo Cheferani)

Farès Bani Hamdan / Fâris banî Hamdân (Niazi Mostafa)

Farewell to the Night / Wadâᵓan ayyouhâ al-layl (Hassan Reda)

His Excellency the Ambassador / Ganâb al-safîr (Niazi Mostafa)

The Idiot / al-ᵓAbît (al-Sayed Bedeir)

Khan al-Khalili / Khân al-Khalîlî (Atef Salem)

Kounouz / Kounouz (Niazi Mostafa)

The Last Born / Âkhir al-ᵓounqoud (Zouheir Bekir)

Life Is Beautiful / al-Hayât houlwah (Helmi Halim)

The Little Adolescent Girl / al-Mourâhiqah al-saghîrah (Mahmoud Zoulficar)

Love in August / Gharâm fî Aghoustous (Hassan al-Saïfi)

Lovers' Tears / Mabkâ al-ᵓouchâq (Hassan al-Saïfi)

A Man and Two Women / Ragoul waimraᵓatân (Nagdi Hafez)

The Man and Women / Houwa wa-l-nisâᵓ (Hassan al-Imam)

My Love in Cairo / Houbbî fî-l-Qâhirah (Adel Sadek)

My Wife Is Managing Director / Mirâtî moudîr ᶜâmm (Fatine Abdel Wahab)

Reserved for Women / Li-l-nisâ faqat (Ali Beheiri)

The Revolution in Yemen / Thawrat al-Yaman (Atef Salem)

Sayyed Darwish / Sayyed Darwich (Ahmed Badrakhan)

Something in My Life / Chayᵓ fî hayâti (Henri Barakat)

The Sphinx's Smile / Ibtisâmat Abou al-Hol (Doccio Tissari)

Take Me Away with You / Khoudnî maʾâk (Abbas Kamel)

The Terrible Children / Chaqâwat riggâlah (Houssam Eddine Mostafa)

Thirty Days in Prison / Thalathoun yawm fî-l-sigʾn (Niazi Mostafa)

The Three Friends / al-Asdiqâ al-thalâthah (Ahmed Diaa Eddine)

Three Thieves / Thalâthat lousous (Fatine Abdel Wahab, Hassan al-Imam, and Kamal al-Cheikh)

Too Young to Love / Saghîrah ʿalâ al-houbb (Niazi Mostafa)

The Victor of Atlantis / Qâhir al-Atlants (Alfonso Breccia)

The Wedding Night / Laylat al-zifâf (Henri Barakat)

Who Do I Love? / Man ouhibb? (Magda al-Sabahi)

A Widow Is Requested / Matloub armalah (Issa Karama)

The Woman's Enemy / ʿAdouww al-marʾah (Mahmoud Zoulficar)

A Woman from Paris / Zawgah min Paris (Atef Salem)

1967

The Beggars' Strike / Idrâb al-chahhâtiin (Hassan al-Imam)

Crime in a Quiet District / Garîmah fî-l-hayy al-hâdiʾ (Houssam Eddine Mostafa)

The Dancer from Soumbat / Ghâziyyah min soumbât (al-Sayed Ziyada)

Driven from Paradise / al-Khouroug min al-gannah (Mahmoud Zoulficar)

Girls Boarding School / Bayt al-Tâlibât (Ahmed Diaa Eddine)

The Girls' Camp / Mouʾaskar al-banât (Khalil Chawki)

Hamza's Suitcase / Chantat Hamzah (Hassan al-Saïfi)

Holiday of Love / Agâzat gharâm (Mahmoud Zoulficar)

The Intruder / al-Dakhîl (Nour al-Demerdache)

The Last Kiss / al-Qoublah al-akhîrah (Mahmoud Zoulficar)

The Long Nights / al-Layâlî al-tawîlah (Ahmed Diaa Eddine)

Love at Karnak / Gharâm fî-l-Karnak (Ali Reda)

A Madman's Loves / Gharâmiyyât magʾnoun (Zouheir Bekir)

The Most Dangerous Man in the World / Akhtar ragoul fî-l-ʾâlam (Niazi Mostafa)

My Wife's Honour / Karâmat zawgatî (Fatine Abdel Wahab)

Noura / Nourâ (Mahmoud Zoulficar)

The Other Half / al-Nisf al-âkhar (Ahmed Badrakhan)

The Palace of Desires / Qasr al-Chawq (Hassan al-Imam)

The Public Idol / Maʾboudat al-gamâhîr (Helmi Rafla)

The Rains Have Dried Up / Gaffat al-amtâr (Sayed Issa),

The Saboteurs / al-Moukharriboun (Kamal al-Cheikh)

The Second Meeting / al-Liqâʾ al-thânî (Hassan al-Saïfi)

The Second Suitor / ul-ʾAris al-thânî (Hassan al-Saïfi)

The Second Wife / al-Zawgah al thâniyah (Salah Abou Seif)

Shame / al-ʾAyb (Galal al-Charkawi)

The Shores of Gaiety / Châti ul-marah (Houssam Eddine Mostafa)

The Students' Flat / Chiqqat al-talabah (Tolba Radwane)

Summer Holiday / Agâzat sayf (Saad Arafa)

That Man Will Drive Me Mad / al-Râguil dah hayganninni (Issa Karama)

Thrushes and Autumn / al-Simân wa-l-kharîf (Houssam Eddine Mostafa)

A Turbulent Girl / Bint chaqiyyah (Houssam Eddine Mostafa)

Very Mad Youth / Chabâb magʾnoun guiddan (Niazi Mostafa)

When We Love / ʿIndamâ nouhibb (Fatine Abdel Wahab)

1968

Adaweyya / ʿAdawiyyah (Kamal Salah Eddine)

Afrah / Afrâh (Ahmed Badrakhan)

Amorous Pursuit / Moutâradah gharmâmiyyah (Nagdi Hafez)

The Beauty of Love / Rawʾat al-houbb (Mahmoud Zoulficar)

The Bravest Man in the World / Achgaʾ ragoul fî-l-âlam (Hassan al-Saïfi)

Chanabo Trapped / Chanabo fî-l-misyadah (Houssam Eddine Mostafa)

The Circus / al-Sîrk (Atef Salem)

A Criminal Put to the Test / Mougrim taht al-ikhtibâr (Abdel Meneim Choukri)

Daddy Wants It Like This / Bâbâ ᶜâyiz kidah (Niazi Mostafa)

Days of Love / Ayyâm al-houbb (Helmi Halim)

Eve and the Gorilla / Hawwâ᾽ wa-l-qird (Niazi Mostafa)

Eve on the Road / Hawwâ᾽ ᶜalâ al-tarîq (Hussein Helmi al-Mouhandès)

The False Millionaire / al-Millionnaire al-mouzayyaf (Hassan al-Saïfi)

The Glass Sphinx / Abou al-Hol al-Zougâguî (Luigi Pescatino)

How to Rob a Millionaire? / Kayfa tasriq million-naire (Nagdi Hafez)

How to Steal an Atomic Bomb / Kayfa tasrouq qounboulah dharriyyah (André Novolcci)

I'm the Doctor / Anâ al-doktor (Abbas Kamel)

Land of Hypocrites / Ard al-nifâq (Fatine Abdel Wahab)

Lost Souls / Noufous hâ᾽irah (Ahmed Mazhar)

Love and Betrayal / Houbb wa khiyânah (al-Sayed Bedeir)

Lovers' Island / Gazîrat al-᾽ouchchâq (Hassan Reda)

Madam Headmaster / al-Sitt al-nâzirah (Ahmed Diaa Eddine)

The Man Who Had Lost His Shadow / al-Ragoul alladhî faqada zillahou (Kamal al-Cheikh)

Modern Marriage / al-Zawâg ᶜalâ al-tarîqah al-hadîthah (Salah Korayyem)

My Wife Is Completely Mad / Mirâtî mag᾽nounah mag᾽nounah (Helmi Halim)

My Wife's Ghost / ᶜIfrît mirâtî (Fatine Abdel Wahab)

One of Those Girls / Bint min al-banât (Hassan al-Imam)

Oum Hatchem's Lantern / Qindîl Oumm Hâchim (Kamal Ateyya)

The Postman / al-Bostaguî (Hussein Kamal)

A Pretty, Boisterous Girl / Hilwah wa chaqiyyah (Issa Karama)

Quiet Honeymoon / Chahr ᶜasal bidoun iz᾽âg (Abdel Meneim Choukri)

The Rebels / al-Moutamarridoun (Tewfik Saleh)

The Schoolgirl and the Professor / al-Tilmîdhah wa-l-oustâdh (Ahmed Diaa Eddine)

Six Girls and One Suitor / Sitt banât wa ᶜarîs (al-Sayed Ziyada)

Son of the District / Ibn al-hittah (Hassan al-Saïfi)

The Story of Three Girls / Hikâyat thalâth banât (Mahmoud Zoulficar)

The Three Prisoners / al-Masâguîn al-thlâthah (Houssam Edine Mostafa)

Three Stories / Thalâth qisas (Ibrahim al-Sahn, Hassan Reda, and Mohamed Nabih)

Trial 68 / al-Qadiyyah 68 (Salah Abou Seif)

A Very Ridiculous World / ᶜÂlam moudhik guid-dan (Houssam Eddine Mostafa)

1969

Agent 77 / al-᾽Amîl sab᾽ah wa sab᾽în (Niazi Mostafa)

Al-Ataba Gazaz / al-᾽Atabah gazâz (Niazi Mostafa)

Al-Sayyed Al-Bolti / al-Sayyed al-Boltî (Tewfik Saleh)

Battle of Professionals / Sirâ᾽ al-mouhtarifîn (Hassan al-Saïfi)

Beautiful Aziza / al-Hilwah ᶜAzîzah (Hassan al-Imam)

The Demon / al-Chaytân (Mohamed Salmane)

Diary of a Deputy Country Prosecutor / Yawmiy-yât nâ᾽ib fî-l-aryâf (Tewfik Saleh)

Eve's Lies / Akâdhîb Hawwâ (Fatine Abdel Wahab)

For a Handful of Children / Min aglhifnât awlâd (Ibrahim Emara)

The Gates of the Night / Abwâb al-layl (Hassan Reda)

Gentlemen Burglars / Lousous lâkin zourafî᾽ (Ibrahim Lotfi)

The Girl from the Music Hall / Fatât al-isti᾽râd (Mahmoud Zoulficar)

Girls' Secrets / Asrâr al-banât (Mahmoud Zoulficar)

Half-an-Hour of Marriage / Nouss sa᾽at zawâg (Fatine Abdel Wahab)

Hello My Dear Wife / Sabâh al-khatr yâ zawgatî al-᾽azîzah (Abdel Meneim Choukri)

How to Get Rid of Your Wife / Kayfa tatakhallas min zawgatik (Abdel Meneim Choukri)

Just One Day's Honeymoon / Yawm wâhid ᶜasal (Ahmed Fouad)

Just One Night / Laylah wâhidah (Saad Arafa)

A Little Suffering / Chay² min al-²adhâb (Salah Abou Seif)

Love in 1970 / al-Houbb sanat as²în (Mahmoud Zoulficar)

Miramar / Miramar (Kamal al-Cheikh)

Mummy's Secretary / Secrétaire mâmâ (Hassan al-Saïfi)

My Father Is Perched in the Tree / Abî fawq al-chagarah (Hussein Kamal)

My Wife, My Mistress and I / Anâ wa mirâtî wa-l-gaww (Abdel Meneim Choukri)

Nadia / Nadia (Ahmed Badrakhan)

People from the Interior / al-Nâs illî gouwwah (Galal al-Charkawi)

Pickpocket in Spite of Himself / Nachchâl raghmâ anfih (Hassan al-Saïfi)

Reserved for Husbands / Li-l-moutazawwiguîn faqat (Ismaïl al-Qadi)

Respectable Families / ²Â²ilât moutaramah (Abdel Rahman al-Khamissi)

Seven Days in Paradise / Sab²ayyâm fî-l-gannah (Fatine Abdel Wahab)

Son of Satan / Ibn al-chaytân (Houssam Eddine Mostafa)

A Story from Home / Hikâyah min baladinâ (Helmi Halim)

The Street of Roundabouts / Châri² al-mahâhî (Abdel Meneim Choukri)

The Terror / al-Rou²b (Mahmoud Farid)

The Thief / al-Harâmî (Nagdi Hafez)

The Three Faces of Love / Thalâth wougouh li-l-houbb (Medhat Bekir, Nagui Riad, and Mamdouh Choukri)

The Three Good Guys / al-Choug²ân al-thalâthah (Houssam Eddine Mostafa)

Three Women / Thalâth nisâ² (Mahmoud Zoulficar, Salah Abou Seif, and Henri Barakat)

A Trace of Fear / Chay² min al-khawf (Hussein Kamal)

A Very Jealous Wife / Zawgah ghayourah guiddan (Helmi Rafla)

The Well of Privation / Bi²r al-hirmân (Kamal al-Cheikh)

Wife without a Man / Zawgah bilâ ragoul (Abdel Rahman Chérif)

The Woman and the Demons / Hiya wa-l-chayâtîn (Houssam Eddine Mostafa)

Young Girls' Frivolity / Dala² al-banât (Hassan al-Saïfi)

1970

Adolescent Girls' Love / Houbb al-mourâhiqât (Mahmoud Zouficar)

Ayn al-hayat / ²Ayn al-hayât (Ibrahim al-Chakankiri)

Dalal the Egyptian Woman / Dalâl al-misriyyah (Hassan al-Imam)

The Devils' End / Nihâyat al-chayâtîn (Houssam Eddine Mostafa)

Dusk and Dawn / Ghouroub wa chourouq (Kamal al-Cheikh)

The Earth / al-Ard (Youssef Chahine)

Evasion / Houroub (Hassan Reda)

The Fire of Desire / Nâr al-chawq (Mohamed Salem)

Flowers and Thorns / Ward wa chuwk (Kamal Salah Eddine)

The Fox and the Chameleon / al-Tha²lab wa-l-harbâ² (Houssam Eddine Mostafa)

Furnished Flat / Chiqqah mafrouchah (Hassan al-Imam)

Honeymoon Trip / Rihlat chahr ²usal (Zouheir Bekir)

I Love You My Beauty / Bahibbik yâ hiulwah (Abdel Meneim Choukri)

The Illusions of Love / Awhâm al-houbb (Mamdouh Choukri)

It Was the Good Time / Kânat ayyâm (Helmi Halim)

It's You Who Killed My Daddy / Inta illî qatalt bâbâyâ (Niazi Mostafa)

The Joyous Troupe / Firqat almarah (Fatine Abdel Wahab)

The Killer of Women / Saffâh al-nisâ² (Niazi Mostafa)

Lost Love / al-Houbb al-dâ²i² (Henri Barakat)

Love and Its Cost / al-Houbb wal-thhaman (Abdel Rahman al-Khamissi)

The Market in Women / Souq al-hârim (Youssef Marzouk)

The Mirage / al-Sarâb (Anwar al-Chennawi)

The Mirror / al-Mirâyah (Ahmed Diaa Eddine)

The Most Difficult Marriage / As²ab gawâz (Mohamed Nabih)

My Husband's Wife / Imra²at zawguî (Mahmoud Zoulficar)

My Life / Hayâti (Fatine Abdel Wahab)

My Wife, the Secretary and Me / Anâ wa zawgatî wa-l-secrétaira (Mahmoud Zoulficar)

No . . . No . . . My Love / Lâ . . . lâ . . . yâ habîbî (Ahmed Diaa Eddine)

One Wife for Five Men / Zawgah li-khamsat riggâlah (Seif Eddine Chawkat)

The Pickpocket / Sâriq al-mihfazat (Zouheir Bekir)

A Quarter of a Dozen Bad People / Rib² dasta achrâr (Nagdi Hafez)

Reda Bond / Ridâ Bond (Nagdi Hafez)

Struggle against Death / Sirâ² ma² al-mawt (Ibrahim Emara)

The Suitor of the Minister's Daughter / ᶜArîs bint al-wâzir (Niazi Mostafa)

The Terrible Hours / al-Sâ²ât al-rahîbah (Abdel-Hamid al-Chazli)

The Thief Who Stole the Lottery Ticket / Harâmîal-waraqah (Ali Reda)

Thieves' Rendezvous / Lousous ᶜalâ Maw²id (Houssam Eddine Mostafa)

Things That Are Not for Sale / Achiyâ² la touchtarâ (Ahmed Diaa Eddine)

The Three Liars / al-Kaddâbîn al-thalâthah (Mounir al-Touni)

The Three Madmen / al-Magânîn al-thalâthah (Hassan al-Saïfi)

The Trickster / al-Ghachchâch (Abdel Rahman Chérif)

We Are Not Angels / Lasnâ malâ²ikah (Mahmoud Farid)

We Don't Plant Thorns / Nahnou lâ nazra² al-chawk (Hussein Kamal)

The Wicked / al-Achrâr (Houssam Eddine Mostafa)

Women Who Flee Love / Hâribât min al-houbb (Adli Khalil)

The Yellow Valley / al-Wâdi al-asfar (Mamdouh Choukri)

Youthful Adventure / Moughâmarat Chabâb (Issa Karama)

1971

Adam and Women / Adam wa-l-nisâ² (al-Sayed Bedeir)

And Then the Sun Rises / Thoumma touchriqou al-chams (Ahmed Diaa Eddine)

The Beauty and the Thief / al-Hasnâ wa-l-liss (Nagdi Hafez)

The Beauty from the Airport / Hasnâ al-matâr (al-Sayed Bedeir)

A Boy, a Girl and the Devil / Walad wa bint wachaytân (Hassan Youssef)

The Choice / al-Ikhtiyâr (Youssef Chahine)

Crime of Honour / Hâdithat charaf (Chafik Chamiyya)

Dangerous Life / Hayât khatirah (Ahmed Fouad)

The Dawn of Islam / Fagr al-Islâm (Salah Abou Seif)

The Deer in the Night / Sab² al-layl (Hassan al-Saïfi)

The Devil's Gang / ᶜIsâbat al-chattân (Houssam Eddine Mostafa)

Discussions on the Nile / Thartharah fawq al-Nîl (Hussein Kamal)

The Elegant, the Noble and the Greedy / al-Zarîf wa-l-charhm wa-l-tammâ² (Nour al-Dermerdache)

The Everyday Toy / Lou²bat koull yawm (Khalil Chawki)

The Fine Thread / al-Khayt al-rafî (Henri Barakat)

5 Love Street / Khamsah chârî²al-habâyib (al-Sayed Bedeir)

Forbidden Love / al-Houbb al-Mouharram (Hassan al-Imam)

Girls at University / Banât fîl-gâmi²ah (Atef Salem)

Homes Have Their Secrets / al-Bouyout asrâr (Al-Sayedd Ziyada)

Innocent at the Gallows / Barî fî-l-machnaqah (Mounir al-Touni)

The Killers / al-Qatalah (Achraf Fahmi)

Love and Money / al-Houb wa-l-foulous (Hassan al-Imam)

Love on an Agricultural Road / Gharâm fî-l-tarîq al-zieâ²î (Abdel Meneim Choukri)

Lovers of Life / ᶜOuchchâq al-hayât (Helmi Halim)

Men Trapped / Rigâl fî-l-misyadah (Mahmoud Farid)

Miss Manal's Diary / Moudhakkarât al-ânisar Manâl (Abbas Kamel)

Mummy's Suitor / Khatîb mâmâ (Fatine Abdel Wahab

Music . . . Love and Espionage / Mousîqâ . . . houbb . . . wa Gâsousiyyah (Nour al-Dermerdache)

My Dearest Daughter / Ibnatî al-ʾazîzah (Helmi Rafla)

My Pretty Schoolteacher / Moudrarrisatî al-hasnâ (Ibrahim Emara)

My Sister / Oukhtî (Henri Barakat)

My Wife and the Dog / Zawgâtî wa-l-kalb (Saïd Marzouk)

One in a Million / Wâhiid fî-l-million (Achraf Fahmi)

The Pardon / al-Ghoufrân (Abdel Rahman Chérif)

A Pleasant Trip / Rihla ladhîdhah (Fatine Abdel Wahab)

The Pleasure and the Suffering / al-Moutʾah wa-l-ʾadhâb (Niazi Mostafa)

The Queen of the Night / Mlikat al-layl (Hassan Ramzi)

Rendezvous with the Beloved / Mawʾid maʾ al-habîb (Helmi Rafla)

Some People Have Two Lives / al-Baʾd yaʾîch marratayn (Kamal Atteya)

Something in My Heart / Chayʾ fî sadrî (Kamal al-Cheikh)

Tender Gesture / Lamsat hanân (Helmi Rafla)

We Men Are Good / Nuhnou al-rigâl tayyiboun (Ibrahim Lotfi)

Without Pity / Bilâ rahmah (Niazi Mostafa)

A Woman and a Man / Imraʾah wa ragoul (Houssam Eddine Mostafa)

A Woman's Confessions / Iʾtirâfât imraʾah (Saad Arafa)

Young People in the Storm / Chabâb fi ʿâsifah (Adel Sadek)

1972

Al-Chaymaa / al-Chaymâʾ (Houssam Eddine Mostafa)

Amacha in the Jungle / ʿAmâchah fî-l-adghâl (Mohamed Salem)

Anger / al-Ghadab (Anwar al-Chennawi)

Badia's Daughter / Bint Badîah (Hassan al-Imam)

The Barrier / al-Hâguiz (Mohamed Radi)

Beware of Zouzou / Khallî bâlak min Zouzou (Hassan al-Imam)

Count Down / Saʾat al-sifr (Hussein Helmi al-Mouhandès)

The Demons of the Sea / Chayâtîn al-bahr (Houssam Eddine Mostafa)

The Devil and Autumn / al-Chaytân wa-l-kharîf (Anwar al-Chennawi)

The Egocentric / ʿÂchiqat nafsihâ (Mounir al-Touni)

The Empire of M / Ambratouriyyat mîm (Hussein Kamal)

Fear / al-Khawf (Saïd Marzouk)

Featureless Men / Rigâl bilâ malâmin (Mahmoud Zoulficar)

Feelings and Body / al-Âtifah wa-l-gasad (Hassan Ramzi)

The Folly of Adolescent Girls / Gounoun al-mourâhiqât (Taysir Abboud)

Forbidden Images / Souwar mamnouʾah (Mohamed Abdel Aziz, Achraf Fahmi, and Madkour Sabet)

From Home to School / Min al-bayt li-l-madrasa (Ahmed Diaa Eddine)

The Haunt of the Wretched / Wakr al-achrâ (Hassan al-Saïfi)

House of Sand / Bayt min al-rimâl (Saad Arafa)

Housing Crisis / Azmat sakun (Helmi Rafla)

Imtithal / Imtithâl (Hassan al-Imam)

The Kidnappers / al-Khattâfin (Houssam Eddine Mostafa)

The Kings of Evil / Moulouk al-charr (Houssam Eddine Mostafa)

The Lights / al-Adwâʾ (Hussein Helmi al-Mouhandès)

The Lights of the City / Adwâ al-madînah (Fatine Abdel Wahab)

Love and Pride / Houbb wa kibriyâʾ (Hassan al-Imam)

Moments of Fear / Lahzât khawf (Hassan Reda)

My Son / Waladî (Nader Galal)

One Last Night of Love / Laylat houbb akhîrah (Helmi Rafla)

One Nose and Three Eyes / Anf wa thalâth ʿouyoun (Hussein Kamal)

The People and the Nile / al-Nâs wa-l-Nîl (Youssef Chahine)

The Return of the Most Dangerous Man in the World / ʿAwdat akhtar ragoul fî-l-ʾâlam (Mahmoud Farid)

Satan Is a Woman / al-Chaytân imraʾah (Niazi Mostafa)

Song on the Passage / Oughniyah ʿâla al-mamarr (Ali Abdel Khalek)

The Story of a Girl Called Marmar / Hikâyat bint ismouhâ Marmar (Henri Barakat)

Tomorrow Love Will Return / Ghadan ya'*oud al-houbb* (Nader Galal)

Under the Sign of the Virgin / Bourg al-'*adhrâ* (Mahmoud Zoulficar)

The Way of Vengeance / Tarîq al-intiqâm (Amine al-Hakim)

Wolves on the Road / Dhi'*âb* '*alâ al-tarîq* (Kamal Salah Eddine)

The Woman Visitor / al-Zâ'*irah* (Henri Barakat)

Word of Honor / Kalimat charaf (Houssam Eddine Mostafa)

A Youth Which Is Eaten Up / Chabâb yahtariq (Mahmoud Farid)

1973

Abou Rabie / Abou Rabî' (Nader Galal)

Al-Soukkariyyah / al-Soukkariyyah (Hassan al-Imam)

The Authentic One / al-Asîl (Abdel Rahman Chérif)

The Beggar / al-Chahhât (Houssam Eddine Mostafa)

The Cheats / al-Moukhâdi'*oun* (Mahmoud Farid)

The City of Silence / Madînat al-samt (Kamel Ateyya)

Desire and Perdition / al-Raghbah wa-l-dayâ' (Ahmed Diaa Eddine)

The Devils and the Balloon / al-Chayâtîn wa-l-kourah (Mahmoud Farid)

The Devils on Holiday / al-Chayâtîn fî agâzah (Houssam Eddine Mostafa)

Foreigners / Ghourabâ' (Saad Arafa)

The Gang of Adolescents / Chillat al-mourâhiqîn (Niazi Mostafa)

The Gang of Swindlers / Chillat al-mouhtâlîn (Helmi Rafla)

The Girls and the Mercedes / al-Banât wal-l-marsîdès (Houssam Eddine Mostafa)

Girls Ought to Get Married / al-Banât lâzim tit-gawwiz (Ali Reda)

Invitation to Life / Da'*wah li-l-hayât* (Medghat Bekir)

A Little Love / Chay' *min al-houbb* (Ahmed Fouad)

Looking for a Scandal / al-Bahth '*an al-fadîhah* (Niazi Mostafa)

Lost Love / Zamân al-houbb (Atef Salem)

Love and Silence / al-Houbb wa-l-samt (Abdel Rahman Chérif)

The Lover of the Soul / '*Âchiq al-rouh* (Ahmed Diaa Eddine)

The Malatilli Baths / Hammâm al-Malâtîli (Sahah Abou Seif)

Men Who Do Not Fear Death / Rigâl lâ yakhâfoun al-mawt (Nader Galal)

The Most Honest of Sinners / Achraf khâti'*a* (Abdel Rahman Cherif)

My Blood, My Tears and My Smile / Damî wa doumou'*î wa ibtisâmatî* (Hussein Kamal)

My Story with Life / Hikâyatî ma' *al-zamân* (Hassan al-Imam)

Night and Barred Windows / Layl wa qoudbân (Achraf Fahmi)

The Obstinate One / al-'*Anîd* (Hassan al-Saïfi)

The Other Man / al-Ragoul al-âkhar (Mohamed Bassiouni)

Past Love / al-Houbb alladhî kân (Ali Badrakhan)

The School for Adolescents / Madrasat al-mourâhiqîn (Ahmed Fouad)

The School for Troublemakers / Madrarsat al-mouchâghibîn (Houssam Eddine Mostafa)

The Service Stairs / al-Soullam al-khalfî (Atef Salem)

Son for Sale / Abnâ li-l-bay' (Niazi Mostafa)

A Student's Love / Gharâm til-mîdhah (Helmi Halim)

Three Adolescent Girls / Thalâth fatayât mourâhiqât (Abdel Rahman Kikkya)

The Voice of Love / Sawt al-houbb (Helmi Rafla)

When Love Sings / '*Indamâ youghanni al-houbb* (Niazi Mostafa)

Wild Flowers / Zouour barriyyah (Youssef Francis)

A Woman from Cairo / Imra'*ah min al-Qâhirah* (Mohamed Abdel Aziz)

The Woman Who Conquered the Devil / al Mar'*ah allatî ghalabat al-chaytân* (Yehya al-Alami)

Woman with a Bad Reputation / Imr'*ah sayyi*'*at al-soum*'*ah* (Henri Barakat)

The Woman with Two Faces / Dhât al-wag'*hayn* (Houssam Eddine Mostafa)

Women of the Night / Nisâ al-layl (Helmi Rafla)

1974

The Ball Is Still in My Pocket / al-Rasâsah lâ tazâl fî gaybî (Houssam Eddine Mostafa)

Bamba Kachar / Bamba Kachchar (Hassan al-Imam)

The Boss's Empire / Ambaratouriyyat al mou'al-lim (Zaki Saleh)

Boudour / Boudour (Nader Galal)

Children of Silence / Abnâ' al-samt (Mohamed Radi)

The Clock Strikes Ten / al-Sâ'ah tadouqq al-âchirah (Henri Barakat)

Devils for Ever / Chayâtîn ilâ al-abad (Mahmoud Farid)

Dounia / Douniâ (Abdel Meneim Choukri)

The Expected Husband / 'Arîs al-hanâ (Mahmoud Farid)

A Forest of Legs / Ghâbah min al-sîqân (Houssam Eddine Mostafa)

The Fugitive / al-Hârib (Kamal al-Cheikh)

Gentle Embrace / al-Ahdân al-dâfi'ah (Nagdi Hafez)

The Giants / al-'Amâliqah (Houssam Eddine Mostafa)

The Grandson / al-Hafîd (Atef Salem)

Great Fidelity / ul-Wafâ' al-azîm (Helmi Rafla)

The Happy Marriage / al-ZawIag al-sa'îd (Helmi Rafla)

The Heroes / al-Abtâl (Houssam Eddine Mostafa)

The Hostile Brothers / al-Ikhwah al-a'dâ' (Houssam Eddine Mostafa)

The Important Thing Is Love / al-Mouhimm al-houbb (Abdel Meneim Choukri)

In Summer You Have to Love / Fî-l-sayf lâzim nihibb (Mohamed Abdel Aziz)

The Innocents / al-Abriyâ' (Mohamed Radi)

It Was Love / Wa kâna al-houbb (Helmi Rafla)

The Language of Love / Loughat al-houbb (Zouheir Bekir)

My Beloved Is Very Mischievous / Habîbatî cha-qiyyah guiddan (Niazi Mostafa)

My Daughter, Love and Me / Anâ wa ibnâtî wa-l-houbb (Mohamed Radi)

My Love / Habîbatî (Henri Barakat)

The Princess of My Love / Amîrat houbbî anâ (Hassan al-Imam)

Resolute Nights / Layâlî lan ta'oud (Taysir Abboud)

Secondary Roads / al-Chawâri' al-khalfiyyah (Kamel Ateyya)

The Slums of the City / Qâ al-madînah (Houssam Eddine Mostafa)

The Sparrow / al-'Ousfour (Youssef Chahine)

Strange O Time / 'Agâyib yâ zaman (Hassan al-Imam)

Suffering on Smiling Lips / al-'Adhâb fawqa chifâh tabtasim (Hassan al-Imam)

Twenty-Four Hours of Love / Arba'ah wa-ichrîn sâ'ah houbb (Ahmad Fouad)

The Voyage of Life / Rihlat al-'oumr (Saad Arafa)

The Voyage of Marvels / Rihlat al-'agâyib (Hassan al-Saïfi)

We Live for Love / 'Aychîn li-l-houbb (Ahmed Diaa Eddine)

Where Is My Reason? / Ayna 'aqlî? (Atef Salem)

Widowed on Her Wedding Night / Armalay lay-lat al-zifâf (al-Sayed Bedeir)

A Woman for Love / Imra'ah li-l-houbb (Ahmed Diaa Eddine)

Woman in Love / Imra'ah 'âchiqah (Achraf Fahmi)

A Woman's Curse / La'nat imra'ah (Niazi Mostafa)

Young Girls and Ladies / Ânisât wa sayyidât (Kamal Salah Eddine)

Young Girls and Love / al-Banât wa-l-houbb (Houssam Eddine Mostafa)

1975

Al-Karnak / al-Karnak (Ali Badrakhan)

And Love Came to an End / Wa intahâ al-houbb (Hassan al-Imam)

And the Train of My Life Passes / Wa madâ qitâr al-'oumr (Atef Salem)

Badia Massabni / Badî'ah Masâbni (Hassan al-Imam)

Beware of Men, Mummy / Ihtarisî min al-rigâl yâ mâmâ (Mahmoud Farid)

Bloody Sunday / Yawm al-ahad al-dâmî (Niazi Mostafa)

Chahira / Chahîrah (Adli Khalil)

The Charmer of Women / Sâ'id al-nisâ (Abdel Meneim Choukri)

The Coward and Love / al-Gabân wa-l-houbb (Hassan Youssef)

Daddy Is the Last to Be Told / Bâbâ âkhir man ya'lam (Hassan Ismaïl)

The Divorced / al-Moutaalaqât (Ismaïl al-Qadi)

Don't Leave Me Alone / La tatroukî wahdî (Hassan al-Imam)

The Evening Visitor / Zâ'ir al-fagr (Mamdouh Choukri)

Everyone Would Like to Fall in Love / al-Koull ᶜâwiz yihibb (Ahmed Fouad)

A Girl Called Mahmoud / Bint ismouhâ Mahmoud (Niazi Mostafa)

Hello, It's Me, the Cat / Allo, anâ al-qittah (Tozri Mahdi)

Hereditary Madness / Magânîn bi-l-wirâthah (Niazi Mostafa)

I Ask for a Solution / Ouridou hallan (Saïd Marzouk)

I Love This One but I Want That One / Hâdhâ ouhibbouh wa hâdhâ ourîdouh (Hassan al-Imam)

I Shall Never Return / Abadan lan aᵓoud (Hassen Ramzi)

The Kings of the Gag / Moulouk al-dahik (Mahmoud Farid)

Let's Love Each Other / Daᵓounâ nouhibb (al-Sayed Ziyada)

The Liar / al-Kaddâb (Salah Abou Seif)

Looking for Problems / al-Bahth ᶜan al-mataâᵓib (Mahmoud Farid)

Lost Women / Nisâᵓ dâᵓiᵓât (Houssam Eddine Mostafa)

Love . . . Even More Beautiful than Love / Houbb ahlâ min al-houbb (Helmi Rafla)

Love Beneath the Rain / al-Houbb tahta al-matar (Hussein Kamal)

Meeting with the Past / Liqâᵓ maᵓ al-mâdî (Yehya al-Alami)

The Mummy aka The Night of Counting the Years / al-Moumyâᵓ (Chadi Abdel Salam)

My First and Last Love / Houbbî al-awwal wa-l-akhîr (Helmi Rafla)

Never Again, Good Heavens / Yâ rabb toubah (Ali Reda)

Nothing Is Important / Lâ chayᵓ yahoumm (Hussein Kamal)

On a Sheet of Cellophane / ᶜAlâ waraq silloufân (Hussein Kamal)

The Queen and I / al-Malikah wa anâ (Atef Salem)

A Question with Love / Souᵓâl fî-l-houbb (Henri Barakat)

Sabrine / Sabrîn (Houssam Eddine Mostafa)

Shadows on the Other Bank / al-Zilâl fî-l-gânib al-âkhar (Ghaleb Chaath)

Shore of Violence / Châti al-ᵓounf (Taysir Abboud)

The Siren / al-Naddahah (Hussein Kamal)

Song of My Life / Nagham fî hayâtî (Henri Barakat)

The Tears Dry Up / Gaffat al-doumouᵓ (Helmi Rafla)

Two Women / Imraᵓatân (Hassan Ramzi)

Until the End of My Life / Hattâ âkhir al-ᵓoumr (Achraf Fahmi)

The Victims / al-Dahâyâ (Houssam Eddine Mostafa)

What a Mess / Moulid yâ douniâ (Hussein Kamal)

The White Dress / al-Ridâᵓ al-abyad (Hassan Ramzi)

Who Are We Shooting At? / ᶜAlâ man noutliq al-rasâs (Kamal al-Cheik)

Who Can Tame Aziza? / Mîn yiqdar ᶜalâ ᶜAzîzah (Ahmed Fouad)

The Woman and the Wolves / al-Ounthâ wa-l-dhiᵓâb (Niazi Mostafa)

Young People Today / Choubbân hâdhihi al-ayyâm (Atef Salem)

1976

An Adolescent Girl from the Country / Mourâhiqah min al-aryâf (al-Sayed Ziyada)

After Love / Mâ baᵓda al-houbb (Kamal Ateyya)

The All-Time Beauty / Qamar al-zamân (Hassan al-Imam)

And Life Returns / Wa ᶜâdat al-hayât (Nader Galal)

Another's Love / Habîbat ghayrî (Ahmed Mazhar)

A Bachelor's Loves / Gharâmiyyât ᶜâzib (Zaki Saleh)

The Beauty and the Crook / al-Fâtinah wa-l-souᵓlouk (Hussein Emara)

Chawq / Chawq (Achraf Fahmi)

The Circle of Vengeance / Dâᵓirat al-intiqâm (Samir Seif)

The Curlew Has Lips / al-Karawân louh chafâyif (Hassan al-Imam)

The Delinquents / al-Mounharifoun (Niazi Mostafa)

Face to Face / Wagᵓhan li wagᵓh (Ahmed Fouad)

Far from the Land / Baᵓîdan ᶜan al-ard (Hussein Kamal)

Farewell for Ever / Wadâᵓan ilâ al-abad (Abdel Rahman Kikkya)

First Year of Love / Sanah oulâ houbb (Salah Abou Seif, Atef Salem, Kamal al-Cheikh, Niazi Mostafa, and Helmi Rafla)

Forbidden during the Wedding Night / Mamnou fî laylat al-doukhlah (Hassan al-Saïfi)

The Gang of Bonviveurs / Chillat al-ouns (Yeyha al-Alami)

Good Children / al-ʾIyâl al-tayyibîn (Mohamed Abdel Aziz)

Heartbeat / Daqqat qalb (Mohamed Abdel Aziz)

His Sisters / Ikhwâtouh al-banât (Henri Barakat)

Home without Tenderness / Bayt bilâ hanân (Ali Abdel Khalek)

I Am neither Reasonable nor Mad / Anâ lâ ʿâqlah wa-lâ magʾnounah (Houssam Eddine Mostafa)

If Only I'd Not Known Love / Laytanî mâ ʿaraftou al-houbb (Anwar Chennawi)

Legs in the Mud / Siqân fî-l-wahl (Atef Salem)

Life Is a Song / al-Hayât naʾham (Abdel Rahman Chérif)

Live Marriage / Gawiz ʿalâ al-hawâ (Ahmed Sarwat)

Love on the Miami Beach / Houbb ʿalâ châtiʾ Miami (Helmi Rafla)

A Meeting Down There / Liqâʾ hounâk (Ahmed Diaa Eddine)

The Music Is in Danger / al-Mazzïkah fî khutar (Mahmoud Farid)

My Lord, It Is Your Will / Hikmituk yâ rab (Houssam Eddine Mostafa)

No Time for Tears / Lâ waqta li-l-doumouʾ (Nader Galal)

No, to You Whom I Loved / Lâ yâ man kounta habîbî (Helmi Rafla)

The Peaceful Nest / al-ʾIchch al-hâdi (Atef Salem)

The Return of the Prodigal Son / ʿAwdat al-ibn al-dâll (Youssef Chahine)

Tawhida / Tawhîdah (Houssam Eddine Mostafa)

The Taxi King / Malik al-taxi (Yehya al-Alami)

Those Who Are at Fault / al-Moudhniboun (Saïd Marzouk)

Thoughtless Husbands / Azwâg tâʾichoun (Niazi Mostafa)

Viva Zalata / Viva Zalata (Hassen Hafez)

The Voyage in Life / Rihlat al-ayyâm (Henri Barakat)

Waves without Border / Amwâg bilâ châtiʾ (Achraf Fahmi)

Where Does the Story Begin? / Nibtidî minîn al-hikâyah (Mohamed Salmane)

With Hot Tears / al-Doumouʾ al-sâkhinah (Yeyha al-Alami)

Women in Love / al-Âchiqât (Mahmoud Farid)

Women under Pressure / Nisâ tahta al-tabʾ (Niazi Mostafa)

A World of Kids / ʿÂlam ʿiyâl ʿiyâl (Mohamed Abdel Aziz)

You Must Venerate Your Parents / Wa bi-l-wâlidayn ihsânan (Hassan al-Imam)

1977

Barefoot on a Golden Bridge / Hâfiyah ʿalâ Guisr min-al-dhahab (Atef Salem)

The Beauty and the Idiot / al-Houlwah wa-l-ghabî (Ahmed Fouad)

Bye-Bye My Pretty One / Bay bay yâ helwah (Atef Salem)

The Cabaret of Life / Kabârîh al-hayât (Mahmoud Farid)

Cat on a Hot Tin Roof / Qittah ʿalâ nâr (Samir Seif)

Come and See What Sokkar Is Doing / Bouss chouf Soukkar bi-taʾmil îh (Achraf Fahmi)

Dearest Uncle Zizou / Oncle Zizou habîbî (Niazi Mostafa)

The Devils / al-Chayâtîn (Houssam Eddine Mostafa)

Exchange of Courtesies / Chayilnî wa achayyilak (Ali Badrakhan)

A Flat in Town / Chaqqah wast al-balad (Mohamed Fadel)

The Follies of Love / Gounoun al-houbb (Nader Galal)

For Life / Min agl al-hayât (Ahmed Sawat)

A Girl Who Is Looking for Love / Fatât tabhath ʿan al-houbb (Nader Galal)

Husbands Are Devils / al-Azwâg al-chayâtîn (Ahmed Fouad)

The Idiot Boy / al-Walad al-ghâbi (Madkour Sabet)

It Was Another Time . . . / Kân wa kân wa kân (Abbas Kamel)

Let's Get Married Quickly My Love / Ilâ al-maʾdhoun yâ habîbî (Mahmoud Farid)

Love . . . in a Dead End / al-Houbb . . . fî tarîq masdoud (Adli Khalil)

Love before Bread Sometimes / al-Houbb qabla al-khoubz ahyânan (Saad Arafa)

The Love Thief / Harâmî al-houbb (Abdel Meneim Choukri)

Love You Are Beautiful / Hilwah yâ douniâ al-houbb (Yehya al-Alami)

The Meeting / al-Talâqî (Sobhi Chafik)

A Million and One Kisses / Alf bousah wa bousah (Mohamed Abdel Aziz)

Mouths and Rabbits / Afwâh wa arânib (Henri Barakat)

My Daughter and the Wolf / Ibnatî wa-l-dhi²b (Sayed Tantawi)

Night and Desire / Layl wa raghbah (Yeyha al-Alami)

Night's Murmurs / Hamsat al-laykl (Hussein Helmi al-Mouhandès)

O Night . . . O Time / Al yâ layl yâ zaman (Ali Reda)

The Oppressed's Prayer / Dou²â²al-madhloumîn (Hassan al-Imam)

The Pretty Liar / al-Bint al-hilwah al-kaddâbah (Zaki Saleh)

Rendezvous with Soussou / Mi²wâd ma² Sousou (Henri Barakat)

The Respectable Husband / al-Zawg al-mouhtaram (Hassan al-Saïfi)

The Sad Bird of Night / Tâ²ir al-layl al-hâzin (Yehya al-Alami)

She Fell into a Sea of Honey / Wa saqatat fî bahr al²asal (Salah Abou Seif)

The Sins of Love / Khatâyâ al-houbb (Yehya al-Alami)

Sonia and the Madman / Sonia wa-l-mag²noun (Houssam Eddine Mostafa)

The Star Maker / Sâni² al-nougoum (Mohamed Radi)

Suffering Is a Woman / al-²Adhâb imra²ah (Ahmed Yehya)

Tears in Eyes That Smile / al-Doumou²fî²ouyoun dIahikah (Ahmed Diaa Eddine)

That's Enough My Heart / Kafânî yâ qalb (Hassan Youssef)

That's How Life Goes / Hâkadhâ al-ayyâm (Atef Salem)

Thirteen and One Lies / Talatata²ch kidbah wa kidbah (Anwar al-Chennawi)

The Violet / Zahrat al-banafsag (Abdel Rahman al-Khamissi)

Virgin, but . . . / ²Adhrâ² wa lâkin (Simon Saleh)

The Watercarrier Is Dead / al-Saqqâ mât (Salah Abou Seif)

The Weaker Sex / Guins nâ²im (Mohamed Abdel Aziz)

When the Body Slides / ²Indamâ yascout al-gasad (Nader Galal)

Where Is the Way Out? Ayna al-Mafarr (Hussein Emara)

With My Love and Tenderness / Ma² houbbî wa achwâqi (Henri Barakat)

Woman of Glass / Imra²ah min Zougâg (Nader Galal)

Women in the City / Nisâ fî-l-madînah (Helmi Rafla)

1978

Al-Akmar / al-Aqmar (Hicham Abou al-Nasr)

All in Hell / Koullouhoum fî-l-nâr (Ahmed al-Sabaawi)

Behind the Sun / Warâ² al-chams (Mohamed Radi)

The Best Days of Life / Ahlâ ayyâm al-²oumr (Hassan al-Saïfi)

Between Them the Devil / Wa thâlithhoum al-chaytân (Kamal al-Cheikh)

The Bill, Miss / al-Hisâb yâ mademoiselle (Anwar al-Chennawi)

A Call after Midnight / Moukâlamah ba²da mountasaf al-layl (Helmi Rafla)

Chafika and Metwalli / Chafîqah wa Mitwallî (Ali Badrakhan)

The Composition of Time / Hisâb al-sinîn (Ahmed al-Sabaawi)

The Criminal / al-Mougrim (Salah Abou Seif)

Desire and Its Cost / al-Raghbah wa-l-thaman (Youssef Chabaane Mohamed)

A Different Girl / Bint ghayr koull al-banât (Kamal Salah Eddine)

The Famous Affair / al-Qadiyyah al-machhourah (Hassan al-Imam)

A Flat and a Woman, Dear Lord / Chiqqah wa ²arousa yia rabb (Zaki Saleh)

The Good Guys / Awlâd al-halâl (Hassan al-Saïfi)

A Heartless Woman / Imra²ah bilâ (Yassine Ismaïl Yassine)

Hearts in a Ocean of Tears / Qouloub fî bahr al-doumou² (Yehya al-Alami)

Hello, Captain / Ahlan yâ kabtin (Mohamed Abdel Aziz)

I Want Love and Tenderness / Ourîd houbban wa hanânan (Nagdi Hafez)

It's Shameful, Lulu . . . Lulu, It's Shameful / ²Eib yâ Loulou . . . Yâ Loulou ²Eib (Sayed Tantawi)

The Judge and the Executioner / al-Qâdî wa-l-gallâd (Nader Galal)

The Last Confession / al-I²tirâf al-akhîr (Anwar al-Chennawi)

Life Is Over, My Son / Dâ᾿ al-oumr yâ waladî (Atef Salem)

Life Is Short / al-᾿Oumr lahzar (Mohamed Radi)

Love on a Volcano / Houbb fawq al-bourkân (Hassan al-Imam)

The Lovers' Route / Sikkat al-᾿âchiqîn (Hassan al-Saïfi)

A Madman's Testimony / Chahâdat mag᾿noun (Talaat Allam)

Masters and Slaves / Asyâd wa ᶜabîd (Ali Reda)

Mounting toward the Abyss / al-Sou᾿oud ilâ al-hâwiyah (Kamal al-Cheikh)

One Smile Is Enough / Ibtismâmah wâhidah takfî (Mohamed Bassiouni)

The Other Woman / al-Mar᾿ah al-oukhrah (Achraf Fahmi)

Our Days Are Numbered / Ayyâm al-᾿oumr ma᾿doudah (Taysir Abboud)

The Purse Is with Me / al-Mihfazah ma᾿âya (Mohamed Abdel Aziz)

Remember Me / Idhkourînî (Henri Barakat)

Remorse / al-Nadam (Nader Galal)

Satan in the City / Iblîs fî-l madîna (Samir Seif)

A Single Life Is Best / Bidoun zawâg afdal (Ahmed al-Sabaawi)

Some People Get Married Twice / al-Ba᾿d yadh-hab ilâ al-ma᾿dhoun marratayn (Mohamed Abdel Aziz)

Step . . . False Step / Wâhdah ba᾿d wâhdah wa nouss (Hussein Emara)

Suzy, Love Merchant / Suzy bâ᾿i᾿at al-houbb (Simon Saleh)

There Are Loves That Kill / Wa min al-houbb mâ qatal (Houssam Eddine Mostafa)

The Thieving Millionnairess / al-Millionnairah al-nachchâlah (Seif Eddine Chawkat)

The Toy / al-Lou᾿bah (Yassine Ismaïl Yassine)

An Unforgettable Night / Laylah lâ tounsâ (Hassan Youssef)

The Voyage of Forgetfulness / Rihlat al-nisyân (Ahmed Yehya)

Voyage to a Woman's Depths / Hihlah dâkhil imra᾿ah (Achraf Fahmi)

A Woman Is a Woman / al-Mar᾿ah hiya al-mar᾿ah (Henri Barakat)

A Woman Killed by Love / Imra᾿ah qatalahâ al-houbb (Achraf Fahmi)

A Woman Who Runs through My Veins / Imra᾿ah fî damî (Ahmed Fouad)

The Wretched / al-Bou᾿asâ᾿ (Atef Salem)

Yasmine's Nights / Layâlî Yasmîn (Henri Barakat)

Youth Dancing on Fire / Chabâb yarqous fawq al-nâr (Yehya al-Alami)

1979

Adventurers Around the World / Moughâmiroun hawl al-᾿âlam (Mahmoud Farid)

Alexandria . . . Why? / Iskandariyyah lîh (Youssef Chahine)

And Sadness Passes / Wa tamdî al-ahzân (Ahmed Yassine)

And the Investigation Continues / Wa Lâ yazâl al-tahqîq moustamirran (Achraf Fahmi)

An Angel's Sin / Khatî᾿at malâk (Yehya al-Alami)

Beware of Your Neighbours / Khallî bâlak min Guîrânak (Mohamed Abdel Aziz)

Conqueror of the Darkness / Qâhir al-zalâm (Atef Salem)

The Cursed / al-Mala᾿în (Ahmed Yassine)

Dirty Hands / al-Aydî al-qadhirah (Ahmed Yehya)

Doubt, My Love / al-Chak yâ habîbî (Henri Barakat)

For Whom the Sun Rises / Liman touchriq al-chams (Hussein Helmi al-Mouhandès)

God Is Patient, but Do Not Forget / Youmhil wa lâ youhmil (Hassan Hafez)

The Hidden Trap / al-Khoud᾿ah al-khafiyyah (Yehya al-Alami)

The Illusion / al-Wahm (Nader Galal)

Let Me Avenge Myself / Da᾿ounî antaqim (Taysir Abboud)

Lovers Younger than Twenty / ᶜOuchchâq tahta al-᾿ichrîn (Henri Barakat)

The Malediction of Time / La᾿nat al-zaman (Ahmed al-Sabaawi)

Men Knowing Nothing of Love / Rigâl lâ ya᾿rifoun al-houbb (Yehya al-Alami)

Migrating Birds / al-Touyour al-mouhîguirah (Hassan Youssef)

A Murderer Who Has Killed No-One / Qâtil mâ qatalch hadd (Mohamed Abdel Aziz)

My Dignity / Karâmatî (Achraf Fahmi)

My Life Is Suffering / Hayâyî ᶜadhâb (Ali Reda)

No Condolences for the Ladies / Wa lâ ᶜazâ li-l-sayyidât (Henri Barakat)

No, Mummy / Lâ yâ oummî (Nasser Hussein)

One Type of Women / Naw᾿ min al-nisâ᾿ (Hassan al-Saïfi)

Paradise Is at His Feet / al-Gannah tahta qada-mayhâ (Hassan al-Imam)

The Queen of Tarab / Soultânat al-tarab (Hassan al-Imam)

Ragab on a Burning Roof / Ragab fawqa safihin sâkhin (Ahmed Fouad)

The Savage / al-Moutawahhichah (Samir Seif)

Save This Family / Anqidhou hâdhini al-ʾâʾilah (Hassan Ibrahim)

Something Frightens Him / Khâʾifah min chayʾin mâ (Yeyha al-Alami)

Storm of Tears / ʿAsifah min al-doumouʾ (Atef Salem)

A Story Behind Every Door / Hikâyah warâʾ koull bâb (Hussein Kamal)

The Story of the West Quarter / Qissat al-hayy al-gharbî (Adel Sadek)

Stronger than Time / Aqwâ mîn al ayyâm (Nader Galal)

Those of Us from the Bus / Ihna, btouʾ al-otobus (Hussein Kamal)

Weep Not, Love of My Life / Lâ tabkî yâ habîb al-ʾoumr (Ahmed Yehya)

With Premeditation / Maʾ sabq al-isrâr (Achraf Fahmi)

A Woman Has Deceived Me / Khadaʾatnî imarʾah (Sayed Tantawi)

1980

Al-Batiniyya / al-Bâtiniyyah (Houssam Eddine Mostafa)

The Alien Brothers / al-Ilhwah al-ghourabâ (Hassan al-Saïfi)

And the Days Pass / Wa tamdî al-ayyâm (Ahmed al-Sabaawi)

A Castle in Spain / Qasr fî-l-hawâʾ (Abdel Halim Nasr)

Chaabane Below Zero / Chaabân tahta al-sifr (Henri Barakat)

The Challenge of the Powerful / Tahaddî al-aqwiyâʾ (Ahmed al-Sabaawi)

The Circle of Doubt / Dâʾirat al-chakk (Zaki Saleh)

The Clumsy Man / Ghâwî machâkil (Mohamed Abdel Aziz)

Desire / al-Raghbah (Mohamed Khan)

The Devils / al-Abâlisah (Ali Abdel Khalek)

Do Not Oppress Women / Lâ tadhlimou al-nisâʾ (Hassan al-Imam)

The Girls' Father / Abou al-banât (Taysir Abboud)

A Glimpse of Sunshine / Darbat chams (Mohamed Khan)

Hell / al-Gahîm (Mohamed Radi)

I Am neither Angel nor Devil / Lastou chaytânan wa-lâ malâkan (Henri Barakat)

Intelligent but Stupid / Adhkiyâ lâkin aghbiyâ (Niazi Mostafa)

Lips Which Do Not Know How to Lie / Chifâh lâ taʾrif al-kadhib (Mohamed Abdel Aziz)

A Love without Sunshine / Houbb lâ yarâ al-chams (Ahmed Yehya)

The Madness of Youth / Gounoun al-chabâb (Khalil Chawki)

A Man Who Has Lost His Mind / Ragoul faqada ʿaqlahou (Mohamed Abdel Aziz)

The Mute / al-Akhras (Ahmed al-Sabaawi)

My Love for Ever / Habîbî dâʾiman (Hussein Kamal)

The Night When the Moon Will Weep / Laylah bakâ fîhâ al-qamar (Ahmed Yehya)

Poor, My Children / al-Fouqarâ awlâdii (Nasser Hussein)

The Suffering of Love / ʿAdhâb al-houbb (Ali Abdel Khalek)

Take Care, Gentlemen / Intabihou ayyouhâ al-sâdah (Mohamed Abdel Aziz)

Tears without Sin / Doumopuʾ bilâ khatâyâ (Hassan Youssef)

The Vagabond / al-Charîdah (Achraf Fahmi)

What Do Girls Want? / al-Banât ʿâyzah îh (Hassan al-Saïfi)

What Love Did to Daddy / ʿAmalîh al-houbb fî bâbâ (Nasserr Hussein)

The Window / al-Choubbâk (Kamal Salah Eddine)

The Woman in Love / al-ʾÂchiqah (Atef Salem)

Women without Chains / Imraʾah bilâ qayd (Henri Barakat)

X Is a Sign of Error / X ʾalâmah maʾnâhâ al-khataʾ (Samir Nawwar)

1981

Bayada / Bayyâdah (Ahmed Sarwat)

Behind the University Walls / Khalf aswâr al-Gâmiʾah (Nagdi Hafez)

A Bird on the Path / Tâʾir ʿalâ al-tartîq (Mohamed Khan)

The Clairvoyant / al-ʾArrâfah (Atef Salem)

Dandach / Dandach (Yehya al-Alami)

A Dangerous Liaison / ʿAlâqah khatirah (Taysir Abboud)

The Devil Preaches / al-Chaytân yaʾîz (Achraf Fahmi)

The Dose of Hashish / al-Qirch (Ibrahim Afifi)

Ever-Opened Eyes / ʿOuyoun lâ tanâm (Raafat al-Mihi)

Fangs / Anyâb (Mohamed Chebl)

Farewell to Suffering / Wadâʾan li-l-ʾadhâb (Ahmed Yehya)

The Fat Cats / al-Qitat al-simân (Hassan Youssef)

4-2-4 / 4-2-4 (Ahmad Fouad)

He Who Has Duped the Devils / Illî dihik ʿalâ al-chayâtîn (Nasser Hussein)

A Hot Summer Night / Laylat chitâʾ dâfiʾah (Ahmed Fouad)

I See Myself in His Eyes / Anâ fî ʿaynayh (Saad Arafa)

I Shall Never Forgive You / Lan aghfir abadan (Sayed Tantawi)

I Shall Return without Tears / Sa aʾoud bilâ doumouʾ (Taysir Abboud)

I'm the Madman / Anâ al-magnoun (Niazi Mostafa)

Journey of Terror / Rihlat al-rouʾb (Mohamed Abdel Aziz)

Judgment Is Given / Hukamat al-Mahkamah (Ahmed Yehya)

Love Alone Is Not Enough / al-Houbb wahdahou lâ yakfî (Ali Abdel Khalek)

The Lovers' Struggle / Sirâʾ al-ʾouchchâq (Yehya al-Alami)

A Man in the True Sense of the Word / Ragoul bimaʾnâ al-kalimah (Nader Galal)

A Man Only Lives Once / al-Insân yaʾîch marrah wâhidah (Simon Saleh)

Moment of Weakness / Lahzat daʾf (Sayed Tantawi)

A Monster Makes Man / al-Wahch dâkhil al-insân (Achraf Fahmi)

Mothers in Exile / Oummahât fî-l-manfâ (Mohamed Radi)

My Greetings to My Dear Professor / Maʾ tahiyyâtî li oustâdhî al-ʾazîz (Ahmed Yassine)

People at the Top / Ahlou al-qimmah (Ali Badrakhan)

Pity / al-Rahman yâ nâs (Kamal Salah Eddine)

Rendezvous for Dinner / Mawʾid ʿalâ al-ʾachâʾ (Mohamed Khan)

Seeds of Evil / Boudhour al-chaytân (Hassan Youssef)

The Suspect / al-Machbouh (Samir Seif)

Take Care, We're the Mad Ones / Ihtaris nahnou al-magânîn (Zaki Saleh)

Tears on a Wedding Night / Doumouʾ fî laylat al-zifâf (Saad Arafa)

The Thieves / al-Lousous (Taysir Abboud)

The Tough Guys from Boulak / Foutouwwât Boulâq (Yehya al-Alami)

Traveler without a Road / Mousâfir bilâ tarîq (Ali Abdel Khalek)

Unidentified Culprit / Wa qouyyidat didd magʾhoul (Medhat al-Sibaï)

The Valley of Memories / Wâdî al-dhikrayât (Henri Barakat)

Vote for Dr. Souleyman Abdel Basset / Intakhibou al-doktor Soulaymân ʿAbd al-Bâsit (Mohamed Abdel Aziz)

Who Will Drive Us Mad? / Mîn yigannin mîn (Ahmed Fouad)

1982

Aggression / Iʾtidâʾ (Saad Arafa)

Al-Salakhana / al-Salakhânah (Ahmed al-Sabaawi)

And My Heart Ended Down There / Wa dâʾa houbbî hounak (Ali Abdel Khalek)

At the Minister's Door / ʿAlâ bâb al-wazîr (Henri Barakat)

Barge 70 / al-ʾAwwâmah sabʿîn (Khaïri Bechara)

Bitter Bread / al-Khoubz al-mourr (Achraf Fahmi)

Blood on the Pink Dress / Dimâʾ ʿalâ al-thawb al-wardî (Hassan al-Imam)

Bloody Fates / al-Aqdâr al-dâmiyah (Kaïri Bechara)

Breakdown / Inhiyâr (Ahmed al-Sabaawi)

Chabrawi the Soldier / al-ʾAskarî chabrâwî (Henri Barakat)

The Degenerate / al-Maʾtouh (Kamal Ateyya)

Disgrace / al-ʾÂr (Ali Abdel Khalek)

An Egyptian Story / Haddoutah masriyyah (Youssef Chahine)

The Execution of a Secondary School Boy / Iʾdâm tâlib thânawî (Ahmed Fouad Darwich)

Fatal Jealousy / al-Ghîrah al-qâtilah (Atef al-Tayeb)

Five in Hell / Khamsah fî-l-gahîm (Ahmed Sarwat)

A Foreigner at Home / Gharîb fî baytî (Samir Seif)

The Girl Who Said No / al-Bint illî ʾâlit laʾ (Ahmed Fouad)

Hamada and Toutou's Gang / ʿIsâbat Hamâdah wa Toutou (Mohamed Abdel Aziz)

*Journey of Suffering and Love / Rihlat al-chaqâ'
wa-l-houbb* (Mohamed Abdel Aziz)

The Last Word / al-Kalimah al-akhîrah (Wasfi
Darwich)

Layal / Layâl (Hassan al-Imam)

The Livelihood / Arzâq yâ douniâ (Nader Galal)

*A Man in the Women's Prison / Ragoul fi sign al-
nisâ'* (Hassan al-Saïfi)

Mawardi's Café / Qahwat al-Mâwardî (Hichem
Abou al-Nasr)

*Morsi from Above, Morsi from Below / Moursî
fawq Moursî taht* (Mohamed Abdel Aziz)

*Moukhaymer Is Always Ready / Moukhaymir
gâhiz dâ'iman* (AhmedSarwat)

*One Fiancée and Two Suitors / 'Arousah wa gouz
'oursân* (Yehya al-Alami)

The Peacock / al-Tâwous (Kamal al-Cheikh)

Poor Mr. Hassan / Hasan bîh al-ghalbân (Henri
Barakat)

The Powerful / al-Aqwiyâ' (Achraf Fahmi)

The Sparkle in Your Eyes / Barîq 'aynayki
(Mohamed Abdel Aziz)

*Sympathy for the Dead Man / Li-l-faqîd al-
rahmah* (Omar Abdel Aziz)

Things against the Law / Achyâ didd al-qânoun
(Ahmed Yassine)

*The Guys from the Mountains / Foutouwwat al-
gabal* (Nader Galal)

The Trial / al-Moukâkamah (Nader Galal)

Vengeance / al-Tha'r (Mohamed Khan)

*A Very Special Invitation / Da'wah khâssah guid-
dan* (Omar Abdel Aziz)

Wekalat al-Balah / Wakâlat al-balah (Houssam
Eddine Mostafa)

*Who Will Extinguish the Fire? / Man youtfî' al-
nâr* (Mohamed Salmane)

Whose Son Is He? / Ibn mîn fî-l-mougtamâ'
(Hassan al-Imam)

1983

The Alleyway of Love / Darb al-hawâ (Houssam
Eddine Mostafa)

Antar Wears His Sword / 'Antar châyil sîfouh
(Ahmed al-Sabaawi)

The Beggar / al-Moutasawwil (Ahmed al-Sabaawi)

The Bus Driver / Sawwâq al-otobus (Atef al-
Tayeb)

The Coachman / al-'Arbaguî (Ahmed Fouad)

A Dog Bite / 'Addat kalb (Hassan al-Saïfi)

The Drug Addict / al-Moudmin (Youssef Francis)

*The End of a Married Man / Nihâyat ragoul
moutazawwig* (Adel Sadek)

The Fences of the Tanneries / Aswâr al-madâbigh
(Chérif Yehya)

Gate Five / Khamsah bâb (Nader Gabal)

*Gentlemen You Are Corrupt / al-Sâdah al-
mourtachoun* (Ali Abdel Khalek)

Gharib Is a Strange Boy / Gharîb walad 'aguîb
(Kamal Salah Eddine)

God Is Great / Yâ mâ inta karîm yâ rabb (Hussein
Emara)

God Watches / Inna rabbaka la-bi-l-mirsâd
(Mohamed Hassib)

Half-a-Million / Nisf arnab (Mohamed Khan)

The Half-Meter Accident / Hâdith al-nisf mitr
(Achraf Fahmi)

I Am Not a Thief / Anâ mouch harâmiyyah
(Hassan al-Saïfi)

The Lout / al-Qifl (Omar Abdel Aziz)

Love in Prison / Houbb fî-l-zinzânah (Mohamed
Fadel)

The Madmen's Strike / Idrâb al-magânîn (Ahmed
Fouad)

*The Man Who Sold the Sun / al-Ragoul alladhî
bâ'a al-chams* (Niazi Mostafa)

*Marriage—It's for the Worthy / al-Gawâz li-l-
guid'ân* (Nagdi Hafez)

Marzouka / Marzouqah (Saad Arafa)

The Monsters of the Port / Wouhouch al-minâ'
(Niazi Mostafa)

*Neither Seen, Nor Recognised / Lâ min châf wa-
lâ min dirî* (Nader Galal)

*Nothing to Do, It's the Way Things Are / Tiguîbhâ
kidah, tiguîlhâ kidah, hiyya kidah* (Omar Abdel
Aziz)

The Ogre / al-Ghoul (Samir Seif)

Prison without Bars / Sig'n bilâ qoudbân (Ahmed
al-Sabaawi)

The Professor and the Dancer / Âlim wa 'âlimah
(Ahmed Yassine)

Raya and Sekina / Rayyâ wa Sakînah (Ahmed
Fouad)

*The Realm of Hallucinations / Mamlakat al-
halwasah* (Mohamed Abdel Aziz)

The Shore of Chance / Châti' al-hazz (Hassan al-
Saïfi)

The Singer / al-Moughannawâti (Sayed Issa)

*Soutouhi Is Perched in the Tree / Soutouhî fawq
al-chagarah* (Nasser Hussein)

Take Care / al-Ihtiyât wâguib (Ahmed Fouad)

Their Wiles Are Great / Kaydahounna ʿadhîm (Hassan al-Imam)

They Steal Rabbits / Innahoum yasriqoun al-arânib (Nader Galal)

Tomorrow I Will Take My Revenge / Ghadan saantaqim (Ahmed Yehya)

The Tough Guys from Bab al-Cheiriyyah / Guyidʾân Bâb al-Chiʾriyyah (Kamal Salah Eddine)

The Tower of the Tanneries / Bourg al-madâbigh (Ahmed al-Sabaawi)

Trial No. 1 / al-Qadiyyah raqam wâhid (Mouhannad al-Ansari)

The Two Tramps / al-Moutacharridân (al-Saïd Mostafa)

The Virgin and the White Hair / al-ʾAdhrâ wa-l-chaʾr al-abyad (Hussein Kamal)

Wedad the Dancer / Widâd al-ghâziyyah (Ahmed Yehya)

Why Is Massoud Happy / Masʾoud saʾîd lîh (Ahmed Sarwat)

The Wolves / al-Dhiʾâb (Adel Sadek)

1984

All Is Well / Koullouh tamân (Ahmed Sarwat)

Al-Labbana Street / Darb al-Labbânah (Ibrahim Baghdadi)

Ayoub / Ayyoub (Hani Lachine)

The Baker's Shop / al-Fourn (Ibrahim Afîfî)

Beauty of the Night / Qamar al-layl (Mohamed Salmane)

Beware of Khott / Ihtaris min al-Khott (Samir Seif)

The Black Panther / al-Nimr al-aswad (Atef Salem)

But There Is Still Something Left / Wa lâkin chayʾan mâ yabqâ (Mohamed Abdel Aziz)

The Crooks / al-Nassaâbîn (Ahmed Yehya)

The Curse / al-Laʾnah (Hussein al-Wakil)

The Dancer and the Percussionist / al-Râqisah wa-l-tabbâl (Achraf Fahmi)

Daughters of Satan / Banât Iblîs (Ali Abdel Khalek)

The Defender of Poor People / Foutouwwat al-nâs al-ghalâbah (Niazi Mostafa)

The Devil Sings / al-Chaytân youghannî (Yassine Ismaïl Yassine)

Do Not Ask Me Who I Am / Lâ tasʾalnî man anâ (Achraf Fahmi)

An Eye for an Eye, a Tooth for a Tooth / Wâhdah bi-Wâhdah (Nader Galal)

Falsification of Official Papers / Tazwîr fî awrâq rasmiyyah (Yehya al-Alami)

The Flute Player / al-Zammâr (Atef al-Tayeb)

Forbidden Games / Alʾâb mamnouʾah (Ahmed Sarwat)

Forbidden to Students / Mamnouʾ li-l-talabah (al-Saïd Mostafa)

The Fox and the Grape / al-Thaʾlab wa-l-ʾinab (Mohamed Abdel Aziz)

Guard Dogs / Kilâb al-hirâsah (Sayed Seif)

Hadi Badi / Hâdî bâdî (Hassan al-Saïfi)

Hamza's Baker's Shop / Tâbounat Hamzah (Ahmed Yassine)

The Hooligans / al-Achqiyâ (Ahmed al-Sabaawi)

The House of Correction / Bayt al-qâsirât (Ahmed Fouad)

I Beg You, Give me this Medecine / Argouk aʾtinî hâdhâ al-dawâ (Hussein Kamal)

It's All My Fault / Anâ illî astâhil (Hassan al-Saïfi)

The Judge's House / Bayt al-qâdî (Ahmed al-Sabaawi)

The Last Respectable Man / Âkhir al-rîgal al-mouhtaramîn (Samir Seif)

The Lawyer / al-Avocato (Raafat al-Mihi)

The Lions of Sinaï / Ousoud Sinâ (Farid Fathallah Manoughehri)

The Lost Plane / al-Tâʾirah al-mafqoudah (Ahmed al-Nahhas)

The Lucky Guy / al-Mahzouz (Omar Abdel Aziz)

The Maidservant / al-Khâdimah (Achraf Fahmi)

Mr Hassan's Flat / Chiqqat al-oustâdh Hasan (Hussein al-Wakil)

Mr Tayyeb / al-Tayyib afandî (Ahmed al-Sabaawi)

Naïma Is a Forbidden Fruit / Naʾîmah fâkihah mouharramah (Ahmed al-Sabaawi)

The Night of Fatima's Arrest / Laylat al-qabd ʿalâ Fatmah (Henri Barakat)

On Close Watch / al-Takhchîbah (Atef al-Tayeb)

Our Daughters Abroad / Banâtounâ fî-l-khârig (Mohamed Abdel Aziz)

The Poor Who Don't Go to Paradise / Fouqarâ la yadkhouloun al-gannah (Medhat al-Sibaï)

The Power of a Woman / Gabarout imraʾah (Nader Galal)

The Prince / al-Prince (Fadel Saleh)

The Professional / al-Hirrîf (Mohamed Khan)

The Promised Night / al-Laylah al-maw'oudah (Yehya al-Alami)

Provided It Is a Son / Yâ rabb walad (Omar Abdel Aziz)

Sammoura and the Pretty Girl / Sammourah wa-l-bint al-'ammourah (Samiur Hafez)

Sea of Illusions / Bahr al-awhâm (Nadia Hamza)

So That the Smoke Doesn't Blow Away / Hattâ lâ yatîr al-doukhân (Ahmed Yehya)

Streets of Fire / Chawârî' min nâr (Samir Seif)

The Terrace / al-Soutouh (Hussein Emara)

They Kill Honest People / Innahoum yaqtouloun al-chourafâ (Nasser Houssein)

To Avenge Ragab / al-Intiqâm la-Ragab (Ahmad Sarwat)

The Traitors / al-Khawanah (Wasfi Darwich)

The Troublemakers in the Army / al-Mouchâghiboun fî-l-gaych (Niazi Mostafa)

Two on the Road / Itnîn 'alâ' al-tarîq (Hassan Youssef)

The Unknown / al-Mag'houl (Achraf Fahmi)

Wanted Dead or Alive / Matloub hayyan aw mayyitan (Adli Khalil)

We Are the Ambulance Men / Ihna boutou' al-is'âf (Salah Korayyem)

When Men Weep / 'Indamâ yabkî al-rigâl (Housam Eddine Mostafa)

Who, of the Two of Us, Is the Thief? / Mîn fînâ al-Harâmî (Mohamed Abdel Aziz)

The Widow and the Devil / al-Armalah wa-l-chaytân (Henri Barakat)

Your Day Will Come, Bey / Lak youm yâ bîh (Mohamed Abdel Aziz)

1985

Al-Darb al-Ahmar / al-Darb al-Ahmar (Abdel Fattah Madbouli)

Ali Bey Mazhar and the Forty Thieves / 'Alî Bîh Mazhar wa-l-arba'în harâmî (Ahmed Yassine)

And Fate Laughs at It / Wa tad'hek al-aqdâr (Hussein Emara)

Angels of the Streets / Malâ'ikat al-chawârî' (Hassan al-Saïfi)

Appeal for Help from the Other World / Istighâthah min al-'âlam al-âkhar (Mohamed Hassib)

Beans Are My Favorite Dish / al-Foul sadîqî (Hussein al-Wakil)

The Beautiful Thieves / al-Nachchalât al-fâtinât (Mahmoud Farid)

Beware of Your Intelligence / Khallî bâlak min 'aqlak (Mohamed Abdel Aziz)

The Cat Was a Lion / al-Qitt aslouh asad (Hassan Ibrahim)

The Celebrity World / 'Âlam al-chouhrah (Mohamed Salmane)

The Days' Struggle / Sirâ' al-ayyâm (Youssef Charaf Eddine)

A Deal Made with a Woman / Safqah ma' imra'ah (Adel al-Aassar)

Deviation / Inhirâf (Taysir Abboud)

The Doorman Is at Your Service / Sâhib al-idârah bawwâb al-'imârah (Nadia Salem)

The Drug / al-Kîf (Ali Abdel Khalek)

The Era of Challenge / Ayyâm al-tahaddî (Adli Youssef)

The Execution of a Dead Man / I'dâm mayyit (Ali Abdel Khalek)

Farewell Bonaparte / al-Wadâ' yâ Bonaparte (Youssef Chahine)

The Flat Goes to the Wife / al-Chiqqah min haqq al-zawgah (Omar Abdel Aziz)

The Flood / al-Tawafân (Bechir al-Dik)

From a Good Family / Awlâd al-Ousoul (Fayek Ismaïl)

The Fugitive / al-Moutârad (Samir Seif)

God's World / Douniâ Allâh (Hassan al-Imam)

The Good and the Bad / al-Âyqah wa-l-dirrîsa (Ahmed al-Sabaawi)

The Hand / al-Kaff (Mohamed Hassib)

Here Is Cairo / Hounâ al-Qâhirah (Omar Abdel Aziz)

The Hippopotamus / al-Sayyed qichtah (Ibrahim Afifi)

Honey Devil / Chaytân min 'asal (Hassan al-Saïfi)

The Hooligans / al-Sa'âlîk (Daoud Abdel Sayed)

Human Beings and Genies / al-Ins wa-l-guinn (Mohamed Radi)

Husbands at Your Service / Zawg taht al-talab (Adel Sadek)

I Am Not a Criminal / Lastou mougriman (Wasfi Darwich)

I'm the One Who Killed al-Hanach / Anâ illî qatalt al-Hanach (Ahmed al-Sabaawi)

Impressions on Water / Basmât fawq al-mâ' (Yassine Ismaïl Yassine)

The Judgment at the End of the Audience / al-Houkm âkhir al-galsah (Mohamed Abdel Aziz)

Khamsa the Genie / al-ʾAbqarî Khamsah (Ahmed Yassine)

The Land Officials / al-Mouwazzafoun fî-l-ard (Ahmed Yehya)

Legitimacy Sweeps It Away / al-Halâl yiksab (Ahmed al-Sabaawi)

The Licit and the Illicit / al-Halâl wa-l-harâm (Sayed Seif)

Living Legitimately / Ayyâm fî-l-halâl (Hussein Kamal)

The Lorry / al-Trîllâ (Salah Serri)

The Louts / al-Awghâd (Ahmed al-Nahhas)

The Mad Woman / al-Magʾnounah (Omar Abdel Aziz)

The Man Who Had Sneezed / al-Ragoul alladhî ʿatas (Omar Abdel Aziz)

The Masters of the Port / Gabâbirat al-minâʾ (Yeyha al-Alami)

Me / Anâ (Ahmed al-Sabaawi)

The Mediocrity / al-Halfout (Samir Seif)

Meghawri at the University / Mighâwrî fî-l-koulliyyah (Hassan al-Saïfi)

The Mild Man's Anger / Ghadab al-halîm (Kamal Ateyya)

The Mountain of Scorpions / Tall al-ʾAqârib (Niazi Mostafa)

The Professor Always Knows More / al-Oustâdh yaʾrif akthar (Ahmed al-Sabaawi)

The Queen's Juice / Chahd al-malikhah (Houssam Eddine Mostafa)

Ragab the Monster / Ragab al-wahch (Kamal Salah Eddine)

Ramadan on a Volcano / Ramadân fawqa al-Bourkân (Ahmed al-Sabaawi)

Reported Missing / Kharaga wa lam ya;oud (Mohamed Khan)

The Resort for Bonviveurs / Mahattat al-ouns (Hassan Ibrahim)

Saad the Orphan / Saʾd al-yatîm (Achraf Fahmi)

Samira's Death / Mawt Samîrah (Mohamed al-Bechir)

Saving What can still be Saved / Inqâdh mâ youmkin inqâdhouh (Saïd Marzouk)

The Slaughterhouse / al-Madbah (Houssam Eddine Mostafa)

The Snake / al-Thouʾbân (Mohamed al-Chami)

Sorry, It's the Law / ʿAfwan ayyouhâ al-qIanoun (Inas al-Deghidi)

The Spider's Web / Khouyout al-ʾankabout (Abdel Latif Zaki)

A Story in Two Words / Hikâyah fî kalimatayn (Hassan Ibrahim)

Ten out of Ten / ʿAchrah ʿalâ ʿachrah (Mohamed Abdel Aziz)

The Thief / al-Nachchâlah (Helmi Rafla)

To Whom by Law / Ilâ man yahoummouhou al-ʾamr (Abdel Hadi Taha)

The Tough Guy from Darb al-Assal / Foutouwwat Darb al-ʾAssâl (Ahmed Sarwat)

The Trial of "The Uncle Ahmed" / Qadiyyat ʿamm Ahmad (Ali Reda)

The Tyrant / al-Tâghiyah (Chérif Yehya)

Uncle Qandil's Scissors / Miqass ʿamm Qandil (Adli Youssef)

The Vengeful Masters / al-Mountaquimoun (Yassine Ismaïl Yassine)

Women / al-Nisâʾ (Nadia Hamza)

The Wounded Man / al-Garîh (Medhat al-Sibaï)

The Years of Danger / Sanawât al-khatar (Nagdi Hafez)

1986

The Alarm Bells / Agrâs al-khatar (Mohamed Abdel Aziz)

Al-Harafish / al-Harâfich (Houssam Eddine Mostafa)

Al-Sakakini / al-Sakâkînî (Houssam Eddine Mostafa)

The Apple and the Skull / al-Touffâhah wa-l-goumgoumah (Mohamed Abou Seif)

The Ballad of Omar / Michwâr ʿOumar (Mohamed Khan)

The Banner / al-Bandîrah (Omar Abdel Aziz)

The Bars of the Harem / Qafas al-harîm (Hussein Kamal)

Before the Farewells / Qabl al-wadâʾ (Hussein al-Wakil)

Beware of the Women's Gang / Ihtaris ʿisâbat al-nisâʾ (Mohamed Abaza)

Bird of the Orient / ʿOusfour al-charq (Youssef Francis)

The Car Thief / Sâriq al-sayyârât (Adli Khalil)

A Citizen's Return / ʿAwdat mouwâtin (Mohamed Khan)

The Commander / al-Komandân (Ismaïl Hassan)

Completely Lost / al-Dâʾiʾah (Atef Salem)

The Cunning / al-Dâhiyah (Abdel Hadi Taha)

Daqqet Zar / Daqqat zâr (Ahmed Yassine)

The Debauched / al-Hanâkîch (Ali Abdel Khalek)

Denunciation of a Woman / Balâgh didd imra²ah (Ahmed al-Sabaawi)

Desire, Malice and Violence / Raghbahj wa hiqd wa intiqâm (Sayed Seif)

Dishonour / Wasmat ᶜâr (Achraf Fahmi)

A Divorced Woman / Imra²ah moutallaqah (Achraf Fahmi)

Do Not Destroy Me Along with Yourself / Lâ tou-dammirnî ma²ak (Mohamed Abdel Aziz)

The Edge of the Sword Blade / Hadd al-sayf (Atef Salem)

Extremely Confidential / Sirrî li-l-ghâyah (Mohamed Abdel Aziz)

Farewell My Child / Wadâ²an yâ waladî (Taysir Abboud)

The Fatal Dream / al-Houlm al-qâtil (Adel al-Aasar)

The Fish Kettle / Châdir al-samak (Ali Abdel Khalek)

Furnished Cemeteries to Let / Madâfin mafrou-chah li-l-îgâr (Ali Abdel Khalek)

Girls and the Unknown / al-Banât wa-l-mag²houl (Hicham Abou al-Nasr)

Hello Friend / Salâm yâ sâhibî (Nader Galal)

Hot Line / al-Khatt al-sâkhin (Kamal Ide)

The House of the Irreproachable / Bayt al-kawâmil (Atef Salem)

The House of the Poisoned Family / Manzil al-²â²ilah al-masmoumah (Mohamed Abdel Aziz)

Hunger / al-Gou² (Ali Badrakhan)

The Hunter / al-Qannâs (Yassine Ismaïl Yassine)

The Informer / al-Moukhbir (Yassine Ismaïl Yassine)

The Inheritors / al-Warathah (Ahmed al-Sabaawi)

The Innocent / al-Barî² (Atef al-Tayeb)

The Innocent Man and the Gallows / al-Barî² wa-l-machnaqah (Nagui Anglo)

It Was Written / Wa²d wa maktoub (Hani Yane)

The Last Chase / al-Moutâradah al-akhîrah (Nagui Anglo)

The Last Love Story / Li-l-houbb qissah akhîrah (Raafat al-Mihi)

The Last Visit / al-Ziyârah al-akhîrah (Chérif Hammouda)

The Liars / Kaddâbîn al-zaffah (Kamal Salah Eddine)

Lord, Deliver Us! / Satrak yâ rab (Hassan al-Saïfi)

Love at the Foot of the Pyramids / al-Houbb fawqa hadabat al-Haram (Atef al-Tayeb)

A Man for These Times / Ragoul li-hâdhâ al-zaman (Nader Galal)

A Man Who Is a Victim of Love / Ragoul qate la-hou al-houbb (Chérif Hammouda)

Melodies / Anghâm (Henri Barakat)

The Midnight Patrol / Dawriyyat nouss al-layl (Kamal Salah Eddine)

The Mixed School Is Banned / al-Ihktilât mam-nou² (Abdel Alim)

The Mulberries and the Cudgel / al-Tout wa-l-babbout (Niazi Mostafa)

My Daughter and the Wolves / Ibnatî wa-l-dhi²âb (Hassan al-Saïfi)

My Friend, My Brother, I Shall Kill You / Akhî wa sadîqî sa-aqtoulak (Yassine Ismaïl Yassine)

Nagwa Madam Chatlata / Nagwâ madame Cha-lâtah (Yehya al-Alami)

The Necklace and the Bracelet / al-Tawk wa-l-iswirah (Khaïri Bechara)

Oh My Country . . . / Ah yâ balad ah . . . (Farid Chawki Hussein)

On the Vice Squad Files / Malaff fî-l-âdâb (Atef al-Tayeb)

The Password / Kalimat al-sirr (Mohamed Abdel Aziz)

Patience in the Salt Mines / al-Sabr fî-l-mallâhât (Ahmed Yehya)

Police Record / Fîch wa tachbîh (Adli Youssef)

Poor but Happy / Fouqarâ² wa lâkin sou²adâ² (al-Saïd Mostafa)

The Poor People / al-Nâs al-ghalâbah (Mahmoud Farid)

The Prey / al-Fârisah (Osman Choukri Selim)

Prison in the Street / Karakoun fî-l-Châri² (Ahmed Yehya)

The Professionals / al-Moutharifoun (Youssef Charaf Eddine)

Rebel Woman / Imra²ah moutamarridah (Youssef Abou Seif)

Rendezvous with Fate / Maw²id ma² al-qadar (Mohamed Radi)

Roots in the Air / Goudhour fî-l-hawâ² (Yehya al-Alami)

Sad Street / Châri² al-sadd (Mohamed Hassib)

Satan's Empire / al-Bidâyah (Salah Abou Seif)

The Secret Session / al-Galsah al-sirriyyah (Mohamed Abdel Aziz)

The Sixth Day / al-Yawm al-sâdis (Youssef Chahine)

The Snakes / al-Thaʾâbîn (Nader Galal)

Some Enjoy and Others Confect / Nâs hâysah wa nâs lâysah (Hassan al-Saïfi)

The Son of Taheya Azouz / Ibn Tahiyyah ʿAzzouz (Ahmed al-Khatib)

The Suicide of the Flat's Owner / Infihâr sâhib al-chiqqah (Ahmed Yeyha)

Terrorized / Ahdân al-khawf (Abdel Meneim Choukri)

The Thugs / al-Awbâch (Ahmed Fouad)

The Time of Love / ʿAsr al-houbb (Hassan al-Imam)

The Time of Wolves / ʿAsr al-dhiʾâb (Samir Seif)

Tomorrow Will Be More Beautiful / Boukra ahlâ min ul-nahâr dah (Hassan al-Imam)

The Train / al-Qitâr (Ahmed Fouad)

The Trainee Lawyer / Mouhâmî taht al-tamrîn (Omar Abdel Aziz)

Under Threat / Taht ul-tahdid (Yassine Ismaïl Yassine)

The Vamp / al-Ounthâ (Hussein al-Wakil)

Vengeance / al-Intiqâm (Fayek Ismaïl)

The Villain Gets It / al-Hidiq yifham (Ahmed Fouad)

A Virgin and Three Men / ʿAdhrâ wa thalâth rigâl (Sayed Seif)

The Virgin Widow / al-Armalah al-ʾadhrâʾ (Hussein Emara)

We Regret This Mistake / Naʾsaf li-hâhhâ al-khataʾ (Hassan Seif Eddine)

Wife on Approval / Imraʾah taht al-ikhtibâr (Mohamed Abaza)

A Woman in Prison / Imraʾah fî-l-sigʾn (Hassan al-Saïfi)

Women Behind Bars / Nisâʾ khalfa al-qoudbân (Nadia Hamza)

The Wretched / al-Safalah (Chérif Hammouda)

1987

The Accusation / al-Ittihâm (Ahmed Sarwat)

Achmawi / ʿAchmâwî (Alaa Mahgoub)

Al-Charabiyyah / al-Charâbiyyah (Salah Serri)

Al-Fahamine / al-Fahhâmîn (Salah Serri)

The Amulet / al-Taʾwîdhah (Mohamed Chebl)

Angels Do Not Live on Earth / al-Malâʾikah lâ taskoun al-ʾard (Saad Arafa)

The Basement / al-Badroun (Atef al-Tayeb)

A Bird with Teeth / ʿOusfour louh anyâb (Hassan Youssef)

A Chance of Thunder / Hazz min al-samâʾ (Abdel Hadi Taha)

The Charlatans / al-Awantaguiyyah (Sayed Tantawi)

The Clerk Caught in a Story of Fraud / alʾArdahâluî fî qadiyyat nasb (Hassan al-Saïfi)

The Confrontation / al-Mouwâgahah (Ahmed al-Sabaawi)

The Conqueror of Time / Qâhir al-zaman (Kamal al-Cheikh)

The Cursed House / al-Bayt al-malʾoun (Ahmed al-Khatib)

The Deer Run / Garî al-wouhouch (Ali Abdel Khalek)

The Doorman / al-Bîh al-bawâb (Hassan Ibrahim)

Drums in the Night / Touboul fî-l-layl (Nasser Hussein)

The Dwarves Arrive / al-Aqzâm qâdimoun (Chérif Arafa)

Fatality / al-Nasîb maktoub (Nasser Hussein)

Fire Woman / Imraʾah min nâr (Ahmed Sarwat)

For Lack of Proof / Li-ʾadam kifâyat al-ʾadillah (Achraf Fahmi)

Four on a Difficult Mission / Arbaʾah fî mouhimmah rasmiyyah (Ali Abdel Khalek)

The Fugitives / al-Hâribât (Nagui Anglo)

The Game of the Great / louʾbat al-kibâr (Saad Arafa)

The Gang / al-ʾIsâbah (Hichem Abou al-Nasr)

The Genie and Love / al-ʾAbqarî wa-l-houbb (Ahmed al-Sabaawi)

A Genie on Stamped Paper / ʿAbqarî ʿalâ warqah damghah (Ahmed Sarwat)

The Giant / al-ʾImlâq (Ahmed al-Sabaawi)

The Girls of Our Alley / Banât haritnâ (Hassan al-Saïfi)

How Much Are You Worth, My Friend? / Yâ sadîqî kam tousâwi (Youssef Francis)

Iron Woman / al-Marʾah al-hadîdiyyah (Abdel Latif Zaki)

Izbat al-Safih / ʿIzbat al-safîh (Ibrahim Afifi)

The Journey's Route / Sikkat safar (Bechir al-Dik)

Khalil after the Changes / Khalîl baʾd al-taʾdîl (Yehya al-Alami)

The Killer / al-Dabbâh (Niazi Mostafa)

The Killer of Karmouz / Sahhâh Karmouz (Hussein Emara)

The Last Look / al-Nazrah al-akhîrah (Chérif Hammouda)

A Madman's Testament / Wasiyyat ragoul mag²noun (Ahmcd Sarwat)

Man Caught in a Women's Trap / Ragoul fî fakh al-nisâ² (Ahmed Saqr)

The Man from Upper Egypt / al-Ragoul al-sa²îdî (Farid Fathallah)

A Man in the Eyes of a Woman / Ragoul fî ᶜou-youn imra²ah (Gamal Ammar)

The Market / al-Souq (Nasser Hussein)

Marriage with Premeditation / Gawâz ma² sabq al-isrâr (Kamal Ide)

Master Stroke / Darbat mou²allim (Atef al-Tayeb)

Meeting during the Honeymoon / Liqâ² fî chahr ᶜasal (Nagui Anglo)

The Monkey Trainer / al-Qirdâtî (Niazi Mostafa)

Mud / al-Wahl (Ali Abdel Khalek)

Nawwara and the Monster / Nawwârah wa-l-wahch (Henri Barakat)

Operation 42 / al-²Amaliyyah tinîn wa arba²în (Adel al-Aassar)

The Past Surges Up Again / ᶜAwdat al-mâdî (Nasseur Hussein)

The Path of Regrets / Sikkat al-naddâmah (Houssam Eddine Mostafa)

The Players / al-La²îbah (Omar Abdel Aziz)

Rawd al-Farag / Rawd al-Farag (Abdel Fattah Madbouli)

The Rhinoceros / al-Khirtît (Ahmed al-Sabaawi)

A Smile in Sad Eyes / Ibtisâmah fî ᶜouyoun hazî-nah (Nasser Hussein)

Sons and Murderers / Abnâ² wa qatalah (Atef al-Tayeb)

The Stabbing / al-Ta²nah (Abdel Hadi Taha)

The Swindle / al-Mal²oub (Osman Choukri)

These Men Are Gentlemen / al-Sâdah al-rigâl (Raafat al-Mihi)

The Thirsty Woman / ᶜAtchânah (al-Saïd Mostafa)

The Three Troublemakers / al-Mouchâghibât al-thalâthah (Houssam Eddine Mostafa)

The Tiger and the Woman / al-Nimr wa-l-ounthâ (Samir Seif)

To Escape from the Asylum / al-Houroub min al-khânkah (Mohamed Radi)

Two Women and a Man / Imra²atân wa ragoul (Abdel Latif Zaki)

The Unfortunate / al-Manhous (Salah Habib)

Very Difficult Mission / Mouhimmah sa²bah guiddan (Hussein Emara)

We Still Have Love / Wa yabqâ al-houbb (Youssef Charaf Eddine)

The Well of Treason / Bi²r al-khiyânah (Ali Abdel Khalek)

The Wife Knows More / al-Zawgah ta²rif akthar (Khalil Chawki)

Witness for the Prosecution / Châdid ithbât (Alaa Mahgoub)

A Woman's Malice / Hiqd imra²ah (Nadia Hamza)

1988

All This Great Love / Koull hâdhâ al-houbb (Hussein Kamal)

Bab al-Nasr / Bâb al-Nasr (Sayed Seif)

Bird in the Sky / Tayr fî-l-samâ (Houssam Eddine Mostafa)

Caught in the Act / Hâlat talabbous (Henri Barakat)

The Challenge / al-Tahaddî (Inas al-Deghidi)

The Claw / al-Kammâchah (Abdel Latif Zaki)

Conqueror of the Horsemen / Qâhir al-foursân (Nasser Hussein)

Cry of Remorse / Sarkat nadam (Mohamed Abdel Aziz)

The Diabolical Plan / Khouttat al-chaytân (Yassine Ismaïl Yassine)

Dreams of Hind and Camellia / Ahlâm Hind wa Kâmîliya (Mohamed Khan)

The Era of Hatem Zahran / Zaman Hâtim Zah-rân (Mohamed el-Naggar)

The Era of Prohibitions / Zaman al-mamnou² (Inas al-Deghidi)

A Father's Revolt / al-Abb al-thâ²ir (Tarek al-Nahri)

Fish, Milk and Tamarind / Samak laban tamr hindî (Raafat al-Mihi)

Golden Girl / Bint min dahab (Mohamed Oussama)

He Returns to Take Revenge / ᶜÂda li-yantaqim (Yassine Ismaïl Yassine)

How's the World Doing? / al-Douniâ garâ fîhâ îh? (Ahmed al-Sabaawi)

I Suffer from Love for You / Anâ wa-l-²adhâb wa hawâk (Mohamed Salmane)

Illusions / al-Awhâm (Ahmed al-Nahhas)

The Killing of a Schoolmistress / Ightiyâl moudarissah (Achraf Fahmi)

A Man against the Law / Ragoul didd al-qânoun (Hatem Radi)

A Man with Seven Lives / Ragoul bi-sab' arwâh (Medhat al-Sibaï)

Money and Monsters / al-Foulous wa-l-wouhouch (Ahmed al-Sabaawi)

The Musician / al-Mazzîkâtî (Mohmaed Abaza)

Nawaem / Nawâ'im (Medhat al-Sibaï)

The Night of Bakiza and Zaghloul's Arrest / Laylat al-qabd 'alâ Bakîzah wa Zaghloul (Mohamed Abdel Aziz)

One July Night / Laylah fî chahr sab'ah (Omar Abdel Aziz)

Paper Hero / Batal min waraq (Nader Galal)

The Rebel / al-Moutamarrid (Henri Barakat)

The River of Fear / Nahr al-khawf (Mohamed Abou Seif)

Samia Chaarawi's Dossier / Malaff Samia Cha'râwî (Nader Galal)

Satan's Friends / Asdiqâ' al-chattân (Ahmed Yassine)

Sergeant Hassan / al-Châwîch Hasan (Ismaïl Hassan)

A Serious Police Record / Arbâb sawâbiq (Mohamed Abaza)

A Seventy-Year-Old Joker / Chaqâwah fî-l-sab'în (Mohamed al-Chami)

A Smile between the Tears / Ibtisâmah fî nahr al-doumou' (Adli Khalil)

Story of Half-a-million Dollars / Hikâyat nisf million dollar (Saad Arafa)

Summer Thefts / Sariqât sayfiyyah (Yousri Nasrallah)

Sweet Day . . . Bitter Day / Yawm mourr . . . yawm hilou (Khaïri Bechara)

Third Class / al-Daragah al-thâlithah (Chérif Arafa)

This Kind of Men / Naw'min al-rigâl (Adli Khalil)

This Marriage Must Not Take Place / al-Gawâzah di mouch lâzim titim (Gamal Ammar)

The Three Tough Guys / al-Guid'ân al-thâlathah (Rachad Abdel Ghani)

Time of Terror / Ayyâm al-rou'b (Saïd Marzouk)

The Troublemakers' Excursion / Rihlat al-mouchâghibîn (Ahmed Sarwat)

The Two Female Prisoners / al-Saguinatân (Ahmed al-Nahhas)

Vipers' Love / Gharâm al-fâ'î (Houssam Eddine Mostafa)

We Share Your Joys / Nouchâtiroukoum al-afrâh (Mohamed Abdel Aziz)

Who Does That Lady Represent? / al-Hânim bi-l-niyâbah (Ahmed Khidr)

The Wife of an Important Man / Zawgat ragoul mouhim (Mohamed Khan)

The Woman and the Law / al-Mar'ah wa-l-qânoun (Nadia Hamza)

A Woman, Alas! / Imra'ah li-l-asaf (Nadia Hamza)

A Woman's Claws / Makhâlib imra'ah (Adel al-Aassar)

The Women's Police / al-Bolîs al-nisâ'i (Abdel Alim)

Youth for All Ages / Chabâb li-koull al-Agyâl (Nasser Hussein)

Youth in Hell / Chabâb fî-l-gahîm (Ahmed al-Sabaawi)

1989

Agent No. 13 / al-'Amîl raqam talata'ch (Medhat al-Sibaï)

Bab Charq / Bâb Charq (Youssef Abou Seif)

The Bad Boy / al-Fatâ al-chirrîr (Mohamed Abdel Aziz)

Berwan Alley / Hârat Bergwan (Hussein Kamal)

Betrayal / Khiyânah (Chérif Hammouda)

Bric-à-brac / Karâkîb (Omar Abdel Aziz)

The Corridor of Death / 'Anbar al-mawt (Achraf Fahmi)

The Cost of Emigration / Thaman al-ghourbah (Nader Galal)

Dearest, We Are All Thieves / Yâ 'azîzî koullounâ lousous (Ahmed Yeyha)

Everything . . . Except My Mother / Illâ . . . oummî (Abdel Alim)

The Execution Squad / Kaîbat al-I'dâm (Atef al-Tayeb)

The Fair / al-Mouled (Samir Seif)

Fratricidal Struggle / Sirâ' al-ahfâd (Abdel Latif Zaki)

Garden of Blood / Boustân al-dam (Achraf Fahmi)

Hell Under Water / Gahîm taht al-mâ³ (Nader Galal)

Help! / Ilhaqounâ (Ali Abdel Khalek)

I Am Not a Killer / Lastou qâtilan (Abdel Hadi Taha)

In the Middle of the Night / Qalb al-layl (Atef al-Tayeb)

The Informer / al-Mourchid (Ibrahim al-Mogui)

The Liar and His Friend / al-Kaddâb wa sahibouh (Ahmed Sarwat)

A Life's Scandal / Fadîhat al-³oumr (Adel al-Aassar)

The Little Monsters / al-Wouhouch al-saghîrah (Abdel Latif Zaki)

Lottery Claimant / ᶜArîs fî-l-yânasîb (Ismaïl Hassan)

Lovers' Lane / Hârat al-habâyib (Hassan al-Saïfi)

The Lucky Ones / Awlâd hazz (al-Saïd Mostafa)

Matron Samah / al-Mou³allimah Samah (Mohamed Abdel Aziz)

A Mother's Mistake / Ghaltat oumm (Ismaïl Hassan)

Nightmare / Kâbous (Mohamed Chebl)

The Old Man and the Crook / al-³Agouz wa-l-baltaguî (Ibrahim Afifi)

Oleich in the Army / ᶜOleich dakhal al-gueich (Youssef Ibrahim)

Playing with Fire / al-Lou³b bi-l-nâr (Mohamed Marzouk)

The Provincials Arrive / al-Sa³âydah goum (Nasser Hussein)

The Puppeteer / al-Aragoz (Hani Lachine)

Rape / Ightisâb (Ali Abdel Khalek)

The Rapists / al-Moughtasiboun (Saïd Marzouk)

Rich Man, Poor Man / al-Ghanâ wa-l-faqîr (al-Saïd Mostafa)

The Secondary School Teacher's Suicide / Intihâr moudarris thâniawî (Nasser Hussein)

Stop / Stop (Mohamed Abaza)

Terrorism / al_Irhâb (Nader Galal)

Those Bastards . . . / Wlad al-îh (Chérif Yehya)

Time of Anger / Ayyâm al-ghadab (Mounir Radi)

The Tough Guys from the Slaughterhouse / Foutouwwat al-Salakhânah (Nasser Hussein)

Unruly Girls in Danger / al-Mouchâghibât fî khatar (Ahmed al-Sabaawi)

A Very Unruly Family / ᶜÂ³ilah mouchâghibah guiddan (Ismaïl Hassan)

We're the Ones Who Robbed the Robbers / Ihna illî saraqnâ al-harâmiyyah (Medhat al-Sibaï)

What Neighbors / Guîrân âkhir zaman (Chérif Hammouda)

Widow of a Living Man / Armalat ragfoul hayy (Henri Barakat)

The World on a Dove's Wing / al-Douniâ ᶜalâ ganâh yamâmah (Atef al-Tayeb)

1990

Alexandria Now and Forever / Iskandariyyah ka-mân we kamân (Youssef Chahine)

An Almost Perfect Crime / Garîmah illâ roub³ (Yassine Ismaïl Yassine)

The Beauty of the Soul / Halâwat al-rouh (Ahmed Fouad Darwich)

Below Zero / Taht al-sifr (Adel Awad)

Captain Nadia's Battle / Ma³rakat al-naqîb Nadiâ (Nadia Hamza)

The Case of an Adolescent Girl / Hâlat mourâhiqah (Sayed Tantawi)

Chawadder / Chawâdir (Ibrahim Afifi)

The Circle of Terror / Halqat al-rou³b (Yassine Ismaïl Yassine)

Crab / Kabouria (Khaïri Bechara)

The Crook and the Dog / al-Nassâb wa-l-kalb (Adel Sadek)

The Dancer and the Politician / al-Râqisah wa-l-siyâsi (Samir Seif)

The Devils / al-³Afârit (Houssam Eddine Mostafa)

The Devil's Island / Gazirat al-chaytân (Nader Galal)

The Egg and the Stone / al-Baydah wa-l-hagar (Ali Abdel Khalek)

The Emperor / al-Ambarâtour (Tarek al-Aryane)

Execution of a Judge / I³dâm qâdî (Achraf Fahmi)

Explosion / Infigâr (Saïd Mohamed Marzouk)

The Faithless Friend / Sahbak min bakhtak (Ismaïl Hassan)

The Fall / al-Souqout (Adel al-Aassar)

The Fool / al-Ahtal (Ahmed al-Sabaati)

Fraud / Iltiyâl (Yassine Ismaïl Yassine)

The Fugitive's Return / ᶜAwdat al-hârib (Youssef Abou Seif)

The Good, the Ugly and the Monster / al-Tayyib, al-charis, al-wahch (Mohamed Marzouk)

Hanafi the Magnificent / Hanafi al-oubbahah (Mohamed Abdel Aziz)

Hell 2 / Gahîm itnîn (Mohamed Abou Seif)

Hello Soussou / Sallim lî ᶜalâ Soussou (Nasser Hussein)

Humiliation / al-Dhoull (Mohamed al-Naggar)

Husbands Beware / Intabihou ayyouhâ al-azwâg (Hassan al-Saïfi)

The Innocent Culprits / al-Moudhniboun al-abriyâ (Mohamed Marzouk)

Insecure Youth / Chabâb ᶜalâ kaff ᶜifrît (Mohsen Mohi Eddine)

It's Fate / Qismah wa nasîb (Hassan al-Saïfi)

Khamis Conquers Cairo / Kharmîs yaghzou al-Qâhirah (Sayed Seif)

Kill My Wife and You'll Have My Gratitude / Iqtil mirâtî we lak tahiyyâti (Hassan Ibrahim)

The Kingdom of God / al-Moulk li Allah (Houssam Eddine Mostafa)

Ladies, Young Ladies / Sayyidâtî ânisâtî (Raafat al-Mihi)

The Last Game / al-Louᵓbah al-akhîrah (Youssef Charaf Eddine)

A Lost Woman / Imraᵓah dallat al-turiq (Nabawi Aglane)

Mahrous the Foreman / al-Oustâ Mahrous (Ismaïl Hassan)

The Network of Death / Chabakat al-mawt (Nader Galal)

Night of Honey / Laylat ᶜasal (Mohamed Abdel Aziz)

Notice to Public Opinion / Balâgh li-l-raᵓî al-ᵓâm (Ahmed al-Sabaati)

One Wife Is Not Enough / Imraᵓah wâhidan lâ takfî (Inas al-Deghidi)

Our Gang Has No Branch / Laysa li-ᵓisâbatinâ farᵓ âktar (Kamal Ateyya)

The Prosecution Pleads Not Guilty / al-Niyâbah tatloub al-barâᵓah (Adli Khalil)

Rendezvous with the President / Mawᵓid maᵓ al-raᵓîs (Mohamed Radi)

The Route of Terror / Darb al-rahbah (Ali Abdel Khalek)

The Samiha Badran Affair / Qadiyyat Samîhah Badrân (Inas al-Deghidi)

Sayyed the Crook / al-Wâd Sayyed al-nassâb (Nasser Hussein)

The Scorpion / al-ᵓAqrab (Adel Awad)

The Servant / al-Khâdim (Ahmed Yeyha)

The She-Devil / al-Chaytânah (Ahmed al-Nahhas)

The She-Devil Who Loved Me / al-Chaytânah al-latî ahabbatnî (Samir Seif)

A Strange Story / Hikâyah laha la-ᵓagab (Hassan al-Saïfi)

Supermarket / Super Market (Mohamed Khan)

The Thief / al-Liss (Saad Arafa)

Three against One / Thalâthah ᶜalâ wâdid (Yassine Ismaïl Yassine)

Three Critical Hours / Talât sâᵓât harigah (Chérif Hammouda)

The Three Idiots / al-Aghbiyâᵓ al-thalâthah (Hassan al-Saïfi)

Traitors in the Night / Layl wa khawanah (Achraf Fahmi)

The Trap / al-Matabb (Hassan al-Saïfi)

The Virgin and the Scorpion / al-ᵓAdhrâᵓ wa-l-ᵓaqrab (Nagui Anglo)

The Volcano / al-Bourkân (Abdel Latif Zaki)

When the Cat's Away, the Mice Play / Mouled w-sâhbouh ghâyib (Nasser Hussein)

The Wounded Bird / al-Tâᵓir al-garîh (Mohamed Abaza)

1991

Abou Kartona / Abou kartounah (Mohamed Hassib)

Adolescent Boys and Girls / Mourâhiqoun wa mourâhiqât (Ahmed Yeyha)

Al-Gablawi / al-Gablâwî (Adel al-Aassar)

Beggars and Proud People / Chahhâtîn wa noubalâᵓ (Asma al-Bakri)

Beware of That Woman / Indharou hâdhihi al-marᵓah (SayedTantawi)

Branded Dangerous / Mousaggal khartar (Samir Seif)

Brigade No. 12 / al-Firqah tnaᵓchar (Abdel Latif Zaki)

The Captain Has Arrived / al-Kâbtin wasal (Ahmed Sarwat)

Citizen Masri / al-Mouwâtin Masrî (Salah Abou Seif)

The City Demons / Chayâtîn al-madînah (Saïd Mohamed Marzouk)

The Corruptors / al-Moufsidoun (Ismaïl Hassan)

Criminal Despite Himself / Mougrim raghm an-fih (Hassan al-Saïfi)

The Crook and the Lady / al-Souᵓlouk wa-l-hânim (Nasser Hussein)

The Cry / al-Sarkhah (Mohamed al-Naggar)

The Dancers' Machinations / Kayd al-awâlim (Ahmed Saqr)

The Devil Finds a Solution / al-Chaytân youqaddim hallan (Mohamed Abdel Aziz)

Dr. Manal Dances / al-Doktorah Nanâl tarqous (Saïd Marzouk)

The Drug Addicts / al-Masâtîl (Hussein Kamal)

The Era of the Powerful / ʿAsr al-qouwwah (Nader Galal)

The Escape / al-Houroub (Atef al-Tayeb)

Female Crooks / Nisâ' sa'âlîk (Nadia Hamza)

Flight Towards Hell / al-Hâribah ilâ al-gahîm (Mohamed Marzouk)

The Fool / al-Ghachîm (Nasser Hussein)

Forbidden Wife / Zawgah mouharramah (Ahmed al-Sabaawi)

The Game of the Wicked / Lou'bat al-achrâr (Henri Barakat)

Half-a-dozen Madmen / Nouss dastat magânîn (Hassan al-Saïfi)

The Heroes of Upper Egypt / Batal min al-Sa'îd (Chérif Hammouda)

Hilali's Grip / Qabdat al-Hilâlî (Ibrahim Afifi)

Humor / al-Mizâg (Ali Abdel Khalek)

The Hunter of Tyrants / Sâ'id al-Gabâbirah (Nasser Hussein)

Hush, They're Listening / Sammi' his (Chérif Arafa)

Ika's Law / al-Qânoun îkâ (Achraf Fahmi)

The Innocent Man and the Executioner / al-Barî' wa-l-gallâd (Mohamed Marzouk)

The Kidnapped Woman / al-Makhtoufah (Chérif Hammouda)

Kit Kat / al-Kît Kât (Daouad Abdel Sayed)

Light in the Eyes / Nour al-'ouyoun (Hussein Kamal)

Looking for Sayyed Marzouq / Al-Bahth ʿan Sayyed Marzouk (Daoud Abdel Sayed)

Madmen on the Road / Magânîn ʿalâ al-tarîq (Chérif Hammouda)

The Midnight Policeman / Châwîch nouss al-leil (Hussein Emara)

The Minister's Daughter / Bint al-Bâchâ al-wazîr (Hassan al-Saïfi)

Moment of Danger / Lahzat khatar (Saïd Amacha)

Oh People / Yâ nâs yâ hou (Atef Salem)

Permission to Kill / Tasrîh bi-l-qatl (Taïmour Serri)

Playing at the Court of the Great / al-Lou'b ma' al-kibâr (Chérif Arafa)

Playing with Demons / al-Lou'b ma' al-chayâtîn (Ahmed Fouad)

Savage Desire / Raghbah moutawahhichah (Khaïri Bechara)

The She-Devils and the Captain / al-Mouchâghibât wa-l-kâbtin (Houssam Eddine Mostafa)

The She-Devils in Prison / al-Mouchâghibât fî-l-sig'n (Nasser Hussein)

The Shepherd and Women / al-Râ'î wa-l-nisâ' (Ali Badrakhan)

The Stroke of My Life / Khabtat al-'oumr (Ismaïl Hassan)

Suspicion / Ichtibâh (Alaa Karim)

Taht al-Rabaa / Tahta al-rab' (Chérif Hammouda)

The Tea Seller / Bâ'i'at al-chây (Ismaïl Hassan)

The Troublemakers No. 6 / al-Mouchâghib sittah (Mohamed Nabih)

A Very Unruly Girl / Bint mouchâghibah guiddan (Ahmed al-Sabaawi)

Women Outlaws / Nisâ' didd al-qânoun (Nadia Hamza)

Ya Mehalabiyyah ya / Yâ mihallabiyyah yâ (Chérif Arafa)

Zanati's Sun / Chams al-Zanâti (Samir Seif)

1992

The Accused Woman / al-Mouttahamah (Henri Barakat)

Against the Government / Didd al-houkoumah (Atef al-Tayeb)

Al-Haggama / al-Haggâmah (Mohamed al-Naggar)

The Battle between the Wives / Sirâ' al-zawgât (Neimat Rouchdi)

Beware of Azouz / Khallî bâlak min ʿAzzouz (Nasser Hussein)

Beware of Charbate / Âh . . . we âh min Charbât (Mohamed Abdel Aziz)

Bitter Love / al-Houbb al-mourr (Houssam Eddine Mostafa)

Blood on the Asphalt / Dimâ' ʿalâ al-isfalt (Atef al-Tayeb)

Bloody Encounter / al-Liqâ' al-dâmî (Ismaïl Gamal)

The Bloody Trace / al-Khoutwah al-dâmiyah (Ahmed al-Sabaawi)

The Bulldozer / *al-Buldozer* (Houssam Eddine Mostafa)

The Cock and His Harem / *Dîk al-barâbir* (Hussein Kamal)

The Courageous / *al-Chougʾân* (Tarek al-Nahri)

Crime at the Bottom of the Sea / *Garîmah fî-l-aʾmâq* (Houssam Eddine Mostafa)

The Dancer and the Devil / *al-Râqisah wa-l-chaytân* (Mahmoud Hanafi)

The Dancer and the Undertaker (*al-Râqisah wa-l-hânoutî* (Nagdi Hafez)

The Deserter / *Hârib min al-tagʾnîd* (Ahmed al-Sabaawi)

Dounia Abdel Gabbar / *Douniâ Abd al-Gabbâr* (Abdel Latif Zaki)

Everyone Deceives Everyone Else / *Loullouh biyilʾab ʿalâ koullouh* (Gamal Ammar)

The Falcon's Eyes / *ʿOuyoun al-saqr* (Ibrahim al-Mogui)

Fallen Woman / *Imraʾah âyilah li-l-souqout* (Medhat al-Sibaï)

Fathiyyah and the Mercedes / *Fathiyyah wa-l-marsîdès* (Saïd Mohamed Marzouk)

Fleshy Lips / *Chifâh ghalîzah* (Chérif Yehya)

Gaber's Resignation / *Istiqâlat Gaber* (Ahmed Saqr)

The Game of Revenge / *Louʾbat al-intiqâm* (Mohamed Abdel Aziz)

Gawhari Alleyway / *Hârat al-gawharî* (Medhat al Sibaï)

Girls in a Jam / *Banât fi wartah* (Ahmed al-Sabaawi)

He Has Finished His Statement / *Wa tammat aqwâlouh* (Magdi Mehrem)

His Majesty's Tears / *Doumouʾ sahibat al-galâlah* (Atef Salem)

Husbands in a Jam / *Azwâg fi wartah* (Hassan al-Saïfi)

Ice Cream in Glim / *Ice cream fi glîm* (Khaïri Bechara)

The Knight of the City / *Fâris al-madînah* (Mohamed Khan)

The Lion's Share / *Nasîb al-asad* (Saïd Saleh)

Love and Cruel Revenge / *Gharâm wa intiqâm bi-l-sâtour* (Mohamed Chebl)

Love and Terror / *al-Houbb wa-l-rouʾb* (Karim Dia Eddine)

Love at Taba / *al-Houbb fî Tâbâ* (Ahmed Fouad)

The Maggot in the Fruit / *al-Fâs fî-l-râs* (Wahid Mekhiemar)

The Man from the Mountains / *Ibn al-Gabal* (Mohamed Marzouk)

Man of Fire / *Ragoul min nâr* (Mohamed Marzouk)

The Massacre of the Honest / *Madhbahat al-chourafâʾ* (Nasser Hussein)

Memories and Regrets / *Dhikrayât wa nadam* (Ahmed Sarwat)

Mission in Tel-Aviv / *Mouhimmah fî Tall Abîb* (Nader Galal)

Mr. Dessouqi on Holiday / *Dessouqi afandî fî-l-masyaf* (Omar Abdel Aziz)

The Murderess / *al-Qâtilah* (Inas al-Deghidi)

My Wife and the Wolf / *Zawgatî wa-l-dhiʾb* (Ahmed al-Sawaabi)

Nagui Al-Ali / *Nâguî al-ʾAlî* (Atef al-Tayeb)

Nannousa / *Nannoussah* (Gamal Ammar)

Nights of Waiting / *Laylâlî al-sabr* (Ahmed Sarwat)

Ouch . . . Ouch . . . / *Aïe . . . Aïe* (Saïd Marzouk)

Peasants Arrive / *al-Fallâhîn ahom* (Nasser Hussein)

The Police Devils / *Chayâtîn al chourtah* (Samir Hafez)

Rare Coins / *alʾImlah al-nâdirah* (Samir Hafez)

The Road to the Asylum / *al-Tarîq li-moustachfâ al-magânîn* (Nasser Hussein)

Samara Al-Amir / *Samârah al-Amîr* (Ahmed Yeyha)

The Scandal / *al-Fadîhah* (Farouk al-Rachidi)

The Slaves' Murmurs / *Hams al-Gawârî* (Nadia Hamza)

The Spy Trap / *Fakhkh al-Gawâsîs* (Achraf Fahmi)

Terrorism and Kebabs / *al-Irhâb wa-l-kabâb* (Cherif Arafa)

The Troublemakers at Nouibi / *Mouchâghiboun fî nouibiʾ* (Nasser Hussein)

The Troublemakers in the Navy / *al-Mouchâghiboun fî-l-bahriyyah* (Nasser Hussein)

Two Outlaws / *Ithnân didd al-qânoun* (Adel Sadek)

The Village of the Greedy / *Kafr al-tammâʾîn* (Wasfi Darwich)

The Wheel Turns / *al-Hagar dâyir* (Mohamed Radi)

The Wicked Person / *al-Charis* (Nader Galal)

The Wolf's Lair / *Wakr al-dhiʾb* (Nasser Hussein)

Woman Prisoner No. 67 / *al-Saguînah sabʾa wa sittîn* (Ahmed Yeyha)

A Woman's Hell / Gahîm imra²ah (Tarek al-Nahri)
Women / al-Sittât (Medhat al-Sibaï)
The Wrongdoer / al-Chaqî (Ibrahim Arayes)
1993
Al-Ghaqana / al-Gharqânah (Mohamed Khan)
America cadabra / Amérika chîkâ bîkâ (Khaïri Bechara)
The Battle of the Beauties / Sirâ² al-hasnâwât (Mohamed Marzouk)
Chase into the Forbidden / Moutâradah f-l-mamnou² (Medhat Bekir)
Christal / Kristâl (Adel Awad)
Dance with Satan / al-Raqs ma² al-chaytân (Alaa Mahgoub)
Dirty Game / al-Lou²bah al-qadhirah (Houssam Eddine Mostafa)
85 at the Crime / 85 Guinâyat (Alaa Karim)
Enquiry with a Citizen / Tahqîq ma² mouwâtinah (Henri Barakat)
Flame of Vengeance / Lahîb al-intiqâm (Samir Seif)
The Forgotten Man / al-Mansî (Chérif Arafa)
The Foxes / al-Tha²âlib (Ahmed al-Sabaawi)
Hard Times / al-Zaman al-sa²b (Mohamed Hassib)
Karawana / Karawânah (Abdel Latif Zaki)
The Knights of Old / Foursân âkhir zaman (Medhat al-Sibaï)
Land of Dreams / Ard al-ahlâm (Daoud Abdel Sayed)
Laughs, Games, Seriousness and Love / Dihk wa lou²b wa gadd wa houbb (Tarek al-Telmessani)
Little Dreams / Ahlâm saghîragh (Khaled al-Hagar)
Love in a Fridge / al-Houbb fî-l-thallâgah (Saïd Hamed)
Maganino / Magânîno (Essam al-Chamma)
Maid Servant, but . . . / Khâdimah wa lâkin (Ali Abdel Khalek)
The Men Are in Danger / al-Rigâl fî khatar (Nagdi Hafez)
Mercedes / Marsîdès (Yousri Nasrallah)
Mister Dollar / Mister Dollar (Ahmed Abdel Salam)
Mister Karate / Mister Karaté (Mohamed Khan)
The Most Courageous / Agda² al-nâs (Medhat al-Cherif)
No to Violence / Lâ yâ ᶜounf (Gamal al-Tabei)
131, Forced Labour / 131 Achghâl (Nader Galal)

The Orphan and Love / al-Yâtim wa-l-houbb (Mahmoud Farid)
The Orphan and the Wolves / al-Yatîm wa-l-dhi²âb (Husssein Emara)
The Pasha / al-Bâchâ (Tarek al-Aryane)
Playing with the Evil / al-Li²b ma² al-achrâr (Tarek al-Nahri)
The Politician / al-Siyâsî (Ismaïl Galal)
Priceless Men / Rigâl bilâ thaman (Abdel Hadi Taha)
A Provincial in the Army / Sa²îdî fî-l-gaych (Nasser Hussein)
Race against Time / Sibâq ma² al-zaman (Anwar Qawadri)
Satan's Gates / Bawwâbat Iblîs (Adel al-Aassar)
Sayyed the Servant / al-Wâd Sayyed al-chaghghâl (Hussein Kamal)
The Shrew / al-Charisah (Ahmed Saqr)
Spicy Taamiyya / Ta²miyyah bi-l-chattah (Abdel Latif Zaki)
The Strongest of Men / Aqwâ al-rigâl (Ahmed al-Sabaawi)
Summons to Reintegrate the Family Home / Indhâr bi-l-Tâ²ah (Atef al-Tayeb)
Three on the Road / Thalâthah ᶜalâ al-tarîq (Mohamed Kamel al-Kalioubi)
Toot Toot / Tout tout (Atef Salem)
The Treasure / al-Kanz (Saïd Chimi)
The Two Fugitives / al-Hâribân (Ismaïl Hassan)
Violets Are Blue / Lîh yâ banafsig (Radwane al-Kachef)
Why Pyramids? / Lîh yâ haram (Omar Abdel Aziz)
The Wicked / al-Chouttâr (Nader Galal)
Without You / Lawlâki (Hassan al-Saïfi)
The Wolves / al-Dhi²âb (Abdel Halim al-Nahhas)
The Woman and the Giant / Hiya wa-l-²imlâq (Ismaïl Hassan)
A Woman Pays the Price / Imra²ah tadfa² al-thaman (Hassan Ibrahim)
1994
Can't Make Up Their Minds (lit. Those Who Dance in the Stairways / Illâ raqasou ᶜalâ al-sillim (Nagui Anglo)
The Dancers' Alley / Darb al-²awâlim (Nasser Hussein)
Danger / al-Khatar (Abdel Latif Zaki)
Desires / Raghbât (Karim Diaa Eddine)
Disco . . . Disco / Disco . . . disco (Inas al-Deghidi)

Disorder / Khaltabîtah (Medhat al-Sibaï)

Either You Love . . . or You Leave / Yâ thibb . . . yâ t'ibb (Abdel Latif Zaki)

The Emigré / al-Moughâguir (Youssef Chahine)

Five-star Thieves / Lousous khamsat nougoum (Achraf Fahmi)

Foxes . . . Rabbits / Ta'âlib . . . arânib (Sayed Seif)

The Game of Crime / Lou'bat al-qatl (Adli Khalil)

The Good, the Ugly and the Beauty / al-Tayyib wa-l-charis wa-l-Gamîlah (Medhat al-Sibaï)

Hekmat Fahmi the Spy / al-Gâsousah Hikmat Fahmî (Houssam Eddine Mostafa)

A Hero of His Time / ʿAntar zamanouh (Taïmour Serri)

I Forgot That I Was a Woman / Wa nasîtou annî imra'ah (Atef Salem)

Jeans / al-Jînz (Cherif Chaaban)

Lifting the Veil / Kachf al-mastour (Atef al-Tayeb)

Madam's Chauffeur / Sawwâq al-hânim (Hassan Ibrahim)

Mr. D / al-Sayyed kâf (Salah Abou Seif)

The Night of the Murder / Laylat al-qatl (Achraf Fahmi)

Our Beautiful Dreams / Ahlâmounâ al-hilwah (Samir Hafez)

The Player / al-Mouqâmir (Chirine Kassem)

The President's Visit / Ziyârat al-Sayyed al-ra'îs (Mounir Radi)

Red Card / Kârt ahmar (Oussama al-Kerdawi)

The Red Flag / al-Râyah al-hamrâ (Achraf Fahmi)

Rubbish / Qadhârah (Adel al-Aassar)

The Strawberry War / Harb al-farâwlah (Khaïri Bechara)

The Terrorist / al-Irhâbî (Nader Galal)

They've Robbed Oum Ali / Saraqou Oumm ʿAlî (Ahmed al-Nahhas)

Three Around a Table of Blood / Thalâthah ʿalâ mâ'idat al-dam (Medhat al-Sibaï)

The Truth Is Called Salem / al-Haqîqah ismouha Sâlim (Ahmed Saqr)

The Wolf Trap / Misyadat al-dhi'âb (Ismaïl Gamal)

A Woman's Revenge / Intiqâm im ra'ah (Ismaïl Gamal)

The Women's Market / Souq al-nisa' (Youssef Francis)

Why Dunia? / Lîh yâ douniâ (Hani Lachine)

1995

Abou Zeid of His Time / Abou Zeid zamanu (Ahmed al-Sabaawi)

Angels Do Not Live on Earth / al-Mala'ika la taskun al-ard (Saïd Arafa)

The Assassination of Faten Tawfik / Ighteyaal Faten Tawfiq (Ismaïl Mourad)

Bekhit and Adila / Bekheet wa ʿAdeela (Nader Galal)

Birds of the Darkness / Tuyour al-zalaam (Cherif Arafa)

Blood after Midnight / Demaa' ba'd muntasaf al-lail (Yassine Ismaïl Yassine)

The Boss-Woman and the Gentleman / al-Me'allemma wal ustaaz (Abdel Halim al-Nahhas)

Boulteyya, a Girl from Bahary / Boulteyya bent Bahary (Salah Serri)

Cheap Flesh / Lahm rakhis (Inas al-Deghidi)

City Dogs / Kelaab al-mudina (Gamal al-Tabei)

Days of Evil / Ayyaam al-charr (Youssef Abou Seif)

Desert Cat / Qett ul-saharaa' (Saïd Marzouk and Youssef Mansour)

Escapee to Prison / Hareb ila al-sign (Yassine Ismaïl Yassine)

Evil Road / Tarik al-charr (Mohammed Marzouk)

The Garage / al-Garage (Alaa Karim)

Goodbye to Bachelorhood / Wada'an lel ʿuzubeyya (Ismaïl Gamal)

Houda and His Excellency the Minister / Huda wa Ma'aal' al-wazir (Saïd Marzouk)

A Little Love, a Lot of Violence / Qaleel mina al-hubb katheer min al-ʿunf (Raafat al-Mihi)

The Man Who Stole Joy / Sarek al-farah (Daoud Abdel Sayed)

Nutshells / Qeshr el bunduk (Khaïri Bechara)

Penalty / Darbet gazza' (Ashraf Fahmi)

Silence of the Sheep / Samt al-kherfaan (Saïd Mohammed)

Stranger at the Harbour / Gharib fil mina (Ismaïl Hassan)

Summer Love Is Crazy / Fil seif al-hubb gonoon (Omar Abdel Aziz)

Tata, Rika and Kazem Bey / Ta'ta wa Reeka wa Kazem Bey (Cherif Chaaban)

The Third Man / al-Ragoul al-thaleth (Ali Badrakhan)

A Very Hot Day / Youm harr gedan (Mohammed Khan)

We Are Children of Today / Ihna welaad el naharda (Sayed Tantawi)

Why Does the Sea Laugh? / al-Bahr beyedhak lih (Mohamed Kamel al-Kalioubi)

A Woman Who Shook Egypt's Throne / Imaraʾa hazzat ʿarsh masr (Nader Galal)

Women's Threshold / ʿAtabet el settaat (Ali Abdel Khalek)

1996

Abou El Dahab / Abou el Dahab (Karim Dia Eddine)

All Hail / Mit foll (Raafat al-Mihi)

As the Heart Loves / al-Qalb wi ma yeʾshaq (Ahmed al-Nahhas)

Assassination / Ighteyaal (Nader Galal)

Caprice / Nazwa (Ali Badrakhan)

The Enraged / al Ghadeboon (Tarek al-Nahri)

Escape to the Summit / al-Horoob ila al-qimma (Adel al-Aassar)

The Fatal Phone Call / al-Mukalama al-qatela (Yassine Ismaïl Yassine)

The Fierce Man / al-Ragoul al-chares (Yassine Ismaïl Yassine)

The Gentleman / el-Gentel (Ali Abdel Khalek)

The Gypsies / al-Ghagar (Ibrahim Afifi)

Hot Night / Laila sakhena (Atef Al-Tayeb)

Jailbird / al-Lumangi (Ismaïl Gamal)

The Jewelry Market / al-Sagha (Ahmed al-Sabaawi)

Lobster / Istakoza (Inas al-Deghidi)

Love in Difficult Circumstances / al-Hubb fi zoroof saʾba (Simon Saleh)

Nasser '56 / Nasser 56 (Mohamed Fadel)

Oh, Life, My Love / Ya donya ya gharamy (Magdi Ahmed Ali)

Railway Switch / al-Tahwila (Amali Bahnasi)

Road Devils / ʿAfarit al-asphalt (Osama Fawzi)

Romantic / Romantica (Zaki Fatin Abdel Wahab)

The Seventh Sin / al-Khatiʾa al-sabeʾa (Abdel Latif Zaki)

Sitting on Their Hands / al-Noum fi al-ʿasal (Cherif Arafa)

Suspicious Liaisons / ʿIlaqaat mashbouha (Adel al-Aassar)

Time and the Dogs / al-Zaman wal kelaab (Samir Seif)

Traffic Light / Isharet muroor (Khaïri Bechara)

The Turtles / al-Salahef (Saïd Mohamed)

A Very Important Man / Ragoul mohemm geddann (Essam al-Chamma)

1997

Apple / Toffaha (Raafat al-Mihi)

Bekhit and Adila: The Bucket and the Coffee Pot / Bekheet wi ʿAdeela: al-Gardal wi al-kanaka (Nader Galal)

The Captain / al-Qubtaan (Sayed Saïd)

Day Devil / ʿAfreet al-nahaar (Adel Al-Aassar)

Destiny / al-Masseer (Youssef Chahine)

A Fish and Four Sharks / Samaka wa arbaʾ quroosh (Cherif Chaaban)

Hassan El Loll / Hassan el loll (Nader Galal)

Ismailia Round Trip / Ismailia rayeh . . . gayy (Karim Dia Eddine)

Mushroom / ʿEish el ghuraab (Samir Seif)

A Police Officer Resigns / Istiqalet dabet shurta (Ashraf Fahmi)

Round Up! / Hallaq hoosh! (Mohamed Abdel Aziz)

Tie the Scarf Around My Hips / Hazzemny ya (Hussein Kamal)

We'll Love and Get Rich / Ha nheb wi nʾeb (Abdel Latif Zaki)

A Woman and Five Men / Imraʾa wa khamas regaal (Alaa Karim)

The Woman and the Cleaver / al-Marʾa wa al-satoor (Saïd Marzouk)

Woman at the Top / Imraʾa fawq al-qemma (Ashraf Fahmi)

1998

Abou Khatwa / Abou Khatwa (Youssef Abou Seif)

The Champion / al-Batal (Magdi Ahmed Ali)

Consolation / Gabr el khawater (Atef al-Tayeb)

Criminal with Honors / Mogrem maʾa martabet el sharaf (Medhat al-Sebaï)

Delicious Killing / al-Katl el laziz (Ashraf Fahmi)

Empire of Evil / Imbratoureyet el sharr (Ismaïl Gamal)

The Female and the Wasp / al-Untha wa al-dabbour (Youssef Abou Seif)

48 Hours in Israel / 48 saʾa fi Israel (Nader Galal)

Gamal Abdel Nasser / Gamal Abdel Nasser (Anwar el-Kawadri)

Harmonica / Harmonica (Fakhr Eddine Negeda)

Hysteria / Hysteria (Adel Adeeb)

Lace / Dantiella (Inas al-Deghidi)

Lady among Ladies / Set el settaat (Raafat al-Mihi)

Mabrouk and Bolbol / Mabrouk wa Bolbol (Sandra Nashaat)

A Message to the Ruler / Resala ela al-wali (Nader Galal)

Pizza Pizza / Pizza pizza (Mazen al-Gabali)

Say Cheese for the Photo to Be Beautiful / Idhak el sourah tetla' helwa(Cherif Arafa)

Surface to Surface / Ard ard (Ismaïl Mourad)

Time for Revenge / Sa'at el-intekam (Ahmed al-Sabaawi)

An Upper Egyptian Goes to the American University / Sa'idi fi el gam'a al-merekeya(Saïd Hamed)

1999

Abboud on the Borders / Abboud 'ala al-hodood (Cherif Arafa)

Al Kafeer / al-Kafeer (Ali Abdel Khalek)

Bluffing / Alabanda (Samir Al-Asfoury and Mohamed Fadel)

Date Wine / 'Ara' el balah (Radwane al-Kachef)

The Empress / al-Imbratoura (Ali Abdel Khalek)

A Girl from Israel / Fatat min Israel (Ihab Radi)

Hammam in Amsterdam / Hammaam fi Amesterdam (Saïd Hamed)

Hassan and Aziza: State Security Case / Hassan wi 'Azeeza, qadeyet amn dawla (Karim Dia Eddine)

I Never Meant to be a . . . / Wa la fi el neyya ab'aa . . . (Karim Dia Eddine)

The Leader / al-Za'eem (Cherif Arafa and Mohamed Fadel)

Mahrous, the Shadow of the Minister / al-Waad Mahrous betaa' el wazeer (Nader Galal)

The Most Elegant Guy in Roxy / Ashyak waad fi roxy (Adel Adeeb)

Night Talk / Kalaam el leel (Inas al-Deghidi)

The Other / al-Akhar (Youssef Chahine)

The Star of the Orient / Kawkab all-sharq (Mohamed Fadel)

State Security / Amn dawla (Nader Galal)

The Unjust and the Wronged / al-Zalim wa al mazloom (Houssam Eddine Mostafa)

Waves of Anger / Amwaag al-ghadab (Ismaïl Gamal)

2000

Action Movie Hero / Shagi' el sima (Ali Ragab)

Al Nims / al-Nims (Ali Abdel Khalek)

All Well and Good / Foll el foll (Medhat al-Sibaï)

All-Girl Band / Ferqet banaat wi bass (Cherif Chaaban)

Cash OK / el-Cash mashi (Tarek Al-Nahri)

The City / al-Madina (Yousri Nasrallah)

Concerto in the Street of Happiness / Concerto fi darb sa'aada (Asma al-Bakri)

Crazy Life / Gonoon al-hayah (Saïd Marzouk)

Cultural Film / Film thaqaafi (Mohamed Amin)

Devils' Paradise / Gannat al-chayatin (Osama Fawzi)

Excuse Me, Debes / La mu'akhza ya de'bes (Ismaïl Hassan)

Fine, Fine / Bono, bono (Ali Abdel Khalek)

First Love / al-Houbb al-awwal (Hamed Saïd)

Going Cheap in Taht El Rab / Taht el rab' be gnih wi rub' (Ismaïl Gamal)

The Heudmaster / al-Nazer (Cherif Arafa)

Hello America / Hallo Amrika (Nader Galal)

Honour / al-Charaf (Mohamed Chaaban)

Land of Fear / Ard el khouf (Daoud Abdel Sayed)

A Man with a Past / Ragoul laho maadi (Ahmed Yehya)

Omar 2000 / Omar 2000 (Ahmed Atef)

Pleasure Market / Souq al-Mut'a (Samir Seif)

The Red Notebook / al-Agenda al-hamraa' (Ali Ragab)

The Red Rose / al-Warda al-hamra (Inas al-Deghidi)

Room to Rent (English, Khaled al-Hagar)

Ruining the Party / Kursi fil koloob (Sameh Al-Bagouri)

Shorts, a T-Shirt and a Cap / Short wa fanella wa cap (Saïd Hamed)

Smart Bilya / Bilya we demagho el 'alya (Nader Galal)

Sons of the Devil / Abna' al-Chaytaan (Ibrahim Afifi)

Talking about Taboos / al-Kalaam fil mamnoo' (Omar Abdel Aziz)

Why Did You Make Me Love You? / Lih khalletny ahebbak? (Sandra Nashaat)

A Woman under Observation / Imra'a taht el muraqba (Ashraf Fahmi)

Zanqet El Settaat / Zanqet el settaat (Alaa Karim)

2001

Abracadabra / Gala gala (Mazen al-Gabali)

Africano / Afrikano (Amr Arafa)

Afrotto / Afrotto (Mohamed Abdel Aziz)

Ambulance 55 / 55 isʾaaf (Magdi Al-Hawwaari)

Anbar and the Colours / ʿAnbar wa al-alwaan (Adel al-Aassar)

A Citizen, a Detective and a Thief / Mowaten wa mukhber wa haraamy (Daoud AbdelSayed)

Closed Doors / al-Abwaab al-mughlaqa (Atef Hetata)

The Costumer / al-Labbeess (Ashraf Fayek)

Days of Sadat / Ayyaam el Sadat (Mohamed Khan)

First Grade, Secondary School / ʿUla thanawy (Mohamed Abou Seif)

Friends or Buisness / Ashaab walla business (Ali Idris)

Fruit Ice / Graneeta (Omar Abdel Aziz)

Girls' Secrets / Asraar el banat (Magdi Ahmed Ali)

A Hero from the South / Batal min al-ganoob (Mohamed Abou Seif)

How to Please God / ʿAlashaan rabbena yehebbak (Raafat al-Mihi)

If This Is a Dream / Law kaan da helm (Tarek al-Nahri)

Journey of Love / Rehlet hubb (Mohamed al-Naggar)

The Lovers / al-ʿAshiqaan (Nour al-Cherif)

Marriage by Presidential Decree / Gawaaz bi qaraar goumhoury (Khaled Youssef)

An Oath of Divorce / Yameen talaq (Ali Abdel Khalek)

Rendezvous / Rendezvous (Ali Abdel Khalek)

Roll Up, Roll Up / Itfarrag ya salaam (Mohamed Kamal al-Kalioubi)

Silence! We're Filming / Sukoot ha nsawwar! (Youssef Chahine)

Snakes and Ladders / al-Sellem wa el teʾbaan (Tarek al-Iryaan)

Son of Ezz the Rich Man / Ibn Ezz (Cherif Arafa)

The Tempest / al-Asefa (Khaled Youssef)

Throwing It About / Rashsha gareeʾa (Saïd Hamed)

Underground Hell / Gaheem that al ʿard (Nader Galal)

An Upper Egyptian Coming and Going / Seʾeedy rayeh gayy (Mohamed al-Naggar)

We Interrupt This Program to Bring You the Following Announcement / Gaʾana al-bayaan al taly (Saïd Hamed)

We Own the Airport / Ihna ashaab el mataar (Cherif Yehya)

Zakeya Zakareya Goes to Parliament / Zakeya Zakareya fi al-barlamaan (Raid Labib)

2002

Adam's Autumn / Kharif Adam (2002, Mohamed Kamal al-Kalioubi)

Al-Lemby / al-Lemby (Wael Ihsaan)

Badr: Enter in Peace / Badr: idkholouha ameneen (Youssef Mansour)

Be Alert / Khalli el demaagh sahi (Mohamed Abou Seif)

Brave Heart / Qalb gareeʾ (Mohamed al-Naggar)

Desire / al-Raghba (Ali Badrakhan)

Diaries of a Teenage Girl / Muzakkeraat muraheqa (Inas al-Deghidi)

Gaafar Al-Masri Disappears / Ikhtifaaʾ Gaafar al-Masri (Adel al-Aassar)

His Excellency the Minister / Maʾaly el wazeer (Samir Seif)

Likewise in Zamalek / Kazalik fi el Zamalk (Ahmed Awad)

Lost in America / Tayeh fi Amrika (Raffi Guirguiss)

Love and Blood / al-ʿIshk wa al-damm (Ashraf Fahmi)

Mafia / Mafia (Cherif Arafa)

Magic of the Eyes / Sehar al-ʿuyoun (Fakhr Eddine Negeda)

The Magician: The Notion of Joy / al-Saher: nazareyet al-bahga (Radwane al-Kachef)

Mediterranean Man / al-Ragoul al-abyad al-mutawasset (Cherif Mandour)

The Ostrich and the Peacock / al-Naʾaama wa al-tawooss (Mohamed Abou Seif)

A Peasant in Congress / Fallah fi el-kongress (Fahmi al-Charkawi)

Prince of Darkness / Ameer al-zalaam (Rami Imam)

Suspicious Journey / Rehala mashbouha (Ahmed Yehya)

Thieves in KG II / Harameya fi kg II (Sandra Nashaat)

A True Friend / Saheb sahbo (Saïd Hamed)
Volcanic Rage / Borkaan al Ghadab (Mazen al-Gabali)
Whale Hunting / Said al-heitaan (Ali Abdel Khalek)
What's Going on? / Howwa feeh eih? (Cherif Mandour)
Woman's Divorce Lawyer / Muhami khol' (Mohamed Yassin)
Youth On Air / Shabaab ʿala el hawa (Adel Awad)
2003
The Actor / al-Meshakhasati (Fakhr Eddine Negeda)
Askar in the Camp / ʿAskar fi el-muʾaskar (Mohammed Yassin)
At First Sight / Min nzret ain (Ihaab Lamei)
The Danish Experiment / al-Tagruba al-Danemarkeya (Ali Idris)
The First Time You Fall in Love / Awwel marra teheb (Alaa Karim)
Fishtail / Deil al-samaka (Samir Seif)
How To Make Girls Love You / I zuay el banat tehebbak (Ahmed Atef)
I Love You; Me Too / Bahebbak; wʾana kamaan (Mohamed Al-Naggar)
I Want My Rights / ʿAwez haqqy (Ahmed Galal)
Indian Movie / Film Hindi (Mounir Radi)
Lovers' Snippets / Qasaqis al-ʿushaq (Saïd Marzouk)
May God Make It Up to Us / ʿAlih al-ʿawad (Ali Abdel Khalek)
Mido the Troublemaker / Mido mashakel (Mohamed al-Naggar)
Mind Your Face! / Iwʾa weshak! (Saïd Hamed)
Runaway Mummy / Horoob mumia (Mourad Aknash)
The Sea-Drill / Haffaar el bahr (Adel al-Aassar)
Sleepless Nights / Sahar al-layali (Hani Khalifa)
Talk to Mom / Kallem Mama (Ahmed Awad)
That's OK / Keda OK (Samir al-Asfouri and Osama al-ʿAsi)
Thieves in Thailand / Harameyya fi Thailand (Sandra Nashaat)
You-Know-Who / Illy baly balak (Wael Ihsaan)
2004
Alexandria-New York / Iskendereya New York (Youssef Chahine)

Aunty Faranssa / Khalty Faranssa (Ali Ragab)
Beach Bum / Sayeʾ bahr (Ali Ragab)
The Best Times / Ahla aliawqaat (Hala Khalil)
Burning Love / Hobbak naar (Ihaab Radi)
Cool, Man! / Ishta yaba (Atef Chukri)
The Day I Fell in Love / Kaan youm houbbak (Ihaab Lamei)
The Day of Dignity / Youm El Karama (Ali Abdel Khalek)
Farah / Farah (Akram Farid)
Great Beans of China / Fuul el sein al-ʿazeem (Cherif Arafa)
Heaven Save Us! / Ashtatan Ashtoot (Omar Abdel Aziz)
I Love the Movies / Baheb el seema (Osama Fawzi)
I'll Let Go if You Will / Seeb wa ana aseeb (Wael Charkas)
In Love / Halet houbb (Saad Hendawi)
Inherently Stupid / Ghaby menno fih (Rami Imam)
Kimo and His Best Friend / Kimo wi antimo (Saïd Hamed)
Okal / ʿOkal (Mohamed al-Naggar)
The Pasha Is a Student / al-Busha telmiz (Wael Ihsan)
Security Police Bridegroom / ʿArees min geha amneya (Ali Idris)
7 Playing Cards / 7 waraqaat kutsheena (Cherif Sabri)
Spicy Kids / Shebr wi nuss (Adel Yehia)
Swindlers, First Grade / Sana ula nasb (Kamla Abou Zikri)
Tito / Tito (Tarek Al-Iryaan)
Women's Love / Houbb al-banaat (Khaled al-Hagar)
2005
Abou Ali / Abu Ali (Ahmed Galal)
Al-Sayyed Abou El-Araby Is Here / al-Sayyed Abu El-Araby wasal (Mohsen Ahmed)
Booha (Rami Imam)
Cholesterol Free / Khaly min al-cholesterol (Mohamed Abou Seif)
Coming Soon / Gayy fil sareeʾ (Gamal Kassem)
Downtown Girls / Banaat wist al-balad (Mohamed Khan)
The Embassy in the Building / al-Sefara fil ʿemara (Amr Arafa)

Excuse Us, We're Being Humiliated / La Mu'akhza iʾna benetbahdel (Cherif Mandour)

The Gate of the Sun / Bab al-Chams [*Departure* (142′) + *Return* (137′)] (Yousri Nasrallah)

Hamada Plays / Hamada yelʾab (Saïd Hamed)*Alexundria Private / Alexandria prive* (Sandra Nashaat)

I Want a Divorce / Ureedo kholʾan (Ahmed Awad)

Italian War /Harb Italia (Ahmed Saleh)

Life Is Delightful / al-Hayat muntaha al-lazza (Manal al-Seifi)

Love Fan / Ghawy hubb (Ahmed al-Badri)

Lover Boys / ʿEyaal habbeeba (Magdi al-Hawwaari)

Karim's Harem / Hareem Kareem (Ali Idris)

Me or My Aunt / Yana ya khalty (Saïd Hamed)

My Soul Mate / Enta omri (Khaled Youssef)

Farhan Mulazem Adam / Farhan Mulazem Adam (Omar Abdel Aziz)

I Love You So /Bahebbak wi bamoot fik (Sayyed Essawy)

The Night Baghdad Fell / Laylat suqoot Baghdaad (Mohamed Amin)

Our Life's Dreams / Ahlaam ʿumrena (Osman Abou Laban)

Private Lesson / Dars khusussi (Sameh Abdel Aziz)

Sentimental Sayyed /Sayyed al-ʿAtify (Ali Ragab)

Seventh Sense / Al-Hassa Al-Sabʾa (Ahmed Mekky)

Spicy Ali / Aly Spicy (Mohamed al-Naggar)

Teach Me How to Love /ʿAllemny al-hubb (Yasser Zayed)

Violence and Hate / alʾUnf wa-l-sukhriya (Asma al-Bakri)

Women in Search of Freedom / al-Bahethaat ʿan al-hurreyya (Inas al-Deghidi)

Zaki Chan / Zaki Chan (Wael Ihsaan)

2006

Abdou Seasons /ʾAbdu mawasem (Wael Charkas)

At Cairo Central Station / Fi mahatet masr (Ahmed Galal)

Chick / Katkoot (Ahmed Awad)

Criminal Countenance / Wesh igraam (Wael Ihsaan)

Criminal Troop 16 / al-Firqa 16 igraam (Hamed Saïd)

Deer's Blood / Damm El-Ghazaal (Mohamed Yassin)

The Diver / al-Ghawwaas (Fakhr Eddine Negeda)

Does He Think That . . . / Ayazun (Akram Farid)

Dunia / Dunia (Jocelyne Saab)

Eighth of a Dozen Thugs / 1/8 Dastet Ashrar (Rami Imam)

Emergency / Zarf Tarek (Wael Ihsaan)

The Game of Love / Leibet al hubb (Mohamed Ali)

Haha and Tuffaha / Hah wa Tuffaha (Akram Farid)

Halim / Halim (Cherif Arafa)

Heads or Tails / Malek wa Ketaba (Kamla Abou Zikri)

The Hostage / al-Rahina (Sandra Nashaat)

I Swear Thrice by Songs / ʾAlayya al-tarab bil talaata (Ahmed al-Badri)

In Arabic, Cinderella / Bil araby Cinderella (Karim Diaa Eddine)

The Kids Ran Away / al-ʿEyaal herbet (Magdi al-Hawwaari)

Legitimate Betrayal / Kheyana mashruʾa (Khaled Youssef)

Leisure Time / Awqat faragh (Mohamed Mostafa Kamal)

Let's Dance / Ma tigi norqus (Inas al-Deghidi)

Like Wishes / Zayy El-Hawa (Akram Farid)

Little Fathers / al-Abaaʾ al-sighaar (Doureid Laham)

Love and Passion / ʿAnn al-ʿishk wal hawa (Kamla Abou Zikri)

Love Talk /Kalaam fil hubb (Ali Idris)

90 Minutes / 90 Daqeeqa (Ismaïl Farouq)

None but That / Mafesh gher kada (Khaled al-Hagar)

Open Your Eyes / Fattah ʾinak (Osman Abou Laban)

An Ordinary Man / Wahid min al naas (Ahmed Galal)

Ouija (Khaled Youssef)

Pay Back My Loan / Rodda qardy (Hishaam Gomʾa)

Perfect / Kamel al-awsaaf (Ahmed al-Badri)

Return of the Wicked Woman / ʿAwdat al-nadla (Saïd Hamed)

She Made Me a Criminal / Gaʾalatny mugreman (Amr Arafa)

Slum Side Story / Qessat al-hayy al-shaʾby (Ashraf Fayek)

Speed Bump / Matabb senaaʾy (Wael Ihsaan)

Touched in the Head / Lakhmet raas (Ahmed al-Badri)

What's the Plan / Ieeh al-nizaam (Hatem Musa)

The Yacoubian Building / Omaret Yacoubian (Marwan Hamed)

Zaza / Zaza (Ali Abdel Khalek)

2007

45 Days / 45 youm (Ahmed Yousri)

A Day of Telling Lies / Sabahu kedb (Mohamed al-Nagggar)

A Lion and Four Cats / Asad wa 4 qitat (Sameh Abdel Aziz)

Agamista / ʿAgamista (Tarek Abdel Muti)

An Account / Kashf hesaab (Amir Ramsis)

Chaos / Heya Fawda (Youssef Chahine & Khaled Youssef)

Code 36 / Code 36 (Ahmed Samir Farag)

Crazy People ½ dot.com / Maganeen ½ com (Ahmed Fahmi)

Cut and Paste / Qass wa lazq (Hala Khalil)

Difficult Task / Mohemma saʾba (Ihab Radi)

Dr. Omar's Gang / ʿIsabet al-Doktoor Omar (Ali Idris)

Dreams of a Reckless Young Man / Ahlam al-fata al taʾish (Sameh Abdel Aziz)

Dukki Nightingale / ʾAndaleeb al-dukki (Wael Ihsaan)

El-Turbini / El-turbini (Ahmed Medhat)

Hide and Seek / Ustughummaaya (Imad Al-Bahhaat)

I Am Not With Them / Ana mush maʾahum (Ahmed al-Badri)

In the Heliopolis Flat / Fi chaqqet masr el gedeeda (Mohammed Khan)

Karkar / Karkar (Ali Ragab)

Magic / Al-magic (Mohamedd Mustafa)

Mind Your Own Business / Khalleek fi halak (Ayman Makram)

Morgan Ahmed Morgan / Morgaan Ahmed Morgaan (Ali Idris)

Number Plate: Alexandria / Malaki Eskandariya (Sandra Nashaat)

Omar and Salma / ʾAmr wa Salma (Tarek al-Iryaan)

Private Affairs / ʿIlaqaat khassa (Ihaab Lamei)

Real Dreams / Ahlaam haqiqeyya (Mohamed Gomʾa)

Such is Love / Al-hubb kida (Akram Farid)

Taymour and Safika / Taymour wa Shafika (Khaled Marie)

That is Satisfactory / Keda reda (Ahmed Galal)

The Clown / Al-beliatshu (Imad al-Bahhaat)

The Devils / Al-chayateen (Ahmed Abou Zeid)

The First Thing in Love / Al-awwela fil gharaa (Mohamed Ali)

The Furthest End of the World / Akher el dunia (Amir Ramsis)

The Ghost / Al-Chabah (Amr Arafa)

Watch out! You Dropped Something / Housh illi weiʾeʾ mennak (Ahmed al-Guendi)

NB Two feature-length works were also shot digitally and not transferred to celluloid by noted Egyptian filmmakers in the 2000s: Mohamed Khan's *The Crook / Klefty* (2004) and Kaïri Bechara's *What's Wrong with You, Sweety / Maal al-amal.*

REFERENCES

Armbrust, Walter. *Mass Culture and Modernism in Egypt.* Cambridge, UK: Cambridge University Press, 1996.

——, ed. *Mass Mediations: New Approaches to Popular Culture in the Middle East and Beyond.* Berkeley: University of California Press, 2000.

Bénard, Marie-Claude, Jean Charles Depaule, and Ayman Salem, ed. *Le Caire et le cinéma égyptien des années 80.* Cairo: CEDEJ, 1990.

Bergmann, Kristina. *Filmkultur und Filmindustrie in Ägypten.* Darmstadt, Germany: Wissenschaftliche Buchgesellschaft, 1993.

Bosséno, Christian, ed. *Youssef Chahine l'alexandrien.* Paris: CinémAction 34, 1985.

Chahine, Youssef. *Alexandrie pourquoi?* (script). Paris: L'Avant-Scène du Cinéma 341, 1985.

——. *Le Destin* (script). Paris: Cahiers du Cinéma, 1997.

Chikhaoui, Tahar, ed. *Chahine, l'enfant prodigue du cinéma arabe.* Tunis: Cinécrits, 2004.

Colla, Elliott. "Shadi Abdal-Salam's *al-Mumiya:* Ambivalence and the Egyptian Nation-State." In *Beyond Colonialism and Nationalism in the Maghrib: History, Culture and Politics,* ed. Ali Abdullatif Ahmida, pp. 109–143. New York: Palgrave, 2000..

Darwish, Mustafa. *Dream Makers on the Nile: A*

Portrait of Egyptian Cinema. Cairo: American University in Cairo Press, 1998.

Elena, Alberto, ed. *Youssef Chahine: el fuego y la palabra / Youssef Chahine: Fire and Word.* Cordoba: Junta de Andalucia, 2007.

Farid, Samir. "Periodisation of Egyptian Cinema." In *Screens of Life: Critical Film Writing from the Arab World,* ed. Alia Arasoughly, pp. 1–18. Quebec: World Heritage Press, 1998.

Fawal, Ibrahim. *Youssef Chahine.* London: British Film Institute, 2001.

Hafez, Sabry. "The Quest for/Obsession with the National in Arabic Cinema." In *Theorising National Cinema,* ed. Valentina Vitali and Paul Willemen, pp. 226–253. London: BFI Publishing, 2006.

Hamzaouli, Hamid. *Histoire du cinéma égyptien.* Paris: Editions Autres Temps, 1997.

Jonassaint, Jean, ed. *Chahine et le cinéma égyptien.* Montreal: *Dérives* 43 (1984).

Jousse, Thierry, ed. *Spécial Youssef Chahine.* Paris: supplement to *Cahiers du Cinéma* 506, 1996.

Khan, Mohamed. *An Introduction to the Egyptian Cinema.* London: Informatics, 1969.

Khayati, Khémais. *Salah Abou Seif: cinéaste égyptien.* Paris: Sindbad, 1993.

Marei, Salah, and Magda Wassef, ed. *Chadi Abdel Salam: le pharaon du cinéma égyptien,* Paris: Institut du Monde Arabe, 1996.

Nicholas, Joe. *Egyptian Cinema.* London: British Film Institute, 1994.

Shadi, Ali Abu. "Genres in Egyptian Cinema." In *Screens of Life: Critical Film Writing from the Arab World,* ed. Alia Arasoughly, pp. 84–129. Quebec: World Heritage Press, 1998.

Shafik, Viola, ed. *Youssef Chahine,* Berlin: *Kinemathek* 74 (1989).

———. "Egyptian Cinema." In *Companion Encyclopedia of Middle Eastern and North African Film,* ed. Oliver Leaman, pp. 23–129. London:New York: Routledge, 2001.

———. *Popular Egyptian Cinema: Gender, Class and Nation.* Cairo: The American University in Cairo Press, 2007.

Thoraval, Yves. *Regards sur le cinéma égyptien.* Beirut: Dar El-Machreq, 1975. Second edition, Paris: Editions L'Harmattan, 1996.

———. *Les Cinémas du Moyen-Orient: Iran, Égypte, Turquie (1896–2000).* Paris: Séguier, 2000.

———. "Égypte, de la littérature au réalisme cinématographique." *Mésogeios* 15 (2002): 107–123.

Wassef, Magda, ed. *Egypte: Cent ans de cinéma.* Paris: Institut du Monde Arabe, 1995.

ETHIOPIA

Output: 10 feature films
Filmmakers: 3
(Yemane Demissie, Haïle Gerima, Teshome Kebede Theodros)

CHRONOLOGY
1976
Bush Mama (Haïle Gerima)
Harvest 3000 Years / Birt sost shi amit (Haïle Gerima)
Wilmington 10—USA 10,000 (documentary) (Haïle Gerima)
1982
Ashes and Embers (Haïle Gerima)
1993
Sankofa (Haïle Gerima)
1996
Tumult / Gir Gir (Yemane Demissie)
1999
Adwa (documentary) (Haïle Gerima)
2003
Kezkaka Wolofen (documentary) (Teshome Kebede Theodros)
2004
Fikir Siferd (documentary) (Teshome Kebede Theodros)
2006
Red Mistake (Teshome Kebede Theodros)

REFERENCES
Demissié, Yemane. Interview with Olivier Barlet, 30 August 2002. www.africultures.com.

Gerima, Haile. "Afterword: Future Directions of South African Cinema." In *To Change Reels: Film and Film Culture in South Africa,* ed.

Isabel Balseiro and Ntongela Masilela, pp. 201–229. Detroit: Wayne State University Press, 2003.

Kandé, Sylvie. "Look Homeward, Angel. Maroons and Mulattos in Haile Gerima's *Sankofa*." In *African Cinema: Post-Colonial and Feminist Readings*, ed. Kenneth W. Harrow, pp. 89–114. Trenton, N.J.: Africa World Press, 1999.

Murashige, Mike. "Haile Gerima and the Political Economy of Cinematic Resistance." In *Representing Blackness: Issues in Film and Video*, ed. Valerie Smith, pp. 183–203. London: Athlone Press, 1997.

Pfaff, Françoise. "Haile Gerima." In *25 Black African Film Makers*, pp. 137–155. New York: Greenwood Press, 1988.

———. "From Africa to the Americas: Interviews with Haile Gerima (1976–2001)." In *Focus on African Films*, pp. 303–220. Bloomington: Indiana University Press, 2004..

Ukadike, Nwachukwu Frank. Interviews with Salem Mekuria and Haile Gerima. In *Questioning African Cinema*, pp. 239–251, 253–279. Minneapolis: University of Minnesota Press, 2002.

GABON

Output: 10 feature films
Filmmakers: 6
(Simon Augé, Pierre-Marie Dong, Imunga Ivanga, Henri-Joseph Koumba Bididi, Charles Mensah, Philippe Mory)

CHRONOLOGY
1971
Where Are You Going, Koumba? / Où vas-tu Koumba? (Simon Augé)
1972
Identity / Identité (Pierre-Marie Dong)
The Tam-Tams Are Silent / Les Tam-tams se sont tus (Philippe Mory)
1976
Obali (Pierre-Marie Dong and Charles Mensah)

1977
Ayouma (Pierre-Marie Dong and Charles Mensah)
1978
Ilombe (Charles Mensah)
Tomorrow Is a New Day / Demain un nouveau jour (Pierre-Marie Dong)
1999
Dôlè (Léon Imunga Ivanga)
2001
The Elephant's Balls / Les Couilles de l'éléphant (Henri-Joseph Koumba Bididi)
2006
The Shadow of Liberty / L'Ombre de Liberty (Léon Ivanga Imunga)
NB A feature-length fictional video was shot in 2006 by André Côme Otonghe: *Nië, the Call / Nië, l'appel.*

REFERENCES
Bachy, Victor. *Le Cinéma au Gabon.* Brussels: OCIC, 1986.

Ivanga, Imunga. "Le Renouveau du cinéma gabonais." In *Cinémas africains, une oasis dans le désert?* ed. Samuel Lelièvre, pp. 226–229. Paris: Corlet/Télérama/*CinémAction* 106, 2003.

Mensah, Charles. "Le prix à payer" (interview with Olivier Barlet). *Africultures* 69 (2007): 157–160.

Pfaff, Françoise. "Pierre-Marie Dong." In *25 Black African Film Makers*, pp. 79–85. New York: Greenwood Press, 1988.

GHANA

Output: 21 feature films
Filmmakers: 14
(Egbert Adjesu, John Akomfrah, King Ampaw, Kwah Paintsil Ansah, Sam Aryeety, Kwame Robert Johnson, Ingrid Metner, Koffi Zokko Nartey, Kwaté Nee Owoo, Bernard Odidja, Kwesi Owusu, Tom Ribeiro, Socrat Safo, Ato Yarney)

CHRONOLOGY
As elsewhere in Africa, locally produced pioneering features were shot by Europeans. Here

in Ghana there were films by two English directors: Sean Graham's *The Boy Kumasenu* (1960) and Terry Bishop's *Tongo Hamile* (a version of Shakespeare's *Hamlet*, 1965)

1968
No Tears for Ananse (Sam Aryeety)
1970
I Told You So (Egbert Adjesu)
1971
Do Your Own Thing (Bernard Odidja)
1972
They Call It Love (King Ampaw)
1977
Genesis Chapter X (Tom Ribeiro)
1980
Love Brewed in the African Pot (Kwah Paintsil Ansah)
1983
Dede (Tom Ribeiro)
His Majesty's Sergeant (Ato Yarney)
Kukurantumi: The Road to Accra (King Ampaw)
Out of Sight (Tom Ribeiro)
The Visitor (Tom Ribeiro)
1994
Black Home Again (Kwame Robert Johnson and Koffi Zokko Nartey)
1986
Juju / Nana Akoto (King Ampaw and Ingrid Metner).
1988
Testament (John Akomfrah)
1989
Heritage . . . Africa (Kwah Paintsil Ansah)
1991
Ama (Kwaté Nee Owoo and Kwesi Owusu)
Who Needs a Heart (John Akomfrah)
1996
Stand by Me (Socrat Safo, video)
1998
Speak Like a Child (documentary, John Akomfrah)
2003
Urban Soul (documentary, John Akomfrah)
2006
The Last Respect (King Ampaw)
NB Beginning with William Akuffo and Richard Quartey's *Zinabu* (1987), over four hundred video features have been shot in Ghana.

REFERENCES
Akomfrah, John. "On the National in African Cinema/s: A Conversation." In *Theorising National Cinema*, ed. Valentina Vitali and Paul Willemen, pp. 274–292. London: BFI Publishing, 2006.
Dadson, Nanabanyin. "Cine in Ghana." Accra, Ghana: *Graphic Showbiz*, 21 May–1 July 1998.
Pfaff, Françoise. "Kwah Ansah." In *25 Black African Film Makers*, pp. 11–18. New York: Greenwood Press, 1988.
Ukadike, Nwachukwu Frank. Interviews with Kwah Ansah and King Ampaw. In *Questioning African Cinema*, pp. 3–17, 203–216. Minneapolis: University of Minnesota Press, 2002.
———. "Video Booms and the Manifestations of 'First' Cinema in Anglophone Africa." In *Rethinking Third Cinema*, ed. Anthony R. Guneratne and Wimal Disanayake, pp. 126–143. New York: Routledge, 2003.
Wendl, Tobias. "Le Miracle vidéo du Ghana." In *Cinémas africains, une oasis dans le désert?* ed. Samuel Lelièvre, pp. 182–191. Paris: Corlet/Télérama/*CinémAction* 106, 2003.

GUINEA

Output: 17 feature films
Filmmakers: 8
(Mohamed Lamine Akin, Cheik Fantamady Camara, Dansogho Mohamed Camara, Mohamed Camara, Moussa Kemoko Diakite, Cheik Doukoure, Gahité Fofana, Mama Keïta)

CHRONOLOGY
1966
Sergeant Bakary Woolen / Le Sergent Bakary Woolen (Mohamed Lamine Akin)
1972
El Haj Million (collective)
The Night Is Lit Up / La Nuit s'illumine (collective)
1977
Give and Take / Du donner et du recevoir (Dansogho Mohamed Camara)

1982
Naitou (Moussa Kemoko Diakite)
1983
Ouloukoro (Dansogho Mohamed Camara)
1990
The Witness / Sere / Le Témon (Dansogho Mohamed Camara)
1991
Ebony White / Blanc d'Ebène (Cheik Doukoure)
1993
The Golden Ball / Le Ballon d'or (Cheik Doukoure)
1997
Destiny / Dakan (Mohamed Camara)
The Eleventh Commandment / Le 11e commandement aka *Choose a Friend / Choisis-toi un ami* (Mama Keïta)
2001
Temporary Registration / I T Immatriculation temporaire (Gahité Fofana)
2002
Paris According to Moussa / Paris Selon Moussa (Cheik Doukoure)
2003
The River / Le Fleuve (Mama Keïta)*
2004
The Snake's Smile / Le Sourire du serpent (Mama Keïta)
2005
Early One Morning / Un matin de bonne heure (Gahité Fofana)
2006
It'll Rain on Conakry / Il va pleuvoir sur Conakry (Cheik Fantamady Camara)

REFERENCE
Spass, Lieve. "Guinea." In *The Francophone Film: A Struggle for Identity*, pp. 224–225. Manchester: Manchester University Press, 2000.

CHRONOLOGY
1987
N'Tturudu (Umban Ukset)
1988
Mortu nega (Flora Gomes)
1990
The Blue Eyes of Yonta / Udju azul di Yonta (Flora Gomes)
1994
Xime (Sana Na N'Hada).
1996
Po di sangui (Flora Gomes)
2002
Nha Fala (Flora Gomes)

REFERENCES
Andrade-Watkins, Claire. "Portuguese African Cinema: Historical and Contemporary Perspectives, 1969–1993." In *Cinemas of the Black Diaspora: Diversity, Dependence and Oppositionality*, ed. Michael T. Martin, pp. 181–203. Detroit: Wayne State University Press, 1995.
———. "Le Cinéma et la culture au Cap Vert et en Guinée-Bissau." In *Cinémas africains, une oasis dans le désert?* ed. Samuel Lelièvre, pp. 148–155. Paris: Corlet/Télérama/*CinémAction* 106, 2003.
Fina, Luciana, Cristina Fina, and António Loja Neves. *Cinemas de África*. Lisbon: Cinemateca Portugesa and Culturgest, 1995.
Rodriguès, Antonio. "Les Cinémas d'Afrique 'lusophone.'" In *Cinémas africains, une oasis dans le désert?* ed. Samuel Lelièvre, pp. 237–238. Paris: Corlet/Télérama/*CinémAction* 106, 2003.
Ukadike, Nwachukwu Frank. Interview with Flora Gomes. In *Questioning African Cinema*, pp. 101–108. Minneapolis: University of Minnesota Press, 2002.

GUINEA-BISSAU

Output: 6 feature films
Filmmakers: 3
(Flora Gomes, Sana Na N'Hada, Umban Ukset)

* completion of a film begun by David Achkar (deceased)

IVORY COAST

Output: 27 feature films
Filmmakers: 13
(Didier Aufort, Sidiki Babaka, Lanciné Diabé, Moussa Dosso, Henri Duparc, Désiré Écaré,

Kramo-Lancine Fadika, Jean-Louis Koula, Gnoan Roger Mbala, Bassori Timité, Kitia Touré, Mory Traore, Kozoloa Yeo)

CHRONOLOGY
1969
It's Up to Us, France / À nous deux France (Désiré Écaré)
The Woman with the Knife / La Femme au couteau (Bassori Timité)
1972
The Family / Abusuan (Henri Duparc)
1975
The Hat / Le Chapeau (Gnoan Roger Mbala)
1977
Wild Grass / L'Herbe sauvage (Henri Duparc)
1979
The Man from Elsewhere / L'Homme d'ailleurs (Mory Traore)
1980
Adja Tio (Jean-Louis Koula)
1981
Djeli (Kramo Lanciné Fadika)
1982
Dalokan / La Parole donnée (Moussa Dosso)
1983
Petanqui (Kozoloa Yeo)
1984
Ablakon (Gnoan Roger Mbala)
Exotic Comedy / Comédie exotique (Kitia Touré)
1985
Women's Faces / Visages de femmes (Désiré Écaré)
1988
Aduefue / Les Guérisseurs (Sidiki Bakaba)
Bal Poussière (Henri Duparc)
Bouka (Gnoan Roger Mbala)
1990
The Sixth Finger / Le Sixième doigt (Henri Duparc)
1992
In the Name of Christ / Au nom du Christ (Gnoan Roger Mbala)
1994
Rue Princesse (Henri Duparc)
Wariko, the Jackpot / Wariko, le gros lot (Kramo Lanciné Fadika)
1996
The Twin Girl / La Jumelle (Lanciné Diabé)

1997
Coffee Coloured / Une couleur café (Henri Duparc)
2000
Adanggaman (Gnoan Roger Mbala)
The Three Bracelets / Les Trois bracelets (Kozoloa Yeo)
2002
Freewheeling / Roues libres (Sidiki Bakaba)
Love's Gamble / Le Pari de l'amour (Didier Aufort)
2005
Caramel (Henri Duparc)

REFERENCES
Bachy, Victor. *Le Cinéma en Côte d'Ivoire.* Brussels: OCIC, 1982 and 1983.
Bonneau, Richard. *Ecrivains, Cinéastes, Artistes Ivoiriens.* Abidjan-Dakar: Nouvelles Éditions Africaines, 1973.
Koffi, Michel. "Le Cas du cinéma ivoirien." In *Cinémas africains, une oasis dans le désert?* ed. Samuel Lelièvre, pp. 138–147. Paris: Corlet/Télérama/*CinémAction* 106, 2003.
Pfaff, Françoise. "Timité Bassori," "Henri Duparc," "Désiré Écare," and "Kramo-Lanciné Fadika." In *25 Black African Film Makers,* pp. 33–42, 87–94, 95–106, 107–113. New York: Greenwood Press, 1988.
Spass, Lieve. "Côte d'Ivoire." In *The Francophone Film: A Struggle for Identity,* pp. 218–223. Manchester: Manchester University Press, 2000.

KENYA

Output: 3 feature films
Filmmakers: 3
(Sao Gamba, Wanjiru Kinyanjui, Anne Mungai)

CHRONOLOGY
1986
Kolormask (Sao Gamba)
1992
Saikati the Enkabaani (Anne Mungai)
1994
The Battle of the Sacred Tree (Wanjiru Kinyanjui)

NB A number of feature-length videos have been shot in Kenya in the 2000s, including Christine Bala's *Babu's Babies* (2003), Robert Bresson's *Help!* (2007), Wanuri Kahiu's *Ras Star* (2007), Judy Kibinge's *Dangerous Affair* (2003) and *Project Daddy* (2004), Mary Migui's *Backlash* (2005) and *Benta* (2007), Catherine Muigai's *Clean Hands* (2006), Jane Munene's *The Price of a Daughter* (2003) and *Behind Closed Doors* (2003), Martin Munyua's *Money and the Cross* (2006), Bob Nyanja's *Malooned* (2007), Brutus Sirucha's *The Green Card* (2004), and Albert Wandago's *Naliaka Is Going* (2003).

REFERENCES

Harding, Frances. "Speaking for Women: Interview with Anne Mungai." In *With Open Eyes: Women and African Cinema*, ed. Kenneth W. Harrow, pp. 81–92. Amsterdam: Rodopi/*Matutu* 19, 1997.

Ondego, Ogova. "Kenya." In *International Film Guide 2005*, ed. Daniel Rosenthal, pp. 203–204. London: Button/Guardian Books, 2005.

———. "Kenya." In *International Film Guide 2006*, ed. Daniel Rosenthal, pp. 199–200. London: Button/Guardian Books, 2006.

LIBYA

Output: 10 feature films
Filmmakers: 9
(Mohamed Ayad Driza, Youssef Chaabane, Mohamed Ali Ferjani, Qassem Hawl, Mohamed Jindi, Khaled Khachim, el-Hadj Rached, Adbellah Rezzoug, Ahmed Toukhi)

CHRONOLOGY

In addition to the films directed by Libyans, the General Organisation for Cinema also co-produced films by other Arab filmmakers: *The Message / al-Risala*, by the Syrian Mustapha Akkad (1976), *The Green Light / al-Daw' al-Akhdar*, by the Moroccan Abdallah Mesbahi (1976), *The Ambassadors / al-Sufara'*, by the Tunisian Naceur Ktari (1976), *Where Are You Hiding the Sun?*

/ Ayna Tukhabi'un al-Shams? also by Abdallah Mesbahi (1979), *Umar al-Mukhtar: The Lion of the Desert / 'Umar al-Mukhtar: Asad al-Sahra*, also by Mustapha Akkad (1980), *A Person Who Lost His Memory / Faqid al-Dhakira*, a Turkish-USSR co-production by Jaji Narlev (1989)

1970
A People's Revolt / Intifadat sh'ab (documentary) (Ahmed Toukhi)

1973
The Road / al-Tariq (Youssef Chaabane)
When Fate Hardens / 'Indama Yaqsu al-Zaman (Adbellah Rezzoug)

1981
The Battle of Taqraft (Taghrift or Taghirfit) / Ma'rakat Taqraft (Khaled Khachim and Mohamed Ayad Driza)

1985
No! (documentary) (el-Hadj Rached)

1986
Love in Narrow Alleys / Hub Fi al-Aziqa al-Dayiqa (Mohamed Jindi)
The Splinter / al-Shaziya (Mohamed Ali Ferjani)

1990
The Four Seasons / al-Fusul al-Arba'a (documentary) (Mohamed AliFerjani)
Searching for Layla al-'Amiriya / al-Bahth 'An Layla al-'Amiriya (Qassem Hawl)

1991
Song of the Rain / Ma'azufatu al-matar (Abdellah Rezzoug)

REFERENCE

Al-'Ubaydi, Amal Sulatman Mahmoud. "Cinema in Libya." In *Companion Encyclopedia of Middle Eastern and North African Film*, ed. Oliver Leaman, pp. 407–419. London: Routledge, 2001.

MADAGASCAR

Output: 7 feature films
Filmmakers: 3
(Raymond Rajaonarivelo, Benoît Ramampy, Ignace-Solo Randrasana)

CHRONOLOGY

1973
Very Remby / Le Retour (Ignace-Solo Randrasana)
1984
Dahalo, Dahalo . . . (Benoît Ramampy)
1987
Mad 47 / Ilo Tsy Very (Ignace-Solo Randrasana)
The Price of Peace / Le Prix de la paix (Benoît Ramampy)
1988
Tabataba (Raymond Rajaonarivelo)
1996
When the Stars Meet the Sea / Quand les étoiles rencontrent la mer (Raymond Rajaonarivelo)
2004
Mahaleo (Raymond Rajaonarivelo)

REFERENCE

Randriamihaingo, Claude. "Le Cinéma documentaire à Madagascar." In *Cinémas africains, une oasis dans le désert?* ed. Samuel Lelièvre, pp. 232–236. Paris: Corlet/Télérama/*Ciném-Action* 106, 2003.

MALI

Output: 27 feature films
Filmmakers: 13
(Abdoulaye Ascofare, Mamo Cisse, Souleymane Cisse, Mambaye Coulibaly, Sega Coulibaly, Kalifa Dienta, Adama Drabo, Alkaly Kaba, Assane Kouyate, Djibril Kouyate, Cheikh Oumar Sissoko, Issa Falaba Traore, Salif Traoré)

CHRONOLOGY

1974
Walanda (Alkaly Kaba)
1975
The Girl / Den muso / La Jeune fille (Souleymane Cisse)
1976
Mogho Dakan / Le Destin (Sega Coulibaly)
Wamba (Alkaly Kaba)
1978
Baara (Souleymane Cisse)
Den Kasso (Sega Coulibaly)

1980
A Banna / C'est fini (Kalifa Dienta)
Am Be Nodo / Nous sommes tous coupables (Issa Falaba Traore)
1982
The Wind / Finye / Le Vent (Souleymane Cisse)
1986
Nyamanton / La Leçon des ordures (Cheikh Oumar Sissoko)
1987
Yeelen (Souleymane Cisse)
1989
A Dance for Heroes / Finzan (Cheikh Oumar Sissoko)
Falato (Mamo Cisse)
1990
Bamunan / Le Pagne sacré (Issa Falaba Traore)
1991
Ta Dona (Adama Drabo)
1992
Yelema (Mamo Cisse)
1993
Tiefing (Djibril Kouyate)
1995
Guimba the Tyrant / Guimba, un tyran, une époque (Cheikh Oumar Sissoko)
Waati (Souleymane Cisse)
1996
Faraw! / Faraw! une mère des sables (Abdoulaye Ascafare)
1997
Taafe Fanga (Adama Drabo)
Yelema II (Mamo Cisse)
1999
Genesis / La Genèse (Cheikh Oumar Sissoko)
2000
Bàttu (Cheikh Oumar Sissoko)
2002
Kabala (Assane Kouyaté)
2006
Faro, Queen of the Waters / Faro, la reine des eaux (Salif Traoré)
Segou's Power / Segu Fanga (animation) (Mambaye Coulibaly)

REFERENCES

Bachy, Victor. *Le Cinéma au Mali.* Brussels: OCIC, 1982 and 1983.
Chikaoui, Tahar, ed. *Souleymane Cisse.* Tunis: *Cinécrits* 16 (1998).

Lelièvre, Samuel. "Enjeux interprétatifs de la féminité dans l'écriture de Souleymane Cissé." In *Ecritures dans les cinémas d'Afrique noire,* ed. De B'béri Boulou Ebanda, pp. 61–76. Montreal: Cinémas, 2000.

MacRae, Suzanne H. "*Yeelen:* A Political Fable of the *Komo* Blacksmiths/Sorcerers." In *African Cinema: Post-Colonial and Feminist Readings,* ed. Kenneth W. Harrow, pp. 127–140. Trenton, N.J.: Africa World Press, 1999.

Pfaff, Françoise. "Souleymane Cissé." In *25 Black African Film Makers,* pp. 51–67. New York: Greenwood Press, 1988.

Sagot-Duvauroux, Jean-Louis. *Kadiatou Konaté.* Montreuil, France: Éditions de l'Oeil, 2005.

Spass, Lieve. "Mali." In *The Francophone Film: A Struggle for Identity,* pp. 191–208. Manchester: Manchester University Press, 2000.

Ukadike, Nwachukwu Frank. Interviews with Souleymane Cisse and Cheick Omar Sissoko. In *Questioning African Cinema,* pp. 19–28, 181–199. Minneapolis: University of Minnesota Press, 2002.

MAURITANIA

Output: 14 feature films
Filmmakers: 3
(Med Hondo, Abderrahmane Sissako, Sidney Sokhona)

CHRONOLOGY
1971
Soleil O (Med Hondo)
1973
The Black Wogs, Your Neighbors / Les Bicots-nègres, vos voisins (Med Hondo)
1975
Nationality: Immigrant / Nationalité: immigré (Sidney Sokhona)
1977
We Have the Whole of Death for Sleeping / Nous avons toute la mort pour dormir (documentary) (Med Hondo)
1978
Safran or the Right to Speak / Safran ou le droit à la parole (Sydney Sokona)

1979
West Indies / West Indies ou les nègres marrons de la liberté (Med Hondo)
1986
Sarraounia (Med Hondo)
1994
Black Light / Lumière noire (Med Hondo)
1997
Watani, a World without Evil / Watani, un monde sans mal (Med Hondo)
1998
Life on Earth / La Vie sur terre (Abderrahmane Sissako)
2002
Waiting for Happiness / Heremakono / En attendant le bonheur (Abderrahmane Sissako)
2004
Fatima, the Algerian Woman from Dakar / Fatima, l'Algérienne de Dakar (Med Hondo)
2006
Bamako / The Court (Abderrahmane Sissako)
2007
First Among Blacks: Toussaint Louverture / Premier des noirs: Toussaint Louverture (Med Hondo)

REFERENCES

Armes, Roy. "Abderrahmane Sissako (Mauritania)." In *African Filmmaking: North and South of the Sahara,* pp. 191–200. Edinburgh: Edinburgh University Press; Bloomington: Indiana University Press, 2006.

Chikhaoui, Tahar. "*La Vie sur terre:* analyse du prégénérique," "Une variante parodoxale du film de Vertov," and an interview with Abderrahmane Sissako and Hajer Bouden, "Sissako ou l'appareil circulatoire." Tunis: *Cinécrits* 17 (1999): 33–71.

Pfaff, Françoise. "Med Hondo." In *25 Black African Film Makers,* pp. 157–172. New York: Greenwood Press, 1988.

Signaté, Ibrahima. *Med Hondo—un cinéaste rebelle.* Paris: Présence Africaine, 1994.

Spass, Lieve. "Mauitania." In *The Francophone Film: A Struggle for Identity,* pp. 208–214. Manchester: Manchester University Press, 2000.

Ukadike, Nwachukwu Frank. Interview with Med Hondo. In *Questioning African Cinema,* pp. 57–72. Minneapolis: University of Minnesota Press, 2002.

MAURITIUS

Output: 5 feature films
Filmmakers: 4
(Brijmohun Brothers, Barlen Pyamootoo, Ramesh Tekoit)

CHRONOLOGY
1975
Lost Dream / Bikre Sapne (Brijmohun Brothers)
1980
And the Smile Returns / Et le sourire revient (Ramesh Tekoit)
1988
The Egotist / Khudgarz (Brijmohun Brothers)
Goodbye My Love (Ramesh Tekoit)
2006
Bénarès (Barlen Pyamootoo)

MOROCCO

OVERALL STATISTICS: 80 filmmakers—
186 feature films
1960s
Output: 3 films
Filmmakers: 5 active
(Larbi Bennani, Latif Lahlou, Ahmed Mesnaoui, Abdelaziz Ramdani, Mohamed B. A. Tazi)

1970s
Output: 16 films
Filmmakers: 10 active, 10 new (*) + 1 collectively made film
(*Hamid Bennani, *Souheil Benbarka, *Ahmed Bouanani, *Mostafa Derkaoui, *Jillali Ferhati, *Nabyl Lahlou, *Ahmed El Maânouni, *Abdellaf Mesbahi, *Mohamed Osfour, *Moumen Smihi)

1980s
Output: 38 films
Filmmakers: 30 active, 21 new (*)
(*Mohamed Abbazi, *Mohamed Aboulbakar, *Abdou Achouba, *Ahmed Kacem Akdi, Souheil Benbarka, *Hamid Benchrif, *Farida Benlyazid, *Mohamed Bensaïd, *Farida Bourquia, *Mohamed Abdelkrim Derkaoui, Mostafa Derkaoui, Ahmed El Maânouni, Jillali Ferhati, *Driss Kettani, *Mustapha Khayat, Latif Lahlou, Nabyl Lahlou, Abdellatif Mesbahi, *Hassan Moufti, *Driss Mrini, *Hakim Noury, *Mohamed Reggab, *Tayeb Saddiki, *Najib Sefioui, Moumen Smihi, *Saïd Souad, *Mohamed Abderrahmane Tazi, Mohamed B. A. Tazi, *Ahmed Yachfine, *Abdallah Zerouali)

1990s
Output: 43 films
Filmmakers: 26 active, 12 new (*) + 1 collectively made film
(Mohamed Abbazi, *Daoud Aouled Sayed, *Nabil Ayouch, Souheil Benbarka, *Hassan Benjelloun, Farida Benlyazid, Hamid Bennani, Larbi Bennani, *Driss Choukha, *Saâd Chraïbi, *Tijani Chrigui, Mohamed Abdelkrim Derkaoui, Mostafa Derkaoui, Jillali Ferhati, *Nour Eddine Gounajjar, *Mohamed Ismaïl, *Fatima Jebli Ouazzani, *Naguib Ktiri-Idrissa, *Abdelkader Lagtaâ, Nabyl Lahlou, *Mohamed Lotfi, Hakim Noury, Moumen Smihi, Mohamed Abderrahman Tazi, Ahmed Yachfine, Abdelllah Zerouali)

2000s
Output: 83 films
Filmmakers: 51 active, 32 new (*)
(*Badr Abdelilah, *Mohamed Asli, Daoud Aoulad Syad, *Hichem Ayouch, Nabil Ayouch, *Hakim Belabbes, *Jamal Belmejdoub, Souheil Benbarka, Hassan Benjelloun, Farida Benlyazid, *Faouzi Bensaidi, *Mourad Boucif, *Ahmed Boulane, Farida Bourquia, Driss Chouika, *Omar Chraïbi, Saâd Chraïbi, Mostafa Derkaoui, Ahmed El Maânouni, *Mohamed Ali El Mejoub *Hamid Faridi, Jillali Ferhati, *Ismaïl Ferroukhi, *Mahmoud Frites, *Hassan Ghanja, Mohamed Ismaïl, *Kamal Kamal, *Yasmine Kasari, Abdelkader Lagtaâ, Latif Lahlou, Nabyl Lahlou, *Nour-Eddine Lakhmari, *Abdelhaï Laraki, *Hassan Legzouli, *Laïla Marrakchi, *Mohamed Mernich, *Imane Mesbahi, *Saïd Naciri, *Narjiss Nejjar, Hakim Noury, *Imad Noury, *Sohael Noury. *Abdelmajid Rchich, Najib Sefioui, *Bachir Skirej, Moumen Smihi, *Saïd Smihi, Saïd Souda, Mohamed Abderrahman Tazi, *Ahmed Ziad, *Mohamed Zineddaine, *Lahcen Zinoun)

CHRONOLOGY

The official Moroccan filmography of feature films begins with Mohamed Osfour's *The Damned Son / Le Fils maudit* (1958), though this is in fact an amateur 16mm film (produced, directed, scripted, shot, and edited by Osfour) and just 50 minutes long. Ahmed Belhachmi, first Moroccan director of the CCM, also made a feature, *The Violin / Le Violin* (1958), which was lost before screening.

1968
Conquer to Live / Vaincre pour vivre (Mohamed B. A. Tazi and Ahmed Mesnaoui)
When the Dates Ripen / Quand murissent les dattes (Abdelaziz Ramdani and Larbi Bennani)
1969
Spring Sunshine / Soleil de printemps (Latif Lahlou)
1970
The Devil's Treasure / Le Trésor infernal (Mohamed Osfour)
Traces / Wechma (Hamid Bennani)
1972
A Thousand and One Hands / Mille et une mains (Souheil Benbarka)
1973
Silence, No Entry / Silence, sens interdit (Abdellah Mesbahi)
1974
About Some Meaningless Events / De quelques événements sans signification (Mostafa Derkaoui)
The Oil War Will Not Take Place / La Guerre du pétrole n'aura pas lieu (Souheil Benbarka)
1975
El Chergui / El Chergui ou le silence violent (Moumen Smihi)
Tomorrow the Land Will Not Change / Demain la terre ne changera pas (Abdellah Mesbahi)
1976
Green Light / Feu vert (Abdellah Mesbahi)
1977
Blood Wedding / Noces de sang (Souheil Benbarka)
Cinders of the Vineyard / Les Cendres du clos (collective)
1978
Al Kanfoudi (Nabyl Lahlou)
The Days, The Days / Oh les jours / Ayyam ayyam (Ahmed El Maânouni)

The Hole in the Wall / La Brèche dans le mur (Jillali Ferhati)
1979
The Mirage / Le Mirage (Ahmed Bouanani)
Where Are You Hiding the Sun? / Où cachez-vous le soleil? (Abdellah Mesbahi)
1980
Amina (Mohamed B. A. Tazi)
The Governor-General of Chakerbakerben Island / Le Gouverneur-général de l'Île de Chakerbakerben (Nabyl Lahlou)
The Postman / Le Facteur (Hakim Noury)
Taghounja / Tarunja (Abdou Achouba)
1981
The Big Trip / Le Grand voyage (Mohamed Abderrahman Tazi)
The Bird of Paradise / L'Oiseau du paradis (Mohamed Bensaïd)
Forty-Four or Tales of the Night / Quarante-Quatre ou le récits de la nuit (Moumen Smihi)
Reed Dolls / Poupées de roseau (Jillali Ferhati)
Trances / Transes (Ahmed El Maânouni)
1982
Amok (Souheil Benbarka)
The Barber of the Poor Quarter / Le Barbier du quartier des pauvres (Mohamed Reggab)
The Beautiful Days of Sheherazade / Les Beaux jours de Chahrazade (Mostafa Derkaoui)
Brahim Who? / Brahim qui? (Nabyl Lahlou)
The Drama of the 40,000 / Le Drame des 40,000 (Ahmed Kacem Akdi)
The Embers / La Braise (Fariqa Bourquia)
From the Other Side of the River / De l'autre côté du fleuve (Mohamed Abbazi)
Medicine Woman / Madame la guérisseuse / Lalla chafia (Mohamed B. A. Tazi)
Steps in the Mist / Des pas dans le brouillard (Hamid Benchrif)
Tears of Regret / Larmes de regret (Hassan Moufti)
1983
Bamou (Driss Mrini)
1984
Dead End / L'Impasse (Mustapha Khayat)
Hadda (Mohamed Aboulouakar)
Nightmare / Cauchemar (Ahmed Yachfine)
Pals for the Day / Les Copains du jour (Abdallah Zerouali)
Provisional Title / Titre provisoire (Mostafa Derkaoui)

The Soul Which Brays / L'Âme qui braît (Nabyl Lahlou)

The Travelling Showman's Day / Le Jour du forain (Mohamed Abdelkrim Derkaoui and Driss Kettani)

What the Winds Have Carried Away / Ce que les vents ont emporté (Ahmed Kacem Akdi)

Zeft (Tayeb Saddiki)

1985

Chams (Najib Sefrioui)

Shadow of the Guardian / L'Ombre du guardien (Saïd Souda)

1986

Abbas or Jouha Is Not Dead / Abbas ou Jouha n'est pas mort (Mohamed B. A. Tazi)

The Compromise / La Compromission (Latif Lahlou)

1987

Caftan of Love / Caftan d'amour (Moumen Smihi)

A Gateway to Heaven / Une porte sur le ciel (Farida Benlyazid)

1988

Badis (Mohamed Abderrahman Tazi)

1989

Komany (Nabyl Laulou)

Land of Challenge / La Terre du défi aka *I Shall Write Your Name in the Sand / J'écrirai ton nom sur le sable* (Abdellah Mesbahi)

1990

The Beach of Lost Children / La Plage des enfants perdus (Jillali Ferhati)

The Hammer and the Anvil / Le Marteau et l'enclume (Hakim Noury)

Other People's Celebrations / La Fête des autres (Hassan Benjelloun)

1991

Aziz and Ito: A Moroccan Wedding / Aziz et Ito, un mariage marocain (Naguib Ktiri-Idrissa)

Chronicle of a Normal Life / Chronique d'une vie normale (Sâad Chraïbi)

The Lady from Cairo / La Dame du Caire (Moumen Smihi)

A Love Affair in Casablanca / Un amour à Casablanca (Abdelkader Lagtaâ)

The Waiting Room / La Salle d'attente (Nour Eddine Gounajjar)

Ymer or The Flowering Thistles / Ymer ou les chardons florifères (Tijani Chrigui)

1992

First Fiction / Fiction première (Mustapha Derkaoui)

The Night of the Crime / La Nuit du crime (Nabyl Lahlou)

1993

Horsemen of Glory / Les Cavaliers de la gloire (a re-edited version of *Drums of Fire / Tambours de feu*, 1991) (Souheil Benbarka)

Looking for My Wife's Husband / A la recherche du mari de ma femme (Mohamed Abderrahman Tazi)

Stolen Childhood / L'Enfance volée (Hakim Noury)

Yarit (Hassan Benjelloun)

1994

(Ga)me in the Past / Je(u) au passé (Mostapha Derkaoui)

The Seven Gates of the Night / Les Sept portes de la nuit (Mostafa Derkaoui)

1995

The Closed Door / La Porte close (Abdelkader Lagtaâ)

The Dream Thief / Le Voleur de rêves (Hakim Noury)

Five Films for a Hundred Years / Cinq films pour cent ans (collective)

I'm the Artist / Moi l'artiste—a completed version of *The Whirlpool / Le Tourbillon* (1980)—(Abdellah Zerouali)

Khafaya (Ahmed Yachfine)

Make-Believe Horses / Chevaux de fortune (Jillali Ferhati)

A Prayer for the Absent One / La Prière de l'absent aka *The Secret of the Milky Way / Le Secret de la voie lactée* (Hamid Bennani)

The Unknown Resistance Fighter / Le Résistant inconnu (Larbi Bennani)

1996

Rhesus—Another Person's Blood / Rhésus, le sang de l'autre (Mohamed Lotfi)

The Shadow of the Pharaoh / L'Ombre du pharaon (Souheil Benbarka)

1997

In My Father's House / In het Huis van mijn Vader (Fatima Jebli Ouazzani)

Lalla Hobby (Mohamed Abderrahman Tazi)

Mektoub (Nabil Ayouch)

A Simple News Item / Un simple fait divers
(Hakim Noury)
The Treasures of the Atlas / Les Trésors de l'Atlas
(Mohamed Abazzi)
Yesterday's Friends / Les Amis d'hier (Hassan
Benjelloun)
1998
Aouchtam (Mohamed Ismaïl)
Cairo Street / Rue le Caire (Mohamed Abdelkrim
Derkaoui)
The Casablancans / Les Casablancais (Abdelkader
Lagtaâ)
Goodbye Traveling Showman / Adieu forain
(Daoud Aouled Sayed)
A Woman's Fate / Destin de femme (Hakim
Noury)
Women . . . and Women / Femmes . . . et Femmes
(Saâd Chraïbi)
1999
Ali Zaoua (Nabil Ayouch)
Mabrouk (Drissa Chouika)
Moroccan Chronicles / Chroniques marocaines
(Moumen Smihi)
Women's Wiles / Ruses de femmes / Keid Ensa
(Farida Benlyazid)
2000
Ali, Rabia and the Others / Ali Rabia et les autres
(Ahmed Boulane)
Braids / Tresses (Jillali Ferhati)
From Heaven to Hell / Du paradis à l'enfer (Said
Souda)
*The Man Who Embroidered Secrets / L'Homme
qui brodait des secrets* (Omar Chraïbi)
*She Is Diabetic and Hypertensive and She Refuses
to Die / Elle est diabétique et hypertendue et elle
refuse de crever* (Hakim Noury)
The Story of a Rose / L'Histoire d'une rose
(Abdelmajid Rchich)
Thirst / Soif (Saâd Chraïbi)
A Woman's Judgment / Jugement d'une femme
(Hassan Benjelloun)
Yacout (Jamal Belmejdoub)
2001
Beyond Gibraltar / Au-delà de Gibraltar (Mourad
Boucif, with Taylan Barman)
Lips of Silence / Les Lèvres du silence (Hassan
Benjelloun)
A Love Story / Une histoire d'amour (Hakim
Noury)

Love without a Visa / Amour sans visa (Najib
Sefrioui)
*The Loves of Hadj Mokhtar Soldi / Les Amours de
Hadj Mokhtar Soldi* (Mostafa Derkaoui)
Mona Saber (Abdelhaï Laraki)
The Wind Horse / Le Cheval de vent (Daoud
Aoulad Syad)
2002
And Afterwards? / Et après? (Mohamed Ismaîl)
Dry Eyes / Les Yeux secs (Narjiss Nejjar)
Kasbah City (Saïd Naciri)
The Lovers of Mogador / Les Amants de Mogador
(Souheil Benbarka)
*A Minute of Sunshine Less / Une minute de soleil
en moins* (Nabil Ayouch)
The Pal / Le Pote (Hassan Benjelloun)
The Paradise of the Poor / Paradis des pauvres
(Imane Mesbahi)
Taif Nizar (Kamal Kamal)
The Years of Exile / Les Années de l'exil (Nabyl
Lahlou)
2003
*Abou Moussa's Neighbours / Les Voisines d'Abou
Moussa* (Mohamed Abderrahmane Tazi)
Casablanca Casablanca (Farida Benlyazid)
Casablanca by Night (Mostafa Derkaoui)
Face to Face / Face à face (Abdelkader Lagtaâ)
Fibres of the Soul / Les Fibres de l'âme (Hakim
Belabbes)
Jawhara (Saâd Chraïbi)
Rahma (Omar Chraïbi)
A Thousand Months / Mille mois (Faouzi Ben-
saidi)
2004
Awakening / Réveil (Mohamed Zineddaine)
The Black Room / La Chambre noire (Hassan
Benjelloun)
Casablanca Daylight (Mostafa Derkaoui)
The Crooks / Les Bandits (Saïd Naciri)
Here and There / Ici et là (Mohamed Ismaïl)
*In Casablanca, Angels Don't Fly / A Casablanca,
les anges ne volent pas* (Mohamed Asli)
The Long Journey / Le Grand voyage (Ismaïl Fer-
roukhi)
The Look / Le Regard (Nour-Eddine Lakhmari)
Memory in Detention / Mémoire en détention
(Jillali Ferhati)
The Sleeping Child / L'Enfant endormi (Yasmine
Kassari)

Tarfya (Daoud Aoulad Syad)

Tenja (Hassan Legzouli)

2005

Bouksasse Boutfounaste (Badr Abdellilah)

The Boy From Tangier / Le Gosse de Tanger (Moumen Smihi)

Broken Wings / Les Ailes brisées (Abdelmajid Rchich)

Heaven's Doors / Les Portes du paradis (Sohael and Imad Noury)

I Saw Ben Barka Get Killed / J'ai vu tuer Ben Barka (Serge Le Péron and Saïd Smihi)

Juanita from Tangier / Juanita de Tanger (Farida Benlyazid)

Marock (Laïla Marrakchi)

Moroccan Symphony / Symphonie marocaine (Kamal Kamal)

She Is Diabetic and Hypertensive and She Still Refuses to Die / Elle est diabétique et hypertendue et elle refuse toujours de crever (Hakim Noury)

2006

Abdou with the Almohades / Abdou chez les Almohades (Saïd Naciri)

Bike, The / Le Vélo (Hamid Faridi)

Broken Hearts / Cœurs brûlés (Ahmed El Maânouni)

Edges of the Heart / Les Arêtes du cœur (Hichem Ayouch)

Game of Love, The / Le Jeu de l'amour (Driss Chouika)

Red Moon, The / La Lune rouge (Hassan Benjelloun)

Tabite or Not Tabite (Nabyl Lahlou)

Tilila (Mohamed Mernich)

Wake Up, Morocco (Narjis Nejjar)

White Wave, The / La Vague blanche (Mohamed Ali El Mejoub)

Why the Sea? / Pourquoi la mer? (Hakim Belabbes)

WWW: What a Wonderful World (Faouzi Bensaidi)

2007

Argana (Hassan Rhanja)

Farewell Mothers / Adieu mères (Mohamed Ismaïl)

Islamour (Saâd Chraïbi)

Moroccan Dream (Jamal Belmejoub)

Nancy and the Monster / Nancy et le monstre (Mahmoud Frites)

Once Upon a Time, Twice Upon a Time / Il était une fois, il était deux fois (Bachir Skiredj)

Real Premonition (Ahmed Ziad)

Samira's Garden / Le jardin de Samira (Latif Lahlou)

Satan's Angels / Les Anges de Satan (Ahmed Boulane)

Scattered Beauty / La Beauté éparpillée (Lahcen Zinoun)

Scent of the Sea / Parfum de mer (Abdelhaï Laraki)

Two Women on the Road / Deux femmes sur la route (Farida Bourquia)

Waiting for Pasolini / En attendant Pasolini (Daoud Aoulad Syad)

Whatever Lola Wants (Nabil Ayouch)

Where Are You Going, Moshe? / Où vas-tu Moshe? (Hassan Benjelloun)

Woven by Hands from Cloth / Tissée de mains et d'étoffe (Omar Chraïbi)

Yasmine and Men / Yasmine et les hommes (Abdelkader Lagtaâ)

REFERENCES

Amar Rodriguez, Victor Manuel, ed. *El Cine marroqui: secuencias para su conocimiento.* Cadiz, Spain: Servicio de Publicaciones de la Universidad de Cadiz, 2006.

Araib, Ahmed, and Eric de Hullessen. *Il était une fois . . . Le cinéma au Maroc.* Rabat, Morocco: EDH, 1999.

Armes, Roy. "Faouzi Bensaidi (Morocco)." In *African Filmmaking: North and South of the Sahara,* pp. 183–190. Edinburgh: Edinburgh University Press; Bloomington: Indiana University Press, 2006.

Bakrim, Mohammed. *Le Désir permanent, chroniques cinématographiques.* Rabat, Morocco: Nourlil Éditeur, 2006.

Belfquih, Mohamed. *C'est mon écran après tout! Réflexions sur la situation de l'audiovisuel au Maroc.* Rabat, Morocco: Infolive, 1995.

Cinéma marocain, filmographie générale longs métrages, 1958–2005. Rabat, Morocco: Centre Cinématographique Marocain, 2006.

Cinquante ans de courts métrages marocains 1947–1997, Rabat, Morocco: Centre Cinématographique Marocain, 1998.

Dahane, Mohamed, ed. *Cinéma Histoire et Société*. Rabat: Publications de la Faculté des Lettres, 1995.

De Hullessen, Eric. *Guide du cinéma et de l'audiovisuel marocain / Guide of Moroccan Cinema and Audiovisual*. Rabat, Morocco: Éditions EDH, 1998.

Du fonds d'aide . . . à l'avance sur recettes. Rabat, Morocco: Centre Cinématographique Marocain, 2006.

Dwyer, Kevin. "'Hidden, Unsaid, Taboo' in Moroccan Cinema: Adelkader Lagtaa's Challenge to Authority." *Framework* 43, no. 2 (2002): 117–133.

———. "Moroccan Filmmaking: A Long Voyage through the Straits of Paradox." In *Everyday Life in the Muslim Middle East*, ed. Donna Lee Bowen and Evelyn A Early, pp. 349–359. Bloomington: Indiana University Press, 2002.

———. *Beyond Casablanca: M.A. Tazi and the Adventure of Moroccan Cinema*. Bloomington: Indiana University Press, 2004.

El Khodari, Khalid. *Guide des réalisateurs marocains*. Rabat, Morocco: El Maarif Al Jadida, 2000.

El Yamlahi, Sidi Mohamed. *Bachir Skiredj: Biographie d'un rire*. Casablanca: Najah el Jadida, 1997.

Elena, Alberto, ed. *Balcón Atlantico: las mil y una imágenes de cine marroqui*. Las Palmas/Madrid: Festival Internacional de Cine de las Palmas de Gran Canaria/T&B Editores, 2007.

Fertat, Ahmed. *Une passion nommée cinéma: vie et oeuvres de Mohamed Osfour*. Tangier: Altopress, 2000.

Jaïdi, Moulay Driss. *Public(s) et cinéma*. Rabat, Morocco: Collection al majal, 1992.

———. *Vision(s) de la société marocaine à travers le court métrage*. Rabat, Morocco: Collection al majal, 1994.

———. *Cinégraphiques*. Rabat, Morocco: Collection al majal, 1995.

———. *Diffusion et audience des médias audiovisuels*. Rabat, Morocco: Collection al majal, 2000.

———. *Histoire du cinéma au Maroc, le cinéma colonial*. Rabat, Morocco: Collection al majal, 2001.

Jibril, Mohamed. "Cinéma marocain, l'improb-able image de soi." In *Le Maroc en mouvement: créations contemporaines*, ed. Nicole de Pontcharra and Maati Kabbal, pp. 179–184. Paris: Maisonneuve and Larose, 2000.

Pour une promotion du cinéma national. Rabat, Morocco: Centre Cinématographique Marocain, 1993.

Regard sur le cinéma au Maroc. Rabat, Morocco: Centre Cinématographique Marocain, 1995.

Souiba, Fouad, and Fatima Zahra el Alaoui. *Un siècle de cinéma au Maroc*. Rabat, Morocco: World Design Communication, 1995.

MOZAMBIQUE

Output: 9 feature films
Filmmakers: 7
(Licínio Azevedo, José Cardoso, Sol de Carvalho, Fernando D'Almeida e Silva, Ruy Guerra, Camilo de Sousa, Fernando Vendrell)

CHRONOLOGY
1979
Mueda, Memory and Massacre / Mueda, memoria e massacre (Ruy Guerra)
1982
Sing, My Brother, Help Me to Sing / Canta meu irmao, ajuda-me a cantar (José Cardoso)
1985
Time of Leopards / O tempo dos leopardos (Camilo de Sousa and Zdravko Velimorovic)
1987
The Wind from the North / O vento sopra do norte (José Cardosa)
1995
The Fight for Water / A guerra de agua (documentry) (Licínio Azevedo)
1996
The Earth's Storm / A tempestade da terra (Fernando D'Almeida e Silva)
2003
Light Drops / O goejar da luz (Fernando Vendrell)
Mixed Up / Estorvo (Ruy Guerra)
2006
O Jardim do Outro Homen (Sol de Carvalho)

REFERENCES

Andrade-Watkins, Claire. "Portuguese African Cinema: Historical and Contemporary Perspectives, 1969–1993." In *Cinemas of the Black Diaspora: Diversity, Dependence and Oppositionality,* ed. Michael T. Martin, pp. 181–203. Detroit: Wayne State University Press, 1995.

Fina, Luciana, Cristina Fina, and António Loja Neves. *Cinemas de África.* Lisbon: Cinemateca Portugesa and Culturgest, 1995.

Pimenta, Pedro. "Il faut investir l'informel" (interview with Olivier Barlet). *Africultures* 69 (2007): 165–171.

Rodriguès, Antonio. "Les Cinémas d'Afrique 'lusophone." In *Cinémas africains, une oasis dans le désert?* ed. Samuel Lelièvre, pp. 237–238. Paris: Corlet/Télérama/*CinémAction* 106, 2003.

NIGER

Output: 13 feature films
Filmmakers: 5
(Mustapha Alassane, Mahamane Bakabe, Mustapha Diop, Oumarou Ganda, Djingary Maiga)

CHRONOLOGY
1970
Le Wazzou polygame (Oumarou Ganda)
1972
FVVA / FVVA: Femme, Villa, Voiture, Argent (Mustapha Alassane)
Saitane (Oumarou Ganda)
1973
Toula or the Water Spirit / Toula ou le génie des eaux (Mustapha Alassane)
1975
The Black Star / L'Étoile noire (Djingary Maiga)
1979
Black Clouds / Nuages noirs (Djingary Maiga)
1980
The Exile / L'Exilé (Oumarou Ganda)
1981
If the Horsemen . . . / Si les cavaliers (Mahamane Bakabe)

1982
The Doctor from Gafiré / Le Médecin de Gafiré (Moustapha Diop)
Kankamba / Kankamba ou le semeur de discorde (Mustapha Alassane)
1983
Black Dawn / Aube noire (Djingary Maiga)
1989
Mamy Wata (Moustapha Diop)
1999
Black Friday / Vendredi noir (Djingary Maiga)

REFERENCES

Ganda, Oumarou. *Cabascabo* (script) (with *Moi un noir*). Paris: *L'Avant-Scène du Cinéma* 265 (1981).

lbo, Ousmane. *Le Cinéma au Niger.* Brussels: OCIC, 1993.

Issa, Maïzama. *Oumarou Ganda, cinéaste nigérien: un regard du dedans sur la société en transition.* Dakar: Enda-Édition, 1991.

Pfaff, Françoise. "Moustapha Alassane" and "Oumarou Ganda." In *25 Black African Film Makers,* pp. 1–9, 125–136. New York: Greenwood Press, 1988.

Spass, Lieve. "Niger." In *The Francophone Film: A Struggle for Identity,* pp. 215–217. Manchester: Manchester University Press, 2000.

Teicher, Gaël. *Moustapha Alassane Cinéaste.* Paris: Les Éditions de l'Oeil, 2003.

NIGERIA

Output: 89 feature films
Filmmakers: 42
(Adewale Adenuga, Bayo Aderohunmu, Afolabi Adesanya, Gbenga Adewusi, Jab Adu, Newton I. Aduaka, Adeyemi Afolayan [also known as Ade Love], Mukaila Ajaga, Tunde Alabi Huneyin, Jimoh Aliu, Segun Alli, Jeta Amata, Saddick Balewa, Baba Balogun, Ola Balogun, Bankole Bello, Omah Diegu, Sanya Dosunmu, Adebayo Faleti, Lola Fani-Kayode, Adamu Halilu, Ladi Ladebo [= Olasubomi Oladipupo Loladere], Dr. Ola Mankinwa, Yussuf Mohamed, Adaora Nwandu, Tubosun Odunsi, Chief Hubert Ogunde, Moyo Ogundipe, Yomi Ogunmola,

Isola Ogunsola, Moses Olaiya Adejumo [also known as Baba Sala], Oyewole Olowomojuore, Tunde Oloyede, Ola Omonitan, Rufus Omotehinse, Ngozi Onwurah, Branwen Okpako, Adebayo Salami, Brendan Shehu, Wole Soyinka, Eddie Ugbomah, Sule Umar)

CHRONOLOGY

The following listing is restricted to films and ignores the many thousands of Nigerian home video features.

As often elsewhere in Africa, true national production was preceded by locally produced features directed by foreigners. In the case of Nigeria, the 1970s began with two English-language features, based on Nigerian literary sources, produced by Francis Oladele's Calpenny Nigeria Films: *Kongi's Harvest* (1970, directed by U.S. filmmaker Ossie Davies) and *Bullfrog in the Sun* (1971, directed by a German filmmaker, Hans Jürgen Pohland). A further Ossie Davies film was *Count Down at Kusini* (1976), produced by Ladi Ladebo.

1972
Alpha (English, Ola Balogun)
1975
Ajani Ogun (Yoruba, Ola Balogun)
Amadi (Ibo, Ola Balogun)
Dinner with the Devil (English, Sanya Dosunmu)
1976
Musik Man (English, Ola Balogun)
Shehu Umar (Hausa, Adamu Halilu)
1977
Bisi Daughter of the River (English, Jab Adu)
The Rise and Fall of Doctor Oyenusi (English, Eddie Ugbomah)
1978
Black Goddess / A Deusa Negra (Portuguese, Ola Balogun)
Ija Ominira (Yoruba, Ola Balogun)
Kanta of Kebbi (Hausa, Adamu Halilu)
1979
Aiye (English, Ola Balogun)
The Mask (English, Eddie Ugbomah)
1980
Jaiyesimi (Yoruba, Chief Hubert Ogunde and Freddie Goode)
Kadara (Yoruba, Adeyemi Afolayan)
1981
Cry Freedom (English, Ola Balogun)

Moment of Truth (English, Adamu Halilu)
Oil Doom (English, Eddie Ugbomah)
1982
Anikura (Yoruba, Oyewole Olowomojuore)
Aropin N'tenia (Yoruba, Chief Hubert Ogunde and Freddie Goode)
Bolus 80 (English, Eddie Ugbomah)
The Boy Is Good (English, Eddie Ugbomah)
Efunsetan Aniwura (Yoruba, Bankole Bello)
Ija Orogun (Yoruba, Adeyemi Afolayan)
Money Power (Yoruba, Ola Balogun)
Orun Mooru (Yoruba, Ola Balogun)
1983
Aare Agbaye (Yoruba, Moses Olaiya Adejumo and Oyewole Olowomojuore)
Ireke Onibudo (Yoruba, Tunde Alabi Hundeyin).
Taxi Driver (Yoruba, Adeyemi Afolayan)
The Wrath of Agbako (English, Rufus Omotehinse)
1984
Blues for the Prodigal (English, Wole Soyinka)
Death of the Black President (English, Eddie Ugbomah)
Iya ni Wura (Yoruba, Adeyemi Afolayan)
Papa Ajasco (Pidgin English, Adewale Adenuga)
Vengeance of the Cult (English, Eddie Ugbomah)
1985
Children of God (English, Ladi Ladebo)
Egunleri (Yoruba, Mukaila Ajaga)
Esan Ake (Yoruba, Eddie Ugbomah)
I Too Sing Nigeria (English Ladi Ladebo)
1986
Apalara (Yoruba, Eddie Ugbomah)
Kanna Kanna (Yoruba, Bayo Aderohunmu)
Lisabi (Yoruba, Oyewole Olowomojuore)
Mosebolatan (Yoruba, Adeyemi Afolayan)
Ogun Ajaye (Yoruba, Ola Omonitan)
Ogun Idile (Yoruba, Segun Alli)
Oju Oro (Yoruba, Olowomujure Oyewole)
The Songbird (English, Moyo Ogundipe)
Taxi Driver II (Yoruba, Adeyemi Afolayan)
1987
Omo Orukan (Yoruba, Adebayo Salami)
1988
Ayanmo (Yoruba, Hubert Ogunde)
Maitatsine (Hausa, Sule Umar)
Omiran (Yoruba, Eddie Ugbomah)
Panpe Aiye (Yoruba, Yomi Ogunmola)
Vendor (English, Ladi Ladebo)

Vigilante (English, Afolabi Adesanya)
1989
Agba Arin (Yoruba, Adebayo Faleti)
Akoni (Yoruba, Mukaila Ajaga)
Eewo / Taboo (English, Ladi Ladebo)
Ejo Ngboro (Yoruba, Tubosun Odunsi *aka* Paadi Mkaila)
Ha! Enia (Yoruba, Yomi Ogunmola)
Iwa (Yoruba, Lola Fani-Kayode)
Ori Olori (Yoruba, Adeyemi Afolayan)
Ruwan bagaja (Hausa, Yussuf Mohamed)
1990
Eri Okan / Conscience (Yoruba, Tunde Oloyede)
1991
Fopomoyo / Chaos (Yoruba, Jimoh Aliu)
Kasarmu Ce (Hausa, Saddick Balewa)
Kirakita (Yoruba, Yomi Ogunmola)
Ose Sango / Sango's Wand (Yoruba, Afolabi Adesanya)
Tori Ade (Yoruba, Eddie Ugbomah)
1992
Ehin Oku (Yoruba, Adeyemi Afolayan)
Itunu (Yoruba, Gbenga Adewusi)
Kulba Na Barna / Blaming the Innocent (Hausa, Brendan Shehu)
Ofa Oro (Yoruba, Segun Alli)
Orogun Orun (Yoruba, Baba Balogun)
1993
Agbo meji / The Two Forces (Dr Ola Mankinwa)
Ogun Laye (Yoruba, Isola Ogunsola)
1994
Pariah (English, Ladi Ladebo)
The Snake in My Bed (English, Omah Diegu)
Welcome II the Terrordome (English, Ngozi Onwurah)
1996
Oselu (Yoruba, Bankole Bello)
1998
Power, aka the Throne (English, Ladi Ladebo)
1999
Baba Zak (English, Ladi Ladebo)
2000
Dreckfresser / Dirt for Dinner (documentary) (German, Branwen Okpako)
Rage (English, Newton I. Aduaka)
2002
Heritage (English, Ladi Ladebo)
2003
Valley of the Innocent (English, Branwen Okpako)

2005
The Amazing Grace (English, Jeta Amata)
2006
Rag Tag (Adaora Nwandu)
2007
Ezra (Newton I. Aduaka)
NB Since the mid-1980s many thousands of feature-length fictional stories have been shot on video in Nigeria: Pierre Barrot estimates 7,000 between 1992 and the beginning of 2005, and it is calculated that a further 1,200 are shot each year.

REFERENCES

Adesanya, Afobali. *The Nigerian Film Index.* Ikeja: A-Production Nigeria, 1994.

———. *Reel Words.* Jos: National Film Institute, 2005.

Ayorinde, Steve. "Nigeria." In *International Film Guide 2006,* ed. Tom Rosenthal, pp. 217–218. London: Button Communications, 2006..

Balogun, Françoise. *Le Cinéma au Nigeria.* Brussels: OCIC, 1984. Translated as *The Cinema in Nigeria.* Enugu, Nigeria: Delta, 1987.

Barlet, Olivier. "Nigeria: la vidéo rêve d'oscars." *Africultures* 68 (2006): 169–175.

Barrot, Pierre, ed. *Nollywood, le phénomène vidéo au Nigeria.* Paris: Éditions L'Harmattan, 2005.

Clark, Ebun. *Hubert Ogunde: The Making of Nigerian Theatre.* Oxford, UK: Oxford University Press, 1979.

Ekwuazi, Hyginus. *Film in Nigeria.* Jos: Nigerian Film Corporation, 1987 and 1991.

———, ed. *Zanani* (screenplay by Irene Carew and Bankole Bello). Jos: National Film Institute, 2003.

———. *Nigerian Cinema: Pioneers and Practitioners.* Jos: National Film Institute, 2004.

Ekwuazi, Hyginus, and Yakubu Nasidi, eds. *No . . . Not Hollywood: Essays and Speeches of Brendan Shehu.* Jos: National Film Institute, 1992.

———, eds. *Operative Principles of the Film Industry: Towards a Film Policy for Nigeria.* Jos: Nigerian Film Corporation, 1992.

Ekwuazi, Hyginus, Mercy Sokomba, and Onyero Mgbejume, eds. *Making the Transition from Video to Celluloid.* Jos: Nigerian Film Corporation, 2001.

Haynes, Jonathan, ed. *Nigerian Video Films*. Jos: Nigerian Film Corporation, 1997.

———. "Nigerian Cinema: Structural Adjustments." In *African Cinema: Post-Colonial and Feminist Readings*, ed. Kenneth W. Harrow, pp. 143–175. Trenton, N.J.: Africa World Press, 1999.

———. "Le Boum du film vidéo au Nigeria." In *Cinémas africains, une oasis dans le désert?* ed. Samuel Lelièvre, pp. 165–173. Paris: Corlet/Télérama/*CinémAction* 106, 2003.

———. "Mobilising Yoruba Popular Culture: *Babangida Must Go*." *Africa* 73, no. 19 (2003): 77–87.

———. "Political Critique in Nigerian Video Films." *African Affairs* 105, no. 421 (2006): 511–583.

Haynes, Jonathan, and Onookome Okome. "Evolving Popular Media: Nigerian Video Films." *Research in African Literatures* 29, no. 3 (1998): 106–128.

Index of Nigerian Motion Picture Industry. Jos: National Film Institute, n.d.

Iyabode, Alakija Funmi. *Problems and Prospects of Filmmaking in Nigeria: Hubert Ogunde Motion Pictures as a Case Study*. Benin, Nigeria: University of Benin, 1985.

Nigerian Film Corporation Handbook. Jos: National Film Corporation, n.d.

Nwachukwu. J. O. J. "Women in Igbo-Language Videos: The Virtuous and the Villainous." In *With Open Eyes: Women and African Cinema*, ed. Kenneth W. Harrow, pp. 67–80. Amsterdam: Rodopi/*Matutu* 19, 1997.

Okome, Onookome. "Ola Balogun et les débuts du cinéma nigérian." In *Cinémas africains, une oasis dans le désert?* ed. Samuel Lelièvre, pp. 158–164. Paris: Corlet/Télérama/*CinémAction* 106, 2003.

Okome, Onookome, and Jonathan Haynes. *Cinema and Social Change in Nigeria*. Jos: Nigerian Film Corporation, 1996.

Opubor, Alfred, and Onura E. Nwuneli. *The Development and Growth of the Film Industry in Nigeria*. Lagos: Third Press International, 1979.

Pfaff, Françoise. "Ola Balogun." In *25 Black African Film Makers*, pp. 19–31. New York: Greenwood Press, 1988.

Ricard, Alain. "Du théâtre au cinéma yoruba: le cas nigérian." In *Cinémas noirs d'Afrique*, ed. Guy Hennebelle, pp. 160–167. Paris: *CinémAction* 23, 1983.

Ukadike, Nwachukwu Frank. Interviews with Eddie Ugbomah and Brendan Shehan. In *Questioning African Cinema*, pp. 85–98, 161–179. Minneapolis: University of Minnesota Press, 2002.

See also the *NFC Film News* (edited quarterly since 2004 at the Nigerian Film Corporation in Jos).

RWANDA

Ouput: 2 feature films
Filmmakers: 2
(Lee Isaac Chung, Nick Hughes)

CHRONOLOGY
2002
100 Days (Nick Hughes)
2007
Munyurangabo (Lee Isaac Chung)
NB A feature-length video was shot in 2006 by Joseph Muganga: *The Kadogo Brothers / Les Frères Kadogo*.

SENEGAL

Output: 50 feature films
Filmmakers: 23
(Moussa Sene Absa, Cheikh Tidiane Aw, Cheikh Ngaïdo Ba, Moussa Yoro Bathily, Ben Diogaye Beye, Clarence T. Delgardo, Massaër Dieng, Djibril Diop Mambety, Safi Faye, Alain Gomis, Cheik N'Diaye, Samba Félix N'Diaye, Joseph Gaye Ramaka, Ababacar Samb-Makharam, Amadou Saalum Seck, Ousmane Sembene, Thierno Faty Sow, Momar Thiam, Amadou Thior, Moussa Touré, Mahama [Johnson] Traore, Paulin Soumanou Vieyra, Mansour Sora Wade)

CHRONOLOGY
1964
Black Girl / La Noire de . . . (Ousmane Sembene)

1968
The Money Order / Mandabi / Le Mandat (Ousmane Sembene)
1970
Diegue-Bi / La Femme (Mahama [Johnson] Traore)
1971
Emitai / Dieu du tonnerre (Ousmane Sembene)
Karim (Momar Thiam)
Kodou (Ababacar Samb-Makharam)
1972
Lambaye / Truanderie (Mahama [Johnson] Traore)
1973
Touki Bouki (Djibril Diop Mambety)
1974
Baks (Momar Thiam)
The Bronze Bracelet / Le Bracelet de bronze (Cheikh Tidiane Aw)
Garga M'Bosse / Cactus (Mahama [Johnson] Traore)
The Option / L'Option (Thierno Faty Sow)
Xala (Ousmane Sembene)
1975
Letter from My Village / Kaddu Beykat / Lettre paysanne (Safi Faye)
Njangaan / N'Diangane (Mahama [Johnson] Traore)
1977
Ceddo (Ousmane Sembene)
1978
Tiyabu Biru / La Circoncision (Moussa Yoro Bathily)
1979
Fad'Jal (Safi Faye)
1980
A Man and Some Women / Sey Seyeti / Un homme, des femmes (Ben Diogaye Beye)
1981
The Eye / L'Oeil (Thierno Faty Sow)
Jom or a People's Story / Jom ou l'histoire d'un peuple (Ababacar Samb-Makharam)
Under House Arrest / En résidence surveillée (Paulin Soumanou Vieyra)
1982
The Certificate / Le Certificat (Cheikh Tidiane Aw)
Sa Dagga Le M'Bandakatt / Le Troubadour (Momar Thiam)

1983
Xew Xew / La Fête commence (Cheikh Ngaïdo Ba)
1988
Camp de Thiaroye (Ousmane Sembene and Thierno Faty Sow)
Saaraba (Amadou Saalum Seck)
1989
White Beans with Cassava or Gombo Sauce / Petits blancs au manioc ou à la sauce gombo (Moussa Yoro Bathily)
1991
Ken Bugul (Moussa Sene Absa)
Niiwan (Clarence T. Delgardo)
Toubab Bi (Moussa Touré)
1992
Guelwaar (Ousmane Sembene)
Hyenas / Hyènes (Djibril Diop-Mambety)
1993
Biliyaane (Moussa Yoro Bathily)
1994
Ngor: The Spirit of the Place / Ngor, l'esprit des lieux (documentary) (Samba Félix N'Diaye)
1996
Mossane (Safi Faye)
Tableau ferraille (Moussa Sene Absa)
1997
TGV (Moussa Touré)
1999
Faat-Kine (Ousmane Sembene)
2000
Almodou (Amadou Thior)
Karmen Geï (Joseph Gaye Ramaka)
2001
L'Afrance (Alain Gomis)
The Price of Forgiveness / Ndeysaan / Le Prix du pardon (Mansour Sora Wade)
2002
A Child's Love / Un amour d'enfant (Ben Diogaye Beye)
Madame Brouette (Moussa Sene Absa)
Moolade (Ousmane Sembene)
2003
Ndobine (Amadou Saalum Seck)
2005
Bul déconne! (Massaër Dieng and Marc Picavez)
Wrestling Grounds / L'Appel des arènes (Cheik Ndiaye)

2006
Teranga Blues (Moussa Sene Absa)

REFERENCES

Armes, Roy. "The Group as Protagonist: *Ceddo.*" In *Action and Image: Dramatic Structure in Cinema*, pp. 155–170. Manchester: Manchester University Press, 1994.

Diagne, Ismaïla. *Les Sociétés africaines au miroir de Sembène Ousmane.* Paris: Éditions L'Harmattan, 2004.

Diop, Papa Samba, Elisa Fuchs, Heinz Hug, and János Riesz. *Ousmane Sembène und die senegalesche Erzählliteratur.* Munich: Edition Text + Kritk, 1994.

Ellerson, Beti. "Africa through a Woman's Eyes: Safi Faye's Cinema." In *Focus on African Films*, ed. Françoise Pfaff, pp. 185–197. Bloomington: Indiana University Press, 2004.

Gadjigo, Samba. "Ousmane Sembene and History on the Screen: A Look Back to the Future." In *Focus on African Films*, ed. Françoise Pfaff, pp. 33–47. Bloomington: Indiana University Press, 2004.

———. *Ousmane Sembene: Une conscience africaine.* Paris: Éditions Homnisphères, 2007.

Gadjigo, Samba, Ralph H. Faulkingham, Thomas Cassirer, and Reinhard Sander, eds. *Ousmane Sembene: Dialogues with Critics and Writers.* Amherst: University of Massachusetts Press, 1993.

Hommage à Paulin Soumanou Vieyra. Paris: *Présence Africaine* 170 (2004): 19–86.

Imbert, Henri-François. *Samba Félix Ndiaye: Cinéaste documentariste africain.* Paris: Éditions L'Harmattan, 2007.

Landy, Marcia. "Folklore, Memory and Postcoloniality in Ousmane Sembene's Films." In *Cinematic Uses of the Past*, pp. 30–66. Minneapolis: University of Minnesota Press, 1996.

Mermin, Elizabeth. "A Window on Whose Reality? The Emerging Industry of Senegalese Cinema." In *African Cinema: Post-Colonial and Feminist Readings*, ed. Kenneth W. Harrow, pp. 201–221. Trenton, N.J.: Africa World Press, 1999.

Mowitt, John. "Ousmane Sembene's *Xala.*" In *Re-takes: Postcoloniality and Foreign Film Languages*, pp. 97–131. Minneapolis: University of Minnesota Press, 2005.

Mulvey, Laura. "The Carapace That Failed: Ousmane Sembene's *Xala.*" In *Fetishism and Curiosity*, pp. 118–136. London: British Film Institute; Bloomington: Indiana University Press, 1996.

Murphy, David. *Sembene: Imagining Alternatives in Film and Fiction.* Oxford: James Currey; Trenton, N.J.: Africa World Press, 2000.

Niang, Sada, ed. *Littérature et cinéma en Afrique francophone: Ousmane Sembene et Assia Djebar.* Paris: Éditions L'Harmattan, 1996.

———. *Djibril Diop Mambety: un cinéaste à contre-courant.* Paris: Éditions L'Harmattan, 2002.

Petty, Sheila, ed. *A Call to Arms: The Films of Ousmane Sembene.* Trowbridge, England: Flicks Books, 1996.

Pfaff, Françoise. *The Cinema of Ousmane Sembene.* Westport, Conn.: Greenwood Press, 1984.

———. "Moussa Bathily," "Safi Faye," "Djibril Diop Mambety," "Ababacar Samb," "Ousmane Sembene," "Momar Thiam," "Mahama Johnson Traoré," and "Paulin Soumanou Vieyra." In *25 Black African Film Makers*, pp. 43–49, 115–124, 217–303. New York: Greenwood Press, 1988.

Sembene, Ousmane. "Filmmakers Have a Great Responsibility to Our People" (interview). In *Art, Politics, Cinema: The Cinéaste Interviews*, ed. Dan Georgakas and Lenny Rubenstein, pp. 41–52. London: Pluto Press, 1985.

Sene, Papa. *Djibril Diop Mambety: la caméra au bout . . . du nez.* Paris: Editions L'Harmattan, 2001.

Serceau, Daniel, ed. *Sembène Ousmane.* Paris: *CinémAction* 34, 1985.

Spass, Lieve. "Senegal." In *The Francophone Film: A Struggle for Identity*, pp. 172–190. Manchester: Manchester University Press, 2000.

Taposa, Clément, ed. "Hommage/Tribute: Djibril Diop Mambety." *Écrans d'Afrique / African Screen* 24 (1998): 1–73.

Turvey, Gerry. "*Xala* and the Curse of Neo-Colonialism: Reflections on a Realist Project." Glasgow: *Screen* 26, no. 3–4 (1995): 75–87.

Ukadike, Nwachukwu Frank. Interviews with Safi Faye and Djibril Diop Mambety. In *Questioning African Cinema,* pp. 29–40, 121–131. Minneapolis: University of Minnesota Press, 2002.

Vieyra, Paulin Soumanou. *Sembène Ousmane cinéaste.* Paris: Présence Africaine, 1972.

———. *Le Cinéma au Sénégal.* Brussels: OCIC, 1983.

———. *Réflexions d'un cinéaste africain.* Brussels: OCIC, 1990.

Wynchant, Anny. *Djibril Diop Mambety, ou le voyage du voyant.* Ivry-Sur Seine: Éditions A3, 2003.

SOMALIA

Output: 4 feature films
Filmmakers: 5
(Idriss Hassan Dirie, Hadj Mohamed Giumale, Soraya Mire, Said Salah, Amar Sneh)

CHRONOLOGY
1968
Town and Village / Miyi Iyo Magaalo (Hadj Mohamed Giumale)
1973
Reality and Myth / Dan Iyo Xarrago (Idriss Hassan Dirie)
1984
The Somali Darwish (Amar Sneh and Said Salah)
1994
Fire Eyes (Soraya Mire)

SOUTH AFRICA

OVERALL STATISTICS: 443 filmmakers—1,434 feature films

Silent: 43 films   13 directors
1930s   5 films   3 active directors,   2 new

1940s	15 films	10 active directors	10 new
1950s	35 films	18 active directors,	17 new
1960s	99 films	52 active directors,	41 new
1970s	236 films	81 active directors,	66 new
1980s	735 films	205 active directors,	179 new
1990s	186 films	100 active directors,	63 new
2000s	80 films	66 active directors,	52 new

Silent Era (1910–1925)

Output:	43 Films
1910	1
1916	14
1917	7
1918	5
1919	5
1920	4
1921	3
1922	1
1923	1
1924	1
1925	1

Filmmakers: 13 active
(Joseph Albrecht, Weston Bowden, B. F. Clinton, Dick Cruikshanks, Leander de Cordova, J. Humphrey, Lorrimer Johnston, Norman V. Lee, H. Lisle Locoque, Denis Santry, Isidore W. Schlesinger, Harold Shaw, M. A. Wertherell)

1930s

Output:	5 films
1931	2
1933	1
1936	1
1938	1

Filmmakers: 3 active—2 new (*)
(Joseph Albrecht, *J. Sinclair, *Berthold Viertel)

1940s

Output:	15 films
1942	3
1944	1
1946	4
1947	3
1949	4

Filmmakers: 10 active—10 new (*)
(*Arthur Bennet, *Thomas Block, *Johannes J. Boonzaaier, *Francis Coley, *Pierre de Wet, *Louis Knobel, *Andries A. Pienaar, *Donald Swanson, *D. W. Uys, *T. A. Wilson-Yelverton)

1950s

Output:	35 films
1950	3
1951	5
1952	1
1953	3
1954	5
1955	3
1956	1
1957	2
1958	5
1959	7

Filmmakers: 18 active—17 new (*)

(*Ken Annakin, *Immel Botha, *Kappie Botha, *Pierre D. Botha, *Franz Cloete, Pierre de Wet, *Werner Grünbauer, *Hyman Kirstein, *Zoltan Korda, *David Macdonald, *David Mullin, *Emil Nofal, *Joo Olwagenol *Bladon Peake, *Gerrie Snyman, *Jamie Uys, *Hennie van den Heever, *Harry Watt)

1960s

Output:	99 films
1960	8
1961	17
1962	13
1963	6
1964	8
1965	8
1966	7
1967	9
1968	11
1969	12

Filmmakers: 52 active—41 new (*)

(Ken Annakin, Kappie Botha, Pierre D. Botha, *Jack Cardiff, *Henning Carlsen, *Don Chaffey, *Franz Conradie, *Richard Daneel, *Dirk de Villiers, Pierre de Wet, *Elmo de Witt, Al Debbo, Cy Enfield, *Werner Grunbauer, *Ivan Hall, *Sandy Howard, *Laurence Huntington, *Anthony Keyser, *Hendrick Kotze, *Robert Lynn, *Alexander Mackendrick, *Basil Mailer, *Paul Martin, *Alfredo Medori, *Lothar Mendes, David Millin, Emil Nofal, *Stanley Norman, *James Norval, *Jan Perold, *Sven Persson, *Truida Pohl, *Peter Prowse, *Jans Rautenbach, *Daan Retief, *Percival Rubens, *Nino Scolaro, *Dennis Scully, *George Sherman, *Mario Schiess, Gerrie Snyman, *Tim Spring, *Herman Stadt, Donald Swanson, *Ivan Tors, Jamie Uys, *Dawie van Heerden, *Gordon Vorster, *Robert Webb, *Cecil Whiteman, *Louis Wiesner, *Cornell Wilde)

1970s

Output:	236 films
1970	16
1971	17
1972	22
1973	20
1974	32
1975	30
1976	28
1977	18
1978	27
1979	26

Filmmakers: 81 active—66 new (*)

(*Willie Alheit, *Gordon Anderson, *Ray Austin, *Viriato Barretto, Kappie Botha, *Jan Breytenbach, *Louis Burke, *George Canes, Don Chaffey, *Morné Coetzer, *Robert Day, Dirk de Villiers, Elmo de Witt, *Louis de Witt, Al Debbo, *Ross Devenish, *Chris du Toit, *Marie du Toit, *James Fargo, *William Faure, *Freddie Francis. *Dianne Ginsberg, *Val Guest, *Chris Halgryn, Ivan Hall, *Ian Hamilton, *Peter Henkel, *Neil Hetherington, *Douglas Hickox, *Peter Hunt, *Ronnie Isaacs, *Gibson Kente, *Kobus Kruger, *Ashley Lazarus, *Franz Marx, *Andrew McLaglan, *Tom Meehan, *Rudi Meyer, *Tommie Meyer, *Grenville Middleton, David Millin, *Donald Monat, *George Montgomery, *Michael Moore, *Jimmy Murray, *Ben Nanoyi, *Anna Neetling-Pohl, Emil Nofal, *Sias Odendaal, Sven Persson, *Harald Phillip, *Stuart Pringle, Jans Rautenbach, *Heinz Reinhl, *Howard Rennie, *Bertrand Retief, Daan Retief, *Koos Roets, *Chris Rowley, Percival Rubens, *Simon Sabela, *Roy Sargeant, Mario Schiess, *Jan Scholtz, Tim Spring, *Wallie Stevens, *Joe Stewardson, *D. B. Steyn, *John Stodel, *Herman Strauss, *François Swart, *Carel Trichardt, Jamie Uys, *Tonie van der Merwe, *Keith G. van der Wat, *Manie van Rensburg, *Albie Venter, *Judex Viljoen, Gordon Vorster, *Sam Williams, *Fred Wilson [Marino Girolami], *Michel Wyn)

1980s

Output:	735 films
1980	27
1981	22

1982	20
1983	34
1984	81
1985	118
1986	57
1987	115
1988	163
1989	98

Filmmakers: 205 active—179 new (*)

(*Catlin Adams, *Jordan Alan, *James Allen, *Gidi Amir, *Yuda Barkan, *Laurens Barnard, *Sean Barton, *David Bensusan, *Robert Bergman, *Johan Bernard, *Charles Biggs, *Allan Birkinshaw, *Johan Blignaut, *Peter Bode, *John Bowey, *Douglas Bristow, Louis Burke, *Bernard Buys, *Gianpietro Calastro, *John Cardos, *Steve Carver, *Bromley Cawood, *Tom Clegg, *Norman Cohen, *Vincent Cox, *Hazel Crampton, *Wayne Crawford, *Chris Curling, *Heinrich Dahms, *Boaz Davidson, *Robert Davies, *Beau Davis, Dirk de Villiers, Elmo de Witt, *Jean Delbeke, Ross Devenish, *Mario Di Leo, *C Dippenaar, *Jay Douwes, Chris du Toit, *M Dyter, *Willam Egan, *Mark Engels, *H Epstein, *James Fargo, *Don Fedler, *Joao Fernandes, *Sam Firstenberg, *Amalia Ford, *Joey Ford, *Lionel Friedberg, *Francis Gerard, *Jeff Gold, *David Goldstein, *Dean Goodhill, *Anton Goosen, *Zika Gravevolik, *Gary Graver, *Chuck Griffith, Ivan Hall, *F. C. Hamman, *Clive Harding, *A Hattingh, *Rod Hay, *Ed Herbst, *Brian Hessler, *Gordon Hessler, Neil Hetherington, *Katinka Heyns, *Douglas Hickox, *Jeno Hodi, *Gray Hofmeyr, *Lance Hool, *Darrell Hood, *John Hookham, *Harry Hope, *Henk Hugo, *Jackson Hunsicker, *Harry Hurwitz, *Mike Inglesby, *Ronnie Isaacs, *Dominique Jones, *Lulu Keating, *Fritz Kiersch, *Gerard Kikoine, *K Kondo, *Hans Kuhle, *Andrew Lane, *Larry Larson, *Don Leonard, *William Levey, *David Lister, *Michele Lupo, *Bruce MacFarlane, *Joanna Mack, *Peter Mackenzie, *Duncan MacNeillie, *Christian Marnham, *Charles Mariott, *Sergio Martino, Franz Marx, *Harry Mayer, *Paul Mayersberg, *Michael McCarthy, *Duncan McLachlan, *Simon Metsing, Rudi Meyer, Tommie Meyer, *Mattys Mocke, *Thomas Mogotlane, Hanro Mohr, *Giuliano Montaldo, *Tara Moore, *John Murlowski, Jimmy Murray,

*Alan Nathanson, *Frans Nel, *Fred Nel, *Gary Nelson, *John Newland, Emil Nofal, *Helena Nogueira, *Aaron Norris, *Charles Norton, Sias Odendaal, *Kenichi Oguri, *Roger Orpen, *Michael Pakleppa, *John Parr, *Hein Pretorius, *David Prior, *Etienne Puren, *Albert Pyun, Jans Rautenbach, Harold Reinl, Daan Retief, *Roland Robinson, Koos Roets, *Darrell Roodt, *Mark Roper, *Thomas Rothig, *Stanley Roup, Christopher Rowley, Percival Rubens, *Terence Ryan, *Jurgen Schadeberg, *Frank Schaeffer, *Oliver Schmitz, Jan Scholz, *Michael Schroeder, *Leon Schuster, *Clive Scott, *Denis Scully, *Michael Shackleton, *Ricki Shelach, *Igal Shilon, *Zvi Shisel, *Barney Simon, *Andrew Sinclair, *John Smallcombe, *Robert Smawley, *Louise Smit, *Neil Sonnekus, *Josh Spencer, Tim Spring, *Oliver Stapleton, *Lynton Stephenson, *Joe Stewardson, *Stuart Stromin, *Juanita Strydom, *Cedric Sundström, *Neal Sundström, *Lourens Swanepoel, *Jane Taylor, *J Lee Thompson, *Joe Tornatore, *Harry Towers, *Clive Turner, *Gerhard Uys, Jamie Uys, *Robert van de Coolwijk, *Regardt van den Bergh, *Philip van der Byl, *Fanie van der Merwe, *Gary van der Merwe, *Japie van der Merwe, *Robert van der Merwe, Tonie van der Merwe, *Wally van der Merwe, Keith van der Wat, Manie van Rensberg, *Johan van Rooyen, *Camilo Vila, *Chuck Vincent, *Roy Walker, *Charles Wallace, *Martin Walters, *Hans Webb, *David Wicht, *Anthony Wilson, *David Winters, *Alain Woolf, *Andrew Worsdale, *Martin Wragge, *Joe Zito)

1990s

Output:	186 films
1990	81
1991	21
1992	13
1993	10
1994	9
1995	7
1996	11
1997	8
1998	11
1999	15

Filmmakers: 100 active—63 new (*)

(*Leonardo August, *Ken Badish, *Laurens Barnard, *Shyam Benegal, David Bensusan, Johan

Bernard, *John Berry, *Les Blair, *Anthony Bond, *John Cherry, *Tom Clegg, *François Coertze, Wayne Crawford, *Chris Crusen, *Tony Cunningham, Heinrich Dahms, *Boaz Davidson, Dirk de Villiers, Elmo de Witt, *Henry Diffenthal, *Allan Eastman, *Nicholas Ellenbogen, *Willie Esterhuizen, *John Eyres, Sam Firstenberg, *Isaac Florentine, Joey Ford, *Wana Fourie, *Athol Fugard, *George Garcia, *Michael Garcia, Francis Gerard, *Robert Ginty, *Peter Goldsmid, Gary Graver, *Michael Hammon, *Larry Harmon, *Dupreez Heunis, Katinka Heyns, Gray Hofmeyr, *Gavin Hood, *Tobe Hooper, *Stephen Hopkins, *Hugh Hudson, *Don Hulette, Harry Hurwitz, *Stefan Ibendroth, *David Irving, *Phil Joannou, *Bernard Joffa, *Danie Joubert, *Ken Kaplan, *Ross Kettle, Larry Larson, *Kristin Levring, David Lister, *Temi Lopez, *Derrick Louw, Bruce MacFarlane, Franz Marx, Duncan McLachlan, Tommie Meyer, *Bob Misiorowski, Frans Nel, Helena Nogueira, John Parr, *Kristine Peterson, *Elaine Proctor, Etienne Puren, Albert Pyun, *Michael Qissi, Koos Roets, *John Rogers, Darrell Roodt, Mark Roper, *Mikael Salomon, Frank Schaeffer, *Michael Schroeder, Leon Schuster, Tim Spring, *Richard Stanley, *Nico Stein, *Rod Stewart, *Ramadan Suleman, Cedric Sundström, Neal Sundström, *David Thompson, *Russell Thompson, Jamie Uys, Robert van de Coolwijk, Regardt van den Berg, Tonie van der Merwe, Manie van Rensburg, *Ntshaveni wa Luruli, *Keoni Waxman [Darby Black], *Yossi Wein, *Thomas Witt, *David Worth, *Alex Wright, *Ralph Zipman)

2000s

Output:	80 films
2000	6
2001	4
2002	3
2003	11
2004	19
2005	16
2006	11

Filmmakers: 70 active, 52 new (*)

(*Billie August, *Caroll Ballard, *John Barker, * Florian Baxmeister, *Uwe Boll, *John Boorman, *Martin Campbell, *Trevor Clarence, François Coertze, Wayne Crawford, *Chris Crusen, *Mark Dornford-May, *Frederick DuChau, Willie Esterhuizen, Anthony Fabian, *Don E. FauntleRoy, *Revel Fox, *Craig Freimond, *Terry George, *Angus Gibson, *Tim Greene, *John Greyson, *Anthony Hickox, *David Hickson, Gray Hofmeyr, Gavin Hood, *Tom Hooper, *Bronwyn Hughes, *Konstandino Kalarytis, *Michael Katelman, *Feroz Khan, *Gustav Kuhn, David Lister, *Norman Maake, *Donovan Marsh, Neil Marshall, *Phillipe Martinez, *Zola Maseko, *Nicholas Mastandrea, *Khaolo Matabane, *Teddy Mattera, *Clive Morris, *Malcolm Needs, *Andrew Niccol, *Phillip Noyce, *Akin Omotso, *Maganthrie Pillay, *Henk Pretorius, *Evelyn Maud Purcell, Koos Roets, Darrell Roodt, *Jean-Pierre Roux, *Oliver Schmitz, Leon Schuster, *Jean Stewart, Ramadan Suleman, Neal Sundstrom, *Stefanie Sycholt, *Ebulus Timothy, *David van Eyssen, Regardt van den Bergh, Ntshaveni Wa Luruli, Alex Wright, *Jason Wulfson, *Jason Xenopoulos, *Ralph Ziman)

CHRONOLOGY

Silent Films
1910
The Kimberley Diamond Robbery / The Star of the South (*Director unknown*)
1916
£20,000 (B. F. Clinton)
An Artist's Inspiration / The Artist's Dream (Harold Shaw and Denis Santry)
De Voortrekkers / Winning a Continent (Harold Shaw)
Gloria (Lorrimer Johnston)
The Gun-Runner (Lorrimer Johnston)
The Illicit Liquor Seller (Lorrimer Johnston)
A Kract Affair (B. F. Clinton)
The Silver Wolf (Lorrimer Johnston)
Sonny's Little Bit (Lorrimer Johnston)
The Splendid Waster (Harold Shaw)
A Story of the Rand (Lorrimer Johnston)
A Tragedy of the Veldt (Norman V. Lee)
The Water Cure (B. F. Clinton)
A Zulu's Devotion (Lorrimer Johnston)
1917
And Then? (J. Humphrey)
A Border Scourge (Joseph Albrecht)
The Major's Dilemma (Dick Cruikshanks)

The Mealie Kids (Dick Cruikshanks)
The Piccanin's Christmas (Dick Cruikshanks)
The Rose of Rhodesia (Harold Shaw)
Zulu-Town Comedies (Dick Cruikshanks)
1918
Bond and Word (Dick Cruikshanks)
The Bridge (Dick Cruikshanks)
King Solomon's Mines (H. Lisle Lucoque)
The Symbol of Sacrifice (Isidore W. Schlesinger)
The Voice of the Waters (Joseph Albrecht)
1919
Allan Quartermaine (H. Lisle Lucoque)
Copper Mask (Joseph Albrecht)
Fallen Leaves (Dick Cruikshanks)
The Stolen Favorite (Joseph Albrecht)
With Edged Tools (Joseph Albrecht)
1920
Isban Israel (Joseph Albrecht)
The Man Who Was Afraid (Joseph Albrecht)
Prester John (Dick Cruikshanks)
Virtue in the City (Norman V. Lee)
1921
Madcap of the Veldt (*Director unknown*)
The Swallow (Leander de Cordova)
The Vulture's Prey (Dick Cruikshanks)
1922
Sam's Kid (*Director unknown*)
1923
The Blue Lagoon (Weston Bowden)
1924
Reef of Stars (Joseph Albrecht)
1925
David Livingstone (M. A. Weatherell)

Sound Films
1931
Moedertjie (Afrikaans, Joseph Albrecht)
Sarie Marais (Afrikaans, Joseph Albrecht)
1933
'n Dogter van die Veld (Afrikaans, J. Sinclair)
1936
Rhodes of Africa (English, Berthold Viertel)
1938
Die Bou van 'n Nasie / They Built a Nation (Afrikaans/English, Joseph Albrecht)
1942
Lig van 'n Eeu (Afrikaans, Andries A. Pienaar)
Newels Oor Mont-Aux-Sources (Afrikaans, Johannes J. Boonzaaier)
Ons Staan 'n Dag Oor (Afrikaans, D. W. Uys)

1944
Donker Spore (Afrikaans, Thomas Block)
1946
Die Skerpioen (Afrikaans, Arthur Bennet)
Die Wildsboudjie (Afrikaans, Arthur Bennet and Louis Knobel)
Geboortegrond (Afrikaans, Pierre de Wet)
Pinkie se Erfenis (Afrikaans, Pierre de Wet)
1947
Kaskenades van Dr Kwak (Afrikaans, Pierre de Wet)
Pantoffelregering (Afrikaans, Arthur Bennet)
Simon Beyers (Afrikaans, Pierre de Wet)
1949
Jim Comes to Jo'burg (English, Donald Swanson)
Kom Saam Vanaand (Afrikaans, Pierre de Wet)
Oom Piet se Plaas (Afrikaans, T. A. Wilson-Yelverton)
Sarie Marais (Afrikaans, Francis Coley)
1950
The Adventurers (English, David Macdonald)
Hier's Ons Weer (Afrikaans, Pierre de Wet)
Zonk (English, Hyman Kirstein)
1951
Alles sal regkom (Afrikaans, Pierre de Wet)
Cry the Beloved Country (English, Zoltan Korda)
Daar Doer in die Bosveld (Afrikaans, Jamie Uys)
Song of Africa (English, Emil Nofal)
Where No Vultures Fly (Harry Watt)
1952
Altyd in my Drome (Afrikaans, Pierre de Wet)
1953
Fifty / Vyftig (Afrikaans/English, Jamie Uys)
Hans-Die-Skipper (Afrikaans, Bladon Peake)
Inspan (Afrikaans, Bladon Peake)
1954
Daar Doer in die Stad (Afrikaans, Jamie Uys)
Die Leeu van Punda Maria / The Lion of Punda Maria (Afrikaans, Gerrie Snyman)
'n Plan is 'n Boerdery (Afrikaans, Pierre de Wet)

Vadertjie Langbeen / Daddy Long-Legs (Afrikaans, Pierre de Wet)
West of Zanzibar (English, Harry Watt)
1955
Geld Soos Bossies / Money to Burn (Afrikaans, Jamie Uys)
Matieland (Afrikaans, Pierre de Wet)
Wanneer die Masker Val (Afrikaans, Hennie Van den Heever)

1956
Paul Kruger (Afrikaans, Werner Grünbauer)
1957
Dis Lekker om te Lewe (Afrikaans, Pierre de Wet)
Donker Afrika (Afrikaans, David Mullin)
1958
Die Bosvelder (Afrikaans, Jamie Uys)
Die Goddelose Stad (Afrikaans, Pierre D. Botha)
Die Sewende Horison (Afrikaans, Franz Cloete)
Fratse van die Vloot (Afrikaans, Pierre de Wet)
Nor the Moon by Night (English, Ken Annakin)
1959
Come Back Africa (English, Lionel Ragosin)
The Desert Inn (English, Immel Botha)
Die Wilde Boere (Afrikaans, J. O. O. Olwagen)
Ek sal Opstaan (Afrikaans, Kappie Botha)
Nooi van my Hart (Afrikaans, Pierre de Wet)
Piet se Tante (Afrikaans, Pierre de Wet)
Satanskoraal (Afrikaans, Elmo de Witt)
1960
Die Bloedrooi Papawer (Afrikaans, Cecil Whiteman)
Die Jagters (Afrikaans, Gordon Vorster)
Die Vlugteling (Afrikaans, Gordon Vorster)
Hou die Blinkkant Bo (Afrikaans, Emil Nofal)
Kyk na die Sterre (Afrikaans, Kappie Botha)
The Last of the Few (English, David Millin)
Oupa en die Plaasnooientjie (Afrikaans, Pierre de Wet)
Rip van Wyk (Afrikaans, Emil Nofal)
1961
Basie (Afrikaans, Gordon Vorster)
Boerboel de Wet (Afrikaans, Al Debbo)
Diamonds Are Dangerous (English, Herman Stadt)
Die Bubbles Schroëder Storie / The Bubbles Schröeder Story (Afrikaans, Pierre D. Botha)
Die Hele Dorp Weet (Afrikaans, Kappie Botha)
Doodkry is Min (Afrikaans, Jamie Uys)
En die Vonke Spat! (Afrikaans, Pierre de Wet)
The Fiercest Heart (English, George Sherman)
Gevaarlike Reis / Heisses Land (Afrikaans, Alfredi Medori and Lothar Lomberg)
Hands of Space (English, Dennis Scully)
Hans en die Rooinek / Sidney and the Boer (English/Afrikaans, Jamie Uys)
The Hellions (English, Ken Annakin)
The Magic Garden / Pennywhistle Blues (English, Donald Swanson)
Moord in Kompartement 1001E (Afrikaans, Pierre D. Botha)

Skadu van Gister (Afrikaans, Hendrick Kotze and Anthony Keyser)
Spore in die Modder (Afrikaans, James Norval)
Tremor / As die Aarde Skeur (English/Afrikaans, Dennis Scully)
1962
As ons Twee eers Getroud is (Afrikaans, Jan Perold)
Die Geheim van Onderplaas (Afrikaans, Al Debbo)
Die Skelm van die Limpopo (Afrikaans, Gerrie Snyman)
Die Tweede Slaapkamer (Afrikaans, Gordon Vorster)
Dilemma (English, Henning Carlsen)
Gevaalike Spel / Dangerous Deals (Afrikaans/English, Al Debbo)
Jy's Lieflik Vanaand (Afrikaans, Gordon Vorster)
Lord Oom Piet / Lord Uncle Pete (Afrikaans, Jamie Uys)
Man in die Donker (Afrikaans, Truida Pohl)
Sammy Going South (English, Alexander MacKendrick)
Stropers van die Laeveld (Afrikaans, David Millin)
Tom, Dirk en Herrie (Afrikaans, Al Debbo)
Voor Sononder (Afrikaans, Emil Nofal)
1963
Die Reen kom Weer (Afrikaans, Pierre D. Botha)
Die Ruiter in die Nag / The Rider in the Night (Afrikaans, Jan Perold)
Gee My Jou Hand (Afrikaans, Tim Spring)
Huis op Horings (Afrikaans, Truida Pohl)
Journey to Nowhere (English, Dennis Scully)
Kimberley Jim (Afrikaans, Emil Nofal)
1964
Die Wonderwêreld van Kammie Kamfer (Afrikaans, Al Debbo)
Dingaka (English, Jamie Uys)
The Forster Gang (English, Percival Rubens)
Piet my Niggie (Afrikaans, Jan Perold)
Rhino (English, Ivan Tors)
Sanders of the River / Death Drums Along the River (English, Lawrence Huntington)
Seven against the Sun (English, David Millin)
Table Bay / Code 7, Victim 5 (English, Robert Lynn)
1965
Coast of Skeletons (English, Robert Lynn)
Debbie (Afrikaans, Elmo de Witt)

Diamond Walkers / Jagd auf die blauen Diamanten (English/German, Paul Martin)

King Hendrik (English, Emil Nofal)

Ride the High Wind / African Gold (English, David Millin)

Sands of the Kalahari (English, Cy Enfield)

Tokolosche (English, Peter Prowse)

Vortreflike Familie Smit (Afrikaans, Kappie Botha)

1966

Africa Shakes (English, Basil Mailer)

All the Way to Paris / After You, Comrade (English, Jamie Uys)

Die Kavaliers / The Cavaliers (Afrikaans, Elmo de Witt)

Mocambique (English, Robert Lynn)

The Naked Prey (English, Cornell Wilde)

Operation Yellow Viper (English, Stanley Norman)

The Second Sin (English, David Millin)

1967

Bennie-Boet (Afrikaans, Kappie Botha)

Die Jakkels van Tula Metsi (Afrikaans, Franz Conradie)

Die Kruger-miljoene / The Kruger Millions (Afrikaans, Ivan Hall)

Die Professor en die Prikkelpop / The Professor and the Beauty Queen (Afrikaans, Jamie Uys)

Escape Route Cape Town (English, Robert R. Webb)

Hoor My Lied / Hear My Song (Afrikaans, Elmo de Witt)

In die Lente van Ons Liefde (Afrikaans, Louis Wiesner)

The Jackals / The Scavengers (English, Robert R. Webb)

Wilde Seisoen / Wild Season (Afrikaans, Emil Nofal)

1968

Die Kandidaat (Afrikaans, Jans Rautenbach)

Dr. Kalie (Afrikaans, Ivan Hall)

Find Livingstone / Finden sie Livingstone (English, Theodore Grädler)

Jy is my Liefling (Afrikaans, Dirk de Villiers)

The Long Red Shadow / Three Days of Fire (English, Percival Rubens)

Majuba (Afrikaans, David Millin)

The Mercenaries / Dark of the Sun (English, Jack Cardiff)

One for the Pot (English, Alfred Travers)

Oupa for Sale (Afrikaans, Richard Daneel)

Raka (Afrikaans, Sven Persson)

Twee Broerders Ry Saam (Afrikaans, Kappie Botha)

1969

Danie Bosman (Afrikaans, Elmo de Witt)

Die Vervlakste Tweeling (Afrikaans, Werner Grunbauer)

Dirkie / Lost in the Desert (Afrikaans, Jamie Uys)

Geheim van Nantes (Afrikaans, Dirk de Villiers)

Katrina (Afrikaans, Jans Rautenbach)

King of Africa / One Step to Hell (English, Sandy Howard and Nino Scolaro)

Petticoat Safari (English, David Millin)

Staal Burger (Afrikaans, Daan Retief)

Stadig oor die Klippe (Afrikaans, Richard Daneel)

Strangers at Sunrise (English, Percival Rubens)

A Twist of Sand (English, Don Chaffey)

Vrolike Vrydag die 13de (Afrikaans, Richard Daneel)

1970

Banana Beach (English, David Millin)

Die Drie van der Merwes (Afrikaans, Dirk de Villiers)

Forgotten Summer (English, Howard Rennie)

Hulda Versteegh MD (Afrikaans, Kappie Botha)

Jannie Totsiens (Afrikaans, Jans Rautenbach)

Knockout (English, Viriato Barretto)

Lied in My Hart (Afrikaans, Ivan Hall)

Onwettige Huwelik (Afrikaans, Mario Schiess)

Satan's Harvest (English, George Montgomery)

Scotty Smith (English, Peter Henkel)

Shangani Patrol (English, David Millin)

Sien Jou Môre (Afrikaans, Elmo de Witt)

Sieraad Uit As (Afrikaans, D. B. Steyn)

Stop Exchange (English, Howard Rennie)

Taxi (English, Joe Stewardson)

Vicki (Afrikaans, Ivan Hall)

1971

Breekpunt (Afrikaans, Daan Retief)

Die Banneling (Afrikaans, David Millin)

Die Erfgenaam (Afrikaans, Koos Roets)

Die Lewe Sonder Jou (Afrikaans, Dirk de Villiers)

Flying Squad (English, Ivan Hall)

Freddie's in Love (English, Manie van Rensburg)

Gold Squad (English, Ivan Hall)

Lindie (Afrikaans, Wallie Stevens)

The Men from the Ministry (English, Tom Meehan)

Mr. Kingstreet's War (English, Percival Rubens)

A New Life (English, Dirk de Villiers)

Pappalap (Afrikaans, Jans Rautenburg)

Pressure Burst (English, George Canes)

Sononder (Afrikaans, Carel Trichardt)

Soul Africa (English, Ashley Lazarus)

Three Bullets for a Long Gun (English, Peter Henkel)

Z.E.B.R.A (Afrikaans, Elmo de Witt)

1972

Boemerang 11.15 (Afrikaans, Ivan Hall)

Creatures the World Forgot (Don Chaffey)

Die Marmerpoel (Afrikaans, Judex C. Viljoen)

Die Skat van Issie (Afrikaans, D. B. Steyn)

Die Wiltemmer (Afrikaans, Elmo de Witt)

K9 Basspatrolliehond (Afrikaans, Kappie Botha)

Kaptein Caprivi (Afrikaans, Albie Venter)

The Last Lion (English, Elmo de Witt)

Leatherlip (English, Stuart Pringle)

Liefde vir Lelik (Afrikaans, Keith G. van der Wat)

Lokval in Venesië (Afrikaans, Ivan Hall)

Makulu / Rogue Lion (English, Sven Persson)

Man van Buite (Afrikaans, Herman Strauss)

The Manipulator (English, Fred Wilson [Marino Girolami])

My Broer se Bril (Afrikaans, Dirk de Villiers)

Next Stop Makouvlei (English, George Canes)

Pikkie (Afrikaans, Sias Odendaal)

Salomien (Afrikaans, Daan Retief)

Spergebied: Diamond Area No. 1 (Afrikaans, Elmo de Witt)

Vlug van die Seemeeu (Afrikaans, Koos Roets)

Weekend (English, Keith G. van der Wat)

The Winners (English, Roy Sargeant and Emil Nofal)

1973

Aanslag op Kariba (Afrikaans, Ivan Hall)

Afspraak in die Kalahari (Afrikaans, Anna Neetling-Pohl)

The Baby Game (English, Joe Stewardson)

The Big Game (English, Robert Day)

Boesman and Lena (Afrikaans/English, Ross Devenish)

The Brave, the Rough and the Raw / Met Murg, Durf en Bloed (English, David Millin)

Die Bankrower (Afrikaans, Manie van Rensburg)

Die Sersant en die Tiger Moth (Afrikaans, Koos Roets)

Die Seun van die Wildtemmer (Afrikaans, Bertrand Retief)

Die Spook van Donkergat (Afrikaans, Diana Ginsberg)

Die Voortrekkers (Afrikaans, David Millin)

Die Wit Sluier (Afrikaans, Dirk de Villiers)

Dog Squad (English, Tim Spring)

Groetnis vir die Eerste Minister (Afrikaans, Bertrand Retief)

House of the Living Dead / Skadus oor Brugplaas (English/Afrikaans, Ray Austin)

Insident of Paradysstrand / Incident on Paradise Beach (Afrikaans, Grenville Middleton and Gordon Anderson)

Jamie 21 (Afrikaans, Daan Retief)

Môre Môre (Afrikaans, Elmo de Witt)

Siener in die Suburbs (Afrikaans, François Swart)

Snip en Rissiepit (Afrikaans, Elmo de Witt)

1974

Babblekous en Bruidegom (Afrikaans, Koos Roets)

Bait (English, Mario Schiess)

Beautiful People (English, Jamie Uys)

Boland! (Afrikaans, Bertrand Retief)

Cry Me a Teardrop (English, Keith G. van der Wat)

Dans van die Vlamink (Afrikaans, Ivan Hall)

Die Afspraak (Afrikaans, Jan Breytenbach)

Die Saboteurs (Afrikaans, Percival Rubens)

Dooie Duikers Deel Nie / No Gold for a Dead Diver (Afrikaans, Heinz Reinhl)

Fraud (English, Donald Monat)

Funeral for an Assassin (English, Ivan Hall)

Geluksdal (Afrikaans, Manie van Rensburg)

Gold (English, Peter Hunt)

Joe Bullet (English, Louis de Witt)

Kwikstertjie (Afrikaans, Elmo de Witt)

Met Liefde van Adele / Wikus en Adele (Afrikaans, Dirk de Villiers)

'n Sonneblom uit Parys (Afrikaans, Sias Odendaal)

Oh Brother / Vinkel en Koljander (English, Roy Sargeant)

Ongewenste Vreemdeling (Afrikaans, Jans Rautenbach)

Pens en Pootjies (Afrikaans, Dirk de Villiers)

The Savage Sport (English, Keith G. van de Wat)

Skadu's van Gister (Afrikaans, François Swart)

Suster Theresa (Afrikaans, David Millin)

Tant Ralie se Losieshuis (Afrikaans, Dirk de Villiers)

They Call Me Lucky (English, Keith G. van der Wat)

Those Naughty Angels (English, Neil Hetherington)

Vang vir my 'n Droom / Catch Me a Dream (Afrikaans, Tim Spring)

The Virgin Goddess (English, Dirk de Villiers)

Voortvlugtige Spioen (Afrikaans, Harald Phillip)

Vreemde Wêreld (Afrikaans, Harald Phillip)

Vrou uit die Nag (Afrikaans, Willie Alheit)

Nogomopho (Zulu, Tonie van der Merwe)

1975

Daan en Doors oppie Diggins (Afrikaans, Dirk de Villiers)

De Wet's Spoor / Guns Across the Veld (Afrikaans, Howard Rennie)

The Diamond Hunters (English, Dirk de Villiers)

Die Square / Hannes Kruger is U Man (Afrikaans, Manie van Rensburg)

Die Troudag van Tant Ralie (Afrikaans, Ivan Hall)

Dingertjie is Dynamite! (Afrikaans, Ivan Hall)

'e Lollipop / Lollipop (English, Ashley Lazarus)

Eendag op in Reëndag / Die Rousseaus van La Rochelle (Afrikaans, Jans Rautenbach)

Gebroke Kontrak (Afrikaans, D. B. Steyn)

Jakalsdraai se Mense (Afrikaans, Franz Marx)

Kniediep (Afrikaans, Roy Sargeant)

Lelik is my Offer (Afrikaans, Joe Stewardson)

Liefste Veertjie (Afrikaans, Elmo de Witt)

Ma Skryf Matriek (Afrikaans, Franz Marx)

Mirage Eskader (Afrikaans, Bertrand Retief)

My Liedjie van Verlange (Afrikaans, Bertrand Retief)

My Naam is Dingertjie (Afrikaans, Dirk de Villiers)

Olie Kolonie (Afrikaans, Neil Hetherington)

Sarah (Afrikaans, Gordon Vorster)

Sell a Million (English, Ian Hamilton and Clive Harding)

Ses Soldate / Six Soldiers (Afrikaans, Bertrand Retief)

Seuns van die Wolke (Afrikaans, Franz Marx)

Soekie (Afrikaans, Daan Retief)

Somer (Afrikaans, Sias Odendaal)

Ter wille van Christine (Afrikaans, Elmo de Witt)

Trompie (Afrikaans, Tonie van der Merwe)

Wat Maak Oom Kallie Daar? (Afrikaans, Jan Breytenbach)

Inkedama (Xhosa, Simon Sabela)

Maxhosa (Xhosa, Lynton Stephenson)

U-Deliwe (Zulu, Simon Sabela)

1976

Daar Kom Tant Alie (Afrikaans, Koos Roets)

Die Rebel / Sending vir 'n Voortvlugtige (Afrikaans, Daan Retief)

Die Ridder van die Grootpad (Afrikaans, Willie Alheit)

Die Vlindervanger Murder on Holiday (Afrikaans, Franz Marx)

Erfgoed is Sterfgoed (Afrikaans, Jan Breytenbach)

Funny People (Afrikaans/English, Kobus Kruger)

Glenda / The Snake Dancer (English, Dirk de Villiers)

Haak Vrystaat (Afrikaans, Al Debbo)

Hank, Hennery and Friend / Hank, Hennery & Vriend (English, Bertrand Retief)

How Long (English, Gibson Kente and Ben Namoyi) [unreleased]

Karate Olympia / Kill or Be Killed (English, Ivan Hall)

Killer Force (English, Val Guest)

Land Apart (English, Sven Persson)

Liefste Madelein (Afrikaans, Franz Marx)

'n Beeld vir Jeannie (Afrikaans, Elmo de Witt)

'n Sondag in September (Afrikaans, Jan Scholz)

Shout at the Devil (English, Peter Hunt)

The South Africans (English, Sven Persson)

Springbok (Afrikaans, Tommie Meyer)

Tigers Don't Cry (English, Peter Collinson)

Vergeet my Nie (Afrikaans, Elmo de Witt)

The Boxer (Zulu, Simon Sabela)

The Eagle (Zulu, Simon Sabela)

I-Kati Elimnyana / The Black Cat (Zulu, Simon Sabela)

Inkunzi (Xhosa, Sam Williams)

Isimanga (Zulu, Tonie van der Merwe)

Mahlomola (Zulu, Tonie van der Merwe)

Ngwanaka (Sotho, Simon Sabela)

1977

Crazy People (English/Afrikaans, Dirk de Villiers)
Die Winter van 14 Julie (Afrikaans, Jan Scholtz)
Dingertjie en Idi (Afrikaans, Dirk de Villers)
En die Dag Ontwaak (Afrikaans, D. B. Steyn)
The Golden Rendezvous (English, Ashley Lazarus and Freddie Francis)
The Guest / Die Besoeker (English/Afrikaans, Ross Devenish)
Kom tot Rus (Afrikaans, Elmo de Witt)
Kootjie Emmer (Afrikaans, Koos Roets)
Lag met Wena (Afrikaans, Morné Coetzer)
Mooimeisiesfonten (Afrikaans, Elmo de Witt)
Netnou Hoor die Kinders (Afrikaans, Franz Marx)
Thaba / Terug na Thaba (Afrikaans, Willie Alheit)
The Winners II / Again My Way (English, Jans Rautenbach)

Inyakanyaka (Zulu, Simon Sabela)
Iziduphunga (Zulu, Tonie van der Merwe)
Mapule (N Sotho, Tonie van der Merwe)
Ngaku (Tswana, Simon Sabela)
Wangenza (Zulu, Tonie van der Merwe)

1978

Billy Boy (English, Tim Spring)
Decision to Die / The Dr. Walters Trial (English, Dirk de Villers)
Diamant en die Dief (Afrikaans, Jan Scholtz)
Die Spaanse Vlieg (Afrikaans, Dirk de Villiers)
Dit was Aand en dit was Môre (Afrikaans, Franz Marx)
Dr. Marius Hugo (Afrikaans, Tim Spring)
The Fifth Season / Die Vyfde Seisoen (Afrikaans/English, Gordon Vorster)
Liefde wat Louter (Afrikaans, D. B. Steyn)
Mr. Deathman (English, Michael Moore)
'n Seder Val in Waterkloof (Afrikaans, Franz Marx)
Nicolene (Afrikaans, Marie du Toit)
Someone Like You / Iemand Soos Jy (Afrikaans/English, Elmo de Witt)
Sonja (Afrikaans, Daan Retief)
Terrorist (English, Neil Hetherington)
The Wild Geese (English, Andrew McLaglan)
Witblits and Peach Brandy (English/Afrikaans, Dirk de Villiers)

Abafana (Zulu, Tonie van der Merwe)
Abashokobezi (Zulu, Dirk de Villiers)
The Advocate (Zulu, Simon Sabela)
Isuvemelwano (Zulu, Simon Sabela)
Luki (Zulu, Tonie van der Merwe)
Moloyi (Zulu, Tonie van der Merwe)
Nofuka (Zulu, Tonie van der Merwe)
Setipana (Sotho, Simon Sabela)
Utotsi (Zulu, Chris Halgryn)
Vuma (Zulu, Tonie van der Merwe)

1979

Charlie Word 'n Ster (Afrikaans, Dirk de Villiers)
Die Eensame Vlug (Afrikaans, Jan Scholtz)
Elsa Se Geheim (Afrikaans, Chris du Toit)
Follow That Rainbow (English, Louis Burke)
Forty Days (English, Franz Marx)
Game for Vultures (English, James Fargo)
Grensbasis 13 (Afrikaans, Elmo de Witt)
Herfsland (Afrikaans, Jan Scholtz)
Marigolds in August (English, Ross Devenish)
Night of the Puppets (English, Daan Reticf)
Phindesela (Zulu, Chris Halgryn)
Plekkie in die Son (Afrikaans, William Faure)
Pretoria O Pretoria (Afrikaans, Betrand Retief)
The Visitors (English, Michel Wyn)
Wat Jy Saai (Afrikaans, Tim Spring)
Weerskant die Nag (Afrikaans, Franz Marx)
Zulu Dawn English, Douglas Hickox)

Botsotso (Zulu, Tonie van der Merwe)
Ingilosi Yekufa (Zulu, Jimmy Murray)
Isoka (Zulu, Rudi Meyer)
Magodu (Zulu, *No director credited*)
Mainstay Cup Final (Zulu, *No director credited*)
Mightyman 1 & 2 (Zulu, Perceval Rubens)
Runaway Melody (English, *No director credited*)
Umunti Akalahlwa (Zulu, Simon Sabela)
Umzingeli (Zulu, Ronnie Isaacs)

1980

April '80 (Afrikaans/English, Jan Scholz)
Burning Rubber (English, Norman Cohen)
The Demon / Midnight Caller (English, Percival Rubens)
Gemini (Afrikaans, Chris du Toit)
The Gods Must Be Crazy (English, Jamie Uys)
Kiepie en Kandas (Afrikaans, Jan Scholtz)
'n Brief vir Simone (Afrikaans, Anton Goosen and F. C. Hamman)

Rally / Safari 3000 (English and Afrikaans, Harry Hurwitz)
Rienie (Afrikaans, Fanie van der Merwe)
Savage Encounter (English, Bernard Buys)
Sing vir die Harlekyn (Afrikaans, F. C. Hamman)
Skelms (Afrikaans, Jan Scholtz)

Amasela (Zulu, *No director credited*)
Baeng (Tswana, Hanro Mohr)
Botsotso II (Zulu, Ronnie Isaacs)
Confetti Breakfast (English, Don Leonard)
Flashpoint Africa (English, *No director credited*)
The Human Experience (English, *No director credited*)
Ighawe (Zulu, Rudi Meyer)
Shadowplay (English, Oliver Stapleton)
Sky Blue (John Hookham)
Umbdhale (Zulu, Ronnie Isaacs)
Umdhlali (Zulu, *No director credited*)
Umnogoloi (Zulu, *No director credited*)
U-Mona (Zulu, Hanro Mohr)
Umonga (Zulu, *No director credited*)
Vimba Isipoko (Zulu, Ronnie Isaacs)
1981
Beloftes van Môre (Afrikaans, Daan Retief)
Birds of Paradise (English, Tommie Meyer and Philip van der Byl)
Blink Stefaans (Afrikaans, Jans Rautenbach)
Kill and Kill Again / Karate Olympia (English, Ivan Hall)
Nommer Asseblief (Afrikaans, Henk Hugo)

Biza Izintombi (Zulu, Ronnie Isaacs)
Castlecroft Service Station (English, *No director credited*)
City Lovers (English, Barney Simon)
Deaf Boy (English, *No director credited*)
Dumela Sam (English/Sotho, Clive Scott and Jimmy Murray)
The Heart of the Matter (English, *No director credited*)
Inkada (Zulu, Gary van der Merwe)
Isigangi (Sotho, Rudi Meyer)
Iwisa (Zulu, Tonie van der Merwe)
So-Mnganga (Zulu, Ronnie Isaacs)
Sonto (Sotho, Jimmy Murray)
Tommy (Zulu, Simon Metsing)
Ukusindiswa (Zulu, Johan van Rooyen)

Umnyakazo (Zulu, Wally van der Merwe)
Ungavimbi Umculo (Zulu, Wally van der Merwe)
Uzenzile Akahalelwa (Zulu, Rudi Meyer)
A Way of Life (English, Rod Hay)
1982
Claws / The Beast (English, Alan Nathanson)
Death of a Snowman (English, Christopher Rowley)
Die Bosveldhotel (Afrikaans, Fred Nel)
Verkeerde Nommer (Afrikaans, Franz Marx)

Blood Money (Zulu/English, Jimmy Murray and Simon Metsing)
Botsotso III (Zulu, Don Fedler)
Bullet on the Run (English, Tonie van der Merwe)
Decor (English, *No director credited*)
Doctor Luke (English, Jimmy Murray)
Impango (Zulu, Tonie van der Merwe)
Isiqwaga (Zulu, Tonie van der Merwe)
Jungle Paradise (English, Harold Reinl)
Pina ya Qetelo (Sotho, Ronnie Isaacs)
Shamwari (English, Clive Harding)
Ubude Abuphangwa (Sotho, Rudi Meyer)
Ukuhlupheka (Sotho, *No director credited*)
Ukulwa (Zulu, Japie van der Merwe)
Umdlalo Umkhulu (Zulu, Wally van der Merwe)
Umjuluko Me Gazi (Zulu, Ronnie Isaacs)
Will to Win (English, Rod Hays)
1983
Funny People II (English, Jamie Uys)
Geel Trui vir 'n Wenner (Afrikaans, Franz Marx)
My Country My Hat (English, David Bensusan)
No One Cries Forever / Tears in the Dry Wind (English, Jans Rautenbach)
The Riverman / Return to Eden (English, Ivan Hall)
Wolhaarstories (Afrikaans, Bromley Cawood)

Amazing Grace (English, Japie van der Merwe)
Children's Games (English, Mattys Mocke)
Herd of Drums (English, *No director credited*)
Imihlolo (Zulu, *No director credited*)
Impumelelo (Sotho, Rudi Meyer)
Inyembezi Zami (Sotho, Rudi Meyer)
Isoduka (Zulu, *No director credited*)
Iziphuku Phuku (Zulu, *No director credited*)
Joe Slaughter (Zulu, Gary van der Merwe)
Johnny Tough (English, Ronnie Isaacs)

Jors Troelie (Afrikaans, *No director credited*)
The Messiah of Peace / Murugadas (English, *No director credited*)
Mmampodi (South Sotho, Gary van der Merwe)
Moloyi (Sotho, Tonie van der Merwe)
Motsumi (Sotho, Johan van Rooyen)
Ndinguwakabani (Tswana, *No director credited*)
Ngavele Ngasho (Zulu, Tonie van der Merwe)
Running Young (English, Johan van Rooyen)
Secret of the Planet Earth (English, Andrew Sinclare)
The Stronger (English, Lynton Stephenson)
Testament to the Bushmen (English, Jane Taylor)
Tommy II / Tommy No Bra Sticks (Zulu, *No director credited*)
Tora ya Raditeble / Boxers Dream (Sotho, *No director credited*)
Umdlalo Umbango (Tswana, Waly van der Merwe)
Vakasha (Zulu/English, Johan van Rooyen)
Washo Ubaba (Sotho, Gary van der Merwe)
Whose Child Am I? (Tawana, *No director credited*)
Why Forsake Me? (English, Wally van der Merwe)

1984

Boetie Gaan Border Toe (Afrikaans, Regardt van den Bergh)
Bomber / The Knock-Out Cop (English, Michele Lupo)
Broer Matie (Afrikaans, Jans Rautenbach)
Die Groen Faktor / The Green Factor (Afrikaans, Jans Rautenbach)
Survival Zone (English, Percival Rubens)
Tewwe Tienies (Afrikaans, Bromley Cawood)

Ababulali (Zulu, *No director credited*)
Ace of Spades (Zulu, Japie van der Merwe)
Bake Mo Motseng (Tswana, *No director credited*)
The Banana Gang (Zulu, David Bensusan)
Bank Busters (Zulu, David Bensusan)
Biophetetso / Revenge (South Sotho, Jimmy Murray)
Bird Boy (English, Ed Herbst)
Blind Justice (English, *No director credited*)
Bobe Mo Motseng (Zulu, Wally van de Merwe)
Bona Manzi (Zulu, Tonie van der Merwe)
Boshodu Ba Sefofo (Sotho, *No director credited*)
Bozo and Bimbo (English, Wally van der Merwe)

Charlie Steel (English, Johan van Rooyen)
Cllaka (Zulu, *No director credited*)
Cold Blood (Zulu, Hein Pretorius)
Crime Doesn't Pay (English, Zika Gravevolik)
The Cross (English, Ed Herbst)
Double Deal (English, A. Hattingh)
Dynamite Jackson (English, *No director credited*)
Fanakalo (Zulu, Ronnie Isaacs)
Fate of the Famous (Zulu, *No director credited*)
Fierce Encounter (Zulu, *No director credited*)
For Money and Glory (English/Sotho, Tonie van der Merwe)
The Hitchhikers (Zulu, C. Dippenaar)
Honor Thy Father (English, *No director credited*)
I Will Repay (English, Wally van der Merwe)
Ighawe II (Zulu, Rudi Meyer)
Imali (Sotho, Regardt van der Bergh and Jimmy Murray)
Impumgu Uhlasa / Green Man (Xhosa, *No director credited*)
Ingwe Ibuyile / Leopard Is Back (Zulu, *No director credited*)
Inyoka (Sotho, H. Epstein and Jimmy Murray)
Isalamusi (Zulu, Gary van der Merwe)
Isithixo Segolide (Zulu, M. Dyter)
Iso Ngeso (Zulu, C. Dippenaar)
Llnga Selwa (Zulu, *No director credited*)
Maphata (Sotho, Zika Gravevolik)
Mathatha: A Hard Life (Sotho/English, Clive Scott and Jimmy Murray)
The Midnight Caller (English, *No director credited*)
Mission Spellbound (English, Wally van der Merwe)
Modise (Tswana, Johan van Rooyen)
Moon Mountain (English, *No director credited*)
Mr. Moonlight (English, Juanita Strydom)
Mr. TNT (Zulu, Darrell Roodt)
The Musicmaker (Zulu/English, C. Dippenaar)
Never Rob a Magician (Zulu, Robert van der Merwe)
Odirang (Sotho, Johan van Rooyen)
One More Shot (Zulu, Ronnie Isaacs)
Playing Dirty (English, Wally van der Merwe)
Point of Return (English/Zulu, M. Dyter)
Prisoners of the Lost Universe (English, Peter Bode)
The Reckoning (English, Wally van der Merwe)
Run for Freedom (English, M. Dyter)

The Sandpiper (English, Lourens Swanepoel)

Sanna / Torn Allegiance (English, Alan Nathanson)

Slow vs. Boner (Zulu, Gary van der Merwe)

Small Budget (*No director credited*)

Snap (Zulu, Ronnie Isaacs)

The Spin of Death (Zulu, Ronnie Isaacs)

Stage Fright (English, *No director credited*)

Stoney the One and Only (English, Rod Hay)

Ulaka (Zulu, Wally van der Merwe)

U-Lindiwe (Sotho, H. Epstein and Jimmy Murray)

Umdobi (Zulu, Ed Herbst)

Umduka (Zulu, *No director credited*)

Umfaan (Zulu, Johan van Rooyen)

Umfaan II (Zulu, Gary van der Merwe)

Umkhovu (Zulu, *No director credited*)

Upondo no Nkinsela (Sotho, Johan van Rooyen)

Usiko Lwabafana (Zulu, M. Dyter)

Uthemba (Zulu, *No director credited*)

Winner Take All (English, Frans Nel)

Yonna Lefatseng (Sotho, Jimmy Murray)

Zero for Zeb (Zulu, Tonie van der Merwe)

1985

Allan Quartermain / The Lost City of Gold (English, Gary Nelson)

Boetie op Manoeuvres / Wild Manoeuvres (Afrikaans, Regardt van den Bergh)

Deadly Passion (English, Larry Larson)

Eendag vir Altyd / Edge of Innocence (Afrikaans, Chris du Toit)

Jane and the Lost City (English, Terence Marcel)

King Solomon's Mines (English, J. Lee Thompson)

The Lion's Share (English, Norman Cohen)

Magic Is Alive My Friends (English, Jan Scholtz)

Mamza (Afrikaans, Johan Blignaut)

Skollie (Afrikaans, Ivan Hall)

Van der Merwe P I (English, Regard van den Bergh)

You're in the Movies (English, Emil Nofal)

Abathakathi (Zulu/Xhosa, *No director credited*)

Abathumbi (Zulu, *No director credited*)

The Ace (English, *No director credited*)

Allegra (Zulu/Xhosa, *No director credited*)

Amagoduka (Zulu/Xhosa, *No director credited*)

Amahlaya (Zulu/Xhosa, *No director credited*)

Amaphayisana (Zulu, *No director credited*)

Bad Company (English, *No director credited*)

Bhema (Zulu, *No director credited*)

Big Land (English, *No director credited*)

Black Magic (English, *No director credited*)

Blue Vultures (English, *No director credited*)

The Comedians (English, *No director credited*)

Contact (English, *No director credited*)

Deadly Obsession (English, Jeno Hodi)

The Dealer (English, *No director credited*)

Diamond Catch (English, *No director credited*)

Diamonds for Dinner (English, *No director credited*)

Die Strandloper (Afrikaans, Lourens Swanepoel)

Emgodini (Zulu, *No director credited*)

The Firegod (Zulu, *No director credited*)

Fist Fighter (English, *No director credited*)

Foul Play (English, *No director credited*)

Getting Lucky (English, Robert van de Coolwijk)

Guquka (Zulu/Xhosa, *No director credited*)

Ihlathi Lezimanga (Zulu/Xhosa, *No director credited*)

Iholide (Zulu/Xhosa, *No director credited*)

Impindiso (Zulu/Xhosa, *No director credited*)

Imusi (Zulu, *No director credited*)

Indlela (Zulu, *No director credited*)

Indlu Yedimoni (Zulu/Xhosa, *No director credited*)

Indodana Yo Lehleko (Zulu, *No director credited*)

Innocent Revenge (English, David Bensusan)

Intaba Yegolide (Zulu, *No director credited*)

Iphutha (Zulu, *No director credited*)

Iqaba (Zulu/Xhosa, *No director credited*)

Isinamuva (Zulu/Xhosa, *No director credited*)

Isipho Sezwe (Zulu/Xhosa, *No director credited*)

Ithlathi Lezimanga (Zulu/Xhosa, *No director credited*)

Johnny Diamini (English, *No director credited*)

Joker (English, *No director credited*)

The Judgment (English, *No director credited*)

The Juggernaut (English, Joey Ford)

Kidnapped (English, *No director credited*)

Lana (Zulu/Xhosa, *No director credited*)

The Last Run (English, *No director credited*)

The Long Run (English, *No director credited*)

Love in the Wood (English, Lourens Swanepoel)

Lucky (English, *No director credited*)

Magic Ring (English, *No director credited*)

The Man (English, *No director credited*)
Mapantsula (Zulu/Xhosa, *No director credited*)
Mapantsula II (Zulu/Xhosa, *No director credited*)
Menzi and Menziwa (Zulu/Xhosa, *No director credited*)
Mesh (English, *No director credited*)
Mmila We Bakwetidi (Sotho, *No director credited*)
Mohlalifi (Sotho, *No director credited*)
The Moment of Truth (Zulu, Ronnie Isaacs)
The Murderer (English, *No director credited*)
Nkululeko (Zulu/Xhosa, *No director credited*)
Phindisela (Zulu/Xhosa, *No director credited*)
Polao e Makatsang (Sotho, *No director credited*)
Rescuers / Umsizi (Zulu/Xhosa, *No director credited*)
Revenge (English, *No director credited*)
Revenge Is Mine (English, *No director credited*)
Rough Nights in Paradise (English, *No director credited*)
Say-Mama (Xhosa, *No director credited*)
The Scoop (English, *No director credited*)
Segana (Zuku/Xhosa, *No director credited*)
Sekehekwa (Sotho, *No director credited*)
Sixpence (English, *No director credited*)
Skating on Thin Uys (English, Bromley Cawood)
Somhlolo (Swazi, *No director credited*)
Somhlolo II (Swazi, *No director credited*)
Sonny (Zulu, *No director credited*)
Spider (English, *No director credited*)
Starbound (Zulu, Ronnie Isaacs)
Stepmother (English, *No director credited*)
Survival I (English, *No director credited*)
Survival II (English, *No director credited*)
The Taste of Blood (Zulu, David Bensusan)
Thor (Zulu/Xhosa, *No director credited*)
Too Late for Heaven (*No director credited*)
Torak (Zulu/Xhosa, *No director credited*)
Treasure Hunters / Umkuzingela (English, *No director credited*)
Tselend ya Bonokwane (Sotho, *No director credited*)
Tusks / Fire in Eden (English, Tara Moore)
Tuxedo Warrior (English, Andrew Sinclare)
Uhlanya / Mad at Somebody (Zulu, *No director credited*)
Ukunvoluka (Zulu, *No director credited*)

Ukuphindisela (Zulu/Xhosa, *No director credited*)
Ukuvuleka (Zulu/Xhosa, *No director credited*)
Ukuzingela (Zulu/Xhosa, *No director credited*)
Ulanga (Zulu, *No director credited*)
Ulunya of Lohlanga (Zulu/Xhosa, *No director credited*)
Umfana Wekarate (Zulu/Xhosa, *No director credited*)
Umoni (Xhosa, *No director credited*)
Umsizi (Zulu/Xhosa, *No director credited*)
Uxolo (Zulu/Xhosa, *No director credited*)
Uzungu (Zulu/Xhosa, *No director credited*)
Vakhashe le U-Satane (English, *No director credited*)
Visitors (Zulu, Chris du Toit)
Vulane (Zulu/Xhosa, *No director credited*)
Wie Laaste Lag / Danger Games (Afrikaans, Koos Roets)
Wind Rider (Zulu/Xhosa, Darrell Roodt)
Witch Doctor (English, *No director credited*)

1986

American Ninja II: The Confrontation (English, Beau Davis and Sam Firstenberg)
Back to Freedom (English, Ivan Hall)
The Big Gag / Candid Camera (English, Yuda Barkan and Igal Shilon)
City of Blood (English, Darrell Roodt)
Freedom Fighters (English, Bruce MacFarlane and Ricki Shelach)
Gor (English, Fritz Kiersch and Harry Towers)
Hostage (English, Hanro Mohr and Percival Rubens)
Jake Speed (English, Andrew Lane and Martin Walters)
Jock of the Bushveld (English, Gray Hofmeyr)
Nag van Vrees / Night of Terror (Afrikaans, Jimmy Murray and Stanley Roup)
Saturday Night at the Palance (English, Robert Davies)
Tenth of a Second (English, Darrell Roodt)
Tojan (Afrikaans, Johan Blignaut)
You Gotta Be Crazy (English, Emil Nofal)
You Must Be Joking (Afrikaans, Elmo de Witt)

Abaphangi / Dish-Ups (*No director credited*)
Danger Coast (English, Hans Kuhle)
Dirty Money (Zulu, *No director credited*)
Doomsday (*No director credited*)

Eyewitness (English, *No director credited*)

Friends' Brothers (*No director credited*)

The Hand (English, *No director credited*)

Hotter than Snow (Zulu, David Bensusan)

I Qunca Lokubulala (Zulu, *No director credited*)

Impumputhe / Blind (Zulu, *No director credited*)

Juluka / Sweat (Zulu, *No director credited*)

Just Desserts / Jungle Paradise (English, Harold Reinl)

Lair of the Hyena (*No director credited*)

Land of the Amazon Queen (English, *No director credited*)

Lindiwe (Zulu, *No director credited*)

Long Distance Runner (*No director credited*)

Love in the Wood II (English, Lourens Swanepoel)

Mobsters (*No director credited*)

Monsters (English, *No director credited*)

Mountain of Hell (Zulu, David Bensusan)

Profit and Loss (*No director credited*)

Raw Terror (English, Hanro Mohr)

Ring of Fire (*No director credited*)

Robin Muir (English, *No director credited*)

Run for Your Life (English, *No director credited*)

Runner Up (*No director credited*)

Satan Shoots (English, David Wicht)

Singabahamabayo / We Are the Movers (Zulu, *No director credited*)

Slip Up (*No director credited*)

Strike Force (English, *No director credited*)

Strikeback (Zulu, Ronnie Isaacs)

Tap and Son (*No director credited*)

The Taste of Blood II (Zulu, David Bensusan)

Taxi War (*No director credited*)

Themba and Thani / Names (Zulu, *No director credited*)

Tholiwe / Found (Zulu, *No director credited*)

The Tiger Kid Gang (*No director credited*)

Tip and Tap in the Haunted House (*No director credited*)

Tip Meets Tap (*No director credited*)

Tommy Le Segotsana (English, *No director credited*)

Vengeance (English, *No director credited*)

The Wedding (English, *No director credited*)

1987

Alien from LA (English, Albert Pyun)

City Wolf (English, Heinrich Dahms)

Davey (English, Louise Smit)

The Devil and the Song (English, Bromley Cawood)

Die Posman (Afrikaans, Anthony Wilson)

Dragonard (English, Dominique Jones and Gerard Kikoine)

The House (Zulu, Roy Walker)

Jewel of the Gods / Grinder's War (English, Robert van de Coolwijk)

Kampus (English, Etienne Puren)

Kill Slade (English, Bruce MacFarlane)

Mapantsula (English, Oliver Schmitz and Thomas Mogotlane)

Master of Dragonard Hill (English, Gerard Kikoine)

My African Adventure (English, Boaz Davidson)

No Hard Feelings / Kick or Die (English, Charles Norton)

Nukie (English, Sias Odendaal and Michael Pakleppa)

Operation Hit Squad (English, Tonie van der Merwe)

Outlaw of Gor (English, John Cardos)

Place of Weeping (English, Darrell Roodt)

Platoon Leader (English, Aaron Norris)

Quest for Love (English, Helena Nogueira)

Quiet Thunder (English, Hans Kuhle)

Rage to Kill (English, David Winters)

Red Scorpion (English, Joe Zito and Joao Fernandes)

Skeleton Coast (English, John Cardos)

The Stay Awake (English, Johan Barnard)

Steel Dawn / Nomads (English, Lance Hool)

The Tangent Affair (English, Neil Hetherington)

Wereld Sonder Grense (Afrikaans, Frans Nel)

You Must Be Joking Too (English, Leon Schuster)

Abadlovi / Loafers (Zulu, *No director credited*)

Alfa (*No director credited*)

Amaphupho ka Zondo / Zondo's Dreams (Zulu, *No director credited*)

Amon (*No director credited*)

Bad Boys (English, *No director credited*)

The Bad Guys (English, *No director credited*)

Bafana / Boys (Zulu, *No director credited*)

Ben's Disappearing Act (*No director credited*)

Black Death (*No director credited*)

Cheap Tricks (*No director credited*)

City of Vice (*No director credited*)
Cobra Force (English, *No director credited*)
The Curse (English, *No director credited*)
Dangerous Curves (English, David Prior)
The Dark Warrior (Zulu, David Bensusan)
Deal for Danger (English, *No director credited*)
Detectives (*No director credited*)
Devil Fish (English, Wayne Crawford)
Diamonds for Danger (English, *No director credited*)
Dizzy Spell (English, *No director credited*)
Enzintandaneni / A Boy Who Needs a Home (Zulu, *No director credited*)
The Evil Below (English, *No director credited*)
Exit (English, *No director credited*)
Face to Face (English, *No director credited*)
Faceless Man (English, *No director credited*)
A Fire in Africa (English, Gerhard Uys)
Freedom Run (English, *No director credited*)
Friends (*No director credited*)
Gangsters (*No director credited*)
The Gold Spear (*No director credited*)
Good and Bad Guys (English, *No director credited*)
The Hat (*No director credited*)
The Hit Team (English, *No director credited*)
Hitman (English, *No director credited*)
Ho Llelo Thuso (Zulu, David Bensusan)
Ifa / Heritage (Zulu, *No director credited*)
Ifa Lami / My Heritage (Zulu, *No director credited*)
Impango II / Provision (Zulu, *No director credited*)
Impilo Entsha / New Health (Zulu, *No director credited*)
Ingozi / Danger (Zulu, *No director credited*)
Jed and Owen Meet Big George (*No director credited*)
Jed and the Bankrobbers (English, *No director credited*)
Journey (English, Albert Pyun)
Journey II (English, Albert Pyun)
Journey to the Center of the Earth (English, Albert Pyun)
Just for the Money / Jungle Paradise (English, Harold Reinl)
Ke-Phiri / It's Wolf (North Sotho, *No director credited*)
Kidnap (*No director credited*)

Kidnapped II (English, *No director credited*)
Killmasters (English, David Winters)
The Last Bullet (Zulu, *No director credited*)
Lola (*No director credited*)
Lucky and Judy (*No director credited*)
Madoda / Men (Zulu, *No director credited*)
Mamalotsi / Name (Tswana, *No director credited*)
Murder in the Veld (*No director credited*)
The Ordeal (*No director credited*)
Paradise at Last (*No director credited*)
The Poacher (English, *No director credited*)
Pop's Oasis (English, Harry Hope)
The Protector (Zulu, *No director credited*)
Red for Danger (*No director credited*)
Return of Borca (*No director credited*)
Revenge of Q (English, David Bensusan)
Room Mates (*No director credited*)
Running Wild (English, *No director credited*)
Scavengers (English, Duncan McLachlan)
Silent Fury (English, *No director credited*)
Sold Out (*No director credited*)
Stealing Time (*No director credited*)
Sticky Fingers (English, Catlin Adams)
The Strange Man (English, *No director credited*)
Sweet Success (*No director credited*)
Sweet Revenge (*No director credited*)
The Third Time (*No director credited*)
To Catch a Rat (English, *No director credited*)
Ubuthi / A Notable Death (*No director credited*)
Umbango / Courtyard (Zulu, *No director credited*)
Umenzi Wobubi / Bad Deeds (Zulu, *No director credited*)
Umnquyi / Biltong (Zulu, *No director credited*)
Umpetha / Sportsman (Zulu, *No director credited*)
The Unforgiving (Zulu, David Bensusan)
White Ghost (English, Beau Davis)
Wipe Out (English, *No director credited*)
Yours Truly (*No director credited*)
Zik's Fortune (English, *No director credited*)
1988
Accidents (English, Gidi Amir)
Act of Piracy (English, John Cardos)
An African Dream (English, John Smallcombe)
African Express (English, Bruce MacFarlane)
American Ninja III: The Cobra Strikes (English, Cedric Sundström)

Any Man's Death (English, Tom Clegg)

Brutal Glory / Kid McCoy (English, Koos Roets)

Buried Alive / Ravenscroft (English, Gerard Kikoine)

Burndown (English, James Allen)

Burns / Under Suspicion (English, Bruce Mac-Farlane)

Circles in the Forest (English, Regardt van den Bergh)

Committed / The Intruder (English, William Levey)

Crazy Camera / Crazy People (English, Boaz Davidson and Zvi Shisel)

Dada en die Flower (Afrikaans, Jan Scholtz)

Dancing in the Forest (English, Mark Roper)

Death Force (English, Frans Nel)

Diamonds High (English, Denis Scully)

Dust (English, Gary Graver)

Easy Kill / Halfway House / Forced Alliance (English, Josh Spencer)

The Emissary (English, Jan Scholtz)

Fair Trade / Flight to Hell (English, Cedric Sundström)

The Fall of the House of Usher (English, Allan Birkinshaw)

Fiela se Kind (Afrikaans, Katinka Heyns)

The Final Alliance (English, David Goldstein and Mario Di Leo)

Final Cut (English, Frans Nel)

Forced Alliance / Halfway House (English, Josh Spencer)

From a Whisper to a Scream (English, Robert Bergman)

Grader Murphy (English, Jim Murray)

Have You Seen Drum Recently? (English, Jurgen Schadeberg)

Headhunter (English, Frank Schaeffer)

Hippo Pool / Big Game (English, Chris du Toit)

Hold My Hand I'm Dying (English, Duncan McLachlan and Terence Ryan)

Hunted (English, John Parr)

In Harm's Way / Dirty Games (English, Gray Hofmeyr)

Jobman / Devil's Island (English, Darrell Roodt)

Laser Mission (English, Beau Davis)

Last Samurai (English, Paul Mayersberg)

The Last Warrior / Coastwatcher (English, Martin Wragge)

Lethal Woman / The Most Dangerous Woman Alive (English, Christian Marnham)

Liewe Hemel, Genis (Afrikaans, Willam Egan)

Merchants of War (English, Peter Mackenzie)

Murphy's Fault (English, Robert Smawley)

Nightslave (English, John Parr)

Options (English, Camilo Vila)

Out on Bail (English, Brian Hessler and Gordon Hessler)

Paradise Road / Traitors (English, Jan Scholtz)

A Private Life / Jack and Stella (English, Francis Gerard)

Purgatory (English, John Newland)

Return of the Family Man (English, John Murlowski)

Return to Justice / The Last Cowboy / White Dust (English, Vincent Cox)

Rhino (English, Ronnie Isaacs)

River of Death (English, Steve Carver)

Saturday Night at the Palance (English, Robert Davies)

The Schoolmaster (English, Jean Delbeke)

The Shadowed Mind (English, Cedric Sundström)

The Short Cut / Time to Kill (English, Giuliano Montaldo)

Shot Down (English, Andrew Worsdale)

The Stick (English, Darrell Hood)

The Survivor (English, Michael Shackleton)

Tattoo Chase / Bottom Line (English, Jeff Gold)

Ten Little Indians / Death on Safari (English, Allan Birkinshaw)

The Trackers / Bush Shrink (English, Ivan Hall)

Tyger Tyger Burning Bright / Autumn Concerto (English, Neal Sundström)

Vulture Is a Patient Bird (English, Gianpietro Calastro)

Vyfster: Die Slot (Afrikaans, Sias Odendaal)

A Kumgani / Honorable (Zulu, *No director credited*)

Abafana a Bahle / Good Boys (*No director credited*)

Abbadon Force (English, *No director credited*)

Adventures of Mr Pips (English, *No director credited*)

Ambushed (English, *No director credited*)

The Bad Guys (English, *No director credited*)

Barracuda (English, John Cardos)

Black Gold (English, Duncan MacNeillie)

Bloodshot (English, Frank Schaeffer)

The Body (English, Amalia Ford)

The Chase (English, *No director credited*)

Cold Sweat (*No director credited*)

The Confrontation (*No director credited*)

Court of Burns (English, *No director credited*)

Cry Vengeance (English, John Parr)

Crystal Eye (English, Douglas Bristow and Joe Tornatore)

Damned River (English, Michael Schroeder)

Dark Forces (English, *No director credited*)

Dark Mountain (English, Robert Davies)

Death Walker (English, Joey Ford)

Dirty Games / In Harm's Way (English, Gray Hofmeyr)

Disco Marathon (Sotho, David Bensusan)

Double Cross (*No director credited*)

Ehlathini / Veld (Zulu, *No director credited*)

The Family Man / Nightmare (English, John Murlowski)

Flashback (English, Jim Murray)

Flight to Hell / Fire with Fire (*No director credited*)

The Gang (*No director credited*)

Great White Hunter (English, *No director credited*)

High Diamonds (English, *No director credited*)

Howling IV / Ghoul (English, Clive Turner)

The Hunter (*No director credited*)

Ilanga Liphuma / Sunrise (Zulu, *No director credited*)

Imali Yiswe / Money Is Everything (Zulu, *No director credited*)

Imidlembe (Zulu, *No director credited*)

In Harm's Way (English, Gray Homeyr)

Indlu Yomthakathi / House of the Witch (Zulu, *No director credited*)

Ingane Ongekhe Wayikohlwa (*No director credited*)

Ingelosi Ephindisebyo / Returned Angels (Zulu, *No director credited*)

Justice Must Be Done (*No director credited*)

Kidnapped III (English, *No director credited*)

Landela / Follow (Zulu, *No director credited*)

A Little Adventure (English, Chuck Griffith)

Live the Easy Way (English, *No director credited*)

Lost and Found (*No director credited*)

Lost Children of the Empire (English, Joanna Mack)

Love and Lobola (*No director credited*)

Love Me Leave Me (English, Allan Birkinshaw and Charles Mariott)

Love Towards Children of Southern Africa (English, Kenichi Oguri)

Lucky Strikes Back (English, Joe Stewardson)

Mad (*No director credited*)

Mad Matrimony (*No director credited*)

Maniac (*No director credited*)

Maniac Cop (*No director credited*)

Manpower (English, *No director credited*)

The Mask (English, *No director credited*)

Medallion (*No director credited*)

Merciless (*No director credited*)

The Midday Sun (English, Lulu Keating)

The Mind Boggles (English, Charles Wallace)

Money Machine (English, *No director credited*)

Moontalk (*No director credited*)

The Most Dangerous Woman Alive (English, Chris Marnham)

The Murderers (English, *No director credited*)

Murdering Maxwell (*No director credited*)

Naughty Camera (English, Lourens Swanepoel)

A New World Travels (English, K Kondo)

The Ninja / American Samurai (English, *No director credited*)

No Easy Choice (*No director credited*)

The Note (*No director credited*)

Nuclear Legacy (English, *No director credited*)

The Pin-Up Girl (Zulu, John Parr)

Practical Jokes (*No director credited*)

The Rat (English, Mike Inglesby)

Raw Vengeance (English, Joey Ford)

Rough Justice (English, Mario Di Leo)

The Run (*No director credited*)

Sakubya / Hallo (Zulu, *No director credited*)

Sam (Sotho, David Bensusan)

Ship of the Desert / Renegades (English, Frank Schaeffer)

Songbirds (*No director credited*)

The Stranger / Ghost Town (English, *No director credited*)

Streets / Death Is a Stranger (English, *No director credited*)

Sweet Justice (English, *No director credited*)

Sweeter than Wine (English, Allan Birkinshaw)

Taxi (*No director credited*)

Terminal Bliss (English, Jordan Alan)

Thlathla Thile / Walk a Long Distance (North Sotho, *No director credited*)

Thrilled to Death (English, Chuck Vincent)

Through Thick and Thin (*No director credited*)

Tiger Kid II (*No director credited*)

Topsy-Turvy (*No director credited*)

True Value (*No director credited*)

Ubudoda Abukhulelwa / Stick Fighter (Xhosa, *No director credited*)

Umbethu (Zulu, *No director credited*)

Umshaya (*No director credited*)

Uvalo / Conscience (Zulu, *No director credited*)

War Movie (*No director credited*)

The Weekend (English, Keith van der Wat)

Whispers (English, Robert Bergman)

Whizz Kid (*No director credited*)

Wild Country (English, *No director credited*)

The Wild Man (*No director credited*)

You're Famous (English, Alain Woolf)

The Zambezi Kid (English, Denis Scully)

1989

American Eagle / Rescue (English, Robert Smawley)

American Ninja IV: The Annihilation (English, Cedric Sundström)

AWOL / The Quarry (English, Neil Sonnekus)

Baby Brown (English, Joey Ford)

Croc (English, Elmo de Witt)

The Curse III: Blood Sacrifice / Panga Chance (English, Sean Barton)

Dark City (English, Chris Curling)

Divided Loyalties (English, Harry Mayer)

Dune Surfer / Kalahari Surfer (English, Heinrich Dahms)

The Endangered (English, Mark Engels)

Fiela's Child (English version, Katinka Heyns)

The Fourth Reich / Operation Weissdorn (English, Manie van Rensberg)

Funny Face (English, Alain Woolf)

The Gods Must Be Crazy II (English, Jamie Uys)

Hellgate / Ghost Town (English, William Levey)

Impact (English, Frans Nel)

In the Name of Blood (English, Robert Davies)

Lambarene / Schweitzer (English, Gray Hofmeyr)

Let the Music Be (English, Frans Nel)

The Masque of Red Death (English, Allan Birkinshaw)

The Native Who Caused All the Trouble (English, Manie van Rensberg)

Odd Ball Hall (English, Jackson Hunsicker)

Oh Schucks It's Schuster (English, Leon Schuster)

Okavango / Wild Country (English, Percival Rubens)

Reason to Die (English, Tim Spring)

The Revenger / Saxman (English, Cedric Sundström)

River of Diamonds (English, Robert Smawley)

Space Mutiny / Southern Son (English, Neal Sundström and David Winters)

Time of the Beast / Mutator (English, John Bowey)

Voice in the Dark (English, Vincent Cox)

Warriors from Hell (English, Ronnie Isaacs)

Abaqophi / Winners (Zulu, *No director credited*)

African Fever (English, Sergio Martino)

An African Journey (English, *No director credited*)

Agent Orange (English, *No director credited*)

The Assassin (English, John Parr)

The Assassin's Bullet (English, *No director credited*)

Backtrack (English/Xhosa, Charles Biggs)

Blood City (English, Hazel Crampton)

Bloodriver (English, Robert van de Coolwijk)

Bloodstone (English, *No director credited*)

Breakout (English, *No director credited*)

Canefields (English, *No director credited*)

Chameleon / Thieves of Fortune (English, Michael McCarthy)

Chasing Namibia (English, Denis Scully)

Dead Ringer (English, Frans Nel)

Death in Camera (English, *No director credited*)

Death of a Witness (English, *No director credited*)

Diamond Gang (English, *No director credited*)

Double Trouble (English, *No director credited*)

Double X / Deadly Licence (English, Larry Larson)

The Drug Smugglers (English, *No director credited*)

Ezimbomeni / Crocodile Creek (Zulu, *No director credited*)

Friday's Ghost (English, *No director credited*)

The Great Pretender (English, Hans Webb)

The Haunted Past (*No director credited*)

Hot Snow (English, Lionel Friedberg)

Killer Instinct (English, David Lister)
King of the Road (Zulu, John Parr)
Knock-Out (Zulu, *No director credited*)
Lobanzi Siphiwe / Broad Given (Xhosa, *No director credited*)
Lost Valley (English, Jay Douwes)
Magic (*No director credited*))
The Magic Bag (*No director credited*)
Mahlokolobe / Pigs' Eyes (Sotho, David Bensusan)
Mark of the Jackal (English, Roger Orpen)
Medallion II (*No director credited*)
The Millionaire (*No director credited*)
Molori / Dreamer (Tswana, David Bensusan)
Moyo Mubi / The Evil Ones (Zulu, *No director credited*)
M'Tandi Ethlathini (*No director credited*)
Murder in the Kraal (Zulu, *No director credited*)
Ngwana (*No director credited*)
Passing Through (*No director credited*)
Pelindara / End of News (Zulu, *No director credited*)
The Pin-Up Girl II (Zulu, John Parr)
The Priest and the Thief (*No director credited*)
Professionals (*No director credited*)
Psycho (*No director credited*)
Ransom (Zulu, Chris du Toit)
The Reds (*No director credited*)
The Refugee (*No director credited*)
Rising Storm (English, *No director credited*)
Run to Freedom (Laurens Barnard)
The Runner (*No director credited*)
Sandman (*No director credited*)
The Search (English, *No director credited*)
Sky Full of Diamonds (Thomas Rothig)
Someone Out There (*No director credited*)
Spice (English, Stuart Stromin)
Spider / Isicabu (Zulu, *No director credited*)
Sweet Murder (English, Percival Rubens)
Tap a Tap / Izilingo (*No director credited*)
Treasure Beach (*No director credited*)
Treasure Hunters (English, Cedric Sundström)
Ufasimba (*No director credited*)
Wastelands / The Wasteland (English, Roland Robinson)
We Were Lucky (English, No director credited)
1990
Agter Elke Man (Afrikaans, Franz Marx)
Au Pair (English, Heinrich Dahms)

The Crime Lords (English, Wayne Crawford and Frank Schaeffer)
Crossing the Line (English, Dean Goodhill and Gary Graver)
Deadly Hunter / Pursuit (English, John Parr)
Déja Vu, Vanessa (English, Laurens Barnard)
Oh Schuks, Here Comes UNTAG / Kwagga Strikes Back (English/Afrikaans, David Lister)
On the Wire (English, Elaine Proctor)
Prey for the Hunter (English, John Parr)
Sandgrass People (English, Koos Roets)
That English Woman (English, Dirk de Villiers)

An African Affair (English, Anthony Bond)
All for Money (*No director credited*)
The Adventures of a Diamond (English, *No director credited*)
The Adventures of a Heidelberg Press (English, Michael Garcia & George Garcia)
The African Precedent (English, Frans Nel)
Barret (English, Tonie van der Merwe)
Benzo No. 2 (*No director credited*)
Beware Tiger (English, *No director credited*)
Black Crusader (Tony Cunningham)
The Black Ninja (English, Wanna Fourie)
Blue Planet (English, *No director credited*)
The Chicken Man (Sotho, David Bensusan)
Choppers (English, *No director credited*)
Coming of Age (Zulu, *No director credited*)
Dance of Death (English, Thomas Witt)
The Deserter (English, David Bensusan)
Diamonds of Death (English, *No director credited*)
Fair Game (English, *No director credited*)
Fast Movers (English, *No director credited*)
Fatal Mission / Kwavinga Run / The Rat (English, Anthony Bond and Tonie van der Merwe)
The Fever / Township Fever (English, David Thompson and Francis Gerard)
Fireside Tales (*No director credited*)
Fishy Stones (English, Tonie van der Merwe)
For Better for Worse / The Gentile Wedding (English, Koos Roets)
Force of the Ninja (English, Cedric Sundström)
The Gift (English, John Rogers)
The Gold Cup (English, Robert van de Coolwijk)
Gone Crazy (*No director credited*)
The Horror (Zulu, *No director credited*)

Kickboxer (English, Frans Nel)

The King's Messenger (English, Larry Larson)

Knock-Out Joe (*No director credited*)

Little Man Big Trouble / Nonpopi Nodambusa (English, Etienne Puren)

The Lucky Find (English, *No director credited*)

Makonrad (*No director credited*)

Mandla / Power (Zulu, *No director credited*)

Midnite Rush (Zulu, David Bensusan)

Mine Boy (English, *No director credited*)

Misfortune (*No director credited*)

Muti / Medecine (Zulu, *No director credited*)

My Brother My Enemy (English, Joey Ford)

Naughty Boys (*No director credited*)

No Choice (*No director credited*)

Oriental Mystery in Africa (Chinese, *No director credited*)

Paranoid (English, Larry Larson)

Pasadenas vs. the Comedians (Zulu, *No director credited*)

The Perfume of the Cyclone (English, David Irving)

The Poachers (Zulu, *No director credited*)

Poison Butterfly (English, Leonardo August)

Poison Minds (English, *No director credited*)

The Prophecy (*No director credited*)

Quest for Gold (English, *No director credited*)

The Red Windmill (English, Frans Nel)

Revenge Is the Name of the Game (English, *No director credited*)

Rich Girl (Tonie van der Merwe)

Run Away (English, *No director credited*)

Runaway Hero (Henry Diffenthal)

Second Time Around (English, *No director credited*)

Sniper (English, *No director credited*)

Super Hero English, *No director credited*)

The Toothman and the Killer (English, Elmo de Witt)

Toxic Heart (English, *No director credited*)

Ukunugcebeleka oku Sabisayo / Horable Finish (Xhosa, *No director credited)*

Under Cover (*No director credited*)

Van der Merwe Strikes Back (English, Elmo de Witt)

Voices in the Wind (English, Bruce MacFarlane)

The Wanderers (*No director credited*)

Wazikazi (*No director credited*)

Wednesday Boy (Zulu, *No director credited*)

Zano's Revenge (*No director credited*)

1991

American Kickboxer (English, Frans Nel)

American Ninja V: The Nostramus Syndrome (English, Joseph [Yossi Wein]

Backlash (English, Michael Qissl)

Chain of Desire (English, Temi Lopez)

Die Nag van die Negentiende (Afrikaans, Koos Roets)

Die Storie van Klara Viljee (Afrikaans, Katinka Heyns)

Dust Devils (English, Richard Stanley)

The Good Fascist (English, Helena Nogueira)

No Hero / Cupid (English, Tim Spring)

Queen of the Castle (English, Derrick Louw)

The Road to Mecca (English, Peter Goldsmid and Athol Fugard)

The Rutanga Tapes (English, David Lister)

Sarafina! (English, Darrell Roodt)

The Sheltering Desert (English, Regardt van den Bergh)

Sonja and Johnny (English, Neal Sundström)

Sport Crazy (English, David Lister)

Sweet 'n Short (English, Gray Hofmeyr)

Taxi to Soweto (Multilingual, Manie van Rensberg)

To the Death (English, Darrell Roodt)

Tolla is Tops (Afrikaans, Elmo de Witt)

Wheels and Deals (English, Michael Hammon)

1992

Adventures in Africa (English, Michael Garcia and Stefan Ibendroth)

American Kickboxer II / The Road Back (English, Albert Pyun and Darrell Roodt)

The Angel, the Bicycle and the Chinaman's Finger (English, Roos Koets and Nicholas Ellenbogen)

Cyborg Cop (English, Sam Firstenberg)

Die Prince van Pretoria / Die Prins van Lichtenstein (Afrikaans, Franz Marx)

Friends (English, Elaine Proctor)

'n Pot Vol Winter (Afrikaans, Johan Bernard)

No Hero (English, Tim Spring)

Orkney Snork Nie—Die Movie (Afrikaans, Willie Esterhuizen)

Point of Impact (English, Bob Misiorowski)

Tolla is Tops II (Afrikaans, Elmo de Witt)

Tough Luck (English, David Lister)

A Woman of Desire (English, Robert Ginty)
1993
Cyborg Cop 2 (English, Sam Firstenberg)
Death Dance (English, Derrick Louw)
A Far Off Place (English, Mikael Salomon)
Fleshtone (English, Harry Hurwitz)
Ipi Tombi (English, Tommie Meyer and Don Hulette)
The Mangler (English, Tobe Hooper)
Orkney Snork Nie 2—Nog 'n Movie (Afrikaans, Willie Esterhuizen)
Running Wild (English, Duncan McLachlan)
Terminator Woman (English, Michael Qissi)
There's a Zulu on My Stoep (English, Gray Hofmeyr)
1994
Armageddon—The Final Challenge (English, Michael Garcia)
Cry the Beloved Country (English, Darrell Roodt)
Human Timebomb (English, Mark Roper)
Kalahari Harry (English, Dirk de Villiers)
Lipstiek, Dipstiek (Afrikaans, Willie Esterhuizen)
Lunar Cop (English, Boaz Davidson)
The Making of the Mahatma (English, Shyam Benegal)
Never Say Die (English, Yossi Wein)
Project Shadowchaser 2 (English, John Eyres)
1995
Cyborg Cop 3 (English, Yossi Wein)
Danger Zone (English, Allan Eastman)
Jock / Jock of the Bushveld (English, Danie Joubert)
Project Shadowchaser 3 (English, John Eyres)
The Redemption (English, Kristine Peterson)
Soweto Green (English, David Lister)
War Head (English, Mark Roper)
1996
Dangerous Ground (English, Darrell Roodt)
Dark Horse (English, Dupreez Heunis)
Fools (English, Ramadan Suleman)
The Ghost and the Darkness (English, Stephen Hopkins)
Hearts and Minds (English, Ralph Zipman)
Jump the Gun (English, Les Blair)
Merchant of Death (English, Yossi Wein)
Operation Delta Force (English, Sam Firstenberg)

Paljas (Afrikaans, Katinka Heyns)
Panic Mechanic (English, David Lister)
A Woman of Color (English, Bernard Joffa)
1997
Delta Force 2—Mayday (English, Yossi Wein)
Delta Force 3—Clear Target (English, Mark Roper)
Ernest in Africa (English, John Cherry)
Ernest in the Army (English, John Cherry)
Kaalgat Tussen Die Daisies (Afrikaans, Dirk de Villiers)
Lenny (English, Nico Stein)
The Sexy Girls (English, Russell Thompson)
Sweepers (English, Keoni Waxman [Darby Black])
1998
After the Rain (English, Ross Kettle)
Bravo Two Zero (English, Tom Clegg)
Cold Harvest (English, Isaac Florentine)
Entropy (English, Phil Joanou)
I Dreamed of Africa (English, Hugh Hudson)
The Last Leprechaun (English, David Lister)
Laurel and Hardy—The Movie (English, Larry Harmon and John Cherry)
The Little Unicorn (English, Paul Matthews)
Pirates of the Plains (English, John Cherry and Ken Badish)
Shark Attack (English, Bob Misiorowski)
Texas Blood Money (English, Scot Spiegel)
1999
Boesman and Lena (English, John Berry)
Chikin Bizniz—The Whole Story (English/ Sotho/Zulu, Ntshaveni wa Luruli)
Desert Diners (English, François Coertze)
Desert Diners (English, François Coertze)
Heel against the Head (English, Rod Stewart)
Inside Out (English, Neal Sundström)
The King Is Alive (English, Kristin Levring)
The Millennium Menace (English, Leon Schuster)
Operation Delta Force 4—Random Fire (English, Yossi Wein)
Operation Delta Force 4—Random Fire (English, Yossi Wein)
Out (English, Neal Sundström)
Pure Blood (English, Ken Kaplan)
A Reasonable Man (English, Gavin Hood)
Shark Attack 2 (English, David Worth)

2000

Final Solution (English, Chris Crusen)

Hijack Stories (English, Oliver Schmitz)

The Long Run (English, Jean Stewart)

Lyk Lollery (English, Francois Coertze)

The Second Skin (English, Darrell Roodt)

Styx (English, Alex Wright)

2001

God Is African (English, Akin Omotso)

Malunde (English, Stefanie Sycholt)

Mr. Bones (English, Gray Hofmeyr)

Othello (English, Ebulus Timothy)

2002

The Piano Player (English, Jean-Pierre Roux)

Promised Land (English, Jason Xenopoulos)

Slash (English, Neal Sundström)

2003

Beat the Drum (English, David Hickson)

Beyond Borders (English, Martin Campbell)

Blast (English, Anthony Hickox)

The Bone Snatcher (English, Jason Wulfson)

Borderline (English, Evelyn Maud Purcell)

A Case of Murder (English, Clive Morris)

Pavement (English, Darrell Roodt)

Snake Island (English, Wayne Crawford)

Soldiers of the Rock (English, Norman Maake)

Stander (English, Bronwyn Hughes)

Sumuru (English, Darrell Roodt)

2004

A Boy Called Twist (English, Tim Greene)

Charlie (English, Malcolm Needs)

Country of My Skull (English, John Boorman)

Dead Easy (English, Neal Sundström)

Dracula 3000 (English, Darrell Roodt)

Drum (English, Zola Maseko)

Duma (English, Caroll Ballard)

Hotel Rwanda (English, Terry George)

The Lord of War (English, Andrew Niccol)

Max and Mona (English, Teddy Mattera)

Oh Schuks I'm Gatvol (English, Leon Schuster and Willie Esterhuizen)

Proteus (English, John Greyson)

Racing Stripes (English, Frederick DuChau)

Red Dust (English, Tom Hooper)

Slipstream (English, David van Eyssen)

The Story of an African Farm (English, David Lister)

Wake of Death (English, Phillipe Martinez)

The Wooden Camera (English, Ntshaveni Wa Luruli)

Yesterday (English, Darrell Roodt)

2005

The Breed (English, Nicholas Mastandrea)

Crazy Monkey Presents: Straight Outta Benoni (English, Trevor Clarence)

Dollars and White Pipes (English, Donovan Marsh)

Faith's Corner (English, Darrell Roodt)

The Flier (English, Revel Fox)

Gums and Noses (English, Craig Freimond)

Mama Jack (English, Gray Hofmeyr)

Mercenary for Justice (English, Don E. Fauntle-Roy)

Number Ten (English, Darrell Roodt)

Ouma Se Slim Kind (Afrikaans, Gustav Kuhn)

Sanctuary (English, Konstandino Kalarytis)

Son of Man / Jezile (English, Mark Dornford-May)

34 South (English, Maganthrie Pillay)

Tsotsi (English, Gavin Hood)

U-Carmen E Khayelitsha (Xhosa, Mark Dornford-May)

Zulu Love Letter (English, Ramadan Suleman)

2006

Bunny Chow (English, John Barker)

Catch a Fire (English, Phillip Noyce)

Conversations on a Sunday Afternoon (English, Khaolo Matabane)

Faith Like Potatoes (English, Regardt van den Bergh)

Footskating 101 (English, *no director credited*)

Goodbye Bafana (English, Billie August)

Heartlines (Angus Gibson)

Jerusalem Entsja (English, Ralph Ziman)

Prey (English, Darrell Roodt)

Primeval (English, Michael Katelman)

Running Riot (English, Koos Roets)

2007

Bakgat (Henk Pretorius)

Doomsday (Neil Marshall)

Ghandhi My Father (Feroz Khan)

Hansie (Regardt van den Berg)

Lullaby (Darrell Roodt)

Poena is Koning! (Willie Esterhuizen)

Rendition (Gavin Hood)

Skin (Anthony Fabian)

The Three Investigators (Florian Baxmeister)
Tunnel Rats (Uwe Boll)

REFERENCES

Balseiro, Isabel, and Ntongela Masilela, eds. *To Change Reels: Film and Film Culture in South Africa.* Detroit: Wayne State University Press, 2003.

Blignaut, Johan, and Martin Botha. *Movies—Moguls—Mavericks: South African Cinema 1979–1991.* Cape Town: Showdata, 1992.

Botha, Martin. "The South African Film Industry: Fragmentation, Identity Crisis and Unification." Ottawa: *Kinema* 2, no. 3 (Spring 1995): 7–19.

———. "The Cinema of Manie van Rensburg: Popular Memories of Afrikanerdom." Ottawa: *Kinema* 8 (Fall 1997): 15–42 (part 1) and *Kinema* 9 (Spring 1998): 43–56 (part 2).

———. "The Song Remains the Same: The Struggle for a South African Audience 1960–2004." Ottawa: *Kinema* 21 (Spring 2004): 67–89.

———. "South African Cinema 1960–2004." In *Festival Cinema Africano di Asia e America Latina* 14, pp. 196–225. Milan: COE and Editrice Il Castoro, 2004.

———. "New Directing Voices in South African Cinema." Ottawa: *Kinema* 23 (Spring 2005): 5–21.

———. "110 Years of South African Cinema." Ottawa: *Kinema* 25 (Spring 2006): 5–26 (part 1) and *Kinema* 26 (Fall 2006): 5–26 (part 2).

———, ed. *Marginal Lives and Painful Pasts: South African Cinema After Apartheid.* Cape Town: Genugtig!, 2007.

Botha, Martin, and Samuel Lelièvre. "*Promised Land:* ou des Afrikaners face à eux-mêmes." *Cahiers d'Études africaines* 44 (2004): 441–445.

Botha, Martin, and Adri van Aswegen. *Images of South Africa: The Rise of the Alternative Film* Pretoria: Human Sciences Research Council, 1992.

Cancel, Robert. "*Come Back Africa:* Cinematic representations of Apartheid over Three Eras of Resistance." In *Focus on African Films,* ed. Françoise Pfaff, pp. 15–32. Bloomington: Indiana University Press, 2004.

Davis, Peter. *In Darkest Hollywood: Exploring the Jungles of Cinema's South Africa.* Johannnesburg: Ravan, 1996.

———. "Cinema in South Africa: The 50s." In *Festival Cinema Africano* 13, pp. 199–243. Milano: COE/Editrice Il Castoro, 2003.

———. *Come Back Africa: Lionel Rogosin: A Man Possessed.* Parktown: STE, 2004.

Gaines, Jane M. "Birthing Nation." In *Cinema and Nations,* ed. Mette Hjort and Scott Mackenzie, pp. 298–316. London: Routledge, 2000.

Gutsche, Thelma. *The History and Social Significance of Motion Pictures in South Africa 1895–1940.* Cape Town: Howard Timmins, 1972.

Maingard, Jacqueline. *South African National Cinema.* London and New York: Routledge, 2007.

Pfaff, Françoise. "Nana Mahomo." In *25 Black African Film Makers,* pp. 195–204. New York: Greenwood Press, 1988.

Tomaselli, Keyan. *The South African Film Industry.* Johannesburg: University of Witwatersrand, 1981.

———, ed. *Le Cinéma sud-africain est-il tombé sur la tête?* Paris: L'Afrique littéraire 78/ *CinémAction* 39, 1986.

———. *The Cinema of Apartheid: Race and Class in South African Film.* London: Routledge, 1989.

———. *Encountering Modernity: Twentieth Century South African Cinemas.* Amsterdam: Rozenberg; Pretoria: UNISA Press, 2006.

Tomaselli, Keyan, and Arnold Shepperson. "Le Cinéma sud-africain après l'apartheid: la restructuration d'une industrie." In *Cinémas africains, une oasis dans le désert?* ed. Samuel Lelièvre, pp. 250–263. Paris: Corlet/Téléram a/*CinémAction* 106, 2003.

Tomaselli, Keyan, Alan Williams, Lynette Steenveld, and Ruth Tomaselli. *Myth, Race and Power: South Africans Imaged on Film and TV.* Belleville, South Africa: Anthropos Publishers, 1986.

Ukadike, Nwachukwu Frank. Interviews with Lionel Ngakane and Ramadan Suleman. In *Questioning African Cinema,* pp. 73–83, 281–299. Minneapolis: University of Minnesota Press, 2002.

SUDAN

Output: 6 feature films
Filmmakers: 3
(Gadalla Gubara, Anouar Hachem, Rachid
Medi)

CHRONOLOGY
1969
Hopes and Dreams (Rachid Medi)
1974
Congratulations / Mabruk alik (Gadalla Gubara)
1982
Tajour (Gadalla Gubara)
1984
Eye Trip (Anouar Hachem)
1988
Viva Sara (Gadalla Gubara)
1998
The Cheikh's Baraka (Gadalla Gubara)

REFERENCE
Ukadike, Nwachukwu Frank. Interview with
Gadalla Gubara. In *Questioning African
Cinema,* pp. 41–55. Minneapolis: University
of Minnesota Press, 2002.

TANZANIA

Output: 1 feature film
Filmmakers: 2
(Martin Mhando, Ron Mulvihill)

CHRONOLOGY
1996
Maangamizi: The Ancient One (Martin Mhando
and Ron Mulvihill)
NB Three feature-length videos have been
shot in Tanzania in the past decade: Geoffrey
Mhagama's *Neema* (1999), George Tyson's *Girl-
friend* (2004), and Beatrix Mugisgagwe's *Tu-
maini* (2005).

TOGO

Output: 2 feature films
Filmmakers: 2
(Kilizou Blaise Abalo, Madjé Ayite)

CHRONOLOGY
1992
Kawilasi (Kilizou Blaise Abalo)
2006
Vanessa et Sosie (Madjé Ayité)

REFERENCE
Mollo Olinga, Jean Marie. "Le Cinéma au Togo:
une image en clair-obscur." www. Africine.
org, 30 October 2006.

TUNISIA

**OVERALL STATISTICS: 51 filmmakers—
102 feature films**
1960s
Output: 4 films
Filmmakers: 3
(Sadok Ben Aicha, Hamouda Ben Halimar,
Omar Khlifi)

1970s
Output: 19 films
**Filmmakers: 14 active, 12 new (*) + 2 collec-
tively made films**
(*Ali Abdelwahab, *Brahim Babaï, *Selma Bac-
car, *Rida Behi, Sadok Ben Aïcha, *Abdellatif
Ben Ammar,*Ferid Boughedir, *Mohamed
Ali El Okbi, *Rachid Ferchiou, *Abderrazak
Hammami, *Mohamed Hammami, *Ahmed
Khechine, Omar Khlifi, *Naceur Ktari)

1980s
Output: 19 films
Filmmakers: 16 active, 12 new (*)
(Ridha Behi, Abdellatif Ben Ammar, *Neija

Ben Mabrouk, *Mahmoud Ben Mahmoud, *Abdelhafidh Bouassida, Ferid Boughedir, *Nouri Bouzid, *Mohamed Damak, *Lotfi Essid, *Fadhel Jaïbi, *Fadhel Jaziri, *Nacer Khemir, Omar Khlifi, *Taïeb Louhichi, *Ali Mansour, *Habib Mselmani)

1990s
Output: 28 films
Filmmakers: 21 active, 11 new (*) + 1 collectively made film
(*Ali Abidi, Brahim Babaï, *Selma Baccar, Ridha Behi, *Fitouri Belhiba, Mahmoud Ben Mahmoud, *Mohamed Ben Smaïl, *Keltoum Bornaz, Ferid Boughedir, Nouri Bouzid, *Moncef Dhouib, *Ahmed Djemaï, *Karim Dridi, Mohamed Ali El Okbi, *Ezzedine Fazaï Melliti, Rachid Ferchiou, Fadhel Jaïbi, Nacer Khemir, Taïeb Louhichi, *Moufida Tlatli, *Mohamed Zran)

2000s
Output: 32 films
Filmmakers: 24 active, 13 new (*)
(*Raja Amari, *Elyes Baccar, Selma Baccar, *Khaled W. Barsaoui, Ridha Behi, *Néjib Belkadhi, Abdellatif Ben Ammar, Mahmoud Ben Mahmoud, Keltoum Bournaz, Nouri Bouzid, *Nidhal Chatta, Mohamed Damak, *Nadia El Fani, *Khaled Ghorbal, *Abdellatif Kechiche, *Moez Kamoen, Nacer Ktari, *Moktar Ladjimi, Taïeb Louhichi, *Jilani Saadi, *Nawfel Saheb-Ettaba, Moufida Tlatli, Mohamed Zran)

CHRONOLOGY

Tunisia has a unique forerunner for its national cinema in Albert Samama Chikly. who made both the pioneering short *Zohra* in 1922 and the feature film *The Girl from Carthage / Aïn el-Ghezal* in 1924.

As elsewhere in the Maghreb, early locally produced post-independence features were directed by foreigners. The government department set up to supervise culture and information (Secrétariat d'Etat aux Affaires Culturelles et à l'Information—SEACI) produced Mario Ruspoli's documentary *Renaissance* (1963) and Jean Michaud-Mailland's fictional feature *H'Mida*

(1965). Jacques Baratier also shot on location there his internationally distributed feature, *Goha* (1958), which was shown at Cannes in 1958 as a "Tunisian" film and which Victor Bachy includes as such in his book *Le Cinéma en Tunisie.*

1964
The Dawn / L'Aube (Omar Khlifi)
1968
Mokhtar (Sadok Ben Aicha)
The Rebel / Le Rebelle (Omar Khlifi)
1969
Khlifa Ringworm / Khlifa le teigneux (Hamouda Ben Halima)
1970
The Fellagas / Les Fellagas (Omar Khlifi)
Murky Death / La Mort trouble (Claude d'Anna and Ferid Boughedir)
Om Abbas / Um 'Abbâs (Ali Abdelwahab)
Such a Simple Story / Une si simple histoire (Abdellatif Ben Ammar)
Under the Autumn Rain / Sous la pluie d'automne (Ahmed Khechine)
1972
And Tomorrow? / Et demain? (Brahim Babai)
In the Land of the Tararani / Au pays de Tararani (collective)
Screams / Hurlements (Omar Khlifi)
Yousra (Rachid Ferchiou)
1973
Omi Traki (Abderrazak Hammami)
1974
Sejnane (Abdellatif Ben Ammar)
1975
The Ambassadors / Les Ambassadeurs (Naceur Ktari)
Children of Boredom / Les Enfants de l'ennui (Rachid Ferchiou)
1977
Hyena's Sun / Le Soleil des hyènes (Ridha Behi)
1978
A Ball and Some Dreams / Un ballon et des rêve (Mohamed Ali El Okbi)
Fatma 75 (Selma Baccar)
The Mannequin / Le Mannequin (Sadok Ben Aicha)
The Wedding / La Noce (collective)
1979
My Village / Mon village (Mohamed Hammami)

1980

Aziza (Abdellatif Ben Ammar)

Two Thieves in Madness / Deux larrons en folie (Ali Mansour)

1981

The Ballad of Mamlouk / La Ballade de Mamlouk (Abdelhafidh Bouassida)

1982

Crossing Over / Traversées (Mahmoud Ben Mahmoud)

Shadow of the Earth / L'Ombre de la terre (Taïeb Louhichi)

1983

African Camera / Caméra d'Afrique (documentary) (Ferid Boughedir)

What Are We Doing This Sunday? / Que fait-on ce dimanche (Lotfi Essid)

1984

The Angels / Les Anges (Ridha Behi)

The Searchers of the Desert / Les Balisseurs du désert (Naceur Khemir)

1986

The Challenge / Le Défi (Omar Khlifi)

The Cup / La Coupe (Mohamed Damak)

Man of Ashes / L'Homme de cendres (Nouri Bouzid)

Sabra and the Monster / Sabra et le monstre de la forêt (Habib Mselmani)

1988

Arab (Fadhel Jaziri and Fadhel Jaibi)

Arab Camera / Caméra arabe (documentary) (Ferid Boughedir)

Bitter Champagne / Champagne amer (Ridha Behi)

The Trace / La Trace (Neija Ben Mabrouk)

1989

Golden Horseshoes / Les Sabots en or (Nouri Bouzid)

Leila My Reason / Layla ma raison (Taïeb Louhichi)

1990

Barg Ellil / Éclair nocturne (Ali Abidi)

The Dove's Lost Necklace / Le Collier perdu de la colombe (Naceur Khemir)

Halfaouine / Halfaouine, l'enfant des terrasses (Ferid Boughedir)

Wandering Heart / Cœur nomade (Fitouri Belhiba)

1991

Autumn '86 / Automne '86 (Rachid Ferchiou)

The Night of the Decade / La Nuit de la décennie (Brahim Babai)

1992

After the Gulf? / La Guerre du Golfe . . . et après? (collective)

Bezness (Nouri Bouzid)

Chichkhan / Poussièrre de diamants (Mahmoud Ben Mahmoud and Fadhel Jaibi)

The Teddy Boys / Les Zazous de la vague (Mohamed Ali El Okbi)

1993

The Sultan of the Medina / Soltane el Medina! (Moncef Dhouib)

Wind of Destinies / Le Vent des destins (Ahmed Djemaï)

1994

The Magic Box / Le Magique (Ezzeddine Fazaï Melliti)

Pigalle (Karim Dridi)

Silences of the Palace / Les Silences du palais (Moufida Tlatli)

Swallows Don't Die in Jerusalem / Les Hirondelles ne meurent pas à Jérusalem (Ridha Behi)

1995

Bye-Bye (Karim Dridi)

Check and Mate / Échec et mat (Rachid Ferchiou)

The Fire Dance / La Danse du feu (Selma Baccar)

One Summer at La Goulette / Un été à La Goulette (Ferid Boughedir)

1996

Essaïda (Mohamed Zran)

1997

Girls from a Good Family / Tunisiennes / Bent familia (Nouri Bouzid)

Keswa: The Lost Thread / Keswa, le fil perdu (Keltoum Bornaz)

Redeyef 54 (Ali Abidi)

1998

Moon Wedding / Noce de lune (Taïeb Louhichi)

Out of Play / Hors jeu (Karim Dridi, in France)

Tomorrow I Burn / Demain je brûle (Mohamed Ben Smaïl)

1999

The Pomegranate Siesta / Les Siestes grenadine (Mahmoud Ben Mahmoud)

2000

Be My Friend / Sois mon amie (Naceur Ktari)

The Men's Season / La Saison des hommes (Moufida Tlatli)
No Man's Love (Nidhal Chatta)
Voltaire's Fault / La Faute à Voltaire (Abdellatif Kechiche)
2001
Fatma (Khaled Ghorbal)
A Thousand and One Voices / Les Mille et une voix (documentary) (Mahmoud Ben Mahmoud)
2002
Bedwin Hacker (Nadia El Fani)
The Bookstore / El-Kotbia (Nawfel Saheb-Ettaba)
Clay Dolls / Poupées d'argile (Nouri Bouzid)
Khorma: Stupidity / Khorma, la bêtise (Jilani Saadi)
The Magic Box / La Boîte magique (Ridha Behi)
The Noria's Song / Le Chant de la noria (Abdellatif Ben Ammar)
Red Satin / Satin rouge (Raja Amari)
2004
Him and Her / Elle et lui (Elyes Baccar)
Men's Words / Parole d'hommes (Moez Kamoen)
Nadia et Sarra (Moufida Tlatli)
An Odyssey / Une odyssée (Brahim Babaï)
The Prince / Le Prince (Mohamed Zran)
The Scam / L'Esquive (Abdellatif Kechiche)
Summer Wedding / Noce d'été / Bab el Arch (Moktar Ladjimi)
The Villa / La Villa (Mohamed Damak)
The Wind Dance / La Danse du vent (Taïeb Louhichi)
2005
Bab-Aziz / Bab-Aziz, le prince qui contemplaît son âme (Nacer Khemir)
Flower of Forgetfulness / Fleur de l'oubli (Selma Baccar)
2006
Beyond the Rivers / Par delà les rivières (Khaled W. Barsaoui)
Madness / Démences (Fadhel Jaïbi)
Making Off (Nouri Bouzid)
The Other Half / L'Autre moitié (Kaltoum Bornaz)
The TV Arrives / La Télé arrive (Moncef Dhouib)
VHS—Kahloucha (Néjib Belkadhi)
Wolf's Kindness / Tendresse du loup (Jilani Saadi)

2007
The Secret of the Grain / La Graine et le mulet (Abdellatif Kechiche)

REFERENCES
Armes, Roy. "Reinterpreting the Tunisian Past: *Les Silences du palais*." In *The Arab-African and Islamic Worlds: Interdisciplinary Studies*, ed. Kevin R. Lacey and Ralph M. Coury, pp. 203–214. New York: Peter Lang, 2000.
———. "The Body in Maghrebian Cinema: Nouri Bouzid's *Man of Ashes*." In Ida Kummer, ed., *Le Corps dans tous ses états*. Saratoga Springs: *Celaan* 4, no. 1–2 (2005): 20–30.
———. "Raja Amari (Tunisia)." In *African Filmmaking: North and South of the Sahara*, pp. 176–182. Edinburgh: Edinburgh University Press; Bloomington: Indiana University Press, 2006,
———. "Taïeb Louhichi's *Shadow of the Earth* and the Role of the Rural in Mahgrebian Film Narrative." In *Representing the Rural: Space, Place and Identity in Films about the Land*, Catherine Fowler and Gillian Helfield, pp. 202–212. Detroit: Wayne State University Press, 2006.
———. "Traversées / Crossing Over." In *The Cinema of North Africa and the Middle East*, ed. Gönül Dönmez-Colin, pp. 70–78. London: Wallflower Press, 2007.
Bachy, Victor. *Le Cinéma de Tunisie*. Tunis: Société Tunisienne de Diffusion, 1978.
Ben Aissa, Anouar, ed. *Tunisie: Trente ans de cinéma*. Tunis: EDICOP, 1996.
Bosséno, Christian. "Le Cinéma tunisien." *La Revue du Cinéma* 382 (1983): 49–62.
Boughedir, Ferid. *Halfaouine, l'enfant des terrasses* (script). Paris: *L'Avant-Scène du Cinéma* 483 (1999).
Bouzid, Nouri. *"Sources of Inspiration"* Lecture: *22 June 1994, Villepreux*. Amsterdam: Sources, 1994.
Chamkhi, Sonia. *Cinéma tunisien nouveau*. Tunis: Sud Éditions, 2005.
Cheriaa, Tahar. *Cinéma et culture en Tunisie*. Beirut: UNESCO, 1964.
Chikhaoui, Tahar. "Le Cinéma tunisien de la maladroite euphorie au juste désarroi." In *Aspects de la civilisation tunisienne*, ed.

Abdelmajid Cherfi et al, pp. 5–33. Tunis: Faculté de Lettres de Manouba, 1998.

———. "Le Cinéma tunisien des années 90: permanences et spécifités." *Horizons Maghrébins* 46 (2002): 113–119.

Gabous, Abdelkrim. *Silence, elles tournent!: Les femmes et le cinéma en Tunisie.* Tunis: Cérès Editions/CREDIF, 1998.

Kchir-Bendana, Kmar. "Ideologies of the Nation in Tunisian Cinema." In *Nation, Society and Culture in North Africa,* ed. James McDougall, pp. 35–42. London: Frank Cass, 2003.

Khalil, Andrea Flores. "Images That Come Out at Night: A Film Trilogy by Moncef Dhouib." Saratoga Springs: *Celaan* 1, no. 1–2 (2002): 71–80.

Khelil, Hédi. *Le Parcours et la trace, témoignages et documents sur le cinéma tunisien.* Salammbô, Tunisia: MediaCon, 2002.

Khlifi, Omar. *L'Histoire du cinéma en Tunisie.* Tunis: Société de Diffusion, 1970.

La Tunisie: Annuaire 1995 (Etats des lieux du cinéma en Afrique). Paris: Association des Trois Mondes/FEPACI, 1995.

Mansour, Guillemette. *Samama Chikly, un tunisien à la rencontre du XXième siècle.* Tunis: Simpact Editions, 2000.

Martin, Florence. "Tunisia." In *The Cinema of Small Nations,* ed. Mette Hjort and Duncan Petrie, pp. 213–228. Edinburgh: Edinburgh University Press, 2007.

Moumen, Touti. *Films tunisiens: longs métrages 1967–98.* Tunis: Touti Moumen, 1998.

Paquet, André. *Cinéma en Tunisie.* Montreal: Bibliothèque Nationale de Québec, 1974.

Salah, Rassa Mohamed. *35 ans de cinéma tunisien.* Tunis: Éditions Sahar, 1992.

Stollery, Martin. "Masculinities, Generations, and Cultural Transformation in Contemporary Tunisian Cinema." *Screen* 42, no. 1 (2001): 49–63.

Tlatli, Moufida. *Les Silences du palais* (script). Paris: *L'Avant-Scène du Cinéma* 536 (2000).

ZIMBABWE

Ouput: 22 feature films
Filmmakers: 10
(Stephen Chigorimbo, Tsitsi Dangarembga, Norbert Fero, Roger Hawkins, Isaac Meli Mabhikwa, Olley Maruma, Godwin Mawuru, Michael Raeburn, John Riber, Ingrid Sinclair)

CHRONOLOGY

1969
Rhodesia Countdown (Michael Raeburn)
1976
Beyond the Plains Where Man Was Born (Michael Raeburn)
Requiem for a Village (Michael Raeburn)
1981
The Grass Is Singing (Michael Raeburn, shot in Zambia)
1990
Jit (Michael Raeburn)
1991
Pfuma Yedu (Stephen Chigorimbo)
Soweto (Michael Raeburn)
1992
More Time (Isaac Meli Mabhikwa)
Neria (Godwin Mawuru)
1994
I Am the Future (Godwin Mawuru)
1995
Everyone's Child (Tsitsi Dangarembga)
1996
Flame (Ingrid Sinclair)
1998
Matters of the Spirit (Norbert Fero)
Winds of Rage (Michael Raeburn)
1999
Home Sweet Home (Michael Raeburn)
2000
Yellow Card (John Riber)
2002
Mama Africa (collective)
2003
The Legend of the Sky Kingdom (animated feature, Roger Hawkins)
Riches (Ingrid Sinclair)
Zimbabwe Countdown (Michael Raeburn)
2004
The Big Time (Olley Maruma)
Kare Kare Zvako / The Survival of the Butchered Woman (Tsitsi Dangarembga)

REFERENCES
Barnes, Teresa. "*Flame* and the Historiography of Armed Struggle in Zimbabwe." In *Black*

and *White on Film: African History on Screen,* ed. Vivian Bickford-Smith & Richard Mendelsohn, pp. 240–255. Oxford: James Currey; Athens: Ohio University Press; Cape Town: Double Storey, 2007.

Burns, James McDonald. *Flickering Shadows: Cinema and Identity in Colonial Zimbabwe.* Athens: Ohio University Press, 2002.

Burns, James. "L'Histoire du cinéma au Zimbabwe." In Samuel Lelièvr, ed. *Cinémas africains, une oasis dans le désert?* Paris: Corlet/Télérama/*CinémAction* 106, 2003, pp. 243–249.

Hungwe, Kedmon Nyasha. "Fifty Years of Film-Making in Zimbabwe." www.ed.mtu.edu/-khungwe/afrika/kedmon-hungwe/index.html.

———. "Southern Rhodesia Propaganda and Education Films for Peasant Farmers (1948–1955)." London: *Historical Journal of Film, Radio and Television* 19, no. 4(1991): 229–241.

———. "Film in Post-Colonial Zimbabwe." *Journal of Popular Film and Television* 19, no. 4 (1992): 165–171.

———. "Narrative and Ideology: 50 Years of Filmmaking in Zimbabwe." London: *Media, Culture and Society* 27, no. 1 (2005): 83–99.

Part Three

Index of
Film Titles

A Banna / C'est fini (Kalifa Dienta, 1974, Mali)

A Casablanca, les anges ne volent pas / In Casablanca, Angels Don't Fly (Mohamed Asli, 2004, Morocco)

A Deusa Negra / Black Goddess (Portuguese, Ola Balogun, 1978, Nigeria)

A guerra de agua / The Fight for Water (Licínio Azevedo, 1995, Mozambique)

A Kumgani / Honorable (Zulu, *No director credited,* 1988, South Africa)

A la recherche du mari de ma femme / Looking for My Wife's Husband (Mohamed Abderrahman Tazi, 1993, Morocco)

A nous deux France / It's Up to Us, France (Désiré Écaré, 1969, Ivory Coast)

A tempestade da terra / The Earth's Storm (Fernando D'Almeida e Silva, 1996, Mozambique)

Aanslag op Kariba (Afrikaans, Ivan Hall, 1973, South Africa)

Aare Agaye (Yoruba, Moses Olaiya Adejumo and Oyewole Olowomojuore, 1983, Nigeria)

Aare Agbaye (Yoruba, Moses Olaiya Adejumo and Oyewole Olowomojuore, 1983, Nigeria)

Ababulali (Zulu, *No director credited,* 1984, South Africa)

Abadlovi / Loafers (Zulu, *No director credited,* 1987, South Africa)

Abafana (Zulu, Tonie van der Merwe, 1978, South Africa)

Abafana a Bahle / Good Boys (*No director credited,* 1988, South Africa)

Abaphangi / Dish-Ups (*No director credited,* 1986, South Africa)

Abaqophi / Winners (Zulu, *No director credited,* 1989, South Africa)

Abashokobezi (Zulu, Dirk de Villiers, 1978, South Africa)

Abathakathi (Zulu/Xhosa, *No director credited,* 1985, South Africa)

Abathumbi (Zulu, *No director credited,* 1985, South Africa)

Abbadon Force (English, *No director credited,* 1988, South Africa)

Abbas or Jouha Is Not Dead / Abbas ou Jouha n'est pas mort (Mohamed B. A. Tazi, 1986, Morocco)

Abbas ou Jouha n'est pas mort / Abbas or Jouha Is Not Dead (Mohamed B. A. Tazi, 1986, Morocco)

Abboud on the Borders / Abboud ʿala al-hodood (Cherif Arafa, 1999, Egypt)

Abdou chez les Almohades / Abdou with the Almohades (Saïd Naciri, Morocco, 2006)

Abdou Seasons / ʾAbdu mawasem (Wael Charkas, 2006, Egypt)

Abdou with the Almohades / Abdou chez les Almohades (Saïd Naciri, 2006, Morocco)

Ablakon (Gnoan Roger M'Bala, 1984, Ivory Coast)

Abnormal Girl, An / Fatât châdhdhah (Ahmed Diaa Eddine, 1964, Egypt)

Abou Ahmed / Abou Ahmad (Hassan Reda, 1960, Egypt)

Abou Al-Dahab / Abou al-Dahab (Helmi Rafla, 1954, Egypt)

Abou Al-Dahab / Abou al-Dahab (Karim Dia Eddine, 1996, Egypt)

Abou Ali / Abu Ali (Ahmed Galal, 2005, Egypt)

Abou Al-Layl / Abou al-Layl (Houssam Eddine Mostafa, 1960, Egypt)

Abou Hadid / Abou Hadîd (Niazi Mostafa, 1958, Egypt)

Abou Halmous / Abou Halmous (Ibrahim Helmi, 1947, Egypt)

Abou Kartona / Abou kartounah (Mohamed Hassib, 1991, Egypt)

Abou Khatwa / Abou Khatwa (Youssef Abou Seif, 1998, Egypt)

Abou Moussa's Neighbors / Les Voisines d'Abou

Moussa (Mohamed Abderrahmane Tazi, 2003, Morocco)

Abou Rabie / Abou Rabî (Nader Galal, 1973, Egypt)

Abou Zarifa / Abou Zarîfah (Alvisi Orfanelli, 1936, Egypt)

Abou Zeid Al-Hilali / Abou Zayd al-Hilâlî (Ezz Eddine Zoulficar, 1947, Egypt)

Abou Zeid of His Time / Abou Zeid zamanu (Ahmed al-Sabaawi, 1995, Egypt)

Abou Zouboul's Prisoner / Saguîn Abou Zou'boul (Niazi Mostafa, 1957, Egypt)

Abouna / Notre Père / Our Father (Mahamat Saleh Haroun, 2001, Chad)

About Some Meaningless Events / De quelques événements sans signification (Mostafa Derkaoui, 1974, Morocco)

Abracadabra / Gala gala (Mazen al-Gabali, 2001, Egypt)

Absent Man's Secret, The / Sirr al-ghâ'îb (Kamal Ateyya, 1962, Egypt)

Absent Woman, The / al-Gâ'ibah (EzzEddine Zoulficar, 1955, Egypt)

Abusuan / The Family (Henri Duparc, 1972, Ivory Coast)

Accident (English, Gidi Amir, 1988, South Africa)

According to Your Means / 'Alâ'ad lihâfak (Fouad Chebl, 1949, Egypt)

Account, An / Kashf hesaab (Amir Ramsis, 2007, Egypt)

Accursed Castle, The / al-Qasr al-mal'oun (Hassan Reda, 1962, Egypt)

Accusation, The / al-Ittihâm (Ahmed Sarwat, 1987, Egypt)

Accusation, The / al-Ittihâm (Mario Volpi, 1934, Egypt)

Accused, The / al-Mouttaham (Kamal Ateyya, 1957, Egypt)

Accused, The / al-Mouttahamah (Henri Barakat, 1942, Egypt)

Accused Woman, The / al-Mouttahamah (Henri Barakat, 1992, Egypt)

Ace, The (English, *No director credited*, 1985, South Africa)

Ace of Spades (Zulu, Japie van der Merwe, 1984, South Africa)

Achmawi / 'Achmâwî (Alaa Mahgoub, 1987, Egypt)

Achour the Lionheart / 'Achur qalb alasad (Hussein Fawzi, 1961, Egypt)

Act of Piracy (English, John Cardos, 1988, South Africa)

Action Movie Hero / Shagi' el sima (Ali Ragab, 2000, Egypt)

Actor, The / al-Meshakhasati (Fakhr Eddine Negeda, 2003, Egypt)

Adam and Eve / Adam wa Hawwâ' (Hussein Sedki, 1951, Egypt)

Adam and Women / Adam wa-l-nisâ' (al-Sayed Bedeir, 1971, Egypt)

Adam's Apple / Touffâhat Adam (Fatine Abdel Wahab, 1966, Egypt)

Adam's Autumn / Kharif Adam (Mohamed Kamal al-Kalioubi, 2002, Egypt)

Adanggaman (Gnoan Roger Mbala, 2000, Ivory Coast)

Adaweyya / 'Adawiyyah (Kamal Salah Eddine, 1968, Egypt)

Adham Al-Charkawi / Adham al-Charqâwi (Houssam Eddine Mostafa, 1964, Egypt)

Adieu forain / Bye Bye Souirty (Daoud Aouled Sayed, 1998, Morocco)

Adieu mères / Farewell Mothers (Mohamed Ismaïl, 2007, Morocco)

Adja Tio (Jean-Louis Koula, 1980, Ivory Coast)

Administrative Council, The / Maglis al-idârah (Abbas Kamel, 1953, Egypt)

Adolescent Boys and Girls / Mourâhiqoun wa mourâhiqât (Ahmed Yeyha, 1991, Egypt)

Adolescent Girl from the Country, An / Mourâhiqah min al-aryâf (al-Sayed Ziyada, 1976, Egypt)

Adolescent Girls, The / al-Mourâhiqât (Ahmed Diaa Eddine, 1960, Egypt)

Adolescent Girls' Love / Houbb al-mourâhiqât (Mahmoud Zouficar, 1970, Egypt)

Adored Soul / 'Âchiq al-rouh (Helmi Rafla, 1955, Egypt)

Aduefue / Les Guérisseurs (Sidiki Bakaba, 1988, Ivory Coast)

Adventurer, The / al-Moughâmir (Hassan Reda, 1948, Egypt)

Adventurers, The (English, David Macdonald, 1950, South Africa)

Adventurers Around the World / Moughâmiroun hawl al-'âlam (Mahmoud Farid, 1979, Egypt)

Adventures in Africa (English, Michael Garcia and Stefan Ibendroth, 1992, South Africa)

Adventures of a Diamond, The (English, *No director credited*, 1990, South Africa)

Adventures of a Heidelberg Press, The (English,

Michael Garcia and George Garcia, 1990, South Africa)

Adventures of a Hero, The / Les Aventures d'un héros (Merzak Allouache, 1978, Algeria)

Adventures of Antar and Abla, The / Moughâmarât 'Antar wa 'Abla (Salah Abou Seif, 1948, Egypt)

Adventures of Mr. Pips (English, *No director credited*, 1988, South Africa)

Advocate, The (Zulu, Simon Sabela, South Africa)

Advocating Slavery / al-Isti'bâd (Youssef Wahbi, 1962, Egypt)

Adwa (documentary) (Haïle Gerima, 1999, Ethiopia)

Afrah / Afrâh (Ahmed Badrakhan, 1968, Egypt)

Afrah / Afrâh (Niazi Mostafa, 1950, Egypt)

Africa I Will Fleece You / Afrique, je te plumerai (Jean-Marie Teno, 1992, Cameroon)

Africa Paradis (Sylvestre Amoussou, 2006, Bénin)

Africa Shakes (English, Basil Mailer, 1966, South Africa)

African Affair, An (English, Anthony Bond, 1990, South Africa)

African Camera / Caméra d'Afrique (documentary) (Ferid Boughedir, 1983, Tunisia)

African Dream, An (English, John Smallcombe, 1988, South Africa)

African Express (English, Bruce MacFarlane, 1988, South Africa)

African Fever (Alphonse Béni, 1985, Cameroon)

African Fever (English, Sergio Martino, 1989, South Africa)

African Gold / Ride the High Wind (English, David Millin, 1965, South Africa)

African Journey, An (English, *No director credited*, 1989, South Africa)

African Precedent, The (English, Frans Nel, 1990, South Africa)

Africano / Afrikano (Amr Arafa, 2001, Egypt)

Afrika! (Afrikaans, Pierre Koep, 1972, South Africa)

Afrique, je te plumerai / Africa I Will Fleece You (Jean-Marie Teno, 1992, Cameroon)

Afrotto / Afrotto (Mohamed Abdel Aziz, 2001, Egypt)

Afspraak, Die (Afrikaans, Jan Breytenbach, 1974, South Africa)

Afspraak in die Kalahari (Afrikaans, Anna Neetling-Pohl, 1973, South Africa)

After Love / Mâ ba'da al-houbb (Kamal Ateyya, 1976, Egypt)

After the Farewells / Ba'da al-wadâ' (Ahmed Dia Eddine, 1953, Egypt)

After the Gulf? / La Guerre du Golfe . . . et après? (collective, 1992, Tunisia)

After the Rain (English, Ross Kettle, 1998, South Africa)

After You, Comrade / All the Way to Paris (English, Jamie Uys, 1966, South Africa)

Again My Way, The Winners II (English, Jans Rautenbach, 1977, South Africa)

Against the Government / Didd al-houkoumah (Atef al-Tayeb, 1992, Egypt)

Agamista / 'Agamista (Tarek Abdel Muti, 2007, Egypt)

Agba Arin (Yoruba, Adebayo Faleti, 1989, Nigeria)

Agbo meji (Dr Ola Mankinwa, 1993, Nigeria)

Agent 77 / al-'Amîl sab'ah wa sab'în (Niazi Mostafa, 1969, Egypt)

Agent No. 13 / al-'Amîl raqam talata'ch (Medhat al-Sibaï, 1989, Egypt)

Agent Orange (English, *No director credited*, 1989, South Africa)

Aggression / l'tidâ' (Saad Arafa, 1982, Egypt)

Agitator, The / al-Mouchâghîb (Niazi Mostafa, 1965, Egypt)

Agter Elke Man (Afrikaans, Franz Marx, 1990, South Africa)

Aicha / 'Âichah (Gamal Madkour, 1953, Egypt)

Aida / 'Aïda (Ahmed Badrakhan, 1942, Egypt)

Ailes brisées, Les / Broken Wings (Abdelmajid Rchich, 2005, Morocco)

Aiye (Yoruba, Ola Balogun, 1979, Nigeria)

Ajani Ogun (Yoruba, Ola Balogun, 1975, Nigeria)

Akoni (Yoruba, Mukaila Ajaga, 1989, Nigeria)

Al-Akmar / al-Aqmar (Hicham Abou al-Nasr, 1978, Egypt)

Alarm Bells, The / Agrâs al-khatar (Mohamed Abdel Aziz, 1986, Egypt)

Al-Ataba Gazaz / al-'Atabah gazâz (Niazi Mostafa, 1969, Egypt)

Al-Atba al-Khadraa / al-'Atbah al-khadrâ' (Fatine Abdel Wahab, 1959, Egypt)

Al-Batiniyya / al-Bâtiniyyah (Houssam Eddine Mostafa, 1980, Egypt)

Albero dei destini sospesi, L / The Tree of Suspended Fates (Mohamed Rachid Benhadj, 1997, Algeria)

Al-Charabiyyah / al-Charâbiyyah (Salah Serri, 1987, Egypt)

Al-Chaymaa / al-Chaymâ² (Houssam Eddine Mostafa, 1972, Egypt)

Al-Darb Al-Ahmar / al-Darb al-Ahmar (Abdel Fattah Madbouli, 1985, Egypt)

Alexandria Now and Forever / Iskandariyyah kamân we kamân (Youssef Chahine, 1990, Egypt)

Alexandria Private / Alexandria prive (Sandra Nashaat, 2005, Egypt)

Alexandria . . . Why? / Iskandariyyah lîh (Youssef Chahine, 1979, Egypt)

Alexandria-New York / Iskendereya New York (Youssef Chahine, 2004, Egypt)

Alfa (*No director credited,* 1987, South Africa)

Al-Fahamine / al-Fahhâmîn (Salah Serri, 1987, Egypt)

Al-Gablawi / al-Gablâwî (Adel al-Aassar, 1991, Egypt)

Alger-Beyrouth, pour mémoire / Algiers-Beirut: In Remembrance (Merzak Allouache, 1998, Algeria)

Algerian Dream, An / Un rêve algérien (documentary) (Jean-Pierre Lledo, 2004, Algeria)

Al-Ghaqana / al-Gharqânah (Mohamed Khan, 1993, Egypt)

Algiers-Beirut: In Remembrance / Alger-Beyrouth, pour mémoire (Merzak Allouache, 1998, Algeria)

Al-Haggama / al-Haggâmah (Mohamed al-Naggar, 1992, Egypt)

Al-Harafish / al-Harâfich (Houssam Eddine Mostafa, 1986, Egypt)

Al-Houseiniyya's Tough Guys / Foutouwwat al-Houseiniyyah (Niazi Mostafa, 1954, Egypt)

Ali au pays des mirages / Ali in Wonderland (Ahmed Rachedi, 1979, Algeria)

Ali Baba and the Forty Thieves / ʿAli Bâbâ wa-l-arbaʾîn harâmî (Togo Mizrahi, 1942, Egypt)

Ali Bey Mazhar and the Forty Thieves / ʿAlî Bîh Mazhar wa-l-arbaʾîn harâmî (Ahmed Yassine, 1985, Egypt)

Ali in Wonderland / Ali au pays des mirages (Ahmed Rachedi, 1979, Algeria)

Ali Rabia et les autres / Ali, Rabia and the Others (Ahmed Boulane, 2000, Morocco)

Ali Zaoua (Nabil Ayouch, 1999, Morocco)

Ali, Rabia and the Others / Ali Rabia et les autres (Ahmed Boulane, 2000, Morocco)

Alien Brothers, The / al-Ilhwah al-ghourabâ (Hassan al-Saïfi, 1980, Egypt)

Alien from LA (English, Albert Pyun, 1987, South Africa)

Al-Kafeer / al-Kafeer (Ali Abdel Khalek, 1999, Egypt)

Al-Kanfoudi (Nabyl Lahlou, 1978, Morocco)

Al-Karnak / al-Karnak (Ali Badrakhan, 1975, Egypt)

All for Money (*No director credited,* 1990, South Africa)

All Hail / Mit foll (Raafat al-Mihi, 1996, Egypt)

All in Hell / Koullouhoum fî-l-nâr (Ahmed al-Sabaawi, 1978, Egypt)

All Is Well / Koullouh tamân (Ahmed Sarwat, 1984. Egypt)

All the Way to Paris / After You, Comrade (English, Jamie Uys, 1966, South Africa)

All This Great Love / Koull hâdhâ al-houbb (Hussein Kamal, 1988, Egypt)

All Well and Good / Foll el foll (Medhat al-Sibaï, 2000, Egypt)

Al-Labbana Street / Darb al-Labbânah (Ibrahim Baghdadi, 1984. Egypt)

Allan Quartermain / The Lost City of Gold (English, Gary Nelson, 1985, South Africa)

Allan Quartermaine (Silent, H. Lisle Lucoque, 1919, South Africa)

Allegra (Zulu / Xhosa, *No director credited,* 1985, South Africa)

Al-Lemby / al-Lemby (Wael Ihsaan, 2002, Egypt)

Alles sal regkom (Afrikaans, Pierre de Wet, 1951, South Africa)

Alley of Miracles, The / Zouqâq al-Midaqq (Hassan al-Imam, 1963, Egypt)

Alleyway of Love, The / Darb al-hawâ (Houssam Eddine Mostafa, 1983, Egypt)

All-Girl Band / Ferqet banaat wi bass (Cherif Chaaban, 2000, Egypt)

All-Time Beauty, The / Qamar al-zamân (Hassan al-Imam, 1976, Egypt)

Al-Mabrouk / al-Mabrouk (Hassan Reda, 1959, Egypt)

Almaz and Abdou al-Hamouli / Almaz wa ʿAbdou al-Hâmoulî (Helmi Rafla, 1962, Egypt)

Almodou (Amadou Thior, 2000, Senegal)

Among the Ruins / Bayn al-Atlâl (Ezz Eddine Zoulficar, 1959, Egypt)

Amorous Bedouin, The / al-Badawiyyah al-ʾâchiqah (Niazi Mostafa, 1963, Egypt)

Amorous Pursuit / Moutâradah gharmâmiyyah (Nagdi Hafez, 1968, Egypt)

Amour interdit / Forbidden Love (Sid Ali Fettar, 1993, Algeria)

Amour sans visa / Love without a Visa (Najib Sefrioui, 2001, Morocco)

Amours de Hadj Mokhtar Soldi. Les / The Loves of Hadj Mokhtar Soldi (Mostafa Derkaoui, 2001, Morocco)

Amulet, The / al-Taʾwîdhah (Mohamed Chebl, 1987, Egypt)

Anbar and the Colours / ʿAnbar wa al-alwaan (Adel al-Aassar, 2001, Egypt)

And Afterwards? / Et après? (Mohamed Ismaïl, 2002, Morocco)

And Fate Laughs at It / Wa tadʾhek al-aqdâr (Hussein Emara, 1985, Egypt)

And Life Returns / Wa ʿâdat al-hayât (Nader Galal, 1976, Egypt)

And Love Came to an End / Wa intahâ al-houbb (Hassan al-Imam, 1975, Egypt)

And Love Returns / Wa ʿâda al-houbb (Fatine Abdel Wahab, 1960, Egypt)

And My Heart Ended Down There / Wa dâʾa houbbî hounak (Ali Abdel Khalek, 1982, Egypt)

And Sadness Passes / Wa tamdî al-ahzân (Ahmed Yassine, 1979, Egypt)

And the Days Pass / Marrat al-ayyâm (Ahmed Diaa Eddine, 1954, Egypt)

And the Days Pass / Wa tamdî al-ayyâm (Ahmed al-Sabaawi, 1980, Egypt)

And the Investigation Continues / Wa Lâ yazâl al-tahqîq moustamirran (Achraf Fahmi, 1979, Egypt)

And the Smile Returns / Et le Sourire revient (Ramesh Tekoit, 1980, Mauritius)

And the Train of My Life Passes / Wa madâ qitâr al-ʾoumr (Atef Salem, 1975, Egypt)

And Then? (Silent, J. Humphrey, 1917, South Africa)

And Then the Sun Rises / Thoumma touchriqou al-chams (Ahmed Diaa Eddine, 1971, Egypt)

And Tomorrow? / Et demain? (Brahim Babaï, 1972, Tunisia)

Angel and Demon / Malâk wa chaytân (Kamal al-Cheikh, 1960, Egypt)

Angel of Mercy (Youssef Wahbi. 1946, Egypt)

Angel, the Bicycle and the Chinaman's Finger, The (English, Roos Koets and Nicholas Ellenbogen, 1992, South Africa)

Angels, The / Les Anges (Ridha Behi, 1984, Tunisia)

Angels Do Not Live on Earth / al-Malaʾika la taskun al-ard (Saad Arafa, 1995, Egypt)

Angels Do Not Live on Earth / al-Malâʾikah lâ taskoun al-ʾard (Saad Arafa, 1987, Egypt)

Angels in Hell / Malâʾikah fî gannam (Hassan al-Imam, 1947, Egypt)

Angels of the Streets / Malâʾikat al-chawârî (Hassan al-Saïfi, 1985, Egypt)

Angel's Sin, An / Khatîʾat malâk (Yehya al-Alami, 1979, Egypt)

Anger / al-Ghadab (Anwar al-Chennawi, 1972, Egypt)

Anges de Satan, Les / Satan's Angels (Ahmed Boulane, 2007, Morocco)

Anges, Les / The Angels (Ridha Behi, 1984, Tunisia)

Anguish of Love / Lawʾat al-houbb (Salah Abou Seif, 1960, Egypt)

Ania's Tea / Le Thé d'Ania (Saïd Ould Khelifa, 2004, Algeria)

Anikura (Yoruba, Oyewole Olowomojuore, 1982, Nigeria)

Anna Makossa (Alphonse Béni, 1980, Cameroon)

Années de l'exil, Les / The Years of Exile (Nabyl Lahlou, 2002, Morocco)

Another's Love / Habîbat ghayrî (Ahmed Mazhar, 1976, Egypt)

Antar and Abla / ʿAntar wa ʿAblah (Niazi Mostafa, 1945, Egypt)

Antar Ibn Chadad / ʿAntar bin chaddâd (Niazi Mostafa, 1961, Egypt)

Antar Wears His Sword / ʿAntar châyil sîfouh (Ahmed al-Sabaawi, 1983, Egypt)

Antar's Son / Ibn ʿAntar (Ahmed Salem, 1947, Egypt)

Any Man's Death (English, Tom Clegg, 1988, South Africa)

Aouchtam (Mohamed Ismaïl, 1998, Morocco)

Apalara (Yoruba, Eddie Ogbumah, 1986, Nigeria)

Au Pair (English, Heinrich Dahms, 1990, South Africa)

Au pays de Tararani / In the Land of the Tararani (collective, 1972, Tunisia)

Au pays des Juliets / In the Land of the Juliets (Mehdi Charef, 1992, Algeria)

Aube des damnés, L' / Dawn of the Damned (Ahmed Rachedi, 1965, Algeria)

Aube noire / Black Dawn (Djingary Maiga, 1983, Niger)

Aube, L' / The Dawn (Omar Khlifi, 1966, Tunisia)

Au-delà de Gibraltar / Beyond Gibraltar (Mourad Boucif, with Taylan Barman, 2001, Morocco)

Aunty Faranssa / Khalty Faranssa (Ali Ragab, 2004, Egypt)

Auprès du peuplier / Beside the Poplar Tree (Moussa Haddad, 1972, Algeria)

Auspicious / Qadam al-khayr (Helmi Rafla, 1952, Egypt)

Authentic One, The / al-Asîl (Abdel Rahman Chérif, 1973, Egypt)

Automne '86 / Autumn '86 (Rachid Ferchiou, 1991, Tunisia)

Automne—octobre à Alger / Autumn—October in Algiers (Malek Lakhdar Hamina, 1991, Algeria)

Autopsie d'un complot / Autopsy of a Plot (Mohamed Slim Riad, 1978, Algeria)

Autopsy of a Plot / Autopsie d'un complot (Mohamed Slim Riad, 1978, Algeria)

Autre Algérie: regards intérieurs, L' / The Other Algeria: Views from Within (collective, 1998, Algeria)

Autre moitié, L' / The Other Half (Kaltoum Bornaz, 2006, Tunisia)

Autre monde, L' / The Other World (Merzak Allouache, 2001, Algeria)

Autumn '86 / Automne '86 (Rachid Ferchiou, 1991, Tunisia)

Autumn Concerto / Tyger Tyger Burning Bright (English, Neal Sundström, 1988, South Africa)

Autumn Song / Chant d'Automne (Mohamed Meziane Yala, 1982, Algeria)

Autumn—October in Algiers / Automne—octobre à Alger (Malek Lakhdar Hamina, 1991, Algeria)

Avenger, The / al-Mountaqim (Salah Abou Seif, 1947, Egypt)

Aventures d'un héros, Les / The Adventures of a Hero (Merzak Allouache, 1978, Algeria)

Awakening / Réveil (Mohamed Zineddine, 2003, Morocco)

Awatef / ʿAwâtif (Hassan al-Imam, 1958, Egypt)

AWOL / The Quarry (English, Neil Sonnekus, 1989, South Africa)

Ayanmo (Yoruba, Hubert Ogunde, 1988, Nigeria)

Ayn al-hayat / ʿAyn al-hayât (Ibrahim al-Chakankiri, 1970, Egypt)

Ayoub / Ayyoub (Hani Lachine, 1984. Egypt)

Ayouma (Pierre-Marie Dong and Charles Mensah, 1977, Gabon)

Aziz and Ito: A Moroccan Wedding / Aziz et Ito, un mariage marocain (Naguib Ktiri-Idrissa, 1991, Morocco)

Aziz et Ito, un mariage marocain / Aziz and Ito: A Moroccan Wedding (Naguib Ktiri-Idrissa, 1991, Morocco)

Aziza (Abdellatif Ben Ammar, 1980, Tunisia)

Aziza / Azîzah (Hussein Fawzi, 1954, Egypt)

Aziza the Ambassadress / al-Safîrah ʿAzîzah (Tolba Radwane, 1961, Egypt)

Baara (Souleymane Cisse, 1978, Mali)

Bab Al-Nasr / Bâb al-Nasr (Sayed Seif, 1988, Egypt)

Bab Aziz (Nacer Khemir, 2005, Tunisia)

Bab Charq / Bâb Charq (Youssef Abou Seif, 1989, Egypt)

Bab el Web (Merzak Allouache, 2005, Algeria)

Bab el-Oued City (Merzak Allouache, 1994, Algeria)

Baba Zak (English, Ladi Ladebo, 1999, Nigeria)

Babblekous en Bruidegom (Afrikaans, Koos Roets, 1974, South Africa)

Baby Brown (English, Joey Ford, 1989, South Africa)

Baby Game, The (English, Joe Stewardson, 1973, South Africa)

Bachelor Husband, The / al-Zawg al-ʾâzib (Hassan al-Saïfi, 1966, Egypt)

Bachelor's Life, A / Hayât ʿâzib (Nagdi Hafez, 1963, Egypt)

Bachelor's Loves, A / Gharâmiyyât ʿâzib (Zaki Saleh, 1976, Egypt)

Barbier du quartier des pauvres, Le / The Barber of the Poor Quarter (Mohamed Reggab, 1982, Morocco)

Barefoot on a Golden Bridge / Hâfiyah ᶜalâ Guisr min-al-dhahab (Atef Salem, 1977, Egypt)

Barg Ellil / Eclair nocturnel (Ali Abidi, 1990, Tunisia)

Barge 70 / al-ᵓAwwâmah sabᵓîn (Khaïri Bechara, 1982, Egypt)

Barracuda (English, John Cardos, 1988, South Africa)

Barret (English, Tonie van der Merwe, 1990, South Africa)

Barricades sauvages / Savage Barricades (Mohamad Benayat, 1975, Algeria)

Barrier, The / al-Hâguiz (1972 Mohamed Radi, 1972, Egypt)

Barrières / Barriers (Ahmed Lallem, 1977, Algeria)

Bars of the Harem, The / Qafas al-harîm (Hussein Kamal, 1986, Egypt)

Basement, The / al-Badroun (Atef al-Tayeb, 1987, Egypt)

Basie (Afrikaans, Gordon Vorster, 1961, South Africa)

Bâton Rouge (Rachid Bouchareb, 1985, Algeria)

Battle between the Wives, The / Sirâ᾿ al-zawgât (Neimat Rouchdi, 1992, Egypt)

Battle of Professionals / Sirâ᾿ al-mouhtarifîn (Hassan al-Saïfi, 1969, Egypt)

Battle of Taqraft / Maᵓrakat Taqraft (Khaled Khachim and Mohamed Ayad Driza, 1981, Libya)

Battle of the Beauties, The / Sirâ᾿ al-hasnâwât (Mohamed Marzouk, 1993, Egypt)

Battle of the Sacred Tree, The (Wanjiru Kinyanjui, 1994, Kenya)

Battle of Tyrants, The / Sirâ᾿ al-gabâbirah (Zouheir Bekir and Raymond Nassour, 1962, Egypt)

Bàttu (Cheikh Oumar Sissoko, 2000, Mali)

Bayada / Bayyâdah (Ahmed Sarwat, 1981, Egypt)

Baya's Mountain / La Montagne de Baya (Azzedine Meddour, 1997, Algeria)

Be Alert / Khalli el demaagh sahi (Mohamed Abou Seif, 2002, Egypt)

Be My Friend / Sois mon amie (Naceur Ktari, 2000, Tunisia)

Beach Bum / Sayeᵓ bahr (Ali Ragab, 2004, Egypt)

Beach of Lost Children, The / La Plage des enfants perdus (Jillali Ferhati, 1991, Morocco)

Beans Are My Favorite Dish / al-Foul sadîqî (Hussein al-Wakil, 1985, Egypt)

Beast, The / Claws (English, Alan Nathanson, 1982, South Africa)

Beat the Drum (English, David Hickson, 2003, South Africa)

Beauté éparpillée, La / Scattered Beauty (Lahcen Zinoun, 2007, Morocco)

Beautiful Aziza / al-Hilwah ᶜAzîzah (Hassan al-Imam, 1969, Egypt)

Beautiful Bedouin Girl, The / al-Badawiyya al-hasnâᵓ (Ibrahima Lama, 1947, Egypt)

Beautiful Days of Sheherazade, The / Les Beaux jours de Chahrazade (Mostafa Derkaoui, 1982, Morocco)

Beautiful Flowers, The / al-Zouhour al-Fâtinah (Gamal Madkour, 1952, Egypt)

Beautiful People (English, Jamie Uys, 1974, South Africa)

Beautiful Thieves, The / al-Nachchalât al-fâtinât (Mahmoud Farid, 1985, Egypt)

Beautiful Woman's Handkerchief, The / Mandîl al-hilou (Abbas Kamel, 1949, Egypt)

Beauty, The / Sitt al-housn (Niazi Mostafa, 1950, Egypt)

Beauty and the Crook, The / al-Fâtinah wa-l-souᵓlouk (Hussein Emara, 1976, Egypt)

Beauty and the Idiot, The / al-Houlwah wa-l-ghabî (Ahmed Fouad, 1977, Egypt)

Beauty and the Students, The / al-Hasnâ wa-l-talabah (Ahmed Diaa Eddine, 1963, Egypt)

Beauty and the Thief, The / al-Hasnâ wa-l-liss (Nagdi Hafez, 1971, Egypt)

Beauty from the Airport, The / Hasnâ al-matâr (al-Sayed Bedeir, 1971, Egypt)

Beauty of Love, The / Rawᵓat al-houbb (Mahmoud Zoulficar, 1968, Egypt)

Beauty of the Night / Qamar al-layl (Mohamed Salmane, 1984. Egypt)

Beauty of the Soul, The / Halâwat al-rouh (Ahmed Fouad Darwich, 1990, Egypt)

Beauty's Cheek, The / Khadd al-gamîl (Abbas Kamel, 1951, Egypt)

Beaux jours de Chahrazade, Les / The Beautiful Days of Sheherazade / Ayyâm chahrazad al-hilwâ (Mostafa Derkaoui, 1982, Morocco)

Bedouin's Love, A / Gharâm badawiyyah (Fouad al-Gazaerli, 1946, Egypt)

Beyond the Plains Where Man Was Born (Michael Raeburn, 1976, Zimbabwe)

Beyond the Rivers / Par delà des rivières (Khaled W. Barsaoui, 2006, Tunisia)

Bezness (Nouri Bouzid, 1992, Tunisia)

Bhema (Zulu, *No director credited*, 1985, South Africa)

Bicots-nègres, vos voisins, Les / The Black Wogs, Your Neighbors (Med Hondo, 1973, Mauritania)

Big Adolescent, The / al-Mourâhiq al-kabîr (Mahmoud Zoulficar, 1961, Egypt)

Big Gag, The / Candid Camera (English, Yuda Barkan and Igal Shilon, 1986, South Africa)

Big Game / Hippo Pool (English, Chris du Toit, 1989, South Africa)

Big Game, The (English, Robert Day, 1973, South Africa)

Big House, The / al-Bayt al-Kabîr (Ahmed Kamel Morsi, 1949, Egypt)

Big Land (English, *No director credited*, 1985, South Africa)

Big Mistake, The / al-Zallah al-koubrâ (Ibrahim Emara, 1945, Egypt)

Big Time, The (Olley Maruma 2004, Zimbabze)

Big Trip, The / Le Grand voyage (Mohamed Abderrahman Tazi, 1981, Morocco)

Bigamist, The / Gouz al-itnîn (Ibrahim Emara, 1947, Egypt)

Bike, The / Le Vélo (Hamid Faridi, 2006, Morocco)

Bikre Sapne / Lost Dream (Brijmohun Brothers, 1975, Mauritius)

Bikutsi Water Blues (Jean-Marie Teno, 1988, Cameroon)

Bilal, the Prophet's Muezzin / Bilâl mouʾadhdhin al-rasoul (Ahmed al-Touhki, 1953, Egypt)

Biliyaane (Moussa Yoro Bathily, 1993, Senegal)

Bill, Miss, The / al-Hisâb yâ mademoiselle (Anwar al-Chennawi, 1978, Egypt)

Billy Boy (English, Tim Spring, 1978, South Africa)

Biltong / Umnquyi (Zulu, *No director credited*, 1987, South Africa)

Biophetetso / Revenge (South Sotho, Jimmy Murray, 1984, South Africa)

Bird Boy (English, Ed Herbst, 1984, South Africa)

Bird in the Sky / Tayr fî-l-samâ (Houssam Eddine Mostafa, 1988, Egypt)

Bird of Paradise, The / L'Oiseau du paradis (Mohamed Bensaïd, 1981, Morocco)

Bird of the Orient / ʿOusfour al-charq (Youssef Francis, 1986, Egypt)

Bird on the Path, A / Tâʾir ʿalâ al-tartîq (Mohamed Khan, 1981, Egypt)

Bird with Teeth, A / ʿOusfour louh anyâb (Hassan Youssef, 1987, Egypt)

Birds of Paradise (English, Tommie Meyer and Philip van der Byl, 1981, South Africa)

Birds of Paradise / ʿAsâfir al-gannah (Seif Eddine Chawkat, 1955, Egypt)

Birds of the Darkness / Tuyour al-zalaam (Cherif Arafa, 1995, Egypt)

Birth of Islam, The / Zouhour al-islâm (Ibrahim Ezz Eddine, 1951, Egypt)

Bisi Daughter of the River (English, Jab Adu, 1977, Nigeria)

Bitter Bread / al-Khoubz al-mourr (Achraf Fahmi, 1982, Egypt)

Bitter Champagne / Champagne amer (Ridha Behi, 1988, Tunisia)

Bitter Grape / alʾInab al-mourr (Farouk Agrama, 1965, Egypt)

Bitter Love / al-Houbb al-mourr (Houssam Eddine Mostafa, 1992, Egypt)

Biza Izintombi (Zulu, Ronnie Isaacs, 1981, South Africa)

Black Candles / al-Choumouʾ al-sawdâʾ (Ezz Eddine Zoulficar, 1962, Egypt)

Black Cat, The / I-Kati Elimnyana (Zulu, Simon Sabela, 1976, South Africa)

Black Clouds / Nuages noirs (Djingary Maiga, 1979, Niger)

Black Crusader (Tony Cunningham, 1990, South Africa)

Black Dawn / Aube noire (Djingary Maiga, 1983, Niger)

Black Death (*No director credited*, 1987, South Africa)

Black Dju (Pol Cruchten, 1997, Cape Verde)

Black Friday / Vendredi noir (Djingary Maiga, 1999, Niger)

Black Girl / La Noire de . . . (Ousmane Sembene, 1964, Senegal)

Black Goddess / A Deusa Negra (Portuguese, Ola Balogun, 1978, Nigeria)

Black Gold (English, Duncan MacNeillie, 1988, South Africa)

Body, The / al-Gasad (Hassan al-Imam, 1955, Egypt)

Body and Soul / al-Rouh wa-l-gasad (Helmi Rafla, 1948, Egypt)

Boemerang 11.15 (Afrikaans, Ivan Hall, 1972, South Africa)

Boerboel de Wet (Afrikaans, Al Debbo, 1961, South Africa)

Boesman and Lena (Afrikaans / English, Ross Devenish, 1973, South Africa)

Boesman and Lena (English, John Berry, 1999, South Africa)

Boetie Gaan Border Toe (Afrikaans, Regardt van den Bergh, 1984, South Africa)

Boetie of Manoeuvres / Wild Manoeuvres (Afrikaans, Regardt van den Bergh, 1985, South Africa)

Boîte magique, La / The Magic Box (Ridha Behi, 2002, Tunisia)

Boland! (Afrikaans, Bertrand Retief, 1974, South Africa)

Bolus 80 (English, Eddie Ugbomah, 1982, Nigeria)

Bomber / The Knock-Out Cop (English, Michele Lupo, 1984, South Africa)

Bona Manzi (Zulu, Tonie van der Merwe, 1984, South Africa)

Bond and Word (Silent, Dick Cruikshanks, 1918, South Africa)

Bone Snatcher, The (English, Jason Wulfson, 2003, South Africa)

Bonnes familles, Les / The Good Families (Djafar Damardji, 1972, Algeria)

Booha (Rami Imam, 2005, Egypt)

Border Scourge, A (Silent, Joseph Albrecht, 1917, South Africa)

Borderline (English, Evelyn Maud Purcell, 2003, South Africa)

Boshodu Ba Sefofo (Sotho, *No director credited*, 1984, South Africa)

Boss's Daughter, The / Bint al-mouʾallim (Abbas Kamel, 1947, Egypt)

Boss's Empire, The / Ambaratouriyyat al mouʾallim (Zaki Saleh, 1974, Egypt)

Boss-Woman and the Gentleman, The / al-Meʾallemma wal ustaaz (Abdel Halim al-Nahhas, 1995, Egypt)

Bosvelder, Die (Afrikaans, Jamie Uys, 1958, South Africa)

Bosveldhotel, Die (Afrikaans, Fred Nel, 1982, South Africa)

Botsotso (Zulu, Tonie van der Merwe, 1979, South Africa)

Botsotso II (Zulu, Ronnie Isaacs, 1980, South Africa)

Botsotso III (Zulu, Don Fedler, 1982, South Africa)

Bottom Line / Tattoo Chase (English, Jeff Gold, 1988, South Africa)

Bou van ʾn Nasie, Die / They Built a Nation (Afrikaans / English, Joseph Albrecht, 1938, South Africa)

Boudour / Boudour (Nader Galal, 1974, Egypt)

Bouka (Gnoan Roger M'Bala, 1988, Ivory Coast)

Bouksasse Boutfounaste (Badr Abdelilah, 2005, Morocco)

Boulboul the Lawyer / al-Mouʾallim Boulboul (Hassan Ramzi, 1951, Egypt)

Boulteyya, a Girl from Bahary / Boulteyya bent Bahary (Salah Serri, 1995, Egypt)

Bouthayna's Love / Gharâm Bouthayna (Galal Mostafa, 1953, Egypt)

Boxer, The (Zulu, Simon Sabela, 1976, South Africa)

Boxers Dream / Tora ya Raditeble (Sotho, *No director credited*, 1983, South Africa)

Boy Called Twist, A (English, Tim Greene, 2004, South Africa)

Boy from Tangier, The / Le Gosse de Tanger (Moumen Smihi, 2005, Morocco)

Boy Is Good, The (English, Eddie Ugbomah, 1982, Nigeria)

Boy Who Needs a Home, A / Enzintandaneni (Zulu, *No director credited*, 1987, South Africa)

Boy, A Girl and the Devil, A / Walad wa bint wachaytân (Hassan Youssef, 1971, Egypt)

Bozo and Bimbo (English, Wally van der Merwe, 1984, South Africa)

Bracelet de bronze, Le / The Bronze Bracelet (Cheikh Tidiane Aw, 1974, Senegal)

Brahim qui? / Brahim Who? (Nabyl Lahlou, 1982, Morocco)

Brahim Who? / Brahim qui? (Nabyl Lahlou, 1982, Morocco)

Braids / Tresses (Jillali Ferhati, 2000, Morocco)

Braise, La / The Embers (Fariqa Bourquia, 1982, Morocco)

Bye-Bye Africa (Mahamat Saleh Haroun, 1999, Chad)

Bye-Bye My Pretty One / Bay bay yâ helwah (Atef Salem, 1977, Egypt)

Bye-Bye Souirty / Adieu forain (Daoud Aouled Sayed, 1998, Morocco)

Cabaret of Life, The / Kabârîh al-hayât (Mahmoud Farid, 1977, Egypt)

Cactus / Garga M'Bosse (Mahama [Johnson] Traore, 1974, Senegal)

Caftan d'amour / Caftan of Love (Moumen Smihi, 1987, Morocco)

Caftan of Love / Caftan d'amour (Moumen Smihi, 1987, Morocco)

Cairo 30 / al-Qâhirah talâtîn (Salah Abou Seif, 1966, Egypt)

Cairo Baghdad / al-Qâhiran Baghdad (Ahmed Badrakahn, 1947, Egypt)

Cairo by Night / al-Qâhirah fii-l-layl (Mohamed Salem, 1963, Egypt)

Cairo Nights / Layâli al-Qâhirah (Ibrahim Lama, 1939, Egypt)

Cairo Street / Rue le Caire (Mohamed Abdelkrim Derkaoui, 1998, Morocco)

Call after Midnight, A / Moukâlamah ba'da mountasaf al-layl (Helmi Rafla, 1978, Egypt)

Call of Love, The / Nidâ' al-houbb (Elhami Hassan, 1956, Egypt)

Call of the Blood / Nidâ al-dam (Ibrahim Lama, 1943, Egypt)

Call of the Blood, The / al-Dam yahinn (al-Sayed Ziyada, 1952, Egypt)

Call of the Heart / Nidâ' al-qaib (Omar Guemei, 1943, Egypt)

Caméra arabe / Arab Camera (documentary) (Ferid Boughedir, 1988, Tunisia)

Caméra d'Afrique / African Camera (documentary) (Ferid Boughedir, 1983, Tunisia)

Cameroon Connection / Cameroun Connection (Alphonse Béni, 1985, Cameroon)

Cameroun Connection / Cameroon Connection (Alphonse Béni, 1985, Cameroon)

Camomile / Camoumille (Mehdi Charef, 1988, Algeria)

Camoumille / Camomile (Mehdi Charef, 1988, Algeria)

Camp de Thiaroye (Ousmane Sembene and Thierno Faty Sow, 1988, Senegal)

Candid Camera / The Big Gag (English, Yuda Barkan and Igal Shilon, 1986, South Africa)

Candle Burns, A / Cham'ah tahtariq (Youssef Wahbi, 1946, Egypt)

Canefields (English, *No director credited*, 1989, South Africa)

Can't Make Up Their Minds (= literally: Those Who Dance in the Stairways) / Illâ raqasou 'alâ al-sillim (Nagui Anglo, 1994, Egypt)

Canta meu irmao, ajuda-me a cantar / Sing My Brother, Help Me to Sing (José Cardoso, 1982, Mozambique)

Caprice / Nazwa (Ali Badrakhan, 1996, Egypt)

Captain Has Arrived, The / al-Kâbtin wasal (Ahmed Sarwat, 1991, Egypt)

Captain Misr / Kabtin Misr (Bahaa Eddine Charaf, 1955, Egypt)

Captain Nadia's Battle / Ma'rakat al-naqîb Nadiâ (Nadia Hamza, 1990, Egypt)

Captain, The / al-Qubtaan (Sayed Saïd, 1997, Egypt)

Car Thief, The / Sâriq al-sayyârât (Adli Khalil, 1986, Egypt)

Caramel (Henri Duparc, 2005, Ivory Coast)

Caravan Passes By, The / al'Qâfilah tasîr (Ibrahim Lama, 1951, Egypt)

Caravan's Return, The / 'Awdat al-qâfilah (Ahmed Badrakhan,1946, Egypt)

Cartouches gaulois / Gallic Cartridges (Mehdi Charef, 2007, Algeria)

Casablanca by Night (Mostafa Derkaoui, 2003, Morocco)

Casablanca Casablanca (Farida Benlyazid, 2003, Morocco)

Casablanca Daylight (Mostafa Derkaoui, 2004, Morocco)

Casablancais, Les / The Casablancans (Abdelkader Lagtaâ, 1998, Morocco)

Casablancans, The / Les Casablancais (Abdelkader Lagtaâ, 1998, Morocco)

Case of an Adolescent Girl, The / Hâlat mourâhiqah (Sayed Tantawi, 1990, Egypt)

Case of Murder, A (English, Clive Morris, 2003, South Africa)

Cash OK / el-Cash mashi (Tarek al-Nahri, 2000, Egypt)

Casino "al-Latafa" / Casino al-latâfah (Gamal Madkour, 1945, Egypt)

Charlie Steel (English, Johan van Rooyen, 1984, South Africa)

Charlie Word 'n Ster (Afrikaans, Dirk de Villiers, 1979, South Africa)

Charmer of Women, The / Sâ'id al-nisâ (Abdel Meneim Choukri, 1975, Egypt)

Charming Postmistresses, The / al-Koumsariyyât al-fâtinât (Hassan al-Saïfi, 1957, Egypt)

Charting Troubled Waters / al-Sâbihah fî-l-nâr (Mohamed Kamel Hassan, 1959, Egypt)

Chase into the Forbidden / Moutâradah f-l-mamnou' (Medhat Bekir, 1993, Egypt)

Chase, The (English, *No director credited*, 1988, South Africa)

Chasing Namibia (English, Denis Scully, 1989, South Africa)

Chawadder / Chawâdir (Ibrahim Afifi, 1990, Egypt)

Chawq / Chawq (Achraf Fahmi, 1976, Egypt)

Cheap Flesh / Lahm rakhis (Inas al-Deghidi, 1995, Egypt)

Cheap Tricks (*No director credited*, 1987, South Africa)

Cheats, The / al-Moukhâdi'oun (Mahmoud Farid, 1973, Egypt)

Cheb (Rachid Bouchareb, 1990, Algeria)

Check and Mate / Échec et mat (Rachid Ferchiou, 1995, Tunisia)

Chef! / Chief! (documentary) (Jean-Marie Teno, 2000, Cameroon)

Cheikh Hassan / al-Chaykh Hasan (Hussein Sedki, 1954, Egypt)

Cheikh's Baraka, The (Gadalla Gubara, 1998, Sudan))

Cherchez la femme / Fattich 'an al-mar'ah (Ahmed Galal, 1939, Egypt)

Cheval de vent, Le / The Wind Horse (Daoud Aoulad Syad, 2001, Morocco)

Chevaux de fortune / Make-Believe Horses (Jillali Ferhati, 1995, Morocco)

Chichkhan / Poussièrre de diamants (Mahmoud Ben Mahmoud and Fadhel Jaibi, 1992, Tunisia)

Chick / Katkoot (Ahmed Awwaad, 2006, Egypt)

Chicken Man, The (Sotho, David Bensusan, 1990, South Africa)

Chief! / Chef! (documentary) (Jean-Marie Teno, 2000, Cameroon)

Chikin Bizniz—The Whole Story (English / Sotho / Zulu, Ntshaveni wa Luruli, 1999, South Africa)

Child Bride (documentary, Adamu Halilu, 1971, Nigeria)

Child from the District, A / Ibn al-hârah (Ezz Eddine Zoulficar, 1953, Egypt)

Child of the Stars / L'Enfant des étoiles (Mohamed Benayat, 1985, Algeria)

Children of Boredom / Les Enfants de l'ennui (Rachid Ferchiou, 1975, Tunisia)

Children of God (English, Ladi Ladebo, 1985, Nigeria)

Children of Silence / Abnâ' al-samt (Mohamed Radi, 1974, Egypt)

Children of the Streets / Awlâd al-chawâri (Youssef Wahbi, 1951, Egypt)

Children of the Wind / Les Enfants du vent (Brahim Tsaki, 1981, Algeria)

Children's Games (English, Mattys Mocke, 1983, South Africa)

Child's Love, A / Un amour d'enfant (Ben Diogaye Beye, 2002, Senegal)

Choice, The / al-Ikhtiyâr (Youssef Chahine, 1971, Egypt)

Choisis-toi un ami / Choose a Friend aka *The Eleventh Commandment / Le 11e commandement* (Mama Keïta, 1997, Guinea)

Choix, Le / Yam Daabo (Idrissa Ouedraogo, 1987, Burkina Faso)

Cholesterol Free / Khaly min al-cholesterol (Mohamed Abou Seif, 2005, Egypt)

Choose a Friend / Choisis-toi un ami aka *The Eleventh Commandment / Le 11e commandement* (Mama Keïta, 1997, Guinea)

Choppers (English, *No director credited*, 1990, South Africa)

Chouchou (Merzak Allouache, 2003, Algeria)

Christal / Kristâl (Adel Awad, 1993, Egypt)

Chronicle of a Normal Life / Chronique d'une vie normale (Sâad Chraïbi, 1991, Morocco)

Chronicle of the Years of Embers / Chronique des années de braise (Mohamed Lakhdar Hamina, 1975, Algeria)

Chronique des années de braise / Chronicle of the Years of Embers (Mohamed Lakhdar Hamina, 1975, Algeria)

Chronique d'une vie normale / Chronicle of a Normal Life (Sâad Chraïbi, 1991, Morocco)

Cœur nomade / Wandering Heart / Regaya (Fitouri Belhiba, 1990, Tunisia)

Cœurs brûlés / Broken Hearts (Ahmed El Maânouni, 2006, Morocco)

Coffee Colored / Une couleur café (Henri Duparc, 1997, Ivory Coast)

Cold Blood (Zulu, Hein Pretorius, 1984, South Africa)

Cold Harvest (English, Isaac Florentine, 1998, South Africa)

Cold Sweat (*No director credited*, 1988, South Africa)

Colère des dieux, La / The Gods' Anger (Idrissa Ouedraogo, 2003, Burkina Faso)

Collier perdu de la colombe, Le / The Dove's Lost Necklace (Nacer Khemir, 1990, Tunisia)

Colline oubliée, La / The Forgotten Hillside (Abderrahmane Bouguermouh, 1996, Algeria)

Colonial Misunderstanding, The / Le Malentendu colonial (documentary) (Jean-Marie Teno, 2004, Cameroon)

Come and Meet / Taʾâla sallim (Helmi Rafla, 1951, Egypt)

Come and See What Sokkar Is Doing / Bouss chouf Soukkar bi-taʾmil îh (Achraf Fahmi, 1977, Egypt)

Come Back Africa (English, Lionel Ragosin, 1959, South Africa)

Come Back Mummy / ʿOudî yâ oummî (Abdel Rahman Chérif, 1961, Egypt)

Comedians, The (English, *No director credited*, 1985, South Africa)

Comédie exotique / Exotic Comedy (Kitia Touré, 1984, Ivory Coast)

Coming of Age (Zulu, *No director credited*, 1990, South Africa)

Coming Soon / Gayy fil sareeʾ (Gamal Kassem, 2005, Egypt)

Commander, The / al-Komandân (Ismaïl Hassan, 1986, Egypt)

Committed / The Intruder (English, William Levey, 1988, South Africa)

Completely Lost / al-Dâʾiʾah (Atef Salem, 1986, Egypt)

Complot d'Aristote, Le / Aristotle's Plot (Jean-Pierre Bekolo, 1996, Cameroon)

Composition of Time, The / Hisâb al-sinîn (Ahmed al-Sabaawi, 1978, Egypt)

Compromise, The / La Compromission (Latif Lahlou, 1986, Morocco)

Compromission, La / The Compromise (Latif Lahlou, 1986, Morocco)

Compulsory Holiday / Agâzah bi-l-ʾâfiyah (Nagdi Hafez, 1966, Egypt)

Conceição Tchimbula, a Day, a Life / Conceição Tchimbula, Um Dia, Uma Vida (António Ole, 1982, Angola)

Conceição Tchimbula, Um Dia, Uma Vida / Conceição Tchimbula, a Day, a Life (António Ole, 1982, Angola)

Concerto in the Street of Happiness / Concerto fi darb saʾaada (Asma al-Bakri, 2000, Egypt)

Concierge, The / Bawwâr al-ʾimârah (Alexandre Farkache, 1935, Egypt)

Confession, The / al-Iʾtirâf (Saad Arafa, 1965, Egypt)

Confessional, The / Koursî al-tirâf (Youssef Wahbi, 1949, Egypt)

Confessions of a Husband / Iʾtirâfât zawg (Fatine Abdel Wahab, 1964, Egypt)

Confetti Breakfast (English, Don Leonard, 1980, South Africa)

Confidences (Cyrille Masso, 2006, Cameroon)

Confrontation, The (*No director credited*, 1988, South Africa)

Confrontation, The / al-Mouwâgahah (Ahmed al-Sabaawi, 1987, Egypt)

Congratulations / Mabrouk (Fouad al-Gazaerli, 1937, Egypt)

Congratulations / Mabrouk ʿalîkî (Abdel Fattah Hassan, 1949, Egypt)

Congratulations / Mabruk alik (Gadalla Gubara, 1974, Sudan)

Conquer to Live / Vaincre pour vivre (Mohamed B. A. Tazi and Ahmed Mesnaoui, 1988, Morocco)

Conqueror of the Darkness / Qâhir al-zalâm (Atef Salem, 1979, Egypt)

Conqueror of the Horsemen / Qâhir al-foursân (Nasser Hussein, 1988, Egypt)

Conqueror of Time, The / Qâhir al-zaman (Kamal al-Cheikh, 1987, Egypt)

Conquest of Egypt, The / Fatʾh Misr (Fouad al-Gazaerli, 1948, Egypt)

Conscience / Uvalo / (Zulu, *No director credited*, 1988, South Africa)

Crime Lords, The (English, Wayne Crawford and Francis Schaeffer, 1990, South Africa)

Crime of Honor / Hâdithat charaf (Chafik Chamiyya, 1971, Egypt)

Crime of Love / Garîmat houbb (Atef Salem, 1959, Egypt)

Criminal, The / al-Mougrim (Kamal Ateyya, 1954, Egypt)

Criminal, The / al-Mougrim (Salah Abou Seif, 1978, Egypt)

Criminal Countenance / Wesh igraam (Wael Ihsaan, 2006, Egypt)

Criminal Despite Himself / Mougrim raghm anfih (Hassan al-Saïfi, 1991, Egypt)

Criminal on Holiday, A / Mougrim fî agâzah (Salah Abou Seif, 1958, Egypt)

Criminal Put to the Test, A / Mougrim taht al-ikhtibâr (Abdel Meneim Choukri, 1968, Egypt)

Criminal Troop 16 / al-Firqa 16 igraam (Hamid Saïd, 2006, Egypt)

Criminal with Honors / Mogrem maʾa martabet el sharaf (Medhat al-Sibaï, 1998, Egypt)

Croc (English, Elmo de Witt, 1989, South Africa)

Crocodile Creek / Ezimbomeni (Zulu, *No director credited*, 1989, South Africa)

Crook, The / al-Nassâb (Niazi Mostafa, 1961, Egypt)

Crook and the Dog, The / al-Nassâb wa-l-kalb (Adel Sadek, 1990, Egypt)

Crook and the Lady, The / al-Souʾlouk wa-l-hânim (Nasser Hussein, 1991, Egypt)

Crook's House, The / Bayt al-nattâch (Hassan Helmi, 1952, Egypt)

Crooked Saint / Saint-Voyou (Alphonse Béni, 1982, Cameroon)

Crooks, The / al-Nassaâbîn (Ahmed Yehya, 1984. Egypt)

Crooks, The / Les Bandits (Saïd Naciri, 2004, Morocco)

Cross, The (English, Ed Herbst, 1984, South Africa)

Crossing Over / Traversées (Mahmoud Ben Mahmoud, 1982, Tunisia)

Crossing the Line (English, Dean Goodhill and Gary Graver, 1990, South Africa)

Cry, The / al-Sarkhah (Mohamed al-Naggar, 1991, Egypt)

Cry Freedom (English, Ola Balogun, 1981, Nigeria)

Cry from the Heart, A / Le Cri de cœur (Idrissa Ouedraogo, 1994, Burkina Faso)

Cry in the Night, A / Sarkhah fî-layl (Ibrahim Lama, 1940, Egypt)

Cry Me a Teardrop (English, Keith G. van der Wat, 1974, South Africa)

Cry of Men, The / Le Cri des hommes (Okacha Touita, 1990, Algeria)

Cry of Remorse / Sarkat nadam (Mohamed Abdel Aziz, 1988, Egypt)

Cry of Stone / Cri de pierre (Abderrahmane Bouguermouh, 1986, Algeria)

Cry the Beloved Country (English, Zoltan Korda, 1951, South Africa)

Cry the Beloved Country (English, Darrell Roodt, 1994, South Africa)

Cry Vengeance (English, John Parr, 1988, South Africa)

Crystal Eye (English, Douglas Bristow and Joe Tornatore, 1988, South Africa)

Cultural Film / Film thaqaafi (Mohamed Amin, 2000, Egypt)

Cunning, The / al-Dâhiyah (Abdel Hadi Taha, 1986, Egypt)

Cunning Man, The / al-Ragoul al-thaʾlab (Nagdi Hafez, 1962, Egypt)

Cup, The / La Coupe (Mohamed Damak, 1986, Tunisia)

Cup of Suffering, The / Kâs al-ʾadhâb (Hassan al-Imam, 1952, Egypt)

Cupid / No Hero (English, Tim Spring, 1991, South Africa)

Curlew Has Lips, The / al-Karawân louh chafâyif (Hassan al-Imam, 1976, Egypt)

Curlew's Call, The / Douʾâʾ al-karawân (Henri Barakat, 1959, Egypt)

Curse, The / al-Laʾnah (Hussein al-Wakil, 1984. Egypt)

Curse, The (English, *No director credited*, 1987, South Africa)

Curse III: Blood Sacrifice, The / Panga Chance (English, Sean Barton, 1989, South Africa)

Cursed, The / al-Malaʾîn (Ahmed Yassine, 1979, Egypt)

Cursed House, The / al-Bayt al-malʾoun (Ahmed al-Khatib, 1987, Egypt)

Dangerous Life / Hayât khatirah (Ahmed Fouad, 1971, Egypt)

Dangerous Woman, A / Imra²ah khatirah (Ahmed Galal, 1941, Egypt)

Danie Bosman (Afrikaans, Elmo de Witt, 1969, South Africa)

Danish Experiment, The / al-Tagruba al-Danemarkeya (Ali Idris, 2003, Egypt)

Dans van die Vlamink (Afrikaans, Ivan Hall, 1974, South Africa)

Danse du feu, La / The Fire Dance (Selma Baccar, 1995, Tunisia)

Danse du vent, La / The Wind Dance (Taïeb Louhichi, 2004, Tunisia)

Danse mon amour / Dance My Love (Alphonse Béni, 1979, Cameroon)

Daqqet Zar / Daqqat zâr (Ahmed Yassine, 1986, Egypt)

Daratt / Dry Season (Mahamat Saleh Haroun, 2006, Chad)

Daresalam (Issa Serge Coelo, 2000, Chad)

Dark City (English, Chris Curling, 1989, South Africa)

Dark Forces (English, *No director credited*, 1988, South Africa)

Dark Glasses / al-Nadhdhârah al-sawdâ² (Houssam Eddine Mostafa, 1963, Egypt)

Dark Horse (English, Dupreez Heunis, 1996, South Africa)

Dark Mountain (English, Robert Davies, 1988, South Africa)

Dark of the Sun / The Mercenaries (English, Jack Cardiff, 1967

Dark Warrior, The (Zulu, David Bensusan, 1987, South Africa)

Dark-Haired Girl from the Sinaï, The / Samrâ² Sinâ² (Niazi Mostafa, 1959, Egypt)

Date Wine / ᶜAra² el balah (Radwane al-Kachef, 1999, Egypt)

Daughter of Aristocrats / Bint al-akâbir (Anwar Wagda, 1953, Egypt)

Daughters of Eve, The / Banât Hawwâ (Niazi Mostafa, 1954, Egypt)

Daughters of Satan / Banât Iblîs (Ali Abdel Khalek, 1984. Egypt)

Davey (English, Louise Smit, 1987, South Africa)

David Livingstone (Silent, M. A. Weatherell, 1925, South Africa)

Dawn, The /L'Aube (Omar Khlifi, 1966, Tunisia)

Dawn Farewells / Wadâ² fî-l-fagr (Hassan al-Imam, 1956, Egypt)

Dawn of a New Day, The / Fagr yawm gadîd (Youssef Chahine, 1965, Egypt)

Dawn of Islam, The / Fagr al-Islâm (Salah Abou Seif, 1971, Egypt)

Dawn of the Damned / L'Aube des damnés (Ahmed Rachedi, 1965, Algeria)

Day I Fell in Love, The / Kaan youm houbbak (Iaab Lamei, 2004, Egypt)

Day of Dignity, The / Youm el karama (Ali Abdel Khalek, 2004, Egypt)

Day of Greatness, A / Yawm fî-l-âlî (Hussein Fawzi, 1946, Egypt)

Day of Judgment / Yawm al-hisâb (Abdel Rahman Chérif, 1962, Egypt)

Day of Telling Lies, The / Sabahu kedb (Mohamed al-Naggar, 2007, Egypt)

Day without Tomorrow / Yawm bilâ ghad (Henri Barakat, 1962, Egypt)

Days, The Days, The / Oh les jours (Ahmed El Maânouni, 1978, Morocco)

Days and Nights / Ayyâm wa layâlî (Henri Barakat, 1955, Egypt)

Day's Business, The / Qadiyyat al-yawm (Kamal Selim, 1943, Egypt)

Days of Evil / Ayyaam al-charr (Youssef Abou Seif, 1995, Egypt)

Days of Glory / Indigènes (Rachid Bouchareb, 2005, Algeria)

Days of Love / Ayyâm al-houbb (Helmi Halim, 1968, Egypt)

Days of Sadat / Ayyaam El Sadat (Mohamed Khan, 2001, Egypt)

Days of Torment / Jours de tourmente (Paul Zoumbara, 1983, Burkina Faso)

Days' Struggle, The / Sirâ² al-ayyâm (Youssef Charaf Eddine, 1985, Egypt)

Days without Love / Ayyâm bilâ houbb (Houssam Eddine Mostafa, 1962, Egypt)

Daytime Devil / ᶜAfreet al-nahaar (Adel al-Aassar, 1997, Egypt)

De Hollywood à Tanarasset / From Hollywood to Tanarasset (Mohamed Zemmouri, 1990, Algeria)

De l'autre côté du fleuve / From the Other Side of the River (Mohamed Abbazi, 1982, Morocco)

De quelques événements sans signification / About

Some Meaningless Events (Mostafa Derkaoui, 1974, Morocco)
De Voortrekkers / Winning a Continent (Silent, Harold Shaw, 1916, South Africa)
De Wet's Spoor / Guns Across the Veld (Afrikaans, Howard Rennie, 1975, South Africa)
Dead among the Living / Bidâyah wa nihâyah (Salah Abou Seif, 1960, Egypt)
Dead Easy (English, Neal Sundström, 2004, South Africa)
Dead End / al-Tarîq al-masdoud (Salah Abou Seif, 1958, Egypt)
Dead End / L'Impasse (Mustapha Khayat, 1984, Morocco)
Dead End of the Two-Palaces, The / Bayn al-qasrayn (Hassan al-Imam, 1964, Egypt)
Dead Ringer (English, Frans Nel, 1989, South Africa)
Dead the Long Night / Morte la longue nuit (collective, 1979, Algeria)
Deadly Hunter / Pursuit (English, John Parr, 1990, South Africa)
Deadly Licence / Double X (English, Larry Larson, 1989, South Africa)
Deadly Obsession (English, Jeno Hodi, 1985, South Africa)
Deadly Passion (English, Larry Larson, 1985, South Africa)
Deaf Boy (English, *No director credited,* 1981, South Africa)
Deal for Danger (English, *No director credited,* 1987, South Africa)
Deal Made with a Woman, A / Safqah ma' imra'ah (Adel al-Aassar, 1985, Egypt)
Dealer, The (English, *No director credited,* 1985, South Africa)
Dearer than My Life / Aghlâ min hayâtî (Mahmoud Zoulficar, 1965, Egypt)
Dearer than the Pupils of My Eyes / Aghlâ min 'aynayya (Ezz Eddine Zoulficar, 1955, Egypt)
Dearest to My Heart / A'azz al-habâyib (Youssef Maalouf, 1961, Egypt)
Dearest Uncle Zizou / Oncle Zizou habîbî (Niazi Mostafa, 1977, Egypt)
Dearest, We Are All Thieves / Yâ 'azîzî koullounâ lousous (Ahmed Yeyha, 1989, Egypt)
Death Dance (English, Derrick Louw, 1993, South Africa)
Death Force (English, Frans Nel, 1988, South Africa)
Death in Camera (English, *No director credited,* 1989, South Africa)
Death Is a Stranger / Streets (English, *No director credited,* 1988, South Africa)
Death of a Snowman (English, Christopher Rowley, 1982, South Africa)
Death of a Witness (English, *No director credited,* 1989, South Africa)
Death of the Black President (English, Eddie Ugbomah, 1984, Nigeria)
Death on Safari / Ten Little Indians (English, Allan Birkinshaw, 1988, South Africa)
Death Walkers (English, Joey Ford, 1988, South Africa)
Debauched, The / al-Hanâkîch (Ali Abdel Khalek, 1986, Egypt)
Debbie (Afrikaans, Elmo de Witt, 1965, South Africa)
December / Décembre (Mohamed Lakhdar Hamina, 1972, Algeria)
Décembre / December (Mohamed Lakhdar Hamina, 1972, Algeria)
Déchirure, La / The Tear (Alphonse Béni, 2005, Cameroon)
Decision to Die / The Dr. Walters Trial (English, Dirk de Villers, 1978, South Africa)
Decor (English, *No director credited,* 1982, South Africa)
Dede (Tom Ribeiro, 1983, Ghana)
Deer in the Night, The / Sab' al-layl (Hassan al-Saïfi, 1971, Egypt)
Deer Run, The / Garî al-wouhouch (Ali Abdel Khalek, 1987, Egypt)
Deer's Blood / Damm El-Ghazaal (Mohamed Yassin, 2006, Egypt)
Defense, The / al-Difâ (Youssef Wahbi, 1935, Egypt)
Defender of Poor People, The / Foutouwwat al-nâs al-ghalâbah (Niazi Mostafa, 1984. Egypt)
Défi, Le / The Challenge (Omar Khlifi, 1986, Tunisia)
Degenerate, The / al-Ma'touh (Kamal Ateyya, 1982, Egypt)
Déja Vu, Vanessa (English, Laurens Barnard, 1990, South Africa)
Délice Paloma / Paloma Sweets (Nadir Moknèche, 2007, Algeria)

Delicious Killing / al-Katl el lazeez (Ashraf Fahmi, 1998, Egypt)

Delinquents, The / al-Mounharifoun (Niazi Mostafa, 1976, Egypt)

Delta Force 2—Mayday (English, Yossi Wein, 1997, South Africa)

Delta Force 3—Clear Target (English, Mark Roper, 1997, South Africa)

Delwende / Delwende, lève-toi et marche (Pierre S. Yaméogo, 2005, Burkina Faso)

Delwende, lève-toi et marche / Delwende (Pierre S. Yaméogo, 2005, Burkina Faso)

Demain je brûle / Tomorrow I Burn (Mohamed Ben Smaïl, 1998, Tunisia)

Demain la terre ne changera pas / Tomorrow the Land Will Not Change (Abdellah Mesbahi, 1975, Morocco)

Demain un nouveau jour / Tomorrow Is a New Day (Pierre-Marie Dong, 1978, Gabon)

Démences / Madness (Fadhel Jaïbi, 2006, Tunisia)

Demon, The / al-Chaytân (Mohamed Salmane, 1969, Egypt)

Demon, The / Midnight Caller (English, Percival Rubens, 1980, South Africa)

Démon au féminin, Le / The Female Devil (Hafsa Zinaï-Koudil, 1993, Algeria)

Demon of the Desert, The / Chaytân al-sahrâ (Youssef Chahine, 1954, Egypt)

Demons of Heaven, The / Chayâtîn al-gaww (Niazi Mostafa, 1956, Egypt)

Demons of the Night / Chayâtîn al-layl (Niazi Mostafa, 1966, Egypt)

Demons of the Sea, The / Chayâtîn al-bahr (Houssam Eddine Mostafa, 1972, Egypt)

Den Kasso (Sega Coulibaly, 1978, Mali)

Den muso / La Jeune fille / The Girl (Souleymane Cisse, 1975, Mali)

Denunciation of a Woman, A / Balâgh didd imraᵓah (Ahmed al-Sabaawi, 1986, Egypt)

Déracinés, Les / The Uprooted (Mohamed Lamine Merbah, 1976, Algeria)

Dernier salaire, Le / Desebagato (Emmanuel Kalifa Sanon, 1987, Burkina Faso)

Dernière image, La / The Last Image (Mohamed Lakhdar Hamina, 1986, Algeria)

Des années déchirées / Shattered Years (Rachid Bouchareb, 1992, Algeria)

Des pas dans le brouillard / Steps in the Mist (Hamid Benchrif, 1982, Morocco)

Desebagato / Le Dernier salaire (Emmanuel Kalifa Sanon, 1987, Burkina Faso)

Desert Ark, The / L'Arche du désert (Mohamed Chouikh, 1997, Algeria)

Desert Cat / Qett al-saharaaᵓ (Saïd Marzouk and Youssef Mansour, 1995, Egypt)

Desert Diners (English, François Coertze, 1999, South Africa)

Desert Horseman, The / Fâris al-sahrâᵓ (Oswaldo Cheferani, 1966, Egypt)

Desert Inn, The (English, Immel Botha, 1959, South Africa)

Desert Rose / Rose des sables / Louss (Mohamed Rachid Benhadj, 1988, Algeria)

Deserter, The (English, David Bensusan, 1990, South Africa)

Deserter, The / Hârib min al-tagᵓnîd (Ahmed al-Sabaawi, 1992, Egypt)

Desire / al-Raghbah (Ali Badrakhan, 2002, Egypt)

Desire / al-Raghbah (Mohamed Khan, 1980, Egypt)

Desire and Its Cost / al-Raghbah wa-l-thaman (Youssef Chabaane Mohamed, 1978, Egypt)

Desire and Perdition / al-Raghbah wa-l-dayâᵓ (Ahmed Diaa Eddine, 1973, Egypt)

Desire, Malice and Violence / Raghbahj wa hiqd wa intiqâm (Sayed Seif, 1986, Egypt)

Desires / Raghbât (Karim Diaa Eddine, 1994, Egypt)

Destin de femme / A Woman's Fate (Hakim Noury, 1998, Morocco)

Destin, Le / Mogho Dakan (Sega Coulibaly, 1976, Mali)

Destiny / al-Masseer (Youssef Chahine, 1997, Egypt)

Destiny / Dakan (Mohamed Camara, 1997, Guinea)

Detectives (*No director credited,* 1987, South Africa)

Deux femmes sur la route / Two Women on the Road (Farida Bourquia, 2007, Morocco)

Deux larrons en folie / Two Thieves in Madness (Ali Mansour, 1980, Tunisia)

Deviation / Inhirâf (Taysir Abboud, 1985, Egypt)

Devil and Autumn, The / al-Chaytân wa-l-kharîf (Anwar al-Chennawi, 1972, Egypt)

Devil and the Song, The (English, Bromley Cawood, 1987, South Africa)

Devil Finds a Solution, The / al-Chaytân youqa-

Discussions on the Nile / Thartharah fawq al-Nîl (Hussein Kamal, 1971, Egypt)

Diseurs de vérité, Les / The Truth Tellers (Karim Traïdia, 2000, Algeria)

Diseurs d'histoires, Les / The Story Tellers (documentary) (Mohamed Soudani, 1998, Algeria)

Disgrace / al-ᵓÂr (Ali Abdel Khalek, 1982, Egypt)

Dishonor / Wasmat ᶜâr (Achraf Fahmi, 1986, Egypt)

Dish-Ups / Abaphangi (No director credited, 1986, South Africa)

Disillusion (Duniyi Areke, 1991, Nigeria).

Disorder / Khaltabîtah (Medhat al-Sibaï, 1994, Egypt)

Dit was Aand en dit was Môre (Afrikaans, Franz Marx, 1978, South Africa)

Dive, The / al-Ghawwaas (Fakhr Eddine Negeda, 2006, Egypt)

Divided Loyalties (English, Harry Mayer, 1989, South Africa)

Divine Justice / ᶜAdl al-samâ (Ahmed Kamel Morsi, 1948, Egypt)

Divine Miracle / Mouᵓguizat al-samâᵓ (Atef Salem, 1956, Egypt)

Divorced, The / al-Moutaalaqât (Ismaïl al-Qadi, 1975, Egypt)

Divorced Woman, A / Imraᵓah moutallaqah (Achraf Fahmi, 1986, Egypt)

Dizziness of Passion, The / Le Vertige de la passion (Armand Balima, 1985, Burkina Faso)

Dizzy Spell (English, No director credited, 1987, South Africa)

Djanta (Tahirou Tasséré Ouédraogo, 2007, Burkina Faso)

Djeli (Kramo Lanciné Fadika, 1981, Ivory Coast)

Djib (Jean Odoutan, 2000, Bénin)

Do Not Ask Me Who I Am / Lâ tasᵓalnî man anâ (Achraf Fahmi, 1984. Egypt)

Do Not Destroy Me Along with Yourself / Lâ toudammirnî maᵓak (Mohamed Abdel Aziz, 1986, Egypt)

Do Not Oppress Women / Lâ tadhlimou al-nisâᵓ (Hassan al-Imam, 1980, Egypt)

Do Your Own Thing (Bernard Odidja, 1971, Ghana)

Doctor, The / al-Doktor (Niazi Mostafa, 1939, Egypt)

Doctor Farhat / al-Doktor Farhât (Togo Mizrahi, 1935, Egypt)

Doctor from Gafiré, The / Le Médecin de Gafiré (Moustapha Diop, 1982, Niger)

Doctor Ibrahim's Secret / Sirr al-doktor Ibrâhîm (Maurice Aptekman, 1937, Egypt)

Doctor Luke (English, Jimmy Murray, 1982, South Africa)

Does He Think That . . . / Ayazun (Akram Farid, 2006, Egypt)

Dog Bite, A / ᶜAddat kalb (Hassan al-Saïfi, 1983, Egypt)

Dog Squad (English, Tim Spring, 1973, South Africa)

Doigt dans l'engrenage, Le / A Finger in the Works (Ahmed Rachedi, 1974, Algeria)

Dôlè (Léon Imunga Ivanga, 1999, Gabon)

Dollars and White Pipes (English, Donovan Marsh, 2005, South Africa)

Don de dieu, Le / Wend Kuuni / God's Gift (Gaston Kaboré, 1982, Burkina Faso)

Don't Be Unjust / al-Dhoulm harâm (Hassan al-Saïfi, 1954, Egypt)

Don't Deny Your Ancestors / Man fâta qadîmouh (Farid al-Guindi, 1943, Egypt)

Don't Extinguish the Sun / Lâ toufiᵓ al-chams (Salah Abou Seif, 1961, Egypt)

Don't Leave Me Alone / La tatrouknî wahdî (Hassan al-Imam, 1975, Egypt)

Don't Tell Anyone / Mâ tᵓoulch li-hadd (Henri Barakat, 1952, Egypt)

Don't Think About It / Ouᵓâ tifakkar (Elhami Hassan, 1954, Egypt)

Don't Think of Me Anymore / Lâ tadhkourînî (Mahmoud Zoulficar, 1961, Egypt)

Donker Afrika (Afrikaans, David Mullin, 1957, South Africa)

Donker Spore (Afrikaans, Thomas Block, 1944, South Africa)

Doodkry is Min (Afrikaans, Jamie Uys, 1961, South Africa)

Dooie Duikers Deel Nie / No Gold for a Dead Diver (Afrikaans, Heinz Reinhl, 1974, South Africa)

Doomsday (No director credited, 1986, South Africa)

Doomsday (Neil Marshall, 2007, South Africa)

Doorman Is at Your Service, The / Sâhib al-idârah bawwâb al-ᵓimârah (Nadia Salem, 1985, Egypt)

Doorman, The / al-Bîh al-bawâb (Hassan Ibrahim, 1987, Egypt)

Dose of Hashish, The / al-Qirch (Ibrahim Afifi, 1981, Egypt)

Douar de femmes / Hamlet of Women (Mohamed Chouikh, 2005, Algeria)

Double Cross (*No director credited*, 1988, South Africa)

Double Deal (English, A. Hattingh, 1984, South Africa)

Double Trouble (English, *No director credited*, 1989, South Africa)

Double X / Deadly Licence (English, Larry Larson, 1989, South Africa)

Doubt, My Love / al-Chakk yâ habîbî (Henri Barakat, 1979, Egypt)

Doubt Which Kills, The / al-Chakk al-qâtil (Ezz Eddine Zoulficar, 1953, Egypt)

Douce France / Sweet France (Malek Chibane, 1995, Algeria)

Dounia / Douniâ (Abdel Meneim Choukri, 1974, Egypt)

Dounia / Douniâ (Mohamed Karim, 1946, Egypt)

Dounia Abdel Gabbar / Douniâ Abd al-Gabhâr (Abdel Latif Zaki, 1992, Egypt)

Dove of Peace, The / Hamâmat al-salâm (Helmi Rafla, 1947, Egypt)

Dove's Lost Necklace, The / Le Collier perdu de la colombe (Nacer Khemir, 1990, Tunisia)

Down with Colonialism / Yasqout al-istiᵓmâr (Hussein Sedki, 1952, Egypt)

Down with Love / Yasqout al-houbb (Ibrahim Lama, 1944, Egypt)

Downtown Girls / Banaat wist al-balad (Mohamed Khan, 2005, Egypt)

Dozen Handkerchiefs, A / Dastit manâdîl (Abbas Kamel, 1954, Egypt)

Dr. Kalie (Afrikaans, Ivan Hall, 1968, South Africa)

Dr. Manal Dances / al-Doktorah Nanâl tarqous (Saïd Marzouk, 1991, Egypt)

Dr. Marius Hugo (Afrikaans, Tim Spring, 1978, South Africa)

Dr. Omar's Gang / ᶜIsabet al-Doktoor Omar (Ali Idris, 2007, Egypt)

Dr. Walters Trial, The / Decision to Die (English, Dirk de Villers, 1978, South Africa)

Dracula 3000 (English, Darrell Roodt, 2004, South Africa)

Dragonard (English, Dominique Jones and Gerard Kikoine, 1987, South Africa)

Drama of the 40,000, The / Le Drame des 40,000 (Ahmed Kacem Akdi, 1982, Morocco)

Drame des 40,000, Le / The Drama of the 40,000 (Ahmed Kacem Akdi, 1982, Morocco)

Dream Princess, The / Amîrat al-ahlâm (Ahmed Galal, 1945, Egypt)

Dream Thief, The / Le Voleur de rêves (Hakim Noury, 1995, Morocco)

Dreamer / Molori (Tswana, David Bensusan, 1989, South Africa)

Dreams of a Reckless Young Man / Ahlam al-fata al taᵓish (Sameh Abdel Aziz, 2007, Egypt)

Dreams of Hind and Camellia / Ahlâm Hind wa Kâmîliya (Mohamed Khan, 1988, Egypt)

Dreams of Love / Ahlâm al-houbb (Fouad al-Gazaerli, 1945, Egypt)

Dreams of Youth / Ahlâm al-chabâb (Kamal Selim, 1942, Egypt)

Drie van der Merwes, Die (Afrikaans, Dirk de Villiers, 1970, South Africa)

Driven from Paradise / al-Khouroug min al-gannah (Mahmoud Zoulficar, 1967, Egypt)

Driven from Paradise / Tarîd al-Fardous (Fatine Abdel Wahab, 1965, Egypt)

Drug Addict, The / al-Moudmin (Youssef Francis, 1983, Egypt)

Drug Addicts, The / al-Masâtîl (Hussein Kamal, 1991, Egypt)

Drug Smugglers, The (English, *No director credited*, 1989, South Africa)

Drug, The / al-Kîf (Ali Abdel Khalek, 1985, Egypt)

Drum (English, Zola Maseko, 2004, South Africa)

Drums in the Night / Touboul fi-l-layl (Nasser Hussein, 1987, Egypt)

Dry Eyes / Les Yeux secs (Narjiss Nejjar, 2002, Morocco)

Dry Season / Daratt (Mahamat Saleh Haroun, 2006, Chad)

Du donner et du recevoir / Give and Take (Dansogho Mohamed Camara, 1977, Guinea)

Du paradis à l'enfer / From Heaven to Hell (Said Souda, 2000, Morocco)

Dukki Nightingale / ᵓAndaleeb al-dukki (Wael Ihsan, 2007, Egypt)

Duma (English, Caroll Ballard, 2004, South Africa)

Dumela Sam (English / Sotho, Clive Scott and Jimmy Murray, 1981, South Africa)

Dune Surfer / Kalahari Surfer (English, Heinrich Dahms, 1989, South Africa)

Dunia / Dunia (Jocelyne Saab, 2006, Egypt)

Dunia / Le Monde (Pierre S. Yaméogo, 1987, Burkina Faso)

Dusk and Dawn / Ghouroub wa chourouq (Kamal al-Cheikh, 1970, Egypt)

Dust Devils (English, Richard Stanley, 1991, South Africa)

Duty / al-Wâguib (Henri Barakat, 1948, Egypt)

Dwarves Arrive, The / al-Aqzâm qâdimoun (Cherif Arafa, 1987, Egypt)

Dynamite Jackson (English, No director credited, 1984, South Africa)

'e Lollipop / Lollipop (English, Ashley Lazarus, 1975, South Africa)

Each According to His Rank / al-Nâs maqâmât (al-Sayed Ziyada, 1954, Egypt)

Each Beat of My Heart / Koull daqqah fî qalbî (Ahmed Diaa Eddine, 1959, Egypt)

Each Household Has Its Man / Koull bayt louh Râguil (Ahmed Kamel Morsi, 1949, Egypt)

Eagle, The (Zulu, Simon Sabela, 1976, South Africa)

Early One Morning / Un matin de bonne heure (Gahité Fofana, 2005, Guinea).

Earth, The / al-Ard (Youssef Chahine, 1970, Egypt)

Earth's Storm, The / A tempestade da terra (Fernando D'Almeida e Silva, 1996, Mozambique)

Easy Kill / Halfway House (English, Josh Spencer, 1988, South Africa)

Ebony White / Blanc d'Ebène (Cheik Doukoure, 1991, Guinea)

Échec et mat / Check and Mate (Rachid Ferchiou, 1995, Tunisia)

Éclair nocturne / Barg Ellil (Ali Abidi, 1990, Tunisia)

Edge of Innocence / Eendag vir Altyd (Afrikaans, Chris du Toit, 1985, South Africa)

Edge of the Sword Blade, The / Hadd al-sayf (Atef Salem, 1986, Egypt)

Edges of the Heart / Les Arêtes du cœur (Hichem Ayouch, 2006, Morocco)

Eendag op in Reëndag / Die Rousseaus van La Rochelle (Afrikaans, Jans Rautenbach, 1975, South Africa)

Eendag vir Altyd / Edge of Innocence (Afrikaans, Chris du Toit, 1985, South Africa)

Eensame Vlug, Die (Afrikaans, Jan Schultz, 1979, South Africa)

Eewo / Taboo (English, Ladi Ladebo, 1989, Nigeria)

Efunsetan Aniwura (Yoruba, Bankole Bello, 1982, Nigeria)

Egg and the Stone, The / al-Baydah wa-l-hagar (Ali Abdel Khalek, 1990, Egypt)

Egocentric, The / ʿÂchiqat nafsihâ (Mounir al-Touni, 1972, Egypt)

Egotist, The / Khudgarz (Brijmohun Brothers, 1988, Mauritius)

Egunleri (Yoruba, Mukaila Ajaga, 1985, Nigeria)

Egyptian in Lebanon, An / Masrî fî Loubnân (Gianni Vernuccio, 1952, Egypt)

Egyptian Story, An / Haddoutah masriyyah (Youssef Chahine, 1982, Egypt)

Ehin Oku (Yoruba, Adeyemi Afolayan, 1992, Nigeria)

Ehlathini / Veld (Zulu, No director credited, 1988, South Africa)

Eighth of a Dozen Thugs / 1/8 Dastet Ashrar (Rami Imam, 2006, Egypt)

85 at the Crime / 85 Guinâyat (Alaa Karim, 1993, Egypt)

Either You Love . . . or You Leave / Yâ thibb . . . yâ tʾibb (Abdel Latif Zaki, 1994, Egypt)

Ejo Ngboro (Yoruba, Tubosun Odunsi, 1989, Nigeria)

Ek sal Opstaan (Afrikaans, Kappie Botha, 1959, South Africa)

El Chergui / El Chergui ou le silence violent (Moumen Smihi, 1975, Morocco)

El Chergui ou le silence violent / El Chergui (Moumen Smihi, 1975, Morocco)

El Goula (Mustapha Kateb, 1972, Algeria)

El Haj Million (collective, 1972, Guinea)

El Manara (Belkacem Hadjadj, 2004, Algeria)

El Moufid / The Benevolent (Amar Laskri, 1978, Algeria)

El Ouelf essaib (Mohamed Hilmi, 1990, Algeria)

El Turbini / El-turbini (Ahmed Medhat, 2007, Egypt)

El-Alamain / al-ʾAlamayn (Abdel Alim Khattab, 1965, Egypt)

Elder Brother, The / al-Akhkh al-kabîr (Fatine Abdel Wahab, 1958, Egypt)

Elegant, the Noble and the Greedy, The / al-Zarîf wa-l-charhm wa-l-tammâʾ (Nour al-Dermerdache, 1971, Egypt)

Elephant's Balls, The / Les Couilles de l'éléphant (Henri-Joseph Koumba-Bididi, 2001, Gabon)

Enquiry with a Citizen / Tahqîq maʾ mouwâtinah (Henri Barakat, 1993, Egypt)

Enraged, The / al Ghadeboon (Tarek al-Nahri, 1996, Egypt)

Entropy (English, Phil Joanou, South Africa, 1998)

Envers du miroir, L' / The Other Side of the Mirror (Nadia Cherabi-Labidi, 2007, Algeria)

Enzintandaneni / A Boy Who Needs a Home (Zulu, *No director credited*, 1987, South Africa)

Epic of Cheikh Bouamama, The / L'Épopée de Cheikh Bouamama (Benamar Bakhti, 1982, Algeria)

Épopée de Cheikh Bouamama, L' / The Epic of Cheikh Bouamama (Benamar Bakhti, 1982, Algeria)

Equal in Misfortune / Fî-l-hawâ sawâ (Youssef Maalouf, 1951, Egypt)

Era of Challenge, The / Ayyâm al-tahaddî (Adli Youssef, 1985, Egypt)

Era of Hatem Zahran, The / Zaman Hâtim Zahrân (Mohamed el-Naggar, 1988, Egypt)

Era of Prohibitions, The / Zaman al-mamnouʾ (Inas al-Deghidi, 1988, Egypt)

Era of the Powerful, The / ʿAsr al-qouwwah (Nader Galal, 1991, Egypt)

Erfgenaam, Die (Afrikaans, Koos Roets, 1971, South Africa)

Erfgoed is Sterfgoed (Afrikaans, Jan Breytenbach, 1976, South Africa)

Eri Okan (Yoruba, Tunde Oloyede, 1990, Nigeria)

Ernest in Africa (English, John Cherry, 1997, South Africa)

Ernest in the Army (English, John Cherry, 1997, South Africa)

Errances / Wanderings—aka Terre en cendres / Land of Ashes (Djafar Damardjji, 1993, Algeria)

Error of My Life, The / Ghaltat al-ʾoumr (Mahmoud Zoulficar, 1953, Egypt)

Esan Ake (Yoruba, Eddie Ugbomah, 1985, Nigeria)

Escape Route Cape Town (English, Robert R. Webb, 1967, South Africa)

Escape to the Summit / al-Horoub ila al-qimma (Adel al-Aassar, 1996, Egypt)

Escape, The / al-Houroub (Atef al-Tayeb, 1991, Egypt)

Escaped from Hell / al-Liss wa-l-kilâb (Kamal al-Cheikh, 1962, Egypt)

Escaped from Life / Hârib min al-hayât (Atef Salem, 1964, Egypt)

Escaped Prisoner, The / al-Hârib (Ibrahim Lama, 1936, Egypt)

Escaped Prisoner, The / Hârb min al-sigʾn (Mohamed Abdel Gawad, 1948, Egypt)

Escapee to Prison / Hareb ila al-sign (Yassine Ismaïl Yassine, 1995, Egypt)

Espoir, L' / Jigi (Kollo Daniel Sanou, 1992, Burkina Faso)

Esquive, L' / The Scam (Abdellatif Kechiche, 2004, Tunisia)

Essaïda (Mohamed Zran, 1996, Tunisia)

Estorvo / Mixed Up (Ruy Guerra, Mozambique, 2003)

Et après? / And Afterwards? (Mohamed Ismaïl, 2002, Morocco)

Et demain? / And Tomorrow? (Brahim Babaï, 1972, Tunisia)

Et le Sourire revient / And the Smile Returns (Ramesh Tekoit, 1980, Mauritius)

Eternal Glory / al-Magd al-khâlid (Youssef Wahbi, 1937, Egypt)

Eternal Love / al-Houbb al-khâlid (Zouheir Bekir, 1965, Egypt)

Eternal Love / Houbb lâ Yamout (Mohamed Karim, 1948, Egypt)

Etoile noire, L' / The Black Star (Djingary Maiga, 1975, Niger)

Étranger, L' / Toungan / The Foreigner (Mamadou Djim Kola, 1992, Burkina Faso)

Evasion / Houroub (Hassan Reda, 1970, Egypt)

Évasion de Hassan Terro, L' / Hassan Terro's Escape (Mustapha Badie, 1974, Algeria)

Eve and the Gorilla / Hawwâʾ wa-l-qird (Niazi Mostafa, 1968, Egypt)

Eve of the Wedding, The / Laylat al-hinnah (Anwar Magdi, 1951, Egypt)

Eve on the Road / Hawwâʾ ʿalâ al-tarîq (Hussein Helmi al-Mouhandès, 1968, Egypt)

Eve's Lies / Akâdhîb Hawwâ (Fatine Abdel Wahab, 1969, Egypt)

Evening Visitor, The / Zâʾir al-fagr (Mamdouh Choukri, 1975, Egypt)

Ever-opened Eyes / ʿOuyoun lâ tanâm (Raafat al-Mihi, 1981, Egypt)

Falcon, The / al-Saqr (Salah Abou Seif, 1950, Egypt)

Falcon's Eyes, The / ʿOuyoun al-saqr (Ibrahim al-Mogui, 1992, Egypt)

Fall, The / al-Souqout (Adel al-Aassar, 1990, Egypt)

Fall of the House of Usher, The (English, Allan Birkinshaw, 1988, South Africa)

Fallen Leaves (Silent, Dick Cruikshanks, 1919, South Africa)

Fallen Woman / Imraʾah âyilah li-l-souqout (Medhat al-Sibaï, 1992, Egypt)

False Bey, The / al-Beh al-mouzayyat (Ibrahim Lama, 1945, Egypt)

False Millionnaire, The / al-Millionnaire al-mouzayyaf (Hassan al-Saïfi, 1968, Egypt)

Falsification of Official Papers / Tazwîr fî awrâq rasmiyyah (Yehya al-Alami, 1984. Egypt)

Fame in the Street / La Gloire dans la rue (Nkieri Ngunia Wawa, 1980, Democratic Republic of Congo)

Family Man / The Nightmare (English, John Murlowski, 1988, South Africa)

Family, The / Abusuan (Henri Duparc, 1972, Ivory Coast)

Famous Affair, The / al-Qadiyyah al-machhourah (Hassan al-Imam, 1978, Egypt)

Fanakalo (Zulu, Ronnie Isaacs, 1984, South Africa)

Fangs / Anyâb (Mohamed Chebl, 1981, Egypt)

Far from the Land / Baʾîdan ʿan al-ard (Hussein Kamal, 1976, Egypt)

Far Off Place, A (English, Mikael Salomon, 1993, South Africa)

Farah / Farah (Akram Farid, 2004, Egypt)

Faraw! / Faraw! une mère des sables (Abdoulaye Ascafare, 1996, Mali)

Faraw! une mère des sables / Faraw! (Abdoulaye Ascafare, 1996, Mali)

Farès Bani Hamdan / Fâris banî Hamdân (Niazi Mostafa, 1966, Egypt)

Farewell Bonaparte / al-Wadâʾ yâ Bonaparte (Youssef Chahine, 1985, Egypt)

Farewell Dance, The / Taqsat al-wadâʾ (Ezz Eddine Zoulficar, 1954, Egypt)

Farewell for Ever / Wadâʾan ilâ al-abad (Abdel Rahman Kikkya, 1976, Egypt)

Farewell Mothers / Adieu mères (Mohamed Ismaïl, 2007, Morocco)

Farewell My Child / Wadâʾan yâ waladî (Taysir Abboud, 1986, Egypt)

Farewell My Love / Wadâʾan yâ gharâmî (Omar Guemei, 1951, Egypt)

Farewell My Love / Waddaʾtou houbbak (Youssef Chahine, 1956, Egypt)

Farewell to Love / Wadâʾan yâ houbb (Houssam Eddine Mostafa, 1960, Egypt)

Farewell to Suffering / Wadâʾan li-l-ʾadhâb (Ahmed Yehya, 1981, Egypt)

Farewell to the Night / Wadâʾan ayyouhâ al-layl (Hassan Reda, 1966, Egypt)

Farhan Mulazem Adam / Farhan Mulazem Adam (Omar Abdel Aziz, 2005, Egypt)

Faro, la reine des eaux / Faro, Queen of the Waters (Salif Traoré, 2006, Mali)

Faro, Queen of the Waters / Faro, la reine des eaux (Salif Traoré, 2006, Mali)

Fast Movers (English, No director credited, 1990, South Africa)

Fat Cats, The / al-Qitat al-simân (Hassan Youssef, 1981, Egypt)

Fatal Dream, The / al-Houlm al-qâtil (Adel al-Aassar, 1986, Egypt)

Fatal Jealousy / al-Ghîrah al-qâtilah (Atef al-Tayeb, 1982, Egypt)

Fatal Mission / Kwavinga Run / The Rat (English, Anthony Bond and Tonie van der Merwe, 1990, South Africa)

Fatal Phone Call, The / al-Mukalama al-qatela (Yassine Ismaïl Yassine, 1996, Egypt)

Fatality / al-Nasîb maktoub (Nasser Hussein, 1987, Egypt)

Fate / al-Mouqaddar wa-l-maktoub (Abbas Kamel, 1953, Egypt)

Fate of the Famous (Zulu, No director credited, 1984, South Africa)

Fate's Laughter / Dihkât al-qadar (Elhami Hassan, 1955, Egypt)

Father, The / al-Abb (Omar Guemei, 1947, Egypt)

Father's Mistake, A / Ghaltat ʿabb (Henri Barakat, 1952, Egypt)

Father's Revolt, A / al-Abb al-thâʾir (Tarek al-Nahri, 1988, Egypt)

Fathiyyah and the Mercedes / Fathiyyah wa-l-marsîdès (Saïd Mohamed Marzouk, 1992, Egypt)

Fatima, l'Algérienne de Dakar / Fatima, the Alge-

Final Solution (English, Chris Crusen, 2000, South Africa)

Final Solution, The / al-Hall al-akhîr (Abdel Fattah Hassan, 1937, Egypt)

Find Livingstone / Finden sie Livingstone (English, Theodore Grädler, 1968, South Africa)

Finden sie Livingstone / Find Livingstone (English, Theodore Grädler, 1968, South Africa)

Fine Thread, The / al-Khayt al-rafî (Henri Barakat, 1971, Egypt)

Fine, Fine / Bono, bono (Ali Abdel Khalek, 2000, Egypt)

Finger in the Works, A / Le Doigt dans l'engrenage (Ahmed Rachedi, 1974, Algeria)

Fintar o Destino (Fernando Vendrell, 1997, Cape Verde)

Finye / Le Vent / The Wind (Souleymane Cisse, 1982, Mali)

Finzan / A Dance for Heroes (Cheikh Oumar Sissoko, 1989, Mali)

Fire Dance, The / La Danse du feu (Selma Baccar, 1995, Tunisia)

Fire Eyes (Soraya Mire, 1994, Somalia)

Fire in Africa, A (English, Gerhard Uys, 1987, South Africa)

Fire in Eden / Tusks (English, Tara Moore, 1985, South Africa)

Fire in My Heart / Nâr fii sadrî (Hassan Reda, 1963, Egypt)

Fire of Desire, The / Nâr al-chawq (Mohamed Salem, 1970, Egypt)

Fire with Fire / Flight to Hell (No director credited, 1988, South Africa)

Fire Woman / Imra'ah min nâr (Ahmed Sarwat, 1987, Egypt)

Fire Woman / Imra'ah min nâr (Gianni Vernuccio, 1950, Egypt)

Firegod, The (Zulu, No director credited, 1985, South Africa)

Fireside Tales (No director credited, 1990, South Africa)

First Among Blacks: Toussaint Louverture / Premier des noirs: Toussaint Louverture (Med Hondo, 2007, Mauritania)

First Day of the Month, The / Awwal al-Chahr (Abdel Fattah Hassan, 1945, Egypt)

First Fiction / Fiction première (Mustapha Derkaoui, 1992, Morocco)

First Glance, The / Awwal nazrah (Niazi Mostafa, 1946, Egypt)

First Grade, Secondary School / 'Ula thanawy (Mohamed Abou Seif, 2001, Egypt)

First Love / al-Houbb al-awwal (Gamal Madkour, 1945, Egypt)

First Love / al-Houbb al-awwal (Hamed Saïd, 2000, Egypt)

First Love / Awwal gharâm (Niazi Mostafa, 1956, Egypt)

First Love, The / Awwal houbb (Abdel Rahman Chérif, 1964, Egypt)

First Step / Premier pas / Al-khutwat al-ula (Mohamed Bouamari, 1979, Algeria)

First Thing in Love, The / Al-awwela fil gharaa (Mohamed Ali, 2007, Egypt)

First Time You Fall in Love, The / Awwel marra teheb (Alaa Karim, 2003, Egypt)

First Year of Love / Sanah oulâ houbb (Salah Abou Seif, Atef Salem, Kamal al-Cheikh, Niazi Mostafa, and Helmi Rafla, 1976, Egypt)

Fish and Four Sharks. A / Samaka wa arba' quroosh (Cherif Chaaban, 1997, Egypt)

Fish Kettle, The / Châdir al-samak (Ali Abdel Khalek, 1986, Egypt)

Fish, Milk and Tamarind / Samak laban tamr hindî (Raafat al-Mihi, 1988, Egypt)

Fisherman's Daughter, The / Bint al-sayyad (Abdel Ghani Qamar, 1957, Egypt)

Fishermen, The / Les Pêcheurs (Ghaouti Bendeddouche, 1976, Algeria)

Fishtail / Deil al-samaka (Samir Seif, 2003, Egypt)

Fishy Stones (English, Tonie van der Merwe, 1990, South Africa)

Fist Fighter (English, No director credited, 1985, South Africa)

Fitna / Fitnah (Mahmoud Ismaïl, 1948, Egypt)

Five Films for a Hundred Years / Cinq films pour cent ans (collective, 1995, Morocco)

Five in Hell / Khamsah fî-l-gahîm (Ahmed Sarwat, 1982, Egypt)

5 Love Street / Khamsah chârî'al-habâyib (al-Sayed Bedeir, 1971, Egypt)

Five Pounds, The / al-Khamsah guinîh (Hassan Helmi, 1946, Egypt)

Five-Star Thieves / Lousous khamsat nougoum (Achraf Fahmi, 1994, Egypt)

5001 / Khamsat âlaf wa wâhid (Togo Mizrahi, 1932, Egypt)

Flame (Ingrid Sinclair, 1996, Zimbabwe)

Flame of Vengeance / Lahîb al-intiqâm (Samir Seif, 1993, Egypt)

Forbidden Love / al-Houbb al-Mouharram (Hassan al-Imam, 1971, Egypt)

Forbidden Love / Amour interdit (Sid Ali Fettar, 1993, Algeria)

Forbidden Story / Qissah mamnou²ah (Tolba Radwane, 1963, Egypt)

Forbidden to Love / Mamnou² al-houbb (Mohamed Karim, 1942, Egypt)

Forbidden to Students / Mamnou² li-l-talabah (al-Saïd Mostafa, 1984. Egypt)

Forbidden Wife / Zawgah mouharramah (Ahmed al-Sabaawi, 1991, Egypt)

Forbidden Women / Nisâ mouharramât (Mahmoud Zoulficar, 1959, Egypt)

Forbidden Zone / Zone interdite (Ahmed Lallem, 1974, Algeria)

Force of the Ninja (English, Cedric Sundström, 1990, South Africa)

Forced Alliance / Halfway House (English, Josh Spencer, 1988, South Africa)

Foreigner at Home, A / Gharîb fî baytî (Samir Seif, 1982, Egypt)

Foreigner, The / Toungan / L'Étranger (Mamadou Djim Kola, 1992, Burkina Faso)

Foreigners / Ghourabâ² (Saad Arafa, 1973, Egypt)

Forest of Legs, A / Ghâbah min al-sîqân (Houssam Eddine Mostafa, 1974, Egypt)

Forget the World / Insâ al-douniâ (Elhami Hassan, 1962, Egypt)

Forgive Me / Samihnî (Hassan Reda, 1958, Egypt)

Forgive Me My Sin / Ighfir lî khatî²atî (al-Sayed Ziyada, 1963, Egypt)

Forgotten Hillside, The / La Colline oubliée (Abderrahmane Bouguermouh, 1996, Algeria)

Forgotten Man, The / al-Mansî (Chérif Arafa, 1993, Egypt)

Forgotten Summer (English, Howard Rennie, 1970, South Africa)

Former Days / Ayyâm zamân (Youssef Wahbi, 1963, Egypt)

Forster Gang, The (English, Percival Rubens, 1964, South Africa)

Forty Days (English, Franz Marx, 1979, South Africa)

45 Days / 45 youm (Ahmed Yousri, 2007, Egypt)

48 Hours in Israel / 48 sa²a fî Israel (Nader Galal, 1998, Egypt)

Forty-Four or Tales of the Night / Quarante-quatre ou le récits de la nuit (Moumen Smihi, 1981, Morocco)

Foul Play (English, No director credited, 1985, South Africa)

Four Girls and an Officer / Arba² banât wa dâbit (Anwar Wagdi, 1954, Egypt)

Four on a Difficult Mission / Arba²ah fî mouhimmah rasmiyyah (Ali Abdel Khalek, 1987, Egypt)

Four Seasons, The / al-Fusul al²Arba²a (documentary) (Mohamed Ali Ferjani, 1990, Libya)

Fourth Reich, The / Operation Weissdorn (English, Manie van Rensberg, 1989, South Africa)

4-2-4 / 4-2-4 (Ahmad Fouad, 1981, Egypt)

Fox and the Chameleon, The / al-Tha²lab wa-l-harbâ² (Houssam Eddine Mostafa, 1970, Egypt)

Fox and the Grape, The / al-Tha²lab wa-l-²inab (Mohamed Abdel Aziz, 1984. Egypt)

Foxes, The / al-Tha²âlib (Ahmed al-Sabaawi, 1993, Egypt)

Foxes . . . Rabbits / Ta²âlib . . . arânib (Sayed Seif, 1994, Egypt)

Fragments de vie / Fragments of Life (François Woukoache, 1998, Cameroon)

Fragments of Life / Fragments de vie (François Woukoache, 1998, Cameroon)

Fratricidal Struggle / Sirâ² al-ahfâd (Abdel Latif Zaki, 1989, Egypt)

Fratse van die Vloot (Afrikaans, Pierre de Wet, 1958, South Africa)

Fraud (English, Donald Monat, 1974, South Africa)

Fraud / Iltiyâl (Yassine Ismaïl Yassine, 1990, Egypt)

Freddie's in Love (English, Manie van Rensburg, 1971, South Africa)

Free from the Days / Hârib min al-ayyâm (Houssam Eddine Mostafa, 1965, Egypt)

Freedom Fighters (English, Bruce MacFarlane and Ricki Shelach, 1986, South Africa)

Freedom Run (English, No director credited, 1987, South Africa)

Freewheeling / Roues libres (Sidiki Bakaba, 2002, Ivory Coast)

Friday Night / Laylat al-goum²ah (Kamal Selim, 1945, Egypt)

Friday's Ghost (English, No director credited, 1989, South Africa)

Friends (English, Elaine Proctor, 1992, South Africa)

Friends (*No director credited*, 1987, South Africa)

Friends or Buisness / Ashaab walla buisiness (Ali Idris, 2001, Egypt)

Friends' Brothers (*No director credited*, 1986, South Africa)

Frivolous Woman, The / al-Moustahtirah (Abdallah Barakat, 1953, Egypt)

From a Good Family / Awlâd al-Ousoul (Fayek Ismaïl, 1985, Egypt)

From a Whisper to a Scream (English, Robert Bergman, 1988, South Africa)

From Heaven to Hell / Du paradis à l'enfer (Said Souda, 2000, Morocco)

From Hollywood to Tanarasset / De Hollywood à Tanarasset (Mohamed Zemmouri, 1990, Algeria)

From Home to School / Min al-bayt li-l-madrasa (Ahmed Diaa Eddine, 1972, Egypt)

From the Other Side of the River / De l'autre côté du fleuve (Mohamed Abbazi, 1982, Morocco)

Frontières / Frontiers (Mostéfa Djadjam, 2000, Algeria)

Frontiers / Frontières (Mostéfa Djadjam, 2000, Algeria)

Fruit Ice / Graneeta (Omar Abdel Aziz, 2001, Egypt)

Fruit of Crime, The / Thamarat al-gârimah (Al-Sayed Ziyada, 1947, Egypt)

Fugitive, The / al-Hârib (Kamal al-Cheikh, 1974, Egypt)

Fugitive, The / al-Hâribah (Hassan Ramzi, 1958, Egypt)

Fugitive, The / al-Moutârad (Samir Seif, 1985, Egypt)

Fugitive from Marriage, The / Hârib min al-zawâg (Hassan al-Saïfi, 1964, Egypt)

Fugitive Woman's Secret, The / Siaa al-hâribah (Houssam Eddine Mostafa, 1963, Egypt)

Fugitives, The / al-Hâribât (Nagui Anglo, 1987, Egypt)

Fugitive's Return, The / ᶜAwdat al-hârib (Youssef Abou Seif, 1990, Egypt)

Funeral for an Assassin (English, Ivan Hall, 1974, South Africa)

Funny Face (English, Alain Woolf, 1989, South Africa)

Funny People (Afrikaans / English, Kobus Kruger, 1976, South Africa)

Funny People II (English, Jamie Uys, 1983, South Africa)

Funny Stories, Stories of People / Histoires drôles, histoires de gens (Jean-Pierre Dikongue-Pipa, 1983, Cameroon)

Furnished Cemeteries to Let / Madâfin mafrouchah li-l-îgâr (Ali Abdel Khalek, 1986, Egypt)

Furnished Flat / Chiqqah mafrouchah (Hassan al-Imam, 1970, Egypt)

Furthest End of the World, The / Akher el dunia (Amir Ramsis, 2007, Egypt)

FVVA: Femme, Villa, Voiture, Argent / FVVA: Woman, Villa, Car, Money (Mustapha Alassane, 1972, Niger)

FVVA: Woman, Villa, Car, Money / FVVA: Femme, Villa, Voiture, Argent (Mustapha Alassane, 1972, Niger)

(Ga)me in the Past / Je(u) au passé (Mostapha Derkaoui, 1994, Morocco)

Gaafar al-Masri Disappears / Ikhtifaaᵓ Gaafar al-Masr (Adel al-Aassar, 2002, Egypt)

Gaber's Resignation / Istiqâlat Gaber (Ahmed Saqr, 1992, Egypt)

Gaiety Station, The / Mahattat al-ouns (Abdel Fattah Hassan, 1942, Egypt)

Gallic Cartridges / Cartouches gaulois (Mehdi Charef, 2007, Algeria)

Gamal Abdel Nasser / Gamal Abdel Nasser (Anwar El-Kawadri, 1998, Egypt)

Gamal and Dalal / Gamâl wa Dalâl (Stephane Rosti, 1945, Egypt)

Game for Vultures (English, James Fargo, 1979, South Africa)

Game of Crime, The / Louᵓbat al-qatl (Adli Khalil, 1994, Egypt)

Game of Love and Marriage, The / Louᵓbat al-houbb-wa-l-zawâg (Niazi Mostafa, 1964, Egypt)

Game of Love, The / Leibet al-hubb (Mohamed Ali, 2006, Egypt)

Game of Love, The / Le Jeu de l'amour (Driss Chouika, 2006, Morocco)

Game of Revenge, The / Louᵓbat al-intiqâm (Mohamed Abdel Aziz, 1992, Egypt)

Game of the Great, The / Louᵓbat al-kibâr (Saad Arafa, 1987, Egypt)

*Game of the Wicked, The / Lou*ʾ*bat al-achrâr* (Henri Barakat, 1991, Egypt)

Gamila the Algerian Girl / Gamîlah (Youssef Chahine, 1958, Egypt)

Gang of Adolescents, The / Chillat al-mourâhiqîn (Niazi Mostafa, 1973, Egypt)

Gang of Bonviveurs, The / Chillat al-ouns (Yeyha al-Alami, 1976, Egypt)

Gang of Swindlers, The / Chillat al-mouhtâlîn (Helmi Rafla, 1973, Egypt)

Gang, The (*No director credited,* 1988, South Africa)

*Gang, The / al-*ʾ*Isâbah* (Hichem Abou al-Nasr, 1987, Egypt)

Gangsters (*No director credited,* 1987, South Africa)

Garage, The / al-Garage (Alaa Karim, 1995, Egypt)

Garden of Blood / Boustân al-dam (Achraf Fahmi, 1989, Egypt)

Garga M'Bosse / Cactus (Mahama [Johnson] Traore, 1974, Senegal)

Gate Five / Khamsah bâb (Nader Gabal, 1983, Egypt)

Gate of the Sun, The / Bab al-Chams [*Departure* (142′) + *Return* (137′)] (Yousri Nasrallah, 2005, Egypt)

Gates of Silence, The / Les Portes du silence (Amar Laskri, 1987, Algeria)

Gates of the Night, The / Abwâb al-layl (Hassan Reda, 1969, Egypt)

Gateway to Heaven, A / Une porte sur le ciel (Farida Benlyazid, 1987, Morocco)

Gawaher / Gawâhir (Mohamed Abdel Gawad, 1949, Egypt)

Gawhara / Gawharah (Youssef Wahbi, 1943, Egypt)

Gawhari Alleyway / Hârat al-gawharî (Medhat al Sibaï, 1992, Egypt)

Geboortegrond (Afrikaans, Pierre de Wet, 1946, South Africa)

Gebroke Kontrak (Afrikaans, D. B. Steyn, 1975, South Africa)

Gee My Jou Hand (Afrikaans, Tim Spring, 1963, South Africa)

Geel Trui vir 'n Wenner (Afrikaans, Franz Marx, 1983, South Africa)

Geheim van Nantes (Afrikaans, Dirk de Villiers, 1969, South Africa)

Geheim van Onderplaas, Die (Afrikaans, Al Debbo, 1962, South Africa)

Geld Soos Bossies / Money to Burn (Afrikaans, Jamie Uys, 1955, South Africa)

Geluksdal (Afrikaans, Manie van Rensburg, 1974, South Africa)

Gemini (Afrikaans, Chris du Toit, 1980, South Africa)

Genèse, La / Genesis (Cheikh Oumar Sissoko, 1999, Mali)

Genesis / La Genèse (Cheikh Oumar Sissoko, 1999, Mali)

Genesis Chapter X (Tom Ribeiro, 1977, Ghana)

*Genetic Tree, The / Chagarat al-*ʾ*â*ʾ*ilah* (Cherif Wali, 1960, Egypt)

*Genie and Love, The / al-*ʾ*Abqarî wa-l-houbb* (Ahmed al-Sabaawi, 1987, Egypt)

Genie on Stamped Paper, A / ᶜAbqarî ᶜalâ warqah damghah (Ahmed Sarwat, 1987, Egypt)

Gensbasis 13 (Afrikaans, Elmo de Witt, 1979, South Africa)

Gentile Wedding, The / For Better for Worse (English, Koos Roets, 1990, South Africa)

*Gentle Embrace / al-Ahdân al-dâfi*ʾ*ah* (Nagdi Hafez, 1974, Egypt)

*Gentle Hands / al-Aydî al-nâ*ʾ*imah* (Mahmoud Zoulficar, 1963, Egypt)

Gentleman Wants to Get Married, The / Bisalamtouh ᶜIawiz yitgawwiz (Alexandre Farkache, 1936, Egypt)

Gentleman, The / al-Gentel (Ali Abdel Khalek, 1996, Egypt)

*Gentlemen Burglars / Lousous lâkin zourafî*ʾ (Ibrahim Lotfi, 1969, Egypt)

Gentlemen You Are Corrupt / al-Sâdah al-mourtachoun (Ali Abdel Khalek, 1983, Egypt)

Getting Lucky (English, Robert van de Coolwijk, 1985, South Africa)

Gevaalike Spel / Dangerous Deals (Afrikaans / English, Al Debbo, 1962, South Africa)

Gevaarlike Reis / Heisses Land (Afrikaans, Alfredi Medori and Lothar Lomberg, 1961, South Africa)

Ghandhi My Father (Feroz Khan, 2007, South Africa)

Gharib Is a Strange Boy / Gharîb walad ᶜaguîb (Kamal Salah Eddine, 1983, Egypt)

Girls in the Sun / Les Filles au soleil (Alphonse Béni, 1975, Cameroon)

Girls of Our Alley, The / Banât haritnâ (Hassan al-Saïfi, 1987, Egypt)

Girls of the Night / Banât al-layl (Hassan al-Imam, 1955, Egypt)

Girls ought to Get Married / al-Banât lâzim titgawwiz (Ali Reda, 1973, Egypt)

Girls' Revolt, The / Yhawrat al-banât (Kamal Ateyya, 1964, Egypt)

Girls' School / Madrasat al-banât (Kamel al-Termessani, 1955, Egypt)

Girls' Secrets / Asraar el banat (Magdi Ahmed Ali, 2001, Egypt)

Girls' Secrets / Asrâr al-banât (Mahmoud Zoulficar, 1969, Egypt)

Gito l'ingrat, / Gito the Ungrateful (Léonce Ngabo, 1992, Burundi)

Gito the Ungrateful / Gito l'ingrat (Léonce Ngabo, 1992, Burundi)

Give and Take / Du donner et du recevoir (Dansogho Mohamed Camara, 1977, Guinea)

Give Me Back My Soul / Roudda qalbî (Ezz Eddine Zoulficar, 1957, Egypt)

Give Me Your Reason / Iddînî ᶜaqlak (Ahmed Kamel Morsi, 1952, Egypt)

Glass and a Cigarette, A / Sigârah wa kâs (Niazi Mostafa, 1955, Egypt)

Glass Sphinx, The / Abou al-Hol al-Zougâguî (Luigi Pescatino, 1968, Egypt)

Glenda / The Snake Dancer (English, Dirk de Villiers, 1976, South Africa)

Glimpse of Sunshine, A / Darbat chams (Mohamed Khan, 1980, Egypt)

Gloire dans la rue, La / Fame in the Street (Nkieri Ngunia Wawa, 1980, Democratic Republic of Congo)

Gloria (Silent, Lorrimer Johnston, 1916, South Africa)

Glory / al-Magd (al-Sayed Bedeir, 1957, Egypt)

Glory and Tears / Magd wa doumouᵓ (Ahmed Badrakhan, 1946, Egypt)

God Is African (English, Akin Omotso, 2001, South Africa)

God Is Great / Allah akbar (Ibrahim al-Sayed, 1959, Egypt)

God Is Great / Yâ mâ inta karîm yâ rabb (Hussein Emara, 1983, Egypt)

God Is Patient, but Do Not Forget / Youmhil wa lâ youhmil (Hassan Hafez, 1979, Egypt)

God Is with Us / Allah maᵓnâ (Ahmed Badrakhan, 1955, Egypt)

God Watches / Inna rabbaka la-bi-l-mirsâd (Mohamed Hassib, 1983, Egypt)

God's Gift / Wend Kuuni / Le Don de dieu (Gaston Kaboré, 1982, Burkina Faso)

God's Hand / Yadu Allah (Youssef Wahbi, 1946, Egypt)

God's World / Douniâ Allâh (Hassan al-Imam, 1985, Egypt)

Goddelose Stad, Die (Afrikaans, Pierre D. Botha, 1958, South Africa)

Gods Must Be Crazy II, The (English, Jamie Uys, 1989, South Africa)

Gods Must Be Crazy, The (English, Jamie Uys, 1980, South Africa)

Gods' Anger, The / La Colère des dieux (Idrissa Ouedraogo, 2003, Burkina Faso)

Goha and Abou Nawwas / Gohâ wa Abou Nawwâs (Manuel Vimance, 1932, Egypt)

Goha and Abou Nawwas Photographers / Gohâ was Abou Nawwâs mousawirân (Manuel Vimance, 1933, Egypt)

Goha and the Seven Girls / Gohâ wa-l-sabᵓbanât (Fouad al-Gazaerli, 1947, Egypt)

Goha's Star Turn / Mismâr Gohâ (Ibrahim Emara, 1952, Egypt)

Going Cheap in Taht El Rab / Taht el rabᵓ be gnih wi rubᵓ (Ismaïl Gamal, 2000, Egypt)

Gold (English, Peter Hunt, 1974, South Africa)

Gold Cup, The (English, Robert van de Coolwijk, 1990, South Africa)

Gold Spear, The (No director credited, 1987, South Africa)

Gold Squad (English, Ivan Hall, 1971, South Africa)

Golden Ball, The / Le Ballon dᵓor (Cheik Doukoure, 1993, Guinea)

Golden Girl / Bint min dahab (Mohamed Oussama, 1988, Egypt)

Golden Horseshoes / Les Sabots en or (Nouri Bouzid, 1989, Tunisia)

Golden Rendezvous, The (English, Ashley Lazarus and Freddie Francis, 1977, South Africa)

Gone Crazy (No director credited, 1990, South Africa)

Green Light / Feu vert (Abdellah Mesbahi, 1976, Morocco)

Green Man / Impumgu Uhlasa (Xhosa, *No director credited*, 1984, South Africa)

Greet Those Whom I Love / Sallim ʿalâ al-habâyib (Helmi Halim, 1958, Egypt)

Grinder's War / Jewel of the Gods (English, Robert van de Coolwijk, 1987, South Africa)

Groen Faktor, Die / The Green Factor (Afrikaans, Jans Rautenbach, 1984, South Africa)

Groetnis vir die Eerste Minister (Afrikaans, Bertrand Retief, 1973, South Africa)

Grotto, Le (Jabob Sou, 1989, Burkina Faso)

Guard Dogs / Kilâb al-hirâsah (Sayed Seif, 1984. Egypt)

Guelwaar (Ousmane Sembene, 1992, Senegal)

Guérisseurs, Les / Aduefue (Sidiki Bakaba, 1988, Ivory Coast)

Guerre de libération, La / The War of Liberation (collective, 1973, Algeria)

Guerre du Golfe . . . et après?, La / After the Gulf? (collective, 1992, Tunisia)

Guerre du pétrole n'aura pas lieu, La / The Oil War Will Not Take Place (Souheil Benbarka, 1974, Morocco)

Guerres sans images / Wars without Images (documentary) (Mohamed Soudani, 2002, Algeria)

Guest House of Surprises, The / Loukândat al-moufâgaʾât (Issa Karama, 1959, Egypt)

Guest, The / Die Besoeker (English / Afrikaans, Ross Devenish, 1977, South Africa)

Guide, The / al-Tourgmân (Hassan al-Saïfi, 1961, Egypt)

Guimba The Tyrant / Guimba, un tyran, une époque (Cheikh Oumar Sissoko, 1995, Mali)

Guimba, un tyran, une époque / Guimba The Tyrant (Cheikh Oumar Sissoko, 1995, Mali)

Gums and Noses (English, Craig Freimond, 2005, South Africa)

Gun-Runner, The (Silent, Lorrimer Johnston, 1916, South Africa)

Guns Across the Veld / De Wet's Spoor (Afrikaans, Howard Rennie, 1975, South Africa)

Guquka (Zulu / Xhosa, *No director credited*, 1985, South Africa)

Guys, the Cops and the Whores, The / Les Mecs les flics et les p . . . aka Les Tringleuses (Alphonse Béni, 1974, Cameroon)

Gypsies, The / al-Ghagar (Ibrahim Afifi, 1996, Egypt)

Ha! Enia (Yoruba, Yomi Ogunmola, 1989, Nigeria)

Haak Vrystaat (Afrikaans, Al Debbo, 1976, South Africa)

Hababa / Habâbah (Niazi Mostafa, 1944, Egypt)

Habits neufs du gouverneur, Les / The Governor's New Clothes (Mwézé D. Ngangura, 2005, Democratic Republic of Congo)

Hada / Houda (Ramsès Naguib, 1959, Egypt)

Hadda (Mohamed Aboulouakar, 1984, Morocco)

Hadi Badi / Hâdî bâdî (Hassan al-Saïfi, 1984. Egypt)

Hadiyyah / Hadiyyah (Mahmoud Zoulficar, 1947, Egypt)

Haha and Tuffaha / Hah wa Tuffaha (Akram Farid, 2006, Egypt)

Halawa / Halâwah (Ibrahim Emara, 1949, Egypt)

Half Virgin / Nisf ʿadhrâʾ (al-Sayed Bedeir, 1961, Egypt)

Half-a-dozen Madmen / Nouss dastat magânîn (Hassan al-Saïfi, 1991, Egypt)

Half-a-Million / Nisf arnab (Mohamed Khan, 1983, Egypt)

Half-an-Hour of Marriage / Nouss saʾat zawâg (Fatine Abdel Wahab, 1969, Egypt)

Halfaouine / Halfaouine, l'enfant des terrasses / (Ferid Boughedir, 1990, Tunisia)

Halfaouine, l'enfant des terrasses / Halfaouine (Ferid Boughedir, 1990, Tunisia)

Half-Meter Accident, The / Hâdith al-nisf mitr (Achraf Fahmi, 1983, Egypt)

Halfway House / Easy Kill / Forced Alliance (English, Josh Spencer, 1988, South Africa)

Halim / Halim (Cherif Arafa, 2006, Egypt)

Hallo / Sakubya (Zulu, *No director credited*, 1988, South Africa)

Hamada and Toutou's Gang / ʿIsâbat Hamâdah wa Toutou (Mohamed Abdel Aziz, 1982, Egypt)

Hamada Plays / Hamada yelʾab (Saïd Hamed, 2005, Egypt)

Heads or Tails / Malek wa Ketaba (Kamla Abou Zikri, 2006, Egypt)

Hamido / Hamido (Niazi Mostafa, 1953, Egypt)

Hamido's Son / Ibn Hamido (Fatine Abdel Wahab, 1957, Egypt)

Hamlet of Women / Douar de femmes (Mohamed Chouikh, 2004, Algeria)

Haunt of Pleasure, The / Wakr al-maladhdhât (Hassan al-Imam, 1957, Egypt)

Haunt of the Wretched, The / Wakr al-achrâ (Hassan al-Saïfi, 1972, Egypt)

Haunted Past, The (*No director credited*, 1989, South Africa)

Have Confidence in God / Khallîk maˀ Allah (Helmi Rafla, 1954, Egypt)

Have Pity on Me / Harâm ˤalayk (Issa Karama, 1953, Egypt)

Have Pity on Me / Irham doumouˀî (Henri Barakat, 1954, Egypt)

Have You Seen Drum Recently? (English, Jurgen Schadeberg, 1988)

He Has Finished His Statement / Wa tammat aqwâlouh (Magdi Mehrem, 1992, Egypt)

He Returns to Take Revenge / ˤÂda li-yantaqim (Yassine Ismaïl Yassine, 1988, Egypt)

He Who Has Duped the Devils / Illî dihik ˤalâ al-chayâtîn (Nasser Hussein, 1981, Egypt)

He Who Is Satisfied with Little . . . / Man radiya bi-qalîhih (Bahaa Eddine Charaf, 1955, Egypt)

He Who Kisses too Much / Sâhib bâlayn (Abbas Kamel, 1946, Egypt)

He's Kidnapped My Wife / Khataf mirâtî (Hassan al-Saïfî, 1954, Egypt)

Headhunter (English, Frank Schaeffer, 1988, South Africa)

Headmaster, The / al-Nazer (Cherif Arafa, 2000, Egypt)

Heads or Tails / Malek wa ketaba (Kamla Abou Zikri, Egypt, 2005)

Hear My Song / Hoor My Lied (Afrikaans, Elmo de Witt, 1967, South Africa)

Heart Has Its Reasons, The / al-Qalb louh ahkâm (Helmi Halim, 1956, Egypt)

Heart Has Only One Love, The / al-Qalb louh wâhid (Henri Barakat, 1945, Egypt)

Heart in the Night / Qalb fî-l-zalâm (Adli Khalil, 1960, Egypt)

Heart of Gold / Qalb min dhadhab (Mohamed Karim, 1959, Egypt)

Heart of the Hunter (English, *Director unknown*, 2005, South Africa) in prod.

Heart of the Matter, The (English, *No director credited*, 1981, South Africa)

Heart to Heart / Min al-qalb li-l-qalb (Henri Barakat, 1952, Egypt)

Heartbeat / Daqqat qalb (Mohamed Abdel Aziz, 1976, Egypt)

Heartless Woman, A / Imraˀah bilâ qalb (Yassine Ismaïl Yassine, 1978, Egypt)

Heartlines (Angus Gibson, 2006, South Africa)

Hearts and Minds (English, Ralph Zipman, 1996, South Africa)

Heart's Elect, The / Ibn al-halâl (Seif Eddine Chawkat, 1951, Egypt)

Hearts in an Ocean of Tears / Qouloub fî bahr al-doumouˀ (Yehya al-Alami, 1978, Egypt)

Heaven and Hell / Gannah wa nâr (Hussein Fawzi, 1952, Egypt)

Heaven Save Us! / Ashtatan ashtoot (Omar Abdel Aziz, 2004, Egypt)

Heaven Watches / al-Samâˀ lâ tanâm (Ibrahim Emara, 1952, Egypt)

Heaven's Doors / Les Portes du paradis (Sohael and Imad Noury, 2005, Morocco)

Heaven's Pity / Rahmah min al-samâˀ (Abbas Kamel, 1958, Egypt)

Heavenly Love, A / Houbb min al-samâ (Abdel Fattah Hussein, 1944, Egypt)

Heel against the Head (English, Rod Stewart, 1999, South Africa)

Heisses Land / Gevaarlike Reis (Afrikaans, Alfredi Medori and Lothar Lomberg, 1961, South Africa)

Hekmat Fahmi the Spy / al-Gâsousah Hikmat Fahmî (Houssam Eddine Mostafa, 1994, Egypt)

Hele Dorp Weet, Die (Afrikaans, Kappie Botha, 1961, South Africa)

Hell / al-Gahîm (Mohamed Radi, 1980, Egypt)

Hell 2 / Gahîm itnîn (Mohamed Abou Seif, 1990, Egypt)

Hell for a Ten-Year-Old / L'Enfer à dix ans (collective, 1968, Algeria)

Hell of Jealousy, The / Gahîm al-gîrah (Kostanof, 1953, Egypt)

Hell Under Water / Gahîm taht al-mâˀ (Nader Galal, 1989, Egypt)

Hellgate / Ghost Town (English, William Levey, 1989, South Africa)

Hellions, The (English, Ken Annakin, 1961, South Africa)

Hello / Nahârak saˀîd (Fatine Abdel Wahab, 1955, Egypt)

His Majesty's Tears / Doumou³ sahibat al-galâlah (Atef Salem, 1992, Egypt)

His Sisters / Ikhwâtouh al-banât (Henri Barakat, 1976, Egypt)

Histoire d'Orokia / Story of Orokia (Jabob Sou, 1987, Burkina Faso)

Histoire d'une rencontre / Story of a Meeting (Brahim Tsaki, 1982, Algeria)

Histoire d'une rose, L' / The Story of a Rose (Abdelmajid Rchich, 2000, Morocco)

Histoires de la révolution / Stories of the Revolution (collective, 1969, Algeria)

Histoires drôles, histoires de gens / Funny Stories, Stories of People (Jean-Pierre Dikongue-Pipa, 1983, Cameroon)

Hit Team, The (English, *No director credited*, 1987, South Africa)

Hitchhikers, The (Zulu, C. Dippenaar, 1984, South Africa)

Hitman (English, *No director credited*, 1987, South Africa)

Ho Llelo Thuso (Zulu, David Bensusan, 1987, South Africa)

Hoda / Houda (Helmi Rafla, 1949, Egypt)

Hold My Hand I'm Dying (English, Duncan McLachlan and Terence Ryan, 1988, South Africa)

Hold Your Tongue / Lisânak hisânak (Abbas Kamel, 1953, Egypt)

Hole in the Wall, The / La Brèche dans le mur (Jillali Ferhati, 1978, Morocco)

Holiday in Hell / Agâzah fî gahannam (Ezz Eddine Zoulficar, 1949, Egypt)

Holiday of Love / Agâzat gharâm (Mahmoud Zoulficar, 1967, Egypt)

Hollow City, Na cidade vazia (Maria João Ganga, 2004, Angola)

Home / Bayt al-Tâ³ah (Youssef Wahbi, 1953, Egypt)

Home Sweet Home (Michael Raeburn, 1999, Zimbabwe)

Home without Tenderness / Bayt bilâ hanân (Ali Abdel Khalek, 1976, Egypt)

Homes Have Their Secrets / al-Bouyout asrâr (Al-Sayedd Ziyada, 1971, Egypt)

Homme d'ailleurs. L' / The Man from Elsewhere (Mory Traore, 1979, Ivory Coast)

Homme de cendres, L' / Man of Ashes (Nouri Bouzid, 1986, Tunisia)

Homme qui brodait des secrets, L' / The Man Who Embroidered Secrets (Omar Chraïbi, 2000, Morocco)

Homme qui regardait les fenêtres, L' / The Man Who Looked at Windows (Merzak Allouache, 1982, Algeria)

Honest Burglar, The / al-Liss al-charîf (Hamada Abdel Wahab, 1953, Egypt)

Honey Devil / Chaytân min ʿasal (Hassan al-Saïfi, 1985, Egypt)

Honeymoon Trip / Rihlat chahr ʿasal (Zouheir Bekir, 1970, Egypt)

Honeymoon, The / Chahr al-³asal (Ahmed Badrakhan, 1945, Egypt)

Honneur de ma famille, L' / My Family's Honor (Rachid Bouchareb, 1997, Algeria)

Honneur du tribu, L' / The Honor of the Tribe (Mahmoud Zemmouri, 1993, Algeria)

Honorable / A Kumgani (Zulu, *No director credited*, 1988, South Africa)

Honorable Family, The / al-³Â³ilah al-kârimah (Fatine Abdel Wahab, 1964, Egypt)

Honor / al-Charaf (Mohamed Chabaan, 2000, Egypt)

Honor Is Precious / al-Charaf ghâli (Ahmed Badrakhan, 1951, Egypt)

Honor of the Tribe, The / L'Honneur du tribu (Mahmoud Zemmouri, 1993, Algeria)

Honor Thy Father (English, *No director credited*, 1984, South Africa)

Hooligans, The / al-Achqiyâ³ (Ahmed al-Sabaawi, 1984. Egypt)

Hooligans, The / al-Sa³âlîk (Daoud Abdel Sayed, 1985, Egypt)

Hoor My Lied / Hear My Song (Afrikaans, Elmo de Witt, 1967, South Africa)

Hope of My Life, The / Amânî al-³oumr (Seif Eddine Chawkat, 1955, Egypt)

Hopes and Dreams (Rachid Medi, 1969, Sudan)

Horable Finish / Ukunugcebeleka oku Sabisayo (Xhosa, *No director credited*, 1990, South Africa)

Horror, The (Zulu, *No director credited*, 1990, South Africa)

Hors jeu / Out of Play (Karim Dridi, 1998, Tunisia)

Horsemen of Glory / Les Cavaliers de la gloire— a re-edited version of *Drums of Fire / Tam-*

Humor / al-Mizâg (Ali Abdel Khalek, 1991, Egypt)

Hunchback, The / al-Ahdab (Hassan Helmi, 1946, Egypt)

Hundred Thousand Pounds, A / Mît alf guinîh (Togo Mizrahi, 1936, Egypt)

Hunger / al-Gouʾ (Ali Badrakhan, 1986, Egypt)

Hunted (English, John Parr, 1988, South Africa)

Hunter of Tyrants, The / Sâʾid al-Gabâbirah (Nasser Hussein, 1991, Egypt)

Hunter, The (*No director credited*, 1988, South Africa)

Hunter, The / al-Qannâs (Yassine Ismaïl Yassine, 1986, Egypt)

Hurlements / Screams (Omar Khlifi, 1972, Tunisia)

Husband for Hire / Zawg li-l-lîgâr (Issa Karama, 1961, Egypt)

Husband for My Sister, A / ʿArîs li-ouktî (Ahmed Diaa Eddine, 1963, Egypt)

Husband of the Four, The / Gouz al-arbbaʾah (Fatine Abdel Wahab, 1950, Egypt)

Husband on Holiday / Zawg fî agâzar (Mohamed Abdel Gawad, 1964, Egypt)

Husbands and Summer / al-Azwâg wa-l-sayf (Issa Karama, 1961, Egypt)

Husbands Are Devils / al-Azwâg al-chayâtîn (Ahmed Fouad, 1977, Egypt)

Husbands at Your Service / Zawg taht al-talab (Adel Sadek, 1985, Egypt)

Husbands Beware / Intabihou ayyouhâ al-azwâg (Hassan al-Saïfi, 1990, Egypt)

Husbands in a Jam / Azwâg fî wartah (Hassan al-Saïfi, 1992, Egypt)

Hush, They're Listening / Sammiʾ his (Cherif Arafa, 1991, Egypt)

Hyena's Sun / Le Soleil des hyènes (Ridha Behi, 1977, Tunisia)

Hyenas / Hyènes (Djibril Diop-Mambety, 1992, Senegal)

Hyènes / Hyenas (Djibril Diop-Mambety, 1992, Senegal)

Hypocrite, The / Dhou al-wagʾhayn (Wali Eddine Saleh and Ahmed Diaa Eddine, 1949, Egypt)

Hysteria / Hysteria (Adel Adeeb, 1998, Egypt)

I Almost Destroyed My Home / Kidtou ahdoumou baytî (Ahmed Kamel Morsi, 1954, Egypt)

I Am Alone / Anâ wahdî (Henri Barakat, 1952, Egypt)

I Am Free / Anâ hourrah (Salah Abou Seif, 1959, Egypt)

I Am Innocent / Anâ barîʾah (Houssam Eddine Mostafa, 1959, Egypt)

I Am Justice / Anâ al-ʾadâlah (Hussein Sedki, 1961, Egypt)

I Am Love / Anâ al-houbb (Henri Barakat, 1954, Egypt)

I Am Neither Angel Nor Devil / Lastou chaytânan wa-lâ malâkan (Henri Barakat, 1980, Egypt)

I Am Neither Reasonable Nor Mad / Anâ lâ ʿâqlah wa-lâ magʾnounah (Houssam Eddine Mostafa, 1976, Egypt)

I Am Not a Criminal / Lastou mougriman (Wasfi Darwich, 1985, Egypt)

I Am Not a Killer / Lastou qâtilan (Abdel Hadi Taha, 1989, Egypt)

I Am Not a Thief / Anâ mouch harâmiyyah (Hassan al-Saïfi, 1983, Egypt)

I Am Not With Them / Ana mush maʾahum (Ahmed al-Badri, 2007, Egypt)

I Am the East / Anâ al-charq (Abdel Hamid Zaki, 1958, Egypt)

I Am the Fugitive / Anâ al-hârib (Niazi Mostafa, 1962, Egypt)

I Am the Future (Godwin Mawuru, 1994, Zimbabwe)

I Am the Past / Anâ al-mâdi (Ezz Eddine Zoulficar, 1951, Egypt)

I Ask for a Solution / Ouridou hallan (Saïd Marzouk, 1975, Egypt)

I Beg You, Give Me This Medicine / Argouk aʾtinî hâdhâ al-dawâʾ (Hussein Kamal, 1984. Egypt)

I Believed in God / Âmint billah (Mahmoud Zoulficar, 1952, Egypt)

I Call You / Banâdî ʿalîk (Ismaïl Hassan, 1955, Egypt)

I Come from a Good Family / Anâ bint nâs (Hassan al-Imam, 1951, Egypt)

I Destroyed My Home / Hadamt baytî (Hussein Fawzi, 1946, Egypt)

I Dreamed of Africa (English, Hugh Hudson, 1998, South Africa)

I Exist / J'existe (Sid Ali Mazif, 1982, Algeria)

I Fear for My Son / Qalbî ʿalâ waladî (Henri Barakat, 1953, Egypt)

I Forgot That I Was a Woman / Wa nasîtou annî imraʾah (Atef Salem, 1994, Egypt)

(Zouheir Bekir and Fatine Abdel Wahab, 1956, Egypt)

I've Killed My Son / Qatalt waladî (Gamal Madkour, 1945, Egypt)

Ice Cream in Glim / Ice cream fî glîm (Khaïri Bechara, 1992, Egypt)

Ici et là / Here and There (Mohamed Ismaïl, 2004, Morocco

Ideal Suitor, The / ʿArîs al-hanâ (Ibrahim Lama, 1944, Egypt)

Identité / Identity (Pierre-Marie Dong, 1972, Gabon)

Identity / Identité (Pierre-Marie Dong, 1972, Gabon)

Identity Papers / Pièces d'identité (Mweze D. Ngangura, 1998, Democratic Republic of Congo)

Idiot Boy, The / al-Walad al-ghâbi (Madkour Sabet, 1977, Egypt)

Idiot, The / al-ʾAbît (al-Sayed Bedeir, 1966, Egypt)

Idle, The / Tanabilat al-soultân (Kamal al-Chennawi, 1965, Egypt)

Iemand Soos Jy / Someone Like You (Afrikaans / English, Elmo de Witt, 1978, South Africa)

If I Were a Man / Law kountou ragoulan (Ahmed Diaa Eddine, 1964, Egypt)

If I Were Rich / Law Kount ghanî (Henri Barakat, 1942, Egypt)

If Only I'd Not Known Love / Laytanî mâ ʿaraftou al-houbb (Anwar al-Chennawi, 1976, Egypt)

If the Horsemen . . . / Si les cavaliers (Mahamane Bakabe, 1981, Niger)

If This Is a Dream / Law kaan da helm (Tarek al-Nahri, 2001, Egypt)

If Youth . . . / Layta al-chabâb (Hassan Abdel Wahab, 1948, Egypt)

Ifa / Heritage (Zulu, *No director credited*, 1987, South Africa)

Ifa Lami / My Heritage (Zulu, *No director credited*, 1987, South Africa)

Ighawe (Zulu, Rudi Meyer, 1980, South Africa)

Ighawe II (Zulu, Rudi Meyer, 1984, South Africa)

Ighraa / Ighrâʾ (Hassan al-Imam, 1957, Egypt)

Ihlathi Lezimanga (Zulu / Xhosa, *No director credited*, 1985, South Africa)

Iholide (Zulu / Xhosa, *No director credited*, 1985, South Africa)

Ija Ominira (Yoruba, Ola Balogun, 1978, Nigeria)

Ija Orogun (Yoruba, Adeyemi Afolayan, 1982, Nigeria)

Ika's Law / al-Qânoun îkâ (Achraf Fahmi, 1991, Egypt)

I-Kati Elimnyana / The Black Cat (Zulu, Simon Sabela, 1976, South Africa)

Il était une fois / Machaho / Once upon a Time / (Belkacem Hadjadj, 1995, Algeria)

Il était une fois, il était deux fois / Once Upon A Time, Twice Upon a Time (Bachir Skiredj, 2007, Morocco)

Il va pleuvoir sur Conakry / It'll Rain on Conakry (Cheik Fantamady Camara, 2006, Guinea)

Ilanga Liphuma / Sunrise (Zulu, *No director credited*, 1988, South Africa)

Ilheu do contenda / Island of Strife (Leão Lopez, 1994, Cape Verde)

Illegal Worker, The / Le Clandestin (José Zeka Laplaine, 1996, Democratic Republic of Congo)

Illicit Liquor Seller, The (Silent, Lorrimer Johnston, 1916, South Africa)

Illusion, The / al-Wahm (Nader Galal, 1979, Egypt)

Illusions / al-Awhâm (Ahmed al-Nahhas, 1988, Egypt)

Illusions of Love, The / Awhâm al-houbb (Mamdouh Choukri, 1970, Egypt)

Ilo Tsy Very / Mad 47 (Ignace-Solo Randrasana, 1987, Madagascar)

Ilombe (Charles Mensah, 1978, Gabon)

Imali (Sotho, Regardt van der Bergh and Jimmy Murray, 1984, South Africa)

Imali Yiswe / Money Is Everything (Zulu, *No director credited*, 1988, South Africa)

Imidlembe (Zulu, *No director credited*, 1988, South Africa)

Imihlolo (Zulu, *No director credited*, 1983, South Africa)

Immortal Song, The / Lahn al-khouloud (Henri Barakat, 1952, Egypt)

Impact (English, Frans Nel, 1989, South Africa)

Impango (Zulu, Tonie van der Merwe, 1982, South Africa)

Impango II / Provision (Zulu, *No director credited*, 1987, South Africa)

Impasse, L' / Dead End (Mustapha Khayat, 1984, Morocco)

Inkada (Zulu, Gary van der Merwe, 1981, South Africa)

Inkedama (Xhosa, Simon Sabela, 1975, South Africa)

Inkunzi (Xhosa, Sam Williams, 1976, South Africa)

Innocent at the Gallows / Barî fî-l-machnaqah (Mounir al-Touni, 1971, Egypt)

*Innocent Culprits, The / al-Moudhniboun al-abriyâ*ᵓ (Mohamed Marzouk, 1990, Egypt)

*Innocent Man and the Executioner, The / al-Barî*ᵓ *wa-l-gallâd* (Mohamed Marzouk, 1991, Egypt)

*Innocent Man and the Gallows, The / al-Barî*ᵓ *wa-l-machnaqah* (Nagui Anglo, 1986, Egypt)

Innocent Revenge (English, David Bensusan, 1985, South Africa)

*Innocent, The / al-Barî*ᵓ (Atef al-Tayeb, 1986, Egypt)

*Innocent's Prayer, The / Da*ᵓ*wat al-mazloum* (Ahmed Kamel Hefnawi, 1956, Egypt)

*Innocents, The / al-Abriyâ*ᵓ (Ahmed Badrakhan, 1944, Egypt)

*Innocents, The / al-Abriyâ*ᵓ (Mohamed Radi, 1974, Egypt)

Insecure Youth / Chabâb ᶜ*alâ kaff* ᶜ*ifrît* (Mohsen Mohi Eddine, 1990, Egypt)

Inside Out (English, Neal Sundström, 1999, South Africa)

Insident of Paradysstrand / Incident on Paradise Beach (Afrikaans, Grenville Middleton and Gordon Anderson, 1973, South Africa)

Insoumis, L' / Si Mohand U M'hand / The Rebel (Liazid Khadja and Rachid Benallel, 2006, Algeria)

Inspan (Afrikaans, Bladon Peake, 1953, South Africa)

*Inspector General, The / al-Moufattich al-*ᵓ*âmm* (Helmi Rafla, 1956, Egypt)

Inspector Tahar's Holiday / Les Vacances de l'Inspecteur Tahar (Moussa Haddad, 1973, Algeria)

Intaba Yegolide (Zulu, *No director credited*, 1985, South Africa)

Intelligence Is a Great Thing / al-Aql zînah (Hassan Redi, 1950, Egypt)

Intelligent but Stupid / Adhkiyâ lâkin aghbiyâ (Niazi Mostafa, 1980, Egypt)

Intelligent Person, The / al-Nâsih (Seif Eddine Chawkat, 1949, Egypt)

Interim Wife / Zawgah bi-l-niyâbah (Ahmed Galal, 1936, Egypt)

Intruder, The / al-Dakhîl (Nour al-Demerdache, 1967, Egypt)

Intruder, The / Committed (English, William Levey, 1988, South Africa)

*Invitation to Life / da*ᵓ*wah li-l-hayât* (Medhat Bekir, 1973, Egypt)

Inyakanyaka (Zulu, Simon Sabela, 1977, South Africa)

Inyembezi Zami (Sotho, Rudi Meyer, 1983, South Africa)

Inyoka (Sotho, H. Epstein and Jimmy Murray, 1984, South Africa)

Iphutha (Zulu, *No director credited*, 1985, South Africa)

Ipi Tombi (English, Tommie Meyer and Don Hulette, 1993, South Africa)

Iqaba (Zulu / Xhosa, *No director credited*, 1985, South Africa)

Ireke Onibudo (Yoruba, Tunde Alabi Hundeyin, 1983, Nigeria)

*Iron Woman / al-Mar*ᵓ*ah al-hadîdiyyah* (Abdel Latif Zaki, 1987, Egypt)

Ironu (François Sourou Okioh, 1985, Bénin)

Is It My Fault? / Anâ dhanbî îh (Ibrahim Ebara, 1953, Egypt)

Isalamusi (Zulu, Gary van der Merwe, 1984, South Africa)

Isban Israel (Silent, Joseph Albrecht, 1920, South Africa)

*Ishmael Yassine and the Ghost / *ᶜ*Ifrîtat Ismâ*ᵓ*îl Yâsîn* (Hassan al-Saïfi, 1954, Egypt)

*Ishmael Yassine as Tarzan / Ismâ*ᵓ*îl Yâsîn Tarazân* (Niazi Mostafa, 1958, Egypt)

*Ishmael Yassine at the Waxworks / Ismâ*ᵓ*îl Yâsîn fî mout*ᵓ*haf al-cham*ᵓ (Issa Karama, 1956, Egypt)

*Ishmael Yassine at the Zoo / Ismâ*ᵓ*îl Yâsîn fî guininet al-haywân* (Seif Eddine Chawkat, 1957, Egypt)

*Ishmael Yassine for Sale / Ismâ*ᵓ*îl Yâsîn li-l-bay*ᵓ (Houssam Eddine Mostafa, 1958, Egypt)

*Ishmael Yassine in Damascus / Ismâ*ᵓ*îl Yâsîn fî Dimachq* (Helmi Rafla, 1958, Egypt)

*Ishmael Yassine in Flying / Ismâ*ᵓ*îl / Yâsîn fî-l-tayarân* (Fatine Abdel Wahab, 1959, Egypt)

Iziduphunga (Zulu, Tonie van der Merwe, 1977, South Africa)

Iziphuku Phuku (Zulu, *No director credited,* 1983, South Africa)

J'ai vu tuer Ben Barka / I Saw Ben Barka Get Killed (Serge Le Péron and Saïd Smihi, 2005, Morocco)

J'écrirai ton nom sur le sable / I Shall Write Your Name in the Sand aka *La Terre du défi / Land of Challenge* (Abdellah Mesbahi, 1989, Morocco)

J'existe / I Exist (Sid Ali Mazif, 1982, Algeria)

Jack and Stella / A Private Life (English, Francis Gerard, 1988, South Africa)

Jackals. The / The Scavengers (English, Robert R. Webb, 1967, South Africa)

Jackpot, The / al-Brimo (Kamel al-Telmessani, 1947, Egypt)

Jagd auf die blauen Diamanten / Diamond Walkers (English / German, Paul Martin, 1965, South Africa)

Jagters, Die (Afrikaans, Gordon Vorster, 1960, South Africa)

Jailbird / al-Lumangi (Ismaïl Gamal, 1996, Egypt)

Jaiyesimi (Yoruba, Chief Hubert Ogunde and Freddie Goode, 1980, Nigeria)

Jakalsdraai se Mense (Afrikaans, Franz Marx, 1975, South Africa)

Jake Speed (English, Andrew Lane and Martin Walters, 1986, South Africa)

Jakkels van Tula Metsi, Die (Afrikaans, Franz Conradie, 1967, South Africa)

Jamie 21 (Afrikaans, Daan Retief, 1973, South Africa)

Jane and the Lost City (English, Terence Marcel, 1985, South Africa)

Jannie Totsiens (Afrikaans, Jans Rautenbach, 1970, South Africa)

Jardin de papa, Le / Daddy's Garden (José Zeka Laplaine, 2003, Democratic Republic of Congo)

Jardin de Samira, Le / Samira's Garden (Latif Lahlou, 2007, Morocco)

Jawhara (Saâd Chraïbi, 2003, Morocco)

Je(u) au passé / (Ga)me in the Past (Mostapha Derkaoui, 1994, Morocco)

Jealousy / al-Ghîrah (Abdel Fattah Hassan, 1946, Egypt)

Jeans / al-Jînz (Cherif Chaabane, 1994, Egypt)

Jed and Owen Meet Big George (*No director credited,* 1987, South Africa)

Jed and the Bankrobbers (English, *No director credited,* 1987, South Africa)

Jerusalem Entsja (English, Ralph Ziman, 2006, South Africa)

Jeu de l'amour, Le / The Game of Love (Driss Chouika, 2006, Morocco)

Jeune fille, La / Den muso / The Girl (Souleymane Cisse, 1975, Mali)

Jeunesse dorée / Gilded Youth (Zaïda Ghorab-Volta, 2001, Algeria)

Jewel of the Gods / Grinder's War (English, Robert van de Coolwijk, 1987, South Africa)

Jewelry, Market, The / al-Sagha (Ahmed al-Sabaawi, 1996, Egypt)

Jezile / Son of Man (English, Mark Dornford-May, 2005, South Africa)

Jigi / L'Espoir (Kollo Daniel Sanou, 1992, Burkina Faso)

Jim Comes to Jo'burg (English, Donald Swanson, 1949, South Africa)

Jit (Michael Raeburn, 1990, Zimbabwe)

Jobman / Devil's Island (English, Darrell Roodt, 1988, South Africa)

Jock / Jock of the Bushveld (English, Danie Joubert, 1995, South Africa)

Jock of the Bushveld (English, Gray Hofmeyr, 1986, South Africa)

Jock of the Bushveld / Jock (English, Danie Joubert, 1995, South Africa)

Joe Bullet (English, Louis de Witt, 1974, South Africa)

Joe Slaughter (Zulu, Gary van der Merwe, 1983, South Africa)

Johnny Diamini (English, *No director credited,* 1985, South Africa)

Johnny Tough (English, Ronnie Isaacs, 1983, South Africa)

Joker (English, *No director credited,* 1985, South Africa)

Jom or a People's Story / Jom ou l'histoire d'un peuple (Ababacar Samb-Makharam, 1981, Senegal)

Jom ou l'histoire d'un peuple / Jom or a People's Story (Ababacar Samb-Makharam, 1981, Senegal)

Jors Troelie (Afrikaans, *No director credited,* 1983, South Africa)

Kanna Kanna (Yoruba, Bayo Aderohunmu, 1986, Nigeria)

Kanta of Kebbi (Hausa, Adamu Halilu, 1978, Nigeria)

Kaptein Caprivi (Afrikaans, Albie Venter, 1972, South Africa)

Karate Olympia / Kill or Be Killed (English, Ivan Hall, 1976, South Africa)

Karate Olympia / Kill or Be Killed (English, Ivan Hall, 1980, South Africa)

Karawana / Karawânah (Abdel Latif Zaki, 1993, Egypt)

Kare Kare Zvako / The Survival of the Butchered Woman (Tsitsi Dangarembga, 2004, Zimbabwe)

Karim (Momar Thiam, 1971, Senegal)

Karim and Sala / Karim et Sala (Idrissa Ouedraogo, 1991, Burkina Faso)

Karim et Sala / Karim and Sala (Idrissa Ouedraogo, 1991, Burkina Faso)

Karim's Harem / Hareem Kareem (Ali Idris, 2005, Egypt)

Karkar / Karkar (Ali Ragab, 2007, Egypt)

Karmen Geï (Joseph Gaye Ramaka, 2000, Senegal)

Kasarmu Ce (Hausa, Saddick Balewa, 1991, Nigeria)

Kasbah City (Saïd Naciri, 2002, Morocco)

Kaskenades van Dr Kwak (Afrikaans, Pierre de Wet, 1947, South Africa)

Kato Kato / Un malheur n'arrive jamais seul (Idrissa Ouédraogo, Burkina Faso, 2006)

Katr al-Nada / Qatr al-nadâ (Anwar Wagdi, 1951, Egypt)

Katrina (Afrikaans, Jans Rautenbach, 1969, South Africa)

Kavaliers, Die / The Cavaliers (Afrikaans, Elmo de Witt, 1966, South Africa)

Kawilasi (Kilizou Blaise Abalo, 1992, Togo)

Keid Ensa / Ruses de femmes / Women's Wiles (Farida Benlyazid, 1999, Morocco)

Keïta, l'heritage du griot / Keita, The Heritage of the Griot (Dani Kouyate, 1994, Burkina Faso)

Keita, The Heritage of the Griot / Keïta, l'heritage du griot (Dani Kouyate, 1994, Burkina Faso)

Keltoum's Daughter / La Fille de Keltoum (Mehdi Charef, 2001, Algeria)

Ken Bugul (Moussa Sene Absa, 1991, Senegal)

Ke-Phiri / It's Wolf (North Sotho, *No director credited*, 1987, South Africa)

Keswa, le fil perdu / Keswa: The Lost Thread (Keltoum Bornaz, 1997, Tunisia)

Keswa: The Lost Thread / Keswa, le fil perdu (Keltoum Bornaz, 1997, Tunisia)

Kezkaka Wolofen (documentary) (Teshome Kebede Theodros, 2003, Ethiopia)

Khadra and Sindbad al-Qibli / Khadrah wa-l-sindibâd al-qiblî (al-Sayed Ziyada, 1951, Egypt)

Khadra's Adventures / Moughâmarât Khadrah (al-Sayed Ziyada, 1950, Egypt)

Khafaya (Ahmed Yachfine, 1995, Morocco)

Khaled Ibn Al-Walid / Khâlid bin al-Walid (Hussein Sedki, 1958, Egypt)

Khalil after the Changes / Khalîl ba'd al-ta'dîl (Yehya al-Alami, 1987, Egypt)

Khamis Conquers Cairo / Kharmîs yaghzou al-Qâhirah (Sayed Seif, 1990, Egypt)

Khamsa the Genie / al-'Abqarî Khamsah (Ahmed Yassine, 1985, Egypt)

Khan Al-Khalili / Khân al-Khalîlî (Atef Salem, 1966, Egypt)

Khlifa le teigneux / Khlifa Ringworm (Hamouda Ben Halima, 1969, Tunisia)

Khlifa Ringworm / Khlifa le teigneux (Hamouda Ben Halima, 1969, Tunisia)

Khorma, la bêtise / Khorma: Stupidity (Jilani Saadi, 2002, Tunisia)

Khorma: Stupidity / Khorma, la bêtise (Jilani Saadi, 2002, Tunisia)

Khouloud / Khouloud (Ezz Eddine Zoulficar, 1948, Egypt)

Khudgarz / The Egotist (Brijmohun Brothers, 1988, Mauritius)

Kick or Die / No Hard Feelings (English, Charles Norton, 1987, South Africa)

Kickboxer (English, Frans Nel, 1990, South Africa)

Kid McCoy / Brutal Glory (English, Koos Roets, 1988, South Africa)

Kidnap (*No director credited*, 1987, South Africa)

Kidnapped (English, *No director credited*, 1985, South Africa)

Kidnapped II (English, *No director credited*, 1987, South Africa)

Kidnapped III (English, *No director credited*, 1988, South Africa)

Kom Saam Vanaand (Afrikaans, Pierre de Wet, 1949, South Africa)

Kom tot Rus (Afrikaans, Elmo de Witt, 1977, South Africa)

Komany (Nabyl Laulou, 1989, Morocco)

Kootjie Emmer (Afrikaans, Koos Roets, 1977, South Africa)

Kounouz / Kounouz (Niazi Mostafa, 1966, Egypt)

Kract Affair, A (Silent, B. F. Clinton, 1916, South Africa)

Krim (Ahmed Bouchaâla, in France, 1995, Algeria)

Kruger Millions, The / Die Kruger-miljoene (Afrikaans, Ivan Hall, 1967, South Africa)

Kruger-miljoene, Die / The Kruger Millions (Afrikaans, Ivan Hall, 1967, South Africa)

Kukurantumi: The Road to Accra (King Ampaw, 1983, Ghana)

Kulba Na Barna (Hausa, Brendan Shehu, 1992, Nigeria)

Kwagga Strikes Back / Oh Schuks, Here Comes UNTAG / (English / Afrikaans, David Lister, 1990, South Africa)

Kwavinga Run / Fatal Mission / The Rat (English, Anthony Bond and Tonie van der Merwe, 1990, South Africa)

Kwikstertjie (Afrikaans, Elmo de Witt, 1974, South Africa)

Kyk na die Sterre (Afrikaans, Kappie Botha, 1960, South Africa)

Laada (Drissa Touré, 1990, Burkina Faso)

Laafi / Tout va bien (Pierre S. Yaméogo, 1990, Burkina Faso)

Lac Sacré, Le / The Sacred Palace (José Zeka Laplaine, 2007, Democratic Republic of Congo)

Lace / Dantiella (Inas al-Deghidi, 1998, Egypt)

Lachine / Lachine (Fritz Kramp, 1938, Egypt)

Ladies, Young Ladies / Sayyidâtî ânisâtî (Raafat al-Mihi, 1990, Egypt)

Ladies' Hairdresser / Hallâq al-sayyidât (Fatine Abdel Wahab, 1960, Egypt)

Lady, The / al-Hânim (Henri Barakat, 1947, Egypt)

Lady among Ladies / Set el settaat (Raafat al-Mihi, 1998, Egypt)

Lady from Cairo, The / La Dame du Caire (Moumen Smihi, 1991, Morocco)

Lady from the Castle, The / Sayyidat al-qasr (Kamal al-Cheikh, 1958, Egypt)

Lady on the Train, The / Sayyidat al-qitâr (Youssef Chahine, 1952, Egypt)

L'Afrance (Alain Gomis, 2001, Senegal)

Lag met Wena (Afrikaans, Morné Coetzer, 1977, South Africa)

Lahalibo / Lahâlibo (Hussein Fawzi, 1949, Egypt)

Lair of the Hyena (No director credited, 1986, South Africa)

Laisse un peu d'amour / Leave a Little Love (Zaïda Ghorab-Volta, 1998, Algeria)

Lalla chafia / Medicine Woman / Madame la guérisseuse (Mohamed B. A. Tazi, 1982, Morocco)

Lalla Hobby (Mohamed Abderrahman Tazi, 1997, Morocco)

Lambarene / Schweitzer (English, Gray Hofmeyr, 1989, South Africa)

Lambaye / Truanderie (Mahama [Johnson] Traore, 1972, Senegal)

Lana (Zulu / Xhosa, No director credited, 1985, South Africa)

Land Apart (English, Sven Persson, 1976, South Africa)

Land of Ashes / Terre en cendres aka *Wanderings / Errances* (Djafar Damardjji, 1993, Algeria)

Land of Challenge / La Terre du défi aka *I Shall Write Your Name in the Sand / J'écrirai ton nom sur le sable* (Abdellah Mesbahi, 1989, Morocco)

Land of Dreams / Ard al-ahlâm (Daoud Abdel Sayed, 1993, Egypt)

Land of Dreams / Ard al-ahlâm (Kamal al-Cheikh, 1957, Egypt)

Land of Fear / Ard el khouf (Daoud Abdel Sayed, 2000, Egypt)

Land of Heroes, The / Ard al-abtâl (Niazi Mostafa, 1953, Egypt)

Land of Hypocrites / Ard al-nifâq (Fatine Abdel Wahab, 1968, Egypt)

Land of Peace / Ard al-salâm (Kamal al-Cheikh, 1957, Egypt)

Land of the Amazon Queen (English, No director credited, 1986, South Africa)

Land of the Nile / Ard al-Nîl (Abdel Fattah Hassan, 1946, Egypt)

Land Officials, The / al-Mouwazzafoun fî-l-ard (Ahmed Yehya, 1985, Egypt)

Landela / Follow (Zulu, No director credited, 1988, South Africa)

Legend of the Sky Kingdom, The (animated feature) (Roger Hawkins, 2003, Zimbabwe)

Legitimacy Sweeps It Away / al-Halâl yiksab (Ahmed al-Sabaawi, 1985, Egypt)

Legitimate Betrayal / Kheyana mashruᵓa (Khaled Yussef, 2006, Egypt)

Legs in the Mud / Siqân fî-l-wahl (Atef Salem, 1976, Egypt)

Leila / Layla (Togo Mizrahi, 1942, Egypt)

Leila and the Others / Leïla et les autres (Sid Ali Mazif, 1978, Algeria)

Leïla et les autres / Leila and the Others (Sid Ali Mazif, 1978, Algeria)

Leila in the Shadows / Layla fî-zalâm (Togo Mizrahi, 1944, Egypt)

Leila My Reason / Layla ma raison (Taïeb Louhichi, 1989, Tunisia)

Leila, Daughter of the Poor / Layla bint al-fouqâra (Anwar Wagdi, 1945, Egypt)

Leila, Daughter of the Rich / Layla bint al-aghniyâ (Anwar Wagdi, 1946, Egypt)

Leila, the American / Layla al-ᵓâmiriyyah (Niazi Mostafa, 1948, Egypt)

Leila, the Bedouin / Layla al-badawiyyah (Bahiga Hafez, 1944, Egypt)

Leila, the Girl from the Beach / Layla bint al-châtiᵓ (Hussein Fawzi, 1959, Egypt)

Leila, the Girl from the Country / Layla bint al-rîf (Togo Mizrahi, 1941, Egypt)

Leila, the Girl from the Desert / Layla bint al-sahrâ (Bahiga Hafez, 1937, Egypt)

Leila, the School Girl / Layla bint al-madâris (Togo Mizrahi, 1941, Egypt)

Leisure Time / Awqat faragh (Mohamed Mostafa Kamal, 2006, Egypt)

Leisure Time / Awqat faragh (Mohamed Mostafa Kamal, 2006, Egypt)

Lelik is my Offer (Afrikaans, Joe Stewardson, 1975, South Africa)

Lend Me Three Pounds / Sallifnî talâtah guinîh (Togo Mizrahi, 1939, Egypt)

Lenny (English, Nico Stein, 1997, South Africa)

Leopard Is Back / Ingwe Ibuyile (Zulu, No director credited, 1984, South Africa)

Let Me Avenge Myself / Daᵓounî antaqim (Taysir Abboud, 1979, Egypt)

Let Me Get Married, Quickly / Ilhaqounî bi-l-maᵓdhoun (Helmi Rafla, 1954, Egypt)

Let Me Live / Daᵓounî aᵓîch (Ahmed Diaa Eddine, 1955, Egypt)

Let Me Sing / Sîbounî aghannî (Hussein Fawzi, 1950, Egypt)

Let the Music Be (English, Frans Nel, 1989, South Africa)

Let's Get Married Quickly My Love / Ilâ al-maᵓdhoun yâ habîbî (Mahmoud Farid, 1977, Egypt)

Let's Love Each Other / Daᵓounâ nouhibb (al-Sayed Ziyada, 1975, Egypt)

Lethal Woman / The Most Dangerous Woman Alive (English, Christian Marnham, 1988, South Africa)

Let's Dance / Ma tigi norqus (Inas al-Deghidi, 2006, Egypt)

Letter from an Unknown Woman / Risâlah min imraᵓah magᵓhoulah (Salah Abou Seif, 1962, Egypt)

Letter from My Village / Kaddu beykat / Lettre paysanne (Safi Faye, 1975, Senegal)

Letter to God / Risâlah ilâ Allah (Kamal Ateyya, 1961, Egypt)

Letters from Algeria / Lettres d'Algérie (Azize Kabouche, 2002, Algeria)

Lettre paysanne / Kaddu beykat / Letter from My Village (Safi Faye, 1975, Senegal)

Lettres d'Algérie / Letters from Algeria (Azize Kabouche, 2002, Algeria)

Lèvres du silence, Les / Lips of Silence / (Hassan Benjelloun, 2001, Morocco)

Lewe Sonder Jou, Die (Afrikaans, Dirk de Villiers, 1971, South Africa)

Liar and His Friend, The / al-Kaddâb wa sahibouh (Ahmed Sarwat, 1989, Egypt)

Liar, The / al-Kaddâb (Salah Abou Seif, 1975, Egypt)

Liars, The / Kaddâbîn al-zaffah (Kamal Salah Eddine, 1986, Egypt)

Licit and the Illicit, The / al-Halâl wa-l-harâm (Sayed Seif, 1985, Egypt)

Lied in My Hart (Afrikaans, Ivan Hall, 1970, South Africa)

Liefde vir Lelik (Afrikaans, Keith G. van der Wat, 1972, South Africa)

Liefde wat Louter (Afrikaans, D. B. Steyn, 1978, South Africa)

Liefste Madelein (Afrikaans, Franz Marx, 1976, South Africa)

Little Demon, The / *al-Chaytân al saghîr* (Kamal al-Cheikh, 1963, Egypt)

Little Devil, The / *al-Chaytânah al-saghîrah* (Hassan al-Imam, 1958, Egypt)

Little Doll, The / *al-ɔArousah al-saghîrah* (Ahmed Badrakhan, 1956, Egypt)

Little Dreams / *Ahlâm saghîragh* (Khaled al-Hagar, 1993, Egypt)

Little Fathers / *al-Abaaɔ al-sighaar* (Doureid Laham, 2006, Egypt)

Little Jerusalem / *La Petite Jérusalem* (Karin Albou, 2005, Algeria)

Little Unicorn, The (English, Paul Matthews, 1998, South Africa)

Little Love, A / *Chayɔ min al-houbb* (Ahmed Fouad, 1973, Egypt)

Little Love, a Lot of Violence, A / *Qaleel mina al-hubb katheer min al-ᶜunf* (Raafat al-Mihi, 1995, Egypt)

Little Magician, The / *al-Sâhirah al-sagghîrah* (Niazi Mostafa, 1963, Egypt)

Little Man Big Trouble / *Nonpopi Nodambusa* (English, Etienne Puren, 1990, South Africa)

Little Millionairess, The / *al-Millionnairah al-saghîrah* (Kamal Barakat, 1948, Egypt)

Little Monsters, The / *al-Wouhouch al-saghîrah* (Abdel Latif Zaki, 1989, Egypt)

Little Senegal (Rachid Bouchareb, 2000, Algeria)

Little Suffering. A / *Chayɔ min al-ɔadhâb* (Salah Abou Seif, 1969, Egypt)

Little Virtues / *Akhlâq li-l-bayɔ* (Mahmoud Zoulficar, 1950, Egypt)

Live marriage / *Gawiz ᶜalâ al-hawâ* (Ahmed Sarwat, 1976, Egypt)

Live the Easy Way (English, *No director credited*, 1988, South Africa)

Livelihood, The / *Arzâq yâ douniâ* (Nader Galal, 1982, Egypt)

Living in Paradise / *Vivre au paradis* (Bourlem Guerdjou, 1998, Algeria)

Living Legitimately / *Ayyâm fî-l-halâl* (Hussein Kamal, 1985, Egypt)

Llnga Selwa (Zulu, *No director credited*, 1984, South Africa)

Loafers / *Abadlovi* (Zulu, *No director credited*, 1987, South Africa)

Lobanzi Siphiwe / *Broad Given* (Xhosa, *No director credited*, 1989, South Africa)

Lobster / *Istakoza* (Inas al-Deghidi, 1996, Egypt)

Lokval in Venesië (Afrikaans, Ivan Hall, 1972, South Africa)

Lola (*No director credited*, 1987, South Africa)

Long Distance Runner (*No director credited*, 1986, South Africa)

Long Journey, The / *Le Grand voyage* (Ismaïl Ferroukhi, 2004, Morocco)

Long Live Art / *Yahyâ al-fann* (Hassan Helmi, 1948, Egypt)

Long Live Love / *Yahyâ al-houbb* (Mohamed Karim, 1938, Egypt)

Long Live Men / *Tahyâ al-riggâlah* (Togo Mizrahi, 1945, Egypt)

Long Live Men! / *Tahyâ al-riggâlah* (Ahmed Kamel Hefnawi, 1954, Egypt)

Long Live Women / *Tahyâ al-sittât* (Togo Mizrahi, 1943, Egypt)

Long Nights, The / *al-Layâlî al-tawîlah* (Ahmed Diaa Eddine, 1967, Egypt)

Long Red Shadow, The / *Three Days of Fire* (English, Percival Rubens, 1968, South Africa)

Long Run, The (English, Jean Stewart, 2000, South Africa)

Long Run, The (English, *No director credited*, 1985, South Africa)

Long-Awaited Day, The / *Yawm sl-mounâ* (Alvisi Orfanelli, 1938, Egypt)

Look, The / *Le Regard* (Nour-Eddine Lakhmari, 2004, Morocco)

Looking for a Scandal / *al-Bahth ᶜan al-fadîhah* (Niazi Mostafa, 1973, Egypt)

Looking for Love / *al-Bâhithah ᶜan al-houbb* (Ahmed Diaa Eddine, 1965, Egypt)

Looking for My Wife's Husband / *A la recherche du mari de ma femme* (Mohamed Abderrahman Tazi, 1993, Morocco)

Looking for Problems / *al-Bahth ᶜan al-mataâɔib* (Mahmoud Farid, 1975, Egypt)

Looking for Sayyed Marzouq / *Al-Bahth ᶜan Sayyed Marzouk* (Daoud Abdel Sayed, 1991, Egypt)

Lord of War, The (English, Andrew Niccol, 2004, South Africa)

Lord Oom Piet / *Lord Uncle Pete* (Afrikaans, Jamie Uys, 1962, South Africa)

Lord Uncle Pete / *Lord Oom Piet* / (Afrikaans, Jamie Uys, 1962, South Africa)

Love at Karnak / Gharâm fî-l-Karnak (Ali Reda, 1967, Egypt)

Love at Taba / al-Houbb fî Tâbâ (Ahmed Fouad, 1992, Egypt)

Love at the Circus / Gharâm fî-l-sîrk (Hussein Fawzi, 1960, Egypt)

Love at the Foot of the Pyramids / al-Houbb fawqa hadabat al-Haram (Atef al-Tayeb, 1986, Egypt)

Love before Bread Sometimes / al-Houbb qabla al-khoubz ahyânan (Saad Arafa, 1977, Egypt)

Love Beneath the Rain / al-Houbb tahta al-matar (Hussein Kamal, 1975, Egypt)

Love Brewed in the African Pot (Kwah Paintsil Ansah, 1980, Ghana)

Love Express, The / Express al-houbb (Hussein Fawzi, 1946, Egypt)

Love Fan / Ghawy hubb (Ahmed al-Badri, 2005, Egypt)

Love for All / Houbb li-l-gamî (Abdel Rahman Chérif, 1965, Egypt)

Love Has No Cure / al-Hawâ mâlouch dawâ (Youssef Maalouf, 1952, Egypt)

Love in 1970 / al-Houbb sanat as°în (Mahmoud Zoulficar, 1969, Egypt)

Love in a Fridge / al-Houbb fî-l-thallâgah (Saïd Hamed, 1993, Egypt)

Love in August / Gharâm fî Aghoustous (Hassan al-Saïfi, 1966, Egypt)

Love in Danger / al-Houbb fî khatar (Helmi Rafla, 1951, Egypt)

Love in Difficult Circumstances / al-Hubb fî zoroof sa°ba (Simon Saleh, 1996, Egypt)

Love in Narrow Alleys / Hub Fi al-Aziqa al-Dayiqa (Mohamed Jindi, 1986, Libya)

Love in Prison / Houbb fî-l-zinzânah (Mohamed Fadel, 1983, Egypt)

Love in the Desert / Gharâm fî-l-sahrâ (Gianni Vernuccio and Léon Klimovski, 1959, Egypt)

Love in the Shadows / Houbb fî-l-zalâm (Hassan al-Imam, 1953, Egypt)

Love in the Wood (English, Lourens Swanepoel, 1985, South Africa)

Love in the Wood II (English, Lourens Swanepoel, 1986, South Africa)

Love Is a Scandal / al-Houbb bahdalah (Salah Abou Seif, 1952, Egypt)

Love Is Beautiful / Yâ halâwat al-houbb (Hussein Fawzi, 1952, Egypt)

Love Judge, The / Qâdî al-gharâm (Hassan al-Saïfi, 1962, Egypt)

Love Letter / Risâlat gharâm (Henri Barakat, 1954, Egypt)

Love Me Leave Me (English, Allan Birkinshaw and Charles Mariott, 1988, South Africa)

Love Nest, The / °Ichch al-gharâm (Helmi Rafla, 1959, Egypt)

Love of My Life, The / Habîb al-°oumr (Henri Barakat, 1947, Egypt)

Love of My Life, The /Habîbî al-asmar (Niazi Mostafa, 1958, Egypt)

Love of My Soul, The / Habîb qalbi (Helmi Rafla, 1952, Egypt)

Love on a Volcano / Houbb fawq al-bourkân (Hassan al-Imam, 1978

Love on an Agricultural Road / Gharâm fî-l-tarîq al-zieâ°î (Abdel Meneim Choukri, 1971, Egypt)

Love on the Miami Beach / Houbb °alâ châtî° Miami (Helmi Rafla, 1976, Egypt)

Love Story / Qissat gharâm (Mohamed Abdel Gawad and Kamal Selim, 1945, Egypt)

Love Story, A / Une histoire d'amour (Hakim Noury, 2001, Morocco)

Love Talk /Kalaam fil hubb (Ali Idris, 2006, Egypt)

Love Taxi, The / Taxi al-gharâm (Niazi Mostafa, 1954, Egypt)

Love Thief, The / Harâmî al-houbb (Abdel Meneim Choukri, 1977, Egypt)

Love towards Children of Southern Africa (English, Kenichi Oguri, 1988, South Africa)

Love without a Visa / Amour sans visa (Najib Sefrioui, 2001, Morocco)

Love without Sunshine, A / Houbb lâ yarâ al-chams (Ahmed Yehya, 1980, Egypt)

Love You Are Beautiful / Hilwah yâ douniâ al-houbb (Yehya al-Alami, 1977, Egypt)

Love, Joy and Youth / Houbb wa-marah wa-chabîb (Nagdi Hafez, 1964, Egypt)

Love, Love / Houbb fî houbb (Seif Eddine Chawkat, 1960, Egypt)

Love . . . Even More Beautiful than Love / Houbb ahlâ min al-houbb (Helmi Rafla, 1975, Egypt)

Love . . . in a Dead End / al-Houbb . . . fî tarîq masdoud (Adli Khalil, 1977, Egypt)

Love's Gamble / Le Pari de l'amour (Didier Aufort, 2002, Ivory Coast)

Mad Matrimony (No director credited, 1988, South Africa)

Mad Woman, The / al-Mag²nounah (Helmi Rafla, 1949, Egypt)

Mad Woman, The / al-Mag²nounah (Omar Abdel Aziz, 1985, Egypt)

Madam Devil / ʿIfrîtah hânim (Henri Barakat, 1949, Egypt)

Madam Feyrouz / Fayrouz hânim (Abbas Kamel, 1951, Egypt)

Madam Headmaster / al-Sitt al-nâzirah (Ahmed Diaa Eddine, 1968, Egypt)

Madam Holds the Power / Sâhibat al-²ismah (Hassan al-Saïfi, 1956, Egypt)

Madam Nawaem / al-Sitt Nawâ²im (Youssef Maalouf, 1958, Egypt)

Madam Osmane's Harem / Le Harem de Mme Osmane (Nadir Moknèche, 2000, Algeria)

Madam Sokkar / Soukkar hânim (al-Sayed Bedeir, 1960, Egypt)

Madam's Chauffeur / Sawwâq al-hânim (Hassan Ibrahim, 1994, Egypt)

Madame Brouette (Moussa Sene Absa, 2002, Senegal)

Madame la guérisseuse / Medicine Woman / Lalla chafia (Mohamed B. A. Tazi, 1982, Morocco)

Madcap of the Veldt (Silent, Director unknown, 1921, South Africa)

Mademoiselle Hanafi / al-Ânissah (Fatine Abdel Wahab, 1954, Egypt)

Madman's Loves, A / Gharâmiyyât mag²noun (Zouheir Bekir, 1967, Egypt)

Madman's Testament, A / Wasiyyat ragoul mag²noun (Ahmed Sarwat, 1987, Egypt)

Madman's Testimony, A / Chahâdat mag²noun (Talaat Allam, 1978, Egypt)

Madmen Are Happy, The / al-Magânîn fî na²îm (Hassan al-Saïfi, 1963, Egypt)

Madmen on the Road / Magânîn ʿalâ al-tarîq (Cherif Hammouda, 1991, Egypt)

Madmen's Strike, The / Idrâb al-magânîn (Ahmed Fouad, 1983, Egypt)

Madness / Démences (Fadhel Jaïbi, 2006, Tunisia)

Madness of Love, The / Gounoun al-houbb (Mohamed Karim, 1954, Egypt)

Madness of Youth, The / Gounoun al-chabâb (Khalil Chawki, 1980, Egypt)

Madoda / Men (Zulu, No director credited, 1987, South Africa)

Mafia / Mafia (Cherif Arafa, 2002, Egypt)

Maganino / Magânîno (Essam al-Chamma, 1993, Egypt)

Magda / Magda (Ahmed Galal, 1943, Egypt)

Maggot in the Fruit, The / al-Fâs fî-l-râs (Wahid Mekhiemar, 1992, Egypt)

Magic (No director credited, 1989, South Africa), 1989, South Africa)

Magic / al-Magic (Mohamed Mustafa, 2007, Egypt)

Magic Bag, The (No director credited, 1989, South Africa)

Magic Box, The / La Boîte magique (Ridha Behi, 2002, Tunisia)

Magic Box, The / Le magique (Ezzeddine Fazaï Melliti, 1994, Tunisia)

Magic Cap, The / Tâqiyyat al-ikhfâ² (Niazi Mostapha, 1944, Egypt)

Magic Garden, The / Pennywhistle Blues (English, Donald Swanson, 1961, South Africa)

Magic Is Alive My Friends (English, Jan Scholtz, 1985, South Africa)

Magic Lamp, The / al-Fânous al-sihrî (Fatine Abdel Wahab, 1960, Egypt)

Magic of the Eyes / Sehar al-ʿouyoun (Fakhr Eddine Negeda, 2002, Egypt)

Magic Ring (English, No director credited, 1985, South Africa)

Magician . . . The Notion of Joy, The / al-Saher . . . nazareyet al-bahga (Radwane al-Kachef, 2002, Egypt)

Magique, Le / The Magic Box (Ezzeddine Fazaï Melliti, 1994, Tunisia)

Magodu (Zulu, No director credited, 1979, South Africa)

Mahaleo (Raymond Rajaonarivelo, 2004, Madagascar)

Mahlokolobe / Pigs' Eyes (Sotho, David Bensusan, 1989, South Africa)

Mahlomola (Zulu, Tonie van der Merwe, 1976, South Africa)

Mahrous the Foreman / al-Oustâ Mahrous (Ismaïl Hassan, 1990, Egypt)

Mahrous, the Shadow of the Minister / al-Waad Mahrous betaa² el wazeer (Nader Galal, 1999, Egypt)

alladhî faqada zillahou (Kamal al-Cheikh, 1968, Egypt)

Man Who Had Sneezed, The / al-Ragoul alladhî ʿatas (Omar Abdel Aziz, 1985, Egypt)

Man Who Has Lost His Mind, A / Ragoul faqada ʿaqlahou (Mohamed Abdel Aziz, 1980, Egypt)

Man Who Is a Victim of Love, A / Ragoul qate lahou al-houbb (Cherif Hammouda, 1986, Egypt)

Man Who Looked at Windows, The / L'Homme qui regardait les fenêtres (Merzak Allouache, 1982, Algeria)

Man Who Sold the Sun, The / al-Ragoul alladhî bâʾa al-chams (Niazi Mostafa, 1983, Egypt)

Man Who Stole Joy, The / Sarek al-farah (Daoud Abdel Sayed, 1995, Egypt)

Man Who Was Afraid, The (Silent, Joseph Albrecht, 1920, South Africa)

Man with a Past, A / Ragoul laho maadi (Ahmed Yehya, 2000, Egypt)

Man with Seven Lives, A / Ragoul bi-sabʾ arwâh (Medhat al-Sibaï, 1988, Egypt)

Man without Sleep / Ragoul lâ yanâm (Youssef Wahbi, 1948, Egypt)

Man, The (English, No director credited, 1985, South Africa)

Mandabi / Le Mandat / The Money Order (Ousmane Sembene, 1968, Senegal)

Mandat, Le / Mandabi / The Money Order (Ousmane Sembene, 1968, Senegal)

Mandla / Power (Zulu, No director credited, 1990, South Africa)

Mangler, The (English, Tobe Hooper, 1993, South Africa)

Maniac (No director credited, 1988, South Africa)

Maniac Cop (No director credited, 1988, South Africa)

Manipulator, The (English, Fred Wilson [Marino Girolami], 1972, South Africa)

Mannequin, Le / The Mannequin (Sadok Ben Aicha, 1978, Tunisia)

Mannequin, The / Le Mannequin (Sadok Ben Aicha, 1978, Tunisia)

Manpower (English, No director credited, 1988, South Africa)

Mapantsula (English / Afrikaans / Zulu / Sotho, Oliver Schmitz and Thomas Mogotlane, 1987, South Africa)

Mapantsula (Zulu / Xhosa, No director credited, 1985, South Africa)

Mapantsula II (Zulu / Xhosa, No director credited, 1985, South Africa)

Mapule (N Sotho, Tonie van der Merwe, 1977, South Africa)

Marathon Tam (Rabie Ben Mokhtar, 1992, Algeria)

Mariage de Moussa, Le / Moussa's Wedding (Tayeb Mefti, 1982, Algeria)

Marie-Line (Mehdi Charef, 2000, Algeria)

Marigolds in August (English, Ross Devenish, 1979, South Africa)

Mark of the Jackal (English, Roger Orpen, 1989, South Africa)

Market in Women, The / Souq al-hârim (Youssef Marzouk, 1970, Egypt)

Market, The / al-Souq (Nasser Hussein, 1987, Egypt)

Marmerpoel, Die (Afrikaans, Judex C. Viljoen, 1972, South Africa)

Marock (Laïla Marrakchi, 2005, Morocco)

Marouf the Bedouin / Maʾrouf al-badawî (Ibrahmin Lama, 1935, Egypt)

Marouf the Shoemaker / Maʾrouf al-iskâfî (Fouad al-Gazaerli, 1947, Egypt)

Marriage—It's for the Worthy / al-Gawâz li-l-guidʾân (Nagdi Hafez, 1983, Egypt)

Marriage by Presidential Order / Gawaaz bi qaraar goumhoury (Khalid Youssef, 2001, Egypt)

Marriage in Danger / Gawâz fî khatar (Issa Karama, 1963, Egypt)

Marriage Photo, The / Sourat al-zifzâf (Hassan Amer, 1952, Egypt)

Marriage with Premeditation / Gawâz maʾ sabq al-isrâr (Kamal Ide, 1987, Egypt)

Marriage, The / al-Zawâg (Fatma Rouchdi, 1933, Egypt)

Marteau et l'enclume, Le / The Hammer and the Anvil (Hakim Noury, 1990, Morocco)

Martyr of the Divine Love / Chahîdat al-houbb al-ilâhî (Abbas Kamel, 1962, Egypt)

Martyrs of Love / Chouhadâʾ al-gharâm (Kamal Selim, 1944, Egypt)

Marzouka / Marzouqah (Saad Arafa, 1983, Egypt)

Mask of an Enlightened Woman, The / Le Masque d'une éclaircie (Mohamed Benayat, 1974, Algeria)

Memories of Our Schoolboy Life, The / Dhikrayât al-talmadhah (Ali Beheiri, 1965, Egypt)

Memory in Detention / Mémoire en détention (Jillali Ferhati, 2004, Morocco)

Memory of a Day / Memoria de um dia (Orlando Fortunato, 1982, Angola)

Men / Madoda (Zulu, *No director credited*, 1987, South Africa)

Men Are in Danger, The / al-Rigâl fî khatar (Nagdi Hafez, 1993, Egypt)

Men from the Ministry, The (English, Tom Meehan, 1971, South Africa)

Men in the Storm / Rigâl fî-l-ʾâsifah (Houssam Eddine Mostafa, 1960, Egypt)

Men Knowing Nothing of Love / Rigâl lâ yaʾrifoun al-houbb (Yehya al-Alami, 1979, Egypt)

Men Never Marry Beautiful Women / al-Rigâl lâ yatazawwagoun al-gamîlîat (Ahmed Farouk, 1965, Egypt)

Men Trapped / Rigâl fî-l-misyadah (Mahmoud Farid, 1971, Egypt)

Men Who Do Not Fear Death / Rigâl lâ yakhâfoun al-mawt (Nader Galal, 1973, Egypt)

Men's Season, The / La Saison des hommes (Moufida Tlatli, 2000, Tunisia)

Men's Words / Parole d'hommes (Moez Kamoen, 2004, Tunisia)

Menzi and Menziwa (Zulu / Xhosa, *No director credited*, 1985, South Africa)

Mercedes / Marsîdès (Yousri Nasrallah, 1993, Egypt)

Mercenaries, The / Dark of the Sun (English, Jack Cardiff, 1967, South Africa)

Mercenary for Justice (English, Don E. Fauntle-Roy, 2005, South Africa)

Merchant of Death (English, Yossi Wein, 1996, South Africa)

Merchants of Death / Touggâr al-mawt (Kamal al-Cheikh, 1957, Egypt)

Merchants of War (English, Peter Mackenzie, 1988, South Africa)

Merciless (*No director credited*, 1988, South Africa)

Merry Widow, The / al-Armalah al-taroub (Helmi Rafla, 1956, Egypt)

Mesh (English, *No director credited*, 1985, South Africa)

Message to the Ruler, A / Resala ela al-wali (Nader Galal, 1998, Egypt)

Messenger from Hell, The / Safîr gahannam (Youssef Wahbi, 1945, Egypt)

Messiah of Peace, The / Murugadas (English, *No director credited*, 1983, South Africa)

Met Liefde van Adele / Wikus en Adele (Afrikaans, Dirk de Villiers, 1974, South Africa)

Met Murg, Durf en Bloed / The Brave, the Rough and the Raw (English, David Millin, 1973, South Africa)

Midday Sun, The (English, Lulu Keating, 1988, South Africa)

Midjeresso (Noukpo Wilannon, 2006, Benin)

Midnight / Nouss al-layl (Hussein Fawzi, 1949, Egypt)

Midnight Caller / The Demon (English, Percival Rubens, 1980, South Africa)

Midnight Caller, The (English, *No director credited*, 1984, South Africa)

Midnight Driver, The / Sawwâq nisf al-layl (Niazi Mostafa, 1958, Egypt)

Midnight Ghost, The / Chabah nisf al-layl (Abdel Fattah Hassan, 1947, Egypt)

Midnight Patrol, The / Dawriyyat nouss al-layl (Kamal Salah Eddine, 1986, Egypt)

Midnight Policeman, The / Châwîch nouss al-leil (Hussein Emara, 1991, Egypt)

Midnight Story, The / Hikâyat nouss al-leil (Issa Karama, 1964, Egypt)

Midnite Rush (Zulu, David Bensusan, 1990, South Africa)

Mido the Troublemaker / Mido mashakel (Mohamed al-Naggar, 2003, Egypt)

Mightyman 1 & 2 (Zulu, Perceval Rubens, 1979, South Africa)

Migrating Birds / al-Touyour al-mouhîguirah (Hassan Youssef, 1979, Egypt)

Mild Man's Anger, The / Ghadab al-halîm (Kamal Ateyya, 1985, Egypt)

Mille et une mains / A Thousand and One Hands (Souheil Benbarka, 1972, Morocco)

Mille et une voix, Les / A Thousand and One Voices (documentary) Mahmoud Ben Mahmoud, 2001, Tunisia)

Mille mois / A Thousand Months (Faouzi Bensaidi, 2003, Morocco)

Millennium Menace, The (English, Leon Schuster, 1999, South Africa)

Million and One Kisses, A / Alf bousah wa bousah (Mohamed Abdel Aziz, 1977, Egypt)

of the Islands (Ruy Duarte de Carvalho, 1989, Angola)

Moia—The Message of the Islands / Moia—O recado das ilhas (Ruy Duarte de Carvalho, 1989, Angola)

Moissons d'acier / Harvests of Steel (Ghaouti Bendeddouche, 1982, Algeria)

Mokhtar (Sadok Ben Aicha, 1968, Tunisia)

Molori / Dreamer (Tswana, David Bensusan, 1989, South Africa)

Moloyi (Sotho, Tonie van der Merwe, 1983, South Africa)

Moloyi (Zulu, Tonie van der Merwe, 1978, South Africa)

Moment of Danger / Lahzat khatar (Saïd Amacha, 1991, Egypt)

Moment of Truth (English, Adamu Halilu, 1981, Nigeria)

Moment of Truth, The (Zulu, Ronnie Isaacs, 1985, South Africa)

Moment of Weakness / Lahzat da²f (Sayed Tantawi, 1981, Egypt)

Moments of Fear / Lahzât khawf (Hassan Reda, 1972, Egypt)

Mon amie ma soeur / My Friend, My Sister (Mohamed Lebcir, 2003, Algeria)

Mon village / My Village (Mohamed Hammami, 1979, Tunisia)

Mona Saber (Abdelhaï Laraki, 2001, Morocco)

Monde est un ballet, Le / The World Is a Ballet (Issa Traoré de Brahima, 2006, Burkina Faso)

Monde, Le / Dunia (Pierre S. Yaméogo, 1987, Burkina Faso)

Money / al-Foulous (Ibrahim Lama, 1945, Egypt)

Money and Children / al-Mâl wa-l-banoun (Ibrahim Emara, 1954, Egypt)

Money and Monsters / al-Foulous wa-l-wouhouch (Ahmed al-Sabaawi, 1988, Egypt)

Money and Women / Mâl wa nisâ² (Hassan al-Imam, 1960, Egypt)

Money Is Everything / Imali Yiswe (Zulu, No director credited, 1988, South Africa)

Money Machine (English, No director credited, 1988, South Africa)

Money Order, The / Mandabi / Le Mandat (Ousmane Sembene, 1968, Senegal)

Money Power (Yoruba, Ola Balogun, 1982, Nigeria)

Money to Burn / Geld Soos Bossies (Afrikaans, Jamie Uys, 1955, South Africa)

Monkey Trainer, The / al-Qirdâtî (Niazi Mostafa, 1987, Egypt)

Monsieur Fabre's Windmill / Le Moulin de Monsieur Fabre (Ahmed Rachedi, 1984, Algeria)

Monster Makes Man, A / al-Wahch dâkhil al-insân (Achraf Fahmi, 1981, Egypt)

Monster, The / al-Wahch (Salah Abou Seif, 1954, Egypt)

Monsters (English, No director credited, 1986, South Africa)

Monsters of the Port, The / Wouhouch al-minâ² (Niazi Mostafa, 1983, Egypt)

Montagne de Baya, La / Baya's Mountain (Azzedine Meddour, 1997, Algeria)

Mooimeisiesfonten (Afrikaans, Elmo de Witt, 1977, South Africa)

Moolade (Ousmane Sembene, 2002, Senegal)

Moon Mountain (English, No director credited, 1984, South Africa)

Moon of Honey and Gall / Chahr ʿasal basal (Issa Karama, 1960, Egypt)

Moon Wedding / Noce de lune (Taïeb Louhichi, 1998, Tunisia)

Moonlighting / Le Clandestin (Benamar Bakhti, 1991, Algeria)

Moontalk (No director credited, 1988, South Africa)

Moord in Kompartement 1001E (Afrikaans, Pierre D. Botha, 1961, South Africa)

More Beautiful than the Moon / Qamar abata²ch (Niazi Mostafa, 1950, Egypt)

Môre Môre (Afrikaans, Elmo de Witt, 1973, South Africa)

More Time (Isaac Meli Mabhikwa, 1992, Zimbabwe)

Morgan Ahmed Morgan / Morgaan Ahmed Morgaan (Ali Idris, 2007, Egypt)

Morituri (Okacha Touita, 2007, Algeria)

Moroccan Chronicles / Chroniques marocaines (Moumen Smihi, 1999, Morocco)

Moroccan Dream (Jamal Belmejoub, 2007, Morocco)

Moroccan Symphony / Symphonie Marocaine (Kamal Kamal, 2005, Morocco)

Morsi from Above, Morsi from Below / Moursî fawq Moursî taht (Mohamed Abdel Aziz, 1982, Egypt)

Mummy's Suitor / Khatîb mâmâ (Fatine Abdel Wahab, 1971, Egypt)

Muna Moto (Jean-Pierre Dikongue-Pipa, 1975, Cameroon)

Munyurangabo (Lee Isaac Chung, 2007, Rwanda)

Murder in the Kraal (Zulu, *No director credited*, 1989, South Africa)

Murder in the Veld (*No director credited*, 1987, South Africa)

Murder on Holiday / Die Vlindervanger (Afrikaans, Franz Marx, 1976, South Africa)

Murderer Who Has Killed No-One, A / Qâtil mâ qatalch hadd (Mohamed Abdel Aziz, 1979, Egypt)

Murderer, The (English, *No director credited*, 1985, South Africa)

Murderers, The (English, *No director credited*, 1988, South Africa)

Murderess, The / al-Qâtilah (Hassan Reda, 1949, Egypt)

Murderess, The / al-Qâtilah (Inas al-Deghidi, 1992, Egypt)

Murdering Maxwell (*No director credited*, 1988, South Africa)

Murderous Mother, The / al-Oumm al-qâtlah (Ahmed Kamel Morsi, 1952, Egypt)

Murky Death / La Mort trouble (Claude d'Anna and Ferid Boughedir, 1970, Tunisia)

Murphy's Fault (English, Robert Smawley, 1988, South Africa)

Murugadas / The Messiah of Peace (English, *No director credited*, 1983, South Africa)

Mushroom / ʿEish el ghuraab (Samir Seif, 1997, Egypt)

Music Is in Danger, The / al-Mazzîkah fî khatar (Mahmoud Farid, 1976, Egypt)

Music . . . Love and Espionage / Mousîqâ . . . houbb . . . wa Gâsousiyyah (Nour al-Demerdache, 1971, Egypt)

Musician, The / al-Mazzîkâtî (Mohamed Abaza, 1988, Egypt)

Musician, The / al-Mousîqar (al-Sayed Ziyada, 1946, Egypt)

Musicmaker, The (Zulu / English, C. Dippenaar, 1984, South Africa)

Musik Man (English, Ola Balogun, 1976, Nigeria)

Must I Kill My Husband? / Hal aqtoul zawguî (Houssam Eddine Mostafa, 1958, Egypt)

Mustapha or The Little Magician / Mostafa aw

al-sâhir al-saghîr (Mahmoud Khalil, 1932, Egypt)

Mutator / Time of the Beast (English, John Bowey, 1989, South Africa)

Mute Girl, The / al-Kharsâʾ (Hassan al-Imam, 1961, Egypt)

Mute, The / al-Akhras (Ahmed al-Sabaawi, 1980, Egypt)

Muti / Medicine (Zulu, *No director credited*, 1990, South Africa)

My African Adventure (English, Boaz Davidson, 1987, South Africa)

My Beloved Is Very Mischievous / Habîbatî chaqiyyah guiddan (Niazi Mostafa, 1974, Egypt)

My Beloved's Fault / Ghaltat habiibî (al-Sayed Bedeir, 1958, Egypt)

My Beloved's Khoulkhal / Khoulkhâl habîbî (Hassan Reda, 1960, Egypt)

My Blood, My Tears and My Smile / Damî wa doumouʾî wa ibtisâmatî (Hussein Kamal, 1973, Egypt)

My Broer se Bril (Afrikaans, Dirk de Villiers, 1972, South Africa)

My Brother My Enemy (English, Joey Ford, 1990, South Africa)

My Brown-Haired Love / Habîbî al-asmar (Hassan al-Saïfi, 1958, Egypt)

My Child / Waladî (Abdallah Barakat, 1949, Egypt)

My Children / Awlâdî (Omar Guemei, 1951, Egypt)

My Companion / Charîk hayâtî (Elhami Hassan, 1953, Egypt)

My Country My Hat (English, David Bensusan, 1983, South Africa)

My Daughter / Ibnatî (Niazi Mostafa, 1944, Egypt)

My Daughter and the Wolf / Ibnatî wa-l-dhiʾb (Sayed Tantawi, 1977, Egypt)

My Daughter and the Wolves / Ibnatî wa-l-dhiʾâb (Hassan al-Saïfi, 1986, Egypt)

My Daughter, Love and Me / Anâ wa ibnâtî wa-l-houbb (Mohamed Radi, 1974, Egypt)

My Daughters and I / Anâ wa banâtî (Hussein Helmi al-Mouhandès, 1961, Egypt)

My Dearest Daughter / Ibnatî al-ʾazîzah (Helmi Rafla, 1971, Egypt)

My Dignity / Karâmatî (Achraf Fahmi, 1979, Egypt)

My Eye Blinks / ʿAynî bi-triff (Abbas Kamel, 1950, Egypt)

My Wife's Honor / Karâmat zawgatî (Fatine Abdel Wahab, 1967, Egypt)

My Wife's Husband / ʿArîs mirâtî (Abbas Kamel, 1959, Egypt)

My Wife's Husband / Gouz mirâti (Niazi Mostafa, 1961, Egypt)

Mysteries of Life, The / Khafâyâ al-douniâ (Ibrahim Lama, 1942, Egypt)

Mystery of the Magic Cap, The / Sirr tâqiyyat al-ikhfâʾ (Niazi Mostafa, 1959, Egypt)

'n Beeld vir Jeannie (Afrikaans, Elmo de Witt, 1976, South Africa)

'n Beeld vir Jeannie (Afrikaans, Elmo de Witt, 1976, South Africa)

'n Brief vir Simone (Afrikaans, Anton Goosen and F. C. Hamman, 1980, South Africa)

'n Brief vir Simone (Afrikaans, Anton Goosen and F. C. Hamman, 1980, South Africa)

'n Dogter van die Veld (Afrikaans, J. Sinclair, 1933, South Africa)

'n Dogter van die Veld (Afrikaans, J. Sinclair, 1933, South Africa)

'n Plan is 'n Boerdery (Afrikaans, Pierre de Wet, 1954, South Africa)

'n Plan is 'n Boerdery (Afrikaans, Pierre de Wet, 1954, South Africa)

'n Plekkie in die Son (Afrikaans, William Faure, 1979, South Africa)

'n Plekkie in die Son (Afrikaans, William Faure, 1979, South Africa)

'n Pot Vol Winter (Afrikaans, Johan Bernard, 1991, South Africa)

'n Pot Vol Winter (Afrikaans, Johan Bernard, 1991, South Africa)

'n Seder Val in Waterkloof (Afrikaans, Franz Marx, 1978, South Africa)

'n Seder Val in Waterkloof (Afrikaans, Franz Marx, 1978, South Africa)

'n Sondag in September (Afrikaans, Jan Scholz, 1976, South Africa)

'n Sondag in September (Afrikaans, Jan Scholz, 1976, South Africa)

'n Sonneblom uit Parys (Afrikaans, Sias Odendaal, 1974, South Africa)

'n Sonneblom uit Parys (Afrikaans, Sias Odendaal, 1974, South Africa)

'n Wereld sonder Grense (Afrikaans, Frans Nel, 1987, South Africa)

Na cidade vazia / Hollow City (Maria João Ganga, 2004, Angola)

Nadia / Nadia (Ahmed Badrakhan, 1969, Egypt)

Nadia / Nâdiâ (Fatine Abdel Wahab, 1949, Egypt)

Nadia et Sarra (Moufida Tlatli, 2004, Tunisia)

Nadouga / Nadougâ (Hussein Fawzi, 1944, Egypt)

Nag van die Negentiende, Die (Afrikaans, Koos Roets, 1991, South Africa)

Nag van Vrees / Night of Terror (Afrikaans, Jimmy Murray and Stanley Roup, 1986, South Africa)

Nagui al-Ali / Nâguî al-ʾAlî (Atef al-Tayeb, 1992, Egypt)

Nagwa Madam Chatlata / Nagwâ madame Chalâtah (Yehya al-Alami, 1986, Egypt)

Nahed / Nâhid (Mohamed Karim, 1952, Egypt)

Nahla (Farouk Beloufa, 1979, Algeria)

Naïma Is a Forbidden Fruit / Naʾîmah fâkihah mouharramah (Ahmed al-Sabaawi, 1984. Egypt)

Naitou (Moussa Kemoko Diakite, 1982, Guinea)

Naked Prey, The (English, Cornell Wilde, 1966, South Africa)

Naked Truth, The / al-Haqîqah al-ʾâriyah (Atef Salem, 1963, Egypt)

Name / Mamalotsi (Tswana, No director credited, 1987, South Africa)

Nancy and the Monster / Nancy et le monstre (Mahmoud Frites, 2007, Morocco)

Nancy et le monstre / Nancy and the Monster (Mahmoud Frites, 2007, Morocco)

Nannousa / Nannoussah (Gamal Ammar, 1992, Egypt)

Narguis / Narguis (Abdel Fattah Hassan, 1948, Egypt)

Nasser '56 / Nasser 56 (Mohammed Fadel, 1996, Egypt)

Nationalité: immigré / Nationality: Immigrant (Sidney Sokhona, 1975, Mauritania)

Nationality: Immigrant / Nationalité: immigré (Sidney Sokhona, 1975, Mauritania)

Native Who Caused All the Trouble, The (English, Manie van Rensberg, 1989, South Africa)

Naughty Boys (No director credited, 1990, South Africa)

Naughty Camera (English, Lourens Swanepoel, 1988, South Africa)

Nawaem / Nawâʾim (Medhat al-Sibaï, 1988, Egypt)

Night of Terror / Nag van Vrees (English, Jim Murray and Stanley Roup, 1984, South Africa)

Night of the Crime, The / La Nuit du crime (Nabyl Lahlou, 1992, Morocco)

Night of the Decade, The / La Nuit de la décennie (Brahim Babai, 1991, Tunisia)

Night of the Murder, The / Laylat al-qatl (Achraf Fahmi, 1994, Egypt)

Night of the Puppets (English, Daan Retief, 1979, South Africa)

Night of Truth, The / La Nuit de la vérité (Régina Fanta Nacro, 2004, Burkina Faso)

Night Talk / Kalaam al-lil (Inas al-Deghidi, 1999, Egypt)

Night Train, The / Qitar al-layl (Ezz Eddine Zoulficar, 1953, Egypt)

Night when the Moon will Weep, The / Laylah bakâ fîhâ al-qamar (Ahmed Yehya, 1980, Egypt)

Night's Dream, A / Hilm laylah (Salah Badrakhan, 1949, Egypt)

Night's Murmurs / Hamsat al-laykl (Hussein Helmi al-Mouhandès, 1977, Egypt)

Nightmare / Cauchemar (Ahmed Yachfine, 1984, Morocco)

Nightmare / Kâbous (Mohamed Chebl, 1989, Egypt)

Nightmare, The / Family Man (English, John Murlowski, 1988, South Africa)

Nights of Love / Layâlî al-houbb (Helmi Rafla, 1955, Egypt)

Nights of Pleasure / Layâli al-Ouns (Niazi Mostafa, 1947, Egypt)

Nights of Waiting / Laylâlî al-sabr (Ahmed Sarwat, 1992, Egypt)

Nights without Sleep / Lâ anâm (Salah Abou Seif, 1957, Egypt)

Nightslave (English, John Parr, 1988, South Africa)

Niiwan (Clarence T. Delgardo, 1991, Senegal)

90 Minutes / 90 Daqeeqa (Ismaïl Farouq, 2006, Egypt)

Ninja III: The Domination (English, Sam Firstenberg, 1988, South Africa)

Ninja, The / American Samurai (English, No director credited, 1988, South Africa)

Njangaan / N'Diangane (Mahama [Johnson] Traore, 1975, Senegal)

Nkululeko (Zulu / Xhosa, No director credited, 1985, South Africa)

No Choice (No director credited, 1990, South Africa)

No Condolences for the Ladies / Wa lâ ʿazâʾ li-l-sayyidât (Henri Barakat, 1979, Egypt)

No Easy Choice (No director credited, 1988, South Africa)

No Gold for a Dead Diver / Dooie Duikers Deel Nie (Afrikaans, Heinz Reinhl, 1974, South Africa)

No Hard Feelings / Kick or Die (English, Charles Norton, 1987, South Africa)

No Hero / Cupid (English, Tim Spring, 1991, South Africa)

No Man's Love (Nidhal Chatta, 2000, Tunisia)

No One Cries Forever / Tears in the Dry Wind (English, Jans Rautenbach, 1983, South Africa)

No Tears for Ananse (Sam Aryeety, 1968, Ghana)

No Time for Love / Lâ waqt li-l-houbb (Salah Abou Seif, 1963, Egypt)

No Time for Tears / Lâ waqta li-l-doumouʾ (Nader Galal, 1976, Egypt)

No to Violence / Lâ yâ ʿounf (Gamal al-Tabei, 1993, Egypt)

No Understanding / Mâ fîch tafâhoum (Atef Salem, 1961, Egypt)

No Way Out / al-Tarîq (Houssam Eddine Mostafa, 1964, Egypt)

No! (documentary) (el-Hadj Rached, 1985, Libya)

No, Mummy / Lâ yâ oummî (Nasser Hussein, 1979, Egypt)

No, to You whom I Loved / Lâ yâ man kounta habîbî (Helmi Rafla, 1976, Egypt)

No . . . No . . . My Love / Lâ . . . lâ . . . yâ habîbî (Ahmed Diaa Eddine, 1970, Egypt)

Noce d'été / Summer Wedding (Moktar Ladjimi, 2004, Tunisia)

Noce de lune / Moon Wedding (Taïeb Louhichi, 1998, Tunisia)

Noce, La / The Wedding (collective, 1978, Tunisia)

Noces de sang / Blood Wedding (Souheil Benbarka, 1977, Morocco)

Nofuka (Zulu, Tonie van der Merwe, 1978, South Africa)

Nogomopho (Zulu, Tonie van der Merwe, 1974, South Africa)

O Night . . . O Time / Al yâ layl yâ zaman (Ali Reda, 1977, Egypt)

O ritmo do N'Gola Ritmos / The Rhythm of Ngola Ritmos (António Ole, 1978, Angola)

O tempo dos leopardos / Time of Leopards (Camilo de Sousa and Zdravko Velimorovic, 1985, Mozambique)

O testamento do Senhor Napumoceno / Señor Napumoceno's Will (Francisco Manso, 1996, Cape Verde)

O vento sopra do norte / The Wind from the North (José Cardosa, 1987, Mozambique)

Oath of Divorce, An / Yameen talaq (Ali Abdel Khalek, 2001, Egypt)

Oath of Love / ʿAhd al-hawâ (Ahmed Badrakahn, 1955, Egypt)

Obali (Pierre-Marie Dong and Charles Mensah, 1976, Gabon)

Obstinate One, The / al-ʾAnîd (Hassan al-Saïfi, 1973, Egypt)

Ocean of Love, An / Bahr al-gharâm (Hussein Fawzi, 1955, Egypt)

Odd Ball Hall (English, Jackson Hunsicker, 1989, South Africa)

Odirang (Sotho, Johan van Rooyen, 1984, South Africa)

Odyssey, An / Une odyssée (Brahim Babaï, 2004, Tunisia)

Oeil, L' / The Eye (Thierno Faty Sow, 1981, Senegal)

Ofa Oro (Yoruba, Segun Alli, 1992, Nigeria)

Ogbori Elemoso (Adebayo Salami, 1991, Nigeria)

Ogre, The / al-Ghoul (Samir Seif, 1983, Egypt)

Ogun Ajaye (Yoruba, Ola Omonitan, 1986, Nigeria)

Ogun Idile (Yoruba, Segun Alli, 1986, Nigeria)

Ogun Laye (Yoruba, Isola Ogunsola, 1993, Nigeria)

Oh Brother / Vinkel en Koljander (English, Roy Sargeant, 1974, South Africa)

Oh les jours / The Days, The Days (Ahmed El Maânouni, 1978, Morocco)

Oh My Country . . . / Ah yâ balad ah . . . (Farid Chawki Hussein, 1986, Egypt)

Oh People / Yâ nâs yâ hou (Atef Salem, 1991, Egypt)

Oh Schucks It's Schuster (English, Leon Schuster, 1989, South Africa)

Oh Schuks I'm Gatvol (English, Leon Schuster and Willie Esterhuizen, 2004, South Africa)

Oh Schuks, Here Comes UNTAG / Kwagga Strikes Back (English / Afrikaans, David Lister, 1990, South Africa)

Oh, Life, My Love / Ya donya ya gharamy (Magdi Ahmed Ali, 1996, Egypt)

Oil Doom (English, Eddie Ugbomah, 1981, Nigeria)

Oil War Will Not Take Place, The / La Guerre du pétrole n'aura pas lieu (Souheil Benbarka, 1974, Morocco)

Oiseau du paradis L' / The Bird of Paradise (Mohamed Bensaïd, 1981, Morocco)

Oju oro (Yoruba, Olowomujore Oyewole, 1986, Nigeria)

Okal / ʿOkal (Mohamed al-Naggar, 2004, Egypt)

Okavango / Wild Country (English, Percival Rubens, 1989, South Africa)

Old Lady and the Child, The / La Vieille dame et l'enfant (Yahia Debboub, 1997, Algeria)

Old Man and the Crook, The / al-ʾAgouz wa-l-baltaguî (Ibrahim Afifi, 1989, Egypt)

Old People's Love / Gharâm al-chouyoukh (Mohamed Abdel Gawad, 1946, Egypt)

Oleich in the Army / ʿOleich dakhal al-gueich (Youssef Ibrahim, 1989, Egypt)

Olie Kolonie (Afrikaans, Neil Hetherington, 1975, South Africa)

Olive Branch, The / Ghousn al-zaytoun (al-Sayed Bedeir, 1962, Egypt)

Olive Tree of Boul'Hilet, The / L'Olivier de Boul'Hilet (Mohamed Nadir Aziri, 1978, Algeria)

Olivier de Boul'Hilet, L' / The Olive Tree of Boul'Hilet (Mohamed Nadir Aziri, 1978, Algeria)

Om Abbas (Ali Abdelwahab, 1970, Tunisia)

Omar 2000 / Omar 2000 (Ahmed Atef, 2000, Egypt)

Omar and Salma / ʾAmr wa Salma (Akram Farid, 2007, Egypt)

Omar Gatlato (Merzak Allouache, 1976, Algeria)

Ombre de la terre, L' / Shadow of the Earth (Taïeb Louhichi, 1982, Tunisia)

Ombre du guardien, L' / Shadow of the Guardian (Saïd Souda, 1985, Morocco)

Ombre du pharaon, L' / The Shadow of the Pharaoh (Souheil Benbarka, 1996, Morocco)

Options (English, Camilo Vila, 1988, South Africa)

Ordeal, The (*No director credited*, 1987, South Africa)

Ordinary Man, An / *Wahid min al naas* (Ahmed Galal, 2006, Egypt)

Ori Olori (Yoruba, Adeyemi Afolayan, 1989, Nigeria)

Oriental Mystery in Africa (Chinese, *No director credited*, 1990, South Africa)

Origine contrôlée / *Control of Origin* (Ahmed and Zakia Bouchaâla, 2001, Algeria)

Orkney Snork Nie—Die Movie (Afrikaans, Willie Esterhuizen, 1992, South Africa)

Orkney Snork Nie 2—Nog 'n Movie (Afrikaans, Willie Esterhuizen, 1993, South Africa)

Orogun Orun (Yoruba, Baba Balogun, 1992, Nigeria)

Orphan and Love, The / *al-Yâtim wa-l-houbb* (Mahmoud Farid, 1993, Egypt)

Orphan and the Wolves, The / *al-Yatîm wa-l-dhi²âb* (Husssein Emara, 1993, Egypt)

Orphan, The / *al-Yatîmah* (Fouad al-Gazaerli, 1946, Egypt)

Orphans' Property / *Amwâl al-yatâmâ* (Gamal Madkour, 1952, Egypt)

Orun Mooru (Yoruba, Ola Balogun, 1982, Nigeria)

Ose Sango (Yoruba, Afolabi Adesanya, 1991, Nigeria)

Oselu (Yoruba, Bankole Bello, 1996, Nigeria)

Ostrich and the Peacock, The / *al-Na²aama wa al-tawooss* (Mohamed Abou Seif, 2002, Egypt)

Othello (English, Ebulus Timothy, 2001, South Africa)

Other Algeria: Views from Within, The / *L'Autre Algérie: regards intérieurs* (collective, 1998, Algeria)

Other Half, The / *al-Nisf al-âkhar* (Ahmed Badrakhan, 1967, Egypt)

Other Half, The / *L'Autre moitié* (Kaltoum Bornaz, 2006, Tunisia)

Other Man, The / *al-Ragoul al-âkhar* (Mohamed Bassiouni, 1973, Egypt)

Other People's Celebrations / *La Fête des autres* (Hassan Benjelloun, 1990, Morocco)

Other People's Courage / *Le Courage des autres* (Christian Richard, 1982, Burkina Faso)

Other Side of the Mirror, The / *L'Envers du miroir* (Nadia Cherabi-Labidi, 2007, Algeria)

Other Woman, The / *al-Mar²ah al-oukhrah* (Achraf Fahmi, 1978, Egypt)

Other World, The / *L'Autre monde* (Merzak Allouache, 2001, Algeria)

Other, The / *Al-akhar* (Youssef Chahine, 1999, Egypt)

Où cachez-vous le soleil? / *Where Are You Hiding the Sun?* (Abdellah Mesbahi, 1979, Morocco)

Où vas-tu Koumba? / *Where Are You Going, Koumba?* (Simon Augé, 1971, Gabon)

Où vas-tu Moshe? / *Where Are You Going, Moshe?* (Hassan Benjelloun, 2007, Morocco)

Ouaga Saga (Dani Kouyate, 2004, Burkina Faso)

Ouch . . . Ouch . . . / *Aïe . . . Aïe* (Saïd Marzouk, 1992, Egypt)

Ouija / *Ouija* (Khaled Youssef, 2006, Egypt)

Ouloukoro (Dansogho Mohamed Camara, 1983, Guinea)

Oum Al-Saad / *Oumm al-Sa²d* (Ahmed Galal, 1946, Egypt)

Oum Hatchem's Lantern / *Qindîl Oumm Hâchim* (Kamal Ateyya, 1968, Egypt)

Oum Ratiba / *Oumm Ratîbah* (al-Sayed Bedeir, 1959, Egypt)

Ouma Se Slim Kind (Afrikaans, Gustav Kuhn, 2005, South Africa)

Oupa en die Plaasnooientjie (Afrikaans, Pierre de Wet, 1960, South Africa)

Oupa for Sale (Afrikaans, Richard Daneel, 1968, South Africa)

Our Beautiful Dreams / *Ahlâmounâ al-hilwah* (Samir Hafez, 1994, Egypt)

Our Best Days / *Ayyâmounâ al-houlwah* (Helmi Halim, 1955, Egypt)

Our Daughter / *Notre fille* (Daniel Kamwa, 1980, Cameroon)

Our Daughters Abroad / *Banâtounâ fî-l-khârig* (Mohamed Abdel Aziz, 1984. Egypt)

Our Days Are Numbered / *Ayyâm al-²oumr ma²doudah* (Taysir Abboud, 1978, Egypt)

Our Father / *Abouna* / *Notre Père* (Mahamat Saleh Haroun, 2001, Chad)

Our Gang Has No Branch / *Laysa li-²isâbatinâ far² âktar* (Kamal Ateyya, 1990, Egypt)

Our Green Land / *Ardounâ al-khadrâ²* (Ahmed Diaa Eddine, 1956, Egypt)

Past Love / al-Houbb alladhî kân (Ali Badra-khan, 1973, Egypt)

Past Surges Up Again, The / ʿAwdat al-mâdî (Nasseur Hussein, 1987, Egypt)

Path of Happiness, The / Rarîq al-saʾâdah (Ahmed Kamel Hefnawi, 1953, Egypt)

Path of Hope, The / Tarîq al-amal (Ezz Eddine Zoulficar, 1957, Egypt)

Path of Regrets, The / Sikkat al-naddâmah (Houssam Eddine Mostafa, 1987, Egypt)

Path of the Demon, The / Tarîq al-chaytân (Kamal Ateyya, 1963, Egypt)

Path Strewn with Thorns, A / Tarîq al-chawk (Hussein Sedki, 1950, Egypt)

Patience in the Salt Mines / al-Sabr fî-l-mallâhât (Ahmed Yehya, 1986, Egypt)

Patience Pays / al-Sabr gamîl (Niazi Mostafa, 1951, Egypt)

Patrol in the East / Patrouille à l'est (Amar Laskri, 1972, Algeria)

Patrouille à l'est / Patrol in the East (Amar Laskri, 1972, Algeria)

Paul Kruger (Afrikaans, Werner Grünbauer, 1956, South Africa)

Pavement (English, Darrell Roodt, 2003, South Africa)

Paweogo / L'Émigrant / The Emigrant (Kollo Daniel Sanou, 1982, Burkina Faso)

Pay Back My Loan / Rodda qardy (Hishaam Gomʾa, 2006, Egypt)

Peaceful Nest, The / al-ʾIchch al-hâdi (Atef Salem, 1976, Egypt)

Peaceful Night / Sagâ al-layl (Henri Barakat, 1948, Egypt)

Peacock, The / al-Tâwous (Kamal al-Cheikh, 1982, Egypt)

Peasant in Congress, A / Fallah fî el-kongress (Fahmi al-Charkawi, 2002, Egypt)

Peasant's Son, A / Ibn al-fallâh (Abdel Fattah Hassan, 1948, Egypt)

Peasants Arrive, The / al-Fallâhîn ahom (Nasser Hussein, 1992, Egypt)

Pêcheurs, Les / The Fishermen (Ghaouti Bendeddouche, 1976, Algeria)

Pelindara / End of News (Zulu, No director credited, 1989, South Africa)

Penalty / Darbet gazzaʾ (Ashraf Fahmi, 1995, Egypt)

Pennywhistle Blues / The Magic Garden (English, Donald Swanson, 1961, South Africa)

Pens en Pootjies (Afrikaans, Dirk de Villiers, 1974, South Africa)

People and the Nile, The / al-Nâs wa-l-Nîl (Youssef Chahine, 1972, Egypt)

People at the Top / Ahlou al-qimmah (Ali Badra-khan, 1981, Egypt)

People from Down There, The / al-Nas illî taht (Kamel al-Telmessani, 1960, Egypt)

People from the Interior / al-Nâs illî gouwwah (Galal al-Charkawi, 1969, Egypt)

People's Revolt, A / Intifadat shʾab (documentary) (Ahmed Toukhi, 1970, Libya)

People's Secets / Asrâr al-nâs (Hassan al-Imam, 1951, Egypt)

Perfect / Kamel al-awsaaf (Ahmed al-Badri, 2006, Egypt)

Perfume of the Cyclone, The (English, David Irving, 1990, South Africa)

Permission to Kill / Tasrîh bi-l-qatl (Taïmour Serri, 1991, Egypt)

Personal Professor / Moudarris khousousî (Ahmed Diaa Eddine, 1965, Egypt)

Petanqui (Kozoloa Yeo, 1983, Ivory Coast)

Petite Jérusalem, La / Little Jerusalem (Karin Al-bou, 2005, Algeria)

Petits blancs au manioc ou à la sauce gombo / White Beans with Cassava or Gombo Sauce (Moussa Yoro Bathily, 1989, Senegal)

Petticoat Safari (English, David Millin, 1969, South Africa)

Pfuma Yedu (Stephen Chigorimbo, 1991, Zimbabwe)

Phindesela (Zulu, Chris Halgryn, 1979, South Africa)

Phindisela (Zulu / Xhosa, No director credited, 1985, South Africa)

Phoenix Code / Code Phénix (Boubakar Diallo, 2005, Burkina Faso)

Piano Player, The (English, Jean-Pierre Roux, 2002, South Africa)

Piccanin's Christmas (Silent, Dick Cruikshanks, 1917, South Africa)

Pickpocket, The / al-Nachchâl (Mahmoud Farid, 1963, Egypt)

Pickpocket, The / Sâriq al-mihfazat (Zouheir Bekir, 1970, Egypt)

Pickpocket in Spite of Himself / Nachchâl raghmâ anfih (Hassan al-Saïfi, 1969, Egypt)

Pièces d'identité / Identity Papers (Mweze D. Ngangura, 1998, Democratic Republic of Congo)

Piet my Niggie (Afrikaans, Jan Perold, 1964, South Africa)

Piet se Tante (Afrikaans, Pierre de Wet, 1959, South Africa)

Pigalle (Karim Dridi, 1994, Tunisia)

Pigs' Eyes / Mahlokolobe (Sotho, David Bensusan, 1989, South Africa)

Pikkie (Afrikaans, Sias Odendaal, 1972, South Africa)

Pina ya Qetelo (Sotho, Ronnie Isaacs, 1982, South Africa)

Pinkie se Erfenis (Afrikaans, Pierre de Wet, 1946, South Africa)

Pin-Up Girl II, The (Zulu, John Parr, 1989, South Africa)

Pin-Up Girl, The (Zulu, John Parr, 1988, South Africa)

Pirates of the Plains (English, John Cherry and Ken Badish, 1998, South Africa)

Pity / al-Rahman yâ nâs (Kamal Salah Eddine, 1981, Egypt)

Pizza Pizza / Pizza pizza (Mazen al-Gabali, 1998, Egypt)

Place of Weeping (English, Darrell Roodt, 1987, South Africa)

Plage des enfants perdus, La / The Beach of Lost Children (Jillali Ferhati, 1991, Morocco)

Platform 5 / Rasîf nimra khamsah (Niazi Mostafa, 1956, Egypt)

Platoon Leader (English, Aaron Norris, 1987, South Africa)

Player, The / al-Mouqâmir (Chirine Kassem, 1994, Egypt)

Players, The / al-Laᵓîbah (Omar Abdel Aziz, 1987, Egypt)

Playing at the Court of the Great / al-Louᵓb maᵓ al-kibâr (Chérif Arafa, 1991, Egypt)

Playing Dirty (English, Wally van der Merwe, 1984, South Africa)

Playing with Demons / al-Louᵓb maᵓ al-chayâtîn (Ahmed Fouad, 1991, Egypt)

Playing with Fire / al-Liᵓb bi-l-nâr (Omar Guemei, 1948, Egypt)

Playing with Fire / al-Louᵓb bi-l-nâr (Mohamed Marzouk, 1989, Egypt)

Playing with the Evil / al-Liᵓb maᵓ al-achrâr (Tarek al-Nahri, 1993, Egypt)

Pleasant Trip, A / Rihla ladhîdhah (Fatine Abdel Wahab, 1971, Egypt)

Pleasure and the Suffering, The / al-Moutᵓah wa-l-ᵓadhâb (Niazi Mostafa, 1971, Egypt)

Pleasure Market / Souq al-Mutᵓa (Samir Seif, 2000, Egypt)

Pledge, The / al-Wadîᵓah (Hussein Helmi al-Mouhandès, 1965, Egypt)

Plot, The / Mouᵓâmarah (Kamal al-Cheikh, 1953, Egypt)

Plunderers, The / Les Spoliateurs (Mohamed Lamine Merbah, 1972, Algeria)

Po di sangui (Flora Gomes, 1996, Guinea-Bissau)

Poacher, The (English, No director credited, 1987, South Africa)

Poachers, The (Zulu, No director credited, 1990, South Africa)

Poena is Koning! (Willie Esterhuizen, 2007, South Africa)

Point of Contact (English, Bob Misiorowski, 1992, South Africa)

Point of Return (English / Zulu, M. Dyter, 1984, South Africa)

Poison Butterfly (English, Leonardo August, 1990, South Africa)

Poison Minds (English, No director credited, 1990, South Africa)

Polao e Makatsang (Sotho, No director credited, 1985, South Africa)

Police Devils, The / Chayâtîn al-chourtah (Samir Hafez, 1992, Egypt)

Police Inspector, The / Moufattich al-mabâhith (Hussein Fawzi, 1959, Egypt)

Police Officer Resigns, A / Istiqalet dabet shurta (Ashraf Fahmi, 1997, Egypt)

Police Record / Fîch wa tachbîh (Adli Youssef, 1986, Egypt)

Police Record / Sahiifat al-sawâbiq (Ibrahim Emara, 1956, Egypt)

Polish Bride, The / De Poolse Bruid / La Fiancée polonaise (Karim Traïdia, 1998, Algeria)

Politician, The / al-Siyâsî (Ismaïl Galal, 1993, Egypt)

Pomegranate Siesta, The / Les Siestes grenadine (Mahmoud Ben Mahmoud, 1999, Tunisia)

Poolse Bruid, De / The Polish Bride / La Fiancée polonaise (Karim Traïdia, 1998, Algeria)

Poor but Happy / Fouqarâ' wa lâkin sou'adâ' (al-Saïd Mostafa, 1986, Egypt)

Poor Man, A / Insân ghalbân (Helmi Rafla, 1954, Egypt)

Poor Millionnaire, The / al-Millionnaire al-faqîr (Hassan al-Saïfi, 1959, Egypt)

Poor Mr. Hassan / Hasan bîh al-ghalbân (Henri Barakat, 1982, Egypt)

Poor People, The / al-Nâs al-ghalâbah (Mahmoud Farid, 1986, Egypt)

Poor Who Don't Go to Paradise, The / Fouqarâ' la yadkhouloun al-gannah (Medhat al-Sibaï, 1984. Egypt)

Poor, My Children / al-Fouqarâ awlâdii (Nasser Hussein, 1980, Egypt)

Pop's Oasis (English, Harry Hope, 1987, South Africa)

Popular and Sympathetic / Baladî wa-khiffah (Hussein Fawzi, 1950, Egypt)

Port Saïd / Port Sa'îd (Ezz Eddine Zoulficar, 1957, Egypt)

Porte close, La / The Closed Door (Abdelkader Lagtaâ, 1995, Morocco)

Portes du paradis, Les / The Gates of Heaven (Sohael and Imad Noury, 2005, Morocco)

Portes du silence, Les / The Gates of Silence (Amar Laskri, 1987, Algeria)

Portrait, Le / The Portrait (Hadj Rahim, 1994, Algeria)

Portrait, The / Le Portrait (Hadj Rahim, 1994, Algeria)

Posman, Die (Afrikaans, Anthony Wilson, 1987, South Africa)

Postman, The / al-Bostaguî (Hussein Kamal, 1968, Egypt)

Postman, The / Le Facteur (Hakim Noury, 1980, Morocco)

Pote, Le / The Pal / (Hassan Benjelloun, 2002, Morocco)

Poupées d'argile / Clay Dolls (Nouri Bouzid, 2002, Tunisia)

Poupées de roseau / Reed Dolls (Jillali Ferhati, 1981, Morocco)

Pour que vive l'Algérie / So That Algeria May Live (collective, 1972, Algeria)

Pour une infidélité / For an Infidelity (Ndomaluele Mafuta Nlanza, 1994, Democratic Republic of Congo)

Pourquoi la mer? / Why the Sea? (Hakim Belabbes, 2006, Morocco)

Pousse Pousse (Daniel Kamwa, 197, Cameroon)

Poussière de vie / Life Dust (Rachid Bouchareb, 1994, Algeria)

Poussièrre de diamants (Mahmoud Ben Mahmoud and Fadhel Jaibi, 1992, Tunisia)

Power / Mandla (Zulu, No director credited, 1990, South Africa)

Power / The Throne (English, Ladi Ladebo, 1998, Nigeria)

Power of a Woman, The / Gabarout imra'ah (Nader Galal, 1984. Egypt)

Powerful, The / al-Aqwiyâ' (Achraf Fahmi, 1982, Egypt)

*Practical Jokes (No director credited, 1988, South Africa)

Prayer for the Absent One, A / La Prière de l'absent aka *The Secret of the Milky Way / Le Secret de la voie lactée* (Hamid Bennani, 1995, Morocco)

Premier des noirs: Toussaint Louverture / First Among Blacks: Toussaint Louverture (Med Hondo, 2007, Mauritania)

Premier pas / First Step (Mohamed Bouamari, 1979, Algeria)

Prends dix mille balles et casse-toi / Take a Hundred Quid and Get Lost (Mahmoud Zemmouri, 1981, Algeria)

President's Visit, The / Ziyârat al-Sayyed al-ra'îs (Mounir Radi, 1994, Egypt)

Pressure Burst (English, George Canes, 1971, South Africa)

Prester John (Silent, Dick Cruikshanks, 1920, South Africa)

Pretoria O Pretoria (Afrikaans, Betrand Retief, 1979, South Africa)

Pretty and Lying / Hilwah wa kaddâbah (Hussein Fawzi, 1962, Egypt)

Pretty Liar, The / al-Bint al-hilwah al-kaddâbah (Zaki Saleh, 1977, Egypt)

Pretty Mothers-in-Law, The / al-Hamawât al-Fâtinât (Helmi Rafla, 1953, Egypt)

Pretty, Boisterous Girl, A / Hilwah wa chaqiyyah (Issa Karama, 1968, Egypt)

Prey (English, Darrell Roodt, 2006, South Africa)

Promise / Wa'd (Ahmed Badrakhan, 1954, Egypt)

Promised Land (English, Jason Xenopoulos, 2002, South Africa)

Promised Night, The / al-Laylah al-maw'oudah (Yehya al-Alami, 1984. Egypt)

Prophecy, The (*No director credited*, 1990, South Africa)

Prophet's Migration to Medina, The / Higrat al-rasoul (Ibrahim Emara, 1964, Egypt)

Prosecution Pleads Not Guilty, The / al-Niyâbah tatloub al-barâ'ah (Adli Khalil, 1990, Egypt)

Prostitute, The / Bint al-hawâ (Youssef Wahbi, 1953, Egypt)

Protector, The (Zulu, *No director credited*, 1987, South Africa)

Proteus (English, John Greyson, 2004, South Africa)

Provided It Is a Son / Yâ rabb walad (Omar Abdel Aziz, 1984, Egypt)

Provincial in the Army, A / Sa'îdî fî-l-gaych (Nasser Hussein, 1993, Egypt)

Provincials Arrive, The / al-Sa'âydah goum (Nasser Hussein, 1989, Egypt)

Provision / Impango II (Zulu, *No director credited*, 1987, South Africa)

Provisional Title / Titre provisoire (Mostafa Derkaoui, 1984, Morocco)

Psycho (*No director credited*, 1989, South Africa)

Public Idol, The / Ma'boudat al-gamâhîr (Helmi Rafla, 1967, Egypt)

Punchinello Street / Châri' al-bahlawân (Salah Abou Seif, 1949, Egypt)

Punishment, The / al-'Iqâb (Henri Barakat, 1948, Egypt)

Pupil, The / al-Timîdhah (Hassan al-Imam, 1961, Egypt)

Pupils' Notes, The / Nimar al-talâmidhah (Issa Karama, 1964, Egypt)

Puppeteer, The / al-Aragoz (Hani Lachine, 1989, Egypt)

Pure Blood (English, Ken Kaplan, 1999, South Africa)

Purgatory (English, John Newland, 1988, South Africa)

Purse Is with Me, The / al-Mihfazah ma'âya (Mohamed Abdel Aziz, 1978, Egypt)

Qaïs and Leila / Qays wa Layla (Ahmed Diaa Eddine, 1960, Egypt)

Quand les étoiles rencontrent la mer / When the Stars Meet the Sea (Raymond Rajaonarivelo, 1996, Madagascar)

Quand murissent les dattes / When the Dates Ripen (Abdelaziz Ramdani and Larbi Bennani, 1968, Morocco)

Quarante-quatre ou le récits de la nuit / Forty-Four or Tales of the Night (Moumen Smihi, 1981, Morocco)

Quarry, The / AWOL (English, Neil Sonnekus, 1989, South Africa)

Quarter of a Dozen Bad People, A / Rib' dasta achrâr (Nagdi Hafez, 1970, Egypt)

Quartier Mozart (Jean-Pierre Bekolo, 1985, Cameroon)

Que fait-on ce dimanche / What Are We Doing This Sunday? (Lotfi Essid, 1983, Tunisia)

Queen and I, The / al-Malikah wa anâ (Atef Salem, 1975, Egypt)

Queen Mother, The / Si-Guériki, la reine-mère (Idrissou Mora-Kpaï, 2001, Bénin)

Queen of Beauty, The / Malikat al-gamâl (Togo Mizrahi, 1946, Egypt)

Queen of Tarab, The / Soultânat al-tarab (Hassan al-Imam, 1979, Egypt)

Queen of the Castle (English, Derrick Louw, 1991, South Africa)

Queen of the Desert, The / Soultânat al-sahrâ (Niazi Mostafa, 1947, Egypt)

Queen of the Night, The / Mlikat al-layl (Hassan Ramzi, 1971, Egypt)

Queen's Juice, The / Chahd al-malikhah (Houssam Eddine Mostafa, 1985, Egypt)

Quest for Freedom (documentary) (Olley Maruma, 1981, Zimbabwe)

Quest for Gold (English, *No director credited*, 1990, South Africa)

Quest for Love (English, Helena Nogueira, 1987, South Africa)

Question d'honneur / Question of Honor (Abderrazak Hellal, 1997, Algeria)

Question of Honor / Question d'honneur (Abderrazak Hellal, 1997, Algeria)

Question of Love, A / Sou'âl fî-l-houbb (Henri Barakat, 1975, Egypt)

Quiet Honeymoon / Chahr 'asal bidoun iz'âg (Abdel Meneim Choukri, 1968, Egypt)

Quiet Thunder (English, Hans Kuhle, 1987, South Africa)

Rabea Al-Adawiyya / Rabi²ah al-²Adawiyyah (Niazi Mostafa, 1963, Egypt)

Rabi (Gaston Kaboré, 1992, Burkina Faso)

Race against Time / Sibâq ma² al-zaman (Anwar Qawadri, 1993, Egypt)

Rachida (Yamina Bachir-Chouikh, 2002, Algeria)

Racing Stripes (English, Frederick DuChau, 2004, South Africa)

Radhia (Mohamed Lamine Merbah, 1992, Algeria)

Rag Tag (Adaora Nwandu, 2006, Nigeria)

Ragab on a Burning Roof / Ragab fawqa safihin sâkhin (Ahmed Fouad, 1979, Egypt)

Ragab the Monster / Ragab al-wahch (Kamal Salah Eddine, 1985, Egypt)

Rage (Newton I. Aduaka, 2000, Nigeria)

Rage to Kill (English, David Winters, 1987, South Africa)

Rahma (Omar Chraïbi, 2003, Morocco)

Raï (Sid Ali Fettar, 1988, Algeria)

Railway Switch / al-Tahwila (Amali Bahnasi, 1996, Egypt)

Rains Have Dried Up, The / Gaffat al-amtâr (Sayed Issa, 1967, Egypt)

Raka (Afrikaans, Sven Persson, 1968, South Africa)

Rally / Safari 3000 (English and Afrikaans, Harry Hurwitz, 1980, South Africa)

Ramadan on a Volcano / Ramadân fawqa al-Bourkân (Ahmed al-Sabaawi, 1985, Egypt)

Rançon d'une alliance, La / The Price of a Marriage (Sébastien Kamba, 1973, Congo)

Ransom (Zulu, Chris du Toit, 1989, South Africa)

Rape / Ightisâb (Ali Abdel Khalek, 1989, Egypt)

Rapists, The / al-Moughtasiboun (Saïd Marzouk, 1989, Egypt)

Rare Coins / al²Imlah al-nâdirah (Samir Hafez, 1992, Egypt)

Rat, The (English, Mike Inglesby, 1988, South Africa)

Rat, The / Fatal Mission / Kwavinga Run (English, Anthony Bond and Tonie van der Merwe, 1990, South Africa)

Ravenscroft / Buried Alive (English, Gerard Kikoine, 1988, South Africa)

Raw Terror (English, Hanro Mohr, 1986, South Africa)

Raw Vengeance (English, Joey Ford, 1988, South Africa)

Rawd Al-Farag / Rawd al-Farag (Abdel Fattah Madbouli, 1987, Egypt)

Rawiya / Râwiya (Niazi Mostafa, 1946, Egypt)

Raya and Sakina / Rayyâ wa Sakînah (Salah Abou Seif, 1953, Egypt)

Raya and Sekina / Rayyâ wa Sakînah (Ahmed Fouad, 1983, Egypt)

Real Dreams / Ahlam haqiqeyya (Mohamed Gom²a, 2007, Egypt)

Real Premonition (Ahmed Ziad, 2007, Morocco)

Reality and Myth / Dan Iyo Xarrago (Idriss Hassan Dirie, 1973, Somalia)

Realm of Hallucinations, The / Mamlakat al-halwasah (Mohamed Abdel Aziz, 1983, Egypt)

Reason and Money, The / al-²Aql wa-l-mâl (Abbas Kamel, 1965, Egypt)

Reason to Die (English, Tim Spring, 1989, South Africa)

Reasonable Man, A (English, Gavin Hood, 1999, South Africa)

Rebel Woman / Imra²ah moutamarridah (Youssef Abou Seif, 1986, Egypt)

Rebel, Die / Sending vir 'n Voortvlugtige (Afrikaans, Daan Retief, 1976, South Africa)

Rebel, The / al-Moutamarrid (Henri Barakat, 1988, Egypt)

Rebel, The / al-Moutamarridah (Mahmoud Zoulficar, 1963, Egypt)

Rebel, The / al-Namroud (Atef Salem, 1956, Egypt)

Rebel, The / Le Rebelle (Omar Khlifi, 1968, Tunisia)

Rebel, The / Si Mohand U M'hand / L'Insoumis (Liazid Khadja and Rachid Benallel, 2006, Algeria)

Rebelle, Le / The Rebel (Omar Khlifi, 1968, Tunisia)

Rebels, The / al-Moutamarridoun (Tewfik Saleh, 1968, Egypt)

Reckless Youth / Âkhir chaqâwah (Issa Karama, 1964, Egypt)

Reckoning, The (English, Wally van der Merwe, 1984, South Africa)

Red Card / Kârt ahmar (Oussama al-Kerdawi, 1994, Egypt)

Red Dust (English, Tom Hooper, 2004, South Africa)

Red Flag, The / al-Râyah al-hamrâ (Achraf Fahmi, 1994, Egypt)

Red for Danger (*No director credited*, 1987, South Africa)

Red Mask, The / al-Qinâal-ahmar (Youssef Wahbi, 1947, Egypt)

Red Mistake (Teshome Kebede Theodros, 2006, Ethiopia)

Red Moon, The / La Lune rouge (Hassan Benjelloun, 2006, Morocco)

Red Notebook, The / al-Agenda al-hamraa³ (Ali Ragab, 2000, Egypt)

Red Rose, The / al-Warda al-hamra (Inas al-Deghidi, 2000, Egypt)

Red Satin / Satin rouge (Raja Amari, 2002, Tunisia)

Red Scorpion (English, Joe Zito and Joao Fernandes, 1987, South Africa)

Red Windmill, The (English, Frans Nel, 1990, South Africa)

Reda Bond / Ridâ Bond (Nagdi Hafez, 1970, Egypt)

Redemption, The (English, Kristine Peterson, 1995, South Africa)

Redeyef 54 (Ali Abidi, 1997, Tunisia)

Reds, The (*No director credited*, 1989, South Africa)

Reed Dolls / Poupées de roseau (Jillali Ferhati, 1981, Morocco)

Reef of Stars (Silent, Joseph Albrecht, 1924, South Africa)

Reen kom Wee, Die (Afrikaans, Pierre D. Botha, 1963, South Africa)

Refugee, The (*No director credited*, 1989, South Africa)

Refus, Le / The Refusal (Mohamed Bouamari, 1982, Algeria)

Refusal, The / Le Refus (Mohamed Bouamari, 1982, Algeria)

Regard, Le / The Look (Nour-Eddine Lakhmari, 2004, Morocco)

Regaya / Wandering Heart / Cœur nomade (Fitouri Belhiba, 1990, Tunisia)

Remains of a Virgin, The / Baqâyâ ʿadhrâ³ (Houssam Eddine Mostafa, 1962, Egypt)

Remember Me / Idhkourînî (Henri Barakat, 1978, Egypt)

Remorse / al-Nadam (Nader Galal, 1978, Egypt)

Remorse / Wakhz al-damir (Ibrahim Lama, 1931, Egypt)

Rendezvous / Rendezvous (Ali Abdel Khalek, 2001, Egypt)

Rendezvous, The / al-Mawʾid (Ahmed Kamel Morsi, 1955, Egypt)

Rendezvous for Dinner / Mawʾid ʿalâ al-ʾachâ³ (Mohamed Khan, 1981, Egypt)

Rendezvous in the Tower / Mawʾid fî-l-bourg (Ezz Eddine Zoulficar, 1962, Egypt)

Rendezvous with Fate / Mawʾid maʾ al-qadar (Mohamed Radi, 1986, Egypt)

Rendezvous with Happiness / Mawʾid maʾ al-saʾâdah (Ezz Eddine Zoulficar, 1954, Egypt)

Rendezvous with Life / Mawʾid maʾ al-hayâh (Ezz Eddine Zoulficar, 1953, Egypt)

Rendezvous with Satan / Mawʾîd ma ʿIblîs (Kamel al-Telmessani, 1955, Egypt)

Rendezvous with Soussou / Miʾwâd maʾ Sousou (Henri Barakat, 1977, Egypt)

Rendezvous with the Beloved / Mawʾid maʾ al-habîb (Helmi Rafla, 1971, Egypt)

Rendezvous with the Past / Mawʾid maʾ al-mâdî (Mahmoud Zoulficar, 1961, Egypt)

Rendezvous with the President / Mawʾid maʾ al-raʾîs (Mohamed Radi, 1990, Egypt)

Rendezvous with the Unknown / Mawʾid maʾ al-magʾhoul (Atef Salem, 1959, Egypt)

Rendition (Gavin Hood, 2007, South Africa)

Renegades / Ship of the Desert (English, Frank Schaeffer, 1988, South Africa)

Reported Missing / Kharaga wa lam yaʾoud (Mohamed Khan, 1985, Egypt)

Requiem for a Village (Michael Raeburn, 1976, Zimbabwe)

Rescue / American Eagle (English, Robert Smawley, 1988, South Africa)

Rescuers / Umsizi (Zulu / Xhosa, *No director credited*, 1985, South Africa)

Reserved for Husbands / Li-l-moutazawwiguîn faqat (Ismaïl al-Qadi, 1969, Egypt)

Reserved for Men / Li-l-rigâl faqat (Mahmoud Zoulficar, 1964, Egypt)

Reserved for Women / Li-l-nisâ faqat (Ali Beheiri, 1966, Egypt)

Resistance Fighters, The / Les Résistants (Yahia Debboub, 1997, Algeria)

Résistant inconnu, Le / The Unknown Resistance Fighter (Larbi Bennani, 1995, Morocco)

Rising Storm (English, *No director credited*, 1989, South Africa)

River of Death (English, Steve Carver, 1988, South Africa)

River of Diamonds (English, Robert Smawley, 1989, South Africa)

River of Fear, The / Nahr al-khawf (Mohamed Abou Seif, 1988, Egypt)

River of Life, The / Nahr al-hayât (Hassan Reda, 1964, Egypt)

River of Love / Nahr al-houbb (Ezz Eddine Zoulficar, 1960, Egypt)

River, The / Le Fleuve (Mama Keïta, 2003, Guinea)

Riverman, The / Return to Eden (English, Ivan Hall, 1983, South Africa)

Road Back, The / American Kickboxer II (English, Albert Pyun and Darrell Roodt, 1991, South Africa)

Road Devils / ʿAfarit al-asphalt (Osama Fawzi, 1996, Egypt)

Road to Mecca, The (English, Peter Goldsmid and Athol Fugard, 1991, South Africa)

Road to the Asylum, The / al-Tarîq li-moustachfâ al-magânîn (Nasser Hussein, 1992, Egypt)

Road, The / al-Tariq (Youssef Chaabane, 1973, Libya)

Robin Muir (English, *No director credited*, 1986, South Africa)

Roll Up, Roll Up / Itfarrag ya salaam (Mohamed Kamal al-Kalioubi, 2001, Egypt)

Romantic / Romantica (Zaki Fatin Abdel Wahab, 1996, Egypt)

Roof a Family, A / Un toit une famille (Rabah Laradji, 1982, Algeria)

Room Mates (*No director credited,* 1987, South Africa)

Room to Rent (English, Khaled al-Hagar, 2000, Egypt)

Roots in the Air / Goudhour fî-l-hawâʾ (Yehya al-Alami, 1986, Egypt)

Rose des sables / Desert Rose / Louss (Mohamed Rachid Benhadj, 1988, Algeria)

Rose of Rhodesia, The (Silent, Harold Shaw, 1917, South Africa)

Roues libres / Freewheeling (Sidiki Bakaba, 2002, Ivory Coast)

Rough Justice (English, Mario Di Leo, 1988, South Africa)

Rough Nights in Paradise (English, *No director credited*, 1985, South Africa)

Round Up! / Hallaq hoosh! (Mohammed Abdel Aziz, 1997, Egypt)

Rousseaus van La Rochelle, Die / Eendag op in Reëndag (Afrikaans, Jans Rautenbach, 1975, South Africa)

Route of Terror, The / Darb al-rahbah (Ali Abdel Khalek, 1990, Egypt)

Rubbish / Qadhârah (Adel al-Aassar, 1994, Egypt)

Rue le Caire / Cairo Street (Mohamed Abdelkrim Derkaoui, 1998, Morocco)

Rue Princesse (Henri Duparc, 1994, Ivory Coast)

Ruining the Party / Kursi fil koloob (Sameh al-Bagouri, 2000, Egypt)

Ruiter in die Nag, Die / The Rider in the Night (Afrikaans, Jan Perold, 1963, South Africa)

Rumor of Love / Ichâʾat houbb (Fatine Abdel Wahab, 1960, Egypt)

Run Away (*No director credited,* 1990, South Africa)

Run for Freedom (English, M. Dyter, 1984, South Africa)

Run for Your Life (English, *No director credited,* 1986, South Africa)

Run to Freedom (Laurens Barnard, 1989, South Africa)

Run, The (*No director credited,* 1988, South Africa)

Runaway Hero (Henry Diffenthal, 1990, South Africa)

Runaway Melody (English, *No director credited,* 1979, South Africa)

Runaway Mummy / Horoob mumia (Mourad Aknash, 2003, Egypt)

Runner Up (*No director credited,* 1986, South Africa)

Runner, The (*No director credited,* 1989, South Africa)

Running Riot (English, Koos Roets, 2006, South Africa)

Running Wild (English, Duncan McLachlan, 1993, South Africa)

Running Wild (English, *No director credited,* 1987, South Africa)

Running Young (English, Johan van Rooyen, 1983, South Africa)

Rupture / Breakdown (Mohamed Chouikh, 1982, Algeria)

Sand Storm / *Vent de sable* (Mohamed Lakhdar Hamina, 1982, Algeria)

Sanders of the River / *Death Drums Along the River* (English, Lawrence Huntington, 1964, South Africa)

Sandgrass People (English, Koos Roets, 1990, South Africa)

Sandman (*No director credited*, 1989, South Africa)

Sandpiper, The (English, Lourens Swanepoel, 1984, South Africa)

Sands of the Kalahari (English, Cy Enfield, 1965, South Africa)

Sang des parias, Le / *Blood of the Outcasts* (Mamadou Djim Kola, 1971, Burkina Faso)

Sango Malo / *The Village Teacher* (Bassek Ba Kobhio, 1991, Cameroon)

Sankofa (Haïle Gerima, 1993, Ethiopia)

Sanna / *Torn Allegiance* (English, Alan Nathanson, 1984, South Africa)

Sarafina! (English, Darrell Roodt, 1991, South Africa)

Sarah (Afrikaans, Gordon Vorster, 1975, South Africa)

Sarie Marais (Afrikaans, Francis Coley, 1949, South Africa)

Sarie Marais (Afrikaans, Joseph Albrecht, 1931, South Africa)

Sarraounia (Med Hondo, 1986, Mauritania)

Satan in the City / *Iblîs fî-l-madîna* (Samir Seif, 1978, Egypt)

Satan Is a Woman / *al-Chaytân imra'ah* (Niazi Mostafa, 1972, Egypt)

Satan Shoots (English, David Wicht, 1986, South Africa)

Satan's Angels / *Les Anges de Satan* (Ahmed Boulane, 2007, Morocco)

Satan's Empire / *al-Bidâyah* (Salah Abou Seif, 1986, Egypt)

Satan's Friends / *Asdiqâ' al-chattân* (Ahmed Yassine, 1988, Egypt)

Satan's Gates / *Bawwâbat Iblîs* (Adel al-Aassar, 1993, Egypt)

Satan's Harvest (English, George Montgomery, 1970, South Africa)

Satanskoraal (Afrikaans, Elmo de Witt, 1959, South Africa)

Satin rouge / *Red Satin* (Raja Amari, 2002, Tunisia)

Saturday Night at the Palance (English, Robert Davies, 1988, South Africa)

Savage Barricades / *Barricades sauvages* (Mohamad Benayat, 1975, Algeria)

Savage Desire / *Rughbah moutawahhichah* (Khaïri Bechara, 1991, Egypt)

Savage Encounter, A (English, *No director credited*, 1980, South Africa)

Savage Sport, The (English, Keith G. van de Wat, 1974, South Africa)

Savage, The / *al-Moutawahhichah* (Samir Seif, 1979, Egypt)

Save this Family / *Anqidhou hâdhini al-'â'ilah* (Hassan Ibrahim, 1979, Egypt)

Saving What Can Still Be Saved / *Inqâdh mâ youmkin inqâdhouh* (Saïd Marzouk, 1985, Egypt)

Saxman / *The Revenger* (English, Cedric Sundström, 1987, South Africa)

Say Cheese for the Photo to Be Beautiful / *Idhak el sourah tetla' helwa* (Cherif Arafa, 1998, Egypt)

Say-Mama (Xhosa, *No director credited*, 1985, South Africa)

Sayyed Darwish / *Sayyed Darwich* (Ahmed Badrakhan, 1966, Egypt)

Sayyed the Crook / *al-Wâd Sayyed al-nassâb* (Nasser Hussein, 1990, Egypt)

Sayyed the Servant / *al-Wâd Sayyed al-chaghghâl* (Hussein Kamal, 1993, Egypt)

Scam, The / *L'Esquive* (Abdellatif Kechiche, 2004, Tunisia)

Scandal at Zamalek / *Fadîhah fî-l-Zamâlik* (Niazi Mostafa, 1959, Egypt)

Scandal Merchant, The / *Tâguir al-fadâ'ih* (Hassan al-Imam, 1953, Egypt)

Scandal, The / *al-Fadîhah* (Farouk al-Rachidi, 1992, Egypt)

Scatterbrain, The / *al-Tâ'ichah* (Ibrahim Emara, 1946, Egypt)

Scattered Beauty / *La beauté éparpillée* (Lahcen Zinoun, 2007, Morocco)

Scavengers (English, Duncan MacLachlan, 1986, South Africa)

Scavengers, The / *The Jackals* (English, Robert R. Webb, 1967, South Africa)

Scent of the Sea / *Parfum de mer* (Abdelhaï Laraki, 2007, Morocco)

Sergent Bakary Woolen, Le / Sergeant Bakary Woolen (Mohamed Lamine Akin, 1966, Guinea)

Serious Police Record, A / Arbâb sawâbiq (Mohamed Abaza, 1988, Egypt)

Sersant en die Tiger Moth, Die (Afrikaans, Koos Roets, 1973, South Africa)

Servant, The / al-Khâdim (Ahmed Yeyha, 1990, Egypt)

Service Stairs, The / al-Soullam al-khalfî (Atef Salem, 1973, Egypt)

Ses Soldate / Six Soldiers (Afrikaans, Bertrand Retief, 1975, South Africa)

Setipana (Sotho, Simon Sabela, 1978, South Africa)

Seun van die Wildtemmer, Die (Afrikaans, Bertrand Retief, 1973, South Africa)

Seuns van die Wolke (Afrikaans, Franz Marx, 1975, South Africa)

Seven against the Sun (English, David Millin, 1964, South Africa)

Seven Days in Paradise / Sabʾayyâm fî-l-gannah (Fatine Abdel Wahab, 1969, Egypt)

Seven Gates of the Night, The / Les Sept portes de la nuit (Mostafa Derkaoui, 1994, Morocco)

Seven Girls / al-Sabʾbanât (Atef Salem, 1961, Egypt)

7 Playing Cards / 7 waraqaat kutsheena (Cherif Sabri, 2004, Egypt)

17 rue Bleue (Chad Chenouga, 2001, Algeria)

Seventeen-Year-Old Girl, The / Bint sabataʾch (Kamal Ateyya, 1958, Egypt)

Seventh Sense / Al-Hassa Al-Sabʾa (Ahmed Mekky, 2005, Egypt)

Seventh Sin, The / al-Khatiʾa al-sabeʾa (Abdel Latif Zaki, 1996, Egypt)

Seventh Wife, The / al-Zawgah al-sâbiʾah (Ibrahim Emara, 1950, Egypt)

Seventy-year-old Joker, A / Chaqâwah fî-l-sabʾîn (Mohamed al-Chami, 1988, Egypt)

Sewende Horison, Die (Afrikaans, Franz Cloete, 1958, South Africa)

Sexy Girls, The (English, Russell Thompson, 1997, South Africa)

Sey Seyeti / Un homme, des femmes / A Man and Some Women (Ben Diogaye Beye, 1980, Senegal)

Shadow of Liberty, The / L'Ombre de Liberty (Léon Ivanga Imunga, 2006, Gabon)

Shadow of the Earth / L'Ombre de la terre (Taïeb Louhichi, 1982, Tunisia)

Shadow of the Guardian / L'Ombre du guardien (Saïd Souda, 1985, Morocco)

Shadow of the Pharaoh, The / L'Ombre du pharaon (Souheil Benbarka, 1996, Morocco)

Shadowed Mind, The (English, Cedric Sundström, 1988, South Africa)

Shadowplay (English, Oliver Stapleton, 1980, South Africa)

Shadows on the Other Bank / al-Zilâl fî-l-gânib al-âkhar (Ghaleb Chaath, 1975, Egypt)

Shame / al-ʾAyb (Galal al-Charkawi, 1967, Egypt)

Shamwari (English, Clive Harding, 1982, South Africa)

Shangani Patrol (English, David Millin, 1970, South Africa)

Shared Bread / al-ʾIch wa-l-milh (Hussein Fawzi, 1949, Egypt)

Shark Attack (English, Bob Misiorowski, 1998, South Africa)

Shark Attack 2 (English, David Worth, 1999, South Africa)

Shattered Years / Des années déchirées (Rachid Bouchareb, 1992, Algeria)

She Fell into a Sea of Honey / Wa saqatat fî bahr alʾasal (Salah Abou Seif, 1977, Egypt)

She Has a Few Pennies / Sâhibat al-malâlîm (Ezz Eddine Zoulficar, 1949, Egypt)

She Is Diabetic and Hypertensive and She Refuses to Die / Elle est diabétique et hypertendue et elle refuse de crever (Hakim Noury, 2000, Morocco)

She Is Diabetic and Hypertensive and She Still Refuses to Die / Elle est diabétique et hypertendue et elle refuse toujours de crever (Hakim Noury, 2005, Morocco)

She Lived for Love / ʿÂchat li-l-houbb (al-Sayed Bedeir, 1959, Egypt)

She Lived in the Shadows / ʿÂchat fî-l-zalâm (al-Sayed Ziyada, 1948, Egypt)

She Made Me a Criminal / Gaʾalatny mugreman (Amir Arafa, 2006, Egypt)

She-Devil Who Loved Me, The / al-Chaytânah al-latî ahabbatnî (Samir Seif, 1990, Egypt)

She-Devil, The / al-Chaytânah (Ahmed al-Nahhas, 1990, Egypt)

She-Devils and the Captain, The / al-

Singabahamabayo / We Are the Movers (Zulu, No director credited, 1986, South Africa)

Singer, The / al-Moughannawâti (Sayed Issa, 1983, Egypt)

Single Life Is Best, A / Bidoun zawâg afdal (Ahmed al-Sabaawi, 1978, Egypt)

Sins / al-Khatâyâ (Hassan al-Imam, 1962, Egypt)

Sins of Love, The / Khatâyâ al-houbb (Yehya al-Alami, 1977, Egypt)

Siraba / Siraba, la grande voie (Issa de Brahima Traore, 2000, Burkina Faso)

Siraba, la grande voie / Siraba (Issa de Brahima Traore, 2000, Burkina Faso)

Siren, The / ʿArousat al-bahr (Abbas Kamel, 1947, Egypt)

Siren, The / al-Naddahah (Hussein Kamal, 1975, Egypt)

Sister Anuarite: A Life for God / Sœur Anuarite, une vie pour dieu (Madenda Kiesse Masekela, 1982, Democratic Republic of Congo)

Sitting on Their Hands / al-Noum fî al-ʿasal (Cherif Arafa, 1996, Egypt)

Six Girls and One Suitor / Sitt banât wa ʿarîs (al-Sayed Ziyada, 1968, Egypt)

Sixième doigt, Le / The Sixth Finger (Henri Duparc, 1990, Ivory Coast)

Sixpence (English, No director credited, 1985, South Africa)

Sixth Day, The / al-Yawm al-sâdis (Youssef Chahine, 1986, Egypt)

Sixth Finger, The / Le Sixième doigt (Henri Duparc, 1990, Ivory Coast)

Skadu van Gister (Afrikaans, Hendrick Kotze and Anthony Keyser, 1961, South Africa)

Skadus oor Brugplaas / House of the Living Dead (English / Afrikaans, Ray Austin, 1973, South Africa)

Skat van Issie, Die (Afrikaans, D. B. Steyn, 1972, South Africa)

Skating on Thin Uys (English, Bromley Cawood, 1985, South Africa)

Skeleton Coast (English, John Cardos, 1987, South Africa)

Skelm van die Limpopo, Die (Afrikaans, Gerrie Snyman, 1962, South Africa)

Skelms (Afrikaans, Jan Scholtz, 1980, South Africa)

Skerpioen, Die (Afrikaans, Arthur Bennet, 1946, South Africa)

Skin (Anthony Fabian, 2007, South Africa)

Skollie (Afrikaans, Ivan Hall, 1985, South Africa)

Sky Blue (John Hookham, 1980, South Africa)

Sky Full of Diamonds (Thomas Rothig, 1989, South Africa)

Sky of Hell / Sirâ fii-l-wâdî (Youssef Chahine, 1954, Egypt)

Sky's Light, The / Nour min al-samâ (Hassan Helmi, 1947, Egypt)

Slash (English, Neal Sundström, 2002, South Africa)

Slaughterhouse, The / al-Madbah (Houssam Eddine Mostafa, 1985, Egypt)

Slave of Her Eyes / Asîr al-ʾouyoun (Ibrahim Helmi, 1949, Egypt)

Slaves of Money / ʿAbîd al-mâl (Fatine Abdel Wahab, 1953, Egypt)

Slaves of the Flesh / ʿAbîd al-gasad (Kamal Ateyya, 1962, Egypt)

Slaves' Murmurs, The / Hams al-Gawârî (Nadia Hamza, 1992, Egypt)

Sleeping Child, The / L'Enfant endormi (Yasmine Kassari, 2004, Morocco)

Sleepless Night / ʿOuyoun sahrânah (Ezz Eddine Zoulficar, 1956, Egypt)

Sleepless Nights / Sahar al-layali (Hani Khalifa, 2003, Egypt)

Slip Up (No director credited, 1986, South Africa)

Slipstream (English, David van Eyssen, 2004, South Africa)

Slow vs Boner (Zulu, Gary van der Merwe, 1984, South Africa)

Slum Side Story / Qessat al-hayy al-shaʾby (Ashraf Fayek, 2006, Egypt)

Slums of the City, The / Qâ al-madînah (Houssam Eddine Mostafa, 1974, Egypt)

Small Budget (No director credited, 1984, South Africa)

Smart Bilya / Bilya we demagho el ʾalya (Nader Galal, 2000, Egypt)

Smile between the Tears, A / Ibtisâmah fî nahr al-doumouʾ (Adli Khalil, 1988, Egypt)

Smile in Sad Eyes, A / Ibtisâmah fî ʿouyoun hazînah (Nasser Hussein, 1987, Egypt)

Snake Dancer, The / Glenda (English, Dirk de Villiers, 1976, South Africa)

Song of My Life / Nagham fî hayâtî (Henri Barakat, 1975, Egypt)

Song of the Rain / Ma²azufatu al-matar (Abdellah Rezzoug, 1991, Libya)

Song on the Passage / Oughniyah ᶜâla al-mamarr (Ali Abdel Khalek, 1972, Egypt)

Songbird, The (English, Moyo Ogundipe, 1986, Nigeria)

Songbirds (*No director credited,* 1988, South Africa)

Sonia and the Madman / Sonia wa-l-mag²noun (Houssam Eddine Mostafa, 1977, Egypt)

Sonja (Afrikaans, Daan Retief, 1978, South Africa)

Sonja and Johnny (English, Neal Sundström, 1991, South Africa)

Sonny (Zulu, *No director credited,* 1985, South Africa)

Sonny's Little Bit (Silent, Lorrimer Johnston, 1916, South Africa)

Sononder (Afrikaans, Carel Trichardt, 1971, South Africa)

Sons and Murderers / Abnâ² wa qatalah (Atef al-Tayeb, 1987, Egypt)

Sons of Africa (Tunde Oloyede, 1971, Nigeria)

Sons of the Devil / Abna² al-Chaytaan (Ibrahim Afifi, 2000, Egypt)

Sonto (Sotho, Jimmy Murray, 1981, South Africa)

Sorry, It's the Law / ᶜAfwan ayyouhâ al-qIanoun (Inas al-Deghidi, 1985, Egypt)

Soul Africa (English, Ashley Lazarus, 1971, South Africa)

Soul Which Brays, The / L'Âme qui braît (Nabyl Lahlou, 1984, Morocco)

Souleyman's Ring / Khâtim Soulaymân (Hassan Ramzi, 1947, Egypt)

Sourire du serpent, Le / The Snake's Smile (Mama Keïta, 2004, Guinea)

Sous la clarté de la lune / Under the Mlight (Apolline Traoré, 2004, Burkina Faso)

Sous la pluie d'automne / Under the Autumn Rain (Ahmed Khechine, 1970, Tunisia)

Sous le signe du vaudon / Under the Sign of the Vaudon (Pascal Abikanlou, 1974, Bénin)

Sous les pieds des femmes / Under Women's Feet (Rachida Krim, 1996, Algeria)

Soussou My Love / Habîbatî Soussou (Niazi Mostafa, 1951, Egypt)

South Africans, The (English, Sven Persson, 1976, South Africa)

Southern Son / Space Mutiny (English, Neal Sundström and David Winters, 1989, South Africa)

Soutouhi Is Perched in the Tree / Soutouhî fawq al-chagarah (Nasser Hussein, 1983, Egypt)

Soweto (Michael Raeburn, 1991, Zimbabwe)

Soweto Green (English, David Lister, 1995, South Africa)

Spaanse Vlieg, Die (Afrikaans, Dirk de Villiers, 1978, South Africa)

Space Mutiny / Southern Son (English, Neal Sundström and David Winters, 1989, South Africa)

Sparkle in Your Eyes, The / Barîq ᶜaynayki (Mohamed Abdel Aziz, 1982, Egypt)

Sparrow, The / al-²Ousfour (Youssef Chahine, 1974, Egypt)

Speak Like a Child (documentary) (John Akomfrah, 1998, Ghana)

Speed Bump / Matabb senaa²y (Wael Ihsaan, 2006, Egypt)

Spergebied: Diamond Area No. 1 (Afrikaans, Elmo de Witt, 1972, South Africa)

Sphinx's Smile, The / Ibtisâmat Abou al-Hol (Doccio Tissari, 1966, Egypt)

Spice (English, Stuart Stromin, 1989, South Africa)

Spicy Ali / Aly Spicy (Mohamed al-Naggaar, 2005, Egypt)

Spicy Kids / Shebr wi nuss (Adel Yehia, 2004, Egypt)

Spicy Taamiyya / Ta²miyyah bi-l-chattah (Abdel Latif Zaki, 1993, Egypt)

Spider (English, *No director credited,* 1985, South Africa)

Spider / Isicabu (Zulu, *No director credited,* 1989, South Africa)

Spider's Web, The / Khouyout al-²ankabout (Abdel Latif Zaki, 1985, Egypt)

Spin of Death, The (Zulu, Ronnie Isaacs, 1984, South Africa)

Splendid Waster, The (Silent, Harold Shaw, 1916, South Africa)

Splinter, The / al-Shaziya (Mohamed Ali Ferjani, 1986, Libya)

Spoliateurs, Les / The Plunderers (Mohamed Lamine Merbah, 1972, Algeria)

bint ismouhâ Marmar (Henri Barakat, 1972, Egypt)

Story of a Life / Hikâyat al'oumr koullouh (Helmi Halim, 1965, Egypt)

Story of a Love / Hikâyat houbb (Helmi Halim, 1959, Egypt)

Story of a Marriage, The / Hikâyat zawâg (Hassan al-Saïfi, 1964, Egypt)

Story of a Meeting / Histoire d'une rencontre (Brahim Tsaki, 1982, Algeria)

Story of a Rose, The / L'Histoire d'une rose (Abdelmajid Rchich, 2000, Morocco)

Story of an African Farm, The (English, David Lister, 2004, South Africa)

Story of Half-a-million Dollars / Hikâyat nisf million dollar (Saad Arafa, 1988, Egypt)

Story of My Love / Qissat houbbî (Henri Barakat, 1955, Egypt)

Story of Orokia / Histoire d'Orokia (Jabob Sou, 1987, Burkina Faso)

Story of the Rand, A (Silent, Lorrimer Johnston, 1916, South Africa)

Story of the West Quarter, The / Qissat al-hayy al-gharbî (Adel Sadek, 1979, Egypt)

Story of Three Girls, The / Hikâyat thalâth banât (Mahmoud Zoulficar, 1968, Egypt)

Story Tellers, The / Les Diseurs d'histoires (documentary) (Mohamed Soudani, 1998, Algeria)

Strandloper, Die (Afrikaans, Lourens Swanepoel, 1985, South Africa)

Strange Era. The / Zaman al-'agâyib (Hassan al-Imam, 1952, Egypt)

Strange Man, The (English, No director credited, 1987, South Africa)

Strange Oh Time / ʿAgâyib yâ zaman (Hassan al-Imam, 1974, Egypt)

Strange Story, A / Hikâyah laha la-'agab (Hassan al-Saïfi, 1990, Egypt)

Stranger at the Harbour / Gharib fil mina (Ismaïl Hassan, 1995, Egypt)

Stranger, The / Ghost Town (English, No director credited, 1988, South Africa)

Strangers at Sunrise (English, Percival Rubens, 1969, South Africa)

Strawberry War, The / Harb al-farâwlah (Khaïri Bechara, 1994, Egypt)

Street of Fools / Darb al-Mahâbîl (Tewfik Saleh, 1955, Egypt)

Street of Love / Chârî' al-houbb (Ezz Eddine Zoulficar, 1958, Egypt)

Street of Roundabouts, The / Chârî' al-mahâhî (Abdel Meneim Choukri, 1969, Egypt)

Street Wife / Zawgah min al-chârî' (Hassan al-Imam, 1960, Egypt)

Streets / Death Is a Stranger (English, No director credited, 1988, South Africa)

Streets of Fire / Chawârî' min nâr (Samir Seif, 1984. Egypt)

Strike Force (English, No director credited, 1986, South Africa)

Strikeback (Zulu, Ronnie Isaacs, 1986, South Africa)

Stroke of My Life, The / Khabtat al'oumr (Ismaïl Hassan, 1991, Egypt)

Stronger than Life / Aqwâ min al-hayât (Mohamed Kamal Hassan, 1960, Egypt)

Stronger than Love / Aqwâ min al-houbb (Ezz Eddine Zoulficar, 1954, Egypt)

Stronger than Time / Aqwâ mîn al ayyâm (Nader Galal, 1979, Egypt)

Stronger, The (English, Lynton Stephenson, 1983, South Africa)

Strongest of Men, The / Aqwâ al-rigâl (Ahmed al-Sabaawi, 1993, Egypt)

Strongest Reason, The / Houkm al-qawî (Hassan al-Imam, 1951, Egypt)

Stropers van die Laeveld (Afrikaans, David Millin, 1962, South Africa)

Struggle against Death / Sirâ' ma' al-mawt (Ibrahim Emara, 1970, Egypt)

Struggle against Life / Sirâ' ma' al-hayât (Zouheir Bekir, 1957, Egypt)

Struggle against the Angels / Sirâ' ma'al-malâ'ikah (Hassan Tewfik, 1962, Egypt)

Struggle in the Mountain / Sirâ' fi-l-gabal (Houssam Eddine Mostafa, 1961, Egypt)

Struggle on the Nile / Sirâ' fî-l-Nîl (Atef Salem, 1959, Egypt)

Student's Love, A / Gharâm til-mîdhah (Helmi Halim, 1973, Egypt)

Students' Flat, The / Chiqqat al-talabah (Tolba Radwane, 1967, Egypt)

Styx (English, Alex Wright, 2000, South Africa)

Such a Simple Story / Une si simple histoire (Abdellatif Ben Ammar, 1970, Tunisia)

Sweet Revenge (*No director credited,* 1987, South Africa)

Sweeter than Wine (English, Allan Birkinshaw, 1988, South Africa)

Swindle, The / *al-Malʾoub* (Osman Choukri, 1987, Egypt)

Swindlers, First Grade / *Sana ula nasb* (Kamla Abou Zikri, 2004, Egypt)

Symbol of Sacrifice, The (Silent, Isidore W. Schlesinger, 1918, South Africa)

Sympathy for the Dead Man / *Li-l-faqîd al-rahmah* (Omar Abdel Aziz, 1982, Egypt)

Symphonie marocaine / *Moroccan Symphony* (Kamal Kamal, 2005, Morocco)

Ta Dona (Adama Drabo, 1991, Mali)

Taafe Fanga (Adama Drabo, 1997, Mali)

Tabataba (Raymond Rajaonarivelo, 1988, Madagascar)

Tabite or Not Tabite (Nabyl Lahlou, 2006, Morocco)

Table Bay / *Code 7, Victim 5* (English, Robert Lynn, 1964, South Africa)

Tableau ferraille (Moussa Sene Absa, 1996, Senegal)

Taboo / *Eewo* (English, Ladi Ladebo, 1989, Nigeria)

Tachera / *Tâhirah* (Fatine Abdel Wahab, 1957, Egypt)

Taghounja / *Tarunja* (Abdou Achouba, 1980, Morocco)

Tahia ya Didou (Mohamed Zinet, 1971, Algeria)

Taht al-Rabaa / *Tahta al-rabʾ* (Cherif Hammouda, 1991, Egypt)

Taif Nizar (Kamal Kamal, 2002, Morocco)

Tajour (Gadalla Gubara, 1982, Sudan)

Take a Hundred Quid and Get Lost / *Prends dix mille balles et casse-toi* (Mahmoud Zemmouri, 1981, Algeria)

Take Care / *al-Ihtiyât wâguib* (Ahmed Fouad, 1983, Egypt)

Take Care, Gentlemen / *Intabihou ayyouhâ al-sâdah* (Mohamed Abdel Aziz, 1980, Egypt)

Take Care, We're the Mad Ones / *Ihtaris nahnou al-magânîn* (Zaki Saleh, 1981, Egypt)

Take Me Away with You / *Khoudnî maʾâk* (Abbas Kamel, 1966, Egypt)

Take Me with My Shame / *Khoudhnî bi-ârî* (al-Sayed Ziyada, 1962, Egypt)

Take Pity on My Heart / *Irham houbbî* (Henri Barakat, 1959, Egypt)

Talk to Mom / *Kallem Mama* (Ahmed Awad, 2003, Egypt)

Talking about Taboos / *al-Kalaam fil mamnooʾ* (Omar Abdel Aziz, 2000, Egypt)

Tam-tams Are Silent, The / *Les Tam-tams se sont tus* (Philippe Mory, 1972, Gabon)

Tam-tams se sont tus, Les / *The Tam-tams Are Silent* (Philippe Mory, 1972, Gabon)

Tangent Affair, The (English, Neil Hetherington, 1987, South Africa)

Tant Ralie se Losieshuis (Afrikaans, Dirk de Villiers, 1974, South Africa)

Tap a Tap / *Izilingo* (*No director credited,* 1989, South Africa)

Tap and Son (*No director credited,* 1986, South Africa)

Tarfya (Daoud Aoulad Syad, 2004, Morocco)

Tartina City (Issa Serge Coélo, 2003, Chad)

Tarunja / *Taghounja* / (Abdou Achouba, 1980, Morocco)

Taste for Profit, The / *L'Appât du gain* (Jules Takam, 1981, Cameroon)

Taste of Blood II, The (Zulu, David Bensusan, 1986, South Africa)

Taste of Blood, The (Zulu, David Bensusan, 1985, South Africa)

Tasuma (Kollo Daniel Sanou, 2002, Burkina Faso)

Tata, Rika and Kazem Bey / *Taʾta wa Reeka wa Kazem Bey* (Cherif Chaaban, 1995, Egypt)

Tattoo Chase / *Bottom Line* (English, Jeff Gold, 1988, South Africa)

Tawhida / *Tawhîdah* (Houssam Eddine Mostafa, 1976, Egypt)

Taxi (English, Joe Stewardson, 1970, South Africa)

Taxi (*No director credited,* 1988, South Africa)

Taxi Driver (Yoruba, Adeyemi Afolayan, 1983, Nigeria)

Taxi Driver II (Yoruba, Adeyemi Afolayan, 1986, Nigeria)

Taxi King, The / *Malik al-taxi* (Yehya al-Alami, 1976, Egypt)

Taxi to Soweto (Multilingual, Manie van Rensberg, 1991, South Africa)

Taxi War (*No director credited,* 1986, South Africa)

Taymour and Safika / Taymour wa Shafika (Khaled Marie, 2007, Egypt)

Tea in the Harem / Le Thé au harem d'Archimède (Mehdi Charef, 1985, Algeria)

Tea Seller, The / Bâ'i'at al-chây (Ismaïl Hassan, 1991, Egypt)

Teach Me How to Love / 'Allemny al-hubb (Yasser Zayed, 2005, Egypt)

Teach Me Love / 'Allimounî al-houbb (Atef Salem, 1957, Egypt)

Tear, The / La Déchirure (Alphonse Béni, Cameroon, 2005)

Tears Dry Up, The / Gaffat al-doumou' (Helmi Rafla, 1975, Egypt)

Tears in Eyes That Smile / al-Doumou'fî'ouyoun dIahikah (Ahmed Diaa Eddine, 1977, Egypt)

Tears in the Dry Wind / No One Cries Forever (English, Jans Rautenbach, 1984, South Africa)

Tears in the Night / Doumou ' fî-l-layl (Ibrahim Emara, 1955, Egypt)

Tears of Blood / Larmes de sang (Ali Akika, with Anne-Marie Autissier, 1980, Algeria)

Tears of Happiness / Doumou' al-farah (Ahmed Salem and Fatine Abdel Wahab, 1950, Egypt)

Tears of Regret / Larmes de regret (Hassan Moufti, 1982, Morocco)

Tears on a Wedding Night / Doumou' fî laylat al-zifâf (Saad Arafa, 1981, Egypt)

Tears without Sin / Doumopu' bilâ khatâyâ (Hassan Youssef, 1980, Egypt)

Teddy Boys, The / Les Zazous de la vague (Mohamed Ali El Okbi, 1992, Tunisia)

Télé arrive, La / The TV Arrives (Moncef Dhouib 2006, Tunisia)

Témon, Le / Sere / The Witness (Dansogho Mohamed Camara, 1990, Guinea)

Tempest, The / al-Asefa (Khaled Youssef, 2001, Egypt)

Temporary Registration / I T Immatriculation temporaire (Gahité Fofana, 2001, Guinea)

Ten Little Indians / Death on Safari (English, Allan Birkinshaw, 1988, South Africa)

Ten Out of Ten / 'Achrah 'alâ 'achrah (Mohamed Abdel Aziz, 1985, Egypt)

Tender Gesture / Lamsat hanân (Helmi Rafla, 1971, Egypt)

Tendresse du loup / Wolf's Kindness (Jilani Saadi, 2006, Tunisia)

Tenja (Hassan Legzouli, 2004, Morocco)

Tenth of a Second (English, Darrell Roodt, 1986, South Africa)

Ter wille van Christine (Afrikaans, Elmo de Witt, 1975, South Africa)

Teranga Blues (Moussa Sene Absa, 2006, Senegal)

Terminal Bliss (English, Jordan Alan, 1988, South Africa)

Terminator Woman (English, Michael Qissi, 1993, South Africa)

Terrace, The / al-Soutouh (Hussein Emara, 1984. Egypt)

Terre du défi, La / Land of Challenge—aka *I Shall Write Your Name in the Sand / J'écrirai ton nom sur le sable* (Abdellah Mesbahi, 1989, Morocco)

Terre en cendres / Land of Ashes aka *Errances / Wanderings* (Djafar Damardjji, 1993, Algeria)

Terrible Children, The / Chaqâwat riggâlah (Houssam Eddine Mostafa, 1966, Egypt)

Terrible Hours, The / al-Sâ'ât al-rahîbah (Abdel-Hamid al-Chazli, 1970, Egypt)

Terror, The / al-Rou'b (Mahmoud Farid, 1969, Egypt)

Terrorised / Ahdân al-khawf (Abdel Mcneim Choukri, 1986, Egypt)

Terrorism / al-Irhâb (Nader Galal, 1989, Egypt)

Terrorism and Kebab / al-Irhâb wa-l-kabâb (Cherif Arafa, 1992, Egypt)

Terrorist (English, Neil Hetherington, 1978, South Africa)

Terrorist, The / al-Irhâbî (Nader Galal, 1994, Egypt)

Terug na Thaba / Thaba (Afrikaans, Willie Alheit, 1977, South Africa)

Testament (John Akomfrah, 1988, Ghana)

Testament to the Bushmen (English, Jane Taylor, 1983, South Africa)

Tewwe Tienies (Afrikaans, Bromley Cawood, 1984, South Africa)

Texas Blood Money (English, Scot Spiegel, 1998, South Africa))

TGV (Moussa Touré, 1997, Senegal)

Thaba / Terug na Thaba (Afrikaans, Willie Alheit, 1977, South Africa)

That English Woman (English, Dirk de Villiers, 1989, South Africa)

That is Satisfactory / Keda reda (Ahmed Galal, 2007, Egypt)

That Man Will Drive Me Mad / *al-Râguil dah hayganninni* (Issa Karama, 1967, Egypt)

That's Enough My Heart / *Kafânî yâ qalb* (Hassan Youssef, 1977, Egypt)

That's How Life Goes / *Hâkadhâ al-uyyâm* (Atef Salem, 1977, Egypt)

That's Love / *Hâdhâ houwa al-houbb* (Salah Abou Seif, 1958, Egypt)

That's OK / *Keda OK* (Samir al-Asfouri and Osama al-ᶜAsi, 2003, Egypt)

That's What Love Is / *al-Houbb kidah* (Mahmoud Zoulficar, 1961, Egypt)

Thé à la menthe, Le / *Mint Tea* (Abdelkrim Bahloul, 1984, Algeria)

Thé au harem d'Archimède, Le / *Tea in the Harem* (Mehdi Charef, 1985, Algeria)

Thé d'Ania, Le / *Ania's Tea* (Saïd Ould Khelifa, 2004, Algeria)

Their Excellencies / *Ashâb al-saᵓâdah* (Mohamed Karim, 1946, Egypt)

Their Wiles Are Great / *Kaydahounna ᶜadhîm* (Hassan al-Imam, 1983, Egypt)

Themba and Thani / *Names* (Zulu, *No director credited,* 1986, South Africa)

There Are Loves That Kill / *Wa min al-houbb mâ qatal* (Houssam Eddine Mostafa, 1978, Egypt)

There's a Zulu on My Stoep (English, Gray Hofmeyr, 1993, South Africa)

There's No Such Thing as Chance / *Le Hasard n'existe pas* (Luzolo Mpwati N'Tima Nsi, 1976, Democratic Republic of Congo)

These Are All My Children / *Koullouhoum awlâdî* (Ahmed Diaa Eddine, 1962, Egypt)

These Men Are Gentlemen / *al-Sâdah al-rigâl* (Raafat al-Mihi, 1987, Egypt)

They Built a Nation / *Die Bou van 'n Nasie* (Afrikaans / English, Joseph Albrecht, 1938, South Africa)

They Call It Love (King Ampaw, 1972, Ghana)

They Call Me Lucky (English, Keith G. van der Wat, 1974, South Africa)

They Have Made Me a Killer / *Gaᵓalounî mougriman* (Atef Salem, 1954, Egypt)

They Kill Honest People / *Innahoum yaqtouloun al-chourafâ* (Nasser Houssein, 1984. Egypt)

They Steal Rabbits / *Innahoum yasriqoun al-arânib* (Nader Galal, 1983, Egypt)

They Will Drive Me Mad / *Hayganninounî* (Fatine Abdel Wahab, 1960, Egypt)

They've Robbed Oum Ali / *Saraqou Oumm ᶜAlîᵓ* (Ahmed al-Nahhas, 1994, Egypt)

Thief Who Stole the Lottery Ticket, The / *Harâmî al-waraqah* (Ali Reda, 1970, Egypt)

Thief, The / *al-Harâmî* (Nagdi Hafez, 1969, Egypt)

Thief, The / *al-Liss* (Saad Arafa, 1990, Egypt)

Thief, The / *al-Nachchâlah* (Helmi Rafla, 1985, Egypt)

Thieves in KG II / *Harameya fî kg II* (Sandra Nashaat, 2002, Egypt)

Thieves in Thailand / *Harameyya fî Thailand* (Sandra Nashaat, 2003, Egypt)

Thieves of Fortune / *Chameleon* (English, Michael McCarthy, 1989, South Africa)

Thieves, The / *al-Lousous* (Taysir Abboud, 1981, Egypt)

Thieves' Rendezvous / *Lousous ᶜalâ Mawᵓid* (Houssam Eddine Mostafa, 1970, Egypt)

Thieving Millionnairess, The / *al-Millionnairah al-nachchâlah* (Seif Eddine Chawkat, 1978, Egypt)

Things against the Law / *Achyâ didd al-qânoun* (Ahmed Yassine, 1982, Egypt)

Things That Are Not for Sale / *Achiyâᵓ la touchtarâ* (Ahmed Diaa Eddine, 1970, Egypt)

Third Act, The / *Le Troisième acte* (Rachid Ben Brahim, 1991, Algeria)

Third Class / *al-Daragah al-thâlithah* (Cherif Arafa, 1988, Egypt)

Third Man, The / *al-Ragoul al-thaleth* (Ali Badrakhan, 1995, Egypt)

Third Time, The (*No director credited,* 1987, South Africa)

Thirst / *Soif* (Saâd Chraïbi, 2000, Morocco)

Thirsty Woman, The / *ᶜAtchânah* (al-Saïd Mostafa, 1987, Egypt)

Thirteen and One Lies / *Talatataᵓch kidbah wa kidbah* (Anwar al-Chennawi, 1977, Egypt)

Thirty Days in Prison / *Thalathoun yawm fî-l-sigᵓn* (Niazi Mostafa, 1966, Egypt)

34 South (English, Maganthrie Pillay, 2005, South Africa)

This Kind of Men / *Nawᵓmin al-rigâl* (Adli Khalil, 1988, Egypt)

This Marriage Must Not Take Place / *al-Gawâzah di mouch lâzim titim* (Gamal Ammar, 1988, Egypt)

Thlathla Thile / *Walk a Long Distance* (North Sotho, *No director credited,* 1988, South Africa)

Three Women / Thalâth nisâ (Mamoud Zoul-ficar, Salah Abou Seif, Henri Barakat, 1969, Egypt)

Thrilled to Death (English, Chuck Vincent, 1988, South Africa)

Throne, The aka *Power* (English, Ladi Ladebo, 1998, Nigeria)

Through Thick and Thin (No director credited, 1988, South Africa)

Throwing It About / Rashsha garee'a (Saïd Hamed, 2001, Egypt)

Thrushes and Autumn / al-Simân wa-l-kharîf (Houssam Eddine Mostafa, 1967, Egypt)

Thugs, The / al-Awbâch (Ahmed Fouad, 1986, Egypt)

Tie the Scarf Around My Hips . . . / Hazzemny ya (Hussein Kamal, 1997, Egypt)

Tiefing (Djibril Kouyate, 1993, Mali)

Tiger and the Woman, The / al-Nimr wa-l-ounthâ (Samir Seif, 1987, Egypt)

Tiger Kid Gang, The (No director credited, 1986, South Africa)

Tiger Kid II (No director credited, 1988, South Africa)

Tiger, The / al-Nimr (Hussein Fawzi, 1952, Egypt)

Tigers Don't Cry (English, Peter Collinson, 1976, South Africa)

Tilai (Idrissa Ouedraogo, 1989, Burkina Faso)

Tilila (Mohamed Mernich, 2006, Morocco)

Time and the Dogs / al-Zaman wal kelaab (Samir Seif, 1996, Egypt)

Time for Revenge / Sa'at el-intekam (Ahmed al-Sabaawi, 1998, Egypt)

Time of Anger / Ayyâm al-ghadab (Mounir Radi, 1989, Egypt)

Time of Leopards / O tempo dos leopardos (Camilo de Sousa and Zdravko Velimorovic, 1985, Mozambique)

Time of Love / 'Asr al-houbb (Hassan al-Imam, 1986, Egypt)

Time of Terror / Ayyâm al-rou'b (Saïd Marzouk, 1988, Egypt)

Time of the Beast / Mutator (English, John Bowey, 1989, South Africa)

Time of Wolves, The / 'Asr al-dhi'âb (Samir Seif, 1986, Egypt)

Time to Kill / The Short Cut (English, Giuliano Montaldo, 1988, South Africa)

Tip and Tap in the Haunted House (No director credited, 1986, South Africa)

Tip Meets Tap (No director credited, 1986, South Africa)

Tissée de mains et d'étoffe / Woven by Hands from Material (Omar Chraïbi, 2007, Morocco)

Tito / Tito (Tarek al-Iryaan, 2004, Egypt)

Titre provisoire / Provisional Title (Mostafa Derkaoui, 1984, Morocco)

Tiyabu Biru / La Circoncision (Moussa Yoro Bathily, 1978, Senegal)

To Avenge Ragab / al-Intiqâm la-Ragab (Ahmad Sarwat, 1984. Egypt)

To Catch a Rat (English, No director credited, 1987, South Africa)

To Escape from the Asylum / al-Houroub min al-khânkah (Mohamed Radi, 1987, Egypt)

To the Death (English, Darrell Roodt, 1991, South Africa)

To Whom by Law / Ilâ man yahoummouhou al-'amr (Abdel Hadi Taha, 1985, Egypt)

To Whom Could I Complain? / Achkî li-mîn (Ibrahim Emara, 1951, Egypt)

Together for Always / Ma'an ilâ al-abad (Hassan Ramzi, 1960, Egypt)

Tojan (Afrikaans, Johan Blignaut, 1986, South Africa)

Tokolosche (English, Peter Prowse, 1965, South Africa)

Tolla is Tops (Afrikaans, Elmo de Witt, 1991, South Africa)

Tolla is Tops II (Afrikaans, Elmo de Witt, 1991, South Africa)

Tom, Dirk en Herrie (Afrikaans, Al Debbo, 1962, South Africa)

Tombola Seller, The / Bayyâ'at al-yânasîb (Abdel Fattah Hassan, 1947, Egypt)

Tommy (Zulu, Simon Metsing, 1981, South Africa)

Tommy II / Tommy No Bra Sticks (Zulu, No director credited, 1983, South Africa)

Tommy Le Segotsana (English, No director credited, 1986, South Africa)

Tommy No Bra Sticks / Tommy II (Zulu, No director credited, 1983, South Africa)

Tomorrow I Burn / Demain je brûle (Mohamed Ben Smaïl, 1998, Tunisia)

Tomorrow I Will Take My Revenge / Ghadan saantaqim (Ahmed Yehya, 1983, Egypt)

Tomorrow Is a New Day / Demain un nouveau jour (Pierre-Marie Dong, 1978, Gabon)

Tomorrow Love Will Return / Ghadan ya'oud al-houbb (Nader Galal, 1972, Egypt)

Tomorrow the Land Will Not Change / Demain la terre ne changera pas (Abdellah Mesbahi, 1975, Morocco)

Tomorrow Will Be Another Day / Ghadan yawmoun âktar (Albert Naguib, 1961, Egypt)

Tomorrow Will Be More Beautiful / Boukra ahlâ min al-nahâr dah (Hassan al-Imam, 1986, Egypt)

Too Late for Heaven (*No director credited*, 1985, South Africa)

Too Young to Love / Saghîrah ʿAlâ al-houbb (Niazi Mostafa, 1966, Egypt)

Toot Toot / Tout tout (Atef Salem, 1993, Egypt)

Toothman and the Killer, The (English, Elmo de Witt, 1990, South Africa)

Topsy-Turvy (*No director credited*, 1988, South Africa)

Tora ya Raditeble / Boxers Dream (Sotho, *No director credited*, 1983, South Africa)

Torak (Zulu / Xhosa, *No director credited*, 1985, South Africa)

Tori Ade (Yoruba, Eddie Ugbomah, 1991, Nigeria)

Torn Allegiance / Sanna (English, Alan Nathanson, 1984, South Africa)

Totor (Daniel Kamwa, 1993, Cameroon)

Toubab Bi (Moussa Touré, 1991, Senegal)

Touched in the Head / Lakhmet raas (Ahmed al-Badri, 2006, Egypt)

Touchia (Mohamed Rachid Benhadj, 1993, Algeria)

Tough Guy from Darb al-Assal, The / Foutouwwat Darb al-'Assâl (Ahmed Sarwat, 1985, Egypt)

Tough Guy, The / al-Foutouwwah (Salah Abou Seif, 1957, Egypt)

Tough Guys from Bab al-Cheiriyyah, The / Guyid'ân Bâb al-Chi'riyyah (Kamal Salah Eddine, 1983, Egypt)

Tough Guys from Boulak, The / Foutouwwât Boulâq (Yehya al-Alami, 1981, Egypt)

Tough Guys from the Mountains, The / Foutouwwat al-gabal (Nader Galal, 1982, Egypt)

Tough Guys from the Slaughterhouse, The / Foutouwwat al-Salakhânah (Nasser Hussein, 1989, Egypt)

Tough Luck (English, David Lister, 1992, South Africa)

Touha / Touhah (Hassan al-Saïfi, 1958, Egypt)

Touki Bouki (Djibril Diop Mambety, 1973, Senegal)

Toula or The Water Spirit / Toula ou le génie des eaux (Mustapha Alassane, 1973, Niger)

Toula ou le génie des eaux / Toula or The Water Spirit (Mustapha Alassane, 1973, Niger)

Toungan / L'Étranger / The Foreigner (Mamadou Djim Kola, 1992, Burkina Faso)

Tourbillon / Silmande (Pierre S. Yaméogo, 1998, Burkina Faso)

Tout va bien / Laafi (Pierre S. Yaméogo, 1990, Burkina Faso)

Towards Fame / Nahw al-magd (Hussein Sedki, 1948, Egypt)

Tower of the Tanneries, The / Bourg al-madâbigh (Ahmed al-Sabaawi, 1983, Egypt)

Town and Village / Miyi Iyo Maagalo (Hadj Mohamed Giumale, 1968, Somalia)

Township Fever / The Fever, The (English, David Thompson and Francis Gerard, 1990, South Africa)

Toxic Heart (English, *No director credited*, 1990, South Africa)

Toy, The / al-Lou'bah (Yassine Ismaïl Yassine, 1978, Egypt)

Trace of Fear, A / Chay' min al-khawf (Hussein Kamal, 1969, Egypt)

Trace, La / The Trace (Neija Ben Mabrouk, 1988, Tunisia)

Trace, The / La Trace (Neija Ben Mabrouk, 1988, Tunisia)

Traces / Wechma (Hamid Bennani, 1970, Morocco)

Traces in the Sand / Âthar fî-l-rimâl (Gamal Madkour, 1954, Egypt)

Trackers, The / Bush Shrink (English, Ivan Hall, 1988, South Africa)

Traffic Light / Isharet muroor (Khaïri Bechara, 1996, Egypt)

Tragedy of the Veldt, A (Silent, Norman V. Lee, 1916, South Africa)

Train, The / al-Qitâr (Ahmed Fouad, 1986, Egypt)

Trainee Lawyer, The / Mouhâmî taht al-tamrîn (Omar Abdel Aziz, 1986, Egypt)

Traitors (English, Jan Scholtz, 1988, South Africa)

Traitors in the Night / Layl wa khawanah (Achraf Fahmi, 1990, Egypt)

Traitors, The / al-Khawanah (Wasfi Darwich, 1984. Egypt)

Trances / Transes (Ahmed El Maânouni, 1981, Morocco)

Transes / Trances (Ahmed El Maânouni, 1981, Morocco)

Trap, The / al-Matabb (Hassan al-Saïfi, 1990, Egypt)

Trap, The / al-Misyadah (Tolba Radwane, 1962, Egypt)

Traveling Showman's Day, The / Le Jour du forain (Mohamed Abdelkrim Derkaoui and Driss Kettani, 1984, Morocco)

Traveller without a Road / mousâfir bilâ tarîq (Ali Abdel Khalek, 1981, Egypt)

Traversées / Crossing Over (Mahmoud Ben Mahmoud, 1982, Tunisia)

Treasure Beach (*No director credited*, 1989, South Africa)

Treasure Hunters (English, Cedric Sundström, 1989, South Africa)

Treasure Hunters / Umkuzingela (English, *No director credited*, 1985, South Africa)

Treasure of Happiness, The / Kanz al-saʾâdah (Ibrahim Lama, 1947, Egypt)

Treasure, The / al-Kanz (Saïd Chimi, 1993, Egypt)

Treasures of the Atlas, The / Les Trésors de l'Atlas (Mohamed Abazzi, 1997, Morocco)

Tree of Suspended Fates, The / L'albero dei destini sospesi (Mohamed Rachid Benhadj, 1997, Algeria)

Tremor / As die Aarde Skeur (English / Afrikaans, Dennis Scully, 1961, South Africa)

Trésor infernal, Le / The Devil's Treasure (Mohamed Osfour, 1970, Morocco)

Trésors de l'Atlas, Les / The Treasures of the Atlas (Mohamed Abazzi, 1997, Morocco)

Tresses / Braids (Jillali Ferhati, 2000, Morocco)

Trial 68 / al-Qadiyyah 68 (Salah Abou Seif, 1968, Egypt)

Trial No. 1 / al-Qadiyyah raqam wâhid (Mouhannad al-Ansari, 1983, Egypt)

Trial of "Uncle Ahmed," The / Qadiyyat ʿamm Ahmad (Ali Reda, 1985, Egypt)

Trial, The / al-Moukâkamah (Nader Galal, 1982, Egypt)

Trickster, The / al-Ghachchâch (Abdel Rahman Chérif, 1970, Egypt)

Tringleuses, Les aka *The Guys, the Cops and the Whores / Les Mecs, les flics et les p . . .* (Alphonse Béni, 1974, Cameroon)

Trip on the Moon / Rihlah ilâ al-qamar (Hamada Abdel Wahab, 1959, Egypt)

Trip to Ouaga / Voyage à Ouga (Camille Mouyeke, 2001, Congo)

Triumph of Islam, The / Intisâr al-islâm (Ahmed al-Toukhi, 1952, Egypt)

Trois bracelets, Les / The Three Bracelets (Kozoloa Yeo, 2000, Ivory Coast)

Trois petits cireurs, Les / The Three Little Shoeblacks (Louis Balthazar Amadangoleda, 1985, Cameroon)

Troisième acte, Le / The Third Act (Rachid Ben Brahim, 1991, Algeria)

Trompie (Afrikaans, Tonie van der Merve, 1975, South Africa)

Troubadour, Le / Sa Dagga Le M'Bandakatt (Momar Thiam, 1982, Senegal)

Troublemakers at Nouibi, The / Mouchâghiboun fî nouibiʾ (Nasser Hussein, 1992, Egypt)

Troublemakers in the Army / al-Mouchâghiboun fî-l-gaych (Niazi Mostafa, 1984. Egypt)

Troublemakers in the Navy, The / al-Mouchâghiboun fî-l-bahriyyah (Nasser Hussein, 1992, Egypt)

Troublemakers No. 6, The / al-Mouchâghib sittah (Mohamed Nabih, 1991, Egypt)

Troublemakers, The / al-Mouchâghiboun (Mahmoud Farid, 1965, Egypt)

Troublemakers' Excursion, The / Rihlat al-mouchâghibîn (Ahmed Sarwat, 1988, Egypt)

Troudag van Tant Ralie, Die (Afrikaans, Ivan Hall, 1975, South Africa)

Truanderie / Lambaye (Mahama [Johnson] Traore, 1972, Senegal)

True Friend, A / Saheb Sahbo (Saïd Hamed, 2002, Egypt)

True Value (*No director credited*, 1988, South Africa)

Truth Is Called Salem, The / al-Haqîqah ismouha Sâlim (Ahmed Saqr, 1994, Egypt)

Truth Tellers, The / Les Diseurs de vérité (Karim Traïdia, 2000, Algeria)

Truth, The / Kalimat al-haqq (Fatine Abdel Wahab, 1953, Egypt)

Ulaka (Zulu, Wally van der Merwe, 1984, South Africa)

Ulanga (Zulu, *No director credited,* 1985, South Africa)

U-Lindiwe (Sotho, H. Epstein and Jimmy Murray, 1984, South Africa)

Ultimate Madness, The / Âkhir guinân (Issa Karama, 1965, Egypt)

Ulunya of Lohlanga (Zulu / Xhosa, *No director credited,* 1985, South Africa)

Umbango / Courtyard (Zulu, *No director credited,* 1987, South Africa)

Umbdhale (Zulu, Ronnie Isaacs, 1980, South Africa)

Umbethu (Zulu, *No director credited,* 1988, South Africa)

Umdhlali (Zulu, *No director credited,* 1980, South Africa)

Umdlalo Umbango (Tswana, Wally van der Merwe, 1983, South Africa)

Umdlalo Umkhulu (Zulu, Wally van der Merwe, 1982, South Africa)

Umdobi (Zulu, Ed Herbst, 1984, South Africa)

Umduka (Zulu, *No director credited,* 1984, South Africa)

Umenzi Wobubi / Bad Deeds (Zulu, *No director credited,* 1987, South Africa)

Umfaan (Zulu, Johan van Rooyen, 1984, South Africa)

Umfaan II (Zulu, Gary van der Merwe, 1984, South Africa)

Umfana Wekarate (Zulu / Xhosa, *No director credited,* 1985, South Africa)

Umjuluko Me Gazi (Zulu, Ronnie Isaacs, 1982, South Africa)

Umkhovu (Zulu, *No director credited,* 1984, South Africa)

Umkuzingela / Treasure Hunters (English, *No director credited,* 1985, South Africa)

Umnogoloi (Zulu, *No director credited,* 1980, South Africa)

Umnquyi / Biltong (Zulu, *No director credited,* 1987, South Africa)

Umnyakazo (Zulu, Wally van der Merwe, 1981, South Africa)

U-Mona (Zulu, Hanro Mohr, 1980, South Africa)

Umonga (Zulu, *No director credited,* 1980, South Africa)

Umoni (Xhosa, *No director credited,* 1985, South Africa)

Umpetha / Sportsman (Zulu, *No director credited,* 1987, South Africa)

Umshaya (*No director credited,* 1988, South Africa)

Umsizi (Zulu / Xhosa, *No director credited,* 1985, South Africa)

Umunti Akalahlwa (Zulu, Simon Sabela, 1979, South Africa)

Umzingeli (Zulu, Ronnie Isaacs, 1979, South Africa)

Un amour à Casablanca / A Love Affair in Casablanca (Abdelkader Lagtaâ, 1991, Morocco)

Un amour à Paris / A Paris Love Story (Merzak Allouache, 1986, Algeria)

Un amour d'enfant / A Child's Love (Ben Diogaye Beye, 2002, Senegal)

Un ballon et des rêves / A Ball and Some Dream (Mohamed Ali El Okbi, 1978, Tunisia)

Un été à La Goulette / One Summer at La Goulette (Ferid Boughedir, 1995, Tunisia)

Un homme, des femmes / Sey Seyeti / A Man and Some Women (Ben Diogaye Beye, 1980, Senegal)

Un malheur n'arrive jamais seul / Kato Kato (Idrissa Ouédraogo, Burkina Faso, 2006)

Un rêve algérien / An Algerian Dream (documentary) (Jean-Pierre Lledo, 2004, Algeria)

Un simple fait divers / A Simple News Item (Hakim Noury, 1997, Morocco)

Un toit une famille / A Roof a Family (Rabah Laradji, 1982, Algeria)

Un vampire au paradis / A Vampire in Paradise (Abdelkrim Bahloul, 1991, Algeria)

Uncle Abdou's Ghost / ʿIfrît ʿamm ʿAbdou (Hussein Fawzi, 1953, Egypt)

Uncle Qandil's Scissors / Miqass ʿamm Qandil (Adli Youssef, 1985, Egypt)

Undecided Hearts / Qouloub hâ'irah (Kamal al-Chennawi, 1956, Egypt)

Under Cover (*No director credited,* 1990, South Africa)

Under House Arrest / En résidence surveillée (Paulin Soumanou Vieyra, 1981, Senegal)

Under Suspicion / Burns (English, Bruce MacFarlane, 1988, South Africa)

Under the Autumn Rain / Sous la pluie d'automne (Ahmed Khechine, 1970, Tunisia)

Uzenzile Akahalelwa (Zulu, Rudi Meyer, 1981, South Africa)

Uzungu (Zulu / Xhosa, *No director credited*, 1985, South Africa)

Vacances de l'Inspecteur Tahar, Les / Inspector Tahar's Holiday (Moussa Haddad, 1973, Algeria)

Vadertjie Langbeen / Daddy Long-Legs (Afrikaans, Pierre de Wet, 1954, South Africa)

Vagabond Souls / Arwâh hâᵓimah (Kamal Barakat, 1949, Egypt)

Vagabond, The / al-Charîdah (Achraf Fahmi, 1980, Egypt)

Vagabond, The / al-Moutacharridah (Mohamed Abdel Gawad, 1947, Egypt)

Vague blanche, La / The White Wave (Mohamed Ali El Mejoub, 2006, Morocco)

Vaincre pour vivre / Conquer to Live (Mohamed B. A. Tazi and Ahmed Mesnaoui, 1988, Morocco)

Vakasha (Zulu / English, Johan van Rooyen, 1983, South Africa)

Vakhashe le U-Satane (English, *No director credited*, 1985, South Africa)

Valley of Memories, The / Wâdî al-dhikrayât (Henri Barakat, 1981, Egypt)

Valley of the Innocent (Branwen Okpako, 2003, Nigeria)

Valse des gros derrières, La / The Waltz of the Fat Bottoms (Jean Odoutan, 2003, Bénin)

Vamp, The / al-Ounthâ (Hussein al-Wakil, 1986, Egypt)

Vampire in Paradise, A / Un vampire au paradis (Abdelkrim Bahloul, 1991, Algeria)

Van der Merwe P I (English, Regard van den Bergh, 1985, South Africa)

Van der Merwe Strikes Back (English, Elmo de Witt, 1990, South Africa)

Vanessa et Sosie (Madjé Atite, 2006, Togo)

Vang vir my 'n Droom / Catch Me a Dream (Afrikaans, Tim Spring, 1974, South Africa)

Veinard, Le / The Lucky Guy (Urbain Dia Mokouri, 1983, Cameroon)

Veld / Ehlathini (Zulu, *No director credited*, 1988, South Africa)

Vélo, Le / The Bike (Hamid Faridi, 2006, Morocco)

Vendor (English, Ladi Ladebo, 1988, Nigeria)

Vendredi noir / Black Friday (Djingary Maiga, 1999, Niger)

Vengeance (English, *No director credited,* 1986, South Africa)

Vengeance / al-Intiqâm (Fayek Ismaïl, 1986, Egypt)

Vengeance / al-Thaᵓr (Mohamed Khan, 1982, Egypt)

Vengeance of the Cult (English, Eddie Ugbomah, 1984, Nigeria)

Vengeance Unfulfilled / Târ bâyit (Abbas Kamel, 1955, Egypt)

Vengeful Masters, The / al-Mountaquimoun (Yassine Ismaïl Yassine, 1985, Egypt)

Vent de sable / Sand Storm (Mohamed Lakhdar Hamina, 1982, Algeria)

Vent des Aurès, Le / The Wind from the Aurès (Mohamed Lakhdar-Hamina, 1966, Algeria)

Vent des destins, Le / Wind of Destinies (Ahmed Djemaï, 1993, Tunisia)

Vent du Sud / Wind from the South (Mohamed Slim Riad, 1975, Algeria)

Vent, Le / Finye / The Wind (Souleymane Cisse, 1982, Mali)

Vergeet my Nie (Afrikaans, Elmo de Witt, 1976, South Africa)

Verkeerde Nommer (Afrikaans, Frans Marx, 1982, South Africa)

Vertige de la passion, Le / The Dizziness of Passion (Armand Balima, 1985, Burkina Faso)

Vervlakste Tweeling, Die (Afrikaans, Werner Grunbauer, 1969, South Africa)

Very Difficult Mission / Mouhimmah saᵓbah guiddan (Hussein Emara, 1987, Egypt)

Very Hot Day, A / Youm harr gedan (Mohammed Khan, 1995, Egypt)

Very Important Man, A / Ragoul mohemm geddann (Essam al-Chamma, 1996, Egypt)

Very Jealous Wife, A / Zawgah ghayourah guiddan (Helmi Rafla, 1969, Egypt)

Very Mad Youth / Chabâb magᵓnoun guiddan (Niazi Mostafa, 1967, Egypt)

Very Remby / Le Retour (Ignace-Solo Randrasana, 1973, Madagascar)

Very Ridiculous World, A / ᶜÂlam moudhik guiddan (Houssam Eddine Mostafa, 1968, Egypt)

Very Special Invitation, A / Daᵓwah khâssah guiddan (Omar Abdel Aziz, 1982, Egypt)

Voice of the Waters, The (Silent, Joseph Albrecht, 1918, South Africa)

Voices in the Wind (English, Bruce MacFarlane, 1990, South Africa)

Voices of the Past / Sawt min al-mâdî (Ataf Salem, 1956, Egypt)

Voie, La / The Way (Mohamed Slim Riad, 1968, Algeria)

Voisine, La / The Neighbor (Ghaouti Bendeddouche, 2002, Algeria)

Voisines d'Abou Moussa, Les / Abou Moussa's Neighbors (Mohamed Abderrahmane Tazi, 2003, Morocco)

Voisins, Voisines / Neighbors (Malik Chibane, 2005, Algeria)

Volcanic Rage / Borkaan al ghadab (Mazen al-Gabali, 2002, Egypt)

Volcano, The / al-Bourkân (Abdel Latif Zaki, 1990, Egypt)

Voleur de rêves, Le / The Dream Thief (Hakim Noury, 1995, Morocco)

Voltaire's Fault / La Faute à Voltaire (Abdellatif Kechiche, 2000, Tunisia)

Voor Sononder (Afrikaans, Emil Nofal, 1962, South Africa)

Voortrekkers, Die (Afrikaans, David Millin, 1973, South Africa)

Voortvlugtige Spioen (Afrikaans, Harald Phillip, 1974, South Africa)

Vortreflike Familie Smit (Afrikaans, Kappie Botha, 1965, South Africa)

Vote for Dr. Soleymane Abdel Basset / Intakhibou al-doktor Soulaymân ᶜAbd al-Bâsit (Mohamed Abdel Aziz, 1981, Egypt)

Voyage à Ouga / Trip to Ouaga (Camille Mouyeke, 2001, Congo)

Voyage en capital / Journey to the Capital (Ali Akiki, with Anne-Marie Autissier, 1977, Algeria)

Voyage in Life, The / Rihlat al-ayyâm (Henri Barakat, 1976, Egypt)

Voyage of Forgetfulness, The / Rihlat al-nisyân (Ahmed Yehya, 1978, Egypt)

Voyage of Life, The / Rihlat al-ᵓoumr (Saad Arafa, 1974, Egypt)

Voyage of Marvels, The / Rihlat al-ᵓagâyib (Hassan al-Saïfi, 1974, Egypt)

Voyage to a Woman's Depths / Hihlah dâkhil imraᵓah (Achraf Fahmi, 1978, Egypt)

Vreemde Wêreld (Afrikaans, Harold Phillip, 1974, South Africa)

Vrolike Vrydag die 13de (Afrikaans, Richard Daneel, 1969, South Africa)

Vrou uit die Nag (Afrikaans, Willie Alheit, 1974, South Africa)

Vulane (Zulu / Xhosa, *No director credited*, 1985, South Africa)

Vulture Is a Patient Bird (English, Gianpietro Calastro, South Africa, 1988)

Vulture's Prey, The (Silent, Dick Cruikshanks, 1921, South Africa)

Vuma (Zulu, Tonie van der Merwe, 1978, South Africa)

Vyfde Seisoen, Die / The Fifth Season (Afrikaans / English, Gordon Vorster, 1978, South Africa)

Vyfster: Die Slot (Afrikaans, Sias Odendaal, 1988, South Africa)

Waalo fendo (Mouhamed Soudani, 1997, Algeria)

Waati (Souleymane Cisse, 1995, Mali)

Wafaa / Wafâ (Ezz Eddine Zoulficar, 1953, Egypt)

Wahiba, Queen of the Gipsies / Wahîba malikat al-ghagar (Niazi Mostafa, 1951, Egypt)

Wahida / Wahîdah (Mohamed Kamel Hassan, 1961, Egypt)

Waiting for Happiness / Heremakono / En attendant le bonheur (Abderrahmane Sissako, 2002, Mauritania)

Waiting for Pasolini / En attendant Pasolini (Daoud Aoulad Syad, 2007, Morocco)

Waiting Room. The / La Salle d'attente (Nour Eddine Gounajjar, 1991, Morocco)

Wake of Death (English, Phillipe Martinez, 2004, South Africa)

Wake Up, Morocco (Narjis Nejjar, 2006, Morocco)

Walanda (Alkaly Kaba, 1974, Mali)

Walk a Long Distance / Thlathla Thile (North Sotho, *No director credited*, 1988, South Africa)

Waltz of the Fat Bottoms, The / La Valse des gros derrières (Jean Odoutan, 2003, Bénin)

Wamba (Alkaly Kaba, 1976, Mali)

Wanderers, The (*No director credited*, 1990, South Africa)

Wandering Heart / Cœur nomade (Fitouri Belhiba, 1990, Tunisia)

We the Students / Ihnâ al-talâmdhah (Atef Salem, 1959, Egypt)

We Want a Wife Straightaway / Matloup zawgah fawran (Mahmoud Farid, 1964, Egypt)

We Were Lucky (English, *No director credited*, 1989, South Africa)

We'll Love and Get Rich / Ha nheb wi n'eb (Abdel Latif Zaki, 1997, Egypt)

We're Human Beings / Nahnou bachar (Ibrahim Emara, 1955, Egypt)

We're the Ones Who Robbed the Robbers / Ihna illî saraqnâ al-harâmiyyah (Medhat al-Sibaï, 1989, Egypt)

Weaker Sex, The / Guins nâ'im (Mohamed Abdel Aziz, 1977, Egypt)

Wechma / Traces (Hamid Bennani, 1970, Morocco)

Wedad the Dancer / Widâd al-ghâziyyah (Ahmed Yehya, 1983, Egypt)

Wedding Night, The / Laylat al-doukhlah (Mostafa Hassan, 1950, Egypt)

Wedding Night, The / Laylat al-zifâf (Henri Barakat, 1966, Egypt)

Wedding, The (English, *No director credited*, 1986, South Africa)

Wedding, The / La Noce (collective, 1978, Tunisia)

Wednesday Boy (Zulu, *No director credited*, 1990, South Africa)

Weekend (English, Keith G. van der Wat, 1972, South Africa)

Weekend, The (English, Keith G. van der Wat, 1988, South Africa)

Weep Not, Love of My Life / Lâ tabkî yâ habîb al-'oumr (Ahmed Yehya, 1979, Egypt)

Weep Not, My Eyes / Kifâyah yâ'ayn (Houssam Eddine Mostafa, 1956, Egypt)

Weerskant die Nag (Afrikaans, Frans Marx, 1979, South Africa)

Weerskant die Nag (Afrikaans, Franz Marx, 1978, South Africa)

Wekalat al-Balah / Wakâlat al-balah (Houssam Eddine Mostafa, 1982, Egypt)

Welcome II the Terrordome (Ngozi Onwurah, 1994, Nigeria)

Well of Privation, The / Bi'r al-hirmân (Kamal al-Cheikh, 1969, Egypt)

Well of Treason, The / Bi'r al-khiyânah (Ali Abdel Khalek, 1987, Egypt)

Well-kept Secret, A / al-Sirr fî bîr (Hassan Helmi, 1953, Egypt)

Wend Kuuni / Le Don de dieu / God's Gift (Gaston Kaboré, 1982, Burkina Faso)

Wendemi / L'Enfant du bon dieu (Pierre S. Yaméogo, 1992, Burkina Faso)

Wereld Sonder Grense (Afrikaans, Frans Nel, 1987, South Africa)

Wesh Wesh—What's Happening / Wesh Wesh, qu'est-ce qui se passe (Rabah Ameur-Zaïmèche, 2002, Algeria)

Wesh Wesh, qu'est-ce qui se passe / Wesh Wesh—What's Happening (Rabah Ameur-Zaïmèche, 2002, Algeria)

West Indies / West Indies ou les nègres marrons de la liberté (Med Hondo, 1979, Mauritania)

West Indies ou les nègres marrons de la liberté / West Indies (Med Hondo, 1979, Mauritania)

West of Zanzibar (English, Harry Watt, 1954, South Africa)

Whale Hunting / Said al-heitaan (Ali Abdel Khalek, 2002, Egypt)

What a Mess / Moulid yâ douniâ (Hussein Kamal, 1975, Egypt)

What Are We Doing This Sunday? / Que fait-on ce dimanche (Lotfi Essid, 1983, Tunisia)

What Do Girls Want? / al-Banât 'âyzah îh (Hassan al-Saïfi, 1980, Egypt)

What Love Did to Daddy / 'Amalîh al-houbb fî bâbâ (Nasserr Hussein, 1980, Egypt)

What Neighbors / Guîrân âkhir zaman (Cherif Hammouda, 1989, Egypt)

What the Winds Have Carried Away / Ce que les vents ont emporté (Ahmed Kacem Akdi, 1984, Morocco)

Whatever Lola Wants (Nabil Ayouch, 2007, Morocco)

What's Going On? / Howwa feeh eih? (Cherif Mandour, 2002, Egypt)

What's the Plan / Ieeh al-nizaam (Hatem Musa, 2006, Egypt)

Wheel Turns, The / al-Hagar dâyir (Mohamed Radi, 1992, Egypt)

Wheels and Deals (English, Michael Hammon, 1991, South Africa)

When Fate Hardens / 'Indama Yaqsu al-Zaman (Adbellah Rezzoug, 1973, Libya)

When I Was Young / Ayyâm chabâbî (Gamal Madkour, 1950, Egypt)

Why the Sea? / Pourquoi la mer? (Hakim Belabbes, 2006, Morocco)

Why, Dunia? / Lîh yâ douniâ (Hani Lachine, 1994, Egypt)

Wicked Person, The / al-Charis (Nader Galal, 1992, Egypt)

Wicked, The / al-Achrâr (Houssam Eddine Mostafa, 1970, Egypt)

Wicked, The / al-Chouttâr (Nader Galal, 1993, Egypt)

Widow and the Devil, The / al-Armalah wa-l-chaytân (Henri Barakat, 1984. Egypt)

Widow and Three Daughters, A / Armalah wa thatlâth banât (Galal al-Charkawi, 1965, Egypt)

Widow Is Requested, A / Matloub armalah (Issa Karama, 1966, Egypt)

Widow of a Living Man / Armalat ragfoul hayy (Henri Barakat, 1989, Egypt)

Widowed on Her Wedding Night / Armalay laylat al-zifâf (al-Sayed Bedeir, 1974, Egypt)

Wie Laaste Lag / Danger Games (Afrikaans, Koos Roets, 1985, South Africa)

Wife for a Day / Zawgah li tawm yâhid (al-Sayed Ziyada, 1963, Egypt)

Wife for My Son, A / Une femme pour mon fils (Ali Ghalem, 1982, Algeria)

Wife Knows More, The / al-Zawgah taʾrif akthar (Khalil Chawki, 1987, Egypt)

Wife No. 13 / al-Zawgah raqam talataʾch (Fatine Abdel Wahab, 1962, Egypt)

Wife of an Important Man, The / Zawgat ragoul mouhim (Mohamed Khan, 1988, Egypt)

Wife on Approval / Imraʾah taht al-ikhtibâr (Mohamed Abaza, 1986, Egypt)

Wife without a Man / Zawgah bilâ ragoul (Abdel Rahman Cherif, 1969, Egypt)

Wife's Confessions, A / Iʾtirâfât zawgah (Hassam al-Imam, 1955, Egypt)

Wikus en Adele / Met Liefde van Adele (Afrikaans, Dirk de Villiers, 1974, South Africa)

Wild Country (English, No director credited, 1988, South Africa)

Wild Country / Okavango (English, Percival Rubens, 1989, South Africa)

Wild Flowers / Zouour barriyyah (Youssef Francis, 1973, Egypt)

Wild Geese. The (English, Andrew McLaglan, 1978, South Africa)

Wild Grass / L'Herbe sauvage (Henri Duparc, 1977, Ivory Coast)

Wild Man, The (No director credited, 1988, South Africa)

Wild Manoeuvres / Boetie of Manoeuvres (Afrikaans, Regardt van den Bergh, 1988, South Africa)

Wild Season / Wilde Seisoen (Afrikaans, Emil Nofal, 1967, South Africa)

Wilde Boere, Die (Afrikaans, J. O. O. Olwagen, 1959, South Africa)

Wilde Seisoen / Wild Season (Afrikaans, Emil Nofal, 1967, South Africa)

Wildsboudjie, Die (Afrikaans, Arthur Bennet and Louis Knobel, 1946, South Africa)

Will to Win (English, Rod Hays, 1982, South Africa)

Wilmington 10—USA 10,000 (documentary) (Haïle Gerima, 1976, Ethiopia)

Wiltemmer, Die (Afrikaans, Elmo de Witt, 1972, South Africa)

Wind Dance, The / La Danse du vent (Taïeb Louhichi, 2004, Tunisia)

Wind from the Aurès, The / Le Vent des Aurès (Mohamed Lakhdar-Hamina, 1966, Algeria)

Wind from the North, The / O vento sopra do norte (José Cardosa, 1987, Mozambique)

Wind from the South / Vent du Sud (Mohamed Slim Riad, 1975, Algeria)

Wind Horse, The / Le Cheval de vent (Daoud Aoulad Syad, 2001, Morocco)

Wind of Destinies / Le Vent des destins (Ahmed Djemaï, 1993, Tunisia)

Wind Rider (Zulu / Xhosa, Darrell Roodt, 1985, South Africa)

Wind, The / Finye / Le Vent (Souleymane Cisse, 1982, Mali)

Window of My Love, The / Choubbâk habîbî (Abbas Kamel, 1951, Egypt)

Window on Paradise / Nâfidhah ʿalâ al-gannah (Ahmed Diaa Eddine, 1953, Egypt)

Window, The / al-Choubbâk (Kamal Salah Eddine, 1980, Egypt)

Windprints (English, David Wicht, 1988, South Africa)

Winds of Rage (Michael Raeburn, 1998, Zimbabwe)

Winner Take All (English, Frans Nel, 1984, South Africa)

Winners / Abaqophi (Zulu, *No director credited*, 1989, South Africa)

Winners II, The / Again My Way (English, Jans Rautenbach, 1977, South Africa)

Winners, The (English, Roy Sargeant and Emil Nofal, 1972, South Africa)

Winning a Continent / De Voortrekkers (Silent, Harold Shaw, 1916, South Africa)

Winter Holidays, The / Agâzat nisf al-sanah (Ali Reda, 1962, Egypt)

Winter van 14 Julie, Die (Afrikaans, Jan Scholtz, 1977, South Africa)

Wipe Out (English, *No director credited*, 1987, South Africa)

Wisdom of the Arabs, The / Ahkâm al-lâthah (Ibrahim Emara, 1947, Egypt)

Wit Sluier, Die (Afrikaans, Dirk de Villiers, 1973, South Africa)

Witblits and Peach Brandy (English / Afrikaans, Dirk de Villiers, 1978, South Africa)

Witch Doctor (English, *No director credited*, 1985, South Africa)

With Edged Tools (Silent, Joseph Albrecht, 1919, South Africa)

With Hot Tears / al-Doumouꞌ al-sâkhinah (Yeyha al-Alami, 1976, Egypt)

With My Love and Tenderness / Maꞌ houbbî wa achwâqi (Henri Barakat, 1977, Egypt)

With No Farewells / Min Ghayr wadâꞌ (Ahmed Diaa Eddine, 1951, Egypt)

With Premeditation / Maꞌ sabq al-isrâr (Achraf Fahmi, 1979, Egypt)

With the Memories / Maꞌ al-dhrikrayât (Saad Afara, 1961, Egypt)

With the People / Maꞌ al-nâs (Kamal Ateyya, 1964, Egypt)

With Time / Maꞌal-ayyâm (Ahmed Diaa Eddine, 1958, Egypt)

With You Always / Dâyman maꞌâk (Henri Barakat, 1954, Egypt)

Without a Rendezvous / Min gheir mîꞌâd (Ahmed Diaa Eddine, 1962, Egypt)

Without Hope / Min gheir amal (Hassan Reda, 1963, Egypt)

Without Pity / Bilâ rahmah (Niazi Mostafa, 1971, Egypt)

Without Return / Bilâ ꞌawdah (Raymond Nassour, 1961, Egypt)

Without Tears / Bilâ doumouꞌ (Mahmoud Zoulficar, 1961, Egypt)

Without You / Lawlâki (Hassan al-Saïfi, 1993, Egypt)

Witness for the Prosecution / Châdid ithbât (Alaa Mahgoub, 1987, Egypt)

Witness, The / Sere / Le Témon (Dansogho Mohamed Camara, 1990, Guinea)

Wolf Trap, The / Misyadat al-dhiꞌâb (Ismaïl Gamal, 1994, Egypt)

Wolf's Kindness / Tendresse du loup (Jilani Saadi, 2006, Tunisia)

Wolf's Lair, The / Wakr al-dhiꞌb (Nasser Hussein, 1992, Egypt)

Wolhaarstories (Afrikaans, Bromley Cawood, 1983, South Africa)

Wolves on the Road / Dhiꞌâb ꞌalâ al-tarîq (Kamal Salah Eddine, 1972, Egypt)

Wolves, The / al-Dhiꞌâb (Abdel Halim al-Nahhas, 1993, Egypt)

Wolves, The / al-Dhiꞌâb (Adel Sadek, 1983, Egypt)

Woman and a Man, A / Imraꞌah wa ragoul (Houssam Eddine Mostafa, 1971, Egypt)

Woman and Demon / Imraꞌah wa chaytân (Seif Eddine Chawkat, 1961, Egypt)

Woman and Five Men, A / Imraꞌa wa khamas regaal (Alaa Karim, 1997, Egypt)

Woman and Men, The / Hiya wa-l-rigâl (Hassan al-Imam, 1965, Egypt)

Woman And the Cleaver, The / al-Marꞌa wa al-satoor (Saïd Marzouk, 1997, Egypt)

Woman and the Demons, The / Hiya wa-l-chayâtîn (Houssam Eddine Mostafa, 1969, Egypt)

Woman and the Giant, The / Hiya wa-l-ꞌimlâq (Ismaïl Hassan, 1993, Egypt)

Woman and the Law, The / al-Marꞌah wa-l-qânoun (Nadia Hamza, 1988, Egypt)

Woman and the Puppet, The / Liꞌbat al-sitt (Wali Eddine Sameh, 1946, Egypt)

Woman and the Wolves, The / al-Ounthâ wa-l-dhiꞌâb (Niazi Mostafa, 1975, Egypt)

Woman at the Top / Imraꞌa fawq al-qemma (Ashraf Fahmi, 1997, Egypt)

Woman for Love, A / Imraꞌah li-l-houbb (Ahmed Diaa Eddine, 1974, Egypt)

Woman from Cairo, A / Imraꞌah min al-Qâhirah (Mohamed Abdel Aziz, 1973, Egypt)

Woman from Paris, A / Zawgah min Paris (Atef Salem, 1966, Egypt)

Woman Has Deceived Me, A / Khada²atnî imar²ah (Sayed Tantawi, 1979, Egypt)

Woman in Love / Imra²ah ᶜâchiqah (Achraf Fahmi, 1974, Egypt)

Woman in Love, The / al-Âchiqah (al-Sayed Ziyada, 1960, Egypt)

Woman in Love, The / al-²Âchiqah (Atef Salem, 1980, Egypt)

Woman in Torment / Imra²ah fî dawwâmah (Mahmoud Zoulficar, 1962, Egypt)

Woman Is a Devil / al-Mar²ah chaytân (Abdel Fattan Hassan, 1949, Egypt)

Woman Is a Woman, A / al-Mar²ah hiya al-mar²ah (Henri Barakat, 1978, Egypt)

Woman Is Everything / al-Mar²ah koull chay² (Helmi Rafla, 1953, Egypt)

Woman Killed by Love, A / Imra²ah qatalahâ al-houbb (Achraf Fahmi, 1978, Egypt)

Woman of Color, A (English, Bernard Joffa, 1996, South Africa)

Woman of Desire, A (English, Roberty Ginty, 1992, South Africa)

Woman of Glass / Imra²ah min Zougâg (Nader Galal, 1977, Egypt)

Woman on the Margins, A / imra²ah ᶜalâ al-hâmich (Hassan al-Imam, 1963, Egypt)

Woman on the Road, A / Imra²as fî-l-tarîq (Ezz Eddine Zoulficar, 1958, Egypt)

Woman Pays the Price, A / Imra²ah tadfa² al-thaman (Hassan Ibrahim, 1993, Egypt)

Woman Prisoner No. 67 / al-Saguînah sab²a wa sittîn (Ahmed Yeyha, 1992, Egypt)

Woman under Observation, A / Imra²a taht el muraqba (Ashraf Fahmi, 2000, Egypt)

Woman Visitor, The / al-Zâ²irah (Henri Barakat, 1972, Egypt)

Woman Who Conquered the Devil, The / al-Mar²ah allatî ghalabat al-chaytân (Yehya al-Alami, 1973, Egypt)

Woman Who Runs through My Veins, A / Imra²ah fî damî (Ahmed Fouad, 1978, Egypt)

Woman Who Shook Egypt's Throne, A / Imara²a hazzat ᶜarsh masr (Nader Galal, 1995, Egypt)

Woman with a Bad Reputation / Imr²ah sayyi²at al-soum²ah (Henri Barakat, 1973, Egypt)

Woman with the Knife, The / La Femme au couteau (Bassori Timité, 1969, Ivory Coast)

Woman with Two Faces, The / Dhât al-wag²hayn (Houssam Eddine Mostafa, 1973, Egypt)

Woman, Alas!, A / Imra²ah li-l-asaf (Nadia Hamza, 1988, Egypt)

Woman, The / al-Mar²ah (Abdel Fattah Hassan, 1949, Egypt)

Woman's Claws, A / Makhâlib imra²ah (Addel al-Aassar, 1988, Egypt)

Woman's Confessions, A / I²tirâfât imra²ah (Saad Arafa, 1971, Egypt)

Woman's Curse, A / La²nat imra²ah (Niazi Mostafa, 1974, Egypt)

Woman's Divorce Lawyer / Muhami khol² (Mohamed Yassin, 2002, Egypt)

Woman's Enemy, The / ᶜAdouww al-mar²ah (Mahmoud Zoulficar, 1966, Egypt)

Woman's Fate, A / Destin de femme (Hakim Noury, 1998, Morocco)

Woman's Hell, A / Gahîm imra²ah (Tarek al-Nahri, 1992, Egypt)

Woman's Imagination, A / Khayâl imra²ah (Hassan Reda, 1948, Egypt)

Woman's Judgment, A / Jugement d'une femme (Hassan Benjelloun, 2000, Morocco)

Woman's Life, A / Hayât imra²ah (Zouheir Bekir, 1958, Egypt)

Woman's Love, A / Gharâmiyyât imra²ah (Tolba Radwane, 1960, Egypt)

Woman's Malice, A / Hiqd imra²ah (Nadia Hamza, 1987, Egypt)

Woman's Revenge, A / Intiqâm im ra²ah (Ismaïl Galal, 1994, Egypt)

Woman's Secret, A / Sirr imra²ah (Atef Salem, 1960, Egypt)

Women / al-Nisâ² (Nadia Hamza, 1985, Egypt)

Women / al-Sittât (Medhat al-Sibaï, 1992, Egypt)

Women and Wolves / nisâ² wa dhi²âb (Houssam Eddine Mostafa, 1960, Egypt)

Women Are Devils / al-Sittât ᶜafrârît (Hassan al-Imam, 1947, Egypt)

Women Are Made Like That / al-Sittât kidah (Hassan Helmi, 1949, Egypt)

Women Behind Bars / Nisâ² khalfa al-qoudbân (Nadia Hamza, 1986, Egypt)

Women Don't Know How to Lie / al-Sittât mâ ya²rafouch yikdibou (Mohamed Abdel Gawad, 1954, Egypt)

Women in Love / al-Âchiqât (Mahmoud Farid, 1976, Egypt)

Yasmine's Nights / Layâlî Yasmîn (Henri Barakat, 1978, Egypt)

Years of Danger, The / Sanawât al-khatar (Nagdi Hafez, 1985, Egypt)

Years of Exile, The / Les Années de l'exil (Nabyl Lahlou, 2002, Morocco)

Years of Love, The / Sanawât al-houbb (Mahmoud Zoulficar, 1963, Egypt)

Yeelen (Souleymane Cisse, 1987, Mali)

Yelbeedo (Abdoulaye Sow, 1990, Burkina Faso)

Yelema (Mamo Cisse, 1992, Mali)

Yelema II (Mamo Cisse, 1997, Mali)

Yellow Card (John Riber, 2000, Zimbabwe)

Yellow Valley, The / al-Wâdi al-asfar (Mamdouh Choukri, 1970, Egypt)

Yesterday (English, Darrell Roodt, 2004, South Africa)

Yesterday's Friends / Les Amis d'hier (Hassan Benjelloun, 1997, Morocco)

Yeux secs, Les / Dry Eyes (Narjiss Nejjar, 2002, Morocco)

Ymer or The Flowering Thistles / Ymer ou les chardons florifères (Tijani Chrigui, 1991, Morocco)

Ymer ou les chardons florifères / Ymer or The Flowering Thistles (Tijani Chrigui, 1991, Morocco)

Yonna Lefatseng (Sotho, Jimmy Murray, 1984, South Africa)

You and Me / Anâ wa anta (Ahmed Badrakhan, 1950, Egypt)

You Are My Life / Hayâtî inta (Youssef Maalouf, 1952, Egypt)

You Are My Love / Anta habîbî (Youssef Chahine, 1957, Egypt)

You Are Thinking of Another Woman / Machghoul bighayrî (Ibrahim Emara, 1951, Egypt)

You Are Witnesses / Ichhadou yâ nâs (Hassan al-Saïfi, 1953, Egypt)

You Deserve It / Halâl ᶜalayk (Issa Karama, 1952, Egypt)

You Gotta Be Crazy (English, Emil Nofal, 1986, South Africa)

You Must Be Joking (Afrikaans, Elmo de Witt, 1986, South Africa)

You Must Be Joking Too (English, Leon Schuster, 1987, South Africa)

You Must Venerate Your Parents / Wa bi-l-wâlidayn ihsânan (Hassan al-Imam, 1976, Egypt)

You Only Live Once / al-ᵓOumr wâhid (Ehsane Farghal, 1954, Egypt)

You're Famous (English, Alain Woolf, 1988, South Africa)

You're in the Movies (English, Emil Nofal, 1984, South Africa)

You've Done Me Wrong / Yâ zâlimnî (Ibrahim Emara, 1954, Egypt)

Youcef, la légende du septième dormant / Youssef—The Legend of the Seventh Sleeper (Mohamed Chouikh, 1993, Algeria)

You-Know-Who / Illy baly balak (Wael Ihsaan, 2003, Egypt)

Young Girls and Ladies / Ânisât wa sayyidât (Kamal Salah Eddine, 1974, Egypt)

Young Girls and Love / al-Banât wa-l-houbb (Houssam Eddine Mostafa, 1974, Egypt)

Young Girls at Auction / ᶜArâyis fî-l-mazâd (Hassan al-Salïfi, 1955, Egypt)

Young Girls' Dreams / Ahlâm al-banât (Youssef Maalouf, 1959, Egypt)

Young Girls' Flirtations / Ghazal al-banât (Anwar Waghi, 1949, Egypt)

Young Girls' Frivolity / Dalaᵓ al-banât (Hassan al-Saïfi, 1969, Egypt)

Young People in the Storm / Chabâb fi ᶜâsifah (Adel Sadek, 1971, Egypt)

Young People Today / Chabâb al-yawm (Mahmoud Zoulficar, 1958, Egypt)

Young People Today / Choubbân hâdhihi al-ayyâm (Atef Salem, 1975, Egypt)

Young Thief, The / Nachchâlah hânim (Hassan al-Saïfi, 1953, Egypt)

Your Day Will Come / Lak Youm yâ zâlim (Salah Abou Seif, 1951, Egypt)

Your Day Will Come, Bey / Lak youm yâ bîh (Mohamed Abdel Aziz, 1984. Egypt)

Your Health! / Fî sihhitak (Abbas Kamel, 1955, Egypt)

Your Horoscope This Week / Hazzak hâdhâ al-ousbouᵓ (Helmi Rafla, 1953, Egypt)

Your Mother-in-Law Loves You / Hamâtak tihibbak (Fouad Chebl, 1950, Egypt)

Your Way / ᶜAlâ keifak (Helmi Rafla, 1952, Egypt)

Yours Truly (*No director credited*, 1987, South Africa)

Yousra (Rachid Ferchiou, 1972, Tunisia)

Youssef—The Legend of the Seventh Sleeper / Youssef, la légende du septième dormant (Mohamed Chouikh, 1993, Algeria)

Youth Dancing on Fire / Chabâb yarqous fawq al-nâr (Yehya al-Alami, 1978, Egypt)

Youth for All Ages / Chabâb li-koull al-Agyâl (Nasser Hussein, 1988, Egypt)

Youth in Hell / Chabâb fî-l-gahîm (Ahmed al-Sabaawi, 1988, Egypt)

Youth On-Air / Shabaab ʿala el hawa (Adel Awad, 2002, Egypt)

Youth Which Is Eaten Up, A / Chabâb yahtariq (Mahmoud Farid, 1972, Egypt)

Youthful Adventure / Moughâmarat Chabâb (Issa Karama, 1970, Egypt)

Zaïna, cavalière de l'Atlas / Zaina, Horsewoman from the Atlas (Bourlem Guerdjou, 2005, Algeria)

Zaina, Horsewoman from the Atlas / Zaïna, cavalière de l'Atlas (Bourlem Guerdjou, 2005, Algeria)

Zakeya Zakareya Goes to Parliament / Zakeya Zakareya fi al-barlamaan (Raid Labib, 2001, Egypt)

Zaki Chan / Zaki Chan (Wael Ihsaan, 2005, Egypt)

Zambezi Kid, The (English, Denis Scully, 1988, South Africa)

Zan Boko (Gaston Kaboré, 1988, Burkina Faso)

Zanati's Sun / Chams al-Zanâti (Samir Seif, 1991, Egypt)

Zannouba / Zannoubah (Hassan al-Saïfi, 1956, Egypt)

Zano's Revenge (*No director credited*, 1990, South Africa)

Zanqet El Settaat / Zanqet el settaat (Alaa Karim, 2000, Egypt)

Zaza / Zaza (Ali Abdel Khalek, 2006, Egypt)

Zazous de la vague, Les / The Teddy Boys (Mohamed Ali El Okbi, 1992, Tunisia)

Zebra (Afrikaans, Elmo de Witt, 1971, South Africa)

Zeft (Tayeb Saddiki, 1984, Morocco)

Zeinab / Zeinab (Mohamed Karim, 1952, Egypt)

Zerda or Songs of Forgetfulness, The / La Zerda ou les chants de l'oubli (Assia Djebar, 1980, Algeria)

Zerda ou les chants de l'oubli, La / The Zerda or Songs of Forgetfulness (Assia Djebar, 1980, Algeria)

Zero for Zeb (Zulu, Tonievan der Merwe, 1984, South Africa)

Zézette / Zézette (Sayed Issa, 1961, Egypt)

Zik's Fortune (English, *No director credited*, 1987, South Africa)

Zimbabwean Countdown (Michael Raeburn, 2003, Zimbabwe)

Zizi's Family / ʿÂʾilat Zizi (Fatine Abdel Wahab, 1963, Egypt)

Zohra / Zohrah (Hussein Fawzi and Kamal Abou el-Ela, 1947, Egypt)

Zondo's Dreams / Amaphupho ka Zondo (Zulu, *No director credited*, 1987, South Africa)

Zone interdite / Forbidden Zone (Ahmed Lallem, 1974, Algeria)

Zonk (English, Hyman Kirstein, 1950, South Africa)

Zulu Dawn (English, Douglas Hickox, 1979, South Africa)

Zulu Love Letter (English, Ramadan Suleman, 2005, South Africa)

Zulu's Devotion, A (Silent, Lorrimer Johnston, 1916, South Africa)

Zulu-Town Comedies (Silent, Dick Cruikshanks, 1917, South Africa)

BIBLIOGRAPHY

Material on specific countries, directors, and films is given at the end of the appropriate national chronology.

BACKGROUND MATERIAL

World Cinema, Colonialism, Immigration

Armes, Roy. *Third World Film Making and the West.* Berkeley: University of California Press, 1987.

Bataille, Maurice-Robert, and Claude Veillot. *Caméras sous le soleil: Le Cinéma en Afrique du nord.* Algiers, 1956.

Benali, Abdelkader. *Le Cinéma colonial au Maghreb.* Paris: Editions du Cerf, 1998.

Benguigui, Yamina. *Mémoires d'immigrés: l'héritage maghrébin.* Paris: Albin Michel, 1997.

Bossaerts, Marc, and Catherine Van Geel, eds. *Cinéma d'en Francophonie.* Brussels: Solibel Edition, 1995.

Bosséno, Christian, ed. *Cinémas de l'Emigration 3.* Paris: Éditions L'Harmattan/*CinémAction* 24, 1983.

Boulanger, Pierre. *Le Cinéma colonial.* Paris: Seghers, 1975.

Burns, James McDonald. *Flickering Shadows: Cinema and Identity in Colonial Zimbabwe.* Athens: Ohio University Press, 2002.

Cameron, Kenneth M. *Africa on Film: Beyond Black and White.* New York: Continuum, 1994.

Chaudhuri, Shohini. *Contemporary World Cinema.* Edinburgh: Edinburgh University Press, 2005.

Convents, Guido. *A la recherche des images oubliés: Préhistoire du cinéma en Afrique, 1897–1918.* Brussels: OCIC, 1986.

Dönmez-Colin, Gönül. *Women, Islam and Cinema.* London: Reaktion Books, 2004.

Downing, John D. H., ed. *Film and Politics in the Third World.* New York: Praeger, 1987.

Elena, Alberto. *El cine del tercer mundo: diccionario de realizadores.* Madrid: Ediciones Turfan, 1993.

———. *"Romancero marroquí": el cine africanista durante la guerra civil.* Madrid: Filmoteca Española, 2005.

Ezra, Elisabeth and Terry Rowden, eds. *Transnational Cinema: The Film Reader.* London and New York: Routledge, 2006.

Frodon, Jean-Pierre, ed. *Au Sud du Cinéma.* Paris: Cahiers du Cinéma/Arte Editions, 2004.

Guneratne, Anthony R., and Wimal Disanayake. *Rethinking Third Cinema.* New York: Routledge, 2003.

Hennebelle, Guy. *Quinze ans de cinéma mondial.* Paris: Éditions du Cerf, 1975.

———, ed. *Cinémas de l'émigration.* Paris: *CinémAction* 8, 1979.

———, ed. *Le Tiers monde en films.* Paris: *CinémAction/Tricontinental,* 1982.

———. *Les Cinémas nationaux contre Hollywood.* Paris: Éditions du Cerf / Éditions Corlet, 2004.

Hennebelle, Guy, and Roland Schneider, eds. *Cinémas métis: De Hollywood aux films beurs.* Paris: *CinémAction* 56/*Hommes et Migrations*/Corlet/Télérama, 1990.

Hennebelle, Guy, and Chantal Soyer, eds. *Cinéma contre racisme.* Paris: *CinémAction* (hors série) and *Tumulte* 7, 1980.

Hjort, Mette, and Scott Mackenzie, eds. *Cinema and Nation.* London: Routledge, 2000.

L'Afrique noire. Perpignan: *Confrontation Cinématographique* 19 (1983).

Landau, Jacob M. *Studies in the Arab Theater and Cinema.* Philadelphia: University of Pennsylvania Press, 1958. Translated into French as *Etudes sur le théâtre et le cinéma arabes.* Paris: G-P Maisonneuve et Larosé, 1965.

Leaman, Oliver, ed. *Companion Encyclopedia of Middle Eastern and North African Film.* London: Routledge, 2001.

Mirzoeff, Nicholas, ed. *Visual Culture Reader.* London: Routledge, 1998.

Mowitt, John. *Re-takes: Postcoloniality and Foreign Film Languages.* Minneapolis: University of Minnesota Press, 2005.

Naficy, Hamid. *An Accented Cinema: Exilic and Diasporic Filmmaking.* Princeton, N.J.: Princeton University Press, 2001.

Nicollier, Valéri. *Der Offene Bruch: Das Kino der Pieds Noirs.* Munich: *Cinim* 34 (1991).

Nowell-Smith, Geoffrey, ed. *The Oxford History of World Cinema*. Oxford, UK: Oxford University Press, 1996.

Sherzer, Dina. *Cinema, Colonialism, Postcolonialism: Perspectives from the French and Francophone Worlds*. Austin: University of Texas Press, 1996.

Shoat, Ella, and Robert Stamm. *Unthinking Eurocentrism: Multiculturalism and the Media*. London: Routledge, 1994.

Slavin, David Henry. *Colonial Cinema and Imperial France, 1919–1939*. Baltimore: Johns Hopkins University Press, 2001.

Spagnoletti, Giovanni, ed. *Il cinema europeo del métissage*. Milan: Editrice Il Castoro, 2000.

Spass, Lieve. *The Francophone Film: A Struggle for Identity*. Manchester: Manchester University Press, 2000.

Steven, Peter, ed. *Jump Cut: Hollywood, Politics and Counter-Cinema*. Toronto: Between the Lines, 1975.

Tarr, Carrie. *Reframing Difference: Beur and Banlieue Filmmaking in France*. Manchester: Manchester University Press, 2005.

Vitali, Valentina, and Paul Willemen, eds. *Theorising National Cinema*. London: BFI Publishing, 2006.

GENERAL STUDIES OF AFRICAN CINEMA

Africa on Africa. London: Channel 4, 1984.

"African Cinema," dossier London. *Sight and Sound*, February 2007, pp. 26–35.

Arab Cinema and Culture: Round Table Conferences (3 volumes). Beirut: Arab Film and Television Center, 1965.

Arasoughly, Alia, ed. *Screens of Life: Critical Film Writing from the Arab World*. Quebec: World Heritage Press, 1998.

Armes, Roy. "Black African Cinema in the Eighties." London: *Screen* 26, no. 3–4 (1985): 60–73.

———. "Cinema." In *The Oxford Encyclopedia of the Modern Islamic World*, ed. John Esposito, pp. 286–290. New York: Oxford University Press, 1995.

———. *Dictionary of North African Film Makers / Dictionnaire des cinéastes du Maghreb*. Paris: Éditions ATM, 1996.

———. "Imag(in)ing Europe: The Theme of Emigration in North African Cinema." In *Mediating the Other: Jews, Christians, Muslims and the Media*, ed. Tudor Parfitt and Yulia Egorova, pp. 68–77. London: RoutledgeCurzon 2004.

———. *Postcolonial Images: Studies in North African Film*. Bloomington: Indiana University Press, 2005.

———. *African Filmmaking: North and South of the Sahara*. Edinburgh: Edinburgh University Press; Bloomington: Indiana University Press, 2006.

Awed, Ibrahim, et al., eds. *First Mogadishu Pan African Film Symposium*. Mogadishu: Mogpafis Management Committee, 1983.

Bachy, Victor. *To Have a History of African Cinema*. Brussels: OCIC, 1987.

Bakari, Umruh, and Mbye Cham, eds. *African Experiences of Cinema*. London: BFI, 1996.

Barlet, Olivier. *Les Cinémas d'Afrique noire: le regard en question*. Paris: L'Harmattan, 1996. English translation: *African Cinemas: Decolonizing the Gaze*. London: Zed Books, 2000.

———. "Les Nouvelles stratégies des cinéastes africains." Paris: *Africultures* 41 (2001): 69–76.

Ben el Haj, Bahri. *Une politique africaine du cinéma*. Paris: Editions Dadci, 1980.

Bensalah, Mohamed. *Cinéma en Méditerranée, une passerelle entre les cultures*. Aix-en-Provence: Édisud, 2005.

Berrah, Mouny, Victor Bachy, Mohand Ben Salama, and Ferid Boughedir, eds. *Cinémas du Maghreb*. Paris: *CinémAction* 14, 1981.

Berrah, Mouny, Jacques Lévy, and Claude-Michel Cluny, eds. *Les Cinémas arabes*. Paris: *CinémAction* 43/Cerf/Institut du Monde Arabe, 1987.

Bickford-Smith, Vivian, and Richard Mendelsohn, eds. *Black and White on Film: African History on Screen*. Oxford: James Currey; Athens: Ohio University Press; Cape Town: Double Storey, 2007.

Binet, Jacques, Ferid Boughedir, and Victor Bachy, eds. *Cinémas noirs d'Afrique*. Paris: *CinémAction* 26, 1983.

Boughedir, Ferid. *Le Cinéma en Afrique et dans le monde*. Paris: Jeune Afrique Plus, 1984.

———. *Le Cinéma africain de A à Z*. Brussels: OCIC, 1987

Brahimi, Denise. *Cinémas d'Afrique francophone et du Maghreb*. Paris: Nathan, 1997.

Canetta, Carlo, and Fiorano Rancati, eds. *Il cinema maghrebino*. Milan: Arci Nova, 1991.

Cent ans de cinéma: Cinéma arabe (Bibliographie de la bibliothèque de l'IMA). Paris: Institut du Monde Arabe, 1995.

CESCA. *Camera nigra: le discours du film africain*. Brussels: OCIC, 1984.

Challouf, Mohamed, Giuseppe Gariazzo, and Alessandra Speciale, eds. *Un posto sulla terra: Cinema per (r)esistere*. Milan: Editrice il Castoro, 2002.

Cham, Mbye B., and Claire Andrade-Watkins, eds. *Blackframes: Critical Perspectives on Black Independent Cinema*. Cambridge, Mass.: MIT Press, 1988.

Cheriaa, Tahar. *Ecrans d'abondance . . . ou cinémas de libération en Afrique?* Tunis: STD, 1979.

Cinéma et libertés: Contribution au thème du Fespaco 93. Paris: Présence Africaine, 1993.

Cinémas de Africa. Lisbon: Cinemeteca Portugesa/Culturgest, 1995.

Cluny, Claude-Michel. *Dictionnaire des nouveaux cinémas arabes.* Paris: Sindbad, 1978.

Colais, Francesca. *Il cinema africano dalla parola all'immagine.* Rome: Bulzoni Editore, 1999.

Convents, Guido. *L'Afrique? Quel cinéma! Un siècle de propagande coloniale et de films africains.* Antwerp: Editions EPO, 2003.

De Arabische Film. Amsterdam: Cinemathema, 1979.

De Fransceschi, Leonardo. *Hudud! Un viaggio nel cinema maghrebino.* Rome: Bulzoni Editore, 2005.

Despierre, P-G., ed. *Le Griot, le psychanalyste et le cinéma africain.* Paris: Grappaf/L'Harmattan, 2004.

Di Martino, Anna, Andrea Morini, and Michele Capasso, eds. *Il cinema dei paesi arabi, Quarta edizione / Arab Film Festival, Fourth Edition.* Naples: Edizioni Magma, 1997.

Diawara, Manthia. "African Cinema Today." London: *Framework* 37 (1989): 110–128.

———. *African Cinema: Politics and Culture.* Bloomington: Indiana University Press, 1992.

Dossier: Spécial Cinémas d'Afrique. Paris: CNC (*Info* 237), 1991.

Ebanda de B'béri, Boulou, ed. *Ecritures dans les cinémas d'Afrique noire.* Montreal: *CiNéMAS,* 2000.

———. *Mapping Alternative Expressions of Blackness in Cinema: A Horizontal Labyrinth of Transgeographical Practices of Identity.* Bayreuth, Germany: *Bayreuth African Studies Series* 80, 2006.

Eke, Maureen N., Kenneth W. Harrow, and Emmanuel Yewah, eds. *African Images: Recent Studies and Text In Cinema.* Trenton, N.J.,: Africa World Press, 2000.

Farid, Samir. *Arab Cinema Guide.* Cairo, 1979.

FEPACI. *L'Afrique et le centenaire du cinéma / Africa and the Centenary of Cinema.* Paris: Présence Africaine, 1995.

Festival: Images du monde arabe. Paris: Institut du Monde Arabe, 1993.

Fina, Luciana, Cristina Fina, and António Loja Neves. *Cinemas de África.* Lisbon: Cinemateca Portugesa and Culturgest, 1995.

Fonkoua, Romuald-Blaise, ed. *Cinquante ans de cinéma Africain/Hommage à Paulin Soumanou Vieyra.* Paris: *Présence Africaine* 170 (2004).

Garcia, Jean-Pierre, ed. *Sous l'arbre à palabres: Guide pratique à l'usage des cinéastes africains.* Amiens: Festival International du Film d'Amiens, 1996.

Second edition, Cottenchy, France: Caravane Éditeurs, 2001.

———. *Itinéraires: les cinéastes africains au festival de Cannes.* Paris: Ministère de la Coopération, 1997.

———, ed. *Spécial Fespaco 2001.* Amiens: *Le Film Africain and Le Film du Sud* 35–36 (2001).

Gardies, André. *Cinéma d'Afrique noire francophone.* Paris: L'Harmattan, 1989.

Gardies, André, and Pierre Haffner. *Regards sur le cinéma négro-africain.* Brussels: OCIC, 1989.

Gariazzo, Giuseppe. *Poetiche del cinema africano.* Turin: Lindau, 1998.

———. *Breve storia del cinema africano.* Turin: Lindau, 2001.

Ghazoul, Ferial J., ed. *Arab Cinematics: Towards the New and the Alternative.* Cairo: *Alif* 15 (1995).

Givanni, June, ed. *Symbolic Narratives/African Cinema: Audiences, Theory and the Moving Image.* London: British Film Institute, 2000.

Gray, John. *Blacks in Film and Television: A Pan-African Bibliography of Films, Filmmakers and Performers.* New York: Greenwood Press, 1990.

Gugler, Josef. *African Film: Re-Imagining a Continent.* London: James Currey, 2003.

Gupta, Dhruba. *African Cinema: A View from India.* Jamshedpur, India: Celluloid Chapter, 1994.

Gutberlet, Marie-Hélène, and Hans-Peter Metzler, eds. *Afrikanisches Kino.* Bad Honnef, Germany: Horlemann/ARTE, 1997.

Gutmann, Marie-Pierre, ed. *Le Partenariat euro-méditerranéen dans le domaine de l'image.* Morocco: Service de coopération de l'action culturelle de l'Ambassade de France au Maroc, 1999.

Haffner, Pierre. *Essai sur les fondements du cinéma africain.* Paris: Nouvelles Éditions Africaines, 1978.

———. *Palabres sur le cinématographe: initiation au cinéma.* Kinshasa, Democratic Republic of Congo: Presses Africaines, 1978.

———. *Kino in Schwarzafrika.* Munich: French Institute (*CICIM* 27–28), 1989.

Harrow, Kenneth W., ed. *With Open Eyes: Women and African Cinema.* Amsterdam: *Matutu* 19 (1997).

———, ed. *African Cinema: Post-Colonial and Feminist Readings.* Trenton, N.J.: Africa World Press, 1999.

———. *Postcolonial African Cinema: From Political Engagement to Postmodernism.* Bloomington: Indiana University Press, 2007.

Hennebelle, Guy, ed. *Les Cinémas africains en 1972.* Paris: Société Africaine d'Edition, 1972.

———, ed. *Cinémas noirs d'Afrique.* Paris: *CinémAction* 23, 1983.

Hennebelle, Guy, and Catherine Ruelle, eds. *Cinéastes*

de l'Afrique noire. Paris: Fespaco/CinémAction 3, 1977.

Hillauer, Rebecca. Freiräume—Lebensträume, Arabische Filmemacherinnen. Unkel am Rhein, Germany: Arte-Edition, 2001. English translation: Encyclopedia of Arab Women Filmmakers. Cairo: American University in Cairo Press, 2005.

Ilboudo, Patrick G. Le Fespaco 1969–1989: Les Cinéastes africains et leurs œuvres. Ouagadougou: Éditions La Mante, 1988.

Image(s) du Maghrébin dans le cinéma français. Paris: Grand Maghreb 47 (1989).

Jung, Fernand. Südlich der Sahara: Filme aus Schwarzafrika. Munich: Kopäd Verlag, 1997.

Kane, Momar Désiré. Marginalité et errance dans la littératue et le cinéma africains francophones. Paris: Éditions L'Harmattan, 2004.

Khayati, Khémais. "La Problématique de la liberté individuelle dans le cinéma arabe." In L'image dans le monde arabe, ed. Gilbert Beaugé and Jean-François Clément, pp. 305–310. Paris: CNRS Éditions, 1995.

———. Cinémas arabes: Topographie d'une image éclatée. Paris: L'Harmattan, 1996.

Khelil, Hédi. Résistances et utopies, essais sur le cinéma arabe et africain. Tunis: Édition Sahar, 1994.

Kummer, Ida, ed. Cinéma Maghrébin. Saratoga Springs: Celaan 1, no. 1–2 (2002).

La Semaine du cinéma arabe. Paris: Institut du Monde Arabe, 1987.

Lanza, Federica. La donna nel cinema maghrebino. Rome: Bulzoni Editore, 1999.

Lazare, Pascal, and Jean-Daniel Simon, eds. Guide du cinéma africain (1989–1999). Paris: Écrans Nord-Sud, 2000.

Le Clap ou à la connaissance des cinéastes africains et de la diaspora. Ouagadougou: Sykif, 2001.

Le Rôle du cinéaste africain dans l'éveil d'une conscience de civilisation noire. Paris: Présence Africaine 90 (1974),

Lelièvre, Samuel, ed. Cinémas africains, une oasis dans le désert? Paris: Corlet/Télérama/CinémAction 106, 2003.

Lequeret, Elisabeth. Le Cinéma africain: un continent à la recherche de son propre regard. Paris: Cahiers du Cinéma/Scérén/CNDP, 2003.

Les Cinémas d'Afrique: Dictionnaire. Paris: Éditions Karthala and Éditions ATM, 2000.

Maarek, Philippe J., ed. Afrique noire: quel cinéma? Paris: Association du Cinéclub de l'Université de Paris X, 1983.

Malkmus, Lizbeth, and Roy Armes. Arab and African Film Making. London: Zed Books, 1991.

Mansouri, Hassouna. De l'identité ou Pour une cer-

taine tendance du cinéma africain. Tunis: Editions Sahar, 2000.

Martin, Angela. African Films: The Context of Production. London: British Film Institute, 1982.

Martin, Michael T., ed. Cinemas of the Black Diaspora: Diversity, Dependence and Oppositionality. Detroit: Wayne State University Press, 1995.

Millet, Raphaël. Cinémas de la Méditerranée, cinémas de la mélancolie. Paris: Éditions L'Harmattan, 2002.

Mondolini, Dominique, ed. Cinémas d'Afrique. Paris: ADPF (Notre Librairie 149), 2002.

Morini, Andrea, Erfan Rashid, Anna Di Martino, and Adriano Aprà. Il cinema dei paesi arabi. Venice: Marsilio Editori, 1993.

Murphy, David, and Patrick Williams. Postcolonial African Cinema: Ten Directors. Manchester and New York: Manchester University Press, 2007.

Ngakane, Lionel, and Keith Shiri. Africa on Film, London: BBC, 1991.

N'Gosso, Gaston Samé, and Catherine Ruelle. Cinéma et télévision en Afrique. Paris: UNESCO, 1983.

Ouédraogo, Hamidou. Naissance et évolution du Fespaco de 1969 à 1973. Ouagadougou: Hamidou Ouédraogo, 1995.

Palmier, Jean Joseph. La Femme noire dans le cinéma contemporain: Star ou faire-valoir? Paris: Éditions l'Harmattan, 2006.

Pfaff, Françoise. 25 Black African Film Makers. New York: Greenwood Press, 1988.

———, ed. Focus on African Films. Bloomington: Indiana University Press, 2004.

Pommier, Pierre. Cinéma et développement en Afrique noire francophone. Paris: Pedone, 1974.

Rancati, Fiorano, and Giuseppe Gariazzo. Il cinema dell'Africa nera. Milan: Arci Nova Metromondo, 1993.

Roitfeld, Pierre. Afrique noire francophone. Paris: Unifrance, 1980.

Ruelle, Catherine, ed. Afriques 50: Singularités d'un cinéma pluriel. Paris: L'Harmattan, 2005.

———, and Antoinette Delafin, eds. Cinémas africains d'aujourd'hui. Paris: Karthala / Radio RFI, 2007.

Russell, Sharon A. Guide to African Cinema. Westport, Conn.: Greenwood Press, 1998.

Sadoul, Georges. The Cinema in the Arab Countries. Beirut: Interarab Center for Cinema and Television/UNESCO, 1966.

Sakr, Naomi, ed. Women and Media in the Middle East: Power through Self-Expression. London: I. B. Tauris, 2004.

Sandrini, Luca, ed. Luminescenze: Panoramiche sui cinema d'Africa. Verona: Cierre Edizoni, 1998.

Schmidt, Nancy. Sub-Saharan Films and Film Makers: *An Annotated Bibliography*. London: Zell, 1988. Second edition, *Sub-Saharan Films and Film Makers, 1987–1992: An Annotated Bibliography*. London: Zell, 1994.

Serceau, Michel, ed. *Cinémas du Maghreb*. Paris: Corlet/Télérama/*CinémAction* 111, 2004.

Shafik, Viola. *Der arabische Film: Geschichte und kulturelle Identität*. Bielefeld: Aisthesis Verlag, 1996. English translation: *Arab Cinema: History and Cultural Identity*. Cairo: American University in Cairo Press, 1998.

Shaka, Femi Okiremuete. *Modernity and the African Cinema*. Trenton, N.J.: Africa World Press, 2004.

Shiri, Keith, ed. *Directory of African Film-Makers and Films*. London: Flicks Books, 1992.

———. *Africa at the Pictures*. London: National Film Theatre, 1993.

———. *Celebrating African Cinema*. London: Africa at the Pictures, 2003.

Speciale, Alessandra, ed. *La Nascita del Cinema in Africa: Il cinema dell'Africa sub-sahariana dalle origini al 1975*. Turin: Lindau, 1998.

Tcheuyap, Alexie. *De l'écrit à l'écran: les réécritures filmiques du roman africain francophone*. Ottawa: Les Presses de l'Université d'Ottawa, 2005.

Thackway, Melissa. *Africa Shoots Back: Alternative Perspectives in Sub-Saharan Francophone African Film*. London: James Currey, 2003.

Thiers-Thiam, Valérie. *À chacun son griot: le mythe du griot-narrateur dans la littérature et le cinéma de l'Afrique de l'Ouest*. Paris: Éditions L'Harmattan, 2004.

Tofetti, Sergio, ed. *Il cinema dell'Africa nera 1963–1987*. Milan: Fabbri Editori, 1987.

Tomaselli, Keyan, ed. *African Cinema*. Natal: *Critical Arts* 7, no. 1–2 (1993).

Ukadike, Nwachukwu Frank. *Black African Cinema*. Berkeley: University of California Press, 1994.

———. *Questioning African Cinema: Conversations with Filmmakers*. Minneapolis: University of Minnesota Press, 2002.

Vieyra, Paulin Soumanou. *Le Cinéma et l'Afrique*. Paris: Présence Africaine, 1969.

———. *Le Cinéma africain des origines à 1973*. Paris: Présence Africaine, 1975.

Zuhur, Sherifa, ed. *Images of Enchantment: Visual and Performing Arts of the Middle East*. Cairo: American University in Cairo Press, 1998.

———, ed. *Colors of Enchantment: Theatre, Dance, Music, and the Visual Arts of the Middle East*. Cairo: American University in Cairo Press, 2001.

MAGAZINES, JOURNALS, AND FESTIVAL PROGRAMS

Actes du Festival International de Montpellier. Montpellier, from 1979.

Adhoua. Paris, 1980–1981 (four issues).

Africa: Film and TV. Harare, Zimbabwe: Z Promotions, from 1993.

Africultures 1–68. Paris: Éditions L'Harmattan, since 1997.

Biennale des cinémas arabes à Paris (catalogues). Paris: Institut du Monde Arabe, from 1992.

Cinéma 3. Casablanca, 1970 (3 issues).

CinémArabe, Paris, 1976–1979 (12 issues).

Cinémathèque Afrique (catalogue). Paris: ADPF, 2004.

Ecrans d'Afrique. Milan: COE, 1992–1999 (24 issues).

Festival Cinema Africano (catalogues). Milan: COE, from 1991.

Festival du film arabe (catalogues). Paris: L'Association pour le film arabe, 1983–1985.

Festival National du Film Marocain (catalogues). Rabat: CCM, from 1982.

Images Nord-Sud. Paris: ATM, from 1988 (68 issues).

International Film Guide. London, annually 1964–2006.

Les Deux écrans. Algiers, from 1978.

SeptièmArt. Tunis, from 1964 (101 issues).

Unir-Cinéma. Saint Louis, Senegal, from 1980s.

ROY ARMES is Professor Emeritus of Film at Middlesex University in the United Kingdom and author of numerous books on film. For twenty years he has specialized in African filmmaking and has published *Postcolonial Images: Studies in North African Film* and *African Filmmaking: North and South of the Sahara* with Indiana University Press. His current project is a companion to this dictionary, a discussion of *Issues in African Film*.